Constructing Correct Software

QA
76.76
.D47
C666
2005

D0882321

BELL LIBRARY-TAMU-CC

John Cooke

Constructing Correct Software

Second Edition

With 100 Figures

Springer

John Cooke, BSc, PhD, CEng, CMath
Department of Computer Studies, Loughborough University, Loughborough, Leicester, LE11 3TU, UK

British Library Cataloguing in Publication Data
Cooke, John, 1947-
Constructing correct software. - 2nd ed.
1. Software engineering 2. Computer software - Development
3. Formal methods (Computer science)
I. Title
005.1

ISBN 1852338202

Library of Congress Cataloging-in-Publication Data
Cooke, John, 1947-
Constructing correct software / John Cooke.
p. cm. -- (Formal approaches to computing and information technology)
Includes bibliographical references and index.
ISBN 1-85233-820-2 (alk. paper)
1. Computer software--Development. 2. Formal methods (Computer science) I. Title. II. Series.

QA76.76.D47C666 2004
005.1--dc22 2004050410

Apart from any fair dealing for the purposes of research or private study, or criticism or review, as permitted under the Copyright, Designs and Patents Act 1988, this publication may only be reproduced, stored or transmitted, in any form or by any means, with the prior permission in writing of the publishers, or in the case of reprographic reproduction in accordance with the terms of licences issued by the Copyright Licensing Agency. Enquiries concerning reproduction outside those terms should be sent to the publishers.

ISBN 1-85233-820-2 2nd edition Springer-Verlag London Berlin Heidelberg
ISBN 3-540-76156-X 1st edition Springer-Verlag London Berlin Heidelberg
Springer Science+Business Media
springeronline.com

© Springer-Verlag London Limited 2005
Printed in the United States of America

First published 1998
Second edition 2005

The use of registered names, trademarks, etc. in this publication does not imply, even in the absence of a specific statement, that such names are exempt from the relevant laws and regulations and therefore free for general use.

The publisher makes no representation, express or implied, with regard to the accuracy of the information contained in this book and cannot accept any legal responsibility or liability for any errors or omissions that may be made.

Typesetting: Camera-ready by author
34/3830-543210 Printed on acid-free paper SPIN 10988084

Abridged Preface to First Edition

The Importance of Software

Today, in almost every piece of machinery or electrical equipment, there is a small computer. We may not be aware of its presence but, more often than not, machines are controlled by a computer system, and computers are controlled by programs. Even if a program is *hard-wired* into a system, so that it cannot be changed, it probably started life as software. Thus you can see how software influences much of our daily activity. When software goes wrong, its effects can be widespread and can wreak havoc in situations that most people would not even associate with computers.

Of course, some computer software is used in situations that are so experimental as to never be repeated. Such 'one off' instances really lie outside the realms of Computing Science; it being expected that those programs might well be changed after each run or even scrapped altogether once a single result has been obtained. *We* are concerned with the production of more general-purpose software — software that will be run with so many different data sets, that we can sensibly regard them as being infinite in number.

It is therefore very important that the software be 'right' — that it *never* gives 'wrong' answers. In most situations[1], it is usually better to get no answer at all than one which is 'incorrect'.

The classical approach to the task of trying to ensure that programs were indeed 'correct' is to test them. This involves writing the program, running it on sample data to generate results, and then checking these results to see if they are as expected. But the number of possible data values is so large that the time needed to perform all the program runs is likely to be considerable (hours, days, or even years), and then all the results need to be checked by some agreed method. This is clearly not practical; all that such an exercise *might* demonstrate is that the program fails, but only if we were fortunate enough to find a suitably discerning piece of data.

[1] The only cases which seem to go contrary to this bold statement are those when an answer might be regarded as 'inaccurate' rather than 'wrong'. In these instances, the specification of what is required — or what 'will do' — must be more carefully defined.

A half-way house in the testing approach is to partition the possible data into classes and test a small number of values from each class. This is better but is still no guarantee of correctness since it depends on the assumption that nothing 'unusual' happens within each class, it therefore merely passes on the responsibility to smaller pieces of program which are presumed to be right — but that is where we came in.

Before any code is written, a programmer needs to know why the software is needed and what it is required to do. As will be illustrated in Chapter 0, the lack of a suitable statement of requirements can cause all sorts of problems and is often very expensive. We argue that what is needed is a *formal* statement of requirements. Even if a completely formal development process is not undertaken, such a description can be used to good effect. The main potential benefits are:

(a) to fully understand the problem to be solved.
 If we cannot describe the problem, then we are unlikely to understand it adequately enough to be able to solve it[2].

(b) as the basis of testing.
 From a proper problem description we should be able to devise acceptance tests — even before programming has begun. We can construct a decision procedure, but this will often only be a *partial* decision procedure — it will tell us either that the software is wrong or that we don't know whether it is right or wrong!

(c) to use in a formal verification.
 We can combine the specification and the program (once written) into a *correctness theorem,* the validity of which can then be investigated. This requires us to perform a mathematical proof and uncovers the fact that proofs are difficult to perform — even for mathematicians, and most programmers are not mathematicians.

(d) as a basis for the construction of software.
 Instead of looking at the specification, writing a program, and then seeing if it is 'correct' relative to the specification, it is possible to transform and refine the specification into a form that is executable (viewed as an expression within a conventional high-level procedural language). This approach is logically equivalent to retrospective verification but does not allow the existence of incorrect programs, which would be wasteful of programmer effort. This constructive approach can be presented so as to be more akin to the evaluation of an expression, and to algebraic manipulation, rather than the discharging of logical assertions by proofs.

[2] We can use incomplete specifications which incorporate appropriate use of approximate answers (to within specified limits!). Such specifications do reflect knowledge of the problem; in particular, the extent to which (in-)accurate results are important. Lack of vital information required in the program will cause the construction process to halt — and for the necessary information to be supplied — before we can continue. So, we can start with an incomplete specification and augment it as we proceed. Providing that no contradictory information is added, we do not have to undo any work already done.

Formal Methods

The *raison d'être* of formal methods is to support reasoning: reasoning about hardware and software, reasoning about their properties and about their construction. Of particular importance is the ability to reason, mathematically, about properties that are required *for all* values from unmanageably large data sets.

The real reason why formal methods are not used as widely as they could be is a general lack of mathematical expertise; hence the lack of confidence and the consequential reluctance to use mathematics even when to do so could be most beneficial. In our presentation, most reasoning is carried out by the evaluation of appropriate expressions; indeed, most mathematical entities are treated in the same way as data values within a programming language. We hope that this will make the mathematical concepts more acceptable to the software engineering community.

Although mathematics is unavoidable, we shall only use it as and when it is needed and not merely in order to make the processes look *more* complicated.

Mathematics will be used first to give descriptions and then to perform calculations upon these descriptions. The descriptions will almost always be in the form of expressions — expressions with which we formulate the specifications (and requirements) of software, characterise properties of data types, and define the programming constructs used. Performing algebra on these expressions allows us to 'mechanise' reasoning and to manipulate specifications and programs.

The degree of formality found within programming *languages* appears acceptable to software engineers (they appreciate why it is needed there) and presenting other aspects of software design in a similar way seems also to make the necessary mathematics more palatable.

Just as in other areas of mathematics, although there are strict sets of rules within which we must work, the solving of problems and the creation of systems are not prescriptive processes. We still need to make choices, to perform certain so-called 'refinement' steps. Indeed, the synthesis process is effectively a mixture of transformations and refinements, which we call ***transfinement***.

Coverage

All software, all programs, include both calculations and communications, and we consider these two aspects separately. It is easier to study each in isolation and then combine them later. Here: the notion of 'calculation' must be viewed sufficiently broadly to include any situation where the answer is computed by evaluating some function of the input. These functions are more powerful than functions that can be coded directly in common programming languages and encompass such tasks as sorting, searching, and the checking for the presence of certain properties within data. Similarly, under 'communications' we include consideration of states and state changes, as well as the more predictable actions associated with input and output. In this introductory text, we shall concentrate on the computational aspects of software and relegate communication issues to one small section.

In a more general scenario, when the software is embedded within a system which provides or controls a 'service', we have to consider the requirements of such a system — expressed in terms of externally observable changes. The software requirements must therefore be expressed relative to other components of the system. Here we are only concerned with software; the design of other components is the concern of engineers from some other discipline (it is *not* software engineering). We don't presume any expertise in such areas and reciprocally, as is apparent from experience, we suggest that serious programming should be left to professional software engineers.

It is most important to recognise that we only claim properties of our derived software designs. Since all software resides within some other system we cannot make any absolute claims about the entire system *per se*; any claims about the software are conditional upon conformance of other components to *their* requirements.

So we do not attempt to venture outside the field of software engineering. This book is primarily concerned with the construction of correct algorithms but in the final chapter we briefly discuss how the relationship between software requirements/specifications to other (hardware?) components may be represented. (This is all part of an overall system design.) The appendix contains a compendium of associated mathematical rules for the manipulation of software descriptions.

Approach

We regard program construction as a form of problem solving and present a basic framework into which new problem-solving tactics and strategies can be slotted as and when they become available. We concentrate on fundamentals and include only the simplest (and most widely applicable) tactics. Then, having investigated some problems from first principles we shall demonstrate how they may be solved more easily — and more immediately — when they are specified in a more abstract fashion. Software requirements and specifications should always be given in the most abstract form possible. This not only makes them simpler to understand but gives the software engineer more flexibility in the way he designs his implementation. Such an approach also supports re-use of components that have been (correctly) constructed earlier.

This is not an Object-Oriented (O-O) approach as such but is consistent with O-O technologies. The novel feature of O-O methods is the concept of inheritance (of data types and, closely related, classes) and is of most benefit when seeking to re-use existing software components. We are *primarily* concerned with the construction of software from scratch.

Just as one might study the principles of programming without having to get embroiled in the specific details of any particular commercially available language and its compiler, we shall present the essence of specification and design of software using logic, a program design language and several varieties of (formal) diagrams. This language being a rational extension and abstraction of proper subsets of other commonly used languages and notations. As will be gleaned from the text, the actual notation used is not important; once you can *read* one notation, it is easy to re-express the same information in another form.

The approach is unashamedly, and necessarily, formal. Formality is *not* theory but is underpinned *by* theory; theory is given and explained only when necessary.

Audience

The presentation is aimed at those who need to regard the production of programs as an end in itself. This includes degree-level students of computer science and software engineering and programmers who have to produce certificated software — those who might be involved in the production of 'critical systems', *whatever* 'critical' means. We treat programming as an intellectual exercise, the context in which the software is (to be) used only being relevant in as much as it is reflected in the requirements (or specification) which the software must satisfy.

Capsule Description

The following questions must be addressed:

- Why is the software needed? (requirements)
- What is the software to do? (specification)
- How does the software work? (implementation)

Formal Methods provide a framework in which correct software can be built.

- Software should meet its requirements.
- As part of the *system* design process,
  its actions must be decided upon and specified.
- The specified actions must then be implemented and controlled.

Ideally, we need a structure in which to apply tactics aimed at 'transfining' specifications and requirements into software designs which are known to be correct. This text focuses on the algorithmic aspects of software; the process of synthesising a design for a procedural program is presented as a sequence of design steps. At each stage, we are typically making decisions or adding details necessary to achieve or maintain the requirements. This is done in such a way as to retain consistency with the immediately preceding, more abstract, design and prevent the introduction of errors. We do this by adhering to various rules.

These are rules associated with

- the data types used
- the logic used, and
- the languages used.

John Cooke
Loughborough University
1997

Preface to Second Edition

Why a New Edition?

This edition has essentially the same content as the first. We have resisted the temptation to 'soup up' the content and to deviate from our original aim of providing a *basic* introduction to formally based software construction. Rather than drastically change the content, we have tried to address the educational conflict between providing lots of detail and giving a very general global overview. Many readers feel the need to have much of the work described in great detail, but others find such detail overwhelming and a distraction from the broader picture. However, 'the devil is in the detail' — all the details must be correct, otherwise all is lost and we gain nothing.

This edition makes greater use of footnotes to qualify the main text and add detail to the exposition. This is done in an attempt to avoid too many distractions whilst trying to be as technically correct as possible.

So, we keep to basics rather than allow ourselves to be tempted to include more advanced material — even though the topics included may not be those chosen by others as their starting point.

Readers should still read the preface to the first edition — it is all still relevant. If you have not already done so, perhaps now is a good time to read it — before continuing here.

What's New?

Although the approach is still constructive rather than retrospective (as is the case with testing or even verification), we do allow for inspiration to be employed within our formal framework. This not only encompasses 'checking', as in the first edition, but also facilitates the use of 'eureka' steps. These effectively start 'in the middle' and requires that we work both backwards, to the problem, and forwards, to an implementation. At a first glance, this 'sideways' technique looks like more work than simply working in a single direction, however, providing that our inspiration works, this approach is very specific to the given problem and moves quickly to a correct design. But here is not the place to tell the full story.

A proper description of the structure of the book, and how the (rest of the) chapters relate to one another, is given in Chapter 0. However, we ought to say something here about the more important changes, which the reader can appreciate without having to delve into the technical material.

In this edition there are more chapters even though some are very small; there is slightly less detailed working in the text and hence more for the reader to do between (printed) steps. The technical appendices have been extended, and more detailed expositions will be placed on the web (www.springeronline.com/uk/1-85233-820-2) where extra, supplementary, material will be added as and when requested / required / available.

There are many small changes and a few major structural ones. At the risk of glossing over some necessary details we aim to 'get to the plot' quickly by including, in Chapter 0, a few brief 'sketches' of the entire synthesis process applied to some simple numerical calculations. However, in order that we can do the job properly, this must be counter-balanced by a very large Part A (Preliminaries), which consists of Chapters 1 and 2 and includes details of the mathematical notions with which the reader should be familiar , but perhaps not the notations — well, almost, there are a few novel twists — and matters related to programming.

Chapter 1 is distilled from four original chapters. This can be skimmed at a first reading, so that the reader is acquainted with its contents, and then relevant sections studied more fully as and when needed in the sequel. (The experience of each reader will be different and hence the need for in-depth study will also be different.)

Chapter 2 is the only one which is completely new. It discusses, in outline, how specifications have been used by others in the construction of software. Although this too can be skipped on the first reading, it is included (in this position) so that the reader is aware of some of the aspirations and problems of earlier work on Formal Methods. This is mainly to provide a basis for comparison with our constructive approach, but the techniques can also be used in a mutually supportive fashion.

In programming we certainly support the idea of using sensible (helpful, indicative, 'meaningful') names when referring to data items, functions etc. but we have serious doubts about the particularly undisciplined use of comments. The use of comments and assertions and their relationship to program correctness is discussed here and provides more motivation for adopting Formal Methods.

The language Pascal was used to illustrate certain points in the initial chapter of the first edition. For those who are unfamiliar with that language — or perhaps did not appreciate its relative unimportance in the overall scheme of the book and felt threatened by its unfamiliarity — we have chosen, in this edition, to use a generic block-structured procedural language. Any similarity with a language known to the reader should provide useful reinforcement. But we shall resist the temptation to wander away from our central topic of study and stray into a formal definition of its semantics. Concepts needed within the language will be discussed in appropriate detail when encountered.

We shall use the same language in the programs constructed as part of our 'methodology' (although that is not a term whose use we would encourage).

Chapters 1 and 2 can be speed read by an experienced and 'mathematically aware' programmer. Chapter 3, in Part B (Fundamentals), is where the real work starts.

Elsewhere, original chapters have been split up so as to permit clearer focussing on important topics that warrant individual discussion and further study. Overall, we aim to compute (correctly derive) programs that perform calculations. Throughout, we have tried to place more emphasis on the relationship between problem breakdown and program assembly. Once mastered, the approach can be applied to 'larger' problems using bigger building blocks; it is not only, as often perceived, for 'programming in the small'.

What this Book is Not About?

This is not a book about Requirements Engineering or about Programming Languages, even though both of these subjects impinge on what we do here. Those topics are closely related to software development and are certainly necessary, but they are not our main concern. And, as already noted, this book is not about 'Programming' — coding — or Data Structures.

Although the book has evolved from taught courses (selected chapters), it is not really a textbook *per se*. (Certainly some exercises are included, and there is a lot of detailed working; but this is to reinforce and emphasize the necessity of paying attention to detail, both in the theory and as the basis of mathematically based software engineering tools.) Neither is it a monograph; it is more of an explication — an extended explanation. We shall try to react to questions received and add extra material in response to readers' needs via the web.

Acknowledgements

The bulk of the material within this book has been distilled from courses presented by the author and his colleagues over a period of some 20 years. During this period of time, researchers and teachers have all been influenced (taught!) by the work of others — sometimes consciously, but often not. Notwithstanding the inevitable omissions from any list, we include, within the bibliography at the end of the book, the more obvious textbooks which have helped form and transform our understanding of Formal Methods. Collectively we share in the ongoing search for better ways of presenting, explaining, and teaching the most recent developments in Formal Methods that have matured sufficiently to warrant wider exposure. (Of course, there are also very many research papers, but to cite any of them would not be appropriate in a basic introduction such as this.)

Regrettably, many of these books are no longer in print, a tragedy of the need for publishers to pander to popular needs for trendy IT books rather than support the Science of Computing or the Engineering of Software. But they all have something to offer, even if you have to borrow a copy from a library.

Interactions, formal and informal, direct and electronic, with colleagues within *BCS-FACS* (the BCS specialist group in Formal Aspects of Computing Science) and fellow members of the editorial board of *Formal Aspects of Computing* are gratefully acknowledged.

Again thanks (and apologies) are due the students who have suffered our attempts to present a topic whilst it was still in its academic infancy. Particular thanks go to my friend and colleague Roger Stone.

The first edition was written largely during a period of study leave from Loughborough University.

I am also indebted to Steve Schuman and Tim Denvir who assisted in honing the first edition, to Mark Withall who reported more errors (typos?) than anyone else, and to Rosie Kemp, Helen Callaghan, Jenny Wolkowicki (and others whose names I do not know) at Springer for their support and patience.

What Next?

At the risk of being unconventional, we mention here some of the more advanced aspects of Formal Methods, which follow on naturally from concepts introduced here and which the reader might pursue next.

The way in which we specify *types* can also be used to derive and present new, composite types and, object-oriented, *classes*. Extra mechanisms need to be introduced so as to facilitate inheritance between hierarchically related classes; but the basic framework for reuse is already in place, and the O-O notion of pattern is merely a generalisation of the tactics introduced here.

Within this text, we meet genuine, non-interfering, parallelism. Other kinds of parallelism are possible and relate naturally to distributed systems that work in a non-deterministic fashion (and can be characterised by non-deterministic eureka rules). Such systems may need to be specified using temporal logic (in which properties change with time). They therefore provide instances of situations where we need to distinguish between (and link) requirements and specifications. And they may well be implemented by multi-processor systems.

As you will see, program transformation plays an important role in our constructions since it allows us to move from recursive functions to iterative statements. But that is all we use it for. When we know more about the target implementation systems (hardware and software) we can study the complexity of the designs we produce and further transform these, correct, programs and systems so as to improve their efficiency.

So there is certainly plenty of scope for development and application of the basic material to be put to use, once it has been fully mastered. Now to work.

John Cooke
Loughborough University
May 2004

Contents

Abridged Preface to First Edition v
Preface to Second Edition xi

0 Introduction 1
0.1 What Is this Book About? 1
0.2 Some Terminology 2
0.3 How Might Programs Fail? 3
0.4 A Way Forward 10
0.5 On Mathematics 12
0.6 Linking Paradigms 13
0.7 Problem Solving 15
0.8 The Book Plan 22

Part A: Preliminaries 29

1 The Technical Background 31
1.0 Introduction 31
1.1 Functions, Relations and Specifications 35
1.1.1 Summary of Features 49
1.1.2 Guidelines for Specifications 50
1.2 Equational Reasoning and Types 51
1.3 The Origin and Application of Rules 55
1.4 Data Types 61
1.4.1 A Glimpse at the Integers 61
1.4.2 Logical Types 66
1.4.2.1 The Boolean Type, $\mathbb{B}$ 66
1.4.2.2 Implication and Deduction 72
1.4.2.3 Boolean Quantifiers 76
1.4.2.4 Extended (3-valued) Logic 78
1.4.3 Sets 91
1.4.4 Integers 96
1.4.4.1 Inequalities 99
1.4.5 Bags 101
1.4.6 Lists 103

1.4.7 Records and n-tuples 107
1.4.8 Union Types 109
1.4.9 Sub-types and Sub-ranges 110
1.4.10 Type Transfer Functions and Casts 111
1.4.11 Data Types and Transformations 114
1.4.12 On Quantification 116
1.5 Applying Unfold/Fold Transformations 118

2 On Programming 125
2.0 Overview 126
2.1 Procedural Programming 127
2.2 'Good' Programming 130
2.3 Structuring and (control) Flowcharts 131
2.4 PDL Overview 134
2.4.1 "Let" and "Where" 138
2.4.2 Scope and Parameters 139
2.5 Comments and Assertions 139
2.6 Verification of Procedural Programs 146
2.6.1 Sequencing 147
2.6.2 Alternation 149
2.6.3 Iteration 150
2.7 Program Derivation 154

Part B: Fundamentals 159

3 Algorithm Extraction 161
3.0 Overview 162
3.1 On Converging Recursion 164
3.2 Design Tactics 169
3.2.1 Checking Perceived Answers 172
3.2.2 Problem Reduction 175
3.2.3 Problem Decomposition 182
3.2.3.1 Structural Splitting 185
3.2.3.2 Predicated Splitting 201
3.2.3.3 Mixed Strategies 201
3.2.3.4 Domain Partitioning 202
3.2.4 The Use of Analogy 203
3.3 'Eureka' Processes 206
Summary 221

4 Recursion Removal 223
4.1 Tail Recursion 225
4.2 Associative Recursion 238

4.3 Up and Down Iteration 249
4.4 Speeding up Iteratons 257
4.5 Recursive Procedures 262
Summary 265

5 Quantifications 267
5.0 Overview 268
5.1 Defining Composite Values 268
5.2 Derived Composite Values 270
5.2.1 1-place Functions 270
5.2.2 2-place Functions 272
5.3 Application to Program Development 277
5.3.1 1-place Functions 278
5.3.2 2-place Functions 280
5.3.3 An Extended Example: The Factorial Function 282
5.4 Some Rules for Quantifications 291
5.4.1 General Rules 292
5.4.2 Special Rules for Logical Quantifiers 298
Summary 300

6 Refinement and Re-use 301
6.1 Operational Refinement 302
6.1.1 On Correctness 302
6.1.2 Some Properties of Design Refinement 307
6.1.3 An Alternative View 309
6.2 Re-using Designs 310

Part C: Developments 315

7 Sorting 317
7.1 Specification and Initial Discussion 317
7.2 Initial Designs 323
7.2.1 Problem Reduction 323
7.2.2 Structural Splitting 326
7.2.3 Predicated Splitting (Partitioning) 333
7.3 Complete Designs 341
7.3.1 Exchange Sorts 341
7.3.2 Merge Sorts 347
7.3.2.1 The Basic Merge Sort 347
7.3.3 Partition Sorts 348
7.3.3.1 Simple Partition Sort 350
7.4 A Quick Design 352

8 Data Refinement 357
8.1 On 'Internal' Data Types 358
8.2 Changing Data Types 358
8.3 Where to next? 370

9 Sorting Revisited 375
9.1 Exchange Sorts 375
9.2 Merge Sorts 383
9.2.1 Variants of the Merge Sort 384
9.3 Partition Sorts 390

10 Failures and Fixes 409
10.1 Inadequate Pre-Conditions 410
10.2 Failures in Structural Splitting 411
10.2.1 Loss of Vital Information 412

11 Further Examples 417
11.1 The 2-D Convex Hull 418
11.2 Topological Sort 424
11.2.1 Experimentation 425
11.2.2 A Proper Formulation 433
11.3 Some 'Extremal' Problems 439

12 On Interactive Software 455
12.1 Specifications Involving Change 457
12.1.1 Specifications of Input/Output 457
12.1.2 Conventional Communications 463
12.1.3 The Enabling of Computations 466
12.2 Pertaining to (Software) Systems 466
12.2.1 System Requirements 467
12.2.2 Specifying Systems 469

Appendix Transformation Digest 473
A.0 Re-write Rule Conventions 473
A.1 Data Manipulation Rules 473
A.1.1 The Type $\mathbb{B}$ 475
A.1.2 Extended Logic and Conditional Expressions 477
A.1.3 Integers 479
A.1.4 Sets 480
A.1.5 Bags 482
A.1.6 Lists 483
A.1.7 Common Conversion Functions 485
A.1.8 Quantifier Rules 486

A.2 Quantifier Properties 490
A.3 'Not Occurs in' 491
A.4 On PDL Structure 492
A.4.1 Scope and Parameters 494
A.5 PDL Transformation Rules 495

Bibliography 501

Index 503

Chapter 0
Introduction

0.1 What is this book about?

It is an introduction to the science of writing programs, the engineering of software. It is not a book concerned with writing programs in a particular programming language, nor is it a collection of standard algorithms for solving common problems. It is about the creation of software designs which are *guaranteed* to meet their requirements, that are *correct* - and correctness cannot be qualified, software is either correct or it isn't.

Software artefacts, programs, are strange things. 'Good' programs often look absolutely trivial, but, like many products of human endeavour, this does not mean that they were easy to create. At a time when virtually all students (of almost all disciplines) are taught "to write computer programs" another book which considers how they should be written may seem unnecessary. Of course there is a whole world of difference between knowing what a programming language looks like (or to be able to understand how a given program might work) and being able to write a program to fulfil a particular need. This difference, this gulf, is analogous to the separation between 'knowing English' and being able to write a good story - in English.

Here we are talking about serious programming - not hacking, not one-off programs to be run on one specific piece of data; but about producing software which is reliable, which will not break, which always does what you expect it to[1].

---

[1] When talking about our expectations about what a program should do, we need to address the concept of robustness. Traditionally, a program is said to be robust if it can cope with 'unexpected' input. As you will see later, part of the specification of a program is devoted to describing which inputs are legal. Handling 'illegal' input, and the extent to which a 'customer' requires you to do this, should be incorporated in the specification so as to include error messages etc. But note that unless the program is reading individual characters (or, possibly, key strokes) then the trapping of certain 'illegal' input is simply not possible when using a high-level language. This has nothing to do with failure of the software, but the failure of someone to use it properly. Likewise, a program which is brought to a halt by an operating system (because of some condition such as overflow) is not necessarily erroneous. It might not be halted at that point when run on a different system - so it has magically corrected itself! We are fundamentally concerned with ensuring that the development of *our* software does not cause errors and that in any context where the other components run correctly, and have adequate capacity, the overall system will deliver results consistent with the specification.

Serious programming requires serious effort and can only be achieved at a cost. That cost has to be considered in the light of the expense incurred when software goes wrong. Of course the nature of such expense depends on the context in which the software is used. Obvious examples include financial implications when a product fails to meet user expectations, the loss of potential new business following the failure of a product, and the more immediate consequences of a program simply giving the wrong answers, giving the wrong advice, issuing wrong instructions to a piece of machinery etc.

0.2 Some Terminology

To indicate how we intend to set about constructing software in a systematic and disciplined manner, it is convenient to limit our comments to particularly simple software artefacts. To this end we introduce some terminology.

- A ***program*** is a piece of software that takes in data, carries out a calculation (executes an algorithm), delivers results, and stops. In principle, all the data is available before execution starts.

- A ***process*** is a piece of software that may never stop; however it might often wait passively to be activated by the receipt of certain stimuli.

- A ***Software systems*** is a collection of inter-linked programs and/or processes controlled externally or by other processes.

All software products include programs (procedures, routines etc.) and hence they are our prime object of study.

We are concerned, only, with the integrity of software that we are constructing. We are allowed to assume that other aspects of the system work in accordance with their specifications and in particular that the programming languages used are properly implemented. The ultimate aim being to be able to claim that "if everything else works as it should, then our software will perform as it should". This is closely allied to the traditional engineering concept of being able to 'sign off' a particular job - effectively taking responsibility for your contribution to a project. It is essentially the basis of a contract which stipulates what your software claims to do and the conditions (assumptions about the context and other provisos) under which it is required to operate. In fulfilling our contract we may also generate new (sub-) contracts for part of the work to be done by others.

0.3 How might programs fail?

To emphasise and illustrate the kind of software error with which we are primarily concerned, consider the following scenario.

'A program[2] is required which will input a sequence of up to 10 real[3] numbers (preceded by an integer value that indicates how many reals are to be processed), and from the sequence generate the 'average' and the 'deviation' - i.e. a measure of the extent to which individual values deviate from the average[4].' Suppose, for the sake of argument, that this problem is given in exactly this level of detail; perhaps over the telephone. This may seem unrealistic but is indicative of the kind of imprecise information that programmers often have to work from.

Our local neighbourhood programmer, who is a physicist by training, recalls that he once met the word 'deviation' in a course on probability and statistics and, after digging around in a text book he came up with a formula for "standard deviation":

$$\text{standard deviation} = \frac{\sqrt[2]{\sum(x-\mu)^2}}{n}$$

where μ is the mean,
and n is the number of integers in the sample.

[The $\sum$ indicates summation of the following bracketed expression over all values of x.]

This seems to be reasonable - and in any case the programmer doesn't want to display his ignorance by asking questions about the problem, which he presumes is fairly easy and the program ought to be straightforward.

---

[2] As already stated, this is not a book about programming in a specific language. Instead of using a real programming language, and running the risk of alienating anyone who has a different 'pet' language, we shall use a generic representation which is similar to many block-structured languages but not intended to be exactly the same as any particular one. We presume that you have knowledge of some such high level programming language so that you will appreciate the situations that we meet. Subsequently we shall develop this into a language for depicting our program designs.

[3] Subsequently we shall not use "real" numbers except for - easy to understand, but perhaps computationally complex - examples such as the current one. To deal with virtually any computation involving real numbers requires knowledge of approximate representations and perhaps a significant excursion into the subject of numerical analysis. In fact most calculations which involve real numbers cannot in the strict sense be computed; most of the numbers involved cannot even be represented within a computer.
Once we get going we shall have no interest in anything to do with this kind of calculation. As you will see, we are mainly concerned with *calculating* programs, i.e. performing calculations, the result of which is a program.

[4] Examples such as the one included here come from the folk lore of programming. No originality is claimed, but no source can be cited.

We now give some programs intended to perform the requested computation.

Program 1

```
program calculation,
begin
        var i,n, integer
        mean, sum: real
        data;array(1,10) of real
        readln(n)
        for i = 1 to n
                readln(data(i))
        sum = 0,
        for i = 1 to n
                sum = sum + data(i)
        mean = sum / n
        writeln(mean),
        sum_of_sq = 0
        for i = 1 to n
                begin
                sum_of_sq = sum_of_sq + sqr(data{i} - mean),
                end
        standard_dev = (sqroot(sum_of_sq)) / n,
        writeln(standard_dev : 1 : 2)
end
```

This 'program' contains many syntax errors. But what is the syntax of this *new* language (Program Design Language, PDL); what are the rules? PDL is discussed in Chapter 2, but here we shall merely make the following points:

a) Semi-colons will be used as sequencing separators. Elsewhere, when no strict order of execution or evaluation is required, we use commas.

b) "=" has been used where the PDL assignment symbol "←" should appear.

c) "{}" brackets have been used to hold the index for the data array. "[ ]" should have been used.

d) Other syntax has been omitted or is incorrect.

e.g "**do**" missing from "**for**...**to**...**do**...**od**" construct.

Here the **do**...**od** are used as brackets which delimit the sequence of commands to be repeated.

The built-in function for square root is "sqrt", not "sqroot", and there is no 'sqr' built in function, x^2 is used to denote x squared.

Some variables have not been declared, etc.
Within a **begin**...**end** block (all) declarations precede (all) commands.
The input / output commands are simply read, write and write_new_line.

In a way, these are 'good' errors because the programming system will find them. We hope that there is no danger of them surviving and producing incorrect answers. Some programmers don't bother checking such details and assume that the programming system will find them. This is dangerous as we shall see.

Program 2

```
program calculation;
begin
      var n, i: integer;
          mean, sum_of_sq, standard_dev, sum: real;
          data: array[1..10] of real;
      read(n);
      for i ← 1 to n do read(data[1]) od;
      sum ← 0;
      for i ← 1 to n do sum ← sum + data[i] od;
      mean ← sum / n;
      write(mean);
      sum_of_sq ← 0;
      for  i ← 1 to n
         do sum_of_sq ← sum_of_sq + (data[i] - mean)^2 od;
      standard_dev ← (sqrt(sum_of_sq)) / n;
      write_new_line;
      write(standard_dev)
end
```

The program is syntactically correct but may be required to perform undefined actions at run time.

The erroneous use of the subscript "1" instead of "i" cannot be detected by the compiler or run time system because it is perfectly valid; but it is perhaps not what was intended.

data[2], *data*[3]..... *data*[10] are uninitialised. Attempts to use these values should result in an error. There would even be a problem with *data*[1] if n was given a negative value.

Program 3

```
program calculation;
begin
        var n, i: integer;
             mean, sum_of_sq, standard_dev, sum: real;
             data: array[1..10] of real;
        read(n);
        for i ← 1 to n do read(data[i]) od;
        sum ← 0;
        for i ← 1 to n do sum ← sum + data[1] od;
        mean ← sum / n;
        write(mean);
        sum_of_sq ← 0;
        for  i ← 1 to n
            do sum_of_sq ← sum_of_sq + sqr(data[i] - mean)^2 od;
        standard_dev ← (sqrt(sum_of_sq)) / n;
        write_new_line;
        write(standard_dev)
end.
```

This program will give the anticipated answer under certain conditions. (Notice that in removing one 'error' we have introduced another.)

This program may be regarded as 'correct' when $n = 1$. It will also perform similarly when $n > 1$ if *data*[*i*] = *data*[1] for enough *i*'s, or the values in the array just happen to give the same answer. The error may not be detected if 'unlucky' test data is used - but if we always knew what data was going to 'break' the program there would be no need to test using such data. What we need is to detect the errors that we don't know about.

Selecting test data by referring to the program under test, or relying purely on chance is another dangerous practice. If you choose to follow the 'build and test' approach, test data should be selected with reference (only) to the problem, not the proposed solution, the program.

Program 4

```
program calculation;
begin
      var n, i: integer;
          mean, sum_of_sq, standard_dev, sum: real;
          data: array[1..10] of real;
      read(n);
      for i ← 1 to n do read(data[i]) od;
      sum ← 0;
      for i ← 1 to n do sum ← sum + data[i] od;
      mean ← sum / n;
      write(mean);
      sum_of_sq ← 0;
      for  i ← 1 to n
         do sum_of_sq ← sum_of_sq + (data[i] - mean)^2 od;
      standard_dev ← (sqrt(sum_of_sq)) / n;
      write_new_line;
      write(standard_dev)
end
```

Arguably the program is getting better. This version is syntactically correct and will run legally when presented with valid data, but there are still latent errors which have still not been removed. With invalid data there will be non-standard operations during execution - the program is not ***robust***[5].

Problems will arise if '$n = 0$' (division by zero), or if '$n > 10$' (the array cannot deal with more than 10 real numbers).

Providing that the run time system is very particular these errors will be detected, but short cuts are often taken and checks omitted. It is possible for a program to run and give results that *look* reasonable but are actually wrong (wrong as opposed to inaccurate - remember this program uses 'real' numbers).

What if we take a different approach? Suppose that we find a program written by someone else which seems to do the required job.

[5] Even with the limited, but common, interpretation in which the type of data is correct but the value is 'unexpected'.

Program 5

```
program calculation;
begin
        var n, i: integer;
             mean, sum_of_sq, standard_dev,mean_sq,
             estimate_std_dev, sum: real;
             data: array[1..10] of real;
        read(n);
        if (n <= 0) or (n > 10)
        then
           write("ERROR!")
        else
           for i ← 1 to n do read(data[i]) od;
           sum ← 0;
           for i ← 1 to n do sum ← sum + data[i] od;
           mean ← sum / n;
           write(mean);
           mean_sq ← mean * mean;
           sum_of_sq ← 0;
           for  i ← 1 to n
             do sum_of_sq ← sum_of_sq + (data[i] - mean)^2 od;
           standard_dev ← (sqrt(sum_of_sq)) / n;
           estimate_std_dev ← (sqrt(sum_of_sq)) / (n - 1);
           write_new_line;
           write(standard_dev)
        fi[6]
end
```

This program is syntactically correct, runs legally with valid data, rejects invalid (but correctly typed) data, but also contains calculations that are not required.

We do not need the calculation of the square of the mean ("mean_sq"), or "estimate_std_dev". There may well be an error within these calculations, indeed this program will crash if $n = 1$. Admittedly a clever optimising compiler might remove the unnecessary code, but probably not before time has been spent in trying to modify it.

Let's see what we get if we strip out all the irrelevant code.

[6] Notice that here we have used 'fi' as a completer for the 'if' construction. In this case **else**...**fi** act as delimiters for the sequence of commands to be executed if the controlling condition is False.

Program 6

```
program calculation;
begin
       var n, i: integer;
           mean, sum_of_sq, standard_dev, sum: real;
           data: array[1..10] of real;
       read(n);
       if (n <= 0) or (n > 10)
       then
         write("ERROR!")
       else
         for i ← 1 to n do read(data[i]) od;
         sum ← 0;
         for i ← 1 to n do sum ← sum + data[i] od;
         mean ← sum / n;
         write(mean);
         sum_of_sq ← 0;
         for  i ← 1 to n
           do sum_of_sq ← sum_of_sq + (data[i] - mean)^2 od;
         standard_dev ← (sqrt(sum_of_sq)) / n;
         write_new_line;
         write(standard_dev)
       fi
end
```

Even a program that is syntactically correct, robust and never fails can still be wrong because the customer wanted something else.

What was actually wanted in this case was the value midway between the minimum and maximum values and half the difference between these extreme values. So, for instance, we might have results x and y which indicate that the input values were in the range $x \pm y$, i.e. from $x - y$ to $x + y$. There was if fact no need for elaborate calculations, and no need to store all the data values. To illustrate that a program is correct we must relate it to the specification of its task. What was actually required here was to find the *max* and *min* values and print $(max + min)/2$ and $(max - min)/2$. (Of course the programmer didn't know this - and that is exactly the point being made.)

As yet you do not know how to write formal specifications. When you do, you will be able to specify what this program *should* have done - this needs to be identified *before* considering how the task may be carried out!

Subsequently you may also be able to prove that a suitable program does indeed satisfy its specification. At least you will be able to formulate the conditions that are necessary for this to be so. Alternatively, and of more practical benefit, you will know how a program can be constructed from a specification in such a way that it will be correct, automatically.

Programs may fail because of:

syntax errors	(context-free syntax)
(compile-time) semantic errors	(context-sensitive syntax errors)
(run-time) semantic errors	(including lack of robustness)

or because it is simply WRONG

The message here is that although the use of certain, modern, languages and sophisticated support systems can prevent the first 3 of these kinds of error, the correctness of a program cannot be judged simply by looking at the program text. So, what can we do?

0.4 A Way Forward

To explain our intentions we consider the words in the book title, albeit in a different order.

Software - Instructions (written in a formal - programming - language) which control the internal actions of a computer with the intention of achieving some desired result/state, or maintaining some relationship between values within the computer's memory.

Correctness - The property that the software satisfies its specification, or meets its requirements. To demonstrate correctness we need the specification (or the requirements - there is a technical difference which will be discussed later) to be expressed unambiguously. Of course, such a specification has always formed the basis of 'testing'. The object of testing being to show that "for all suitable data, the outcome that it produces is consistent with the specification".

Construction - Hitherto it has been the tradition that software was written and then, retrospectively, 'tested'. With the advent of program verification, a theory was developed whereby, in principle, a procedure could be set up so that the "correctness theorem" might be formulated and, hopefully, proven; the aim being the *same* as testing, namely to show that "for all suitable data, the outcome that it produces is consistent with the specification". Such mathematical proofs can be inordinately complex, even when theorem proving *tools* are available; and if the theorem is shown to be false - i.e. the software is wrong - there may be no useful clues as to where it fails and how to fix it. In contrast, taking the constructive approach we work directly on the specification and manipulates it in an attempt to make it executable (ultimately in a procedural fashion). This process might not succeed - some requirements may be unattainable, for various reasons - but at each stage the current software 'design' is always consistent with the specification.

Basics - Obviously there is a limit to what can be covered in an introductory text on software construction. We shall concentrate on exposing the problem, setting up a framework for the synthesis of correct software designs from adequate descriptions and introducing appropriate mathematical machinery to (a) support the description of requirements and (b) allow us to reason about relationships between requirements and designs.

We seek ways of developing software

so that it is *consistent with its specification*,

so that it is *correct by construction*.

The approach adopted here might best be described as

***calculating a program from its specification*.**

How do we go about this?

Although we are not primarily interested in solving 'mathematical' problems, the mere fact that we are going to perform some rather special calculations means that we do need to to use (a different kind of) mathematics. This needs a few words of explanation.

0.5 On Mathematics

Regardless of the kind of data being processed, and how it is processed, all computing activity can be characterised mathematically. This is crucial to our purposes since we wish to be able to reason about the problem and, hopefully, how we might solve it. Any suitably precise notation having 'well-defined' meaning and amenable to value-preserving manipulations *is* mathematics. To benefit from the problem being expressed in a mathematical fashion, we need to understand how that mathematics works.

As we proceed mathematics will be used:

- as a language in which to express specifications and requirements
    - we need to know how to read (and speak) it
    - we need to know exactly what it says (what it means)
- as rules which govern how we are allowed to manipulate information
    - we need to know what to aim for
      (i.e. to identify the goal of our manipulation).

The need to *read* mathematics ranges from coping with peculiar (but easy to process) syntax such as 'atom(x)' - spoken as 'x is_an_atom'[7] - to the more esoteric symbols such as $\Rrightarrow$,▸,$\forall$,and $\forall'$. These relate to well-defined operations and provide a precise and concise shorthand which can subsequently be manipulated. A set of manipulation rules are collected together in the appendix, but all the concepts will also be discussed informally when they are first encountered, and we shall indicate how the notation should be *spoken*.

It is often the case that, when 'writing' a procedural program, a programmer will start coding directly into the appropriate target language. We adopt a different stance, seeking first to derive a functional representation from which a procedural program can often be obtained in a fairly routine fashion. Proceeding in this way delays the need to consider state changes, assignment statements, and iterations; indeed many of these, usually tedious and 'hard to verify' procedural language features, can subsequently be handled in a very simple way using transformational methods. It also provides forms of program which can be used as intermediate goals in our mathematical manipulations.

So how should we set about constructing programs that calculate functions? That is the problem addressed by this book - the complete answer will not emerge for some time but, so as to give you a glimpse of how we shall proceed, we give a handful of simple examples. These will first be discussed informally and will be revisited later when the necessary formalities have been introduced, and we can do it *properly*.

[7] You can even write it in exactly this form! - without the quotes.

Throughout the book it is *not* our intention to consider specialist problem domains. To do this would take us away from general methods and would require the reader to have specialist knowledge. We are primarily interested in explaining general techniques and illustrating them (in detail) by applying them to a handful of familiar problems. Obviously we need a vehicle for our initial illustrations; where necessary we shall use natural numbers (1,2,3,4,...) and presume some familiarity with simple arithmetic. Having said that, it must be stressed that the techniques that we shall study are not mathematical in the commonly used sense of the word, they are not limited to or biased to the calculation of mathematical[8] functions.

Within the overall approach there are two major strands, the first is the linked use of the logic(al), functional[9] and procedural paradigms.

0.6 Linking Paradigms

We illustrate with a very simple example.

Example 0.1 Suppose we have a logical description which links the input value x to the output value y by the expression:

$$x = y - 2$$

Now rearrange to give y as the subject

◆ $y = x + 2$

Or, without the y, so the answer is simply the result of evaluating an expression.

▸▸ $[y =] \quad x + 2$

And finally, make the delivery of the result to y explicit.

▸▸ $y \leftarrow x + 2$

In a more complex situation we might introduce a function name in the last two phases to give,

$$[y =] \quad F(x) \text{ where } F(x) \triangleq x + 2$$

[8] There is a paradox here. *All* the manipulations carried out in computers under the control of software can be viewed as mathematical but do not necessarily use *everyday* mathematics, such as calculus or common arithmetic.

[9] Our main development path only skirts the possibilities afforded by full-blown functional programming. To follow alternative paths may prove fruitful but would distract from our current purpose. Apologies to devotees of functional programming.

⏩

$$F(x) \triangleq x + 2;$$
$$y \leftarrow F(x)$$

❑

Here the symbols ⧏⧐ and ⏩, which will be properly explained later, indicate that an expression has been manipulated in a reversible way, or that there has been a change in the type of program (written in a different programming paradigm). We trace the derivation, the calculation, of the final procedural program by a sequence of expressions.

The expression

$x = y - 2$ is a logical expression, implicitly defining y in terms of x,

the expression

$x + 2$ is a numerical expression, and

the expression

$$F(x) \triangleq x + 2;$$
$$y \leftarrow F(x)$$

represents the definition of the function F, followed by the evaluation of $F(x)$ and the assigning of its result to y.

Each of these expressions obeys appropriate structuring rules and has an unambiguous meaning. Manipulation of these well-structured, strongly-typed, expressions provides a basis for our formal derivation / development of programs.

Of course most calculations are far more complicated than the above illustration. By virtue of the intermediate functional form we usually encounter recursion. Indeed the logical-functional-procedural (LFP) progression might also be described as recursion introduction and (often) subsequent removal. This is pivotal to the method which we will put forward, so much so that a large section of Chapter 3 is devoted to the topic.

The LFP scheme of development is fairly mechanical - but not totally, it does need human intervention to 'steer' the process[10] - and it gives some intermediate goals to aim at when constructing the program. But how do we start to manipulate a (logical) specification into a corresponding function? The second strand of 'method' is the use of general problem solving tactics within this phase of the construction. To do this properly requires that we introduce some necessary background material but, as above, we shall first try to give a flavour of the ideas involved.

[10] We can therefore have many different programs which perform the same computation.

0.7 Problem Solving

As with all problems, we need to have some 'domain knowledge', i.e. we need to know something about the kind of data items involved, and their properties. Regardless of how it may be solved using a computer; we need (at least in principle) to be able to solve the problem 'by hand'. As already noted, our introductory illustrations will use natural numbers and simple arithmetic in an attempt to get started without having to explain the *problems* in great detail. Having said that, we shall use this occasion to gently introduce some of the notation which will be routinely used in subsequent chapters (the notation will also be properly described and explained, at length, when we meet the technical issues for real). Notice that the program schemes derived in these examples are recursive. This is an important characteristic of intermediate forms of program design which we evolve and plays a major role in avoiding error introduction.

Example 0.2: The Greatest Common Divisor[11]
Given natural numbers m and n we have to find the largest integer (actually another natural number) which exactly divides both of them.

First of all we define (declare!) $\mathbb{N}$ as the name for the set, or type[12], of natural numbers. $\mathbb{N}$ (pronounced, 'n', or 'the naturals' or 'the natural numbers' depending on how brief you wish to be - but you must be unambiguous). Here we have another 'n' but, even when spoken rather than written, the context should make it clear which you mean, the type or (the name of) a number.

$\mathbb{N}$ is the set { 1, 2, 3, 4, ... (to 'infinity') ..}.

The values, n and m, represent values of type $\mathbb{N}$. We indicate this by writing

$m{:}\mathbb{N},\ n{:}\mathbb{N}$

or

$m,n{:}\mathbb{N}$ that is "m and n are of type $\mathbb{N}$" - this is the same idea as declarations in many modern programming languages.

Now for the function,

$gcd(m,n{:}\mathbb{N}) \triangleq$ the largest $i{:}\mathbb{N}$ such that $i|m$ and $i|n$.

"the function gcd ....($\triangleq$) is defined to be ... ($i|m$) i divides m and .... ."

We will not go into all the details but pick out some of the relevant factors used in the proper mathematical calculation (of the program scheme, not the answer to the gcd problem).

---

[11] Also called the Highest Common Factor (HCF).

[12] Types are also called 'sorts' or 'kinds', but we shall not use these terms for types.

Notice if $i|m$ then $m = i*j$, for some integer j i.e. m is a multiple of i (with i,j:ℕ). Similarly

if $i|n$ then $n = i*k$ (for some k:ℕ).

Moreover $1 \le i \le m$, $1 \le j \le m$
and
$1 \le i \le n$, $1 \le k \le n$.

Obviously, if we were only asked to find any divisor of m and n, the number 1 would do.

$1|m$ since $m = 1*m$ etc.

Finding the *largest* divisor (of both m and n) is a little more tricky; let's defer that problem for a while and look at some special cases.

What if $m = n$? Then $n|m$ and $n|n$ (because $n = 1*n$) so n is a common divisor; it is also the largest since all divisors of n are '$\le n$'.
So

$gcd(n,n) = n$

Similarly, since m and n are interchangeable in the definition of $gcd(m,n)$, it must be the case that

$gcd(m,n) = gcd(n,m)$.

Let us now assume that $m \le n$. If this is not so then we can simply swap the values of m and n.

Notice also that if $m < n$ and $i|m$ and $i|n$, then

$$n - m = i*k - i*j$$
$$= i*(k - j) \quad \text{and } (k - j):\mathbb{N}.$$

so i is a divisor of $(n - m)$.

Hence, any divisor of m and n , and hence also the greatest divisor (whatever it is, we certainly don't know yet) is also a divisor of $(n - m)$. So, $gcd(m, n)$ divides n - (and m) and therefore is $\le gcd(m,n - m)$. By a similar argument $gcd(m,n - m)$ divides m and n and is therefore $\le gcd(m,n)$. Hence they are equal and we may write:
When $m \ne n$,

$gcd(m,n)$ = if $m>n$ then $gcd(n,m)$
else $gcd(m,n\text{-}m)$ fi

and $n\text{-}m$ is smaller[13] than n.

[13] This is certainly true but in general we need to be a little more careful; see Chapter 3.

So, by way of illustration:

$$\begin{aligned} gcd(15,9) &= gcd(9,15) \\ &= gcd(9,6) \\ &= gcd(6,9) \\ &= gcd(6,3) \\ &= gcd(3,6) \\ &= gcd(3,3) \\ &= 3 \end{aligned}$$

A full (functional) scheme for the calculation of *gcd* is thus:

```
gcd(m, n) ≜ if m=n  then n
                    else  if m>n then gcd(n, m)
                                 else gcd(m, n-m)
                          fi
            fi
```
[14]

Notice that the right-hand side of this expression is simply a recursive expression.

❑

What should we notice from this example which might be of more general use?

1 We use cases (such as $m > n$ and $m \leq n$) to break the problem into similar, but simpler or smaller, problems which together solve the original.
2 We make use of simple instances of the problem (such as when $m=n$).
3 We have used a way of reducing the problem to another instance of the same problem acting on 'smaller' data value (by replacing $gcd(m, n)$ by $gcd(m, m\text{-}n)$ when appropriate).

Of course, the detailed reasoning used here depends on the properties of integer operations and tests. We shall seek similar properties of other data types so that design principles can be used in many different situations.

Example 0.3: Integer Division Function
We are asked to derive a program to compute:

$$div(p,q{:}\mathbb{N}) \triangleq n{:}\mathbb{Z} \mid n \leq p/q < n+1$$

"the division of p and q, both natural numbers, is defined to be n, an integer ($\mathbb{Z}$), such that (written as '|') $n \leq$ (the fraction) p divided by q which is less than $n + 1$."

[14] Remember that we use "fi" to close the 'if then else' construct. Thus **else**...**fi** act as brackets and avoids ambiguity in similar but more complex situations.

Notice that since the answer for *div*(2, 5) is zero, the type of the result cannot be $\mathbb{N}$. $\mathbb{Z}$ is the set, the type, of *all* integers.

$$\mathbb{Z} \triangleq \{ \ldots, -3, -2, -1, 0, 1, 2, 3, \ldots. \}$$

Notice also that p/q represents the exact fractional answer but the answer to the *div*(p, q) function evaluation is n, an integer.

In fact $n = p \div q$

so

$3 \div 2 = 1$	remainder 1		
$2 \div 3 = 0$	remainder 2		
$7 \div 3 = 2$	remainder 1	etc.	

In integers

$$1 \leq 3 \div 2 < 2$$

i.e., multiplying through by 2,

$$1*2 = 2 \leq 3 < 4 = 2*2$$

and in general

$$n*q \leq p < (n+1) * q$$

Similarly,

$$0*3 \leq 2 < (0+1) * 3$$

and

$$2*3 \leq 7 < (2+1) * 3.$$

How can we derive a program design to compute *div*?

Are there any simple cases which give rise to simpler sub-problems? And which might be useful in finding an answer to the overall problem.

Although there is no guarantee of success, reasonable things to try might be looking at the problem when $p=q$, $p<q$ and when $p>q$.
When $p=q$ we should surely get $p \div q = 1$. We can check that this does in fact hold by substituting 1 for n (and q for p) in the definition.

i.e. $1*q \leq q < (1 + 1)*q$

or $q \leq q < 2*q$ which holds since $0 < 1 \leq q$ and $0 + q < q + q$.

So 1 is a valid result. In fact it is the only valid result when $p=q$ but that does not really matter (see the next example).

Now what if $p < q$? What if we are dividing by a number larger than p? Clearly the fractional answer from dividing p by q will be less than 1 and, since p and q are both positive p/q will not be negative. So zero seems to be a reasonable value to expect for *div*(p, q) when $p<q$. Again we need to check.

$$0*q \leq p < (0+1) * q$$

simplifies to

$$0 \leq p < q \qquad \text{which holds since } 0<p \text{ and, by assumption, } p<q.$$

Now for the hard bit. Suppose $p>q$ and let $r = p - q$. (Since $q>0$ then $r<p$ and, if we keep subtracting more q's, to get $p - 2*q$, $p - 3*q$, $p - 4*q$ etc., we will eventually reach a value which is $\leq q$. Moreover we get there in less than p moves, since the smallest possible value of q is 1. Knowing how many moves is not important here, we simply need to know that we will get there in a finite number of steps.) But how does this help with the evaluation of *div*(p, q)?

Try this; suppose that *div*(r, q) = m.

Then $\quad m \leq r/q < m + 1$

so

$$m*q \leq r < (m + 1)*q$$

and

$$m*q \leq p - q < (m + 1)*q$$

Thus

$$m*q + q \leq p < (m + 1)*q + q$$

and

$$(m + 1)*q \leq p < (m + 1 + 1)*q.$$

But this says that $m + 1$ is an acceptable value for *div*(p, q). Put another way

$$div(p, q) = div(p - q, q) + 1 \qquad [div(p, q) = div(p - q, q) + div(q, q) \;!]$$

Thus we can extract an executable expression - to use as the body of a function implementation:

```
div(p, q) ≜ if p<q then 0
                   else if p=q then 1
                               else 1 + div(p - q, q)
                        fi
            fi
```

Let's just illustrate this by means of two specimen evaluations.

$$\begin{aligned} div(14, 3) &= 1 + div(11, 3) \\ &= 2 + div(8, 3) \\ &= 3 + div(5, 3) \\ &= 4 + div(2, 3) \\ &= 4 \end{aligned}$$

and

$$\begin{aligned} div(4, 2) &= 1 + div(2, 2) \\ &= 1 + 1 \\ &= 2 \end{aligned}$$

❑

Despite some similarities with the previous example, this design is not based on problem reduction but problem decomposition. If we regard the size of the initial problem as p (with $p > q$), then we have replaced it with a combination of two smaller problems, of sizes $p - q$ and q. This worked for this problem because $div(q, q)$ gives an exact answer.

Example 0.4: Greater_than

The two preceding examples were deterministic (i.e. for each valid input - and *all* inputs of the appropriate type were valid - there was exactly one answer). This, by definition is what should happen with (the implementation of) a function. But the specification of a function (or more properly a class of functions) need not be so restrictive. It might also be the case that some input values may not yield valid results even though they are of the right type. This example illustrates both these possibilities.

First we need a description of what is required of this *greater_than* function[15].

The input and output values for this function are drawn from the type 0..10, that is the set of integers between 0 and 10 inclusive. If the function is given the value x as input and delivers the result y, then all we require is that $x<y$ should be true. Of course any particular implementation will give the same value y whenever it is presented with a specific input x. On the face of it we can therefore write

$$greater\_than(x{:}0..10) \triangleq y{:}0..10 \mid x<y$$

A few minutes thought will reveal potential problems with this "definition". Given the x value 7, *greater_than*(x) could deliver 8 or 9 or 10 as valid answers. Similarly, *greater_than*(5) should deliver one of the values 6 or 7 or 8 or 9 or 10, but which? Well, from the given requirement we really don't care - providing that we always get the same answer every time we try the same evaluation. What is

[15] This is *not* the function which takes two numbers and delivers the value True if the first is 'greater than' the second.

more worrying is what do we do with greater_than(10)? There is *no* value in the set 0..10 which is greater than 10 so no answer is possible, the computation is impossible and we would have best been advised never to have tried to carry it out. So we need to include, as part of the specification, some proviso which tells us that 10 is not a good input value.

You might regard this as a strange example when compared with the others. True, it doesn't really have a nice formula[16] associated with it but in many ways it is more typical of (under specified) computations which are carried out by programs. Even though there is some scope for variation in the way that the above problems can be programmed, all the program designs will be 'similar'. Here there is much room for diversity.

Although we shall soon be able to write the necessary information in a much more systematic way, let us first include the relevant conditions in the description.

$$greater\_than(x{:}0..10 \mid x<10) \triangleq y{:}0..10 \mid x<y$$

i.e. given a value x of type 0..10, which is less than 10, deliver a value y, of the same type such that x<y.

Now we give a few of the possible, correct, implementation schemes:

$$greater\_than(x) \triangleq x + 1$$

$$greater\_than(x) \triangleq 10$$

$$greater\_than(x) \triangleq \text{ if } x<5 \text{ then } x + 2 \text{ else } x + 1 \text{ fi}$$

```
greater_than(x) ≜ if x = 0 then 9
                       else if x = 2 then 3
                                 else if x = 7 then 9
                                           else 10
                                 fi
                       fi
                  fi
```

Of course there may be many different ways a certain function can be implemented. There is also another degree of variability which follows from having intentional (logically) weak specification, such as that given above for *greater_than*. In general we specify sets of functions, each of which will adequately fulfil the needs of a particular requirement.

[16] A formula which tells how to compute y directly from a given x.

0.8 The Book Plan

Procedural programs - such as programs written in Pascal, or C, or C++, or Java - are the most common; they are also the most difficult to verify, i.e. to prove that they actually satisfy their specifications - that they ***never*** give wrong answers. Other, less well-known programming paradigms (ways of expressing the computations to be undertaken) are much easier to verify and that is why they are so important in serious programming.

Adopting a fairly traditional approach to programming, even with these more esoteric kind of languages, still requires something to be proved if we are to guarantee correctness - and proofs are ***hard*** - hence the reason why program verification is seldom carried out by practitioners. The overall approach underpinning the development method presented here hides many of the proofs. It uses calculations and 'checks' but is, nevertheless, proper.

Program development is concerned with the constructing of a program that will run using an available language/machine combination and which can ***be shown to carry out the desired calculation***. These 'calculations' include all situations where the answer can be derived/deduced from the input data by manipulation; so they include sorting, file updating etc., and are certainly not restricted to numerical computations. In fact these numerical programs are of little general interest in Computing Science.

Our prime concern is correctness (at the procedural level) and factors such as efficiency and optimisation are only considered to a very limited extent - they are *important* but are *secondary* to correctness; a 'small', 'fast' program which is wrong is easy to write but utterly useless.

How the various components and processes fit together is shown in Figure 0.1. Here, the demarcation line, between the customer and the software engineer comes at the level of formal specifications. This means that 'testing' (which includes exercising, rapid prototyping etc.) should be targeted at getting the initial description as near 'correct' as possible before investing software engineering effort to build a proper, a more acceptable, program *from* this description.

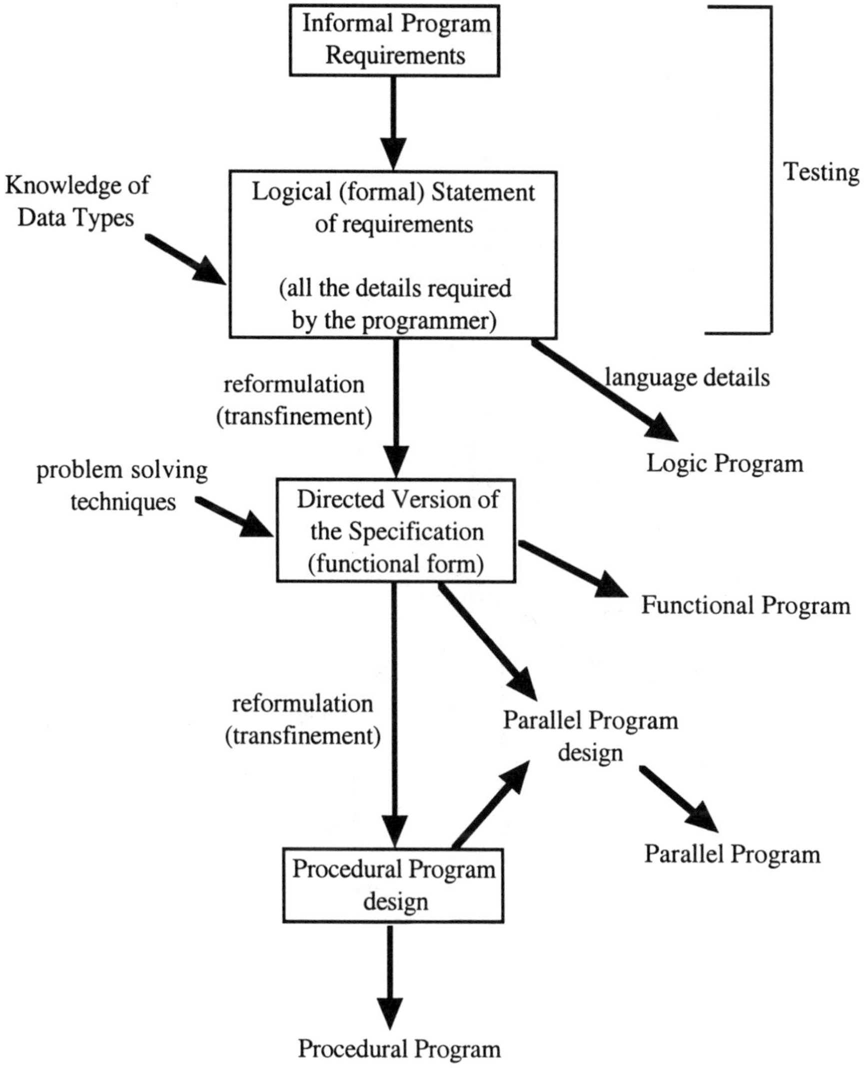

Figure 0.1

One activity which occurs twice in the scheme is 'transfinement'. Although this means the same as the more commonly used term 'refinement', we choose to use this new term (derived from 'refinement' and 'transformation') to emphasise the technical differences between transformations - which are reversible - and strict refinement or reduction, which is not reversible and generally indicates a loss of information or the rejection of certain alternatives. The word 'reification' is also sometimes, and more properly, used instead of refinement; it means "to make more 'like stone' ", more firm, more deterministic, in this context, more like a program.

How do we translate this scheme into a programme of study, into the chapters of a book? The master plan is set out in Figure 0.2.

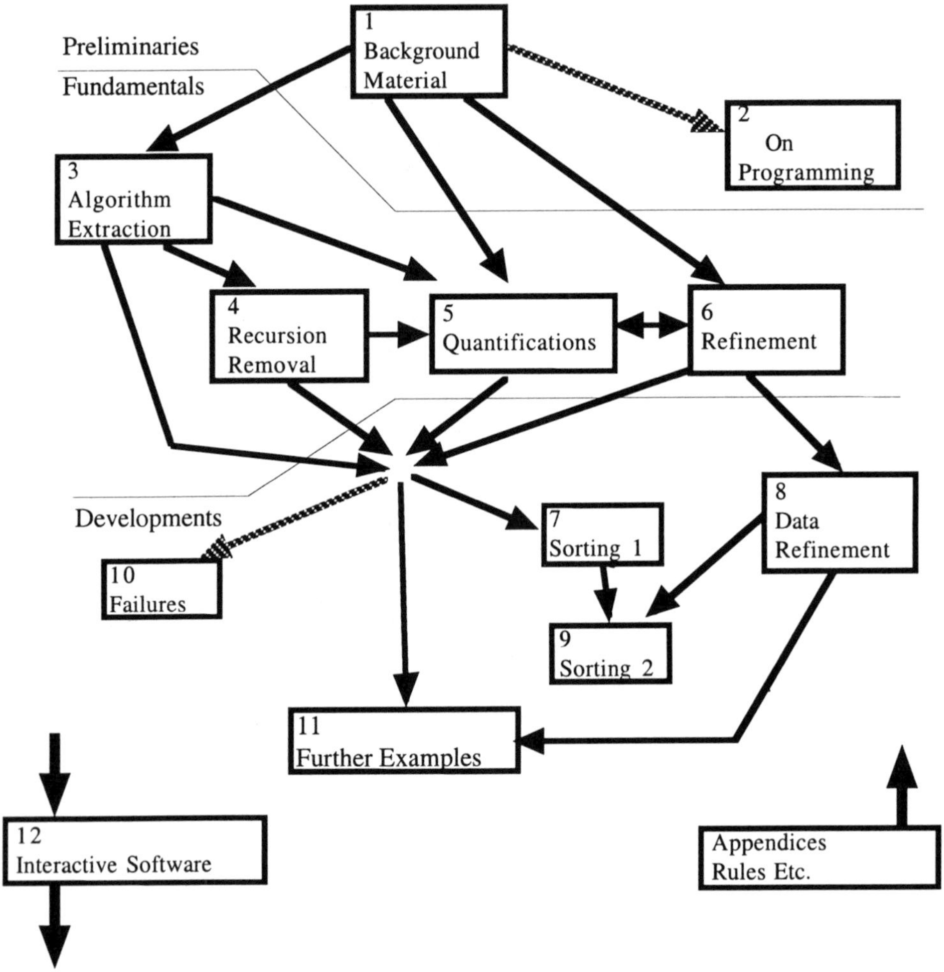

Figure 0.2

Before we can begin with the main task of program generation we must introduce appropriate technical 'machinery'. We do this in Chapter 1, and start by introducing the way in which we present specifications - these say what are the *essential* properties of the calculation which we are required to perform. A specification tells us *what* has to be done, not *how* it can be achieved, and here no *changes* are specified. It begins with explaining the various components necessary to specify a function[17]. These kinds of specifications are expressed as a relation between an input (a single value) and an output (again a single value). However, these values may be of arbitrarily complicated *types* - exactly in the same way that complex data types can be built within high-level programming languages - and so the inputs and outputs are not as restricted as they might first appear. We therefore move on to define the basic data types and constructors for building more complex types from already existing ones. This is done by giving sets of legal algebraic transformations[18] that can be applied to expressions involving data values of these types - expressions which can then form part of our specifications. How new rules may be derived is covered, as is the proper justification of how the rules are applied to transform expressions so as to preserve their value.

Although detailed manipulations will eventually be necessary, we discuss most of these types and constructors in outline only. More extensive rule sets are given in the appendices for subsequent reference.

[It is essential that the reader is familiar with the possibility and practice of rearranging information into a required form - and doing it within the 'rules of the game' i.e. algebraically. Remember we eventually want to be able to calculate a program from a specification and to do this, as with any other calculation, we need to be able to perform the calculations for ourselves before even entertaining the possibility of computer-assisted mechanisation.]

Chapter 2, which can be skipped without interrupting the main flow of the presentation, discusses traditional wisdoms about programming and established formal approaches which link programs with formal specifications.

This material, some of which can fruitfully integrated with the subject matter of later chapters, is included here in order to illustrate and emphasize the alternative stance adopted in Chapter 3 - Chapter 2 is, in part , retrospective; Chapter 3 seeks to be constructive. Having said this, there are some sections which might seem out of place; there is no clear dividing line.

Chapter 3 contains the pivotal material of this book. It deals with the first part of the LFP sequence of programming paradigms; it covers the introduction of recursion, and the formalisation of various problem solving strategies which help us in constructing these recursive designs for solutions. The end products of this

[17] In fact we specify non-empty sets of functions, any one of which will adequately deliver acceptable results.

[18] The transformation rules associated with the data types covered in Chapter 1 may also be thought of as specifications of those types, algebraic specifications. So as not to confuse and overload this word we shall try to avoid using it in this way.

chapter are procedural programs which embody function calls, usually recursive functions, and no loops. [The notion of (loop) invariants, commonly found in other books on formal methods and discussed briefly in Chapter 2, is hidden - it is still there of course but is not *needed.*]

Adopting a purely constructive approach to producing an implementation of a function often involves considerable amounts of very detailed calculation and manipulation. Having seen how a function - a calculation - can be specified and how we are allowed to manipulate the expressions within the specification, we are now in a position to 'twist' and (legally) 'trim' the specification into an executable form which can be used as a program design which, by construction, will be consistent with the specification; we *calculate* a program design from the specification of a function. To do this usually requires much detailed manipulation. Although such detail cannot be avoided, it need not subsequently be *repeated.* There are two major ways to handle this. One is by 'checking' the correctness of a result which is thought to be 'obvious'; this is introduced in Chapter 3; the other, component reuse, is considered in Chapter 6. Examples of this technique - essentially simple instances of retrospective verification carried out by evaluation of appropriate expressions - are to be found in various places throughout the remainder of the text.

Although the construction process can be used in different ways it is perhaps best to regard it initially as evolving the structure of software in a top-down fashion. One way to visualise this is to consider that, starting from a single 'black box' which contains a specification, we replace it either by a segment of executable code, or by a (structured) flowchart which includes lower level specification boxes. By virtue of the rules used, each replacement is 'correct' and the development of each box can be done independently (independent of other boxes but sensitive to its own context and thus using properties of the data values which arise from preceding computations).

Having derived (calculated, computed) a correct recursive program might not be enough in some situations. It could be that the target language which we have to use for implementation does not support recursion. In Chapter 4 we present a way of transforming certain common forms of recursion into familiar looping commands.

[The reader who is unhappy with the thought of recursion introduction can read Chapter 4 *before* Chapter 3 and (hopefully) convince himself that the recursions which are introduced can, usually, subsequently be removed. But using these intermediate recursive forms and deferring iteration, allows us to avoid side-effects and the notion of values which change as the program is executed.]

Prompted by the possibility of extracting program designs from certain forms of 'specification'[19] Chapter 5 returns briefly to the subject of specifications. This also means that we can fill a few gaps in the formal descriptions encountered (and admitted) earlier. We look at certain forms of specification which readily lend themselves to more immediate extraction of program designs; thus we can take bigger steps in the synthesis process (but here there is a price to pay, namely having less possibility of exploiting features which occur to the current situation but not in general). These forms not only include the logical quantifiers "for all" and "there exists" and their generalisation to other data types but also the extension of unary and binary functions to act on collections of data items. To benefit from these 'big' rules often requires substantial reformulation of the initial specification and may be regarded as seeking a more abstract representation.

When using transformation rules all the manipulations are reversible. However it is not uncommon for us not to need all the information presented to us and hence selections can be made and here the manipulations are generally not reversible. Technically we move on to the topic of refinement (or reduction) which is addressed in Chapter 6. Principally there are two kinds of refinement, operational refinement and data refinement. Here we present operational refinement which deals with the removal of alternative ways of processing data without altering the set of valid inputs. It might seem strange to start off with a non-deterministic specification of a function - the implementation of which, by definition, *has* to be deterministic. That is a fair observation, but we often introduce intermediate calculations and, so as to delay design decisions as long as possible, the specification of *these* can be non-deterministic. This chapter also discusses the possibility of re-use and puts in a formal context; essentially we ask whether a design which satisfies one specification can be used to satisfy another.

In Chapter 7 we apply many of the transfinement techniques to the familiar - and important, easy to understand but non-trivial - problem of sorting. This chapter is extensive and includes much detailed manipulation of large expressions. It is important to emphasise that although such *expressions* (intermediate representations of program segments) are long, the actual changes between one version and the next are often very small. As a consequence, the presentation of a handful of simple manipulations often takes up several pages. So don't take these transformation sequences at face value. In particular, don't be put off by the length of some of the derivation sequences.

In Chapter 8 we deal Data Refinement. Essentially this addresses the possibilities of using (internal) data types different from those used in the specification - either input/output types or within the pre- or post-conditions.

[19] Later we shall refer to certain 'specifications' as 'designs' so as not be thought to be *changing* a specification.

We illustrate data refinement, data transformation, data structure replacement by returning (in Chapter 9) to the topic of sorting. Although we make no pretence that this is a book on data structures, we are able to draw out some useful comparisons between the use of different structures in certain situations.

Of course, not all tactics are applicable to any given problem. In Chapter 10 we discuss how the key tactics might fail and how they can be made to succeed. The price paid to 'fix' the failure involves retaining more data than might strictly be necessary. We briefly consider the removal of (some of) this data, and generally try to store the necessary data more efficiently.

As noted earlier, we are not concerned with large, complicated and very specialised calculations (problems) as such but with explaining how to process a specification which you may be given. Having said this, it is often useful to interact with a customer to clarify the problem/specification and express it in a mutually acceptable form. Chapter 11 includes two further large examples. Although these are much less familiar then sorting, they are easy to understand (and can be explained graphically) and further illustrate important aspects of algorithm synthesis in areas perhaps unfamiliar to most readers. The chapter also includes a brief section on some common classes of problems to which formal techniques have been applied and which have served as a sounding board for the development of formal methods.

Finally we have two stand alone modules, Chapter 12 and the Appendix. Chapter 12 essentially describes (the building of) bridges between the computation of functions and other activities undertaken by software and software systems. Our order of presentation means the notion of a variable changing value could be deferred until very late in the construction process, initially we had only to reason about constant (but unknown) values. We can easily easily extend the work of Chapter 1 to handle the *specification* of operations which necessitate changes of state; and this includes conventional input/output operations.

But the development of a software system does not *start* with the specification of the operations that it might perform but from a statement of the requirements that it should meet. To do this we need new logical forms with which to state these requirements and another level of design (between requirements and specifications), and associated notions of refinement etc. We cannot deal with these topics in this book but we include a brief discussion of the ideas which need to be considered within the formal synthesis of software *systems*.

The Appendix comprises a collection of the more important mathematical rules so that the reader can cross-reference from elsewhere in the text. These include transformation rules for manipulating program segments. They can be applied like other rules but their derivation (justification) is not included.

Part A
Preliminaries

Here we present, in some detail, because detailed working will be necessary later, the common underlying structure of expressions that are found both in mathematics and in programs. This also allows us to introduce a unified notational framework which is used for all these expressions. The reader with an appropriate background may defer detailed study of this part, merely checking that he is familiar with the notation and reading individual sections in detail only when he feels the need to fill in, reinforce or revise specific topics.

Chapter 1
The Technical Background

1.0 Introduction

Computationally, we are concerned here with any segment of code which carries out a calculation and is executed *between* successive state changes (often in the guise of input or output instructions). Performing a calculation is synonymous with evaluating a function. Mathematically, a function is something that generates a *unique* result from each acceptable data value. Regarded as a complete program, it should be possible in principle to read all the required input into some 'variable' called x, evaluate $f(x)$ — spoken "f of x" — and then 'write' the answer. Throughout Chapters 1 to 11, we shall only be concerned with the second of these three phases. In particular, within the *specifications*, we will not be interested in any *changes* of value. Most of our reasoning will involve values which are constant but unknown.

So, computationally, an entire program can be regarded as a single assignment statement such as $y \leftarrow f(x)$, where x represents all the data, y all the results (distinct from x and initially undefined, and hence this assignment is more properly an initialisation of y, not a change or update) but f is perhaps not yet known explicitly.

The purpose of this chapter is to lay down the mathematical framework that is required in order to make our program constructions well-founded. In essence, what we shall do is produce a program by performing mathematical manipulations upon a formal specification of that program. To a reader with experience of modern mathematics, particularly algebra, most of this lengthy chapter should be plain sailing. However, one must be familiar with our terminology and notation. Sections (and corresponding parts of the appendix) which are skipped may need to be consulted later when detailed mathematical manipulations are undertaken in subsequent chapters.

Initially, we try to avoid large amounts of detailed manipulation — though it will be needed later — by introducing general concepts and giving a few instances; further details can be found in the appendix.

In Section 1.1, we introduce functions, since functions are what programs compute, and (binary) relations, since these will be used to specify functions. Also included are details of the special notations we shall use to define specifications. Implicit within these topics is the notion of a set. We shall use set notation but avoid lots of technical detail. Here sets are merely collections of relevant items that can be used as data and results of functions. Later, in Section 1.2, we shall extend these sets into types (as found in programming languages) and define them by giving the rules which can be used in manipulating descriptive expressions; these manipulations form the basis of logical reasoning to justify that what we are doing is legal and defensible. As will be apparent from this attempt at describing the technical contents of this chapter, we really need *all* these ideas before we can start to describe *any* of them. Hence there will be parts of the development which may not be fully clear until later notions have been encountered. Please be patient — to make the explanations completely, mathematically, water-tight would be to render it extremely difficult for the newcomer to read.

Finally, in Section 1.3, we shall give a few examples and illustrations of what we can do with the mathematical machinery we have introduced.

But first we make a few points concerning the need to pay attention to detail and clarity in what we write, in English or mathematics.

The Need for Clarity

Computer Scientists (like pure mathematicians) are often accused of interpreting language too literally. Whilst this often causes annoyance if used in inappropriate circumstances, the subject of formal logic — which embraces the formal methods of software construction — is one area where it *should* always be applied. Everything we say about a piece of software should be capable of only one interpretation, so ambiguity and unintended and unnecessary lack of precision has to be avoided. Initial requirements and specifications of software often arise from a non-computing context and are prone to imprecision. Before we can start constructing software, we need an agreed and sufficiently precise description of what is wanted. This is more properly the concern of a Requirements Engineer, but the dividing line[1] is very unclear. Suffice it to say that if through consultation with the customer — the person for whom you are developing the software — you can identify and resolve misunderstandings and vagaries, then we can save much wasted time and effort. It serves nobody well to spend time solving the wrong problem or building the wrong system. We must also avoid over-specification and not include any unnecessary constraints.

[1] Between requirements and a specification.

We do allow non-determinism and intended vagueness where detail does not matter (i.e., don't be more specific than necessary; allow for choice and variation when possible).

In a very simplistic way, this can be identified with the sloppy use of natural language. Below we give some 'silly' examples. They are silly because we can easily see what the problem is. In extensive textual descriptions of software requirements (which may occupy many pages or even volumes of detailed explanations), similar situations will not be so obvious. Indeed, such lengthy descriptions may be so long that *nobody* ever reads them fully and hence they may be a complete waste of time. What we need are descriptions that tell us all we need to know in as concise a fashion as possible. The following examples illustrate inexact statements and questions which can be resolved either by more careful use of English (or any other natural language, but we shall use English) or by using a more stylised, more formal and mathematical, representation.

> Did it rain in Trafalgar Square on January 1st 1997, or not?

Regardless of how we define 'is raining', the answer to this question is always "yes" since it either did rain or it did not, and thus the question is of no use. The question which should have been asked was:

> Did it rain in Trafalgar Square on January 1st 1997?

The answer "yes" tells us that it did indeed rain, and the answer "no" that it did not.

Now look at the following. It is a notice that used to appear in a local cafeteria.

<u>TRAY SYSTEM</u>

PLEASE DO NOT REMOVE
YOUR MEAL FROM THE TRAY
PLEASE PUT THE TRAY ON TO THE
CONVEYOR AFTER YOUR MEAL

THANK YOU

You really can have some fun with this. How can you eat a meal without removing it from the tray? (Is the meal the same as the food?) If you put the tray onto the conveyor after your meal, does this imply that you have already put your meal onto the conveyor? (And the meal is still on the tray, remember.) Can you devise an unambiguous (punctuated!) directive which defines a possible and sensible course of action?

Proper punctuation is very important. If it helps to disambiguate a sentence and bind some parts of it more strongly together, you can employ brackets.

Now consider the use of the same linguistic construct in two different contexts. If you ride a motorcycle, then you must abide by the instruction

> "Helmets must be worn."

When travelling on the London Underground, you will see the sign

> "Dogs must be carried on the escalator."

Clearly the word "must' is used in a different way; other, unstated assumptions come into play. Can you imagine the chaos that would ensue if you had to find a dog to carry before you stepped onto an escalator, or you were to be excused from wearing a helmet when riding your motor cycle simply because you didn't have one?

The fix is quite easy; you merely need to change the second instruction to

> "When on the escalator, if you have a dog with you then it should be carried."

You will doubtless be able to think of many other situations which include logical nonsense or rely upon unstated assumptions in order to make sense. As we introduce more mathematically descriptive notations, you should be able to re-express them in formal, and concise, terms which encapsulate the essential information in a compact fashion. It is crucially important that all statements about software only have one interpretation, which can be clearly and quickly(?) deduced by all those who need to consult it.

The drawing up of specifications (and requirements) is *not* the concern of the current text; it is, however, necessary that appropriate specifications be available to us *before* we embark on the construction of software. Our principal aim is to build software that is correct with reference to a given specification (or a statement of requirements), that no errors are *introduced* as the software artefacts are engineered.

Intentionally, most of our examples are simple so that we don't have to spend much time investigating the problem but can concentrate on deriving solutions.

The techniques presented are applicable to problems which are more complicated[2] (harder to describe) and perhaps presented in a textual form. Whenever such (potentially ambiguous, incomplete, or just plain wrong) descriptions are given, you must spend time ascertaining what is really meant and, perhaps in negotiation with its originator, modify them as necessary so that they mean exactly what was intended. Ultimately, using notations similar to those to be found in the sequel, you should be able to express these descriptions in a formal ('mathematical') fashion susceptible to manipulation and computation.

1.1 Functions, Relations and Specifications

These three entities are introduced in an order that is convenient to us. It is not the conventional order in which they would be presented in a mathematical text, and we only include directly relevant material. Remember that although our presentation is necessarily much more formal than that found in other areas of computing, this is not a maths text.

The fundamental property of a function is that, given an acceptable input value, it delivers a *unique* result. Pictorially, skating over other details, we *cannot* have the situation represented in Figure 1.1:

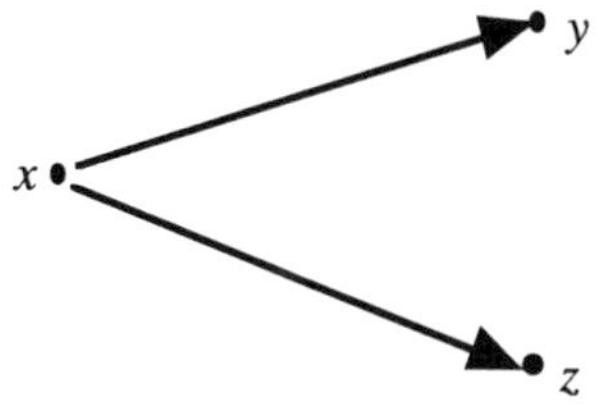

Figure 1.1

So, if f is a *function* and we are told that y is a value of $f(x)$ and also that z is a value of $f(x)$, then it must be the case that y and z are actually the same.

[2] In much the same way that structured programming was initially thought by many programmers to be applicable only to certain classes of 'nice' ('toy'?) problems, you may think that these statements apply only to a restricted collection of problems. This is not so, but to apply what we have to say to more complex problems does require that you understand such problems much more deeply than when using less formal, less scientific, less mathematical methods. Formal methods bring any lack of understanding to the fore.

Making sure that we don't have situations like that above, the full picture for f might be:

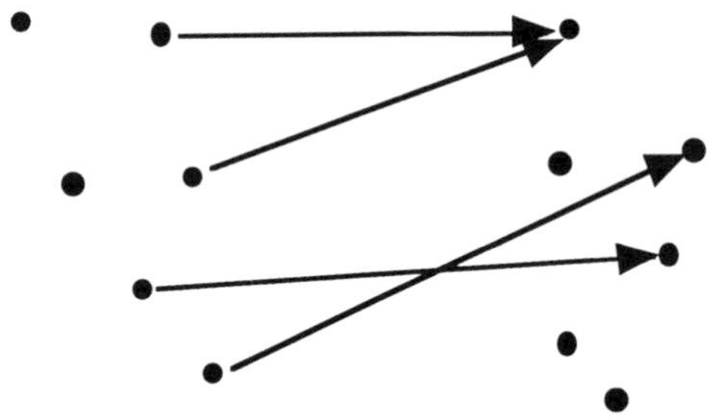

Figure 1.2

We draw all the arrows from right to left. This in itself is not important but what in general *is* important is that we can distinguish the values which can be placed at the start of an arrow (the input values) and those at the sharp end (result values). Notice that two arrows might point to the same result, and not all of the data points or result points are necessarily used.

Other kinds of diagram are sometimes used, as we shall see. Here, so as not to mix up data and results, we often enclose the two sets (yes sets) of values in non-overlapping closed curves such as ovals, as in Figure 1.3. [If the same value is required as both an input and output, then we make two copies and put one in the input set and one in the output set.]

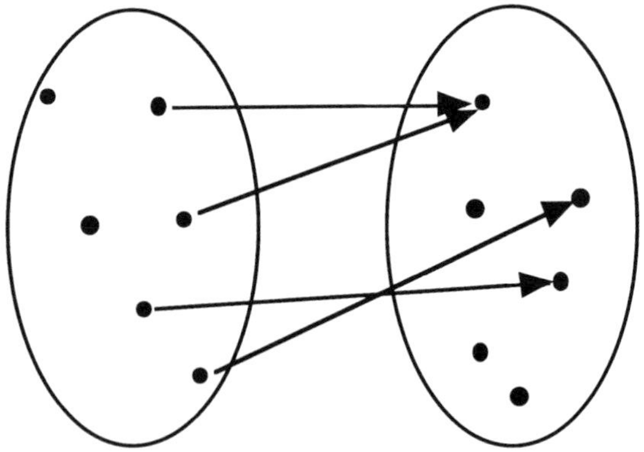

Figure 1.3

For the function *f* to be consistent with a specification, the specification must include all the 'arrows' of *f* but might also have many others. The specification of a function is in fact a ***binary relation***[3]. As far as we are concerned, this can be regarded as a generalisation of a function. (Of course we shall want eventually to start with the relation and reduce it to a function, but more on that later. Here we are only introducing concepts, terminology and notation — if the pictures make sense, all is well).

[Note that many programming languages have a so-called 'random' function which can apparently give different results. Of course it does not give random results at all but is driven by input values that are hidden from us, and for each input it gives the same result every time.]

So, the ***specification*** of a function is a binary relation which may be represented by *arrows* as in Figure 1.4. So as to make it easier to talk about the arrows, we now label the input (data) set and output (results) set. Suppose that we use the names *X* and *Y* for the sets in this example.

Although the relation (the arrows) in Figure 1.4 could be reversed — by simply turning all the arrows around — to give a perfectly valid relation, the direction is usually important; we want to derive results from data values, not vice versa.

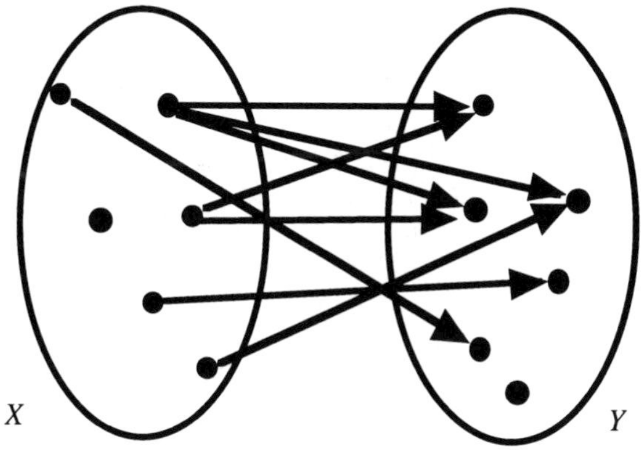

Figure 1.4

[3] We make no distinction between specifications and binary relations. Associated terminology can be interchanged. The word "binary" simply indicates that there are two sets involved, *X* and *Y* in Figure 1.4.

Now consider Figure 1.5.

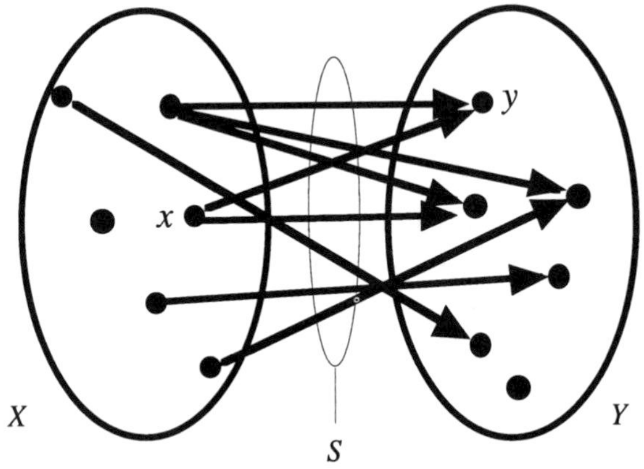

Figure 1.5

Stand by for a blast of terminology and notation.

- The arrow, from x to y, is represented by an ordered pair, written $\langle x,y \rangle$ (spoken as "the pair x,y" or simply "x y").
- The set of all possible arrows between X and Y is written as $X \times Y$ (this is the ***Cartesian product*** of X and Y, and is spoken "X cross Y")

So $\langle x,y \rangle \in X \times Y$ (i.e. "the 'arrow' x,y is an ***element*** of the set X cross Y"), and therefore $x \in X$ and $y \in Y$.

Now the specification S, as shown on Figure 1.5, is simply a collection of arrows in $X \times Y$. Hence we can also write

$S \subseteq X \times Y$. (that is "S is a ***subset***[4] of $X \times Y$")

Although we can represent certain ideas and principles using pictures (diagrams), most actual cases involve very large sets, and hence we can never adequately represent the situation in all its detail by a picture. In principle, we could define a particular specification by writing down all the arrows (all the ordered pairs) that it contained. Some relations, for instance the relations that are held in a relational database, *have* to be represented in this way. Within software requirements and specifications, it is more often the case, and it is much more convenient, to define a relation, S (say), by a test (a condition, a predicate) so that the pair $\langle x,y \rangle$ satisfies the test exactly when $\langle x,y \rangle \in S$.

[4] i.e. all the elements of S are also elements of $X \times Y$.

We have one last link to put into place before we can write down some proper examples of specifications. Notice that "$\langle x,y \rangle \in S$" is a mathematical expression which may either be True or False. [The values "true" and "false" are of particular importance and, so as to distinguish them from normal English usage we shall, when using them mathematically, begin them with a capital letter.]

$\langle x,y \rangle \in S$ is True if S *does* contain the arrow $\langle x,y \rangle$.

$\langle x,y \rangle \in S$ is False if S *does not* contain the arrow $\langle x,y \rangle$.

This second case can also be written:

$\langle x,y \rangle \notin S$ (spoken "x,y is not (an element) in S").

In certain situations, we wish to indicate that an element *is*, by definition, included in a given set. Indeed, this is a way of introducing a new identifier, a named value. Referring back to Figure 1.5, instead of asking whether x was an element of X (i.e., if $x \in X$ is True), we could write $x{:}X$ and say "*x is* of type X". This fits with the common usage of this syntax in many programming languages and, as we shall see in Section 1.2, a type *is* a set (together with some extra machinery).

In much the same way as ":" is used to identify the type of a new value or name, we can use "$\triangleq$" (an equals symbol together with the Greek capital delta) to indicate that a new name *is,* by definition, equal to some known value; the value possibly indicated by an expression. We can now introduce the notation associated with the concept of a set, already mentioned informally in passing. Sets can be defined in several ways, and here we shall use two. Firstly, a (small) set can be defined *explicitly*; for example:

$A \triangleq \{1,2,3,5,7,9\}$ All the elements of the set are written out.

"*A* is (defined to be) the set (of all the numbers) 1,2,3,5,7 and 9."

Similarly, let B be defined by:

$B \triangleq \{1,2,4,6,8\}$

Then we can define T, *implicitly*, by

$T \triangleq \{\langle x,y \rangle{:}A \times B \mid x < y\}$

"*T* is the set of all x,y pairs (of type $A \times B$) such that ('|') $x<y$."

Following on from these definitions we can write $A \times B$ and T explicitly:

$$\begin{array}{lllllll}
A \times B \text{ is the set } \{ & \langle 1,1\rangle, & \langle 2,1\rangle, & \langle 3,1\rangle, & \langle 5,1\rangle, & \langle 7,1\rangle, & \langle 9,1\rangle, \\
 & \langle 1,2\rangle, & \langle 2,2\rangle, & \langle 3,2\rangle, & \langle 5,2\rangle, & \langle 7,2\rangle, & \langle 9,2\rangle, \\
 & \langle 1,4\rangle, & \langle 2,4\rangle, & \langle 3,4\rangle, & \langle 5,4\rangle, & \langle 7,4\rangle, & \langle 9,4\rangle, \\
 & \langle 1,6\rangle, & \langle 2,6\rangle, & \langle 3,6\rangle, & \langle 5,6\rangle, & \langle 7,6\rangle, & \langle 9,6\rangle, \\
 & \langle 1,8\rangle, & \langle 2,8\rangle, & \langle 3,8\rangle, & \langle 5,8\rangle, & \langle 7,8\rangle, & \langle 9,8\rangle \}
\end{array}$$

and

$$\begin{array}{llllll}
T \text{ is the set } \{ & & & & & \\
 & \langle 1,2\rangle, & & & & \\
 & \langle 1,4\rangle, & \langle 2,4\rangle, & \langle 3,4\rangle, & & \\
 & \langle 1,6\rangle, & \langle 2,6\rangle, & \langle 3,6\rangle, & \langle 5,6\rangle, & \\
 & \langle 1,8\rangle, & \langle 2,8\rangle, & \langle 3,8\rangle, & \langle 5,8\rangle, & \langle 7,8\rangle \quad \}
\end{array}$$

or, in a more usual, but perhaps less comprehensible, form[5]:

$$\{ \langle 1,2\rangle, \langle 1,4\rangle, \langle 2,4\rangle, \langle 3,4\rangle, \langle 1,6\rangle ; \langle 2,6\rangle, \langle 3,6\rangle, \\ \langle 5,6\rangle, \langle 1,8\rangle, \langle 2,8\rangle, \langle 3,8\rangle, \langle 5,8\rangle, \langle 7,8\rangle \}$$

Notice that the relation T, and in fact *any* relation, is also a set. Notice also that the implicit form is usually much more compact and will be more suitable for 'manipulation' than the explicit form.

Although not yet expressed in the usual form for a specification, we now have all the essential information. The general form of a (***binary***) ***relation*** between A and B looks like:

$$\{\langle x,y\rangle : A \times B \mid p(x,y)\}$$

where p is a ***predicate***, here written as an expression involving x and y. This is required to evaluate to True or False for *all* values $x{:}A$ and $y{:}B$ (for all values x of type A and values y of type B). So p is really a decision procedure, and within a relation used as a specification, it is exactly *the* decision procedure that we would need to test "whether y is an acceptable result from the input x".

Gradually, we want to formalise expressions so that they are properly structured (their syntax is well-defined) and all components are of acceptable types. The predicate p used above has a function type. The inputs to p are of the type $A \times B$ and its outputs are drawn from the set {True, False}. The set {True, False} has a special name, the Booleans, and is denoted by the symbol $\mathbb{B}$. The type information for p can then be represented as:

$$p{:}\ A \times B \to \mathbb{B}$$

The "→" is spoken as "to" so p is of type "A cross B to Boolean".

[5] A layout which helps you see the real structure of data, or of an expression, can be very useful. Just like 'pretty printing' program texts.

[Lest we forget to include all relevant type information, we give here the notation and terminology associated with relations. Most relations that we shall encounter will be binary relations, and hence we shall not explicitly mention that fact.

$\mathcal{P}(A)$ is defined to be the set of all subsets of (the set or type) A and is called the ***powerset*** of A, so

$$x \in \mathcal{P}(A) \text{ is the same as } x \subseteq A.$$

Now if X and Y are given types, T, a relation between X and Y (in that order) we indicate its type by:

T: $\mathcal{P}(X \times Y)$

"T is of type 'powerset of X cross Y' ", or more simply,
"T is a subset of $X \times Y$", or even
"T is a relation between X and Y"

— but remember that this is *type* information.

Without the type of any entity, we do not know what operations/functions can be applied to it.]

Now for a few simple numerical examples. For these we introduce the (local) types X and Y and assume the usual, as yet unjustified, properties of numbers.

$X \triangleq \{1,2,3,4\}$
$Y \triangleq \{1,2,3,4,5,6\}$

Consider the following three binary relations (specifications):

$R_1 \triangleq \{\langle x,y \rangle : X \times Y \mid x = y + 1\}$
$R_2 \triangleq \{\langle x,y \rangle : X \times Y \mid x - 1 < y \leq x + 1\}$
$R_3 \triangleq \{\langle x,y \rangle : Y \times Y \mid x = y + 1\}$

These are all very straightforward and simple, and are subtly different. To illustrate and emphasize the differences we shall introduce another kind of diagram — similar to the traditional graphs used to depict functions of a real variable. This will also serve as a vehicle to introduce more terminology.

In relation R_1, the input value, x, is of type X. X is the ***source*** of R_1 (the set from which input values may be selected). Similarly, Y is the ***target*** of R_1 (the set of potential results). It is important to know that, even if these sets are the same as one another, different source and target sets can give rise to different relations even when the 'same formula' is used in the definition.

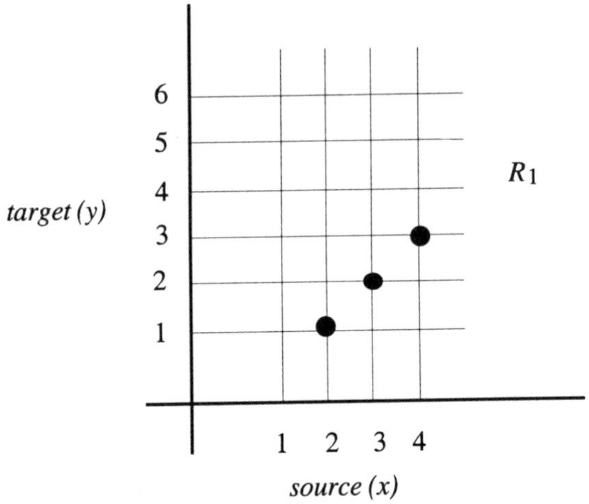

Figure 1.6

The interpretation of Figure 1.6 is quite straightforward. The dot at the intersection of lines representing $x = 2$ and $y = 1$ represents the arrow from 2 to 1 and indicates that $\langle 2,1 \rangle \in R_1$.

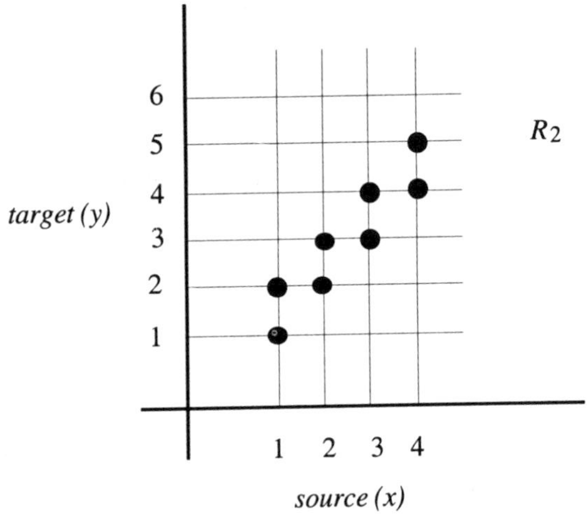

Figure 1.7

$$R_2 \triangleq \{\langle x,y \rangle : X \times Y \mid x - 1 < y \leq x + 1\}$$

Notice that this relation is not a function since $\langle 2,2 \rangle \in R_2$ and $\langle 2,3 \rangle \in R_2$ but $2 \neq 3$, (see Figure 1.7).

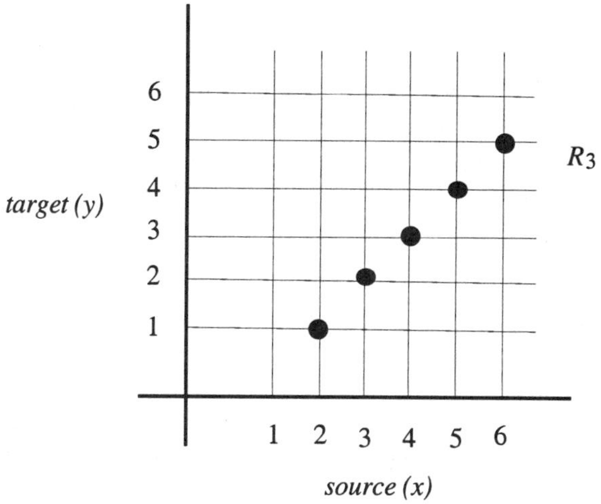

Figure 1.8

$R_3 \triangleq \{\langle x,y \rangle : X \times Y \mid x = y + 1\}$

Notice that R_3 (in Figure 1.8) is not the same as R_1. Even though the same 'formula' is used in both relations[6]. Their targets are different and hence their types are different.

So much for specifications purely as relations. Computationally, we wish to proceed from left to right (as in Figure 1.5), from input to output, and we need to avoid taking a source value *x* and failing to find any '*x* to *y*' pair in the relation. Therefore, we shall want to take notice of the direction of the arrows. To make the distinction, we must first identify the set of all source values which *do* correspond to a proper connection within the (binary) relation. This is called the ***domain*** of the relation. The domain of *R*, denoted by $\mathcal{D}_R$ and read as "the domain of *R*", might be thought of as:

$$\mathcal{D}_R \triangleq \{x:X \mid \langle x,y \rangle \in R\} \qquad \text{where } R:\mathbb{P}(X \times Y)$$

(i.e., the set of all possible values, *x*, in *X*, such that there is an *x y* "arrow" in *R*)

This is basically right, but *y* seems to have just materialised out of thin air. Is *y* a new value, a new name, or has it been introduced somewhere else? What would we assume if such a construction appeared within a program? Actually, what we want to say is that *y* is an appropriate value from the target set *Y* and is a new name.

[6] These two relations are in fact functions — no point in the source corresponds to more than one point in the target. Another way of representing the point-to-point connections in a function is by using ***maplets*** as i.e., $R_3 = \{ 2 \mapsto 1, 3 \mapsto 2, 4 \mapsto 3, 5 \mapsto 4, 6 \mapsto 5 \}$.

Even if another y exists, this one is *new*. In programming terms, its scope is "| .... }" and it does not exist outside of these symbols, and within them it *hides* any other y which might have been introduced earlier. This is a notation from logic that corresponds exactly to this familiar concept of scope from block-structured programming languages. Fuller explanations will be given later; for now this is simply helping to describe what the y is all about.

$$\mathcal{D}_R \triangleq \{x{:}X \mid (\exists y{:}Y)(\langle x,y\rangle \in R)\ \} \qquad \text{where } R{:}\mathcal{P}(X \times Y)$$

"The domain of R is the set of all x's (of type X) such that, for each x, *there exists* a y of type Y, '$(\exists y{:}Y)$', where the pair $\langle x,y\rangle$ is in R"

The syntax (the layout) used here will probably be strange to anyone who has not encountered formal logic. The brackets are merely to help indicate the scope in which y can be used.

$(\exists y{:}Y)\ \ (\langle x,y\rangle \in R)$ - usually written *without* the gap in the middle -

means "that there is some value of type Y, we call it 'y', such that the expression '$\langle x,y\rangle \in R$' is True".

[The logical notion of "existential quantification" (the symbol $\exists$) works in exactly the same way as local variables in block-structured programming languages — no more, no less. Here the brackets surrounding "$\langle x,y\rangle \in R$" indicate the scope of the new y, and again the layout is slightly different.]

Also defined is the mirror-image concept of the ***range*** of the relation R. This is written $\mathcal{R}_R$ and is defined:

$$\mathcal{R}_R \triangleq \{y{:}Y \mid (\exists x{:}X)(\langle x,y\rangle \in R)\ \} \qquad \text{where } R{:}\mathcal{P}(X \times Y)$$

This gives the set of all values in Y that are to be found at the pointed end of the arrows which comprise R. The relationships between these different sets are illustrated in Figure 1.9. In this figure, the relation R_1 is used as the example.

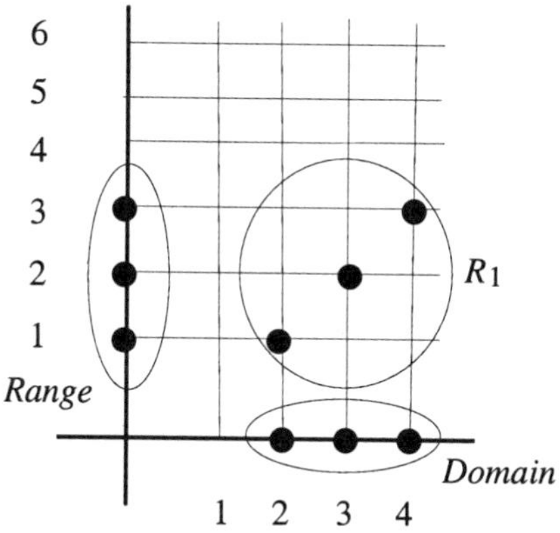

Figure 1.9

Referring to the figure and definition of R_1,

$$R_1 \triangleq \{ \langle x,y \rangle : X \times Y \mid x = y + 1 \}$$

it is clear that it is fruitless to attempt to find an answer (an answer compatible with R_1) starting from the value 1 as input. The condition that the data value x *does* 'work', i.e. that x is in the domain, is:

$$x > 1 \quad .$$

This condition, often called the ***weakest pre-condition*** and denoted by $wp(R_1)$, is the least restrictive condition upon values of the appropriate source type for which the specification includes 'answers'. Notice that this condition is derived from the relation and hence is, in some sense, 'going backwards', from output values to inputs. Whilst in general it is absolutely necessary that this condition be met — and sometimes, when it is not known from the outset exactly what this condition is, it may only become clear as software development is under way — we might use a stronger condition derived from the context in which an implementation of R_1 is to be used.

[Some asides: (1). We shall encounter situations where one function is applied after another. There is a special notation for this, and here is a convenient place to give it. "$g \circ f$" is spoken "g over f"or "g of f" and is defined by:

$$(g \circ f)(x) \triangleq g(f(x)) \qquad \text{where} \quad f : X \to Y$$
$$g : Y \to Z$$
$$\text{and} \quad \mathcal{R}_f \subseteq \mathcal{D}_g$$

We can then apply (the function) g to any result given by applying (the function) f to any value x where $x \in \mathcal{D}_f$, and hence have "g of f (of x)".

(2). Two functions, f and $g{:}X \rightarrow Y$ are equal if $\mathcal{D}_f = \mathcal{D}_g$ and $f(x) = g(x)$ for all $x \in \mathcal{D}_f$, written '$f = g$'.

(3). An important property of '$\circ$', of functional composition, is that when (say) $f{:}A \rightarrow B$, $g{:}B \rightarrow C$, and $h{:}C \rightarrow D$ and $\mathcal{R}_f \subseteq \mathcal{D}_g$ and $\mathcal{R}_g \subseteq \mathcal{D}_h$, so that when $x \in \mathcal{D}_f$, $h(g(f(x)))$ is properly defined. It follows that $(h \circ g) \circ f = h \circ (g \circ f)$. We say that functional composition is ***associative***. (We shall meet this term again in familiar circumstances.)

(4). It is also convenient here to give the definition of the graph of a function. The distinction between a function and its graph is often blurred, but here goes.

Given a function f of type $X \rightarrow Y$, the ***graph*** of f is the relation (which is of type $\mathcal{P}(X \times Y)$) consisting of the pairs $\langle x, f(x) \rangle$ for all x for which $f(x)$ exists.]

Suppose now that x, the input value for R_1, is known to be greater than 2. This is OK since "if $x > 2$ then $x > 1$" and the *wp* condition is met, but so we don't spend effort working out a result for $x = 2$ (which will never be used) we can use the relation

$$\{\langle x,y \rangle : X \times X \mid x > 2 \ \textit{and} \ x = y + 1\}$$

Of course, *and* is a logical connective, a logical operator, and we shall say much more about such things later. Here we concentrate on the bare minimum.

The values of $x > 2 \ \textit{and} \ x = y + 1$ and $x = y + 1 \ \textit{and} \ x > 2$ should surely be the same. But if we investigate the '$x = y + 1$' component first, we have gained nothing, we may have derived a value which must now be rejected (i.e., the $y = 1$ associated with $x = 2$, but $2 > 2$ is False). For the constraint on the source values to be of benefit, it must be examined *first*. In the context of a Boolean expression, we write this as:

$x > 2 \ \blacktriangle \ x = y + 1$ spoken "$x > 2$ *and_then* $x = y + 1$".

In full, this is interpreted as:

"if $x > 2$
then
if $x = y + 1$ then True else False fi[7]
else
False
fi".

[7] So as to avoid potential parsing - bracketing - problems 'fi' is used to indicate the end of the 'if then else' construction; the 'fi' indicating the end of the 'else' part of the expression.

The order of evaluation is strictly left to right and if '$x > 2$' is False then no further evaluation is done; the answer is False and the '$x = y + 1$' component is *ignored*. As will become apparent later on, an expression in this position may fail to be either True or False and hence would generate an error if we actually tried to work it out (needlessly).

So, after going around the houses and discussing the mathematical entities involved we can represent the relation

$$\{\langle x,y\rangle : X \times Y \mid x > 2 \ \wedge\ x = y + 1\}$$

in a more usual (specification) form as:

$$
\begin{aligned}
&\mathit{function\_name}: X \to Y \\
&\text{pre-}\mathit{function\_name}(x) \triangleq x > 2 \\
&\text{post-}\mathit{function\_name}(x,y) \triangleq x = y + 1
\end{aligned}
$$

The first line introduces the name of the function being specified and tells us the source and target. Next we have the pre-condition (so called because it can be checked before execution of the function commences); it must be possible to evaluate this for *all* values x of the relevant type, here X[8].

So the pre-condition is a function and its type is indicated by:

$$\text{pre-}\mathit{function\_name}: X \to \mathbb{B}$$

For all values of x for which pre-*function_name*(x) = True, and all values of y (of type Y), we should be able to evaluate the post-condition. This tells us, implicitly, which values of y would be acceptable results from *function_name*(x) once we know that the value of x is acceptable. It is a partial logical function (a predicate) of two variables. Its type is indicated thus:

$$\text{post-}\mathit{function\_name}: X \times Y \to \mathbb{B}$$

These specification components are sufficient in any situation that is not required to indicate a desired *change* of value.

Mathematically, for the purposes of actually performing calculations, we have:

$$\text{spec-}\mathit{function\_name}^{9} \triangleq \{\langle x,y\rangle : X \times Y \mid x > 2 \ \wedge\ x = y + 1\}$$

which is an instance of the general situation
i.e.,

$$
\begin{aligned}
&\text{spec-}\mathit{function\_name} \triangleq \\
&\qquad \{\langle x,y\rangle : X \times Y \mid \text{pre-}\mathit{function\_name} \ \wedge\ \text{post-}\mathit{function\_name}\}.
\end{aligned}
$$

[8] A function of type $X \to Y$ with $\mathcal{D} f = X$ is said to be a ***total*** function or ***mapping***. When f is a mapping, pre-$f(x) \triangleq$ True, and the pre-condition may be omitted without information loss.

[9] So clearly the specification is a subset of $X \times Y$ and is of type $\mathcal{P}(X \times Y)$.

For documentation purposes, other ways of displaying the components are used, such as:

$function\_name: x{:}X \rightarrow y{:}Y$
pre $\triangleq$ $x > 2$
post $\triangleq$ $x = y + 1$

or

spec-*function_name* $\triangleq$ [pre-*function_name*, post-*function_name*]

where pre-*function_name*$(x{:}X) \triangleq x > 2$
post-*function_name*$(x{:}X, y{:}Y) \triangleq x = y + 1$

or

spec-*function_name*:$\mathcal{P}(X \times Y) \triangleq$ [pre-*function_name*, post-*function_name*]

where pre-*function_name*$(x) \triangleq x > 2$
post-*function_name*$(x,y) \triangleq x = y + 1$

or even, using an alternative notation for functions[10]

spec-*function_name* $\triangleq$ [pre-*function_name*, post-*function_name*]

where pre-*function_name* $\triangleq (\lambda x{:}X)(x > 2)$
post-*function_name* $\triangleq (\lambda \langle x,y\rangle{:}X \times Y)(x = y + 1)$

Exercises

Although we have only met a very limited collection of operators so far, try the following exercises.

1.1 Assuming that x and y are of type 0..10 i.e. {0,1,2,3,4,5,6,7,8,9,10}, consider the post-conditions below:

post-*double*$(x,y) \triangleq y = 2*x$
post-*is_even*(x,b)[11] $\triangleq b \Leftrightarrow (\exists z{:}0..10)(x = 2*z)$
post-*half*$(x,y) \triangleq x = 2*y$
post-*different*$(x,y) \triangleq y \neq x$
post-*greater*$(x,y) \triangleq y > x$
post-*two_away*$(x,y) \triangleq y = x - 2 \ or \ y = x + 2$

For each, identify the domain and range and give the (weakest) pre-condition.

[10] If you have not met this notation before then skip this paragraph. It will be defined later.

[11] If the symbol '$\Leftrightarrow$' is new to you just consider it to be '='. All will be explained in Section 1.2.

1.2 Now, using the type 0..10 for inputs and $\mathbb{B}$ for outputs, have a go at specifying the functions below. The intended meaning should be clear from the name, but can you formalise it?

greater_than_5
divisible_by_3
is_prime
is_product_of_two_distinct_primes

Now repeat the exercises, using the same post-conditions but with $\mathbb{Z}$, the integers — all the whole numbers — instead of 1..10.

❑

1.1.1 Summary of Features

The purpose of 'pre' is to reassure the evaluation mechanism that if the input value satisfies this condition, then the calculation can proceed satisfactorily. The logical link between pre-f and post-f is something like:

if pre-$f(x)$ then $(\exists y{:}Y)($ post-$f(x,y))$ fi

but finding a suitable y can be problematic and involve an extensive search, even one that gives rise to error situations, since the post-condition may not be defined for all values in $X \times Y$. To avoid such errors requires that y be introduced *only* when the pre-condition is True. To achieve this, we need to know the rules associated with the '$\wedge$' operator; and is therefore deferred until section 1.4.2.4. However, we can use this link as an implicit definition of y, and this is the stance we shall adopt in synthesising programs from specifications.

Now suppose we had a specification of a function f, of type $X \rightarrow Y$, and we were given:

pre-$f(x) \triangleq (\exists y{:}Y)($post-$f(x,y))$

Here, the need to know if there is an answer is logically equivalent to being able to find one. (Just *read* this pre-condition. It says "x is a valid input if there exists a y which is a valid answer from the input x".) But this implies that we have to do the calculation to find out whether we can get *an* answer before we begin the calculation to get *the* answer.

We should therefore not knowingly utilise f within its own pre-condition. We can attempt to circumvent this by running the test on the acceptability of the data and working on the calculation at the same time. Of course, if the data turns out to be unacceptable, then the calculation will fail. We shall return to this discussion several times in the sequel.

1.1.2 Guidelines for Specifications

Within the development process, we are not allowed to ignore (or contravene) *any* of the constraints included in the specification. Therefore, it is extremely important that the specification should be as abstract as possible. Essentially, the specification provides the means by which the correctness of the derived software will be judged. Put another way, the creation of the specification, from an informal statement of the requirement, is where testing should be done[12]. It is human nature to repeat the same mistakes over and over again; we see exactly what we want to see. Therefore, it is good practice to get someone else to try to 'break' your specification. In a learning situation, this is easy to arrange — work in pairs and try to find errors in, and construct counter-examples to, each others specifications. In other situations, it is perhaps a good idea to leave a (part of a) specification, do something else, and return to it after your mind has been occupied with another problem.

One problem which we have already encountered concerns the robustness of a program or system. As part of the specification for a program, we need to know the set of values (not necessarily numerical values, just the set of all valid inputs) to which the program is required to respond. Anything else may cause it to fail and is not our concern!

Removing logical redundancy within a specification means that it is 'smaller' and easier to check and to manipulate. [Subsequently we may wish to transform a mathematical expression into a particular form for a particular purpose, seemingly 'going backwards'. But this will be for a specific reason and will be under *our* control, not inflicted by the customer.] Being as concise as possible (without being needlessly cryptic) is also desirable, as you will see.

It may seem that we are making a meal of this, *but* it is very important that the terminology be understood (and memorised). Notation is less important (within software engineering, many different notations are used for the same concept) but how to read the notation *is* important. If you come across some notation which you cannot remember, then look it up and remind yourself how it should be "spoken". Otherwise you will eventually come across a combination that you might only interpret as "an upside down *a*, an *x*, a *v* with an arrow at the right-hand side, a *b*, and ...." and which you have absolutely no chance of understanding.

[12] By whatever means is deemed appropriate, the creator of the specification needs to assure himself that the 'arrows' or 'dots' in the relation that underlies the specification *do* correspond to allowed/desired pairs and that any pair *not* required is *not* included. This *is* passing the buck, but the specification is much simpler than any software that results from the synthesis process and hence easier to 'test'. Our purpose is to ensure that no errors are introduced from here on.

1.2 Equational Reasoning and Types

We now look at how expressions used to define functions or specifications, expressions of 'any' type, can be manipulated[13]. So this is really algebra; we develop the 'machinery' of transformation and present sets of equational rules sufficient to explain the manipulations used in our synthesis of programs. Having said that, it is not our intention to give a fully constructive basis for all the mathematical entities used. We could start with *any* set of rules; it need not be the smallest, most fundamental set possible.

We introduce a powerful and general mathematical device that will facilitate both algebraic calculations and proofs. It is based on the notion of textual substitution and in a logical (reasoning) situation is called ***equational reasoning***[14].

When the basic idea has been mastered, it can be used time and time again. Initially it will probably be regarded as very tedious, extremely long-winded, and even 'obvious' — and it is! But there are two important points that must be made. Firstly, we cannot bail out and claim that something *is* 'obvious'; that word is strictly forbidden in any argument about correctness. If a claim really is obvious, then it should be easy to justify. If it cannot be justified by a short formal argument, then perhaps it is not obvious and may even be wrong. Secondly, if we find ourselves repeating essentially the same work on numerous occasions, then we can do some side-work and create a new rule which can then be used to cut out this repetition. This is a simple instance of the concept of re-use — re-use of a piece of logic, a piece of program design development and so on.

As with most concepts associated with computing, equational reasoning is a simple idea but can be difficult to express and explain in its most general form. Before attempting a technical definition, we give a simple example of a transformation sequence. This may be regarded as a 'simplification' but here we shall make no pronouncement about what is simple and what is complex. These 'calculation' are presented as a list of equivalent expressions separated by '◆' symbols.

Suppose that x and y are two (constant but unknown) integers. This information is represented as $x,y{:}\mathbb{Z}$. We need to know that x and y are integers because only "integer rules" can be used in their manipulation. Now we take the expression $(x + y) + (x - y)$. This should simplify to $2x$ (or in more familiar computer-oriented syntax, $2*x$), but why, how? We 'walk through' the sequence of algebraic expressions and annotate the derivation with mathematical justifications.

---

[13] At a first reading we suggest that you sample the major types (Integers, as a familiar beginning, and then Booleans and Lists). Other types and operators can be studied as required.

[14] This is also called 'Term Re-writing' or, more simply 'algebraic manipulation'.

$(x + y) + (x - y)$

— read "◆" as "..has the same value as.."
(for + we can re-bracket but keep the numbers in

◆ (the same order and position.

(This is called ***associativity.***

$x + (y + (x - y))$

— " ^-y represents 'negative y' "
(replace subtraction by addition and negation.

◆ (^-y is the number which you need to

(add to y to get zero.

$x + (y + (x + {}^-y))$

(now we can swap the order of two adjacent

◆ (numbers which are to be added together.

(This is called ***commutativity***.

$x + (y + ({}^-y + x))$

(now we can use associativity (of +) again, so as

◆ (to get y and ^-y next to each other.

$x + ((y + {}^-y\ ) + x)$

(now we can use the property of ^-y to combine

◆ (with y and get 0.

$x + (0 + x)$

(now '+ing' 0 to a number has no effect,

◆ (so '0 +' effectively disappears.

(This is exactly what subtraction is all about.

$x + x$

(Having just removed 0 we now go in the
(opposite direction and introduce the number 1,

◆ (which behaves in the same way with *

(multiplication as 0 did with +.

$(1 * x) + (1 * x)$

(now factorise so as to do the addition before

◆ (multiplication.

$(1 + 1) * x$

(this is simple arithmetic, with known constants.

◆ (2 is *defined* to be the result of adding 1 to 1.

$2 * x$

You should convince yourself that each line is an 'acceptable' re-formulation of the previous one[15]. (The juggling of brackets might seem to be rather arbitrary and unnecessarily tedious. Draw the structure/type tree associated with each line and you will see that the changes are quite significant — a significance often hidden in the textual form.) Thus far, the example is merely to illustrate the way in which equational reasoning, or a transformational sequence, is presented.

Of course all the steps involved in these 'calculations' need to be explained and justified. There is actually a lot going on here, most of which we take for granted, probably without fully understanding the properties of the operators and relations within the expressions.

Lists of the major properties of the common data types are given in the Appendix.

Notice that these 'calculations' are presented as a progression of expressions of the same type and all having the same value.
So we may write:

$$a \blacktriangleleft\!\blacktriangleright b \blacktriangleleft\!\blacktriangleright c \blacktriangleleft\!\blacktriangleright d \blacktriangleleft\!\blacktriangleright e$$

which means

$$a \blacktriangleleft\!\blacktriangleright b$$

and

$$b \blacktriangleleft\!\blacktriangleright c$$

and

$$c \blacktriangleleft\!\blacktriangleright d$$

and

$$d \blacktriangleleft\!\blacktriangleright e$$

Now the operator $\blacktriangleleft\!\blacktriangleright$ between expressions (of the same type) is ***transitive***. Put simply, this means that if

$$a \blacktriangleleft\!\blacktriangleright b \blacktriangleleft\!\blacktriangleright c \blacktriangleleft\!\blacktriangleright d \blacktriangleleft\!\blacktriangleright e.$$

then a has the same value (and is of the same type) as b, which has the same value as c, which has the same value as d, which has the same value as e. Thus a has the same value as c, a has the same value as d, and a has the same value as e.
So, symbolically,

$$a \blacktriangleleft\!\blacktriangleright c$$

$$a \blacktriangleleft\!\blacktriangleright d$$

$$a \blacktriangleleft\!\blacktriangleright e$$

---

[15] At this stage, the mathematical 'justifications' are not so important, but eventually it will be very convenient to use such terminology. These and other terms will be used to describe rules within the definitions of (data) types. We shall not usually include explicit justification or explanation when rules are applied, but you should always be able to cite such a rule if challenged.

We can omit the intermediate working (once we know that there are valid 'stepping stones') and replace this sequence with the single transformation

$$a \;◆\; e$$

Moreover, we can save the derived transformation (perhaps together with its derivation, just for reference) and re-use it in any appropriate context. So, we could now write:

$$(x + y) + (x - y) \;◆\; 2*x$$

and use this as a perfectly valid transformation rule in its own right. We need not repeat the earlier working.

Any global assumption p can be used as a rule, represented in the form:

$$p \;◆\; \text{True}$$

And in rule sets, inclusion of the Boolean *expression p* indicates validity of the *rule*

$$p \;◆\; \text{True.}$$

Also, we may have conditional rules such as

$$x * y = x * z \;◆\; y = z \qquad \text{provided that } x \neq 0.$$

We write this as:

$(x \neq 0)$ $\qquad x * y = x * z \;◆\; y = z$

Similarly, if the property p is conditional upon c being True, we represent it thus:

(c)[16] $\qquad p \qquad (\;◆\; \text{True}\;)$

If the condition does not hold, then the rule is simply not available.

Other (expected?) properties of '◆' include

$a \;◆\; a$ $\qquad$ for any a $\qquad$ '◆' is ***reflexive***

and

if $\quad a \;◆\; b$

then $\quad b \;◆\; a.$ $\qquad$ '◆' is ***symmetric.***

[16] If c is a complex condition, it may only be partially evaluated. See Section 1.4.2.4 and/or Section A.0 of the Appendix for more details.

Given a set of rules such as this, the basic idea is to replace a sub-expression with another (of the same type) which, when evaluated with any legal (allowed) and consistent substitutions, always gives the same value as the original sub-expression. We discuss and justify such manipulations below.

Of course '◆' is closely related to '=' but we use '◆' so as to be different (i.e., so as not to use a symbol which that legitimately appear in any specification or program. The poor old '=' symbol is greatly overused anyway so we don't want to contribute further to the confusion that already exists. The '=' sign may be indicating that two quantities are equal (or even asking the question, "are they equal?"), whereas the '◆' symbol is used to separate the two parts of a rewrite rule, or to indicate that such a (transformation) rule is being applied so that one expression is transformed into another (of the same type and, when fully evaluated, the same value). Additionally (and implicitly) we also need to have syntactic equality (i.e., exactly the same sequence of significant characters — omitting irrelevant spaces, etc.) and this covers equality of values when their representations are unique. We shall also presume the existence of the universal rule

"text" = "text" ◆ True

for *any*[17] piece of text which represents a valid — well-formed — expression.

Brackets will rarely be mentioned within the syntax but can be used with all types so as to clarify or disambiguate the linear textual form associated with a particular structure/type tree.

1.3 The Origin and Application of Rules

Most rules that are used within a transformation sequence are not rules which have been given explicitly, nor are they applied to entire expressions. They are more often rules derived from some "meta-rule" (a more 'general' rule) and applied to just a part of the expression under consideration. Rule sets associated with particular data types are outlined later in this chapter and given more fully in the Appendix. First we say something about other ways of introducing transformation rules and explain how the substitutions are carried out. An understanding of this process is necessary to appreciate how some software engineering tools work and to resolve any conflicts which might arise when trying to justify a particular piece of calculation.

Suppose we are given expressions x and y (which contain only constants, and both evaluate to a value of the same type, T), then we say that $x = y$ (by definition!) if

[17] There is one exception, which will be discussed in Section 1.4.2.4.

they both evaluate to the *same value*, which will be of type T. Thus we have the general conditional rules:

$$(x \triangleq y) \qquad x \blacktriangleleft\!\blacktriangleright y$$ (see[18])

and

$$(x = y) \qquad x \blacktriangleleft\!\blacktriangleright y$$

The way in which '=' is evaluated depends on either textual equivalence or the rules that define the type T. Rules for common types will be given later.

Now suppose that we have two functions f and g of the same type $X \to Y$. From the definition of a function, it follows that

$$(x = y) \qquad f(x) \blacktriangleleft\!\blacktriangleright f(y)$$

Moreover, from the definition of equality between functions

$$f = g \triangleq (\forall x{:}X)^{19} \; (f(x) = g(x))$$ see[20]

we have

$$(f = g) \qquad f(x) \blacktriangleleft\!\blacktriangleright g(x)$$

Recall also that we can introduce new data names as well as our own macro and function definitions, and functions can be thought of as parameterised expressions. And once we have introduced a new name for something, we can swap between the old and new representations at will by using the conditional rule (conditional upon the definition '$x \triangleq y$', where x is some new entity, perhaps having parameters and y is an expression). We now apply this process to justify general substitutions within a larger expression.

Given the definition

$$inc\_by\_2(x) \triangleq x + 2$$

the value of '$inc\_by\_2(x)$' is defined to be equal to the value of '$x + 2$' and we immediately have the rule

$$inc\_by\_2(x) \blacktriangleleft\!\blacktriangleright x + 2$$

---

[18] Note that this is *not* a proper conditional rule, it merely looks like one. $x \triangleq y$ is not a Boolean expression but an agreed statement of fact, a declaration of the meaning of x, and hence $x = y$ is True by definition.

[19] '$\forall x{:}X$' is read as 'for all x of type X'. '$\forall$' is the universal quantifier and will be discussed further when needed.

[20] From this definition it follows that $\mathcal{D}f = \mathcal{D}g$. If f is total (i.e. if $\mathcal{D}f = X$) then function equality follows from the equality defined on type Y; however, if $x \in X \setminus \mathcal{D}f$, — that is, $x \in X$ and $x \notin \mathcal{D}f$, see Section 1.4.3 — then we say that $f(x)$ is identified with a special value $\bot_Y$, called 'the undefined value of type Y' — not to be confused with the value of type $\mathbb{E}$ to be discussed shortly. This is a technical fix which we can now ignore until Chapter 12. There is also an alternative formulation in the appendix which uses other, as yet undefined, operators.

Associated with function definitions and their application, we have two familiar, and computationally very important, processes — so important that they have their own terminology. Using the current example, we can ***unfold*** by replacing

'$inc\_by\_2(x)$' by '$x + 2$'.

In the reverse direction, we can perform a ***fold*** by replacing

'$x + 2$' by '$inc\_by\_2(x)$'.

We can even replace

'$y + 2$' by '$inc\_by\_2(y)$'.

Why we would want to do either, or even both, of these transformations will become clear later on in Section 1.5. Currently, it will simply prove to be a useful mechanism to facilitate partial substitutions. But before we put them to use, and while we are discussing functions, we explain an alternative representation of a function. In the definition

'$inc\_by\_2(x) \triangleq x + 2$'

we are not really defining the function 'inc_by_2' but the expression '$inc\_by\_2(x)$'. What we introduce now is a notational device for separating 'inc_by_2' from the '(x)' part.

First notice that the type of 'inc_by_2' is $\mathbb{Z} \rightarrow \mathbb{Z}$, whereas the type of '$inc\_by\_2(x)$' is $\mathbb{Z}$. Something happens to get from one to the other, and that something is the substitution, the delivering, of an argument (of type $\mathbb{Z}$) and the subsequent evaluation of the expression to give a result, here again of type $\mathbb{Z}$. The new notation makes the substitution explicit and corresponds to the substitution of an actual parameter for a formal parameter in the same way as occurs in a computer implementation of a function call. The notation is called ***lambda notation*** (λ is the Greek lower case letter lambda)[21] and, using the same example, is written thus:

$$inc\_by\_2 \triangleq (\lambda x{:}\mathbb{Z})(x + 2)$$

- meaning "substitute a value, of type $\mathbb{Z}$, for x in '$x + 2$' "

and then, following the textual substitution rules[22], since

$$inc\_by\_2 \Leftrightarrow (\lambda x{:}\mathbb{Z})(x + 2)$$

[21] This notation may also be used to relate the formal and actual parameters of 'macros' — functions/operators written in a more computing-oriented fashion — about which we shall say more, in passing, later.

[22] Although this instance might look rather complicated, all this means is that if $f \Leftrightarrow g$ is a rule, then $f(a) \Leftrightarrow g(a)$ is also a rule. The only difference here is that one of the functions is represented by a 'formula' instead of a simple name.

we have

$$inc\_by\_2(z) \blacklozenge (\lambda x:\mathbb{Z})(x + 2)(z).$$

The form of the expression '$(\lambda x:\mathbb{Z})(x + 2)(z)$' will be new to most readers. It has three components, which are referred to in the order 'third, first, second', and means

"substitute the value z for x in '$x + 2$' ", to give

'$z + 2$'.

Here, z is the actual parameter, x is the formal parameter (used in the definition as an integer place holder), and '$x + 2$' is the body of the function/routine.

Now suppose that we have some expression that involves one or more instances of the (free)[23] variable x, and let this expression define the function f,

$$f(x) \triangleq \underline{\quad\quad} x \underline{\quad\quad} \quad \text{(an expression in } x)$$

Then we have

$$\underline{\quad\quad} x \underline{\quad\quad}$$

$\blacklozenge$ — fold using $f(x)$ $\blacklozenge$ $\underline{\quad\quad} x \underline{\quad\quad}$

$\quad f(x)$

$\blacklozenge$ — $x \blacklozenge y$

$\quad f(y)$

$\blacklozenge$ — unfold using $f(y)$ $\blacklozenge$ $\underline{\quad\quad} y \underline{\quad\quad}$

$\underline{\quad\quad} y \underline{\quad\quad}$

                                        (the *same* expression, in terms of y)

(This is exactly the scenario which typifies the substitution of x by y in an arbitrary well-formed expression, so our sub-expression replacements have been justified.)

There are other notations that are used to indicate substitution. One which is commonly encountered and which we shall find convenient to use is the following:

$$P(x) [x \leftarrow y] \triangleq (\lambda x:)(P(x))(y)$$
$$\blacklozenge P(y)$$

So, the result is $P(x)$ with all (free) occurrences of x replaced by y.

---

[23] Free variables are those that we may regard as already existing; bound variables are effectively new, local, variables. Thus far we have encountered bound variables in conjunction with universal and existential quantifiers.

Before moving on to look at rule sets for specific types of data, we extend λ-notation to facilitate the change of variables within rewrite rules. One rule associated with integer addition (of type $\mathbb{Z} \times \mathbb{Z} \to \mathbb{Z}$) is

$$a + b \;\;◆\;\; b + a$$

We wish to be able to use this rule to manipulate integers other than a and b; they are only to be interpreted as place holders. Hence we write

$$(\lambda a,b{:}\mathbb{Z}) \qquad a + b \;\;◆\;\; b + a$$

i.e., for any integers a and b, $a + b$ can be replaced by $b + a$.
This rule can then be ***instantiated***[24] using x and y in place of a and b to give the rule

$$x + y \;\;◆\;\; y + x \qquad \text{as expected.}$$

So the λ construction is used to indicate the allowed substitution of values (or names of unknown values) into expressions and rules. An extension to this permits the substitution of types, but to indicate the difference in the 'kind' of entity being manipulated, we use the syntax "(λ ::)" as in "(λ*X*::Type)". This means that we can substitute any, non-empty, type for X in whatever follows.

The transformation rules may therefore be parameterised over types and values (names) and may be universally applicable or conditional. These rules will be used primarily to substitute one sub-expression for another within the current 'working' expression. The rules may be given, by way of the definition of the data types used, or arise from user-defined functions and relations.

To summarise, we can can express these important generic properties associated with functions, and two such properties can be expressed as the highly parameterised rules

$(\lambda X{::}\text{Type}, Y{::}\text{Type})$ -- see[25]

  $(\lambda f{:}X \to Y)$

    $(\lambda x,y{:}X)$

      $(x = y) \quad f(x) \;◆\; f(y)$

and

$(\lambda X{::}\text{Type}, Y{::}\text{Type})$

  $(\lambda f,g{:}X \to Y)$

    $(\lambda x{:}X)$

      $(f = g) \quad f(x) \;◆\; g(x)$

---

[24] All this means here is that x and y are substituted for a and b, but the word *instantiate* is often used.

[25] And these Types may be different.

The second of these reads as: "Given types X and Y, we can take functions f and g (each of type $X \to Y$) such that for any given value of $x{:}X$, if $f = g$ then $f(x)$ can be replaced by $g(x)$. Notice how the rule is presented in a structured fashion, each layer adding a level of abstraction.

[In reverse,

$$(\forall x{:}X)(\, f(x) = g(x)) \qquad\qquad f \;◆\; g \qquad\qquad]$$

The same form of rule may also be derived from certain properties which might be possessed by relations and functions, where these properties are themselves defined by means of universally quantified equalities. Some of these are included in the Appendix, but here we give an illustration, based on a characterisation[26] of the property that a function is associative.

$$is\_assoc(f) \triangleq (\forall x,y,z{:}T) \quad f(f(x,y),z) = f(x,f(y,z))$$

where $f{:}T \times T \to T$ for some T::Type.

Thus

$$(is\_assoc(f))$$
$$(\lambda x,y,z{:}T)$$
$$f(f(x,y),z) \;◆\; f(x,f(y,z)).$$

This says that if f is associative then we can use the rule $f(f(x,y),z)$ ◆ $f(x,f(y,z))$ with any substitutions of type T values for the place holders x, y and z..

Similarly, if we have an infix binary operator $\otimes$ acting on type T, then

$$(is\_assoc(\otimes))$$
$$(\lambda x,y,z{:}T)$$
$$(x \otimes y) \otimes z \;◆\; x \otimes (y \otimes z).$$

Of course we are interested in specifying the calculation of functions that use data items more complicated than single integers. Actually, the theory of computable functions tells us that there really is nothing else which *can* be computed — all computations and data values can be encoded into single integers. But not all data *looks* like a single integer, and we want to be able to perform calculations which act on (uncoded) data in the form that we commonly see it.

There are basically two ways to go: we can either have more complicated data types or we can base the specification on a more complicated Boolean expression, a more complicated predicate, and we can utilise both these 'extensions' within the same specification.

---

[26] We can use the notation *is_assoc(f)*, or a pre-fix operator *is_assoc f*, or even a post-fix operator, and write *f is_assoc*.

1.4 Data Types

We now collect together some primitive operations on basic data types and then take a look at how we build more complex data types. This is done in a constructive fashion, literally building new types from existing ones. At the same time, we say something about the manipulation rules that underpin the meanings of the types. It turns out that these rules are sufficient to define the types (*any* implementation which behaves in accordance with the given rules will be acceptable) but remember that here we are primarily concerned with describing and defining *what* is to be done, not *how* it is to be done.

Types, not only the data types commonly found in programming languages but also more abstract types, comprise a set of values together with operations and predicates which act on these values. To be able to use these (named) values, operations and predicates, we need to know how they should be written and what they mean.

We need to describe the kinds of values used as data and results, as well as other types[27] that may be used *within* the pre- and post-conditions and, since these functions are both predicates, we obviously need to involve Booleans — regardless of the types of values manipulated by the program. Booleans are the most fundamental type, but we shall start by taking a quick look at the integers (which we shall consider more extensively later).

1.4.1 A Glimpse at the Integers

Our 'toy' examples in the earlier part of this chapter involved integers in a very simplistic way. The types used there were based on small finite sets and we assumed that the operators '=' and '–' worked in the usual fashion (but didn't give results outside the prescribed types) and the inequalities '<' and '≤', and indeed '=', gave the expected Boolean answers. So far, so good, but we really need to pin down exactly what is going on within a specification.

[27] These types may never truly exist. They might be used simply to aid descriptions and not be implemented within the final software.

Suppose that we have a specification for some function *f*, given by

$$\text{pre-}f\colon \mathbb{Z} \rightarrow \mathbb{B}$$
$$\text{post-}f\colon \mathbb{Z} \times \mathbb{Z} \rightarrow \mathbb{B},$$

where $\mathbb{Z}$ denotes the integer type and pre-$f(x{:}\mathbb{Z}) \triangleq x > 3$. The '>' symbol represents an 'operation' or a function of *type* $\mathbb{Z} \times \mathbb{Z} \rightarrow \mathbb{B}$. It takes two $\mathbb{Z}$ values, *x* and 3 and delivers a Boolean result. Moreover, the '>' symbol is placed *between* the *x* and the 3, and is called an ***infix*** operator[28].

We represent all this information in the ***signature*** of '>' which we write as

$$\mathbb{Z} > \mathbb{Z} \rightarrow \mathbb{B}.$$

Similarly we have:

$$\mathbb{Z} = \mathbb{Z} \rightarrow \mathbb{B}$$
$$\mathbb{Z} \geq \mathbb{Z} \rightarrow \mathbb{B}$$

Shortly we shall see how the meaning, the semantics, of these operators can be defined axiomatically by rules such as

$$x \geq y \;\;⧏⧐\;\; x > y \textit{ or } x = y$$ see[29]

and

$$x \leq y \;\;⧏⧐\;\; y \geq x$$

But first we consider the structure and type information associated with expressions which we can build using these operators.

The set of (all) integers is infinite, but in any implementation, in any system, we can only represent a finite subset of them. Both of these, contradictory, views must be considered but can be used to advantage. The notation for the set of integers is '$\mathbb{Z}$'. The 'Z', written in what is often called "Blackboard capitals"[30], comes from the German word 'zahlen', meaning number.

$$\mathbb{Z} \triangleq \{.., {}^{-}2, {}^{-}1, 0, 1, 2, \;\; ,...\}$$

where the sequence of numbers extends to infinity in both direction.

---

[28] Strictly 'operators' are defined so as to take input values — ***operands*** — and results from the *same* type, but here it makes no sense to worry about such things. Of more importance is to note that symbols such as '>' denote functions, but they are so commonly used that an alternative representation has been devised; 'greater_than(*x*,3)' is a little bit cumbersome.

[29] Recall that the symbol ⧏⧐ indicates that two expressions are of equal value and can be read as "is the same as" or "can be replaced by". The same symbol will be used to indicate (i) that expressions *are* equal, by definition, and (ii) that we have deduced, or calculated, such an equality.

[30] We shall adopt the convention of using other Blackboard capitals to denote other 'standard' sets and types but not as type constructors.

Here '$^-1$' is "negative 1" (minus 1), it has nothing yet to do with subtraction, just "counting down" from zero. The high '$^-$' symbol is used to distinguish negation (a unary operation) from the infix binary subtraction operator.

We assume that if a calculation ever overflows, then an error occurs and no valid answer (certainly no answer of type $\mathbb{Z}$) is delivered. This is consistent with our overall maxim that applying legal manipulations to a given expression should achieve an equivalent expression. Generating an error obviously contravenes this.

We shall exploit the boundedness of implementations by arguing that, *in principle*, we could write out the set display in full. This would then allow us to apply various operations to individual integers or to pairs of them as appropriate. Conversely, we shall eventually want to apply algebraic arguments so that we need not *in practice* carry out all individual evaluations — there are simply too many.

Later we shall consider the construction of the set (and type) $\mathbb{Z}$, but now our concern is with structure and type information. As in programming languages, just because an expression is well-formed and type-consistent does not guarantee that its evaluation is always valid and would succeed. Mathematically, valid syntax and type consistency are necessary, but they may not be sufficient. Other checks (such as that required so as not to try to carry out division by zero) will need to be incorporated, but these are semantic considerations. As a first move, you should ensure that all expressions are properly structured and type-compatible. One way to check this is to construct a tree representation of how sub-expressions are linked and incorporate type information into this. Two possible representations of the expression "$x > 3$" over $\mathbb{Z}$ are given in Figures 1.10 and 1.11.

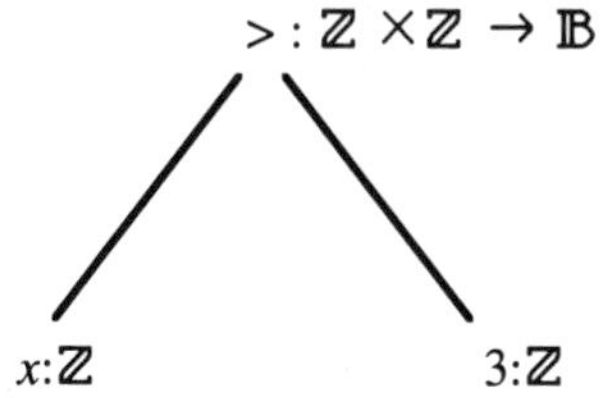

Figure 1.10

In Figure 1.10 the tree is simple and perhaps as expected but with type information attached to the nodes — particularly the operator node — makes the annotation rather complex. Placing an extra line (upwards, from the old root) and attaching type information to the arcs rather than the nodes, we get the less cluttered representation in Figure 1.11.

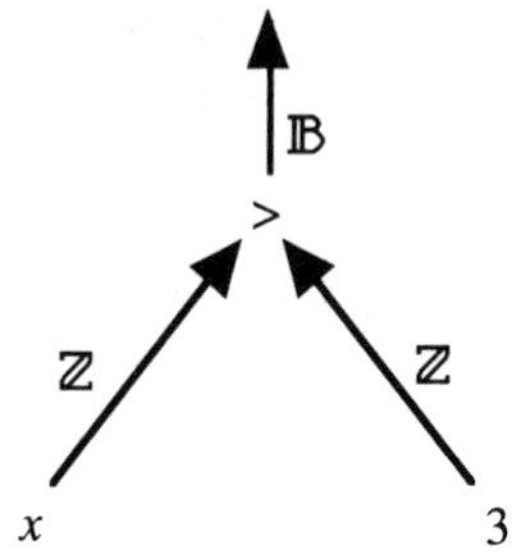

Figure 1.11

More complicated expressions are represented simply by plugging these trees together. Generally brackets are not required in the trees — unless we have some really strange syntactic constructs, and we do — but they are often needed to resolve ambiguities within the *textual* versions of expressions. Of course, some 'trees' look a little strange (such as Figure 1.12, which corresponds to the expression ^-x, the negation of x) but still carry the desired information.

We shall say little more about these tree representations, but if you ever get confused about how to decipher an expression, they are a very good first move in trying to resolve your problem; and if you can't draw a corresponding tree, or if you can draw more than one, then you need look no further for something that must be fixed before you can go on.

Figure 1.12

Assuming familiarity with integer arithmetic and therefore skipping explanations of the common operations and predicates (equality and the inequalities), the signatures are as follows:

$$\mathbb{Z} > \mathbb{Z} \rightarrow \mathbb{B}$$
$$\mathbb{Z} \geq \mathbb{Z} \rightarrow \mathbb{B}$$
$$\mathbb{Z} = \mathbb{Z} \rightarrow \mathbb{B}$$

and

$$\mathbb{Z} < \mathbb{Z} \rightarrow \mathbb{B}$$
$$\mathbb{Z} \leq \mathbb{Z} \rightarrow \mathbb{B}$$
$$\mathbb{Z} \neq \mathbb{Z} \rightarrow \mathbb{B}$$

$$\mathbb{Z} + \mathbb{Z} \rightarrow \mathbb{Z}$$
$$^{-}\mathbb{Z} \rightarrow \mathbb{Z}$$ (the negative high '¯')
$$\mathbb{Z} - \mathbb{Z} \rightarrow \mathbb{Z}$$

$$\mathbb{Z} * \mathbb{Z} \rightarrow \mathbb{Z}$$
$$\mathbb{Z} \div \mathbb{Z} \rightarrow \mathbb{Z}$$ (where $3 \div 2 = 1$, $2 \div 3 = 0$, etc.)

For completeness, we also need to include (the signatures of) constants. These are functions of zero variables. There are infinitely many of these so we could be here for some time. In fact, as will be explained we only *need* one constant, 0, but short of having infinitely many, it will also be convenient to identify 1 as a special constant. These constants are indicated thus:

$$0 \rightarrow \mathbb{Z}$$
$$1 \rightarrow \mathbb{Z}$$

For the purpose of building expression trees, you may assume all the other integer constants can be treated similarly. Notice also that 'declarations' like $x{:}\mathbb{Z}$ correspond to the introduction of signatures such as

$$x \rightarrow \mathbb{Z}$$

(i.e., as far as we are concerned, x is an integer constant)

1.4.2 Logical Types

Having introduced some basic notation using the type $\mathbb{Z}$, we now move to the formal definitions of basic types and ways of constructing composite types.

1.4.2.1 The Boolean Type, $\mathbb{B}$

Here there are only two values: two constants, 'True' and 'False', and the basic operators *not*, *and*, and *or*. As might be expected, there are special notations associated with these operators: *not* is written as $\neg$, *and* as $\wedge$ (remembered using $\wedge$nd), and *or* as $\vee$, and their signatures are

$$\begin{aligned} \text{True} &\to \mathbb{B} \\ \text{False} &\to \mathbb{B} \\ \neg\,\mathbb{B} &\to \mathbb{B} \\ \mathbb{B} \wedge \mathbb{B} &\to \mathbb{B} \\ \mathbb{B} \vee \mathbb{B} &\to \mathbb{B} \end{aligned}$$

These don't look very exciting since all input and output values are of type $\mathbb{B}$ and the set $\mathbb{B}$ is only {True, False}, but the type $\mathbb{B}$ (i.e., the set $\mathbb{B}$ together with the operations *not*, *and* and *or*) forms the basis of all logical arguments, reasoning, and deduction.

Formal characterisations of the operators (operations) follow soon, but just to provide a touchstone for any reader who has not met them before, we give some informal descriptions[31]. The $\neg$ operator simply 'flips' its argument, so these rules should be valid:

$$\neg\,\text{True} \;\blacktriangleleft\!\!\blacktriangleright\; \text{False}$$

and

$$\neg\,\text{False} \;\blacktriangleleft\!\!\blacktriangleright\; \text{True}.$$

This can then be used to give direct definitions to 'secondary' operators such as

$$a \neq b \triangleq \neg(a = b)$$

The other two operators can be described more concisely.

$a \wedge b$ is True if and only if both a and b are True.
$a \vee b$ is True if and only if either a or b (or both) are True.

Now for a proper definition of the type $\mathbb{B}$. It is important that the reader understands not only the content of the section but also the framework used to deliver the information.

[31] In the proper definition which follows we take care to avoid circularity. For our purposes, it is sufficient to take all our type definitions (and their rule sets) in their entirety.

Mathematically, a common starting point for the study of Boolean Algebras is the following list of ten identities/axioms, which we now write as re-write rules.

Recall that the *set* $\mathbb{B}$ is {True, False}, the operators $\neg$, $\wedge$ and $\vee$ are *not*, *and* and *or*, respectively and the syntax and type information of the operators for $\mathbb{B}$ is indicated by the following signatures:

$\neg\ \mathbb{B} \rightarrow \mathbb{B}$	*not* is a prefix operator.
$\mathbb{B} \wedge \mathbb{B} \rightarrow \mathbb{B}$	*and* is an infix operator
$\mathbb{B} \vee \mathbb{B} \rightarrow \mathbb{B}$	*or* is an infix operator

($\lambda a,b,c$:$\mathbb{B}$)

1	$a \vee b$	◆	$b \vee a$	*or* is commutative[32]
2	$a \vee (b \vee c)$	◆	$(a \vee b) \vee c$	*or* is associative
3	$a \vee$ False	◆	a	False is an identity element for *or*
4	$a \vee \neg a$	◆	True	
5	$a \wedge b$	◆	$b \wedge a$	*and* is commutative
6	$a \wedge (b \wedge c)$	◆	$(a \wedge b) \wedge c$	*and* is associative
7	$a \wedge$ True	◆	a	True is an identity element for *and*
8	$a \wedge \neg a$	◆	False	
9	$a \wedge (b \vee c)$	◆	$(a \wedge b) \vee (a \wedge c)$	*and* distributes over *or*
10	$a \vee (b \wedge c)$	◆	$(a \vee b) \wedge (a \vee c)$	*or* distributes over *and*

In much the same way that λ can be used to indicate the substitution of actual parameters for formal parameters (used in the definition of a function); λ is used here to indicate that the quoted names (a, b and c) are merely place holders in the rules, and can be replaced by any required expressions of the appropriate type, here $\mathbb{B}$.

[32] All these terms relate to ways in which the expression can be manipulated. They can also be defined as transformations on the underlying tree structure of the expression. See the appendix for illustrations of the most common forms.

From the given set of ten rules, we can deduce many others which may prove very useful. In particular, they can be used as 'short cuts' to avoid the need to repeat lots of tedious and distracting 'side work'. For example:

$a \vee \text{True}$

◆ True is the identity element for $\wedge$

$(a \vee \text{True}) \wedge \text{True}$

◆ Property of $\neg a$

$(a \vee \text{True}) \wedge (a \vee \neg a)$

◆ Distributivity of $\vee$ over $\wedge$, factorization

$a \vee (\text{True} \wedge \neg a)$

◆ True is the identity element for $\wedge$

$a \vee \neg a$

◆ Property of $\neg a$

True

so we have the (new) rule

$a \vee \text{True}$ ◆ True

Similarly, we can derive the rule

$a \wedge \text{False}$ ◆ False

These are called the ***null*** rules since '$\vee$ ing' with True nullifies the effect of a within the expression $a \vee \text{True}$, and similarly with $\wedge$ and False in the second rule. These are probably familiar to the reader, but they are not in the given set, and their derivations — though easy to follow — are not particularly easy to 'invent'. We certainly wouldn't like to have to spend a long time trying to re-derive them (and probably going round in circles) in the midst of a serious piece of program synthesis. Two other rules which are less familiar, and perhaps somewhat 'suspicious' are the ***absorption*** rules.

$a \vee (a \wedge b)$ ◆ a[33]
$a \wedge (a \vee b)$ ◆ a

Here the terms involving b are absorbed into a and effectively disappear. The calculations are straightforward now that we have the null rules. We leave justification of these to the reader.

---

[33] Compare this with *x max* (*x min y*) or *max*(*x*, *min*(*x*, *y*)), where *x* and *y* are integers and *max* and *min* compute maximum and minimum values.

But surely there is something missing! We would definitely expect that the deMorgan rules should be included, i.e.,

$$\neg(a \wedge b) \;\Leftrightarrow\; (\neg a) \vee (\neg b)$$

and

$$\neg(a \vee b) \;\Leftrightarrow\; (\neg a) \wedge (\neg b)$$

Not only are these absent from the list but there is no *direct* way of obtaining them. Searching through the rules, you will see that no rule can be applied to '$\neg(a \wedge b)$' which will move the $\neg$ operation.

Derivation and justification of these rules requires that we use the uniqueness of complements.

If $x,y{:}\mathbb{B}$ are values or expressions which satisfy the two rules

$$x \wedge y \;\Leftrightarrow\; \text{False} \qquad\qquad x \vee y \;\Leftrightarrow\; \text{True}$$

then y is called a ***complement*** of x.

Given the Boolean (variable with the) value a, suppose there are Boolean values b and c such that the following rules hold:

$$a \wedge b \;\Leftrightarrow\; \text{False} \qquad\qquad a \vee b \;\Leftrightarrow\; \text{True}$$
$$a \wedge c \;\Leftrightarrow\; \text{False} \qquad\qquad a \vee c \;\Leftrightarrow\; \text{True}$$

From these assumptions, we can show (another exercise for the reader) that

$$b \;\Leftrightarrow\; c$$

Therefore any two complements of a given value are equal and complements are *unique*.

Since we also have

$$a \vee \neg a \;\Leftrightarrow\; \text{True} \quad \text{and} \quad a \wedge \neg a \;\Leftrightarrow\; \text{False}$$

and these two rules together tell us that $\neg a$ is *the* complement of a.

It follows therefore that

$$b \;\Leftrightarrow\; \neg a$$

Any Boolean (variable or expression) with these properties, relative to a, is equivalent to the complement of a. It is merely a different way of writing $\neg a$.

Let's put this result to use immediately.

Notice that

$$\text{True} \vee \text{False} \Leftrightarrow \text{True}$$

and, after some manipulation,

$$\text{True} \wedge \text{False} \Leftrightarrow \text{False}$$

Hence we *do* have the rules

$$\neg\text{True} \Leftrightarrow \text{False}$$

and

$$\neg\text{False} \Leftrightarrow \text{True}$$

Similarly

$$(a \wedge b) \wedge (\neg a \vee \neg b) \Leftrightarrow \text{False}$$

and

$$(a \wedge b) \vee (\neg a \vee \neg b) \Leftrightarrow \text{True}$$

So $\neg a \vee \neg b$ is *the* complement of $a \wedge b$
and hence

$\neg(a \wedge b) \Leftrightarrow (\neg a \vee \neg b)$ can be used as a rule.

Other rules, which can be derived as exercises by the reader who feels the need to develop his manipulative skills, include

$$\neg(a \vee b) \Leftrightarrow (\neg a \wedge \neg b)$$

$(a \wedge a) \Leftrightarrow a$
and the ***idempotent*** laws
$(a \vee a) \Leftrightarrow a$

and $\neg\neg a \Leftrightarrow a$ the ***involution*** law.

We can now collect together various parts and present a definition of the *type* $\mathbb{B}$. It is not the smallest, most compact, definition that could be given, but it does contain most of the commonly used Boolean rules and illustrates how we shall define types, axiomatically, from now on. Additionally, we also include terminology (which describe common properties of the operators) that is easier to quote than to give in symbolic form.

Type/Class $\mathbb{B}$ (Boolean)
values $\mathbb{B}$ $(\triangleq \{\text{True},\text{False}\})$
operations:

$$\begin{aligned} \text{True} &\to \mathbb{B} \\ \text{False} &\to \mathbb{B} \\ \neg\mathbb{B} &\to \mathbb{B} \\ \mathbb{B} \wedge \mathbb{B} &\to \mathbb{B} \\ \mathbb{B} \vee \mathbb{B} &\to \mathbb{B} \end{aligned}$$

rules: $(\lambda a,b,c{:}\mathbb{B})$

$a \vee b \Leftrightarrow b \vee a$	$\vee$ is commutative
$a \vee a \Leftrightarrow a$	$\vee$ is idempotent
$a \vee (b \vee c) \Leftrightarrow (a \vee b) \vee c$	$\vee$ is associative
$a \vee \text{False} \Leftrightarrow a$	False is an identity element for the $\vee$ operation
$a \vee (\neg a) \Leftrightarrow \text{True}$	$\neg a$ is a complement[34] of a
$a \vee \text{True} \Leftrightarrow \text{True}$	True is a null element for $\vee$
$a \wedge b \Leftrightarrow b \wedge a$	$\wedge$ is commutative
$a \wedge a \Leftrightarrow a$	$\wedge$ is idempotent
$a \wedge (b \wedge c) \Leftrightarrow (a \wedge b) \wedge c$	$\wedge$ is associative
$a \wedge \text{True} \Leftrightarrow a$	True is an identity element for the $\wedge$ operation
$a \wedge (\neg a) \Leftrightarrow \text{False}$	$\neg a$ is a complement of a
$a \wedge \text{False} \Leftrightarrow \text{False}$	False is a null element for $\wedge$
$\neg\text{True} \Leftrightarrow \text{False}$	
$\neg\text{False} \Leftrightarrow \text{True}$	
$\neg\neg a \Leftrightarrow a$	involution
$a \wedge (b \vee c) \Leftrightarrow (a \wedge b) \vee (a \wedge c)$	$\wedge$ distributes over $\vee$
$a \vee (b \wedge c) \Leftrightarrow (a \vee b) \wedge (a \vee c)$	$\vee$ distributes over $\wedge$
$a \vee (a \wedge b) \Leftrightarrow a$	absorption law
$a \wedge (a \vee b) \Leftrightarrow a$	absorption law
$\neg(a \wedge b) \Leftrightarrow (\neg a \vee \neg b)$	deMorgan's law
$\neg(a \vee b) \Leftrightarrow (\neg a \wedge \neg b)$	deMorgan's law

[34] Note that both the rules $a \vee (\neg a) \Leftrightarrow \text{True}$ and $a \wedge (\neg a) \Leftrightarrow \text{False}$ are needed to fully determine complements.

1.4.2.2 Implication and Deduction.

There are other logical connectives which may be defined, but for our purposes the following two are the most relevant.

$$x \textit{ implies } y$$

is written as

$$x \Rightarrow y$$

and informally this can be thought of as

"if x then y (else True) fi".

The idea behind this operator is that we can deduce y from x; that is, we can deduce that y is True when we know that x is True.

Also we have

$$x \textit{ is\_equivalent\_to } y$$

which is written as

$$x \Leftrightarrow y$$

meaning that

"x and y have the same (Boolean) value".

As there are only two possible results, this can also be verbalised as "(x is True) if and only if (y is True)", which is often abbreviated to "x *iff* y".

Of course, the signatures are

$$\mathbb{B} \Rightarrow \mathbb{B} \rightarrow \mathbb{B}$$
$$\mathbb{B} \Leftrightarrow \mathbb{B} \rightarrow \mathbb{B}$$

These two operators relate to the notion of 'deduction' and are not only useful in specification but allow us to derive other Boolean equivalences in a more straightforward manner and play an important part when it comes to strict refinement (i.e., reduction) as opposed to (reversible) transformations. But more on that later.

Jumping straight in we have

$$a \Rightarrow b \triangleq (\neg a) \vee (a \wedge b)$$

The motivation behind this definition is as follows: a may be False, in which case the implication tells us nothing about b, but if a is True we require that b also be True. Hence we have this (non-standard) definition.

Similarly, we have

$$a \Leftrightarrow b \triangleq (a \Rightarrow b) \wedge (b \Rightarrow a)$$

The properties of equivalence thus follow from those of implication.

When introducing new operators or new macros, we must take care to preserve consistency (i.e., to avoid any situation where, using rules in ways that now become available, an expression can be evaluated in different orders to give different values which are not intended to be equivalent). Here there should be no such difficulties since the bridge between each new operator and old ones is achieved by a *single* rule, The rules are

$$a \Rightarrow b \;\blacktriangleleft\!\blacktriangleright\; (\neg a) \vee (a \wedge b)$$

and

$$a \Leftrightarrow b \;\blacktriangleleft\!\blacktriangleright\; (a \Rightarrow b) \wedge (b \Rightarrow a)$$

The reason for our non-standard definition of implication will become clear when we extend the set of truth values. However, notice that by using existing rules we have

$$\begin{aligned} a \Rightarrow b \;&\blacktriangleleft\!\blacktriangleright\; (\neg a) \vee (a \wedge b) \\ &\blacktriangleleft\!\blacktriangleright\; ((\neg a) \vee a) \wedge ((\neg a) \vee b) \\ &\blacktriangleleft\!\blacktriangleright\; \text{True} \wedge ((\neg a) \vee b) \\ &\blacktriangleleft\!\blacktriangleright\; (\neg a) \vee b \end{aligned}$$

This is the more commonly seen form, and we can use it in manipulations. It is simpler (shorter) but can often cause confusion when first encountered. It is not immediately obvious how it relates to the notion behind implication.

The implication operator has many interesting and useful properties: These can be obtained by 'translating' $\Rightarrow$ into $\wedge$, $\vee$ and $\neg$. The most immediate are:

For all a (i.e., for an arbitrary a)

$$(a \Rightarrow a) \;\blacktriangleleft\!\blacktriangleright\; \text{True} \qquad (\Rightarrow \text{ is reflexive})$$

and

$$(a \Rightarrow b \wedge b \Rightarrow c) \qquad (a \Rightarrow c) \qquad (\Rightarrow \text{ is transitive})$$

The implication operator, '$\Rightarrow$', can be associated with deduction sequences of the form 'if assumption .... then conclusion'. We demonstrate this by showing the equivalence of the evaluation of the expression '$a \Rightarrow b$' to give True and the evaluation of b under the assumption that a holds.

Following our definition of $a \Rightarrow b$, we note the following argument:

if a is False (so $\neg a$ is True), then trivially it follows that $a \Rightarrow b$,
if a is True, then all we have to do is to show that b is True.

Hence, proving that

$$a \Rightarrow b \;\text{◆}\; \text{True}$$

is the same as showing that[35]

$$(a) \qquad b \qquad (\;\text{◆}\; \text{True}\;)$$

given that a is True, it follows that b is True.

We shall use it as justification for switching between these different ways of showing the validity of conditional claims; we can either

assume a and evaluate b

or

evaluate '$a \Rightarrow b$'.

Hence our 'formula' for $a \Rightarrow b$ does fit with the idea of deducing b from a.

[Although we shall need to insist on one further technical requirement, we should point out here that '$\Rightarrow$' is particularly important in program derivation because, given the specification for some function $f{:}X \to Y$, the necessary logical link between its data and result values is

$$(\forall x{:}X)\ (\text{pre-}f(x) \Rightarrow (\exists y{:}Y)\ (\text{post-}f(x,y)\ )$$

i.e., given a suitable x there *is* an appropriate y.]

The discussion above is related to what logicians call *Modus Ponens*, a method of reasoning which forms the basis of many deductive arguments.

In our notation, this is something like

$$(a \wedge (a \Rightarrow b)) \Rightarrow b$$

[35] That is $(a) \qquad b \;\text{◆}\; \text{True}$

Other '$\Rightarrow$' rules which can easily be derived, and used to simplify expression involving '$\Rightarrow$' include

$$(a \wedge b) \Rightarrow a$$
$$a \Rightarrow (a \vee b).$$

$$(\text{True} \Rightarrow q) \blacktriangleleft\!\blacktriangleright q$$
$$(\text{False} \Rightarrow q) \blacktriangleleft\!\blacktriangleright \text{True}$$
$$(p \Rightarrow \text{True}) \blacktriangleleft\!\blacktriangleright \text{True}$$
$$(p \Rightarrow \text{False}) \blacktriangleleft\!\blacktriangleright \neg p$$

$$(p \Rightarrow q) \blacktriangleleft\!\blacktriangleright (\neg q \Rightarrow \neg p)$$
$$p \Rightarrow q) \Rightarrow (p \Rightarrow (q \vee r)) \qquad (\blacktriangleleft\!\blacktriangleright \text{True})$$
$$(p \Rightarrow q) \Rightarrow ((p \wedge r) \Rightarrow q) \qquad (\blacktriangleleft\!\blacktriangleright \text{True})$$
$$((p \Rightarrow q) \wedge (\neg p \Rightarrow \neg q)) \blacktriangleleft\!\blacktriangleright (p \Leftrightarrow q)$$

Less expected are the following rules which may be regarded as absorption rules. That is, under appropriate conditions, part of an expression 'disappears'.

$$(a \Rightarrow b) \qquad a \blacktriangleleft\!\blacktriangleright a \wedge b$$

$$(a \Rightarrow b) \qquad b \blacktriangleleft\!\blacktriangleright a \vee b$$

$$a \wedge (a \Rightarrow b) \wedge b \blacktriangleleft\!\blacktriangleright a \wedge (a \Rightarrow b)$$

$$a \wedge b \blacktriangleleft\!\blacktriangleright a \wedge (a \Rightarrow b)$$

[So we also have

$$a \wedge b \blacktriangleleft\!\blacktriangleright b \wedge (b \Rightarrow a)$$

and hence

$$a \wedge (a \Rightarrow b) \blacktriangleleft\!\blacktriangleright b \wedge (b \Rightarrow a) \qquad !!$$

]

By comparison '$\Leftrightarrow$' is more straightforward and less interesting. Its main rules are

$$a \Leftrightarrow a \blacktriangleleft\!\blacktriangleright \text{True}$$

$$b \Leftrightarrow a \blacktriangleleft\!\blacktriangleright a \Leftrightarrow b$$

$$(a \Leftrightarrow b \wedge b \Leftrightarrow c) \qquad a \Leftrightarrow c \blacktriangleleft\!\blacktriangleright \text{True}$$

So $\Leftrightarrow$ is a value equivalence relation, just like '=', and hence we can also use it as the basis of re-write rules and replace it with '$\blacktriangleleft\!\blacktriangleright$' whenever we have a valid logical equivalence that we wish to use as a rule:

$$(a \Leftrightarrow b) \qquad a \blacktriangleleft\!\blacktriangleright b$$

We also have

$$a \Leftrightarrow b \;\blacktriangleleft\!\blacktriangleright\; (a \wedge b) \vee (\neg a \wedge \neg b)$$

Now we can extend the definition of $\mathbb{B}$ to include the declaration of these new operators and derived rules. These are given in the Appendix.

1.4.2.3 Boolean Quantifiers

We have already met the existential quantifier, "there exists", written "$\exists$", within specifications. So

$$(\exists x{:}\mathbb{Z})(\ x + 3 = 0\ )$$

means that "there exists an integer x such that $x + 3 = 0$".

This is a simple example, where the expression "$x + 3 = 0$" should be thought of as a mechanism for obtaining a Boolean value from the integer x. The "$(\exists x{:}\mathbb{Z})$" then causes the expression to be evaluated for each value in $\mathbb{Z}$ and the results combined appropriately[36]. The *calculation* of this final step requires infinitely many values be combined, and the tree relating to this will be rather wide; however, we can still use a more compact tree to indicate the *types* involved (as in Figure 1.13).

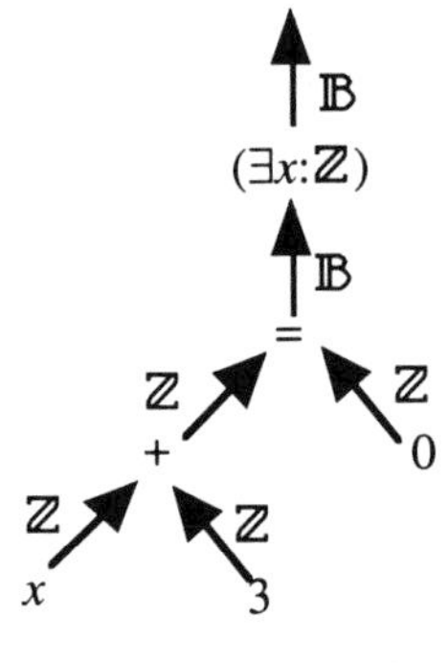

Figure 1.13

When a logically quantified expression is *fully* evaluated, it delivers a Boolean result. But x is not a single constant, and "$x + 3 = 0$" does not represent a Boolean value, it is a function of type $\mathbb{Z} \rightarrow \mathbb{B}$.

[36] Actually by using the $\vee$ connective, but more about that later.

Linking the x's in Figure 1.13 (to give Figure 1.14) clarifies the fact that x is not an 'input' value and in fact the expression "$(\exists x{:}\mathbb{Z})(\ x + 3 = 0\ )$" is a Boolean constant; it is a rather complicated way of writing "True". x is a ***bound variable***, an internal variable. Think of it as a local variable. Such linking within 'trees' is useful in simple cases, but it is perhaps not worthwhile taking this idea much further.

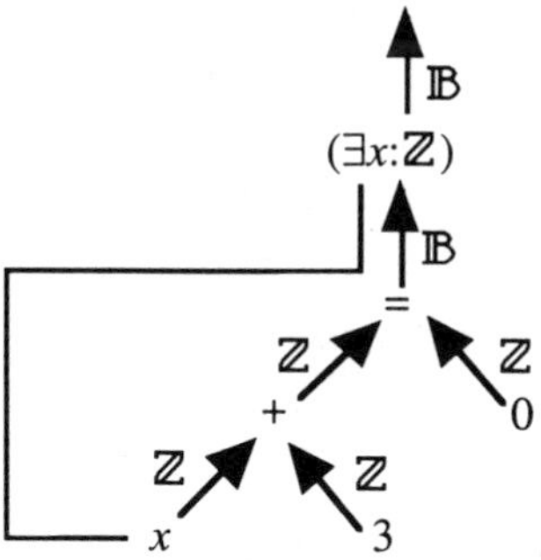

Figure 1.14

Finally, consider

$$(\exists x{:}\mathbb{Z})(\ x + y = 0\ ) \qquad\qquad \text{where } y{:}\mathbb{Z}$$

This gives the picture in Figure 1.15, which clearly shows that we have a function of type $\mathbb{Z} \to \mathbb{B}$.

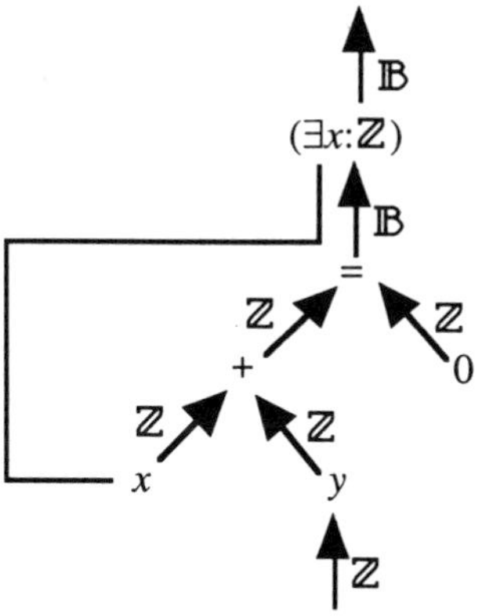

Figure 1.15

1.4.2.4 Extended (3-valued) Logic

Apart from the Boolean type based on the set {True, False}, there are situations where a seemingly innocuous expression gives rise to errors and hence we want, at all costs, to prevent an attempt to complete the evaluation of certain 'Boolean' expressions. To avoid using a post-condition in a situation where the pre-condition failed (i.e., gave False, indicating that the data was invalid), we used the sequential, or *conditional*, *and* operator. This works in exactly the same way as the normal *and* when used with Boolean inputs but also allowed us to have an undefined input for the second operand provided that, when that happened, the first one was False. This condition guaranteed that the resulting expression was 'well-formed' and never gave an undefined result. We therefore have the informal definition

$$a \wedge b \triangleq \text{if } a \text{ then } b \text{ else False fi}$$

but the result must be of type $\mathbb{B}$.

Similarly, we have a *conditional or*,

$$a \vee b \triangleq \text{if } a \text{ then True else } b \text{ fi}$$

and again the result must be of type $\mathbb{B}$.

Representing the extended truth set/type by $\mathbb{E} \triangleq$ {True, False, Undefined[37]}, we have the signatures

$$\mathbb{B} \wedge \mathbb{E} \rightarrow \mathbb{B}$$
$$\mathbb{B} \vee \mathbb{E} \rightarrow \mathbb{B}$$

Of course, we are not really interested in situations where *final* results are Undefined or Unknown, but we need to know what to do with them if and when they occur *within* expressions. We shall try to deal with such 'values' in a minimal way.

Before giving the formal (but implicit) definitions of these operators, we note the distinction between False and Undefined.

The expression	$1 / 0 < 6$ is Undefined	– it is neither True nor False,
whereas	$1 < 6 * 0$ is False	– it reduces to $1 < 0$.

To prevent unnecessary operand evaluation and restrict the range of valid results from evaluating these operations, we require that $\wedge$ and $\vee$ satisfy the following rules. As will be seen, these are consistent with similar operations over $\mathbb{B}$.

[37] This value can also be regarded as 'Unknown' or 'Error' – which is distinct from either True or False. It is not the same as saying that the value is either True or False but we don't know which one. It is sometimes more natural to use one of these names rather than 'Undefined'.

The rules are:

$$\text{True} \curlywedge b \;\blacktriangleleft\!\blacktriangleright\; b \qquad \text{with } b{:}\mathbb{B}$$
$$\text{False} \curlywedge b \;\blacktriangleleft\!\blacktriangleright\; \text{False}$$

and

$$\text{True} \curlyvee b \;\blacktriangleleft\!\blacktriangleright\; \text{True}$$
$$\text{False} \curlyvee b \;\blacktriangleleft\!\blacktriangleright\; b \qquad \text{with } b{:}\mathbb{B}$$

and, for completeness[38],

$$\text{Undefined} \curlywedge b \;\blacktriangleleft\!\blacktriangleright\; \text{Undefined}$$
$$\text{True} \curlywedge \text{Undefined} \;\blacktriangleleft\!\blacktriangleright\; \text{Undefined}$$

and

$$\text{Undefined} \curlyvee b \;\blacktriangleleft\!\blacktriangleright\; \text{Undefined}$$
$$\text{False} \curlyvee \text{Undefined} \;\blacktriangleleft\!\blacktriangleright\; \text{Undefined}$$

Of course, since $\mathbb{E}$ is an extension of $\mathbb{B}$ (this follows because $\mathbb{B} \subseteq \mathbb{E}$ and the results coincide when common values are used as operands), the Boolean operators are also available on the appropriate values in $\mathbb{E}$ (i.e., on True and False).

So, if $a,b{:}\mathbb{B}$, then

$$a \curlywedge b \;\blacktriangleleft\!\blacktriangleright\; a \wedge b$$

and

$$a \curlyvee b \;\blacktriangleleft\!\blacktriangleright\; a \vee b$$

It also follows that

$$\neg(a \curlywedge b) \;\blacktriangleleft\!\blacktriangleright\; (\neg a \curlyvee \neg b)$$

and

$$\neg(a \curlyvee b) \;\blacktriangleleft\!\blacktriangleright\; (\neg a \curlywedge \neg b).$$

These are the $\mathbb{E}$ variants of deMorgan's laws. Here $\neg$ Undefined is not defined. Remember, consequential parts of the expressions are only evaluated when necessary; and '$\neg$' is defined only over $\mathbb{B}$.

So, in certain circumstances we can replace $\curlywedge$ by $\wedge$, and $\curlyvee$ by $\vee$, and $\neg$ reacts in the expected way with $\curlywedge$ and $\curlyvee$.

The situation becomes less clear when both conditional and 'normal' connectives are used together (and where we allow the possibility of unknown values and hence we cannot simply replace the conditional operators with the Boolean versions).

[38] These rules are not those to be found elsewhere. They are included only for completeness, and we shall not have cause to use them. To omit them might only have led the reader to ask "but what if...?" Indeed, for them to be valid we would have to extend the operator signatures to: $\mathbb{E} \curlywedge \mathbb{E} \rightarrow \mathbb{E}$ and $\mathbb{E} \curlyvee \mathbb{E} \rightarrow \mathbb{E}$. To do this would admit expressions which we regard as ill-formed.

Note also that Undefined = Undefined $\blacktriangleleft\!\blacktriangleright$ Undefined (the right-hand side is Undefined, *not* True)

Although the $\dot\wedge$ and $\dot\vee$ connectives will be new to most readers, we shall not digress into an extensive development of the associated algebra but merely quote some results, work out some others directly from the definitions, and derive only a few by algebraic manipulation.

For example, we have

$$x \mathbin{\dot\wedge} (y \mathbin{\dot\wedge} a) \Leftrightarrow (x \mathbin{\dot\wedge} y) \mathbin{\dot\wedge} a \qquad \text{where } x{:}\mathbb{B},\ y,a{:}\mathbb{E}$$
$$x \mathbin{\dot\wedge} (y \mathbin{\dot\wedge} a) \Leftrightarrow (x \wedge y) \mathbin{\dot\wedge} a \qquad \text{where } x,y{:}\mathbb{B},\ a{:}\mathbb{E}$$
$$x \wedge (y \mathbin{\dot\wedge} a) \Leftrightarrow (x \wedge y) \mathbin{\dot\wedge} a \qquad \text{where } x,y{:}\mathbb{B},\ a{:}\mathbb{E}$$

$$p \mathbin{\dot\wedge} (x \vee y) \Leftrightarrow (p \mathbin{\dot\wedge} x) \vee (p \mathbin{\dot\wedge} y) \qquad \text{where } p{:}\mathbb{B},\ x,y{:}\mathbb{E}$$

$$(p \vee q) \mathbin{\dot\wedge} a \Leftrightarrow (p \mathbin{\dot\wedge} a) \vee (q \mathbin{\dot\wedge} a) \qquad \text{where } p,q{:}\mathbb{B},\ a{:}\mathbb{E}$$

Less obvious, and utilising normal Boolean algebra in their derivation, are:

$$(p \mathbin{\dot\wedge} a) \vee (\neg p \mathbin{\dot\wedge} q \mathbin{\dot\wedge} a) \qquad \text{where } p,q{:}\mathbb{B},\ a{:}\mathbb{E}$$

$\Leftrightarrow$

$$(p \mathbin{\dot\wedge} a) \vee ((\neg p \wedge q) \mathbin{\dot\wedge} a)$$

$\Leftrightarrow$

$$(p \vee (\neg p \wedge q)) \mathbin{\dot\wedge} a$$

$\Leftrightarrow$

$$((p \vee \neg p) \wedge (p \vee q)) \mathbin{\dot\wedge} a$$

$\Leftrightarrow$

$$(\text{True} \wedge (p \vee q)) \mathbin{\dot\wedge} a$$

$\Leftrightarrow$

$$(p \vee q) \mathbin{\dot\wedge} a$$

There are more useful identities involving these conditional operators. These include

$$(p \mathbin{\dot\wedge} a) \wedge (q \mathbin{\dot\wedge} b) \Leftrightarrow (p \wedge q) \mathbin{\dot\wedge} (a \wedge b)$$

a special case of which is

$$(p \mathbin{\dot\wedge} a) \wedge (\neg p \mathbin{\dot\wedge} b) \Leftrightarrow \text{False}$$

We also have

$$(p \mathbin{\dot\wedge} a) \vee (q \mathbin{\dot\wedge} b) \Rightarrow (p \vee q) \mathbin{\dot\wedge} (a \vee b)$$

$$(p \mathbin{\dot\vee} a) \vee (q \mathbin{\dot\vee} b) \Leftrightarrow (p \vee q) \mathbin{\dot\vee} (a \vee b)$$

$$(p \wedge q) \mathbin{\dot\vee} (a \wedge b) \Rightarrow (p \mathbin{\dot\vee} a) \wedge (q \mathbin{\dot\vee} b)$$

$$a \wedge (b \mathbin{\Lambda} c) \Leftrightarrow (a \wedge b) \mathbin{\Lambda} c$$

and hence

$$a \wedge (a \mathbin{\Lambda} c) \Leftrightarrow a \mathbin{\Lambda} c$$

The forms above relate specifically to conditional expressions (as in programs) and subsequently to conditional statements. Hence, instead of just noting them, we look at their derivation. First we examine

$$(p \mathbin{\Lambda} a) \wedge (q \mathbin{\Lambda} b) \Leftrightarrow (p \wedge q) \mathbin{\Lambda} (a \wedge b).$$

If $(p \wedge q) \Leftrightarrow \text{True}$, then $p \Leftrightarrow \text{True}$ and $q \Leftrightarrow \text{True}$, so

$$(p \wedge q) \mathbin{\Lambda} (a \wedge b) \Leftrightarrow (a \wedge b)$$

and

$$(p \mathbin{\Lambda} a) \wedge (q \mathbin{\Lambda} b) \Leftrightarrow (a \wedge b).$$

On the other hand, if either $p \Leftrightarrow \text{False}$ or $q \Leftrightarrow \text{False}$, then

$(p \mathbin{\Lambda} a) \Leftrightarrow \text{False}$ or $(q \mathbin{\Lambda} b) \Leftrightarrow \text{False}$, so

$$(p \mathbin{\Lambda} a) \wedge (q \mathbin{\Lambda} b) \Leftrightarrow \text{False}.$$

Similarly,

$$(p \wedge q) \Leftrightarrow \text{False}$$

so

$$\begin{aligned}(p \wedge q) \mathbin{\Lambda} (a \wedge b) &\Leftrightarrow \text{False}\\ &\Leftrightarrow (p \mathbin{\Lambda} a) \wedge (q \mathbin{\Lambda} b),\end{aligned}$$

and so the rule holds.

For the implication

$$(p \mathbin{\Lambda} a) \vee (q \mathbin{\Lambda} b) \Rightarrow (p \vee q) \mathbin{\Lambda} (a \vee b),$$

we assume the truth of the left-hand side and evaluate the right-hand side.

If $(p \mathbin{\Lambda} a) \vee (q \mathbin{\Lambda} b) \Leftrightarrow \text{True}$, then without loss of generality we can suppose that $(p \mathbin{\Lambda} a) \Leftrightarrow \text{True}$ (i.e., $p \Leftrightarrow \text{True}$ and $a \Leftrightarrow \text{True}$) so

$$\begin{aligned}&(p \vee q) \mathbin{\Lambda} (a \vee b)\\ \Leftrightarrow\ &\text{True} \mathbin{\Lambda} \text{True}\\ \Leftrightarrow\ &\text{True}\end{aligned}$$

Hence the implication holds.

Once we have these two rules, the others follow by the straightforward algebraic manipulation. We just do one further derivation:

$$(p \mathbin{\dot\vee} a) \vee (q \mathbin{\dot\vee} b)$$

$\blacktriangleleft\!\blacktriangleright$

$$\neg\neg((p \mathbin{\dot\vee} a) \vee (q \mathbin{\dot\vee} b))$$

$\blacktriangleleft\!\blacktriangleright$

$$\neg(\neg(p \mathbin{\dot\vee} a) \wedge \neg(q \mathbin{\dot\vee} b))$$

$\blacktriangleleft\!\blacktriangleright$

$$\neg((\neg p \mathbin{\dot\wedge} \neg a) \wedge (\neg q \mathbin{\dot\wedge} \neg b))$$

$\blacktriangleleft\!\blacktriangleright$

$$\neg((\neg p \wedge \neg a) \mathbin{\dot\wedge} (\neg q \wedge \neg b)) \qquad \text{by the first of these new rules.}$$

$\blacktriangleleft\!\blacktriangleright$

$$\neg(\neg p \wedge \neg a) \mathbin{\dot\vee} \neg(\neg q \wedge \neg b)$$

$\blacktriangleleft\!\blacktriangleright$

$$(\neg\neg p \vee \neg\neg a) \mathbin{\dot\vee} (\neg\neg q \vee \neg\neg b)$$

$\blacktriangleleft\!\blacktriangleright$

$$(p \vee a) \mathbin{\dot\vee} (q \vee b)$$

It is also convenient, when defining conditional programming statements to have a version of implication in which evaluation is 'lazy' and which thus prevents us from attempting to evaluate sections of expressions or commands that are, at best not required and at worst would give rise to needless errors. Thus we have the conditional/sequential/lazy implication operator '$\Rrightarrow$', defined as

$$a \Rrightarrow b \triangleq (\neg a) \vee (a \mathbin{\dot\wedge} b).$$

Note that in many situations where '$\Rightarrow$' would commonly be used, and hence give rise to failures in evaluation, the lazy version should be used.

The signature of lazy implication is $\qquad \mathbb{B} \Rrightarrow \mathbb{E} \to \mathbb{B}$.

As with the simple, Boolean, case, there is a simpler equivalent. This is predictably

$$\neg a \mathbin{\dot\vee} b$$

That both expressions are value equivalent can be seen by considering the two values which a might have. If a is True, then both expressions evaluate to b. If a is False, then we have the result True for both expressions.

It also follows that

$$(a \Rrightarrow b) \wedge (b \Rrightarrow a) \blacktriangleleft\!\blacktriangleright (a \Leftrightarrow b)$$

and

$$((a \Rrightarrow b) \wedge (b \Rrightarrow c)) \Rightarrow (a \Rrightarrow c)$$

Conditional Expressions

Having used a set of rules (axioms) to define $\dot{\wedge}$ and $\dot{\vee}$, rather than a formula in which we might well have been tempted to use an "if .. then..." construct, we can now use these operators to give a proper definition to "if...then..." and thus avoid circular definitions:

$$\text{if } a \text{ then } b \text{ else } c \text{ fi} \triangleq (a \Rrightarrow b) \wedge (\neg a \Rrightarrow c)$$

To be of use within transformation sequences, conditional expressions must be *well-formed*. By this we mean that it must give a Boolean result. Its signature is:

$$\text{if } \mathbb{B} \text{ then } \mathbb{E} \text{ else } \mathbb{E} \text{ fi} \rightarrow \mathbb{B}.$$

In practice, this means that if the first operand (the test) gives True, then the second operand (the 'then' value) must be Boolean; and if the test yields False, then the 'else' operand must be Boolean.

We have a definition of '$\Rrightarrow$' but no manipulation rules. Note the following derivation:

$$(a \Rrightarrow b) \wedge (\neg a \Rrightarrow c)$$

$\blacktriangleleft\!\blacktriangleright$

$$((\neg a) \vee (a \mathbin{\dot{\wedge}} b)) \wedge ((a) \vee (\neg a \mathbin{\dot{\wedge}} c))$$

$\blacktriangleleft\!\blacktriangleright$

$$\begin{array}{ll} & (\neg a \wedge a) \\ \vee & (\neg a \wedge (\neg a \mathbin{\dot{\wedge}} c)) \\ \vee & (a \wedge (a \mathbin{\dot{\wedge}} b)) \\ \vee & ((a \mathbin{\dot{\wedge}} b) \wedge (\neg a \mathbin{\dot{\wedge}} c)) \end{array}$$

$\blacktriangleleft\!\blacktriangleright$

$$\begin{array}{ll} & \text{False} \\ \vee & (\neg a \mathbin{\dot{\wedge}} c) \\ \vee & (a \mathbin{\dot{\wedge}} b) \\ \vee & \text{False} \end{array}$$

$\blacktriangleleft\!\blacktriangleright$

$$(a \mathbin{\dot{\wedge}} b) \vee (\neg a \mathbin{\dot{\wedge}} c)$$

So we have

$$\text{if } a \text{ then } b \text{ else } c \text{ fi} \;\blacktriangleleft\!\blacktriangleright\; (a \mathbin{\dot{\wedge}} b) \vee (\neg a \mathbin{\dot{\wedge}} c)$$

We can now utilise some of the rules for conditional operators to derive rules for manipulating "if...then...else...fi" expressions.

The first is trivial:

$$\begin{aligned}\text{if } a \text{ then } b \text{ else } c \text{ fi} \;&\blacktriangleleft\!\blacktriangleright\; (a \mathbin{\Lambda} b) \vee (\neg a \mathbin{\Lambda} c)\\ &\blacktriangleleft\!\blacktriangleright\; (\neg a \mathbin{\Lambda} c) \vee (\neg\neg a \mathbin{\Lambda} b)\\ &\blacktriangleleft\!\blacktriangleright\; \text{if } \neg a \text{ then } c \text{ else } b \text{ fi}\end{aligned}$$

Next, with $p{:}\mathbb{B}$, $a_1,a_2,b_1,b_2{:}\mathbb{E}$, provided that the following expressions are well-formed

$$(\text{if } p \text{ then } a_1 \text{ else } b_1 \text{ fi}) \;\wedge\; (\text{if } p \text{ then } a_2 \text{ else } b_2 \text{ fi})$$

$$\blacktriangleleft\!\blacktriangleright$$

$$\text{if } p \text{ then } (a_1 \wedge a_2) \text{ else } (b_1 \wedge b_2) \text{ fi}$$

This is derived by straightforward calculation:

$$(\text{if } p \text{ then } a_1 \text{ else } b_1 \text{ fi}) \;\wedge\; (\text{if } p \text{ then } a_2 \text{ else } b_2 \text{ fi})$$

$$\blacktriangleleft\!\blacktriangleright$$

$$((p \mathbin{\Lambda} a_1) \vee (\neg p \mathbin{\Lambda} b_1)) \;\wedge\; ((p \mathbin{\Lambda} a_2) \vee (\neg p \mathbin{\Lambda} b_2))$$

$$\blacktriangleleft\!\blacktriangleright$$

$$\begin{aligned}&((\;p \mathbin{\Lambda} a_1) \wedge (\;p \mathbin{\Lambda} a_2))\\ \vee\; &((\;p \mathbin{\Lambda} a_1) \wedge (\neg p \mathbin{\Lambda} b_2))\\ \vee\; &((\neg p \mathbin{\Lambda} b_1) \wedge (\;p \mathbin{\Lambda} a_2))\\ \vee\; &((\neg p \mathbin{\Lambda} b_1) \wedge (\neg p \mathbin{\Lambda} b_2))\end{aligned}$$

$$\blacktriangleleft\!\blacktriangleright$$

$$\begin{aligned}&((\;p \wedge \;p) \mathbin{\Lambda} (a_1 \wedge a_2))\\ \vee\; &((\;p \wedge \neg p) \mathbin{\Lambda} (a_1 \wedge b_2))\\ \vee\; &((\neg p \wedge \;p) \mathbin{\Lambda} (b_1 \wedge a_2))\\ \vee\; &((\neg p \wedge \neg p) \mathbin{\Lambda} (b_1 \wedge b_2))\end{aligned}$$

$$\blacktriangleleft\!\blacktriangleright$$

$$\begin{aligned}&(\;p \quad \mathbin{\Lambda} (a_1 \wedge a_2))\\ \vee\; &(\text{False} \mathbin{\Lambda} (a_1 \wedge b_2))\\ \vee\; &(\text{False} \mathbin{\Lambda} (b_1 \wedge a_2))\\ \vee\; &(\neg p \quad \mathbin{\Lambda} (b_1 \wedge b_2))\end{aligned}$$

$$\blacktriangleleft\!\blacktriangleright$$

$$(p \mathbin{\Lambda} (a_1 \wedge a_2)) \vee (\neg p \mathbin{\Lambda} (b_1 \wedge b_2))$$

$$\blacktriangleleft\!\blacktriangleright$$

$$\text{if } p \text{ then } (a_1 \wedge a_2) \text{ else } (b_1 \wedge b_2) \text{ fi}$$

Similarly, we have

if p then (if p then a else b fi) else c fi

$\Leftrightarrow$

if p then a else c fi

This follows since

if p then (if p then a else b fi) else c fi

$\Leftrightarrow$

$(p \wedge ((p \wedge a) \vee (\neg p \wedge b))) \vee (\neg p \wedge c)$

$\Leftrightarrow$

$(p \wedge p \wedge a) \vee (p \wedge \neg p \wedge b) \vee (\neg p \wedge \mathrm{c})$

$\Leftrightarrow$

$(p \wedge a) \vee (\mathrm{False} \wedge b) \vee (\neg p \wedge c)$

$\Leftrightarrow$

$(p \wedge a) \vee (\neg p \wedge c)$

$\Leftrightarrow$

if p then a else c fi

and

if p then a else (if q then a else b fi) fi

$\Leftrightarrow$

if $(p \vee q)$ then a else b fi

By calculation

if p then a else (if q then a else b fi) fi

$\Leftrightarrow$

$(p \wedge a) \vee (\neg p \wedge ((q \wedge a) \vee (\neg q \wedge b)))$

$\Leftrightarrow$

$(p \wedge a) \vee (\neg p \wedge q \wedge a) \vee (\neg p \wedge \neg q \wedge b)$

$\Leftrightarrow$

$(p \wedge a) \vee ((\neg p \wedge q) \wedge a) \vee ((\neg p \wedge \neg q) \wedge b)$

$\Leftrightarrow$

$((p \vee (\neg p \wedge q)) \wedge a) \vee (\neg(p \vee q) \wedge b)$

$\Leftrightarrow$

$(((p \vee \neg p) \wedge (p \vee q)) \wedge a) \vee (\neg(p \vee q) \wedge b)$

$\Leftrightarrow$

$((\mathrm{True} \wedge (p \vee q)) \wedge a) \vee (\neg(p \vee q) \wedge b)$

$\Leftrightarrow$

$((p \vee q) \wedge a) \vee (\neg(p \vee q) \wedge b)$

$\Leftrightarrow$

if $(p \vee q)$ then a else b fi

Recall also that

$$(p \mathbin{\dot\wedge} a) \vee (q \mathbin{\dot\wedge} a) \;\Leftrightarrow\; (p \vee q) \mathbin{\dot\wedge} a$$

so

$$\begin{aligned}(p \mathbin{\dot\wedge} a) \vee (\neg p \mathbin{\dot\wedge} a) \;&\Leftrightarrow\; (p \vee \neg p) \mathbin{\dot\wedge} a\\ &\Leftrightarrow\; \text{True} \mathbin{\dot\wedge} a\\ &\Leftrightarrow\; a\end{aligned}$$

That is,

if p then a else a fi $\Leftrightarrow$ a. as should be expected.

Of course, in many cases the whole point of using a conditional expression is to prevent the (illegal?)[39] evaluation of certain sub-expressions.

Also notice that, again with $a,b:\mathbb{B}$,

$$\begin{aligned}&\text{if } a \text{ then } b \text{ else True fi}\\ \Leftrightarrow\;& (a \Rrightarrow b) \wedge (\neg a \Rrightarrow \text{True})\\ \Leftrightarrow\;& (a \Rrightarrow b) \wedge (a \mathbin{\dot\vee} \text{True})\\ \Leftrightarrow\;& (a \Rrightarrow b) \wedge (a \vee \text{True})\\ \Leftrightarrow\;& (a \Rrightarrow b) \wedge \text{True}\\ \Leftrightarrow\;& (a \Rrightarrow b)\end{aligned}$$

This piece of calculation goes some way to justify the often mistrusted definition of the 'incomplete' conditional, which, in any case only makes sense with logical operands:

$$\text{if } a \text{ then } b \text{ fi} \triangleq \text{if } a \text{ then } b \text{ else True fi}$$

Embedded Conditional Expressions

Despite our insistence that the type of the 'if' operand of the 'if ... then ... else ... fi' construct should be Boolean, there are cases when allowing it to be 'undefined' *does* makes sense[40]. In these situations, the surrounding logical context only allows access to this operand when it is guaranteed to evaluate to True or to False.

So, consider the following expressions in which $p:\mathbb{B}$, $q:\mathbb{E}$ and $b,c:\mathbb{E}$.

---

[39] Uses of "(...?)", such as here, indicate possible alternative terminology, or interpretations or views — probably thought provoking.

[40] Without extra qualifications (such as context information - see below) a conditional 'predicated' on 'undefined' cannot be evaluated.

Notwithstanding the questionable type of q, notice the following two derivations:

Let $X \triangleq (\neg p \vee \neg q) \wedge (p \wedge b)$.

If $p \Leftrightarrow$ True and $q \Leftrightarrow$ True, then $X \Leftrightarrow$ False. If $p \Leftrightarrow$ True and $q \Leftrightarrow$ False then $X \Leftrightarrow b$. And if $p \Leftrightarrow$ False, then $X \Leftrightarrow$ False.

Similarly, let $Y \triangleq p \wedge \neg q \wedge b$.

If $p \Leftrightarrow$ True and $q \Leftrightarrow$ True, then $Y \Leftrightarrow$ False. If $p \Leftrightarrow$ True and $q \Leftrightarrow$ False then $Y \Leftrightarrow b$. And if $p \Leftrightarrow$ False, then $Y \Leftrightarrow$ False.

So we have the rule $(\neg p \vee \neg q) \wedge (p \wedge b) \Leftrightarrow p \wedge \neg q \wedge b$.

By a similar argument, we can also derive the rule

$$(\neg p \vee \neg q) \wedge (\neg p \wedge c) \Leftrightarrow (\neg p \wedge c).$$

We now use these rules in a straightforward calculation:

if $p \wedge q$ then a
  else if p then b else c fi
fi

$\Leftrightarrow$ $((p \wedge q) \wedge a) \vee$
$(\neg (p \wedge q) \wedge ((p \wedge b) \vee (\neg p \wedge c)))$

$\Leftrightarrow$ $(p \wedge q \wedge a) \vee$
$((\neg p \vee \neg q) \wedge ((p \wedge b) \vee (\neg p \wedge c)))$

$\Leftrightarrow$ $(p \wedge q \wedge a) \vee$
$((\neg p \vee \neg q) \wedge (p \wedge b)) \vee$
$((\neg p \vee \neg q) \wedge (\neg p \wedge c))$

$\Leftrightarrow$ $(p \wedge q \wedge a) \vee$
$((p \wedge \neg q \wedge b)) \vee (\neg p \wedge c))$

$\Leftrightarrow$ $((p \wedge q \wedge a) \vee (p \wedge \neg q \wedge b)) \vee (\neg p \wedge c)$

$\Leftrightarrow$ $(p \wedge ((q \wedge a) \vee (\neg q \wedge b))) \vee (\neg p \wedge c)$

$\Leftrightarrow$ if p then if q then a else b fi
  else c
fi

So

if $p \curlywedge q$ then a
    else if p then b else c fi
fi

⧓

if p then if q then a else b fi
    else c
fi

In both these expressions, the evaluation of q follows an evaluation of p that results in True (either by the 'sequential and' or by the hierarchical structure imposed by the nested conditional expressions). Hence, when p ⧓ False, q can be undefined (i.e., q is allowed to be of type $\mathbb{E}$, it is not confined to $\mathbb{B}$). Therefore, the signature for conditional expressions can be extended, in certain circumstances, to

if $\mathbb{E}$ then $\mathbb{E}$ else $\mathbb{E}$ fi $\rightarrow$ $\mathbb{E}$.

The situations when this type 'extension' is acceptable are characterised by a predicate p so that the conditional

if q then a else b fi

can only be evaluated if

$(p \Leftrightarrow \text{True}) \Rrightarrow q{:}\mathbb{B}$.   ($q$ is of type $\mathbb{B}$, see Section 1.4.8 on unions below)

Here p is the context (the assumption, which is known to be True) when q is evaluated.

An outer condition, c, may be implicit but can be carried forward into the current calculation (and made explicit) by use of the rules

(c)	$c \wedge b$ ⧓ b		$b{:}\mathbb{B}$
(c)	$c \curlywedge p$ ⧓ p		$p{:}\mathbb{E}$

[Moreover, when we have complex conditions that involve a sequence of conjuncts, such as

$(a \curlywedge b)$ x ⧓ y

we represent this in abbreviated form as:

(a, b) x ⧓ y

]

The *sequential implication* operator now gives us another way to express the relationship between pre- and post-conditions: Recall that the purpose of the pre-condition is to identify those input values for which it is possible (and for which we *wish*) to compute the specified function. It is therefore tempting to write

$$\text{pre-}f(x) \Rightarrow (\exists y{:}Y)(\ \text{post-}f(x,y)\ )$$

That is, if x satisfies the pre-condition then there is some value y — and there may be more than one value — such that $\langle x,y \rangle$ satisfies the post-condition.

This seems reasonable, but in the definition of '$\Rightarrow$' the two operands are expanded independently. Therefore, the evaluation of $(\exists y{:}Y)(\text{post-}f(x,y))$ is unrelated to pre-$f(x)$ and hence might require us to evaluate post-$f(x,y)$ for a value of x for which post-$f(x,y)$ is False, and this violates the whole purpose of having a pre-condition. To circumvent this logical problem, we bridge the two sides of the implication by using

$$\text{pre-}f(x) \Rrightarrow (\exists y{:}Y)(\ \text{post-}f(x,y)\ )$$

Henceforth, in the synthesis of (implementations of) f, we shall assume the existence of x and y and manipulate post-$f(x,y)$ under the presumption that its value (and that of pre-$f(x)$) is True. Remember that post-$f(x,y)$ is an implicit definition of y in terms of x.

Conditional Expressions with Arbitrary Types

Providing that the conditional expressions are well-formed, we can extend the signature of the conditional expression from

$$\text{if } \mathbb{B} \text{ then } \mathbb{E} \text{ else } \mathbb{E} \text{ fi} \rightarrow \mathbb{B}$$

to

$$\text{if } \mathbb{B} \text{ then } X \text{ else } X \text{ fi} \rightarrow X \qquad \text{with } X \neq \mathbb{E}.$$

We do this by using the existence of '=' on the type X:

$$a = (\text{if } p \text{ then } b \text{ else } c \text{ fi}) \triangleq \text{if } p \text{ then } (a = b) \text{ else } (a = c) \text{ fi}.$$

From the right-hand side, which uses the signature 'if $\mathbb{B}$ then $\mathbb{E}$ else $\mathbb{E}$ fi $\rightarrow \mathbb{B}$', it follows that if p is True then the value of the right-hand side is $a = b$. Then, on the left-hand side we also have $a = b$, so the value of (if p then b else c fi) is b.

Similarly, if p is False, we find that $a = c$ and so (if p then b else c fi) evaluates to c, so:

$$\text{if True then } b \text{ else } c \text{ fi} \quad \blacklozenge \quad b$$
$$\text{if False then } b \text{ else } c \text{ fi} \quad \blacklozenge \quad c$$

(p) $a = (\text{if } p \text{ then } b \text{ else } c \text{ fi}) \quad \blacklozenge \quad a = b$
$(\neg p)$ $a = (\text{if } p \text{ then } b \text{ else } c \text{ fi}) \quad \blacklozenge \quad a = c$

By a similar argument, we can mix conditionals with a function application, so if $f:X \rightarrow Y$, we have

$$f(\text{if } p \text{ then } b \text{ else } c \text{ fi}) \quad \blacklozenge \quad \text{if } p \text{ then } f(b) \text{ else } f(c) \text{ fi}$$

and the functions may be predicates (e.g., $f:X \rightarrow \mathbb{B}$ where $f(y) \triangleq a = y$) and again we have

$$a = (\text{if } p \text{ then } b \text{ else } c \text{ fi}) \quad \blacklozenge \quad \text{if } p \text{ then } (a = b) \text{ else } (a = c) \text{ fi}$$

which generalises to any predicate. Any parameter of a function can be conditional, and this justifies the use of conditional terms within an expression. So, for instance if a, c and $d:\mathbb{Z}$ and $b:\mathbb{B}$, we can have

$$a + (\text{if } b \text{ then } c \text{ else } d \text{ fi}) \quad \blacklozenge \quad \text{if } b \text{ then } (a + c) \text{ else } (a + d) \text{ fi}$$

This follows from the definition of $add(x,y) \triangleq x + y$ by the progression

$$a + (\text{if } b \text{ then } c \text{ else } d \text{ fi}) \quad \blacklozenge \quad add(a, \text{if } b \text{ then } c \text{ else } d \text{ fi })$$
$$\blacklozenge \quad \text{if } b \text{ then } add(a,c) \text{ else } add(a,d) \text{ fi}$$
$$\blacklozenge \quad \text{if } b \text{ then } (a + c) \text{ else } (a + d) \text{ fi}$$

Finally, notice that for $x:X$

$$\text{True}$$
$$\blacklozenge \quad \text{if } b \text{ then True else True fi}$$
$$\blacklozenge \quad \text{if } b \text{ then } x = x \text{ else } x = x \text{ fi}$$
$$\blacklozenge \quad x = (\text{if } b \text{ then } x \text{ else } x \text{ fi})$$

Therefore, $x = (\text{if } b \text{ then } x \text{ else } x \text{ fi})$ holds and thus $x \; \blacklozenge \; (\text{if } b \text{ then } x \text{ else } x \text{ fi})$ is a universal rule.

So, we get the expected rules for conditional expressions, but now they have been explained and have a formal foundation; they have not just been plucked out of thin air. The rules discussed here are collected together in the Appendix.

Take particular notice how this major piece of syntax[41] can be overloaded by virtually any type and hence not only the rules but almost the entire data type specification is parameterised. As always, we need to know exactly the type of data being manipulated. [The conditional operators are included for completeness and used to define the "if then else fi" forms. Elsewhere they can be used to indicate sequential actions within the specification of more complex software.]

1.4.3 Sets

Although not having as high a profile as in some other areas of mathematics, sets are the fundamental entities from which relations and functions are constructed. In program specification and design, sets are mainly used to describe internal links between more concrete objects.

We assume that the reader is familiar with sets — this section merely to introduces the rules for formal manipulation of expressions involving sets — but we include a simple example as a reminder.

Suppose $W \triangleq \{1, 2, 3, 4, 5, 6\}$
and

$$A \triangleq \{2, 3\}$$
$$B \triangleq \{1, 2, 3, 4\}$$
$$C \triangleq \{2, 4, 5\}$$

Clearly

$A \subseteq W$, $B \subseteq W$ and $C \subseteq W$ — A,B,C are subsets of W,

and

$2 \in A$ whereas $4 \notin A$.

Moreover,

$B \cup C$ ◆ the set of all elements in B *or* C (or both)
◆ $\{1, 2, 3, 4, 5\}$

$B \cap C$ ◆ the set of all elements both in B *and* C
◆ $\{2,4\}$

$B \setminus C$ ◆ the set of all elements in B but *not* in C (the set '*B without C*')
◆ $\{1, 3\}$

$A \subseteq B$ ◆ True whereas $C \subseteq B$ ◆ False

and

$\#A$ ◆ 2 and $\#B$ ◆ 4.

❑

[41] The 'if ... then ... else ... fi' construct.

In a general setting, recall that for some arbitrary type, X, $\mathcal{P}(X)$ is the set of all subsets of X (including $\emptyset$, the empty set, and the set X itself) and is the ***Powerset*** of X. Most of the common set operations on $\mathcal{P}(X)$ are directly related to Boolean operations, and their properties (rules) follow from that correspondence.

From the seemingly non-sensical equivalence

$$A \Leftrightarrow \{ x{:}X \mid x \in A \}$$

(i.e., A is the set (the subset of X) which includes all the elements in A) we can define

$$A \cap B \triangleq \{ x{:}X \mid (x \in A) \wedge (x \in B) \}. \qquad \text{intersection}$$

But

$$A \cap B \Leftrightarrow \{ x{:}X \mid x \in (A \cap B) \}$$

so

$$x \in (A \cap B) \Leftrightarrow (x \in A) \wedge (x \in B).$$

Similarly,

$$x \in (A \cup B) \Leftrightarrow (x \in A) \vee (x \in B) \qquad \text{union}$$

and

$$x \in (A \setminus B) \Leftrightarrow (x \in A) \wedge (x \notin B). \qquad \text{difference}$$

Then, for example,

$$\begin{aligned}
& x \in A \cap (B \cup C) \\
\Leftrightarrow\ & \\
& (x \in A) \wedge x \in (B \cup C) \\
\Leftrightarrow\ & \\
& (x \in A) \wedge ((x \in B) \vee (x \in C)) \\
\Leftrightarrow\ & \qquad\qquad\qquad\qquad \text{distributivity} \\
& ((x \in A) \wedge (x \in B)) \vee ((x \in A) \wedge (x \in C)) \\
\Leftrightarrow\ & \\
& (x \in (A \cap B)) \vee (x \in (A \cap C)) \\
\Leftrightarrow\ & \\
& x \in ((A \cap B) \cup (A \cap C))
\end{aligned}$$

So

$$\begin{aligned}
& A \cap (B \cup C) \\
\Leftrightarrow\ & \\
& \{ x{:}X \mid x \in A \cap (B \cup C) \} \\
\Leftrightarrow\ & \qquad\qquad\qquad\qquad \text{---- see}^{42} \\
& \{ x{:}X \mid x \in ((A \cap B)) \cup (A \cap C)) \} \\
\Leftrightarrow\ & \\
& ((A \cap B)) \cup (A \cap C))
\end{aligned}$$

[42] '$x \in A \cap (B \cup C)$' is a sub-expression of '$\{ x{:}X \mid x \in A \cap (B \cup C) \}$' and normal substitution rules apply.

Of course,

$$\varnothing \triangleq \{\, x{:}X \mid x \in \varnothing \}$$
$$\Leftrightarrow \{\, x{:}X \mid \text{False} \}$$

and

$$X \triangleq \{\, x{:}X \mid x \in X \}$$
$$\Leftrightarrow \{\, x{:}X \mid \text{True} \} \qquad \text{— since } x{:}X \Rightarrow x \in X$$

and, using set difference instead of complementation, we have

$$x \in (X \setminus (A \cap B))$$
$$\Leftrightarrow$$
$$(x \in X) \wedge \neg (x \in (A \cap B))$$
$$\Leftrightarrow$$
$$(x \in X) \wedge \neg (x \in A \wedge x \in B)$$
$$\Leftrightarrow$$
$$(x \in X) \wedge (x \notin A \vee x \notin B)$$
$$\Leftrightarrow$$
$$(x \in X \wedge x \notin A) \vee (x \in X \wedge x \notin B)$$

so

$$X \setminus (A \cap B) \Leftrightarrow (X \setminus A) \cup (X \setminus B)$$

the set version of one of deMorgan's laws.

For a given set X, all sets within $\mathbb{P}(X)$ are bounded, by X, and to be useful in computations, we also need them to be finite. Even when X is infinite (or even uncountable), we can pick out finite subsets. They even have a special notation, $\mathbb{F}(X)$, and for any element, Y, of $\mathbb{F}(X)$, we can find $\#Y$, the *size* of Y (the number of elements in Y). The other operations on $\mathbb{F}(X)$ are derived from those on $\mathbb{P}(X)$.

Notice that ',' is used as shorthand within set displays so that $\{x,y\}$ represents the result of $\{x\} \cup \{y\}$ when $x \neq y$, and $\{x,x\}$ is usually written as $\{x\}$. Duplicates have no significance, and (via the rule $A \cap (X \setminus A) \Leftrightarrow \varnothing$) no element of X can be both included in, and excluded from, A when $A{:}\mathbb{P}(X)$.

The Boolean combinators can be used to build new sets from existing ones, but we also need a way of building sets from scratch. As is typical in many situations, we can start with the simplest objects imaginable and build up from there. In the case of sets, we have the empty set, $\varnothing$, and singletons $\{x\}$ for each element x of type X.

We can illustrate this directly by relating it to the containment operator '$\in$':

$$\begin{aligned} x \in \emptyset &\;\Leftrightarrow\; \text{False} \\ x \in \{y\} &\;\Leftrightarrow\; x = y \\ x \in (A \cup B) &\;\Leftrightarrow\; x \in A \lor x \in B \end{aligned}$$

The ***size*** (#) of finite subsets of X (sets of type $\mathcal{F}(X)$) is also found inductively by addition of positive integers, and we have

$$\begin{aligned} \#\emptyset &\;\Leftrightarrow\; 0 \\ \#\{x\} &\;\Leftrightarrow\; 1 \\ \#D + \#E &\;\Leftrightarrow\; \#(D \cup E) + \#(D \cap E) \end{aligned}$$

We can also use Boolean algebra to derive the operators that relate pairs of set. Given $A,B{:}\mathcal{P}(X)$,

$$A \subseteq B \triangleq (\forall x{:}X)(\,(x \in A) \Rightarrow (x \in B)\,) \qquad \text{'}A \text{ is a } \textbf{\textit{subset}} \text{ of } B\text{'}$$

therefore, we have the rule

$$\begin{array}{l} (\lambda x{:}X) \\ \qquad (x \in A) \Rightarrow (x \in B) \end{array}$$

and the other subset rules follow accordingly. Strict (as in '<') subset and equality between sets are defined in predictable ways:

$$\begin{aligned} A = B &\triangleq A \subseteq B \land B \subseteq A \\ A \neq B &\triangleq \neg (A = B) \\ A \subset B &\triangleq A \subseteq B \land A \neq B \end{aligned}$$

An extensive collection of rules for set manipulation is to be found in the Appendix.

Readers familiar with sets might be surprised that we have not mentioned the complementation operator, often written as A'. Well, unless we are extremely careful with types, set complements are not always well-defined. If in doubt about any construction or operation, then perhaps it is best avoided if at all possible.

Given $A{:}\mathcal{P}(X)$ it would seem obvious to define its complement by

$$A' \triangleq X \setminus A$$

But now suppose that we also have $X \subset Y$ (i.e., X is a proper subtype of Y). Then $Y \setminus X \neq \emptyset$ so $(\exists z{:}Y)(z \in (Y \setminus X))$.

Pictorially, we have the situation in Figure 1.16.

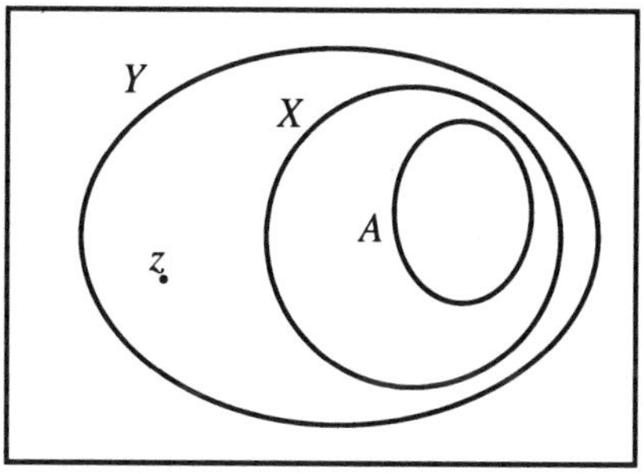

Figure 1.16

The problem is that A can be thought of as being of type $\mathcal{P}(X)$ or of type $\mathcal{P}(Y)$ and, as can be seen from the diagram, we will get different results depending on from which set (X or Y) we 'subtract' A. We can actually prove this.

Notice that

$$A \subseteq X$$
$$\Leftrightarrow$$
$$(Y \setminus X) \subseteq (Y \setminus A)$$

and

$$z \in (Y \setminus X) \text{ so } z \in (Y \setminus A).$$

On the other hand,

$$(X \setminus A) \subseteq X$$
$$\Leftrightarrow$$
$$(Y \setminus X) \subseteq (Y \setminus (X \setminus A))$$

So

$$\begin{aligned} z \in (Y \setminus X) &\Rightarrow z \in (Y \setminus (X \setminus A)) \\ &\Rightarrow (z \in Y) \wedge (z \notin (X \setminus A)) \\ &\Rightarrow z \notin (X \setminus A) \end{aligned}$$

Therefore, $(Y \setminus A) \neq (X \setminus A)$, and it is safer to use explicit set differences such as $X \setminus A$ rather than A', which is ill-defined unless we insist on strict typing so that even when $A : \mathcal{P}(X)$ and $X \subseteq Y$, A was not of type $\mathcal{P}(Y)$ even though $A \subseteq Y$!! This would be harsh. If we really want to create a set (with the same 'value' as A but having type $\mathcal{P}(Y)$), this can be achieved by using $\mathcal{P}(Y)$ as type the transfer function, also called a ***cast***, but care must be taken in converting rules from a subtype (X) to the super-type (Y). More about this later.

[In these situations, mathematicians introduce a so-called 'universe of discourse' — a problem-dependent superset that contains everything relevant to the given problem, typically written $\mathfrak{C}$ — and then take all complements relative to $\mathfrak{C}$. (i.e., $\mathfrak{C} \setminus X$). For us to do this would undermine the whole purpose of introducing types.]

1.4.4 Integers

We have already met the set on which the integer type is based,

$$\mathbb{Z} \triangleq \{.., {}^{-}2, {}^{-}1, 0, 1, 2, \quad ,...\}$$

But this is not just a set of (names of) unrelated values; they have meanings that are inductively derived from operations which are defined *on* the set itself. This is important. It explains why we did not even try to introduce more constants and shows how a mathematical structure can be defined by the use of axioms (properties that we require should hold) and conventions (which allow the introduction of more manageable shorthand). $\mathbb{Z}$ is a structured type, and other types can be constructed in a similar (but much more direct) fashion.

In our earlier glimpse at the integers, we only bothered with the distinct constants 0 and 1 (see[43]), so $0{:}\mathbb{Z}$ and $1{:}\mathbb{Z}$. Here we quickly outline how $\mathbb{Z}$ can be constructed, from sets! The idea is that we start with the empty set and a procedure for constructing, from any given set[44], another which has 'one more element'.

Suppose we have the function $next{:}X \mapsto X \cup \{X\}$. Here X represents the input *value*, not the type. (Don't even *try* to devise a suitable type.) Now, starting with $\emptyset$, we can in principle compute the sequence

$$\emptyset,\ next(\emptyset),\ next(next(\emptyset)),\ next(next(next(\emptyset))),\ next(next(next(next(\emptyset)))),\ \text{etc.}$$

This goes on for ever. Each term is a set; the first few are

$\emptyset$,
$\emptyset \cup \{\emptyset\}$ (◆ $\{\emptyset\}$),
$\{\emptyset\} \cup \{\{\emptyset\}\}$,
$\{\emptyset\} \cup \{\{\emptyset\}\} \cup \{\{\{\emptyset\}\}\}$, etc.

---

[43] Indeed, after reading the next couple of pages, you should conclude that we only really need zero. The relevance of 1, or any other integer distinct from 0, will become clear later.

[44] A 'proper' set, which does not contain itself. Such constructs lead to circular reasoning and some logical paradoxes.

This progression can be used to define the set of positive numbers which can be used for counting[45]. We shall not follow the (pure) mathematical tradition of actually using numbers for the names of these sets but link them together by means of the 'size of' operator '#'.

So

$$0 \triangleq \#(\varnothing),$$
$$1 \triangleq \#(\{\varnothing\}),$$
$$2 \triangleq \#(\{\varnothing\} \cup \{\{\varnothing\}\}),$$
$$3 \triangleq \#(\{\varnothing\} \cup \{\{\varnothing\}\} \cup \{\{\{\varnothing\}\}\}), \text{ etc.}$$

Now, for any number n, we can *define* $n + 1$ (the result of adding one and the *name* of the next number in the sequence. Hence we can '+ 1', and adding 2 is achieved by adding one twice. It is tedious, but it all works and provides an inductive construction of $\mathbb{P}$, which, in more familiar (but questionable) notation, is

$$\mathbb{P} \triangleq \{n{:}\mathbb{Z} \mid n = 0 \lor n = m + 1 \text{ where } m{:}\mathbb{P}\}$$

so $\mathbb{P}$ is the set of ***positive*** integers and is the infinite set which starts

$$\{0, 1, 2, 3, 4, 5, 6, \; ....\}$$

We (or the mathematicians) can work out the following properties of addition on $\mathbb{P}$:

$$x + 0 \Leftrightarrow x$$
$$x + y \Leftrightarrow y + x \qquad \text{(and therefore } 0 + x \Leftrightarrow x\text{)}$$
$$(x + y) + z \Leftrightarrow x + (y + z)$$

Similarly, for use in counting, we have the set $\mathbb{N}$ of ***natural*** (i.e. counting) numbers.

$$\mathbb{N} \triangleq \{n{:}\mathbb{Z} \mid n = 1 \lor n = m + 1 \text{ where } m{:}\mathbb{N}\}$$

and so

$$\mathbb{N} \Leftrightarrow \{1, 2, 3, 4, 5, 6, \; ....\}$$

We shall refer to these types only when necessary. Most of their operations are 'cut down' versions of the corresponding operations on $\mathbb{Z}$.

Now for addition on the type $\mathbb{Z}$, so far we only have 'half' of $\mathbb{Z}$, there are as yet no negative numbers.

---

[45] You might think that counting is trivial and of no relevance to programming (certainly not to 'non-mathematical' programs). Although we shall not go into any of the theory, *all* programs are mathematical in some sense, and counting is essentially the same as computing. To be able to compute a function requires that a related set of values be countable — so hang on in there.

For a given integer x, we want there to be another, y, such that when they are added together they give 0.

So, given $x{:}\mathbb{Z}$, we require that there exists $y{:}\mathbb{Z}$ such that the rule $x + y$ ◆ 0 holds.

For a given value of x, the corresponding value y is unique[46] and is usually written as ^-x, and is called the *additive inverse* of x. The correspondence $x \mapsto {}^-x$ therefore defines a function, and we may regard it as a monadic operation.

So $^-\mathbb{Z} \to \mathbb{Z}$ is the signature of the *negate* operation and it is defined by the single axiom (rule)

$$x + {}^-x \ ◆ \ 0 \qquad\qquad \text{(and it then follows that } {}^-x + x \ ◆ \ 0)$$

By definition

$$^-x + {}^-({}^-x) \ ◆ \ 0 \qquad\qquad \text{since } {}^-({}^-x) \text{ is an additive inverse of } {}^-x$$

and

$$^-x + x \ ◆ \ 0 \qquad\qquad \text{since } x \text{ is also an additive inverse of } {}^-x$$

So, both $^-({}^-x)$ and x are additive inverses of ^-x and hence are equal, i.e.,

$$^-({}^-x) \ ◆ \ x$$

We can now define *subtraction*, with syntax and type information given by

$$\mathbb{Z} - \mathbb{Z} \to \mathbb{Z}$$

and the evaluation defined by

$$x - y \triangleq x + ({}^-y)$$

Next, *multiplication*. This has the signature $\mathbb{Z} * \mathbb{Z} \to \mathbb{Z}$, and its evaluation is related to addition by the rules

$$a * 1 \ ◆ \ a$$
$$a * (b + c) \ ◆ \ (a * b) + (a * c)$$

Note the shape of this implicit definition. We have a base case that gives a result directly, and an 'extender' which, when used 'backwards', reduces multiplication by larger values to the summation of smaller products. So, for example,

$$x * 7 \ ◆ \ (x * 3) + (x * 4)$$

but then integer multiplication is really only shorthand for repeated addition.

---

[46] The reasoning is similar to that concerning the uniqueness of complements in Boolean algebra.

From the basic definitions other properties can be deduced. We shall not give their full construction; they provide interesting and challenging exercises.

However, notice that multiplication is commutative (i.e., $a*b \Leftrightarrow b*a$) as illustrated below.

$$
\begin{aligned}
2 * 3 &\Leftrightarrow 2 * (1 + 1 + 1) \\
&\Leftrightarrow (2 * 1) + (2 * 1) + (2 * 1) \\
&\Leftrightarrow 2 + 2 + 2 \\
&\Leftrightarrow (1 + 1) + (1 + 1) + (1 + 1) \\
&\Leftrightarrow (1 + 1 + 1) + (1 + 1 + 1) \\
&\Leftrightarrow 3 + 3 \\
&\Leftrightarrow (3 * 1) + (3 * 1) \\
&\Leftrightarrow 3 * (1 + 1) \\
&\Leftrightarrow 3 * 2
\end{aligned}
$$

So the *commutativity* of * comes from the *associativity* of +.

1.4.4.1 Inequalities

In much the same way that addition gave rise to negation and (subsequently) subtraction and multiplication, we can build the inequality tests (predicates) from subtraction and the positive integers $\mathbb{P}$.

First notice that for any $x{:}\mathbb{Z}$, exactly one of the following is True $x \in \mathbb{P}\backslash\{0\}$, $x = 0$, or $^-x \in \mathbb{P}\backslash\{0\}$. Note that we take 0 to be included in $\mathbb{P}$. So, for example, if $y{:}\mathbb{Z}$ and $y \notin \mathbb{P}$, then $^-y \in \mathbb{P}\backslash\{0\}$. Moreover, using the notation of inequalities,

$$0 \leq x \triangleq x \in \mathbb{P}$$

and $\quad 0 < x \triangleq x \in \mathbb{N} \qquad$ and $\mathbb{N} \Leftrightarrow \mathbb{P}\backslash\{0\}$

Further, $\mathbb{P}$ is closed under + and *; i.e.,

$$x \in \mathbb{P} \wedge y \in \mathbb{P} \Rightarrow (x + y) \in \mathbb{P} \wedge (x*y) \in \mathbb{P}$$

This can also be expressed in a more familiar fashion as conditional rules:

$(0 \leq x \wedge 0 \leq y) \qquad 0 \leq (x + y)$

$(0 \leq x \wedge 0 \leq y) \qquad 0 \leq (x*y)$

The bridge between the subtraction operation and the '≤' predicate is immediate:

$$a \leq b \triangleq 0 \leq (b - a)$$

whence we have

$$a = b \triangleq (a \leq b) \wedge (b \leq a),$$
$$a \neq b \triangleq \neg(a = b),$$
$$a < b \triangleq (a \leq b) \wedge (a \neq b),$$
$$a \geq b \triangleq b \leq a$$

and

$$a > b \triangleq b < a$$

From these definitions and basic properties, we can deduce more common manipulation rules for inequalities.

Example 1.1

For $a,b,c{:}\mathbb{Z}$

$$a \leq b \wedge b \leq c \Rightarrow a \leq c$$

Suppose that $a \leq b \wedge b \leq c$ and then consider $a \leq c$.
First notice that if $a \leq b$, then $0 \leq (b - a)$ and if we let $x = (b - a)$, then $0 \leq x$. Similarly. let $y = (c - b)$, and since $b \leq c$ we have that $0 \leq y$ and hence that $0 \leq x + y$;

or, by a more formal calculation,

$a \leq c$

◆

$0 \leq c - a$

◆

$0 \leq c + (b + {}^{-}b) - a$

◆

$0 \leq c + ({}^{-}b + b) - a$

◆

$0 \leq (c + {}^{-}b) + (b - a)$

◆

$0 \leq (c - b) + (b - a)$

◆

$0 \leq y + x$

◆

True

That is,

$$a \leq b \wedge b \leq c \Rightarrow a \leq c$$

❑

For completeness, we can now include a definition of *integer* division:

$$\neg(b = 0) \qquad \vdash ((a \div b) = c \triangleq (\exists d{:}\mathbb{Z})(a = (b * c) + d \wedge (\quad (0 \le d \wedge d < b) \vee (b < d \wedge d \le 0)\,)\,)$$

Here *d* is the remainder. The formula is so complicated because it has to cope with both positive and negative values of *a* and *b*. Notice that *b* cannot be zero.

The reader is again referred to the appendix for an extensive set of rules for operations and predicates associated with $\mathbb{Z}$ (and the subtypes $\mathbb{P}$ and $\mathbb{N}$).

1.4.5 Bags

From finite sets, we move on to another structure in which (finitely many) repeats are allowed. These are bags, or multi-sets, and the set of all bags constructible from a given base type *X* is denoted by $\mathfrak{B}(X)$. Like finite subsets, bags are also finite, but they can contain duplicate elements and use a different kind of syntax; bag brackets are written $\{\!|\ |\!\}$. With sets the essential question is, "given a set *S* and an 'element' *x*, is *x* in *S*?" With a bag *B*, the question is "how many *x*s are there in *B*?".

So, if $X \triangleq \{\!|\ a, b, c, d\ |\!\}$, then

$$\{\!|a, a, a, b, a, b, a, c, a, c, c, c, a|\!\} \in \mathfrak{B}(X)$$

and $$\{\!|b, a, a, a, a, a, a, c, c, c, c|\!\} \in \mathfrak{B}(X).$$

The bag operations are generalised from the corresponding set operations, the bag union operation adds[47] the number of instances of each element, and the bag intersection is associated with the least number of occurrences of each element in the given bags. Again, examples illustrate this:

$$\{\!|a, a, a, b, b, c, c, c, c|\!\} \uplus \{\!|a, b, c, c|\!\} \Leftrightarrow \{\!|a, a, a, a, b, b, b, c, c, c, c, c, c|\!\}$$

and

$$\{\!|a, a, a, b, b, c, c, c, c|\!\} \cap \{\!|a, b, c, c, c, c, c, c|\!\} \Leftrightarrow \{\!|a, b, c, c, c, c|\!\}$$

[47] Since this is not consistent with the set operation, there is a variation in notation.

One bag is a sub-bag of another if it contains no more instances of any element, so

$$\{\!|a, a, b, b, c, c|\!\} \subseteq \{\!|a, a, a, b, b, c, c, c, c|\!\}.$$

As with sets and lists, we use # as a 'size of' operator; but here there is also an infix version. As a prefix operator, it delivers the size of (i.e., number of elements in) the bag. As an infix operator, it is used to indicate the number of instances of a particular element within the bag, so

$$\begin{aligned}
\#\{\!|a, a, a, b, b, c, c, c, c|\!\} &\blacktriangleleft\!\blacktriangleright 9\\
a\#\{\!|a, a, a, b, b, c, c, c, c|\!\} &\blacktriangleleft\!\blacktriangleright 3\\
b\#\{\!|a, a, a, b, b, c, c, c, c|\!\} &\blacktriangleleft\!\blacktriangleright 2\\
c\#\{\!|a, a, a, b, b, c, c, c, c|\!\} &\blacktriangleleft\!\blacktriangleright 4\\
d\#\{\!|a, a, a, b, b, c, c, c, c|\!\} &\blacktriangleleft\!\blacktriangleright 0
\end{aligned}$$

The type and syntax information associated with the common bag operations is presented in the usual fashion:

$(\lambda X{::}\mathrm{Type})$

$$\begin{aligned}
\emptyset &\to \mathfrak{B}(X) &&\text{(the empty bag)}\\
\{\!|X|\!\} &\to \mathfrak{B}(X)\\[1ex]
\mathfrak{B}(X) \uplus \mathfrak{B}(X) &\to \mathfrak{B}(X)\\
\mathfrak{B}(X) \cap \mathfrak{B}(X) &\to \mathfrak{B}(X)\\
\mathfrak{B}(X) \subseteq \mathfrak{B}(X) &\to \mathbb{B}\\[1ex]
\#\mathfrak{B}(X) &\to \mathbb{P}\\
X\#\mathfrak{B}(X) &\to \mathbb{P} &&(a\#B \text{ represents the number of } a\text{'s in } B)
\end{aligned}$$

Bags are of particular importance because of their close relationship with lists (see the following section), and lists are important by virtue of their serial nature.

The empty bag has the same value as the empty set, and the same notation is used. (So $\emptyset{:}\mathfrak{B}(X)$, as well as $\emptyset{:}\mathfrak{F}(X)$ and $\emptyset{:}\mathfrak{P}(X)$. We say that the notation $\emptyset$ is 'overloaded'.) The conventions that apply to bags are similar to those used with sets. The enclosing punctuation is $\{\!|\ldots|\!\}$, and $\{\!|x,y|\!\}$ represents the outcome of the bag union operation $\{\!|x|\!\} \uplus \{\!|y|\!\}$ but notice that $\{\!|x|\!\} \uplus \{\!|x|\!\} \blacktriangleleft\!\blacktriangleright \{\!|x,x|\!\}$ not $\{\!|x|\!\}$ and $\{\!|x,x|\!\}$ may[48] be written as $\{\!|x2|\!\}$.

[48] Providing that there is no ambiguity.

We forego any further preliminaries and dive straight into the type specification. The two variants of '#' are defined inductively by

$$x\#\varnothing \;\Leftrightarrow\; 0$$
$$x\#\{\!|y|\!\} \;\Leftrightarrow\; \text{if } x = y \text{ then } 1 \text{ else } 0 \text{ fi}$$
$$x\#(B \uplus C) \;\Leftrightarrow\; (x\#B) + (x\#C)$$

$$\#\varnothing \;\Leftrightarrow\; 0$$
$$\#\{\!|y|\!\} \;\Leftrightarrow\; 1$$
$$\#(B \uplus C) \;\Leftrightarrow\; \#B + \#C$$

Then we have

$$x\#(B \cap C) \;\Leftrightarrow\; \min(x\#B, x\#C)$$
$$x\#(B \setminus C) \;\Leftrightarrow\; (x\#B) \text{ minus } (x\#C)$$

where

$$m \text{ minus } n \;\Leftrightarrow\; \text{if } n \le m \text{ then } m - n \text{ else } 0 \text{ fi} \qquad ([49])$$
$$\min(m,n) \;\Leftrightarrow\; \text{if } n \le m \text{ then } n \text{ else } m \text{ fi}$$

Also

$$A \sqsubseteq B \;\Leftrightarrow\; (\forall x{:}X)(\,(x\#A) \le (x\#B)\,)$$

whence

$$A = B \;\Leftrightarrow\; (\forall x{:}X)(\,(x\#A) = (x\#B)\,)$$

Other rules follow in a predictable way. As usual, the Appendix contains a fairly extensive collection of these rules.

1.4.6 Lists

When we execute a conventional procedural program, we always process input,and generate output in a specific order. We read and write ***lists***. Lists are finite sequences of elements. We represent a list by enclosing its elements in angled brackets and separating them with commas. The order of the elements *is* important. Instead of asking whether an element is contained (once or more than once) in a set or bag, with a list L, a more appropriate question might be "where in L is there an instance of x?".

So, using the set of characters $\{a, b, c, d\}$ as a base, $\langle b, a, d \rangle$ is a list and $\langle d, a, b \rangle$ is a different list. The list $\langle a, a, a, a, d, a, b \rangle$ is also valid (repeats are allowed), as is the empty list, which is written as $\langle\ \rangle$.

Given a data type X, the set of all lists which use elements from X is denoted by X^*, and again we can replace X with any required type.

---

[49] 'minus' is an infix operator (or macro) where

$$\_ \text{ minus } \_ \;\triangleq\; (\lambda x,y{:}\mathbb{P})\,(\text{ if } x \le y \text{ then } y - x \text{ else } 0 \text{ fi})$$

so

$$m \text{ minus } n \;\triangleq\; (\lambda x,y{:}\mathbb{P})\,(\text{ if } x \le y \text{ then } y - x \text{ else } 0 \text{ fi})\,(m,n) \;.$$

Thus we can have

$$\langle\, 1, 2, 1, 3 \,\rangle \in \mathbb{Z}^*$$

Lists can be built using the following operators. For any $x{:}\mathbb{Z}$, we can build a ***singleton*** list and represent (the outcome of) this operation by $\langle x \rangle$; and given lists $L,M{:}\mathbb{Z}^*$ then $L^\frown M$ represents the list that is the ***concatenation*** of L and M in the order given, so

$$\langle 1, 2\rangle \frown \langle 3, 4\rangle \;\;◆\;\; \langle 1, 2, 3, 4\rangle.$$

We also have a 'size of' function, which is again denoted by the operator #, so

$$\#\langle 1, 2, 4, 6, 7\rangle \;\;◆\;\; 5$$

and

$$\#\langle\rangle \;\;◆\;\; 0$$

In much the same way that we have a predicate which tests whether an element is contained within a set, there is one for testing for inclusion in a list. The following statements are True:

$$2 \in \{1, 2, 3\}$$

$$2 \text{ in } \langle 1, 2, 3\rangle$$

Other tests include

$$L \text{ is\_empty} \triangleq L = \langle\rangle$$

and

$$L \text{ is\_atomic} \triangleq (\exists x{:}X)(L = \langle x\rangle)$$

and, to complete these definitions, we need the predicate '$L = M$' which has quite a complex definition but requires that the lists have the same elements in the same order.

List variables in programs are not the same as conventional arrays. One difference is that they may change in length. Absolute positions within a list are not very meaningful; recognition of the end elements and sub-lists is of far more relevance. Traditionally, the operators head_of and tail_of have been defined to act on non-empty lists so that, for example,

$$\text{head\_of}(\langle 1, 2, 3\rangle) \;\;◆\;\; 1$$

and

$$\text{tail\_of}(\langle 1, 2, 3\rangle) \;\;◆\;\; \langle 2, 3\rangle \;.$$

But these are indicative of how lists were initially implemented. There are no names which might relate in a similar way to the other end of the list, so we use the names first_of, rest_of, last_of and front_of, so that

$$\begin{aligned}
\text{first_of}(\langle 1, 2, 3\rangle) &\blacklozenge 1 \\
\text{rest_of}(\langle 1, 2, 3\rangle) &\blacklozenge \langle 2, 3\rangle \\
\text{last_of}(\langle 1, 2, 3\rangle) &\blacklozenge 3 \\
\text{front_of}(\langle 1, 2, 3\rangle) &\blacklozenge \langle 1, 2\rangle
\end{aligned}$$

Now for the signatures. Again they are parameterised by an underlying type:

$(\lambda X{::}\text{Type})$

$$\begin{aligned}
\langle\rangle &\rightarrow X^* \\
\langle X\rangle &\rightarrow X^* \\
X^* \frown X^* &\rightarrow X^* \\
\#X^* &\rightarrow \mathbb{P} \\
X \text{ in } X^* &\rightarrow \mathbb{B}
\end{aligned}$$

$$\begin{aligned}
X^* \text{ is_empty} &\rightarrow \mathbb{B} \\
X^* \text{ is_atomic} &\rightarrow \mathbb{B} \quad \text{(True if the operand is a singleton list)} \\
X^* = X^* &\rightarrow \mathbb{B}
\end{aligned}$$

$$\begin{aligned}
\text{first_of}(X^*) &\rightarrow X && (\\
\text{rest_of}(X^*) &\rightarrow X^* && \text{(note that the target types} \\
\text{last_of}(X^*) &\rightarrow X && \text{(of these are } \textit{not} \text{ the same} \\
\text{front_of}(X^*) &\rightarrow X^* && (
\end{aligned}$$

Finally, since we often have cause to exclude empty lists, it is convenient to use the notation X^+ for the set (type) of non-empty X-lists.

[Note that the use of 'decorations' such as * and $^+$ (corresponding to an arbitrary number of repetitions and to one or more repetitions, respectively)[50] is a concept that crops up in many areas of Computer Science. Similarly, the use of the same style of print, such as blackboard capitals ($\mathbb{B}$, $\mathbb{Z}$, etc.) for 'standard' sets/types, is to be encouraged, and we shall try to promote their use whenever they do not go against historically entrenched usage. More problematic is the use of 'directed' symbols (which incorporate an arrow and are not symmetric), such as $\frown$, when operations are not commutative. For example, given arbitrary lists L and M, $L \frown M \neq M \frown L$; but this is difficult to apply uniformly since there are many symmetric symbols commonly used to indicate non-commutative operations, such as '–' in $x - y$, but for arbitrary $x,y{:}\mathbb{Z}$, $x - y \neq y - x$.]

The construction of arbitrary lists (and all lists are finite) can then achieved inductively using singletons and concatenation.

[50] They are *not*, as in many mathematical contexts, used as arbitrary (local) notation.

These satisfy the rules

$(\lambda L,M,N{:}X^*)$

$$
\begin{array}{rcl}
(L^\frown M)^\frown N & \Leftrightarrow & L^\frown(M^\frown N) \\
L^\frown\langle\,\rangle & \Leftrightarrow & L \\
\langle\,\rangle^\frown L & \Leftrightarrow & L
\end{array}
$$

But notice that the notation $\langle x,y\rangle$ is a shorthand convention for $\langle x\rangle^\frown\langle y\rangle$. The ',' is not a list operator, and its use is merely a *shorthand* convention.

Other common list operators are also generated inductively, as will be seen from the rules given below, but the operator pairs first/rest and front/last are specified implicitly but are relational combinations of other operators.

$$
\begin{array}{rcl}
\#\langle\,\rangle & \Leftrightarrow & 0 \\
\#\langle x\rangle & \Leftrightarrow & 1 \\
\#(L^\frown M) & \Leftrightarrow & \#L + \#M
\end{array}
$$

$$
\begin{array}{rcl}
x \text{ in } \langle\,\rangle & \Leftrightarrow & \text{False} \\
x \text{ in } \langle y\rangle & \Leftrightarrow & x = y \\
x \text{ in } L^\frown M & \Leftrightarrow & x \text{ in } L \;\vee\; x \text{ in } M
\end{array}
$$

$$
\begin{array}{rcl}
\langle\rangle \text{ is\_empty} & \Leftrightarrow & \text{True} \\
\langle x\rangle \text{ is\_empty} & \Leftrightarrow & \text{False} \\
L^\frown M \text{ is\_empty} & \Leftrightarrow & L \text{ is\_empty} \;\wedge\; M \text{ is\_empty}
\end{array}
$$

and

$$
\begin{array}{lrcl}
 & \langle\rangle = \langle\rangle & \Leftrightarrow & \text{True} \\
 & \langle\rangle = \langle x\rangle^\frown L & \Leftrightarrow & \text{False} \\
\neg(L = \langle\rangle) \wedge \neg(M = \langle\rangle) & L = M & \Leftrightarrow & \text{first\_of}(L) = \text{first\_of}(M) \\
 & & & \quad\wedge\; \text{rest\_of}(L) = \text{rest\_of}(M) \\
 & L = M & \Leftrightarrow & M = L
\end{array}
$$

whereas

$$
\begin{array}{lrcl}
\neg(L = \langle\rangle) & L & \Leftrightarrow & \langle \text{first\_of}(L)\rangle^\frown \text{rest\_of}(L) \\
\neg(L = \langle\rangle) & L & \Leftrightarrow & \text{front\_of}(L)^\frown\langle \text{last\_of}(L)\rangle
\end{array}
$$

1.4.7 Records and n-tuples.

In contrast to lists, which are not of fixed length, we can also have records or n-tuples (consisting of n ordered data values, which may be of different types). These are very similar to lists but have special notations for their types and data values. There are many variations on the actual syntax used; some languages use yet another kind of bracket, but we shall use forms closely associated with conventional procedural programming languages.

The idea here is simply that the composite values are constructed by taking values from a fixed number of (not necessarily distinct) types, in a prescribed order. Again this is a concept that we have already met when we discussed the relations that underpin the specifications of functions. There we were concerned with pairs of input and output values. Typically, in a mathematical scenario, we might have $A \times B$ representing the set of all pairs $\langle a,b \rangle$ where $a{:}A$ and $b{:}B$. This concept can be extended to triples, quadruples, ... , and n-tuples for any integer value n where $n \geq 1$. Of course, the sets/types used in such a construction need not be distinct, and hence we can use a contracted notation for the type denotation and replace $A \times A$ by A^2 and A^n for n-tuples drawn from A. To access the components of *these* structures, we need only count up to a certain position, so if x is declared as $x{:}A^n$, then the ith element can be referenced by $x[i]$, where $1 \leq i \leq n$. In other situations it might be more convenient simply to name the components; read on.

A familiar mathematical example is the representation of points in the plane — ordinary, 2-dimensional, geometry. So we might define

$$Point \triangleq \mathbb{R} \times \mathbb{R} \ .$$

and model the plane as the set of all its points, each characterised by two real[51] numbers, usually referred to as the x and y co-ordinates. In a computational context, we will need to access the individual components, or *fields*, so it is convenient to name them in the expected fashion and extend the type definition above to

$$Point \triangleq x{:}\mathbb{R} \times y{:}\mathbb{R}.$$

[51] We shall use $\mathbb{R}$, the set of *real* numbers — which includes all the integers, all the rational (fractional) numbers, and all the irrational numbers such as the square root of 2, etc. — in selected examples. This is because they are familiar, but we must be careful when even suggesting that we can perform calculations with them. Much to the annoyance of certain groups of would-be computer users, real numbers are *not* computable. One fundamental problem is that absolute equality between two reals is not decidable; 0.99 re-occurring and 1.00 re-occurring represent the same number. Another difficulty is that between any two distinct real numbers there are infinitely many other reals, but any computer system can only store a finite number of values!! Also, mainly within specifications, we shall allow the set/type, $\mathbb{Q}$, of rational numbers (Q for quotients). For any technical work with rationals, we can regard them as pairs of integers subject to various extra rules concerning common factors.

Switching examples again, and intentionally re-using the same names so as to stress that these names are nothing special[52], suppose we had the type declaration/ definition

$$R \triangleq A \times B \times C$$

or

$$R \triangleq a{:}A \times b{:}B \times c{:}C.$$

Now introduce a name relating to a value of type R and call it x (i.e. $x{:}R$). Suppose further that we 'give' x a value and write $x \triangleq \langle p, q, r\rangle$, or, more explicitly, $x \triangleq R{:}\langle p, q, r\rangle$, to force[53] the triple to take on the structure of the type R, together with its field selectors.
Thus we have

a of $x = p$ $\quad$ b of $x = q$ $\quad$ c of $x = r$, $\quad$ and each of these can then be processed in ways permissible for data of type A, B or C, respectively.

Our use of record structures is limited (and is really included only for completeness) but the availability of such structures allows the specification of more realistic problems and hence extends the domain in which the techniques can be used. For example, we typically want to sort records which consist of a key and some other data even though, as far as sorting is concerned, we are primarily interested only in the key. So, we might have

Key $\triangleq \mathbb{Z}$
Data $\triangleq$??? (something appropriate to the particular data set)

and

Record $\triangleq$ *key*:*Key* $\times$ *data*:*Data*
File $\triangleq$ *Record**

This models a sequential file of records, each of which consists of an integer key and some data. When sorting integers, we would typically use the predicate $x \leq y$, where $x,y{:}\mathbb{Z}$; moving to the sorting of records in the *File* as defined above, this would become *key* of $x \leq$ *key* of y, where x,y:*Record*.

Record types do not normally permit empty structures, and therefore it is convenient — and in some contexts, essential — to allow the inclusion of such an empty 'list' to facilitate termination of a recursively defined structure and associated processing. For example, we might define a binary tree structure (holding integers) as follows:

Bin_tree $\triangleq$ *left*:*Bin_tree* $\times$ *number*:$\mathbb{Z}$ $\times$ *right*:*Bin_tree*

However, to be able to use structures like this, we require a 'way out'; otherwise, the structures are infinite. Such 'alternatives' are facilitated by union types, as we shall soon see.

[52] Here we are just playing with the mathematics. In any actual computing context we would try to use meaningful names which would help comprehension, but remember that, from the technical point of view, *any* names would do.

[53] Technically called a ***coercion***. More about this in section 1.4.10.

There is one other piece of notation that we shall use later but logically is best introduced here. Recall that, for some given A,

$A^2 \triangleq \{\langle a,b\rangle \mid a,b{:}A\}$
$A^3 \triangleq \{\langle a,b,c\rangle \mid a,b,c{:}A\}$ etc.

Obviously, this generalises upwards to longer n-tuples, but we can also go down to include:

$A^1 \triangleq \{\langle a\rangle \mid a{:}A\}$

and, by convention,

$A^0 \triangleq \{\langle\rangle\}$.

1.4.8 Union Types

Whilst staying within a regime of strong typing, we can allow variables (obviously not constants) to be one of several types. To characterise this situation, we build union types from unions of their base sets. Of course, when it comes to performing operations on (values derived from) these variables, we need to know exactly what type it actually is; this is the main problem, and it is solved by using conditional constructs.

If $x{:}X$ and $X \triangleq A \cup B$, then we can check the type of x (i.e., check whether it is an A variant or a B variant) by the construction

if $x{:}A$? then ... i.e., if x is of type A then ...

A classical example associated with compiler construction is

$Exp \triangleq Var \cup Val \cup Binary\_exp \cup Unary\_exp$

where:

$Binary\_exp \triangleq (left{:}Exp \times op{:}infix\_op \times right{:}Exp)$
$Unary\_exp \triangleq (op{:}prefix\_op \times exp{:}Exp)$

If we then have a value *e* of type *Exp*, it can be processed by

if *e*:*Var*? then process as a variable (i.e., an identifier)
else_if[54] *e*:*Val*? then process as a value (of a type specified elsewhere)
else_if *e*:*Binary_exp*?
then extract the *left*, *right* and *op* components and combine the intermediate results as appropriate.
else (*e* must be of type *Unary_exp*)
extract the *exp* and *op* components, process and combine fi.

[54] This is a syntactic extension defined by
if *a* then *b* else if *c* then *d* else *e* fi fi $\triangleq$ if *a* then *b* else_if *c* then *d* else *e* fi

We can also relate the union operator to the construction of the list types X^* and X^+. These use the 'big' version of the union operator (just like Σ and Π are often used for the summation and products of numerical sequences):

$$X^* \triangleq \bigcup_{(0 \leq n \leq \infty)} X^n$$

$$X^+ \triangleq \bigcup_{(1 \leq n \leq \infty)} X^n$$

So X^* is the, infinite, union of all 0-tuples, 1-tuples, 2-tuples, etc., from X. Of course, in any specific situation, we need only go up to some finite limit[55]. When $X \neq \emptyset$, X^* is an infinite set/type but all its elements are finite.

1.4.9 Sub-Types and Sub-Ranges

There are other ways of deriving new data types. Suppose that we had some type B, that $A \subseteq B$, and that '*', an operation of type $B * B \rightarrow B$. If $x * y \in A$ whenever $x,y \in A$, then we say that '*' is closed on A and $(A,*)$ — the set A on which the operator $A * A \rightarrow A$ is defined — A is a type — a ***sub-type*** of $(B,*)$ — with the '*' operation ***induced*** (imported) from B. This idea can be extended to include cases when there are more operations defined on B. In such cases, all the operations on B have to be closed on A.

Common examples are when operations on $\mathcal{F}(X)$ are induced from $\mathcal{P}(X)$ for any X. Likewise we can take $\mathbb{N}$ (natural numbers, integers greater than or equal to 1) and $\mathbb{P}$ (positive[56] integers greater than or equal to 0) as subtypes of $(\mathbb{Z},+,*)$, but $0 \notin \mathbb{N}$. Similarly $\mathbb{Z}$ can be regarded as a subtype of $\mathbb{Q}$ and of $\mathbb{R}$, but there are tricky problems of representation, so we should not get carried away and try to do clever things without proper recourse to the relevant numerical analysis.

Also, if $D = \{x:\mathbb{Z} \mid (\exists y:\mathbb{Z})(x = 2*y) \}$ — the set of all even integers — then $(D,+,*)$ is also a subtype of $(\mathbb{Z},+,*)$, but notice here that $1 \notin D$.

Sub-ranges (sets of adjacent values from a super-set of integers and lying between two specified end points) are a special case of this situation in which results that fall outside the required (sub-)set are treated as errors.

A typical situation, given $a,b:\mathbb{Z}$ with $a \leq b$, is $a..b \triangleq \{x:\mathbb{Z} \mid a \leq x \wedge x \leq b\}$. This can be generalised to other situations where $a,b:X$ and X is some finite ordered type.

---

[55] Indeed, some theoreticians would argue that to include infinity in this definition is wrong. So, to be safe, always assume some finite limiting value (limited by the eventual implementation).

[56] Recall that the definition of $\mathbb{P}$ requires that it be closed under multiplication and addition (adding or multiplying elements of $\mathbb{P}$ gives results in $\mathbb{P}$, and multiplication of two negative numbers (in $\mathbb{Z} \setminus \mathbb{P}$) is positive.

So, the basic idea when $A \subseteq B$, is to do the calculation in B and keep only the results within A. In general, keep proper results and ignore the rest — don't include *unknowns*; make sure that you avoid them.

1.4.10 Type Transfer Functions and Casts

To ensure that we know exactly which transformation rules may be applied to any given expressions, we demand strong typing[57]. However, sometimes the types don't quite match and we need to 'force' a type change in order to be totally consistent. When this can be done (it is not always possible even when all the required data is available), we may either invent a suitable function or use the more general notation

$$< \text{new type} > : < \text{old value} >.$$

The < new type > coerces or ***casts***[58] the < old value > into a new form. Think of this as moulding the given data into a new shape.

For example

$$\text{if } a{:}X \text{ then } \mathfrak{F}(X){:}\ a = \{a\}$$

and

$$\text{if } \langle\, a,b,c\, \rangle{:}X^* \text{ then } \mathfrak{B}(X){:}\langle\, a,b,c\, \rangle = \{\!\!\{\, a,b,c \,\}\!\!\}$$

These say "make an X set from the X element a" and " make an X bag from the X list $\langle\, a,b,c\, \rangle$". The implied bracketing of these combinations must be

$$(\mathfrak{F}(X){:}\ a) = \{a\} \qquad \text{and} \qquad (\mathfrak{B}(X){:}\langle\, a,b,c\, \rangle) = \{\!\!\{\, a,b,c \,\}\!\!\}$$

The whole point of such constructions is that $\mathfrak{F}(X){:}\ (a = \{a\})$ makes no sense since a and $\{a\}$ are values of *different* types and cannot be compared, and even if this were possible, a Boolean result could not be cast into an X set.

We must ensure that the conversion gives a well-defined result, so, for instance, $X^*{:}\{\!\!\{\, a,b,c \,\}\!\!\}$ would not work since there are six different lists that can be obtained from the bag $\{\!\!\{\, a,b,c \,\}\!\!\}$. However, within specifications we *could* write

$$\mathfrak{B}(X){:}\ A = \mathfrak{B}(X){:}\ B \qquad\qquad \text{where } A,B{:}X^*$$

to indicate that the lists A and B have the same elements. Thus, we must avoid the temptation to write something like

$$A = X^*{:}\ \mathfrak{B}(X){:}\ B \quad \text{which is not well-defined.}$$

[57] This need not be over-restrictive. Remember that we have union types.

[58] In much the same way that iron can be cast into a particular shape.

If it means anything, the right-hand side of the 'test' says "take B, obtain the bag of its elements, and from this make a new list — and determine whether this list is the same as A". Notice that even $A = X^*: \mathfrak{B}(X): A$ is undefined, since it may give the value True or the value False when $\#A > 1$.

Of course we have already met this notion before. Recall that if we have the type declaration $R \triangleq a{:}A \times b{:}B \times c{:}C$ and $x{:}R$, and $\langle p, q, r\rangle{:}A \times B \times C$, then $x = R{:}\langle p, q, r\rangle$ not only connects the values x, p, q, and r but also links the selectors, so a of $x = p$, etc. As in languages such as Pascal, R and $A \times B \times C$ are regarded as distinct types.

For emphasis, we can always attach explicit type information to any value and write $x{:}T_1$ (for the appropriate type T_1) instead of the more usual x. In certain situations, the value x can be 'widened' to produce an equivalent value which is subsequently regarded as being of a super-type (of some type T_2, where $T_1 \subseteq T_2$). Although we must take care so as not to create impossible constructions (i.e., to create expressions which cannot be evaluated unambiguously), expressions of type T_1 can often be converted into expressions of type T_2, and thus strict type consistency is preserved.

The notation $T_2{:}\,x{:}T_1$ is interpreted as follows: take the value x (of type T_1) and create a *new* object, of type T_2, having the *same* value. (This may be extended to use types which are not subtypes but for which there exists an appropriate, reversible, relational connection, or some useful notion of 'embedding' — see the examples below.) We shall restrict discussion to very common cases and to operations which are constructive, in the sense that they build up new values from atomic values. Also, because type names are used as operators (casts), we will need to devise special conventions within the specification of the term re-writing rules to distinguish between these operators and the usual representation of the types of data being manipulated; within the formal presentation of the rules, we surround the operators with quotes " ". We shall also include the optional indication of the result type when this may not be clear.

We consider five situations, the conversion of

(i) Booleans to the integers $\{0,1\}$

(ii) $\mathfrak{F}(X)$ to $\mathfrak{P}(X)$

(iii) $\mathfrak{F}(X)$ to $\mathfrak{B}(X)$

(iv) $\mathfrak{P}(X)$ to $\mathfrak{P}(Y)$, when $X \subseteq Y$

and

(v) X^* to $\mathfrak{B}(X)$.

We first give a few simple illustrations and then the appropriate transformation rules.

$\mathbb{P}$: True ◀▶ 1 where 1:$\mathbb{P}$

so we can 'force' True to become the integer 1.

Notice that the full form of this rule is

$\mathbb{P}$: True :$\mathbb{B}$ ◀▶ 1 :$\mathbb{P}$

where the cast appearing at the left-hand side (here "$\mathbb{P}$:") is mirrored at the right-hand side (:$\mathbb{P}$), where it optionally indicates the type of the result. This is common and reinforces the similarity in the syntax, and the difference in meaning, of these constructs.

Of perhaps more obvious application,

$\mathcal{B}(X)$: $\{x\}$ ◀▶ $⦃x⦄$

or more fully

$\mathcal{B}(X)$: $\{x\}$:$\mathfrak{F}(X)$ ◀▶ $⦃x⦄$:$\mathcal{B}(X)$.

and

$\mathcal{B}(X)$: $L^\frown M$ ◀▶ $\mathcal{B}(X)$: L $\uplus$ $\mathcal{B}(X)$: M

which again can be written more fully as

$\mathcal{B}(X)$: $L^\frown M{:}X^*$ ◀▶ $\mathcal{B}(X)$: $L{:}X^*$ $\uplus$ $\mathcal{B}(X)$: $M{:}X^*$

As usual, these operators can be defined inductively. We give some examples below and refer the reader to the appendix for a more comprehensive collection.

eqns: $(\lambda a,b{:}\mathbb{B}, x{:}X, m,n{:}\mathbb{P}, A,B{:}\mathfrak{F}(X), C,D{:}\mathcal{P}(X), L,M{:}X^*)$

"$\mathbb{P}$:" True ◀▶ 1
"$\mathbb{P}$:" False ◀▶ 0
"$\mathbb{P}$:" $a \vee b$ ◀▶ max("$\mathbb{P}$:" a , "$\mathbb{P}$:" b)

where

max(m,n) ◀▶ if $n \le m$ then m else n fi

"$\mathcal{P}(X)$:" $\varnothing$:$\mathfrak{F}(X)$ ◀▶ $\varnothing$:$\mathcal{P}(X)$
"$\mathcal{P}(X)$:" $\{x\}$:$\mathfrak{F}(X)$ ◀▶ $\{x\}$:$\mathcal{P}(X)$
"$\mathcal{P}(X)$:" $A \cup B$:$\mathfrak{F}(X)$ ◀▶ "$\mathcal{P}(X)$:" A :$\mathfrak{F}(X)$ $\cup$ "$\mathcal{P}(X)$:" B :$\mathfrak{F}(X)$

$$\text{“}\mathcal{B}(X)\text{:”}\ \varnothing : \mathcal{F}(X) \ \blacktriangleleft\!\blacktriangleright\ \varnothing : \mathcal{B}(X) \qquad (\blacktriangleleft\!\blacktriangleright\ \{\!|\,|\!\})$$
$$\text{“}\mathcal{B}(X)\text{:”}\ \{x\} : \mathcal{F}(X) \ \blacktriangleleft\!\blacktriangleright\ \{\!|x|\!\}$$

$$(\text{“}\mathcal{B}(X)\text{:”}\ A \cup B : \mathcal{F}(X)) \uplus (\text{“}\mathcal{B}(X)\text{:”}\ A \cap B : \mathcal{F}(X))$$
$$\blacktriangleleft\!\blacktriangleright\ (\text{“}\mathcal{B}(X)\text{:”}\ A : \mathcal{F}(X)) \uplus (\text{“}\mathcal{B}(X)\text{:”}\ B : \mathcal{F}(X))$$

$$\text{“}\mathcal{B}(X)\text{:”}\ \langle\rangle \ \blacktriangleleft\!\blacktriangleright\ \varnothing \qquad (\blacktriangleleft\!\blacktriangleright\ \{\!|\,|\!\})$$
$$\text{“}\mathcal{B}(X)\text{:”}\ \langle x\rangle \ \blacktriangleleft\!\blacktriangleright\ \{\!|x|\!\}$$
$$\text{“}\mathcal{B}(X)\text{:”}\ L \frown M \ \blacktriangleleft\!\blacktriangleright\ \text{“}\mathcal{B}(X)\text{:”}\ L \uplus \text{“}\mathcal{B}(X)\text{:”}\ M$$

Removing the optional type indicators and the quotes, the rules look much simpler. For instance

$$\mathcal{P}(X)\text{: } \varnothing \ \blacktriangleleft\!\blacktriangleright\ \varnothing$$

and

$$\mathcal{P}(X)\text{: } \{x\} \ \blacktriangleleft\!\blacktriangleright\ \{x\}$$

Notice that without the extra, emphatic, type information, these type change operations seem to be without purpose. Only when prompted by an appropriate CASE[59] tool might you be aware of their necessity.

1.4.11 Data Types and Transformations

We now have the basis for what is known as a term re-writing system based on sets of equations; the rules which define the operations on the different data types are going to be given by identities (equations) which must always hold. Our specifications not only give type information but also indicate the syntactic structure of expressions. In this Chapter, we have also seen how the manipulation rules give the meaning to expressions (this is again done implicitly — two expressions are equivalent, and are defined to have the same meaning, if one can be transformed into the other using the rules).

Remember, our main concern is in writing down properties which define the functions to be constructed (from the basic values and operations provided by the underlying programming language support system).

The notation (name) for $\mathbb{Z}$ is fairly standard, but $\mathbb{N}$ and $\mathbb{P}$ are not. (Mathematicians are quite fond of introducing their own notations and, unfortunately, since the mathematics associated with Computer Science has been derived from numerous different disciplines there are often clashes of notation. So be careful to check what notational conventions are being used.)

[59] CASE, Computer Assisted Software Engineering.

Mathematicians like to 'decorate' names, often in ways which differ from day to day, from problem to problem. In computing, we are usually restricted by the syntax that text-processing programs (such as compilers) will accept. Nevertheless, there is considerable deviation — particularly in areas where hand-written representations are common, such as theory. The freedom to use whatever notation seems appropriate is to be fiercely defended but can be confusing to most of us, particularly if we have to read and understand something very quickly. Throughout this book we shall attempt not to introduce further confusion and try to be consistent in our use of conventions and decorations (so from $\mathbb{Z}$ we can have $\mathbb{Z}^*$, $\mathbb{Z}^+$, $\mathbb{Z}^2$, etc., and even $\mathbb{Z}_2$ is possible but we won't use it) and the use of $*$ and $^+$ in other, non-arithmetic, contexts will have closely related meanings.

When we use transformations to derive program designs from specifications, we shall work on a post-condition and assume it to be True. Ideally it will be in conjunctive form (i.e., one or more sub-expressions '$\wedge$ed' together). Since, to give the answer True, all the terms of a conjunction must be True, we can use the information in one term to simplify another. We call this ***rationalisation***.

So, for example, $x = y \wedge p(x)$ can be replaced by $p(y)$ and we can remove x (if this is a sensible move).

1.4.12 On Quantification

So far, we have encountered the logical quantifiers ($\forall$ and $\exists$) *within* specifications and *within* certain rules, but we do not yet have any rules for the manipulation of the quantifiers themselves. The whole of Chapter 5 is devoted to an extensive treatment of quantifications and similar 'big' operations on composite data types. However we shall need some quantification scope rules almost as soon as we start transforming specifications; hence this Section. The main rules introduced within the text are collected together in the Appendix for easy reference, so, if we need to use a rule before it has been properly explained, we can consult the Appendix. Hence, we do not wish to go into details here but we ought to say something about the kinds of quantified situations we have already met. They stem from the two (so far unjustified) implications

$(\forall x{:}T)(p(x)) \Rightarrow p(a)$ where $a{:}T$

and

$q(b) \Rightarrow (\exists x{:}T)(q(x))$ where $b{:}T$.

The first of these gives rise to the legal substitution of $a{:}T$ for x in $(\lambda x{:}T)(p(x))$ and the second to the so-called 'one-point' rule which amounts to $(\exists x{:}T)(q(x))$ ◆ True providing that you can find some value $b{:}T$ that 'works' (i.e., $q(b)$ ◆ True.

A concept that is familiar to programmers in procedural languages, but quite alien to most mathematicians, is ***scope***. Within the classic quantifier syntax, such as

$(\exists x{:}T)(\ \ldots\ )$ the second pair of brackets represents the scope of x, (i.e., the only part of any surrounding expression where x is defined). Any occurrence of the identifier x outside of the (....)(....) construction refers to a different quantity. The analogous situation in block-structured programs is

begin var $x{:}T$; .... end

where the scope of x is 'begin .... end'.

The ways in which quantifiers interact with other (typically binary) operators are determined by rules which are given later, but we briefly mention how the scope of the existential quantifier ($\exists$) can be changed and introduced.

Given two Boolean expressions p and q, .

$(x \setminus p)^{60}$ $(\exists x:T)(q) \wedge p \quad \blacklozenge \quad (\exists x:T)(q \wedge p)$

and

$(T \neq \emptyset \wedge x \setminus p)$ $(\exists x:T)(p) \quad \blacklozenge \quad p$

If $T = \emptyset$, then
$$(\exists x:T)(p) \quad \blacklozenge \quad \text{False}$$
regardless of the value of p.

The corresponding programming situation

      begin var $x:\emptyset$; .... end

                  is, at best, useless and perhaps should be treated as illegal by the language support system.

Exercises

Specify the following functions. Within the specifications use the name given in italics on the right.

1.3   Find the maximum of two real numbers.   *max_of_2*

1.4   Find the maximum element in a set of integers.   *MAXS*

1.5   Find a maximal element of a list of integers.   *Listmax*

1.6   Find the positive square root of a positive real number to within a tolerance of 1/100.

                                  ASR (approximate square root)

1.7   Produce the list of the corresponding squares of the elements of a given list of integers.

                                  squares

1.8   Determine whether a list of integers vary in value by no more than 10.

                                  within_10

---

[60] This is read "x does not occur in p" and means that x is not free for substitution in p. See Section A3 of the Appendix. In practice this means that either x simply does not occur at all within the expression or it is itself a bound variable of some other, interior, quantification and hence is a different x.

1.9 Test whether a list of integers is in (strictly) ascending order.

strict_ascend

1.10 Reverse a given list of integers.

reverse

Suppose now that we have some data type, D, and records of structure $Key \times D$ (or $key{:}Key \times d{:}D$), where $Key \triangleq \mathbb{N}$. Sequential files are modelled as lists of such records.

1.11 Obtain a sorted (by increasing key order) version of a given file.

sort

1.12 Insert a record into an appropriate position in an ordered file.

insert

1.13 Given a specific key, known to be used in a given file, deliver a file with the relevant record(s) removed.

delete

1.14 Merge two ordered files. *merge*

❑

1.5 Applying Unfold/Fold Transformations

As we move towards the task of 'calculating' programs from functions, we shall encounter many kinds of manipulation, some of which are very specialised and others that, had we been performing the transformations by hand, we might not even notice.

Probably the most important transformation (important in the sense that it plays a part in many program derivations) was first identified by Darlington and is basically used to (re-)introduce recursion. The specifications we have met so far have not been sufficiently complex or abstract to warrant the introduction of recursion, but we illustrate the power of the unfold/fold transformation by showing how it can be used to reduce an instance of double recursion to a single recursion.

Suppose that we are given the functions *sum*: $\mathbb{Z}^* \rightarrow \mathbb{Z}$, which sums the elements of an integer list, and *keep_evens*: $\mathbb{Z}^* \rightarrow \mathbb{Z}^*$, which creates a copy of a given integer list in which the odd values have been deleted. These functions may be defined recursively as follows. (Here we use the function *odd*: $\mathbb{Z} \rightarrow \mathbb{B}$ and presume that it has been defined elsewhere.)

```
sum(L) ≜ if L = ⟨ ⟩
         then 0
         else first_of(L) + sum(rest_of(L))
         fi

keep_evens(L) ≜ if L = ⟨ ⟩
                then ⟨ ⟩
                else if odd(first_of(L))
                     then keep_evens(rest_of(L))
                     else ⟨first_of(L)⟩⌢keep_evens(rest_of(L))
                     fi
                fi
```

Now we wish to introduce a new function which is defined directly in terms of these two. It takes an integer list and delivers the sum of its even elements, i.e.,

even_sum(*L*) ≜ *sum*(*keep_evens*(*L*)) see[61]

To illustrate how programs, written as functions, can be manipulated we offer the following unfold/fold transformation. Thus far transformations have not been 'directed', there has been no clearly identified goal. So as to give some justification for the calculation that follows, notice that, on the face of it, the evaluation of *even_sum* from its definition suggests that we take a list, apply *keep_evens* to it, and then process the resulting list with the *sum* function. We access even list values twice. The outcome of the transformation gives us a way of evaluating *even_sum* which only visits each list item only once and no longer requires the functions *keep_evens* or *sum*.

[61] Using quantifications (Chapter 5), this function can be specified in a particularly neat way from which several program designs can be quickly derived.

Here goes.

First notice that

```
sum(⟨⟩) ◆ if ⟨⟩ = ⟨⟩
          then 0
          else first_of(⟨⟩) + sum(rest_of(⟨⟩))
          fi

        ◆ if True
          then 0
          else first_of(⟨⟩) + sum(rest_of(⟨⟩))
          fi

        ◆ 0
```

Now

```
      even_sum(L)
◆
      sum(keep_evens(L))
◆
      sum( if L = ⟨⟩
           then ⟨⟩
           else  if odd(first_of(L))
                 then keep_evens(rest_of(L))
                 else ⟨first_of(L)⟩⁀keep_evens(rest_of(L))
                 fi
           fi  )
◆
      if L = ⟨⟩
      then  sum(⟨⟩)
      else  sum(  if odd(first_of(L))
                  then keep_evens(rest_of(L))
                  else ⟨first_of(L)⟩⁀keep_evens(rest_of(L))
                  fi )
      fi

◆
      if L = ⟨⟩  then 0
      else  sum(  if odd(first_of(L))
                  then keep_evens(rest_of(L))
                  else ⟨first_of(L)⟩⁀keep_evens(rest_of(L))
                  fi )
      fi
```

◆

```
if L = ⟨⟩ then 0
else   if odd(first_of(L))
       then sum( keep_evens(rest_of(L)) )
       else sum( ⟨first_of(L)⟩⁀keep_evens(rest_of(L)) )
       fi
 fi
```

◆

```
if L = ⟨⟩ then 0
else   if odd(first_of(L))
       then even_sum(rest_of(L))
       else sum( ⟨first_of(L)⟩⁀keep_evens(rest_of(L)) )
       fi
 fi
```

◆

```
if L = ⟨⟩ then 0
else   if odd(first_of(L))
       then even_sum(rest_of(L))
       else   if ⟨first_of(L)⟩⁀keep_evens(rest_of(L)) = ⟨⟩
              then 0
              else first_of(⟨first_of(L)⟩⁀keep_evens(rest_of(L))) +
                   sum(rest_of(⟨first_of(L)⟩⁀keep_evens(rest_of(L))))
              fi
       fi
 fi
```

◆

```
if L = ⟨⟩ then 0
else   if odd(first_of(L))
       then even_sum(rest_of(L))
       else   if False
              then 0
              else first_of(⟨first_of(L)⟩⁀keep_evens(rest_of(L))) +
                   sum(rest_of(⟨first_of(L)⟩⁀keep_evens(rest_of(L))))
              fi
       fi
 fi
```

◆

```
if L = ⟨⟩  then 0
else  if odd(first_of(L))
      then even_sum(rest_of(L))
      else  first_of(⟨first_of(L)⟩⁀keep_evens(rest_of(L))) +
            sum(rest_of(⟨first_of(L)⟩⁀keep_evens(rest_of(L))))
      fi
fi
```

◆

```
if L = ⟨⟩  then 0
else  if odd(first_of(L))
      then  even_sum(rest_of(L))
      else  first_of(L) + sum(keep_evens(rest_of(L)))
            fi
fi
```

◆

```
if L = ⟨⟩  then 0
else  if odd(first_of(L))
      then  even_sum(rest_of(L))
      else  first_of(L) + even_sum(rest_of(L))
      fi
fi
```

◆

```
if L = ⟨⟩  then 0
else  if odd(first_of(L))
      then  0 + even_sum(rest_of(L))
      else  first_of(L) + even_sum(rest_of(L))
      fi
fi
```

◆

```
if L = ⟨⟩
then 0
else
   if odd(first_of(L)) then 0 else first_of(L)  fi
                              + even_sum(rest_of(L))
fi
```

Thus, we have the promised version of *even_sum*. The functions *keep_evens* and *sum* used in the original specification have been removed and we only have a single recursive call left (to *even_sum*).

Although the manipulation above may seem rather complex — and lengthy — it is not really all that difficult. You need to be able to work through it, identify the main steps — namely the unfolding and subsequent folding and the necessary bits of re-arrangement — convince yourself that it works, and convince yourself that *you* could do it.

As already mentioned, one reason for showing the unfold/fold transformation is because it is a particularly useful one in practice. However, an equally important reason is to show that transformations of mathematical specifications are *possible*. It is just not possible to manipulate English language specifications and procedural programs in this way.

Exercises

1.15 From the recursive definitions of $sum:\mathbb{Z}^* \rightarrow \mathbb{Z}$ and $square:\mathbb{Z}^* \rightarrow \mathbb{Z}^*$ (given below), derive a representation for $sum\_square:\mathbb{Z}^* \rightarrow \mathbb{Z}$ which uses a single recursive call.

$$
\begin{aligned}
sum(L) \triangleq\ & \text{if } L = \langle\rangle \text{ then } 0 \\
& \qquad\qquad \text{else first\_of}(L) + sum(\text{rest\_of}(L)) \\
& \text{fi}
\end{aligned}
$$

$$
\begin{aligned}
square(L) \triangleq\ & \text{if } L = \langle\rangle \text{ then } \langle\rangle \\
& \qquad\qquad \text{else } \langle(\text{first\_of}(L))^2\rangle \frown square(\text{rest\_of}(L)) \text{ fi}
\end{aligned}
$$

$$sum\_square(L) \triangleq sum(square(L))$$

(This is a classic example which *has* to be included in any discussion of unfold/fold transformations.)

1.16 Using a recursive realisation of '$length:\mathbb{Z}^* \rightarrow \mathbb{P}$' (i.e., the operator #),

$$
\begin{aligned}
length(L) \triangleq\ & \text{if } L = \langle\rangle \text{ then } 0 \\
& \qquad\qquad \text{else } 1 + length(\text{rest\_of}(L)) \\
& \text{fi}
\end{aligned}
$$

and the direct definition of $average:\mathbb{Z}^+ \rightarrow \mathbb{Q}$,

$$average(L) \triangleq sum(L) \,/\, length(L),$$

derive a function $sum\_length:\mathbb{Z}^+ \rightarrow \mathbb{Z} \times \mathbb{P}$, so that

$$sum\_length(L) \triangleq \langle sum(L), length(L)\rangle$$

and then

$$average(L) \triangleq x/y, \text{ where } \langle x,y\rangle = sum\_length(L)\,.$$

❑

Chapter 2
On Programming

We are *not* going to try to 'teach programming' in the sense that the reader might understand the term. In this chapter, we are going to make some observations on programs and programming — and on ways in which programmers have tried to 'guarantee' that their programs were 'right'. In Chapter 3, we shall set about the formal derivation of programs from specifications. In some sense, therefore, these chapters are competing. We make no pretence that the competition is fair. For the reader who skips through this chapter, some common elements are repeated in Chapter 3.

Of course, not all programs are written by professional or even trainee or student programmers[1]; and not all programmers are Computer Scientists or Software Engineers. Many of those involved in training or examining student programmers will often advocate the use of well-commented, well-structured code which uses meaningful identifiers. Nobody would argue with this, but it is certainly not enough. Merely adhering to these maxims produces programs which look pretty; programming is more properly about the way in which a program (denoted by the program text) is derived, how it is built, how it is constructed. What most people regard as a program — the final text or what it does when it is loaded into a computer and executed — is merely the output of the programming process.

Paradoxically, most good programs look simple (the converse need not be true), but it is how you get the program — and how you know that it does what it is required to do — which is important, not its appearance *per se*.

[1] But by workers in other professions who have decided to, or have been asked to, 'write a program'. The mere fact that this situation arises frequently confirms the commonly held — but certainly erroneous — belief that programming is easy and can be undertaken by almost anybody. There is more to playing chess (well) than simply knowing the moves.

2.0 Overview.

We start, in Section 2.1, with a discussion about the essential features of procedural programs and procedural programming. This is the kind of programming which is most common (so common that the qualification 'procedural' is usually omitted). Other terms are sometimes included (such as object-oriented, or user-centered), but these do not contradict the fact that much of the central code is still procedural and hence all that we have to say is still relevant. This is followed with a brief digression on what some people regard as 'good' programming.

Then, in Section 2.3, we start to get a little more technical and introduce the notion of flowcharts and their structure. We then introduce the PDL language, which we use for the code of examples throughout the book. Although we give a reasonably complete description of the syntax (which includes some features that might be unfamiliar to the reader), the semantics — the meaning — is described less formally. There is sufficient information to allow the reader to construct and interpret PDL programs but perhaps not enough for someone to construct a compiler.

We move, gradually, to the important question of the required and actual effects of a program by discussing (in Section 2.5) comments and then the related, but more formal, notion of assertions — executable comments! Assertions can be used to demonstrate program correctness but are expensive to evaluate. (Essentially each assertion is a small program, written in another kind of language, and we shall return to this idea in Chapter 3.) In Section 2.6, we go 'all technical' and introduce the concept of program verification. Here, in principle, we can take a program together with a formal specification of what it is supposed to compute, and justify, mathematically, that they fit together in the required way; namely, that for each valid data input value, the result produced by the program (together with the data) satisfies the specification. We only consider the verification of PDL 'structured programs' and give the basic verification rules; we do not develop the theory or illustrate its use. The main reason for this is that using assertions, or verification (or indeed testing[2]) is a retrospective process; we have to build a program and then try to demonstrate that it is 'right'. And if it is *not* then we are stuck.

We wish to adopt an alternative approach and move in the opposite direction; we want to write a program so that it is 'correct by construction'. This is the central theme of our book, and hence we go into it in some considerable detail. As a way of 'breaking the ice', we discuss the idea briefly in Section 2.7.

[2] As we shall say many times, for programs which are used with many different inputs, testing is simply not a serious option. Unless you can apply exhaustive test methods (which take more time than any of us have in a single lifetime), testing can only demonstrate program failure, not correctness.

2.1 Procedural Programming

In procedural programming, the programmer indicates, explicitly, how the execution of the program should proceed; or how a collection of procedures should be sequenced, controlled. Most programmers (certainly most 'occasional' programmers and indeed many professional programmers) equate all 'programs' with 'procedural programs' — they are simply not aware of other programming paradigms.

So, we are not teaching programming, in the sense of coding. We assume that the reader is familiar with some (possibly object-oriented) procedural programming language. Here we merely make observations on 'style', typical features, and later (cursory remarks on) their verification.

Procedural programs are thought of as being easy to write because they only do simple things — essentially assignments. But, it is the ways in which these simple actions can be combined which cause difficulties in keeping track of the overall effect caused by these actions.

Characteristically, procedural programs work by causing changes in 'state'. The state (of a computation at a particular place in the program, when execution has reached this point, at this time) can be thought of as the current set of values associated with the 'variables' to which the program has access at that point.

The name x might refer to different locations (and possibly different types of values) in different parts of the program. Moreover, a given x might be required to change in value as the execution proceeds, and the value of x at a given place in the program will often be different when the execution passes through the same place on a subsequent occasion.

A lot *can* change, and indeed we require that some values *do* change, but keeping track of these changes, and reasoning about them, can be complicated. It is specifically to avoid (or at least to defer) the complexity of state changes that we shall adopt the LFP[3] scheme for program derivation in Chapter 3. It is also for this reason that we do not include much detail when describing the (direct) verification and construction of procedural programs.

In any procedural language (such as our PDL — Program Design Language — in Section 2.4), there are three basic kinds of components: declarations, expressions and commands. Declarations introduce new (local) names which will be associated with entities within the surrounding block. These entities are typically locations — 'variables' in colloquial, but erroneous, terminology — in which we may store

[3] Logic, Functions and Procedures, or Logical, Functional and Procedural.

values of a given type. This type is given in the declaration. We can also declare functions (see 'expressions' below — a function call, here, is little more than a parameterised expression). A block, in many languages delimited by 'begin ... end', is really a compound command and consists of an optional list of declarations followed by a list of commands. Declarations perform no computation; they merely introduce entities which can be used in subsequent expressions and commands.

Expressions can be evaluated to compute values, and change nothing (in our language we do not allow 'unexpected' side effects). They are well-formed mathematical expressions and as such follow certain syntactic and semantic rules — the rules are those given as type specifications in Chapter 1. The evaluation of an expression gives a value which can be used in a command. Expressions cannot occur in isolation[4]. (In PDL, expressions can be conditional, and again the forms introduced in Chapter 1 are used.) Function calls yield values, and hence may such calls may occur within expressions.

In general terms, commands are language components which have the facility to change the values stored in named locations[5], to import a value from the input stream into a named location, export the value of an expression (to the output stream), or influence the flow of program control.

Though not regarded as essential, we also admit the existence of labels (which label, identify, commands). Indeed, although very messy, we could regard all commands as a labelled 'proper' command followed by a conditional or unconditional "goto" statement[6] which then directs the program to the labelled command to be executed next. Fortunately we can do much better than this — but flow of control is important and should not be taken for granted or disregarded.

Alternatively, a procedural program could be regarded as a description of journeys which can be taken around a (control) flowchart. The program text is simply a description of that flowchart. The route of this journey is sometimes referred to as the locus of control.

The fundamental building blocks of flowcharts are: one start point, and (for convenience) one stop point, (optionally labelled) 1-in, 1-out rectangles representing computational commands[7], and diamond shapes with one in path and two out paths (labelled True and False), the diamond containing a Boolean

[4] There is one exception in the shorthand form: the expression which delivers the result of a function evaluation.

[5] They may not *always* cause a change. For example, when executing the sequence '$x \leftarrow 1$; $x \leftarrow 1$', the second statement never causes a state change; it replaces the 'value of x' with 'the value of x', which is 1.

[6] 'Statement' is simply another name for 'command'.

[7] 'Leaning' parallelograms are also often used to indicate input/out commands. We shall ignore them since we presume that all input precedes proper processing and output comes last.

expression. These facilitate the switching of control flow between two alternatives. Graphically, these are typically as depicted in Figure 2.1.

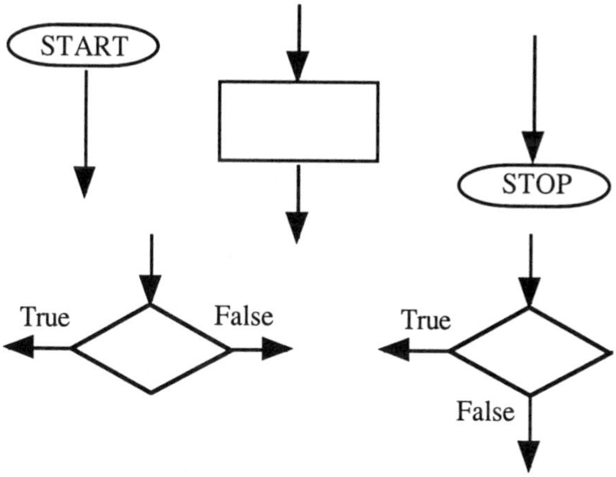

Figure 2.1

More problematic is how components are put together. We take one START node, one STOP node and as many computation rectangles and test diamonds as required. The rectangles can be inscribed with a description of a computational step (a command) and the diamonds with a Boolean expression. So far, so good. Now join up the arrows, but preserve the number of inward and outward arrows shown in the illustration. The only other ways of linking arrows is by means of joining points, at which several (but usually two) incoming arrows link up with one outgoing arrow, such as in Figure 2.2.

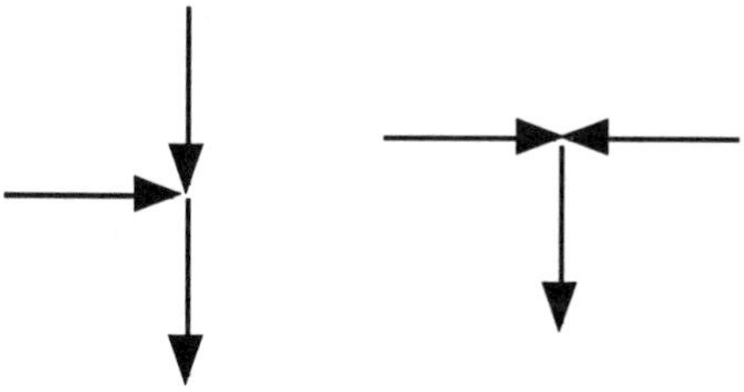

Figure 2.2

Absolutely *any* configuration is possible. We certainly are not going to give an example. Try it for yourself and see exactly why we can end up with what have been called 'spaghetti' programs.

Execution of a flowchart program is as follows. Control starts at the START node and follows the arrows until we reach STOP. Upon encountering a rectangle, we carry out the enclosed command (usually resulting in a state change) and follow the 'out' arrow. On reaching a test, we evaluate the enclosed Boolean expression and follow either the True arrow or the False arrow depending on the result of that evaluation. Yes, it sounds easy — after all, computers can only perform simple tasks (but very many, very quickly).

A procedural program (or, more properly, the text of such a program) is simply a representation of one such flowchart.

By virtue of having only a single way in and a single way out, the entire flowchart can be regarded as another higher-level 'rectangle'. Adding extra entry points and extra (abnormal?) exit points will usually complicate any description of what the program actually does. It is for the same reason, at a lower level, that the computational rectangles are restricted to having unique entry and exit points. We will say more about program structure in Section 2.3.

Other features commonly found in procedural language include recursive expressions (achieved by means of recursive functions) and blocks which can be named (and parameterised) to give procedures which may or may not be recursive. There are also array types, but these are not central to *our* exposition and will only be used in certain (small) sections.

2.2 'Good' Programming

Today, most programming is done in so-called high-level languages. One characteristic of such languages is that they allow the programmer to devise and use 'long' names. [But it may not be easy to invent enough names which are meaningful, distinct, and not too long. Some language implementations have in the past permitted the use of very long names but then only took notice of the first '*n*' characters — not so clever!]. They also have English[8] keywords that are fixed in the language and are supposed to convey the appropriate semantic meaning. The upshot of these possibilities is that the program text can be made more 'readable', less cryptic. In the reverse direction, there is the desire to make the written form of the program reasonably compact. This is the same argument as applied to specifications. They should not be needlessly verbose: otherwise, you cannot see what is there because there is too much 'noise'.

---

[8] We expect that the reader will encounter these situations, but, for example, French would be perfectly acceptable for a French reader or writer of programs.

So, for instance, in place of

"evaluate *E* and store the result in *L*"

we may write

"put *E* in *L*"

or

"$E \rightarrow L$" — yes there are languages where assignment statements are strictly from left to right.

rather than

"$L := E$" — the ':=' combination being an accident of (the lack of) technology.

We shall use

"$L \leftarrow E$". — location *L* is given the value of expression *E*.

Within the body of this text[9], '=' means 'equals' — the predicate, the test — and nothing else. It certainly has nothing to do with the assignment command *per se*.

Making the program text more readable reduces the need for comments. Certainly comments that merely describe adjacent commands in a program are a waste of time and effort (but see Section 2.5).

[Similar principles can be used when using systems-programming languages. These look like high-level languages but also have lower level operations.]

2.3 Structuring and (Control) Flowcharts

Any 1-in, 1-out block can be thought of as a state-to-state assignment. Any part of a flowchart having this 1-in, 1-out property can be regarded as a logical sub-program and can, for documentation purposes and to aid reasoning, be drawn separately as a stand-alone flowchart and referenced — in the appropriate position — in the 'main' flowchart by means of a labelled (named) rectangle as shown in Fgure 2.3.

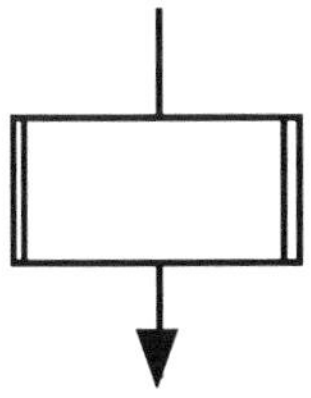

Figure 2.3

9 Except for brief segments where we try to draw similarities (or familiarity) with more traditional manipulations.

In so-called structured programs, only certain ways of combining components into higher-level 1-in, 1-out 'structures' are used. These assist in breaking down the overall problem/solution into fewer pieces, the computational elements of which are again 1-in, 1-out. Moreover, the meanings of the components are 'easily' related logically to the combination. These are not independent, nor are they exhaustive. The major ones used are shown, in flowchart form, in Figure 2.4. At the top left we have the conditional construct "if ... then ... else ... fi". The test is performed and either the left or right fork taken, depending on whether the result is True or False. In the top right of Figure 2.4, we have the often forgotten sequence construct. This is represented by the ";" operator, the "go - on" symbol. Here we simply execute the upper command first and then the lower one. Notice that we use the semi-colon as a *separator*, not a terminator. In the lower two diagrams in Figure 2.4, we have two kinds of loop configurations. On the left is a "while .. do ... od" loop in which the test is performed and, if - and *only* if - the result is True, the body of the loop is performed and we return (hopefully with a changed state) to the beginning of the loop and execute the construct again. The loop exits when the test evaluation yields False. [Remember that the evaluation of a test — and indeed any expression — causes no change in state.] On the right is a "repeat ... until ... " construct. Here we start by executing the enclosed command and then we evaluate the test. We loop back to the start, with the current state, if the result from the test is False.

The 'while' loop is also called a pre-check loop because the test comes before the body; the body of the loop may not be executed at all. Executed zero times. On the other hand, the 'repeat' loop — a post-check loop because the test comes after the body — always executes the body at least once.

Notice that by default flow is from top to bottom and left to right, and therefore many arrowheads can be omitted. But put them in if you feel that any confusion might arise.

Using only these ways of combining commands and tests within a program means that there is no technical need for gotos, but labels can still be used to assist in documentation (comments etc.).

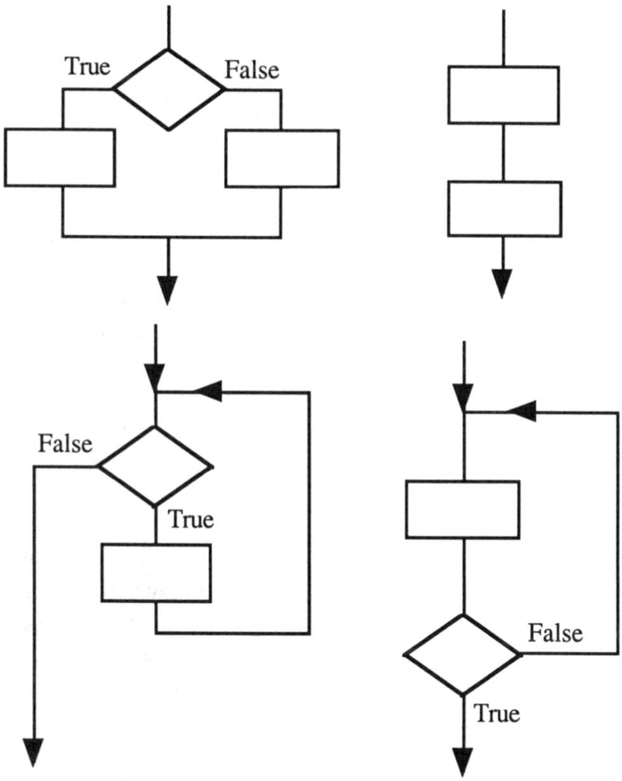

Figure 2.4

2.4 PDL Overview

The language we use to express implementation designs is PDL, which stands for Program Design Language. It is like many actual languages but is not intended to be exactly the same as *any* of them. Indeed, you may also regard it as a pseudo-code which then needs to be translated into a locally available (supported and implemented) language.

PDL has deterministic control (it does not have, as is commonly seen in similar texts, guarded commands, which are loop structures with the possibility of different execution sequences from a given initial state).

We shall follow the common practice of using the notation $A[i]$ to represent the ith location of the array A, with A subscripted by i. This is the location, offset by an amount associated[10] with i, relative to the location of (the array base address) A. Some languages make this more explicit, and perhaps more confusing but technically correct, by using the notation for a function call; i.e., $A.i$ or $A(i)$.

We do not give a fully formal description of PDL. We do not intend that it necessarily be implemented, and hence such a definition is not required[11]. Instead, we describe its syntactic structures in a variant of BNF[12] which avoids the need for more new symbols.

Our style of presenting the syntax of PDL uses capitals to name syntactic classes. The occurrence of such a name as part of a definition must be expanded using one of the possible alternatives in *its* definition. Symbols used as part of the language (and which therefore might appear within the text of a program) are delimited by double quotation marks. The lowest level of detail is omitted. Explanations of related semantic notions are given in italic text.

The syntax is recursive, and hence the syntactic classes have no natural ordering. We use an ordering that approximates to 'bottom up'; that is, we describe the smaller units first and then assemble them into larger units and ultimately an entire program. Remember, this description is precisely that — a description. In an attempt to keep the description readable and hence useful, some details have been omitted.

---

[10] The precise details depend on the layout of the computer store and the type of date held in the array.

[11] We shun the temptation to include huge amounts of material quite tangential to the main theme of our text. It is certainly true that programming languages do need formal specifications, which may be thought of as specifications of compilers, and compilers *are* programs. But they are very special programs and best specified using techniques other than the general ones discussed elsewhere in this book.

[12] Backus Naur (or Backus Normal) Form, with which we assume the reader has at least a passing acquaintance. The more traditional form of BNF is used in the Appendix.

IDENT — an identifier

is

a meaningful(?) name consisting of a string of letters, digits and the symbol "_", starting with a letter

IDENTS — a list of IDENTs

is

IDENT "," IDENTS

or

IDENT

EXP — an expression

is

any well-formed expression using the types defined in Chapter 1

or

IDENT "("EXPS ")" — a function call

or

"if" EXP "then" EXP "else" EXP "fi" — a conditional expression

the first expression is of type Boolean; if it yields True, then the middle expression delivers the result, if False then the third expression gives the result. (Here and elsewhere, there is no specific connection between the different occurrences of the same class name, such as 'EXP'.)

or

EXP "where:" EXP — *the second* EXP *yields a Boolean value — see later in this section.*

or

"if" EXP "then" EXP
"else_if" EXP "then" EXP "else" EXP "fi"

one contracted form of nested conditional expressions

or

CAST ":" EXP

The result from the EXP *is 'coerced' into the type indicated by the* CAST. *Refer to Section 1.4.10*

CAST

is

TYPE

TYPE type

here undefined but includes all the type indicators given in Chapter 1

TYPES

is

TYPE "," TYPES

or

TYPE

EXPS an expression list

is

EXP "," EXPS *the "," is a list separator*

or

EXP

DEC a declaration[13]

is

"var" IDENTS ":" TYPE a 'variable'[14] declaration

or

IDENT "(" IDENTS ")" "≙" EXP a function declaration

or

IDENT "(" IDENTS ")" "≙" "(" EXP ")" *alternative form*

or

IDENT "(" IDENTS ")" "≙" BLOCK a function / procedure declaration

a form of function declaration in which each flow through the BLOCK *terminates in an* EXP, *implicitly or explicitly assigned to the 'result'. Without a 'result', this is a procedure*

or

IDENT "≙" BLOCK[15] a procedure declaration

a procedure with no parameters

or

"var" IDENT "[" TYPES "]" ":" TYPE an array declaration

the TYPES *are index types and must be subranges.* TYPE *is the type of the data held in the array.*

[13] Other contracted forms are also allowed by way of 'syntactic sugar'.

[14] These are names of constant locations, but the contents can be changed. Hence they are often described as 'variables'.

[15] Or a statement other than a 'goto' statement.

DECS		declarations
is		
	DEC ";" DECS	
or		
	DEC	
STMT		a statement
is		
	IDENT ":" STMT	*the identifier is a label*
or		
	BLOCK	
or		
	STMT "‖" STMT	*parallel execution*
or		
	"skip"	*the* skip *command, change nothing*
or		
	IDENT "←" EXP	*assignment, evaluate the* EXP *and pass the value to the location associated with* IDENT
or		
	IDENT "[" EXPS "]" "←" EXP	*assignment to an array element*
or		
	⟨ IDENTS ⟩ "←" ⟨ EXPS ⟩	*parallel assignment. The lists are of equal length and of corresponding types. All the* EXPS *are evaluated. Then the values are deposited in the locations named by the corresponding* IDENTS.
or		
	"if" EXP "then" STMT "else" STMT "fi"	conditional statement
or		
	"if" EXP "then" STMT "fi"	*contracted form, presumes* "else skip"
or		
	"if" EXP "then" STMT "else_if" EXP "then" STMT "else" STMT "fi"	*one contracted version of one form of the nested conditional statement.*
or		
	"while" EXP "do" STMT "od"	'while' loop[16], EXP *is* Boolean
or		
	"repeat" STMT "until" EXP	'repeat' loop, EXP *is* Boolean
or		
	"goto" IDENT	IDENT *is a label in the same* BLOCK

[16] We could also have 'for' commands as syntactic sugar for certain 'while' loops.

or

"result" "←" EXP	delivers the result of a function evaluation ["result ←"] *denotes optionality*

or

IDENT "(" EXPS ")"	procedure call

or

IDENT	procedure call *with no parameters*

BLOCK[17]
is

"begin" DECS ";" STMTS "end"

or

"begin" STMTS "end"

STMTS
is

STMT ";" STMTS

or

STMT

PROG — a program
is

BLOCK

We also have comments and assertions. These may be placed between statements.

COMMENT

any sequence of characters (other than quotation marks) delimited by " *and* ".

ASSERTION

"$" EXP "$"

or — *where* EXP *is of type* Boolean

"$" "assert" EXP "$"

These syntax rules can be used either in the generation of programs or the analysis of strings (as part of the process of determining whether you have a valid program). They can also be regarded as rewrite rules, albeit in a context different from that found throughout the rest of this book.

2.4.1 "Let" and "Where". Conventionally, and for very good practical reasons, most procedural languages require that all named entities, functions etc., be declared before use. This is the 'let' style of presentation, even if the word 'let' is not used

[17] And "(...)" can be used in place of "begin ... end" as delimiters.

explicitly. This is available in PDL, but for use in intermediate forms we also have the 'where' style, which allows the use of incomplete (or general) expressions that are then completed (or restricted) by quoting additional Boolean information, definitions or specifications.

For example:

$$x + f(y) \qquad \text{where: } x = a + b \ \text{ and } \ f \triangleq (\lambda x{:}X)(x + 3)$$

which means $a + b + y + 3$

2.4.2 Scope and Parameters. 'Variables' referenced within a block but not declared within that block are those declared within the smallest surrounding block. Within function and procedure calls, that block is a block surrounding the call rather than the declaration. Notice also that parameters are passed by value and are therefore constants, which cannot be changed within a function or procedure.

2.5 Comments and Assertions

Programs written in modern programming languages should be very nearly self-documenting and hence there is less need for comments. Nevertheless, comments, if up-to-date and related to the code, can be very useful. However, they *may* not have anything to do with the code. They may be out of date, or just plain wrong.

Comments are sometimes written at the same time as the code and hence are likely to be related to the code (in a meaningful and relevant way). When code is modified, since the comments are ignored by the compiler and need not be changed in order to make the code work, it is probable that the comments are *not* modified. Hence the comments, even if helpful once, may not always be so. The fewer the comments, the easier it is to ensure that they *are* up-to-date.

Of course, they are only there for the benefit of the human reader; they are totally ignored by the compiler.

Instead of comments, we could use ***assertions*** — executable comments. If the evaluation of an assertion (the body of an assertion, is a Boolean expression) gives the value False, then the program is aborted (halted) preferably with some indication of where the failure took place. If the assertion yields True, indicating that some property you thought ought to hold (at that point in the program) was actually true, and execution of the program continues, albeit at some computational cost. Using the pre-condition[18] as an assertion immediately after the input phase reflects the assumptions made about acceptable input values[19].

[18] Part of the specification of the function which the program is supposed to compute.

[19] Together with the data type constraints imposed by the read command is as far as we can go to cope with robustness.

Similarly, if we keep a copy of the input values (and that means making no subsequent changes to the relevant 'variables'), then, just before the output phase, we can include the post-condition as another assertion. This would then check that the answer which we had computed was in fact an acceptable answer for the given input.

This sounds fine, and it is much easier than doing lots of technical work with specifications and programs, but evaluating assertions can be very expensive and take huge amounts of time and other (machine) resources. Moreover, placing assertions between every pair of commands and including all information that the programmer thinks *may* be of relevance would make the text completely unreadable. Of course, the assertions which are True immediately before a certain command are logically related to those that are True immediately afterwards, and hence not everything need be repeated.

The see how these assertions are connected mathematically, we consider the three basic computational components of a flowchart. These are depicted (with assertions) in Figure 2.5.

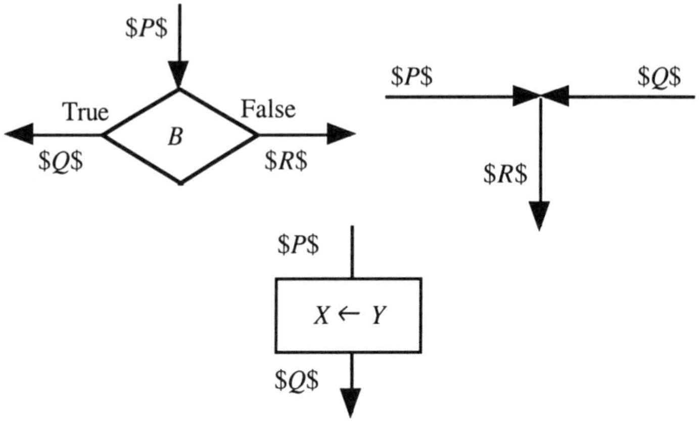

Figure 2.5

The three kinds of component are tests, joins and assignments. The first two are often forgotten because nothing seems to be happening, but they are crucially important. In Figure 2.5 the assertions (annotations?) are Boolean expressions but we shall also treat P, Q and R as being synonymous with labels at the positions indicated on the segments of the flowchart.

In the test flowchart, any facts within P are clearly also within Q and R since we have done nothing to change that information(?). Here we assume that the test B was useful within the program and hence that either outcome of the test was possible. If this is not so, then we could simply always go from P to Q, or always go from P to R, and remove the test. By similar reasoning, Q and R should be different; otherwise it makes no sense to 'follow' them with different program segments. So what is the difference? The difference is that at Q we know that the value of B is True and, if we get to R then the value of B is False. Hence we can write

$$Q \Leftrightarrow P \wedge B \qquad \text{and} \qquad R \Leftrightarrow P \wedge \neg B$$

These are the strongest assertions which can be used in positions Q and R. We may not wish to retain all this information; we may simply not need it, and hence some of the information could be discarded without compromising further reasoning. However, in all cases we *do* know the following:

$$P \wedge B \Rightarrow Q \qquad \text{and} \qquad P \wedge \neg B \Rightarrow R$$

This helps in appreciating the inter-relationships between the assertions associated with the join flowchart. Here, we have:

$$P \Rightarrow R \qquad \text{and} \qquad Q \Rightarrow R$$

These implications always hold. The (logically) strongest assertion we can use for R is

$$R \Leftrightarrow P \vee Q$$

— we simply do not know which branch we followed on our way to R.

Now for explicit computation steps, as indicated by rectangles within flowcharts. First notice that we have written an assignment command to represent the computational process between $ P $ and $ Q $. Any command[20] can be regarded as an assignment, albeit, in general, a parallel multiple assignment (in which n expressions are evaluated and then placed in the corresponding named locations), with the possibility of conditional expressions and/or recursive function calls. So, in restricting consideration to an assignment, we lose nothing.

Obviously, with complex expressions, logical reasoning is more complicated; we shall content ourselves with simple illustrations to introduce the necessary relationships.

The situation depicted in Figure 2.5 can be written as

$ P $
$X \leftarrow Y$
$ Q $

[20] Other than a 'goto' command.

If we need Q to be True, what can we say about P? That is, what do we need to be True at P in order to guarantee that Q will be True after we have executed the assignment statement? Suppose either that P is initially absent or that it is present but tells us nothing (it provides no information, no reason for halting the program), in which case it is logically, identically, True.

Example 2.1

$$\$\ P?\ \$$$
$$z \leftarrow x + 9$$
$$\$\ z > 0\ \$$$

For P we could have $x + 9 > 0$ since the final value of z is equal to $x + 9$ and hence the properties of z must be equivalent to the properties of the expression $x + 9$. In fact, here we can say more:

$$\$\ x + 9 > 0\ \$$$
$$z \leftarrow x + 9$$
$$\$\ z = x + 9 \ \wedge\ z > 0\ \$$$

❑

Of course, it gets rather involved if values change (and we often need them to) as in

$$\$\ x + 9 > 0\ \$$$
$$x \leftarrow x + 9$$
$$\$\ x > 0\ \$$$

In general, if we have

$$\$\ P\ \$$$
$$X \leftarrow Y$$
$$\$\ Q\ \$$$

then, given Q, we have that

$$P \Rightarrow Q[\ X \leftarrow Y\ ]$$

That is, given P (is True) we can deduce the expression Q in which X has been replaced by Y. P must logically include $Q[\ X \leftarrow Y\ ]$.

Of course, the coincidental use of this notation is not accidental. If P initially tells us nothing (so it is identically True) then we can have $P \Leftrightarrow Q[\ X \leftarrow Y\ ]$ and hence

$$\$\ Q[\ X \leftarrow Y\ ]\ \$$$
$$X \leftarrow Y$$
$$\$\ Q\ \$$$

Example 2.2 We can extend this idea in a natural way; for instance

```
$ ( x + 9 ) * 2 – 1 > 0 $
x ← x + 9;
$ ( x * 2 ) – 1 > 0 $
x ← x * 2 – 1
$ x > 0 $
```

Consequently, we can remove the intermediate working and simply write

```
$ ( x + 9 ) * 2 – 1 > 0 $
x ← x + 9;
x ← x * 2 – 1
$ x > 0 $
```

❑

Working backwards from the final required predicate, the post-condition, we can[21] — in principle — move through a finite sequence of statements (each equivalent to an assignment statement) with the aim of obtaining an initial assertion (which logically follows, using '⇛', from the post-condition).

But there *are* problems. Very few procedural programs are totally sequential but involve some repetition, such as loops, a possibility which we consider below.

More serious is the possibility of including an inappropriate assignment which effectively destroys information, making it impossible to complete the calculation. [If a program is wrong, there is no way that assertions can be inserted which prove it correct!] Moreover, an assertion is applicable at one specific point in the program code (although that point may be revisited on numerous occasions), but a specification, in particular the post-condition part of a specification, refers to the input *and* output of a (sub-) calculation. Hence, to use assertions to enforce/affirm/check adherence to a specification requires that we keep a copy of the original input values to the corresponding segment of code.

We need to address the possibility of state changes (which are fundamental to the philosophy of procedural languages) and slip from a classical function, f, to a (computational) operation[22], F. To illustrate this, consider the pair of assignment commands

$$y \leftarrow f(x)$$

and

$$\langle x', y' \rangle \leftarrow F(\langle x, y \rangle)$$

---

[21] There is an extra technicality involved here, which means that we may need to refer to an earlier 'state'.

[22] These are akin to commands in programming languages, not traditional mathematical operations, which are merely alternative syntactic forms for common functions.

For these to represent the same action, we need to interpret the second as

$$y' \leftarrow f(x)$$

and

$$x' \leftarrow x \qquad\qquad \text{assuming that } x \text{ and } y \text{ are different.}$$

or, more generally,

$$\sigma' \leftarrow F(\sigma)$$

where σ (lower case Greek letter sigma) denotes the state, which can be thought of as the n-tuple of (allowed/accessible) locations, and σ' (and, as required, σ_1, σ_2 etc.) represents the same n-tuple at another point in the program. Remember that we are usually dealing with changes in value, and hence σ may represent different values even within the *same* command.

So, instead of

$$\sigma' \leftarrow F(\sigma)$$

we would usually write (in PDL)

$$\sigma \leftarrow F(\sigma)$$

which represents the context shown in Figure 2.6.

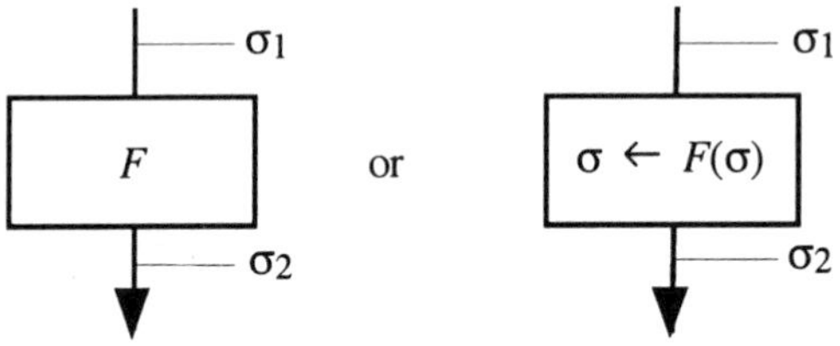

Figure 2.6

Here, the state σ_2 can be calculated from σ_1 using

$$\sigma_2 \;\blacktriangleleft\!\blacktriangleright\; F(\sigma_1) \qquad \text{derived from} \qquad \sigma_2 \triangleq F(\sigma_1)$$

Having set up the necessary notation, we can explain the basic concept of correctness. Suppose we had program P, which was intended to compute some function F specified using pre-F and post-F. The program (or program segment) P is linked to states σ_1 and σ_2 as in Figure 2.7.

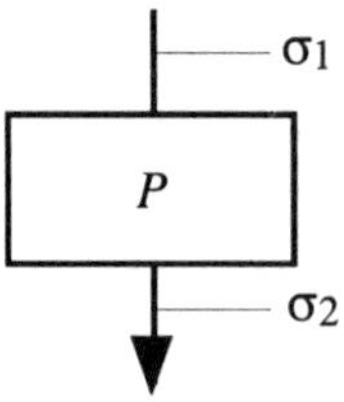

Figure 2.7

For P to correctly compute the specified function, F, we must be able to demonstrate the truth of the implication:

$$\begin{array}{ll} & \text{pre-}F(\sigma_1) \\ \Rrightarrow & \\ & \text{post-}F(\sigma_1, \sigma_2) \qquad \text{where } \sigma_2 = P(\sigma_1) \end{array}$$

Therefore, in terms of assertions, we need

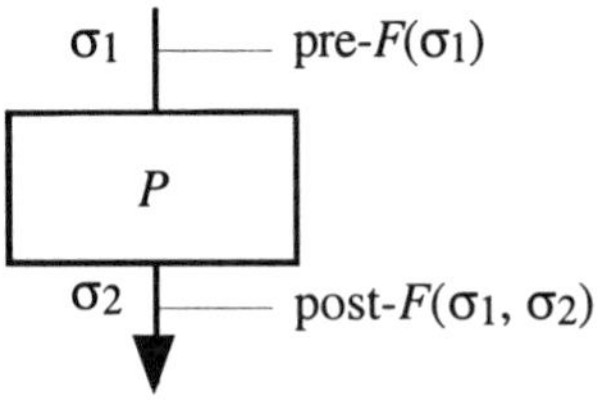

Figure 2.8

To implement such (post-) assertions we need to allocate extra storage to save the value of σ_1 for future use. Clearly, the problem of extra storage and its management can get out of hand, particularly when we try to decompose P into smaller parts more closely resembling primitive (rather than multiple) assignments. However, this is more manageable when we insist on the discipline of structured programming, as in the next section.

So, we can relate assertions within programs to the specifications of the functions/operations they are intended to compute. We have seen a simple example of how an intermediate assertion can be removed once it has been used to establish the logical link between earlier and later ones.

Verification (the next section) may thus be seen as removing the need for assertions, and hence because, for valid input, the output is correct, the post-condition (which is usually very expensive to calculate/evaluate) does not need to be included explicitly. All predicates used in the verification proof obligations (in Section 2.6) may be 'implemented' as assertions (and, by some, regarded as more practical than theoretical)[23] but at considerable cost and risk.

We make one final observation on assertions. Very many true but irrelevant pieces of information can be included within acceptable assertions. These add nothing to our understanding of the computational processes and can be very distracting and misleading. They also make the evaluation of assertions more complex and time consuming to compute. Therefore, to be informative to the reader, assertions should be as concise as possible, whilst providing adequate information to enable the logical links with the specifications to be established.

2.6 Verification of Procedural Programs

Verification of a program is the process of justifying that it is correct with respect to (wrt) its specification.

This means that

"for every valid input, the program runs to completion
and delivers an acceptable (correct) result".

Using the formal notation introduced in Chapter 1, we can express this requirement as a theorem, the correctness theorem:

f is a correct implementation (of its specification) if

$$(\forall x{:}X)(\text{pre-}f(x) \Rrightarrow \text{post-}f(x, f(x)))$$

where

$\text{pre-}f(x) \triangleq \ldots$	the test for valid input x
$\text{post-}f(x,y) \triangleq \ldots$	the test that y is a valid output for input x

Another way to look at verification is to regard it as justification for the removal of *all*[24] assertions (because, for valid input, the output is correct, so the usually very expensive post-condition does not need to checked/evaluated)

[23] This is, of course, not true. The only difference is that failure in verification prevents a program being 'delivered' and used; failure in the evaluation of a run-time assertion would cause the program to fail/abort/halt at run time, and this may be catastrophic.

[24] With the possible exception of that associated with the pre-condition to address the problem of the robustness of a program.

Reasoning (constructing useful assertions and hence eventually including the pre- and post-conditions) with an arbitrary flowchart program can be very hard. Fortunately, Structured Programming comes to the rescue.

Identifying states by σ_1, etc., as in Section 2.5, we give the required logical relationships between various points (positions, 'line segments') in the flowcharts of non-atomic structured program components.

Note that here we are not concerned with how a program is created but presume that a program has (somehow) been written and the task is to verify that it satisfies a given specification — retrospectively!

The structure of a 'structured program' is defined so that any 1-in, 1-out segment is either a single, atomic, command or can be decomposed into smaller components using one of the following forms[25], which we have already met:

(1) Sequencing $P; Q$

(2) Alternation (choice) if b then P
else Q
fi

(3) Iteration while b
do P od

For each of these we attach 'state markers' and then quote the so-called 'proof obligations' which when discharged (i.e., proven to be True) guarantee correctness of the overall combination, provided that its proper sub-components are correct (relative to their own specifications).

2.6.1 Sequencing

We refer to the flowchart in Figure 2.9.

P is a correct implementation of (the specification of) F_1

$$\text{if } (\forall \sigma_1) \qquad \text{pre-}F_1(\sigma_1) \Rrightarrow \text{post-}F_1(\sigma_1, \sigma_2)$$

$$\text{where: } \sigma_2 = P(\sigma_1)$$

So, taking the $(\forall \sigma_1)$ as implicit,

$$\text{pre-}F_1(\sigma_1) \Rrightarrow \text{post-}F_1(\sigma_1, P(\sigma_1))$$

[25] Others are possible, but they can be derived from the three given here; they are syntactic sugar.

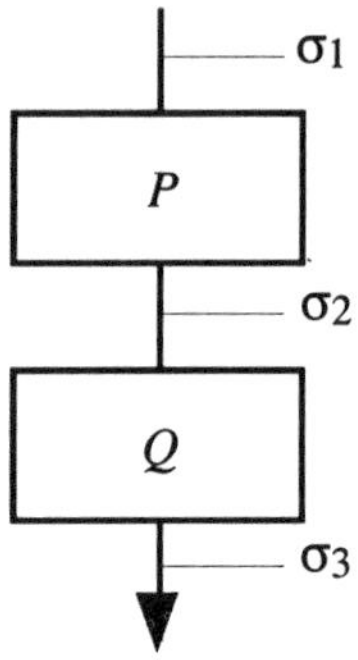

Figure 2.9

Similarly, Q is correct wrt F_2 if

$$\text{pre-}F_2(\sigma_2) \Rightarrow \text{post-}F_2(\sigma_2, Q(\sigma_2))$$

We require that the sequential combination P; Q be correct wrt F,

i.e., $$\text{pre-}F(\sigma_1) \Rightarrow \text{post-}F(\sigma_1, Q \circ P(\sigma_1))$$ see[26]

Instead of trying to tackle this directly (which could be quite difficult since we may not know explicitly the details of P and Q, but merely that they are correct implementations of F_1 and F_2 respectively), we consider the inter-relationships between states and take our lead from the flowchart.

The logical links (rules) are:

D_1: $$\text{pre-}F(\sigma_1) \Rightarrow \text{pre-}F_1(\sigma_1)$$

D_2: $$\text{pre-}F_1(\sigma_1) \wedge \text{post-}F_1(\sigma_1, \sigma_2) \Rightarrow \text{pre-}F_2(\sigma_2)$$

R_1: $$\text{pre-}F(\sigma_1) \wedge \text{post-}F_1(\sigma_1, \sigma_2) \wedge \text{post-}F_2(\sigma_2, \sigma_3) \Rightarrow \text{post-}F(\sigma_1, \sigma_3)$$

Notice that these rules do not mention P and Q explicitly; we only need to know that they satisfy their respective specifications. These rules together justify that P; Q satisfies F.

D_1 and D_2 are domain (or data) rules. D_1 says that we can start to execute P if we can start to execute $P; Q$.

[26] Recall the change in order, which is necessary so as to fit with the 'function of a function' notation.

D_2 says that, after executing P, the state reached (σ_2) is suitable for input to Q.

R_2 is a range (or result) rule. This says that with a suitable initial state (σ_1) we can first derive σ_2 and then σ_3, which is a correct output for $P;Q$ relative to the initial state σ_1 and (the specification of) F.

Already[27] we know something about how σ_2 is related to σ_3 (in such a way that Q always works correctly), but working forward is more difficult.

❑

2.6.2 Alternation

For this, see Figure 2.10.

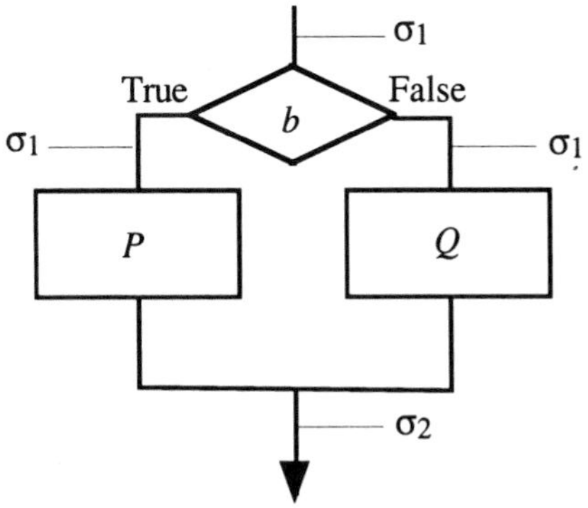

Figure 2.10

With the previous assumptions about P and Q, we now consider the requirements for the construction:

if b then P else Q fi satisfies the specification G.

Using the same kind of diagrammatic/logical reasoning, we have

D_1: pre-$G(\sigma_1) \wedge b(\sigma_1) \Rightarrow$ pre-$F_1(\sigma_1)$

D_2: pre-$G(\sigma_1) \wedge \neg b(\sigma_1) \Rightarrow$ pre-$F_2(\sigma_1)$

R_1: pre-$G(\sigma_1) \wedge b(\sigma_1) \wedge$ post-$F_1(\sigma_1, \sigma_2) \Rightarrow$ post-$G(\sigma_1, \sigma_2)$

R_2: pre-$G(\sigma_1) \wedge \neg b(\sigma_1) \wedge$ post-$F_2(\sigma_1, \sigma_2) \Rightarrow$ post-$G(\sigma_1, \sigma_2)$

[27] See Section 2.5.

Here the D rules check that σ_1, the initial state, is a valid input for the combination, together with b being either True or False ensure that P or Q can be executed correctly wrt their own specifications. The R rules then check that the results / changes produced by P and Q, respectively, fit with those required by G.

❑

2.6.3 Iteration. This is the most complex construct. For total correctness[28] a 'while' loop can pass through a finite but unbounded number of states[29].

We first deal with partial correctness. By this we mean that, *if* we get to the end, the result is acceptable, but ... . The reasoning here is similar to that used for the previous constructs but with two extra (seemingly unproductive but logically useful) predicates which provide a link between one iteration and the next. The implications can be deduced by the use of recursion together with sequencing and alternation, but we shall go straight to the rules.

We want to use the construct

while b do P od   to implement H.

Again we appeal to a flowchart with some named states; see Figure 2.11.

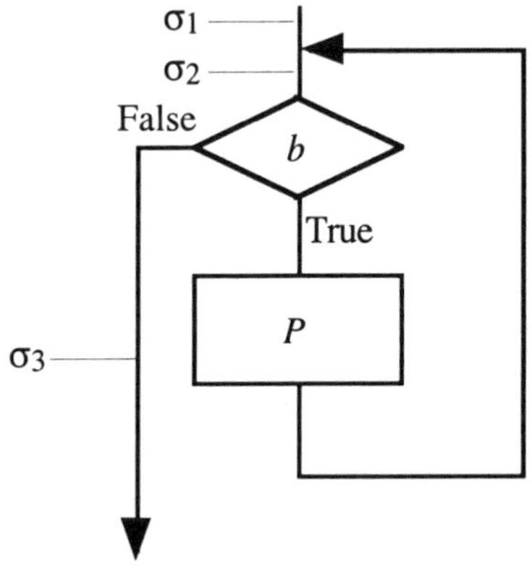

Figure 2.11

Notice that although σ_1 and σ_3 are visited only once, σ_2 may be visited many times. Here is where *invar* is evaluated.

[28] Here 'total' correctness stresses what we have implicitly taken for granted — that the evaluation of an expression or command terminates, concludes, in a finite number of steps.

[29] Each loop will exit legally in n steps, for some $n{:}\mathbb{P}$, but we can always construct a case where we will need more than n steps.

Now, 'out of the hat' we postulate the predicates:

$$invar\text{: state} \rightarrow \mathbb{B}$$

and

$$to\text{-}end\text{: state} \times \text{state} \rightarrow \mathbb{B}.$$

The rules which allow us to join the three marked places and the computational/test components are:

D_1: pre-$H(\sigma_1) \Rightarrow invar(\sigma_1)$ enter the loop

(pre-$H(\sigma_1) \Rightarrow invar(\sigma_2)$ but no calculation takes place, so on the first time through $\sigma_1 = \sigma_2$)

D_2: $invar(\sigma_2) \wedge b(\sigma_2) \Rightarrow$ pre-$F_1(\sigma_2)$
remember that P satisfies F_1

D_3: pre-$F_1(\sigma_2) \wedge$ post-$F_1(\sigma_2, \sigma_2') \Rightarrow invar(\sigma_2')$
round again, σ_2' is σ_2 on the next iteration.

R_1: $invar(\sigma_2) \wedge \neg b(\sigma_2) \Rightarrow to\text{-}end(\sigma_2, \sigma_3)$
no change has taken place here so, at this stage of the iteration we could write
$invar(\sigma_2) \wedge \neg b(\sigma_2) \Rightarrow to\text{-}end(\sigma_2, \sigma_2)$

R_2: pre-$F_1(\sigma_2) \wedge$ post-$F_1(\sigma_2, \sigma_2') \wedge to\text{-}end(\sigma_2', \sigma_3) \Rightarrow to\text{-}end(\sigma_2, \sigma_3)$
link the final state to a σ_2 state which is one iteration further back, if there is one.

R_3: pre-$H(\sigma_1) \wedge to\text{-}end(\sigma_1, \sigma_3) \Rightarrow$ post-$H(\sigma_1, \sigma_3)$
link back to initial state, σ_1.

The justification that this does prove partial correctness of the loop follows from 'joining up' segments of any execution path through the flowchart. For each rule, track it through the relevant part of the flowchart (Figure 2.11). We shall not attempt an inductive proof that the rules are suitable; In Chapter Four you will see that these rules are not necessary. They are included here for completeness and because it is via such rules that the science of verification was developed[30].

[30] The thesis of this book is that we should construct a program to be correct, not that we write a program and then, retrospectively, (try to) prove it to be correct.

But we have not yet finished. We provide a mechanism to show termination of an iterative loop. Technically, we need a 'well-ordering' on the different σ_2 states as the iteration progresses. We require a function:

$$term\text{: state} \rightarrow \mathbb{P} \qquad \text{(at the } \sigma_2 \text{ point in the flowchart)}$$

Evaluation of *term* on successive iterations of the loop must yield strictly reducing integer values, reaching zero when we eventually exit from the loop. Hence the rules are:

T_1: $\quad \text{pre-}H(\sigma_1) \Rrightarrow term(\sigma_1) \geq 0$ $\qquad$ initial value

T_2: $\quad invar(\sigma_2) \wedge (term(\sigma_1) > 0) \Rrightarrow b(\sigma_2)$

T_3: $\quad invar(\sigma_2) \wedge (term(\sigma_1) = 0) \Rrightarrow \neg b(\sigma_2)$

(so $(term(\sigma) = 0) \Leftrightarrow \neg b(\sigma_2)$,
term is a measure of how close we are to the exit condition)

T_4: $\quad \text{pre-}F_1(\sigma_2) \wedge \text{post-}F_1(\sigma_2, \sigma_2') \Rrightarrow term(\sigma_2') < term(\sigma_2)$

Again you should check the rules against segments of Figure 2.11. In practice, given the code, the selection of a suitable expression with which to define *term* is usually quite straightforward, providing that the loop actually *does* terminate.

The analogue of *term* in the recursive situation will be seen as very important (Section 3.1). It cannot be avoided, but once it has been successfully handled, it will guarantee that derived loops terminate automatically.

❑

So that is how (logically and physically) components (commands) can be assembled and linked to their specifications. But what are the 'atomic' units from which they are constructed? They are Boolean expressions, about which we shall say nothing further, and either composite processes (which logically add nothing new) or multiple assignments such as

$$\langle x, y, \ldots \rangle \leftarrow C(\langle x, y, \ldots \rangle) \qquad \text{where } C \text{ denotes a computation, a function.}$$

or

$$\sigma \leftarrow C(\sigma)$$

whence

$$\$\ P(\sigma)\ \$$$
$$\sigma \leftarrow C(\sigma)$$
$$\$\ P(\sigma) \ \wedge\ \sigma' = C(\sigma)\ \$$$

where σ is the state before the assignment and σ' is the state immediately after its execution.

But is the assignment correct? What is *P*?

Essentially, both these questions relate to a specification; let's suppose it is [pre, post]. Using assertions, we could require that

$$\$\ \text{assert pre}(\sigma)\ \$$$
$$\sigma \leftarrow C(\sigma)$$
$$\$\ \text{assert post}(\ \sigma, C(\sigma)\ )\ \$$$

If σ represents *all* the data to which the program has access, then this works perfectly well and we can use these relationships (again) but now we write them as proof obligations.

The assignment $\sigma \leftarrow C(\sigma)$

is a correct implementation of the specification *J* if

D_1: $\text{pre-}J(\sigma) \Rightarrow \text{pre-}C(\sigma)$

R_1: $\text{pre-}J(\sigma) \wedge \text{post-}C(\sigma, \sigma') \Rightarrow \text{post-}J(\sigma, \sigma')$

Often, by design, the calculation, *C*, can always be evaluated, and hence pre-$C(\sigma)$ is True and therefore D_1 holds. Moreover, R_1 can often be simplified to

$$\text{pre-}J(\sigma) \Rightarrow \text{post-}J(\sigma, C(\sigma))$$

So, for example, if *J* is $[\ x > 0\ ,\ y' > x + 3\ ]$ and we have the assignment

$$y \leftarrow x + 6 \qquad \text{where: } x,y{:}\mathbb{Z}$$

Namely

$$\langle x, y\rangle \leftarrow \langle x, x + 6\rangle$$

so

$$\langle x', y'\rangle = \langle x, x + 6\rangle$$

then, since the validity of $x > 0$ implies that x must have some valid $\mathbb{Z}$ value,

$$D_1 \Leftrightarrow \text{True}$$

and

$$\begin{aligned} R_1 &\Leftrightarrow \text{pre-}J(\sigma) \Rightarrow \text{post-}J(\sigma, C(\sigma)) \\ &\Leftrightarrow \text{pre-}J(\sigma) \Rightarrow \text{post-}J(\langle x, y\rangle, \langle x', y'\rangle) \\ &\Leftrightarrow x > 0 \Rightarrow y' > x + 3 \\ &\Leftrightarrow x > 0 \Rightarrow x + 6 > x + 3 \\ &\Leftrightarrow x > 0 \Rightarrow 6 > 3 \\ &\Leftrightarrow x > 0 \Rightarrow \text{True} \\ &\Leftrightarrow \text{True} \end{aligned}$$

So, that is all we want to say about verification. Theorists would say that this is all we need, but finding feasible predicates and then showing that they work — by discharging the proof obligations given above — is very time consuming, even with a tame theorem prover to do all the calculations, hopefully in an error-free way. And what if one of the required obligations is False? There is no routine way of correcting an error even when we have located it. The actual problem may be elsewhere in the program, not where it has caused a problem.

Can we do anything about this? Can we apply the basic theory in a different way? Yes, as we will show in the next section.

2.7 Program Derivation

Just as we usually assume 'correctness' of computer hardware when we run a program, we must also presume that the language support systems are also 'correct'. We are therefore more properly concerned with contextual correctness (or relative correctness), so running the hardware system, the run-time system (etc.), and the user program together, in parallel, works in accordance with the specification. Of course, the only component within this parallel combination on which we have any influence is our own program. If any of the other components is 'wrong' in some way, there is nothing that we can do to fix the error. We can only try to ensure that our contribution is error-free.

Given a program, we could attempt to argue its correctness using assertions. But, apart from the assertions which express the pre- and post-conditions (as supplied within the given specification), other, intermediate, *assertions* can be difficult to find. And once we have found them and used them to substantiate adequate logical connections between the program components, since they could be expensive to evaluate, we may remove[31] them or convert them into comments.

[31] Adequate (minimal) assertions can be deleted, or transformed (using $\Leftrightarrow$) but not otherwise changed.

An alternative approach is to start with the specification and use it to *create* a program design. One way to view this process is to begin with a single unknown command (one which is totally lacking in detail), as in Figure 2.12, and try to 'fill it in'.

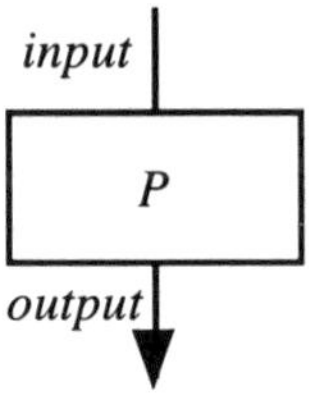

Figure 2.12

A general technique for the construction of program *P* is to 'divide and conquer' the problem and build it from smaller 'sub-programs' which solve 'parts' of the problem; but in a way that is consistent with the logical requirements within the specification.

Two (of the many) ways in which this could be done are by 'vertical decomposition' and by 'horizontal decomposition'. These can be illustrated as in Figures 2.13 and 2.14

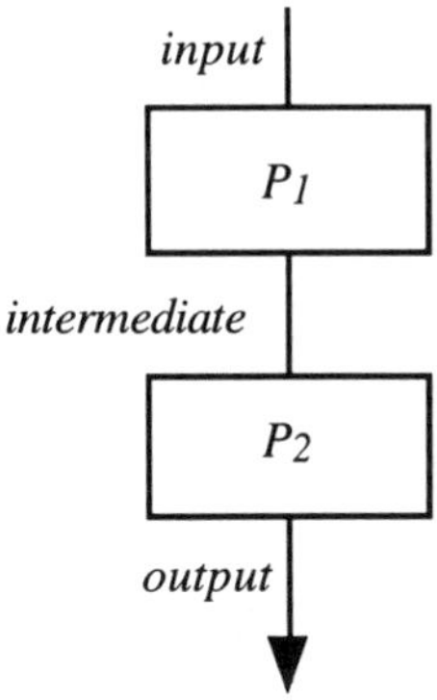

Figure 2.13 Vertical Decomposition

In vertical decomposition, P_1 takes the input and produces an intermediate result (or state), which then acts as input to P_2. Execution of P_2 then delivers the final result. This can be written as:

$$output \Leftrightarrow P_2(P_1(input))$$

which fits exactly with the concept of a 'function of a function'. But, again, determining a suitable intermediate *state* is not always easy.

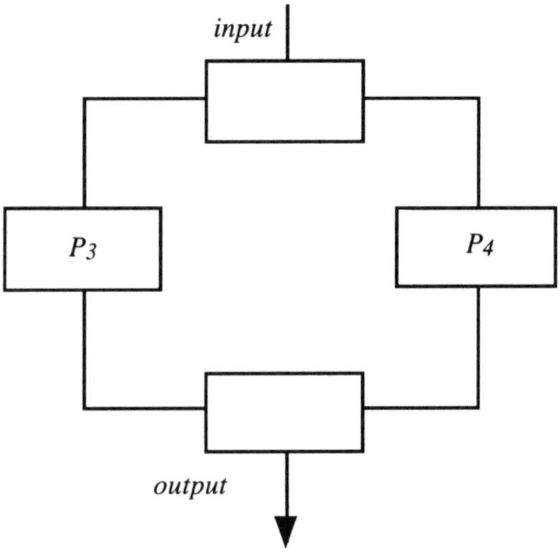

Figure 2.14 Horizontal Decomposition (i)

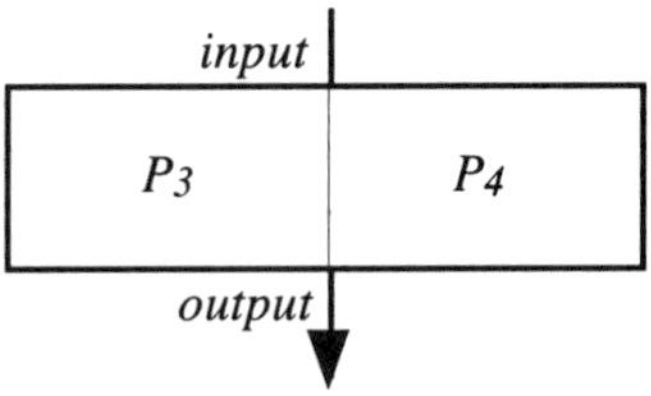

Figure 2.15 Horizontal Decomposition (ii)

In horizontal[32] decomposition, the input is divided up (somehow), each part is processed separately, and the two (or more) intermediate results from P_3 and P_4 are combined to give the overall result, from P.

[32] Of course, drawing the diagrams so that the flow is left to right would mean that the use of alternative (opposite?) terminology would seem 'natural'. Be careful. As in many situations, the terminology is *not* 'standard'.

Much of the material presented in Chapter 3 concerns variants of horizontal (de-) composition. In practice, most program derivations involve a mix of the two approaches, applying vertical decomposition whenever an opportunity (usually a clear case of 'function of a function') presents itself.

Part B
Fundamentals

Being devoted to the application of tactics for the creation of correct program designs from the specifications of (sets of) functions, this work mirrors certain common problem-solving strategies appropriately formalised.

We also study transformations for the extraction of iterative program schemes, the derivation of 'quick' methods that can be applied to certain high-level forms of specifications, and how intuition may be harnessed within the formal framework. Non-reversable (operational) refinement is also included.

Chapter 3
Algorithm Extraction

We are now in a position to start assembling a chain of processes which can be used to ***transfine*** the specification of a function into a scheme for the implementation of a program that, given suitable data, can be executed to calculate the function. In most cases, we shall have to use a mix of different design strategies for transformation and refinement. So far we have only met (reversible) transformations[1] (refinement comes later), and so we shall have to make specific structure choices which will preserve the deterministic nature of our specifications. In Chapters 5 and 6, we shall be able to handle non-deterministic specifications and introduce general decomposition methods (which must then be particularised to make the resultant design deterministic, i.e., we must choose from a set of alternatives, and this then involves an irreversible step in which some superfluous information is, intentionally, discarded).

In this chapter we examine the first part of the program construction process: we derive a recursive program scheme. In Chapter 4, we derive (conditional) rules which can be used to replace recursion by the more familiar iterative program constructs, primarily *while* loops. This order of presentation is logically correct, but if the reader is worried about introducing recursion into a program, then Chapter 4 should reassure him that it can often be removed and replaced by iteration. Chapter 4 results in program designs which look more like conventional procedural programs, which we hope are more familiar to the reader. At the risk of encountering a few unexpected back references, the reader could study these chapters in reverse order without any great loss.

---

[1] Using '◀▶' replacement rules to rearrange expressions.

3.0 Overview

Suppose that we have the specification

$$\text{spec-}f: \mathcal{P}(X \times Y) \triangleq [\text{pre-}f, \text{post-}f]$$

where

$$\text{pre-}f(x) \triangleq \dots$$
$$\text{post-}f(x,y) \triangleq \dots$$

The correctness theorem for any implementation, f, which satisfies this specification is

$$(\forall x{:}X)(\text{pre-}f(x) \Rrightarrow \text{post-}f(x, f(x)))$$

This says that the implementation f is correct if for any $x{:}X$ which satisfies the pre-condition (so that x is 'good data') the pair of values x and $f(x)$, the result obtained from x when processed by f, together satisfy the post-condition. Recall f is a function so, for given x, the value $f(x)$ is *unique*.

In the classical approach to program verification as discussed briefly in Chapter 2, an implementation f has to be obtained and then the correctness theorem proved: i.e., we must first find some f and then show

$$(\forall x{:}X)(\text{pre-}f(x) \Rrightarrow \text{post-}f(x, f(x))) \quad \blacklozenge \text{ True.}$$

We adopt a fundamentally different approach.

We assume that an answer, an implementation of f, does exist, that x is an input value (any valid input), so that pre-$f(x)$ ◆ True (see[2]), and that y is the result delivered by applying f to x.

The conditional expression

$$(\text{pre-}f(x)) \qquad \text{post-}f(x,y)$$

                                         is then presumed to be True and regarded as a *logic* program in which y is defined *implicitly* in terms of x using the predicates pre-f and post-f.

Of course, there may be no such answer; the set of acceptable implementations may be empty. To test for this in advance is not always possible; however, problems with the specification — including the lack of acceptable answers, which we strive to eliminate — should give rise to technical problems during development, derivation, and hence, albeit later than is desirable, cause the specification to be revisited and revised.

---

[2] If pre-$f(x)$ is False, then x is unsuitable data for f and we will not try to compute $f(x)$.

Notice also that taking as given the set of all ⟨x,y⟩ pairs which give True from this expression can itself be viewed as an *implicit* description of any function(s) *f* which correctly implement this specification. Essentially our job is to derive an *explicit* representation, a formula if you like, for one of these functions. So that we may use (reversible) equivalences (i.e., ◆ rules), we shall initially assume specifications are deterministic and therefore only specify one function.

[As noted above, until we have introduced the notion of (operational) refinement, we can only cope with deterministic specifications. We shall not make a big thing out of this but merely use deterministic examples throughout and cope with non-determinism later.]

Being deterministic, for any value of $x{:}X$ which satisfies pre-*f*, there is only a single value $y{:}Y$ such that post-$f(x,y)$ is True. The first, and most complicated, stage in the synthesis is to transform the post-condition from its given form into what we call a ***functional*** form, in which the evaluation of *y* is *explicit*; i.e., the post-condition is expressed in the form "$y = \ldots$", where *y* only appears on the left-hand side of the "=" sign. To achieve this, we use common problem-solving strategies (see Section 3.2). For any non-trivial calculation, this form of the program will involve recursion and so the 'logic to functional' phase of the derivation process can also be regarded as ***recursion introduction***. As already hinted in Chapter 1, the initial specification ought not to involve explicit recursion, as it encourages bias towards certain designs. We wish to defer for as long as possible any influences on the way in which the design evolves. In Chapter 5 we shall encounter more (quantified rather than recursive) constructs which can be used in specifications.

The final step will be to treat the (now functional) design as a function within a ***procedural*** language[3] and, where appropriate, transform the function declaration and its call into an iterative design. This is ***recursion removal***. Hence recursion is used within an intermediate form and provides a goal for the first part of our transfinement manipulations. One of the advantages of proceeding this way is that we avoid the need to find loop invariants[4]. The transformation into iterative form, where possible and desirable, is completely systematic, and the associated correctness proof is implicit.

Recursion removal is not considered in detail until Chapter 4, but we shall reserve the right to apply results from there, as the last phase of a program derivation, to show what the final form of the program might look like.

[3] We shall not use a proprietary programming language but one of our own invention, which we call PDL, Program Design Language. This is basically a high-level block-structured language with complex types. It was described in Chapter 2 and its 'rules' are summarised in Sections A.4 and A.5 of the Appendix. However, it should look sufficiently familiar so as to require little explanation as we go along.

[4] Though we still do need to find something akin to a loop variant.

In Section 3.1, we describe the kinds of intermediate recursions which are acceptable for our needs. In Section 3.2, we tackle the more fundamental problem of transforming the original logical specification into the 'functional' form. This will be based on a formal presentation of common problem-solving strategies.

3.1 On Converging Recursion

In our "logical-functional-procedural" (LFP) program synthesis strategy, recursion plays a very important bridging role. Ideally, we replace quantification[5] by recursion and, later, recursion by iteration.

Recall from Section 1.5 that recursions can be created by folding. The same idea can be extended to act on certain quantified expressions (see in Chapter 5).

So if

$$f(x) \triangleq exp(x)$$

or, more properly

$$f \triangleq (\lambda x{:}X)(\ exp(x)\ )$$

where f is presumed to be total,

then, we have the rule

$$(\lambda x{:}X) \qquad f(x) \;◀▶\; exp(x)$$

so we can replace $f(y)$ by $exp(y)$ using *unfolding*, or in the reverse direction, by *folding*.

We must ensure that any recursion that we create actually does converge, i.e., we must eventually reach a non-recursive part of the specification, and we must get there in a finite number of steps.

To formalise this requirement, consider

$$
\begin{array}{l}
f{:}X \to Y \\
\text{pre-}f(x) \triangleq \text{True} \qquad\qquad\qquad\qquad \text{(say)} \\
\text{post-}f(x,y) \triangleq y = \text{if} \;....\; \text{then } g(x) \\
\qquad\qquad\qquad\qquad\qquad \text{else } comb(f(f_1(x)), f(f_2(x)), \ldots, f(f_n(x))) \\
\qquad\qquad\qquad\qquad \text{fi}
\end{array}
$$

Here $n{:}\mathbb{P}$ and each f_i 'reduces' x somehow, and *comb* combines the intermediate results.

---

[5] For now, just think of this as meaning the logical quantifiers $\forall$ and $\exists$. Other forms will be introduced in Chapter 5.

So each evaluation can be represented by a tree of the form given in Figure 3.1.

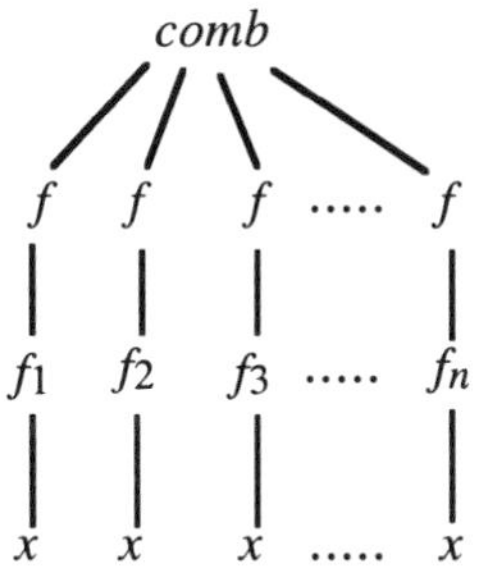

Figure 3.1

The crucial point here is that although the branches of such a tree may be of different lengths, they are all finite. Typically, the leftmost one will be as depicted in Figure 3.2. Other branches will involve a mix of the functions f_1, f_2, etc.

If X was $\mathbb{P}$, then we could use the ordering of $\mathbb{P}$ insisting that $f_i(x) < x$ for appropriate i's. The classical example of this is the good old factorial function where x and y are related by

$$y \; = \; \text{if } x = 0 \text{ then } 1 \text{ else } x * f(x-1) \text{ fi}$$

i.e., '$f_1(x)$' $\triangleq x - 1$ and $x - 1 < x$

More generally, we need to devise[6] some measure m (of type $X \rightarrow \mathbb{P}$) so that $m(f_i(x)) < m(x)$; i.e., f_i (which is of type $X \rightarrow X$) reduces the 'size' of the problem.

We should never perform a fold using f unless we have a function such as m that guarantees that the resulting recursion terminates.

This will then guarantee that any derived iterations, 'while' loops and so forth, do not continue executing forever.

Recall how the recursions introduced in the example of Section 1.5 used 'rest_of(L)' as the parameter within a call embedded in the expression derived from the definition of $even\_sum(L)$. Using the length of the list as a size measure, this clearly converges to zero and the recursion terminates.

[6] This is one of the few places where we cannot routinely apply 'automation'.

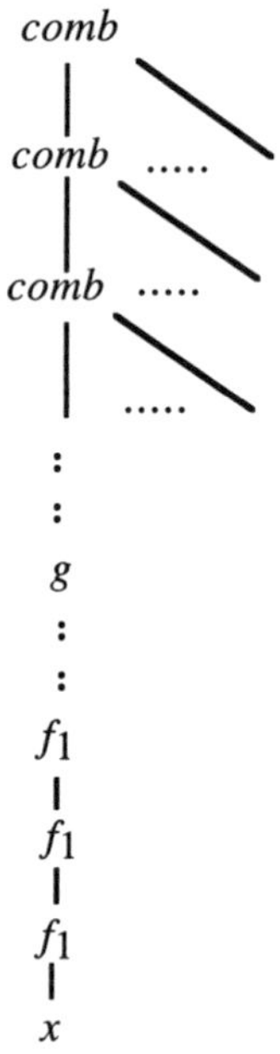

Figure 3.2

What we need to check is clear.

'Within the development of $f(x)$, we can only apply

(pre-$f(y)$) $f(y) \Leftrightarrow exp(y)$

so as to achieve a fold and re-introduce f, if $m(y) < m(x)$,
where $m{:}X \rightarrow \mathbb{P}$ is a suitable measure on X'.

Example 3.1 To illustrate this situation, we consider the function *all_same*. We make no pretence of justifying how this design has been arrived at; it is merely given as an illustration of an unusual recursive decomposition of a problem.

Given the specification:

$all\_same{:}X^{*} \rightarrow \mathbb{B}$
pre-$all\_same(L) \triangleq$ True
post-$all\_same(L,b) \triangleq b \Leftrightarrow (\exists x{:}X)(\forall y{:}X)(y \text{ in } L \Rightarrow x=y)$

then

$all\_same(L) \blacklozenge \text{True}$ when $\#L \leq 1$

$all\_same(\langle w,z \rangle) \blacklozenge w = z$ where all the actual calculation is done

and

$$\text{post-}all\_same(L \frown M \frown N, b) \blacklozenge b \Leftrightarrow (all\_same(L \frown M) \wedge all\_same(M \frown N))$$

where $L,M,N{:}X^{+}$

In this case it follows that since $\#L \geq 1$, then $\#(M \frown N) < \#(L \frown M \frown N)$, and similarly, since $\#N \geq 1$, $\#(L \frown M) < \#(L \frown M \frown N)$. Hence, using the length of the lists as a measure, the recursion converges even though

$$\#(L \frown M \frown N) \neq \#(L \frown M) + \#(M \frown N).$$

❑

Example 3.2 Now assume that we do not have integer addition but only *inc* and *dec*, which deliver a result one higher or one lower than their given integer argument.

We can then compute *add* (of type $\mathbb{P} \times \mathbb{Z} \rightarrow \mathbb{Z}$) by

$$add(x,y) \triangleq \text{if } x = 0 \text{ then } y \text{ else } add(dec(x), inc(y)) \text{ fi}$$

But what about

$$\text{if } x = 0 \text{ then } y \text{ else } add(inc(x), dec(y)) \text{ fi} \qquad ?$$

The use of the *inc* function here causes the x value to diverge *away* from the exit condition '$x = 0$' and the calculation never terminates. We can, however, modify the function so that its signature is $\mathbb{Z} \times \mathbb{Z} \rightarrow \mathbb{Z}$ and has the 'formula'

```
if x = 0 then y
         else  if x > 0 then add(dec(x), inc(y))
                        else add(inc(x), dec(y))
               fi
fi
```

This is based on the same idea but always works.

❑

Example 3.3 Now consider

$$tricky\_1(x{:}\mathbb{R}, n{:}\mathbb{N}) \triangleq \text{if } x \leq 0 \text{ then } 0 \text{ else } tricky\_1(x - 1/n, n+1) + 1 \quad \text{fi}$$

This works (try some *small* values of x and n), but finding a suitable measure is hard and requires that we know quite a lot about numbers. ❑

Even more problematic is:

Example 3.4 Suppose

$tricky\_2(x{:}\mathbb{R}, n{:}\mathbb{N}) \triangleq$ if $x \le 0$ then 0
else $tricky\_2(x - 1/n, 2*n) + 1$ fi

Can you identify the pre-condition for *tricky_2*?

Look what happens when we try to calculate *tricky_2*(3,1). We get the progression:

$tricky\_2(3, 1)$

$\Leftrightarrow$

$tricky\_2(3-1, 2*1) + 1$

$\Leftrightarrow$

$tricky\_2(2, 2) + 1$

$\Leftrightarrow$

$tricky\_2(2 - 0.5, 2*2) + 1 + 1$ ---see[7]

$\Leftrightarrow$

$tricky\_2(1.5, 4) + 2$

$\Leftrightarrow$

$tricky\_2(1.25, 8) + 3$

$\Leftrightarrow$

$tricky\_2(1.125, 16) + 4$

$\Leftrightarrow$

$tricky\_2(1.0625, 32) + 5$

etc.

With the input value pair $\langle 3,1 \rangle$, the calculation never terminates, and hence this pair is not in the domain of *tricky_2* and should be excluded by the pre-condition.

❑

The purpose of these last two examples was firstly to caution the reader against jumping to conclusions about expressions (specifications etc.) which look similar but behave very differently and secondly to emphasise the importance of using the set $\mathbb{P}$ rather than $\mathbb{Q}$ (or, worse still, $\mathbb{R}$). When 'counting down' to an exit value, we must always move towards zero and must take big enough steps so as to guarantee that we get there in a finite number of steps. Essentially the only way to do this is to use $\mathbb{P}$ and to strictly reduce the measure at each stage.

(It is also possible to allow a finite number of steps where no change is made between the strict reduction steps. This is akin to 'stuttering', which will be referred to in the sequel. We shall, wherever possible, avoid 'nasties' like this until we have dealt with the central ideas in 'better behaved' situations.)

[7] The reason for using these exact decimal representations will become clear as we proceed. To use rational numbers (fractions) here would just get out of hand, but binary fractions would be very illuminating.

3.2 Design Tactics

Although there are new (variations on) problem-solving techniques being evolved all the time, there are certain key strategies which characterise the vast majority of ways in which problems are solved and, correspondingly, solutions are sought (or programs, which solve the problems, are developed). In broad terms, we either seek to reduce the problem to a 'similar' one which is somehow easier to solve or to break the problem down into several parts, which are again easier to solve and from the solutions to which we can derive a solution to the original problem (commonly known as the "divide and conquer" strategy). These approaches are studied in Sections 3.2.2 and 3.2.3, respectively, but alone they cannot solve *any* problem. We need also to be able to cope with instances of problems which, because they are too small, cannot be further reduced or split up. Often, in such situations, the problem is so 'small' that the answer is 'easily seen' (but of course we still need to justify that our intuition is well-founded and to show that what we believe to be an answer actually works). We consider this scenario in Section 3.2.1. It may also be the case that the problem is structurally similar to another one for which we already have a solution or a partly completed design. This is the most complex situation to describe in general terms, but we discuss the basic principle in Section 3.2.4. And in Section 3.3 we look at some situations where we attempt to justify correct constructions based on inspiration.

As we progress through this chapter, we shall use small excerpts from larger problems to illustrate the different tactics. Subsequently these ideas will be brought together to construct more substantial, and more complete, program designs.

Before proceeding, it must be stressed that problem solving, of which program construction is an instance, is *not* an automatic process. Although parts of what we shall describe can be mechanised, you will still need to select what you believe to be an appropriate tactic for finding the 'solution' of each problem. Very often a 'standard' tactic, or a slight variant, will work, but you will still encounter situations that demand the creation of a new tactic or, even worse, problems which cannot be solved in the form presented. They are just insolvable, but a closely related problem may not be. This section merely presents a small collection of tactics, one or more of which will bear fruit in very many cases.

To set the scene more formally, recall the form of a specification:

$$
\begin{aligned}
& f{:}X \to Y \\
& \text{pre-}f(x) \triangleq \quad .... \\
& \text{post-}f(x,y) \triangleq \quad ....
\end{aligned}
$$

The post-condition is really only an implicit definition of y (or possibly a collection of acceptable y's) in terms of an x value which satisfies the pre-condition. The move from a logical form (as in the specification) to a functional form requires that we rearrange (the information in) the post-condition into the form

$$y = exp \ ,$$

where *exp* is an expression involving the input x (but not y) and, for interesting programs, recursive references to f. These recursions must be such that there is always 'a way out'. As discussed in Section 3.1, we need to find a reduction function (of type $X \rightarrow X$) and an associated measure (of type $X \rightarrow \mathbb{P}$).

Our initial specifications involve predicates, quantifiers etc. and can be quite complex, though not as complex as some would have us believe. Keep them as simple as possible, remove any redundancy — making them logically as weak as possible — and anything that relates to implementation rather than the problem. We need to be able to break the problem into smaller, more manageable, parts. Unfortunately, what is considered to be more acceptable in a specification — usually interpreted as 'more easily understood' — is unlikely to be structurally similar to a useful design for a procedural program.

To illustrate the structural extremes, a specification of the form

$$\ldots \wedge \ldots \wedge \ldots \wedge \ldots$$

where each of the terms is logically independent (or orthogonal), is likely to be easier to understand than more general expressions, but the direct 'coding' of any one of these terms might result in unbounded amounts of calculation and never yield results. On the other hand, in a 'straight line' procedural program we ultimately end up with a sequence of intermediate values, such as z where

$$(\exists z{:}T)\ (z = g(x) \wedge y = f(z))$$

which might be encoded as

```
        (result) y ← f(g(x))

or      begin  var z:T;
               z ← g(x);
               y ← f(z)
        end
```

or

```
begin  var z:T;
       read x;
       G(x,z);
       F(z,y);
       write y
end
```

depending on the language used.

However, as noted in Chapter 2, the direct search for z (and f and g) is usually quite difficult. It proves much easier to take a different approach in which suitable states and functions 'come out in the wash'. This is one of the situations in which we may be able to apply a 'eureka' process, but that must wait until Section 3.3.

Our program constructions may be regarded as constructive proofs (that the derived program is 'correct'). Logically they are equivalent to verification proofs, but they usually differ in the effort required and in their productivity. Often, performing a construction is easier than a retrospective verification proof (which, of course, might fail), but there are exceptions. If we really *do* know the answer or we are very confident that we know a possible answer, then, in simple cases, it may be easier to demonstrate that this answer does indeed work rather than try to re-derive it from the specification. We are not advocating full-blown complex proofs, but only the kind of proof which can be discharged by the direct (and simple and relatively short) evaluation of a Boolean expression.

Now let us look at the details. We shall concentrate on a small collection of data-driven tactics that are derived directly from well-known approaches to problem solving and are often used in combination. Here they are first described in isolation and in very general terms, and they will then be illustrated by simple examples.

(Note that the names associated with the various tactics are not standard but are indicative of their underlying motivation.)

3.2.1 Checking Perceived Answers

Take the generic case of

$$\text{spec-}f:\mathcal{P}(X \times Y) \triangleq [\text{pre-}f, \text{post-}f]$$

Suppose that for a given input value $v:X$ (such that pre-$f(v)$ ◀▶ True, so v is a *valid* input) and we believe that $z:Y$[8] is an acceptable answer for $f(v)$[9].

If z works as an answer for $f(v)$, then post-$f(v,z)$ must be True, and that is exactly what we have to show (indeed it is the *only* thing we have to show). In practice, we *back substitute* the solution into the problem (here the specification) and evaluate post-$f(v,z)$.

Providing that this evaluation gives the result True, then we may write

$$\langle v,z\rangle \in \{\ \langle x,y\rangle:X \times Y \mid \text{post-}f(x,y)\ \}$$

Moreover, since pre-$f(v)$ is True,

$$\langle v,z\rangle \in \{\ \langle x,y\rangle:X \times Y \mid \text{pre-}f(x) \wedge \text{post-}f(x,y)\ \}$$

i.e.,

$$\langle v,z\rangle \in \text{spec-}f.$$

We can then partially define an implementation of the specification by requiring that

$$f(v) \triangleq z.$$

Of course, if v was perfectly general so we could extend this to all input values in the domain of spec-f, we would have found the whole of f and could write

$$\text{spec-}f \blacktriangleright \{\ \langle v,z\rangle:X \times Y \mid z = f(v)\ \}$$

This means that $\{\langle v,z\rangle:X \times Y \mid z = f(v)\}$ is a (correct) refinement of spec-f. And notice that $\{\langle v,z\rangle:X \times Y \mid z = f(v)\}$ could be written $\{\langle v, f(v)\rangle:X \times Y\}$ or $\{v \mapsto f(v):X \to Y\}$; it is merely the graph of (a particular implementation of) the function f. However, it is unlikely that we could treat the whole of the domain (all valid inputs) in one fell swoop.

---

[8] More generally, z can be any expression — such as '*exp*' — in which v may be a parameter and which gives a result of type Y.

[9] Notice that although f, an implementation of spec-f, is deterministic (so that for a given f and a valid x, $f(x)$ is unique), it may not be the case that f is the *only* implementation of spec-f. Therefore, to use the notation spec-f ◀▶ f (or even the more technically correct form spec-f ◀▶ graph(f), where the graph of f is the relation consisting of all the maplets of the form $x \mapsto f(x)$) would be inappropriate. Because there may be loss of information, we write spec-f ▶ graph(f) and say that graph(f) is an operational ***refinement*** of spec-f. Operational refinement is an operation between binary relations and is more properly addressed in Chapter 6; here we merely need to explain why we use the notation. Notice also that graph(f:$X \to Y$) $\triangleq$ $\{\langle x,y\rangle:X \times Y \mid y = f(x)\ \}$.

More commonly, we would treat those values of v satisfying some extra condition (*cond*, say) and claim only that

$(cond)^{10}$ spec-f ▶ $\{v \mapsto f(v):X \rightarrow Y\}$

This would only work when *cond* holds. In Section 3.2.3.4, we shall see how to partition the domain so that all relevant cases are covered.

All that may sound overly complicated. The processing isn't but the description probably is. Let's look at what it means in practice.

Example 3.5 Take the specification

$Listmax:\mathbb{Z}^* \rightarrow \mathbb{Z}$
pre-$Listmax(L) \triangleq \#L \neq 0$
post-$Listmax(L,m) \triangleq m \text{ in } L \wedge (\forall z:\mathbb{Z})(z \text{ in } L \Rightarrow z \leq m)$

Recall that if *Listmax* is an *implementation* (which will be deterministic) of the specification and m denotes the output, then we can write $m = Listmax(L)$.

Suppose that (following consideration of how we might solve the overall problem) we have decided that the length of L is a suitable measure of the size of the problem (technically, if the recursion is to exit when the measure equals zero then we need $\#L - 1$, but to worry about that here as it would be an unwelcome distraction).

Consider the case when $\#L = 1$; i.e., L ◀▶ $\langle x \rangle$ for some $x:\mathbb{Z}$.
Here

pre-$Listmax(L)$ ◀▶ $1 \neq 0$
◀▶ True
so, of course, the data is valid.

First, for comparison, let us see how we might actually *calculate* the answer from the specification. Remember, we are assuming that $\#L = 1$.

[10] We ought to explain more fully how this conditional refinement should be interpreted. We shall ultimately wish to filter such conditions through conditional expressions, therefore we need only explain the interpretation when the condition holds. Clearly, on the right-hand side we should have $\{v \mapsto f(v):X \rightarrow Y \mid cond(v)\}$. What to do on the left-hand side is not so obvious since v does not appear, even implicitly: however, the restriction must be consistent with that on the right-hand side and so the conditional expansion of spec-f should be

$$\{ \langle x,y \rangle :X \times Y \mid cond(x) \wedge \text{pre-}f(x) \wedge \text{post-}f(x,y) \}.$$

In other words, we intersect both sides with the set $\{\langle x,y \rangle :X \times Y \mid cond(x)\}$. This simply imposes the constraint on the input (X) values.

$$\text{post-}Listmax(L,m)$$
◆
$$\text{post-}Listmax(L,m) \land \text{True}$$
◆
$$\text{post-}Listmax(L,m) \land (\#L = 1)$$
◆
$$\text{post-}Listmax(L,m) \land (\exists x{:}\mathbb{Z})(L = \langle x \rangle)$$
◆
$$(\exists x{:}\mathbb{Z})(\text{post-}Listmax(L,m) \land (L = \langle x \rangle))$$
◆
$$(\exists x{:}\mathbb{Z})(m \text{ in } L \land (\forall z{:}\mathbb{Z})(z \text{ in } L \Rightarrow z \le m) \land (L = \langle x \rangle))$$
◆
$$(\exists x{:}\mathbb{Z})(m \text{ in } \langle x \rangle \land (\forall z{:}\mathbb{Z})(z \text{ in } \langle x \rangle \Rightarrow z \le m) \land (L = \langle x \rangle))$$
◆
$$(\exists x{:}\mathbb{Z})(m = x \land (\forall z{:}\mathbb{Z})(z \text{ in } \langle x \rangle \Rightarrow z \le m) \land (L = \langle x \rangle))$$
◆
$$(\exists x{:}\mathbb{Z})(m = x \land (\forall z{:}\mathbb{Z})(z \text{ in } \langle m \rangle \Rightarrow z \le m) \land (L = \langle x \rangle))$$
◆
$$(\exists x{:}\mathbb{Z})(m = x \land (\forall z{:}\mathbb{Z})(z = m \Rightarrow z \le m) \land (L = \langle x \rangle))$$
◆
$$(\exists x{:}\mathbb{Z})(m = x \land \text{True} \land (L = \langle x \rangle))$$
◆
$$(\exists x{:}\mathbb{Z})(m = m \land (L = \langle m \rangle))$$
◆
$$(\exists x{:}\mathbb{Z})(\text{True} \land (L = \langle m \rangle))$$
◆
$$(\exists x{:}\mathbb{Z})(L = \langle m \rangle)$$
◆
$$L = \langle m \rangle$$
◆
$$m = \text{first\_of}(L) \land \langle\,\rangle = \text{rest\_of}(L)$$
◆
$$m = \text{first\_of}(L) \land 0 = \#\text{rest\_of}(L)$$
◆
$$m = \text{first\_of}(L) \land 1 = \#L$$
◆
$$m = \text{first\_of}(L) \land \text{True}$$
◆
$$m = \text{first\_of}(L)$$

i.e., $(\#L = 1)$ $\quad Listmax(L)$ ◆ $\text{first\_of}(L)$

so $(\#L = 1)$ $\quad \text{post-}Listmax(L,\text{first\_of}(L))$ ◆ True

That's how to *work out* the answer. [Study this derivation and identify exactly what is being done at each stage and why it is being done.] Now, instead of going through the calculation, which often will be more involved than in this example, we merely have to *check* that the 'apparently obvious' answer does in fact work.

To do this, we evaluate

post-*Listmax*$(\langle x\rangle, x)$

◆ (we already know that pre-*Listmax*$(\langle x\rangle)$ ◆ True)

x in $\langle x\rangle \wedge (\forall z{:}\mathbb{Z})(z$ in $\langle x\rangle \Rightarrow z \le x)$

◆

$x = x \;\wedge\; (\forall z{:}\mathbb{Z})(z = x \Rightarrow z \le x)$

◆

True $\wedge$ $(\forall z{:}\mathbb{Z})$(True)

◆

True

Here we use essentially the same basic reasoning, but the manipulation is shorter and easier (since we don't have to *find* the answer).

We have therefore concluded that

$(\#L = 1)$ spec-*Listmax* ▸ $\{L \mapsto \text{first\_of}(L){:}\mathbb{Z}^* \to \mathbb{Z}\}$

This can then be used within the construction

m = if $\#L = 1$ then first_of(L)
else ... fi

but more of that later.

❑

Put simply, if we believe that we know an 'answer', we just plug it into the post-condition and evaluate. If the evaluation yields True, then we have a valid (conditional) refinement and can proceed to the next part of the construction. But remember that our answer might not be the only one, so what we have here is potentially a refinement rather than a reversible transformation.

3.2.2 Problem Reduction

As hinted at in the previous example, within the initial analysis of a problem to be solved (or of a calculation to be performed), we must consider the notion of 'size'. In general terms, we can only be rather vague about what constitutes the size of a problem or even the size of a piece of data. Typical measures of size which *might* be useful in certain situations are the length of a list, the size of a finite set or bag, or even the magnitude (value) of a positive number[11]. Of course, the measure of problem size must be directly related to the problem being solved, and hence a numerical characterisation of 'unsortedness' and 'being more sorted' (to be used within a sorting algorithm) might be more indicative of the kind of measure, and associated reduction function, which must be sought.

Technically, the data (input) value supplied to a function can always be regarded as a single entity, even if it is a list or set or whatever. With this in mind, ***problem reduction*** can be simply expressed as "given a suitably 'large' data item, create a 'smaller' data value for which the program should give the *same* answer". Of course, this all hinges on the notion of size, which is problem-specific.

Problem reduction is rarely used directly but occurs in some way in the derivation of virtually all iterative programs. This is hardly surprising since problem reduction leads straight to tail recursion, which, in its pure form, is not commonly found. As you will see in Chapter 4, it can get quite involved.

This is the first instance of recursion introduction and is based on the relationship

$$f(x) = f(reduce(x))$$

Of course, this would never terminate/converge, but the following conditional expression incorporates the same concept.

$f(x)$ ◀▶ if ...
then ...
else $f(reduce(x))$
fi

With a suitable *measure* function, then all we require is that

$$measure(reduce(x)) < measure(x).$$

So, we solve/compute $f(x)$ by finding $f(y)$, where y is a reduced problem obtained from x.

Example 3.6
Again we use the *Listmax* function. The insight behind the reduction here is simply that if we have the list L, which includes at least two elements x and y, then we can throw away the smaller of these and then find *Listmax* of the list which remains.

[11] This need not be from the set $\mathbb{P}$. It could be a real number, but in this case the associated reduction function must 'change' the value in such a way as to guarantee that the exit value (usually zero) is reached in a finite number of steps.

In the general situation the list L has the form $A^\frown\langle x\rangle^\frown B^\frown\langle y\rangle^\frown C$ and, depending on whether $x \le y$ or not, we replace this list with either $A^\frown B^\frown\langle y\rangle^\frown C$ or $A^\frown\langle x\rangle^\frown B^\frown C$. But the x and y values can be chosen in many different ways; and this introduces algorithmic non-determinism. To avoid this perfectly valid[12] but distracting situation, we select a *particular* pair of x,y values within L.

Specifically, we shall view L as $\langle x,y\rangle^\frown C$, i.e., we name the first two elements. Let's plug this expression into the post-condition and see what happens.

If m is an acceptable result for *Listmax*(L), then

$$\text{post-}Listmax(\langle x,y\rangle^\frown C, m)$$

$$\Leftrightarrow$$

$$m \text{ in } (\langle x,y\rangle^\frown C) \wedge (\forall z{:}\mathbb{Z})(z \text{ in } (\langle x,y\rangle^\frown C) \Rightarrow z \le m)$$

$$\Leftrightarrow$$

$$((m = x) \vee (m = y) \vee m \text{ in } C) \wedge (\forall z{:}\mathbb{Z})(z \text{ in } (\langle x,y\rangle^\frown C) \Rightarrow z \le m)$$

$$\Leftrightarrow$$

$$((m = x) \vee (m = y) \vee m \text{ in } C) \wedge \\ \quad ((x \le m) \wedge (y \le m) \wedge (\forall z{:}\mathbb{Z})(z \text{ in } C \Rightarrow z \le m))$$

$$\Leftrightarrow$$

True

For the sake of argument, let us now assume that $x \le y$. (Of course, in the fullness of time we must also consider the case when $x > y$. Constructions will be introduced so that we cannot forget such possibilities.) The intuition is that *Listmax*($\langle y\rangle^\frown C$) is the same as *Listmax*($\langle x,y\rangle^\frown C$). Then we would be able to write

$$Listmax(\langle x,y\rangle^\frown C) \Leftrightarrow \text{if } x \le y \text{ then } Listmax(\langle y\rangle^\frown C) \text{ else } \ldots \text{ fi}$$

Let us see what we get from *Listmax*($\langle y\rangle^\frown C$) and then see how it relates to the original problem. If *Listmax*($\langle y\rangle^\frown C$) $= n$, then

$$\text{post-}Listmax(\langle y\rangle^\frown C, n)$$

$$\Leftrightarrow$$

$$n \text{ in } (\langle y\rangle^\frown C) \wedge (\forall z{:}\mathbb{Z})(z \text{ in } (\langle y\rangle^\frown C) \Rightarrow z \le n)$$

$$\Leftrightarrow$$

$$((n = y) \vee n \text{ in } C) \wedge (\forall z{:}\mathbb{Z})(z \text{ in } (\langle y\rangle^\frown C) \Rightarrow z \le n)$$

[12] Taking such a general view is the desired way to proceed. The choice of exactly which selection to make from the set of alternatives then constitutes a further design decision, and such decisions should ideally be delayed for as long as possible.

⟺

$((n = y) \vee n \text{ in } C) \wedge (y \le n) \wedge (\forall z{:}\mathbb{Z})(z \text{ in } C \Rightarrow z \le n)$

⟺

True

What is the connection between *m* and *n*? We want them to be equal. Instead of deriving an expression for each and checking to see whether they are equal, we can check for compatibility in a single step.

Still working with the assumption that $x \le y$, we need to evaluate

$$\text{post-}Listmax(\langle x,y\rangle \frown C \,,\, Listmax(\langle y\rangle \frown C))$$

or, put another way, evaluate

$$\text{post-}Listmax(\langle x,y\rangle \frown C \,,\, n) \qquad \text{where post-}Listmax(\langle y\rangle \frown C \,,\, n).$$

So, using $((n = y) \vee n \text{ in } C) \wedge (y \le n) \wedge (\forall z{:}\mathbb{Z})(z \text{ in } C \Rightarrow z \le n)$ ⟺ True;

i.e., $((n = y) \vee n \text{ in } C)$ ⟺ True,
$(y \le n)$ ⟺ True
and $(\forall z{:}\mathbb{Z})(z \text{ in } C \Rightarrow z \le n)$ ⟺ True and $x \le y$ ⟺ True

we evaluate

$$\text{post-}Listmax(\langle x,y\rangle \frown C, n).$$

Here goes:

$\text{post-}Listmax(\langle x,y\rangle \frown C, n)$

⟺

$n \text{ in } (\langle x,y\rangle \frown C) \wedge (\forall z{:}\mathbb{Z})(z \text{ in } (\langle x,y\rangle \frown C) \Rightarrow z \le n)$

⟺

$((n = x) \vee (n = y) \vee n \text{ in } C) \wedge (\forall z{:}\mathbb{Z})(z \text{ in } (\langle x,y\rangle \frown C) \Rightarrow z \le n)$

⟺

$((n = x) \vee (n = y) \vee n \text{ in } C) \wedge$
$\quad ((x \le n) \wedge (y \le n) \wedge (\forall z{:}\mathbb{Z})(z \text{ in } C \Rightarrow z \le n))$

⟺

$((n = x) \vee \text{True}) \wedge ((x \le n) \wedge (y \le n) \wedge (\forall z{:}\mathbb{Z})(z \text{ in } C \Rightarrow z \le n))$

⟺

$\text{True} \wedge ((x \le n) \wedge (y \le n) \wedge (\forall z{:}\mathbb{Z})(z \text{ in } C \Rightarrow z \le n))$

⟺

$(x \le n) \wedge (y \le n) \wedge (\forall z{:}\mathbb{Z})(z \text{ in } C \Rightarrow z \le n)$

⟺

$(x \le n) \wedge (y \le n) \wedge \text{True}$

⟺

$(x \le n) \wedge (y \le n)$

◆

$(x \le n) \wedge \text{True} \wedge (y \le n)$

◆

$(x \le n) \wedge (x \le y) \wedge (y \le n)$

◆ $(x \le y) \wedge (y \le n) \Rightarrow (x \le n)$

and using the rule $(A \Rightarrow B) \quad A \wedge B$ ◆ A

$(x \le y) \wedge (y \le n)$

◆

$\text{True} \wedge \text{True}$

◆

True[13]

So post-*Listmax*(⟨*x*,*y*⟩⁀*C* , *Listmax*(⟨*y*⟩⁀*C*)) ◆ True

and we can write[14]

post-*Listmax*(⟨*x*,*y*⟩⁀*C*,*m*)

▸

m = if $x \le y$ then *Listmax*(⟨*y*⟩⁀*C*)
else ... fi

By a similar — but subtly different — piece of calculation, we can obtain

post-*Listmax*(⟨*x*,*y*⟩⁀*C*,*m*)

▸

m = if $x \le y$ then ...
else *Listmax*(⟨*x*⟩⁀*C*) fi

Putting these together, we have

post-*Listmax*(⟨*x*,*y*⟩⁀*C*,*m*)

▸

m = if $x \le y$ then *Listmax*(⟨*y*⟩⁀*C*)
else *Listmax*(⟨*x*⟩⁀*C*) fi

and then

post-*Listmax*(⟨*x*,*y*⟩⁀*C*,*m*)

▸

m = *Listmax*(⟨if $x \le y$ then *y* else *x* fi⟩⁀*C*)

---

[13] Again, check that you understand this derivation. Identify the difference between consecutive expressions, confirm that they are equivalent and that you understand why the transformation was performed.

[14] We use '▸' rather than '◆' because an implementation '*Listmax*(⟨*y*⟩⁀*C*)' is used and implementations are generally *refinements* of specifications. Valid alternatives may have been discarded and hence the step might not be reversible. This is discussed more fully in later Chapter 6.

To place this result back into the general form quoted at the beginning of this section

post-*Listmax*(L, m)

▶

$$m = (\text{if } \#L < 2 \text{ then } \ldots$$
$$\text{else } Listmax(\langle \text{if } x \le y \text{ then } y \text{ else } x \text{ fi}\rangle \frown C) \text{ fi})$$
$$\text{where } L = \langle x,y \rangle \frown C$$

[Notice that

$$Listmax(\langle \text{if } x < y \text{ then } y \text{ else } x \text{ fi}\rangle \frown C)$$
$$\text{where } L = \langle x,y \rangle \frown C$$

can be written as

$$Listmax(\langle \text{ if first\_of}(L) \le \text{first\_of(rest\_of}(L))$$
$$\text{then first\_of(rest\_of}(L))$$
$$\text{else first\_of}(L) \text{ fi } \rangle \quad \frown \text{rest\_of(rest\_of}(L)))$$

To say the least, this is rather messy. A neater alternative is

$$Listmax(reduce(L)),$$

where

$$reduce(\langle x,y \rangle \frown C) \triangleq \langle \text{if } x \le y \text{ then } y \text{ else } x \text{ fi}\rangle \frown C.\ ]$$

Just to remind the reader of our objective, we can take the working from the *previous* example and incorporate the current working to give

$$m = (\text{if } \#L < 2 \text{ then first\_of}(L)$$
$$\text{else } Listmax(reduce(L)) \text{ fi})$$

from which we get two function declarations and a function call:

$$Listmax(L) \triangleq (\text{if } \#L < 2 \text{ then first\_of}(L)$$
$$\text{else } Listmax(reduce(L)) \text{ fi});$$
$$reduce(\langle x,y \rangle \frown C) \triangleq \langle \text{if } x \le y \text{ then } y \text{ else } x \text{ fi}\rangle \frown C;$$
$$Listmax(L)$$

The last line could also be written as

$$m = Listmax(L),$$

to indicate the link between the calculated value and the name m used in the specification, or as

$$m \leftarrow Listmax(L)$$

to explicitly indicate the delivery of the value to m. We shall use the third alternative, as it conveniently bridges the move from the functional form — the pure function call — to the procedural assignment statement.

Removing the recursion by means of the standard transformation (see Chapter 4), we can replace $m \leftarrow Listmax(L)$

by:

```
begin  var v:ℤ*;
           v ← L;
           while #v ≥ 2
             do v ← reduce(v)
             od;
           m ← first_of(v)
end
```

❑

Again we have used checking, but here we have more structure to play with and we achieve a more computationally useful result. The amount of work involved here is untypically large. Taking a less direct approach, and showing that the function *max* is associative,

so $$max(a,max(b,c)) = max(max(a,b),c)$$

would allow us to derive a similar design with less work. But we cannot yet justify such a step.

Exercises

3.1 Following the lead given above, deduce the following:

post-$Listmax(\langle x,y\rangle \frown C\ , m)$

▶

$m =$ if $x \le y$ then ...
else $Listmax(\langle x\rangle \frown C)$ fi

❑

3.2.3 Problem Decomposition

When confronted with problems involving a 'small' amount of data (by which we mean capable of being 'seen' as a whole or fully comprehended as a "head full of information")[15], there is an understandable desire to dive straight in, to get on with the job in hand and not to spend time organising *how* to proceed. This is not unreasonable since the task is perceived as being so simple as not to require such things.

Although extra considerations, such as how to store and access the data, need eventually to be taken into account, it is often fruitful from the very outset to assume that the program is going to be used with *huge* inputs, so that a degree of organisation is essential. Such approaches are akin to using multiple resources (parallel computers or even a team of human helpers). Indeed, for machine processing of data, organisation is arguably more important than the actual (atomic) calculations, which are often trivial in comparison.

As noted in the previous section, pure problem reduction is rarely applicable to an initial specification; we therefore seek ways in which the given problem can be broken down (rather than reduced) into smaller (easier?) problems, the solutions of which lead us to a solution of the given problem.

What constitutes a smaller, or 'easier', problem depends not only on the problem but also on how we are attempting to solve it. It should therefore be expected that very many problems (genuinely different - dissimilar - problems) will best be solved by *variants* of general methods rather than by straightforward 'handle turning'. Consequently, it is also reasonable to expect that general techniques on their own will yield solution schemes which are correct (and proved to be correct) but perhaps not optimal. But optimality depends on properties over which the software designer may have no control, such as the speed of certain operations on a particular machine, and is secondary to correctness. It may be possible to improve the efficiency of a correct program; there is no point in doing anything with a program which is not known to be correct.

Essentially the tactics given below range from using the (pure) *structure* of the data to using the atomic data values and disregarding the structure in which they are held, or include a mix of both, or use selected properties of data (viewed as a single entity) to divide up the problem domain. We shall describe these tactics in terms of the main composite types defined earlier but focus mainly on lists. They not only form the basis from which all internal data types are constructed in modern

[15] The analogy which we are attempting to draw out here is similar to that which advocates that any flowchart should fit onto a single piece of A4 paper and yet use notations and descriptions which can be easily read. There is a certain limiting amount of information, which is almost impossible to quantify and is very subjective, that can be easily understood and mentally 'processed' without the use of any aids.

programming languages, they are also the way in which sets and bags are represented within computer systems.

In general, what we are searching for is a pair of functions, which we shall generically call *split* and *combine* (but these names will also be used in specific examples, and other locally appropriate names will also be used so beware), so that we can:

replace (refine) $f(A)$ by $combine(f(B), f(C))$ where $\langle B, C \rangle = split(A)$.

This can be denoted by

$(\langle B, C \rangle = split(A)) \quad f(A) \blacktriangleright combine(f(B), f(C))$

A dataflow[16] diagram (Figure 3.3) will more clearly show what we are trying to do. This basic diagram will occur with almost monotonous regularity from now on. It is therefore very important that you see exactly what is going on.

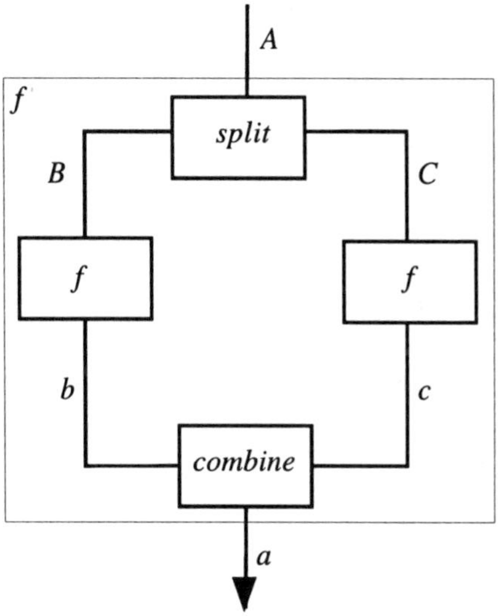

Figure 3.3

We want to *split* the input A into B and C, so that f can be performed on values B and C independently to yield answers b and c. These are then combined to give a, which is a valid answer for the original calculation, namely $f(A)$.

[16] Despite a degree of similarity with the 'if then else fi' flowcharts in Chapter 2, remember that this is a dataflow diagram. Data flows down both branches.

Forgetting for the moment about the details of the *split/combine* part of the scheme, if f is to be a valid implementation of spec-f applied to A, we require that

$$\text{pre-}f(A) \; \blacklozenge\!\!\blacktriangleright \; \text{True}$$

and

$$\text{post-}f(A, a) \; \blacklozenge\!\!\blacktriangleright \; \text{True}$$

i.e., that the data A is valid and the answer a works.

So, if the connections within the outer 'f box' in the diagram are to provide a correct replacement for $f(A)$, the following inter-relationships must hold. (Check that you understand how they relate to the lines and boxes in Figure 3.3.)

$$(A \text{ is large enough}) \qquad \text{pre-}f(A) \;\Rrightarrow\; \text{pre-}split(A) \qquad\qquad (1)$$

so that *split*ting A is legal and desirable,

$$(split(A) = \langle B,C \rangle) \;\Rrightarrow\; (\,\text{pre-}f(B) \wedge \text{pre-}f(C)\,) \qquad (2)$$

so that the evaluations of $f(B)$ and $f(C)$ are legal,

$$\text{post-}f(B,b) \; \blacklozenge\!\!\blacktriangleright \; \text{True} \quad \text{and} \quad \text{post-}f(C,c) \; \blacklozenge\!\!\blacktriangleright \; \text{True} \qquad (3)$$

so the two sub-calculations give the valid results b and c,

$$\text{pre-}combine(\langle b,c \rangle) \; \blacklozenge\!\!\blacktriangleright \; \text{True} \qquad\qquad (4)$$

so *combine*ing b and c is legal,

$$\text{post-}combine(\langle b,c \rangle, a) \; \blacklozenge\!\!\blacktriangleright \; \text{True} \qquad\qquad (5)$$

and gives the valid answer a, and

$$\text{post-}f(A, a) \; \blacklozenge\!\!\blacktriangleright \; \text{True} \qquad\qquad (6)$$

which is also a valid answer for $f(A)$.

In total, given a value A for which pre-$f(A)$ is True and A is 'large enough' to require splitting, if these six conditions hold, $combine(f(B), f(C))$ is a correct replacement for $f(A)$. We write this as

$$f(A) \; \blacktriangleright \; combine(f(B), f(C))$$

namely $f(A)$ is refined to $combine(f(B), f(C))$.

or $f(A)$ can be implemented by $combine(f(B), f(C))$.

But this looks like hard work, we have six properties to check. Fortunately, some or all of these will often involve little or no work. What we seek is to reduce the overall task by looking for special ways of *split*ting data so that the conditions always hold and *combine* is easy to specify or define. Indeed, it may even be the case that the main check can simply be performed by evaluating

$$\text{post-}f(A, combine(f(B), f(C))) \qquad \text{with suitable substitutions.}$$

There are other approaches to dealing with this situation. We could 'guess' the *split* and *combine* components and then try to show that they fit into the scheme. Alternatively, we could invent a *split* and then try to calculate a *combine* function that fits the conditions; this is more in keeping with our desire to calculate all but the most obvious details (which we simply check). Of course, for a bad choice of a *split*ting function, it may not be possible to find *any combine* function. In such a situation, it might be possible to find a suitable scheme for a different, but closely related, specification and then devise code to link the two. We address this possibility in Chapter 10. Alternatively, if we can reformulate the specification to use certain kinds of functions, such as quantifiers, then 'divide and conquer' schemes can be obtained in a single step. This scenario is investigated further in Chapter 5, but here we intentionally develop constructions from first principles.

3.2.3.1 Structural Splitting

Arguably this is the most important technical instance of problem decomposition, and consequently we devote a considerable amount of time to it. Structural splitting amounts to dividing a suitably large data item into two or more smaller parts without reference to individual items within the input. As always, an appropriate measure of size needs to be found so as to give some meaning to 'large' and 'smaller' but, using the length of lists and the size of (i.e., the number of elements in) a finite set or bag, we can illustrate the general intent.

Suppose that the input to function $f{:}X^* \rightarrow Y$ is $L{:}X^*$ and we decide to decompose it into sub-lists $M{:}X^*$ and $N{:}X^*$, where L ◆ $M {}^\frown N$. In order to make progress in solving the problem, we must have that $\#M < \#L$ and that $\#N < \#L$, and, since $\#L$ ◆ $\#M + \#N$, this means that $\#N \geq 1$ and $\#M \geq 1$. This is a requirement for making progress even if $\langle\rangle$ is a valid input for the function being computed.

To indicate how the components of the sought-after design fit together, we refer to the usual dataflow diagram appropriately annotated (Figure 3.4).

Notice that since f has type $X^* \rightarrow Y$, it follows that

split has type $X^* \rightarrow X^* \times X^*$
and *combine* is of type $Y \times Y \rightarrow Y$.

Typically we will be considering situations where pre-$f(L)$ is defined either to be 'True' or '$\#L > 0$'. What then can be said about the functions *split* and *combine*?

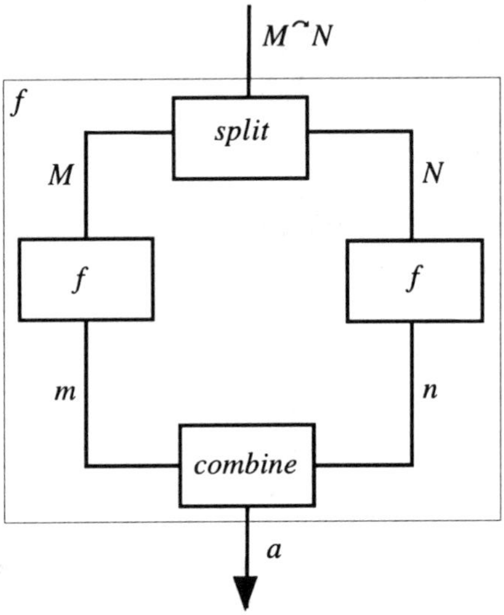

Figure 3.4

(1) We already know from the discussion above that $\#M \geq 1$ and $\#N \geq 1$, so it would be reasonable to include '$\#L \geq 2$' within pre-*split*, indeed this is often the condition under which splitting is required.

So defining

$$\text{pre-}split(L) \triangleq \#L \geq 2 \wedge \text{pre-}f(L),$$

we have

($\#L \geq 2$) $\quad$ pre-$f(L) \Rrightarrow$ pre-$split(L)$

$\Leftrightarrow$

pre-$f(L) \Rrightarrow (\#L \geq 2 \wedge$ pre-$f(L))$

$\Leftrightarrow$

pre-$f(L) \Rrightarrow$ (True $\wedge$ pre-$f(L)$)

$\Leftrightarrow$

pre-$f(L) \Rrightarrow$ pre-$f(L)$

$\Leftrightarrow$

True

Therefore condition (1) is valid by construction.

(2) Now we need to formulate post-*split*. Again, from the preceding discussion we already have the requirement

$$\text{post-}split(L,\langle M,N\rangle) \;\Rrightarrow\; \#M \geq 1 \;\wedge\; \#N \geq 1 \;\wedge\; L = M^\frown N$$

This has all the essentials that we require of a *split* function specification. However, it does not specify a unique function but a *set* of functions, and hence it introduces non-determinism. Clearly, given M and N, $M^\frown N$ represents a unique value, but the reverse is not always True. Notice that

$$\langle\, 1, 2, 3 \,\rangle \;\blacklozenge\; \langle 1, 2 \rangle \;^\frown\; \langle 3 \rangle$$
$$\blacklozenge\; \langle 1 \rangle \;^\frown\; \langle 2, 3 \rangle$$

so, if $M^\frown N = \langle\, 1, 2, 3 \,\rangle$, M and N are not uniquely determined.

To make *split* deterministic we must add extra constraints to ensure that the 'break point' (between M and N) is well-defined. Three commonly used possibilities are

(i) $\#M = 1$ (which suggests serial right-to-left processing)

(ii) $\#N = 1$ (left-to-right processing)

(iii) $(\#M = \#N) \;\vee\; (\#M = \#N + 1)$
             (which supports equi-parallel processing).

We shall assume that *some* choice has been made in order that *split* is deterministic (ideally such a choice be deferred, but we want to avoid non-determinism), but we shall only use the essential information; i.e., we work with

$$\text{post-}split(L,\langle M,N\rangle) \;\triangleq\; \#M \geq 1 \;\wedge\; \#N \geq 1 \;\wedge\; L = M^\frown N$$

and with this condition (2) holds trivially if pre-$f \triangleq (\lambda L{:}X^*)(\text{True})$ and almost trivially if pre-$f \triangleq (\lambda L{:}X^*)(\#L \geq 1)$.

Condition (3) is where induction on the length or size of the data value is *hidden* away. Recall that $\#M < \#L$ and $\#N < \#L$, the data values input to the two sub-calculations, are strictly smaller than that submitted to the overall calculation. Put another way, we are assuming that $f(M)$ and $f(N)$ can be correctly calculated and we are attempting to use them to build a correct answer for $f(L)$ to define a correct implementation for f when applied to (the bigger input value) L. The upshot is that, we do not need to check condition (3); we can legitimately assume that it holds. If it does not, then the fault lies within the construction that handles smaller input values and is not our immediate concern.

Now, for condition (4), this checks that the results produced by the two sub-calculations *can* be combined. Clearly, this should (logically) contain

$$(\exists M,N:X^*)(\ m = f(M) \ \wedge \ n = f(N)\ )$$

indeed, since the inputs to the sub-calculations must be non-void, we could define

$$\text{pre-}combine(m,n) \triangleq (\exists M,N:X^+)(\ m = f(M) \wedge n = f(N)\ )$$

Notice that M and N are non-empty.

In many situations, there is no actual constraint on inputs to *combine*; any value of type Y is a valid result for some input to f, and then we must have

$$\text{pre-}combine(m,n) \triangleq \text{True}$$

Often it is convenient to use 'True' even if not strictly necessary, but then we run the risk of having to devise an implementation for *combine*, part of which will never be used; but this is often done. Provided that no 'special cases' have to be considered when designing code to implement *combine*, this is no real penalty.

Finally, conditions (5) and (6) together link the answer given by *combine* to that required by the specification of f and which will work for $f(L)$. The processing carried out by the scheme in Figure 3.4 and using four *functions* (i.e., implementations of the specifications) should give a valid answer for $f(L)$, but it may not be the only answer allowed by the specification; therefore, instead of equivalence, there is a weaker logical connection, namely

$$\text{post-}combine(\langle f(M), f(N)\rangle, a) \Rrightarrow \text{post-}f(M^\frown N, a)$$

If a is a valid answer from the *split / f / f / combine* scheme, then it is also valid for the overall evaluation.

This can also be checked by evaluating

$$\begin{array}{lll} \text{post-}f(M^\frown N,a) & \text{where} & \text{post-}combine(\langle m, n\rangle,a) \\ & \text{where} & \text{post-}f(M,m) \text{ and post-}f(N,n) \end{array}$$

This is the pivotal step in showing that the scheme works — *if* it does.

Remember that what we would *like* to do, and are *attempting* to do, is to replace $f(N^\frown M)$ by $combine(f(N),f(M))$. This amounts to *defining* $f(L)$ in terms of $f(M)$ and $f(N)$ and requires that we show

$$combine(f(N),f(M)) \quad \text{is a correct result for} \quad f(N^\frown M)$$

If this works, we can write

$$f(L) \blacktriangleright combine(f(N),f(M)) \qquad \text{where } \langle N,M\rangle = split(L).$$

The construction of the *split* function is straightforward, as is pre-*combine*, but there is no guarantee that the result delivered by *combine* will work for $f(L)$. So the construction of *combine* is the focus of this tactic. We give three examples. The first uses checking, the second addresses the same function but uses calculation, and the third illustrates a situation for which the tactic fails.

Example 3.7
Again we use the *Listmax* function.

$$Listmax{:}\mathbb{Z}^* \to \mathbb{Z}$$
$$\text{pre-}Listmax(L) \triangleq \#L \geq 1$$
$$\text{post-}Listmax(L,x) \triangleq x \text{ in } L \wedge (\forall z{:}\mathbb{Z})(z \text{ in } L \Rightarrow z \leq x)$$

If $\#L \geq 2$, then suppose we split L into M and N where $\#M \geq 1$, $\#N \geq 1$, and $L = M^\frown N$, and then calculate $m = Listmax(M)$ and $n = Listmax(N)$. It would then seem feasible that the maximum of m and n would give x.

Now we formalise this and identify exactly what has to be checked.

$$split{:}\mathbb{Z}^* \to \mathbb{Z}^* \times \mathbb{Z}^*$$
$$\text{pre-}split(L) \triangleq \#L \geq 2$$
$$\text{post-}split(L,\langle M,N\rangle) \triangleq \#M \geq 1 \wedge \#N \geq 1 \wedge L = M^\frown N$$
$$[\wedge\ ((\#M = \#N) \vee (\#M = \#N + 1))]$$

— the last clause is included so as to avoid non-determinism.

$$combine{:}\mathbb{Z} \times \mathbb{Z} \to \mathbb{Z}$$
$$\text{pre-}combine(\langle m,n\rangle) \triangleq \text{True}$$
$$\text{post-}combine(\langle m,n\rangle,x) \triangleq x = max(m,n)$$

$$\text{where } max(m{:}\mathbb{Z},n{:}\mathbb{Z}) \triangleq \text{if } m > n \text{ then } m \text{ else } n \text{ fi}$$

By construction, the following hold:

$$(\#L \geq 2) \qquad \text{pre-}Listmax(L) \Rrightarrow \text{pre-}split(L) \qquad (1)$$

$$(split(L) = \langle M,N\rangle) \Rrightarrow \text{pre-}Listmax(M) \wedge \text{pre-}Listmax(N) \qquad (2)$$

$$\text{post-}Listmax(M,m) \Leftrightarrow \text{True and post-}Listmax(N,n) \Leftrightarrow \text{True} \qquad (3)$$

$$\text{pre-}combine(\langle m,n\rangle) \Leftrightarrow \text{True} \qquad (4)$$

$$\text{post-}combine(\langle m,n\rangle,x) \Leftrightarrow \text{True} \qquad (5)$$

These claims are quickly verified, but you should go through the details for yourself.

Now comes the crunch. Does it all fit? We plug the assumptions that follow from the working above and evaluate. We shall try to substitute 'backwards' from x, m, n, etc.

$\text{post-}Listmax(L, x)$

where $\text{post-}combine(\langle m,n\rangle,x) \Leftrightarrow \text{True}$
$\text{post-}Listmax(M,m) \Leftrightarrow \text{True}$
$\text{post-}Listmax(N,n) \Leftrightarrow \text{True}$
$split(L) \Leftrightarrow \langle M,N\rangle$ and
$(\#L \geq 2)$

$\Leftrightarrow$

$x \text{ in } L \wedge (\forall z{:}\mathbb{Z})(z \text{ in } L \Rightarrow z \leq x)$

$\Leftrightarrow$

$max(m,n) \text{ in } L \wedge (\forall z{:}\mathbb{Z})(z \text{ in } L \Rightarrow z \leq max(m,n))$

Next consider the two possibilities either $(m > n)$ or $(m \leq n)$.

Since $(m > n \vee m \leq n) \Leftrightarrow$ True, we could introduce this clause and then proceed with

if $m > n$ then $max(m,n) \text{ in } L \wedge (\forall z{:}\mathbb{Z})(z \text{ in } L \Rightarrow z \leq max(m,n))$
else $max(m,n) \text{ in } L \wedge (\forall z{:}\mathbb{Z})(z \text{ in } L \Rightarrow z \leq max(m,n))$ fi

This is equivalent to continuing first with the assumption that $m > n$ and then with $m \leq n$ and then combining the results. How best to do this is largely a matter of preference or of how a CASE tool is prepared to assist you. We shall proceed with the extra assumption $m > n$ and leave the other case as an exercise.

$max(m,n) \text{ in } L \wedge (\forall z{:}\mathbb{Z})(z \text{ in } L \Rightarrow z \leq max(m,n))$

$\Leftrightarrow$

$m \text{ in } L \wedge (\forall z{:}\mathbb{Z})(z \text{ in } L \Rightarrow z \leq m)$

$\Leftrightarrow$

$m \text{ in } (M\frown N) \wedge (\forall z{:}\mathbb{Z})(z \text{ in } (M\frown N) \Rightarrow z \leq m)$

$\Leftrightarrow$

$(m \text{ in } M \vee m \text{ in } N) \wedge (\forall z{:}\mathbb{Z})(z \text{ in } (M\frown N) \Rightarrow z \leq m)$

$\Leftrightarrow$

$(\text{True} \lor m \text{ in } N) \land (\forall z{:}\mathbb{Z})(z \text{ in } (M^\frown N) \Rightarrow z \le m)$

$\Leftrightarrow$

$\text{True} \land (\forall z{:}\mathbb{Z})(z \text{ in } (M^\frown N) \Rightarrow z \le m)$

$\Leftrightarrow$

$(\forall z{:}\mathbb{Z})(z \text{ in } (M^\frown N) \Rightarrow z \le m)$

$\Leftrightarrow$

$(\forall z{:}\mathbb{Z})(z \text{ in } M \Rightarrow z \le m) \land (\forall z{:}\mathbb{Z})(z \text{ in } N \Rightarrow z \le m)$

$\Leftrightarrow$

$\text{True} \land (\forall z{:}\mathbb{Z})(z \text{ in } N \Rightarrow z \le m)$

$\Leftrightarrow$

$(\forall z{:}\mathbb{Z})(z \text{ in } N \Rightarrow z \le m)$

$\Leftrightarrow$

$\text{True} \land (\forall z{:}\mathbb{Z})(z \text{ in } N \Rightarrow z \le m)$

$\Leftrightarrow$

$(\forall z{:}\mathbb{Z})(z \text{ in } N \Rightarrow z \le n) \land (n < m) \land (\forall z{:}\mathbb{Z})(z \text{ in } N \Rightarrow z \le m)$

$\Leftrightarrow$ since $((\forall z{:}\mathbb{Z})(z \text{ in } N \Rightarrow z \le n) \land (n < m)) \Rightarrow (\forall z{:}\mathbb{Z})(z \text{ in } N \Rightarrow z \le m)$

$(\forall z{:}\mathbb{Z})(z \text{ in } N \Rightarrow z \le n) \land (n < m)$

$\Leftrightarrow$

True

So,

$max(m,n) \text{ in } L \land (\forall z{:}\mathbb{Z})(z \text{ in } L \Rightarrow z \le max(m,n))$

$\Leftrightarrow$

if $m > n$ then $max(m,n) \text{ in } L \land (\forall z{:}\mathbb{Z})(z \text{ in } L \Rightarrow z \le max(m,n))$
else $max(m,n) \text{ in } L \land (\forall z{:}\mathbb{Z})(z \text{ in } L \Rightarrow z \le max(m,n))$ fi

$\Leftrightarrow$

if $m > n$ then True
else $max(m,n) \text{ in } L \land (\forall z{:}\mathbb{Z})(z \text{ in } L \Rightarrow z \le max(m,n))$ fi

and, when you have done the other part,

$\Leftrightarrow$

if $m > n$ then True
else True fi

$\Leftrightarrow$

True

Thus, the proposed scheme does work and, subject to L being long enough, we can use the replacement

$$Listmax(L) \blacktriangleright max(Listmax(M),Listmax(N)) \quad \text{where: } split(L) = \langle M,N\rangle$$

As before, this can be slotted into a higher-level construction to give

$$Listmax(L) \blacktriangleright \text{if } \#L \geq 2 \text{ then } max(Listmax(M),Listmax(N)) \quad \text{where: } \langle M,N\rangle = split(L) \quad \text{else first\_of}(L) \text{ fi}$$

❑

The transformation sequence given above (used to carry out an evaluation and thus perform a check) looks like a lot of work. It is *equivalent* to a verification proof and hence obviates the need to *test* that the scheme works for *all* valid data. Moreover, compared with how a piece of everyday school algebra would look if we included all the details, it is not really very long. Indeed, if you had a mathematically aware editor, then each line could be obtained from its predecessor by selecting (highlighting) an appropriate sub-expression, choosing a rule and hitting the 'apply' button. Having said that, the main aim from here on is to seek ways of cutting down the effort required by developing 'bigger' rules. These would make the transfinement sequences shorter but, at the same time, reduce the ability to exercise control over the fine details that influence the characteristics of the final design.

Example 3.8

Now, again by way of comparison, we shall outline how we can *derive* (calculate?) the *combine* component of the previous scheme. We start in the same way from the specifications of *Listmax* and *split*.

$$Listmax{:}\mathbb{Z}^{*} \rightarrow \mathbb{Z}$$
$$\text{pre-}Listmax(L) \triangleq \#L \geq 1$$
$$\text{post-}Listmax(L,x) \triangleq x \text{ in } L \land (\forall z{:}\mathbb{Z})(z \text{ in } L \Rightarrow z \leq x)$$

$$split{:}\mathbb{Z}^{*} \rightarrow \mathbb{Z}^{*} \times \mathbb{Z}^{*}$$
$$\text{pre-}split(L) \triangleq \#L \geq 2$$
$$\text{post-}split(L,\langle M,N\rangle) \triangleq \#M \geq 1 \land \#N \geq 1 \land L = M^\frown N \quad [\land \; ((\#M = \#N) \lor (\#M = \#N + 1))]$$

— but we shall again ignore the last clause.

Now we need to find (the specification of) a *combine* function. Let us take the following as a starting point:

$combine{:}\mathbb{Z} \times \mathbb{Z} \rightarrow \mathbb{Z}$
pre-$combine(\langle m,n \rangle) \triangleq$ True
post-$combine(\langle m,n \rangle,x) \triangleq$?

And additionally, we assume $\#L \geq 2$.

Starting with post-$Listmax(L,x)$ we try to manipulate this expression into a form that has local (existentially quantified) values M, N, m and n and in which the only inter-relationships between them correspond to the evaluation of *split* (linking L, M and N), of the two instances of *Listmax* (linking M with m and N with n), and of *combine* (m, n and x). To do this we can call upon the assumptions made about L, about the correct implementations of *split* and *Listmax* (acting on M and N) and that these implementations are guaranteed to deliver results from valid data values.

In transforming the expressions, we may introduce or remove any terms which can be derived from other terms. Predictably, these will often involve implication and use the rule

$(A \Rightarrow B) \qquad A \wedge B \Leftrightarrow A$

You may have thought that the previous example was long, but this is longer[17]. So we shall only give selected intermediate forms (and leave the filling in of details as a very useful exercise in manipulation) and concentrate on explaining how the transformation sequence is developed.

post-$Listmax(L,x)$

$\Leftrightarrow$

$x \text{ in } L \wedge (\forall z{:}\mathbb{Z})(z \text{ in } L \Rightarrow z \leq x)$

Now, by assumption, $\#L \geq 2 \Leftrightarrow$ True, so

$\Leftrightarrow$

$x \text{ in } L \wedge (\forall z{:}\mathbb{Z})(z \text{ in } L \Rightarrow z \leq x) \wedge \#L \geq 2$

$\Leftrightarrow$

$x \text{ in } L \wedge (\forall z{:}\mathbb{Z})(z \text{ in } L \Rightarrow z \leq x) \wedge$ pre-$split(L)$

and if we can perform *split* on L, then there must be answers since

pre-$split(L) \Rightarrow (\exists M,N{:}\mathbb{Z}^*)($post-$split(L,\langle M,N \rangle))$

[17] Typically we have a lot of steps, each of which makes some small change within the expression. With a suitable software engineering tool, each of these would be similar to a simple edit.

◆

$$x \text{ in } L \wedge (\forall z{:}\mathbb{Z})(z \text{ in } L \Rightarrow z \leq x) \\ \wedge \text{ pre-}split(L) \wedge (\exists M,N{:}\mathbb{Z}^*)(\text{post-}split(L,\langle M,N\rangle))$$

The pre- and post-conditions together give the overall specification of *split* and can eventually be refined to ('replaced' by) its implementation, but for now we need to use clauses within post-*split* to process the rest of the expression.

◆

$$(\exists M,N{:}\mathbb{Z}^*)\ (x \text{ in } L \wedge (\forall z{:}\mathbb{Z})(z \text{ in } L \Rightarrow z \leq x) \\ \wedge \text{ pre-}split(L) \wedge \text{post-}split(L,\langle M,N\rangle)\ )$$

◆

$$(\exists M,N{:}\mathbb{Z}^*)\ (x \text{ in } L \wedge (\forall z{:}\mathbb{Z})(z \text{ in } L \Rightarrow z \leq x) \\ \wedge \text{ pre-}split(L) \wedge \#M \geq 1 \wedge \#N \geq 1 \wedge L = M^\frown N\ )$$

Notice that we have a conjunction of six terms and we can use any to rationalise the others. We use L ◆ $M^\frown N$ to remove all instances of L except those occurring in the specification of *split*. (We must retain the link with the input, L.)

◆

$$(\exists M,N{:}\mathbb{Z}^*)\ (x \text{ in } (M^\frown N) \wedge (\forall z{:}\mathbb{Z})(z \text{ in } (M^\frown N) \Rightarrow z \leq x) \\ \wedge \text{ pre-}split(L) \wedge \#M \geq 1 \wedge \#N \geq 1 \wedge L = M^\frown N\ )$$

similarly,

◆

$$(\exists M,N{:}\mathbb{Z}^*)\ (x \text{ in } (M^\frown N) \wedge (\forall z{:}\mathbb{Z})(z \text{ in } (M^\frown N) \Rightarrow z \leq x) \\ \wedge \text{ pre-}split(L) \wedge \#M \geq 1 \wedge \#N \geq 1 \wedge L = M^\frown N \\ \wedge \#M \geq 1 \wedge \#N \geq 1\ )$$

◆

$$(\exists M,N{:}\mathbb{Z}^*)\ (x \text{ in } (M^\frown N) \wedge (\forall z{:}\mathbb{Z})(z \text{ in } (M^\frown N) \Rightarrow z \leq x) \\ \wedge \text{ pre-}split(L) \wedge \#M \geq 1 \wedge \#N \geq 1 \wedge L = M^\frown N \\ \wedge \text{ pre-}Listmax(M) \wedge \text{pre-}Listmax(N)\ )$$

◆

$$(\exists M,N{:}\mathbb{Z}^*)\ (x \text{ in } (M^\frown N) \wedge (\forall z{:}\mathbb{Z})(z \text{ in } (M^\frown N) \Rightarrow z \leq x) \\ \wedge \text{ pre-}split(L) \wedge \#M \geq 1 \wedge \#N \geq 1 \wedge L = M^\frown N \\ \wedge \text{ pre-}Listmax(M) \wedge (\exists m{:}\mathbb{Z})(\text{post-}Listmax(M,m)) \\ \wedge \text{ pre-}Listmax(N) \wedge (\exists n{:}\mathbb{Z})(\text{post-}Listmax(N,n))\ )$$

◆

$$(\exists M,N{:}\mathbb{Z}^*,m,n{:}\mathbb{Z}) \\ (\ x \text{ in } (M^\frown N) \wedge (\forall z{:}\mathbb{Z})(z \text{ in } (M^\frown N) \Rightarrow z \leq x) \\ \wedge \text{ pre-}split(L) \wedge \text{post-}split(L,\langle M,N\rangle) \\ \wedge \text{ pre-}Listmax(M) \wedge \text{post-}Listmax(M,m) \\ \wedge \text{ pre-}Listmax(N) \wedge \text{post-}Listmax(N,n)\ )$$

We have the specifications of three of the parts and two other clauses which link M and N to x. As we used post-*split* earlier, we now need to use post-*Listmax* to establish a link between x and m rather than between x and M, and similarly for N and n.

$\Leftrightarrow$

$$
\begin{aligned}
&(\exists M,N{:}\mathbb{Z}^*,m,n{:}\mathbb{Z})\\
&\qquad(\ x \text{ in } (M^\frown N) \wedge (\forall z{:}\mathbb{Z})(z \text{ in } (M^\frown N) \Rightarrow z \le x)\\
&\qquad\wedge \text{ pre-}split(L) \wedge \text{post-}split(L,\langle M,N\rangle)\\
&\qquad\wedge \text{ pre-}Listmax(M)\\
&\qquad\wedge\ m \text{ in } M \wedge (\forall z{:}\mathbb{Z})(z \text{ in } M \Rightarrow z \le m)\\
&\qquad\wedge \text{ pre-}Listmax(N)\\
&\qquad\wedge\ n \text{ in } N \wedge (\forall z{:}\mathbb{Z})(z \text{ in } N \Rightarrow z \le n)\ )
\end{aligned}
$$

Now we must start playing with inequalities.

Key facts are

$$m \text{ in } M \Rightarrow m \text{ in } (M^\frown N) \text{ and } m \text{ in } (M^\frown N) \Rightarrow m \le x$$

so

$$m \text{ in } M \Rightarrow m \le x$$

Similarly, $\quad n \text{ in } N \Rightarrow n \le x$

and hence we go on

$\Leftrightarrow$

$$
\begin{aligned}
&(\exists M,N{:}\mathbb{Z}^*,m,n{:}\mathbb{Z})\\
&\qquad(\ x \text{ in } (M^\frown N) \wedge (\forall z{:}\mathbb{Z})(z \text{ in } (M^\frown N) \Rightarrow z \le x)\\
&\qquad\wedge \text{ pre-}split(L) \wedge \text{post-}split(L,\langle M,N\rangle)\\
&\qquad\wedge \text{ pre-}Listmax(M)\\
&\qquad\wedge\ m \text{ in } M \wedge (\forall z{:}\mathbb{Z})(z \text{ in } M \Rightarrow z \le m)\\
&\qquad\wedge \text{ pre-}Listmax(N)\\
&\qquad\wedge\ n \text{ in } N \wedge (\forall z{:}\mathbb{Z})(z \text{ in } N \Rightarrow z \le n)\\
&\qquad\wedge\ m \le x \wedge n \le x)
\end{aligned}
$$

So far, we have used rationalisation directly, but now it starts to be a little more difficult. We need to cope with $M^\frown N$ and take one instance at a time.

First notice that

$$
\begin{aligned}
(\forall z{:}\mathbb{Z})(z \text{ in } (M^\frown N) \Rightarrow z \le x) \quad \Leftrightarrow \quad &(\forall z{:}\mathbb{Z})(z \text{ in } M \Rightarrow z \le x)\\
&\wedge (\forall z{:}\mathbb{Z})(z \text{ in } N \Rightarrow z \le x)
\end{aligned}
$$

So

$$(\exists M,N:\mathbb{Z}^*,m,n:\mathbb{Z})$$
$$\begin{aligned}
&(\ \ x \text{ in } (M^\frown N) \land (\forall z:\mathbb{Z})(z \text{ in } (M^\frown N) \Rightarrow z \le x)\\
&\land \text{pre-}split(L) \land \text{post-}split(L,\langle M,N\rangle)\\
&\land \text{pre-}Listmax(M)\\
&\land m \text{ in } M \land (\forall z:\mathbb{Z})(z \text{ in } M \Rightarrow z \le m)\\
&\land \text{pre-}Listmax(N)\\
&\land n \text{ in } N \land (\forall z:\mathbb{Z})(z \text{ in } N \Rightarrow z \le n)\\
&\land m \le x \land n \le x)
\end{aligned}$$

⧫

$$(\exists M,N:\mathbb{Z}^*,m,n:\mathbb{Z})$$
$$\begin{aligned}
&(\ \ x \text{ in } (M^\frown N)\\
&\land (\forall z:\mathbb{Z})(z \text{ in } M \Rightarrow z \le x)\\
&\land (\forall z:\mathbb{Z})(z \text{ in } N \Rightarrow z \le x)\\
&\land \text{pre-}split(L) \land \text{post-}split(L,\langle M,N\rangle)\\
&\land \text{pre-}Listmax(M)\\
&\land m \text{ in } M \land (\forall z:\mathbb{Z})(z \text{ in } M \Rightarrow z \le m)\\
&\land \text{pre-}Listmax(N)\\
&\land n \text{ in } N \land (\forall z:\mathbb{Z})(z \text{ in } N \Rightarrow z \le n)\\
&\land m \le x \land n \le x\ )
\end{aligned}$$

and now we can start 'throwing parts away',

⧫ $$(\ (\forall z:\mathbb{Z})(z \text{ in } M \Rightarrow z \le m) \land m \le x\ ) \Rightarrow (\forall z:\mathbb{Z})(z \text{ in } M \Rightarrow z \le x)$$

$$(\exists M,N:\mathbb{Z}^*,m,n:\mathbb{Z})$$
$$\begin{aligned}
&(\ \ x \text{ in } (M^\frown N)\\
&\land \text{pre-}split(L) \land \text{post-}split(L,\langle M,N\rangle)\\
&\land \text{pre-}Listmax(M)\\
&\land m \text{ in } M \land (\forall z:\mathbb{Z})(z \text{ in } M \Rightarrow z \le m)\\
&\land \text{pre-}Listmax(N)\\
&\land n \text{ in } N \land (\forall z:\mathbb{Z})(z \text{ in } N \Rightarrow z \le n)\\
&\land m \le x \land n \le x\ )
\end{aligned}$$

Now for the tricky bit. We need to remove 'x in $(M^\frown N)$', if we can. But expanding this term gives rise to a disjunction (an 'or' operation) rather than a conjunction, and hence we must consider different cases if we wish to use rationalisation.

The first step is easy:

$$
\begin{array}{l}
\Leftrightarrow \\
\quad (\exists M,N{:}\mathbb{Z}^*,m,n{:}\mathbb{Z}) \\
\qquad (\ (x \text{ in } M \ \vee\ x \text{ in } N) \\
\qquad \wedge\ \text{pre-}split(L) \wedge \text{post-}split(L,\langle M,N\rangle) \\
\qquad \wedge\ \text{pre-}Listmax(M) \\
\qquad \wedge\ m \text{ in } M \wedge (\forall z{:}\mathbb{Z})(z \text{ in } M \Rightarrow z \le m) \\
\qquad \wedge\ \text{pre-}Listmax(N) \\
\qquad \wedge\ n \text{ in } N \wedge (\forall z{:}\mathbb{Z})(z \text{ in } N \Rightarrow z \le n) \\
\qquad \wedge\ m \le x \wedge n \le x\ )
\end{array}
$$

The term 'x in M $\vee$ x in N' has to be True, so either 'x in M' or 'x in N', or both. We consider two cases, (x in M) and $\neg$(x in M), and then use

$$\text{True} \Leftrightarrow (x \text{ in } M) \vee \neg(x \text{ in } M)$$

If (x in M), then $x \le m$ and since $m \le x$ we deduce $x = m$. Moreover, the term 'x in M $\vee$ x in N' can be deduced from $x = m$ and 'm in M'.

So, in this case

$$
\begin{array}{l}
\qquad (\ (x \text{ in } M \ \vee\ x \text{ in } N) \\
\qquad \wedge\ \text{pre-}split(L) \wedge \text{post-}split(L,\langle M,N\rangle) \\
\qquad \wedge\ \text{pre-}Listmax(M) \\
\qquad \wedge\ m \text{ in } M \wedge (\forall z{:}\mathbb{Z})(z \text{ in } M \Rightarrow z \le m) \\
\qquad \wedge\ \text{pre-}Listmax(N) \\
\qquad \wedge\ n \text{ in } N \wedge (\forall z{:}\mathbb{Z})(z \text{ in } N \Rightarrow z \le n) \\
\qquad \wedge\ m \le x \wedge n \le x\ ) \\
\Leftrightarrow \\
\qquad (\ \text{pre-}split(L) \wedge \text{post-}split(L,\langle M,N\rangle) \\
\qquad \wedge\ \text{pre-}Listmax(M) \\
\qquad \wedge\ m \text{ in } M \wedge (\forall z{:}\mathbb{Z})(z \text{ in } M \Rightarrow z \le m) \\
\qquad \wedge\ \text{pre-}Listmax(N) \\
\qquad \wedge\ n \text{ in } N \wedge (\forall z{:}\mathbb{Z})(z \text{ in } N \Rightarrow z \le n) \\
\qquad \wedge\ m \le x \wedge n \le x \wedge m = x\ )
\end{array}
$$

Similarly, if $\neg$(x in M), then (x in N), $x \le n$, and hence $x = n$, etc.

So

$$
\begin{aligned}
&(\ \ (x \text{ in } M \ \ \vee\ x \text{ in } N)\\
&\wedge \text{pre-}split(L) \wedge \text{post-}split(L,\langle M,N\rangle)\\
&\wedge \text{pre-}Listmax(M)\\
&\wedge m \text{ in } M \wedge (\forall z{:}\mathbb{Z})(z \text{ in } M \Rightarrow z \le m)\\
&\wedge \text{pre-}Listmax(N)\\
&\wedge n \text{ in } N \wedge (\forall z{:}\mathbb{Z})(z \text{ in } N \Rightarrow z \le n)\\
&\wedge m \le x \wedge n \le x\ )
\end{aligned}
$$

◆

$$
\begin{aligned}
&(\ \ \text{pre-}split(L) \wedge \text{post-}split(L,\langle M,N\rangle)\\
&\wedge \text{pre-}Listmax(M)\\
&\wedge m \text{ in } M \wedge (\forall z{:}\mathbb{Z})(z \text{ in } M \Rightarrow z \le m)\\
&\wedge \text{pre-}Listmax(N)\\
&\wedge n \text{ in } N \wedge (\forall z{:}\mathbb{Z})(z \text{ in } N \Rightarrow z \le n)\\
&\wedge m \le x \wedge n \le x \wedge n = x\ )
\end{aligned}
$$

Putting the two parts together, we have the transformation

$$
\begin{aligned}
&(\exists M,N{:}\mathbb{Z}^*,m,n{:}\mathbb{Z})\\
&\qquad(\ \ (x \text{ in } M \ \ \vee\ x \text{ in } N)\\
&\qquad\wedge \text{pre-}split(L) \wedge \text{post-}split(L,\langle M,N\rangle)\\
&\qquad\wedge \text{pre-}Listmax(M)\\
&\qquad\wedge m \text{ in } M \wedge (\forall z{:}\mathbb{Z})(z \text{ in } M \Rightarrow z \le m)\\
&\qquad\wedge \text{pre-}Listmax(N)\\
&\qquad\wedge n \text{ in } N \wedge (\forall z{:}\mathbb{Z})(z \text{ in } N \Rightarrow z \le n)\\
&\qquad\wedge m \le x \wedge n \le x\ )
\end{aligned}
$$

◆

$$
\begin{aligned}
&(\exists M,N{:}\mathbb{Z}^*,m,n{:}\mathbb{Z})\\
&\qquad(\ \ \text{pre-}split(L) \wedge \text{post-}split(L,\langle M,N\rangle)\\
&\qquad\wedge \text{pre-}Listmax(M)\\
&\qquad\wedge m \text{ in } M \wedge (\forall z{:}\mathbb{Z})(z \text{ in } M \Rightarrow z \le m)\\
&\qquad\wedge \text{pre-}Listmax(N)\\
&\qquad\wedge n \text{ in } N \wedge (\forall z{:}\mathbb{Z})(z \text{ in } N \Rightarrow z \le n)\\
&\qquad\wedge m \le x \wedge n \le x \wedge (n = x \ \ \vee\ m = x)\ )
\end{aligned}
$$

◆

$$
\begin{aligned}
&(\exists M,N{:}\mathbb{Z}^*,m,n{:}\mathbb{Z})\\
&\qquad(\ \ \text{pre-}split(L) \wedge \text{post-}split(L,\langle M,N\rangle)\\
&\qquad\wedge \text{pre-}Listmax(M) \wedge \text{post-}Listmax(M,m)\\
&\qquad\wedge \text{pre-}Listmax(N) \wedge \text{post-}Listmax(N,n)\\
&\qquad\wedge m \le x \wedge n \le x \wedge (n = x \ \ \vee\ m = x)\ )
\end{aligned}
$$

To round off the construction, we could now define the *function*

$$combine(\langle m,n\rangle) \triangleq x \qquad \text{where: } m \le x \wedge n \le x \wedge (n = x \ \vee\ m = x)$$

from which we see that $combine(\langle m,n\rangle) \Leftrightarrow x = \text{if } m > n \text{ then } m \text{ else } n \text{ fi}$
$\Leftrightarrow max(\langle m,n\rangle)$

as before.

Then we can insert implementations:

$$\blacktriangleright \quad (\exists M,N:\mathbb{Z}^*,m,n:\mathbb{Z})\ (\ \langle M,N\rangle = split(L) \wedge m = Listmax(M) \wedge n = Listmax(N) \wedge x = max(m,n)\ )$$

❑

After lots of expression juggling[18] and a final jump to implementations, we have something that is recognisable as a scheme which corresponds to four sub-calculations linked by the appropriate variables. But what happens if we get stuck and fail to achieve this form of expression? The first three parts follow mechanically providing that we have constructed *split* as described. The problems usually arise because we cannot remove unwanted data dependencies, either because we simply lack the skill to remove them (even though they can legitimately be removed) or because they are necessary links and cannot be taken out.

In either case, no incorrect (or correct but unjustified) answer is found. This might be frustrating, but it is safe.

Now for an example for which this tactic can be shown to fail.

Example 3.9
Consider the specification

$all\_same:\mathbb{Z}^* \to \mathbb{B}$
pre-$all\_same(L) \triangleq \text{True}$
post-$all\_same(L,b) \triangleq b \Leftrightarrow (\exists x:\mathbb{Z})(\forall y:\mathbb{Z})(y \text{ in } L \Rightarrow x = y)$

Just in case you are perplexed by the pre-condition, we take the stand that *all_same*(L) would be False only if it contained two integers which were different.

From the specification, the elements of L are *all_same* if there is some value x such that every element in L is equal to x. If $L = \langle\rangle$, then any integer will do for x; and if $L = \langle y\rangle$, then y would suffice for x.

[18] Again, the reader needs to check that he fully understands the 'what and why' of each step.

Now if $\#L \geq 2$, then we can replace L by $M^\frown N$, where $\#M \geq 1$ and $\#N \geq 1$ as before; but since the results obtained from *all_same*(M) and *all_same*(N) are Boolean, no record of the contents of M and N is preserved, and hence structural splitting fails.

As in traditional testing, a single 'wrong' instance can demonstrate failure. But *sometimes* we get the 'right' answer, so

$$\begin{aligned} all\_same(\langle 2,2\rangle) &\Leftrightarrow combine(all\_same(\langle 2\rangle), all\_same(\langle 2\rangle)) \\ &\Leftrightarrow combine(\text{True},\text{True}) \end{aligned}$$

and

$$\begin{aligned} all\_same(\langle 2,3\rangle) &\Leftrightarrow combine(all\_same(\langle 2\rangle), all\_same(\langle 3\rangle)) \\ &\Leftrightarrow combine(\text{True},\text{True}) \end{aligned}$$

Clearly, we need

$$all\_same(\langle 2,2\rangle) \Leftrightarrow \text{True}$$

and

$$all\_same(\langle 2,3\rangle) \Leftrightarrow \text{False}$$

But for a given input, the result returned by a function is unique; therefore there can be no *combine* function.

❑

Hence, the basic technique fails when applied to certain specifications. It may be possible to slightly modify the strategy so that it succeeds, but we shall not consider that here (but see Chapter 10).

Although, because of our desire to defer the introduction of non-deterministic splits, we have included extra — but unused — clauses within their specification,

$$\begin{aligned} \text{post-}split(L,\langle M,N\rangle) \Rightarrow \#M \geq 1 \wedge \#N \geq 1 \wedge L = M^\frown N \\ [\wedge\ ((\#M = \#N) \vee (\#M = \#N + 1))] \end{aligned}$$

it is clear that the bracketed '[..]' clause could have been omitted and introduced much later. Indeed, since the concatenation operator "$^\frown$" is associative, splitting the list L *anywhere*[19] would give the same answer to a terminating computation; this property is exploited in Chapter 5 when we consider a class of 'more abstract' operations[20]. Notice also, that even though we can take a sufficiently large data item, *split* it, process its constituent parts and build an 'answer' from the results of these processes, there is no guarantee that the answer will fit the original problem.

[19] That is consistent with the rest of the specification.

[20] (Which you might regard as either non-recursive or super-recursive depending on your point of view.)

As in the *Listmax* example, if the tactic is to succeed, we need certain implications (the strictly Boolean '$\Rightarrow$') to hold in order that superfluous clauses can be legally 'thrown away' so as to leave us with the required four components depicted in Figure 3.4. This is the most complicated part of this construction but, again, associative operators can often 'come to the rescue' and make the processing easier.

3.2.3.2 Predicated Splitting

As an extreme contrast to Structural Splitting, a Predicated Split completely ignores the structure of the input, so the input can generally be regarded as a bag, being the most unstructured way of holding finite amounts of data whilst allowing duplicates. Using a predicated split simply involves dividing up the input bag into two or more sub-bags, the contents of which satisfy extra properties (dictated by predicates) which we can choose.

Sensible examples will come later, but to indicate the general scenario, suppose we have a specification of a function as follows:

$$
\begin{aligned}
& f{:}X^* \to Y \\
& \text{pre-}f\ldots \\
& \text{post-}f(L, y) \triangleq (\forall x{:}X)(x \text{ in } L \Rightarrow \textit{property}(x, y))
\end{aligned}
$$

Now choose some discriminating condition, $cond{:}X \to \mathbb{B}$, and proceed thus:

$$
\begin{aligned}
\text{post-}f(L, y) \;&\Leftrightarrow\; (\forall x{:}X)(x \text{ in } L \Rightarrow \textit{property}(x, y)) \\
&\Leftrightarrow\; (\forall x{:}X)((x \text{ in } L \wedge \text{True}) \Rightarrow \textit{property}(x, y)) \\
&\Leftrightarrow\; (\forall x{:}X)((x \text{ in } L \wedge (\textit{cond}(x) \vee \neg\, \textit{cond}(x)) \Rightarrow \textit{property}(x, y)) \\
&\Leftrightarrow\; \quad (\forall x{:}X)((x \text{ in } L \wedge \textit{cond}(x)) \Rightarrow \textit{property}(x, y)) \\
&\qquad \wedge\; (\forall x{:}X)((x \text{ in } L \wedge \neg\, \textit{cond}(x)) \Rightarrow \textit{property}(x, y))
\end{aligned}
$$

These two parts can then be developed separately, the intention being that knowing that $cond(x)$ ($\Leftrightarrow$ True) or $\neg\, cond(x)$ makes the evaluation of $property(x, y)$ simpler.

To be a little more concrete, suppose that X was $\mathbb{Z}$ and *disc* was *is_even*, so that we could process *even* and *odd* values as two cases.

3.2.3.3 Mixed Strategies

Whereas the first two variants of the problem decomposition tactic either deal exclusively with the structure of the input or completely ignore the overall structure in favour of the constituent items *within* the input, here we split the input into parts. However, the way in which this is done depends (to some extent) on the actual values within the input.

For example, we might want to split a list at a point where a particular relationship exists between consecutive values, say $x = y$, $x \neq y$, or $x > y$, where the input is regarded as $N^\frown M$ and N ◆ $\langle \ldots ,x\rangle$, and M ◆ $\langle y, \ldots\rangle$.

Example 3.10 Perhaps the most immediate example of this situation concerns lists of numbers (say, integers) in which we are interested in sequences of non-decreasing values. When we do not have this situation, then the list can be written as $N^\frown M$, where $N,M{:}\mathbb{Z}^*$ and N ◆ $\langle \ldots , x\rangle$, and M ◆ $\langle y , \ldots\rangle$ and $x > y$.

❑

3.2.3.4 Domain Partitioning

This is another kind of problem decomposition. It is not concerned with breaking up single input values but with dividing up the *set* of valid inputs (which constitutes the domain of the function being implemented).

Typically this tactic uses a 'property' of the input, seen as a single entity, to introduce different 'cases' — enough cases to cover *all* eventualities. A common situation is to use it to separate simple cases from more complex ones. This may well be seen as 'putting it all together'.

Generically we might have

if *input_is_small*
then *solve_problem_directly*
else *decompose_input_further*
fi

Here the notion of size is related to a suitable measure which, of course, is problem-dependent. Familiar examples are

$L = \langle\,\rangle$
$\#L = 1$
$A = \emptyset$
in_order L   where: $L{:}\mathbb{Z}^*$

This tactic is an almost inevitable part of any derivation. Indeed, it is used every time recursion is involved to identify the exit/termination condition. It is certainly no big deal and is mentioned here only for the sake of completeness and to emphasise that choosing to recurse further or to process in some other (direct?) way *is* a design decision, albeit one which might be taken almost subconsciously.

Example 3.11 Following on from the previous example, we can identify the existence of N, M, x, y with the list not being 'in_order'.

❑

3.2.4 The Use of Analogy

The tactics given earlier all suppose that we are trying to solve a problem (construct a program) *'ab initio'* — from scratch. Often, this will not be the case. There will be some similarity with other programs already known to the software engineer. Here we seek to cut down the work required in a full, step-by-step synthesis by drawing an analogy between the current problem and another for which we know a correct transformation[21].

In general terms, there is little more that can be said about the use of analogies, but by reference to Figure 3.5 we point out the connection between two analogous design steps and a (more abstract) transfinement *rule*. [This is described as being a specification-to-design step, but it can be equally well be applied to a pair of designs, one of which is an operational transfinement of the other.]

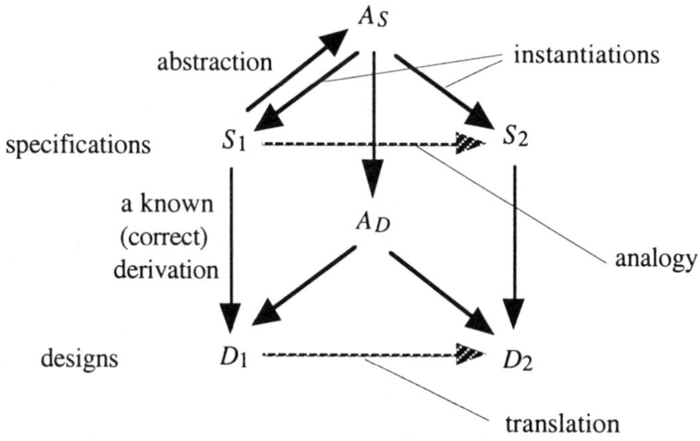

Figure 3.5

The typical situation is as follows. We know of an existing (correct) transfinement step $S_1 \blacktriangleright D_1$ (simply regard D_1 as an implementation of S_1 if this helps to understand the situation) and *notice* some similarity between S_1 and a 'new' specification S_2. It must be similar to the extent that we can perform a translation, changing names, types, operations etc. from S_1 to S_2 and the translation is reversible. Moreover, the properties used in the transfinement $S_1 \blacktriangleright D_1$ are also present in S_2. One way to check this requirement is to abstract from S_1 to A_S, a specification of a more general function in which the common elements of S_1 and S_2 are included directly and the different components are replaced by generalisations

[21] This tactic is applicable not only to transformations but also to refinements (as will be discussed in Chapter 6). We shall therefore use the transfinement notation '▶'. The symbol '▶' can be replaced throughout by '◀▶'.

which have the properties essential for the application of the $S_1 \blacktriangleright D_1$ step. Then, applying the same transfinement step to A_S yields (by definition) A_D, a design for A_S. Then $A_S \blacktriangleright A_D$ is a rule which, with suitable substitutions will give us back the transfinement $S_1 \blacktriangleright D_1$; it will also give us $S_2 \blacktriangleright D_2$ by using other substitutions.

Analogy is a very vague notion, but, as you will see from the example below, it is not new. It is precisely by recognising analogous situations that useful rules are identified and formalised to an appropriate level of parameterisation.

If a given transfinement can only be employed occasionally, then the extraction of the associated rule is perhaps not worth serious consideration. If, however, the same kind of situation arises very often, then it *is* worthwhile deriving a suitably abstract rule. The rule can then be applied directly without reference to earlier instances of its use. Indeed it makes good sense for software engineers to build their own library of these rules.

Example 3.12 For the 'known' transfinement[22] we linking the recursive program scheme R_1 to the iterative (looping) scheme L_1, where[23]:

$R_1 \triangleq$ $S{:}\mathbb{Z} \leftarrow sum\_of(L{:}\mathbb{Z}^*)$
where: $sum\_of(L) \triangleq$ if $L = \langle\rangle$ then 0
else first_of(L) + sum_of(rest_of(L)) fi

$L_1 \triangleq$ begin var $N{:}\mathbb{Z}^*$, $res{:}\mathbb{Z}$;
$N \leftarrow L$;
$res \leftarrow 0$;
while $N \neq \langle\rangle$
do $res \leftarrow res$ + first_of(N);
$N \leftarrow$ rest_of(N)
od;
$S \leftarrow res$
end

We are now presented with R_2 defined by

$P{:}\mathbb{Z} \leftarrow product(W{:}\mathbb{Z}^*)$
where: $product(W) \triangleq$ if $W = \langle\rangle$ then 1
else first_of(W) * $product$(rest_of(W)) fi

The 'known' transfinement $R_1 \blacktriangleright L_1$ utilises the associativity of addition and the fact that 0 is an identity element for addition. These properties also hold for

[22] This will be derived in Chapter 4.

[23] Here, R_1 and L_1 correspond to S_1 and D_1 in the general formulation.

multiplication (and the constant value 1) in R_2. So by analogy we can *write down* L_2 by translating L_1 in a way consistent with the differences between R_1 and R_2 to give

```
L2 ≜ begin  var N:ℤ*, res:ℤ;
            N ← W;
            res ← 1;
            while N ≠ ⟨⟩
               do  res ← res * first_of(N);
                   N ← rest_of(N)
               od;
            P ← res
     end
```

The underlying rule that gives rise to these steps, and many others, can be expressed as

$(\forall a,b,c{:}\mathbb{Z})\,(\ a \blacklozenge (b \blacklozenge c) = (a \blacklozenge b) \blacklozenge c\ )$

where $\blacklozenge$ is an infix operator of type $\mathbb{Z} \times \mathbb{Z} \rightarrow \mathbb{Z}$

$(\exists e{:}\mathbb{Z})$

$(\forall a{:}\mathbb{Z})\,(\ a \blacklozenge e = a \ \wedge\ e \blacklozenge a = a\ )$

$(\forall L{:}\mathbb{Z}^*)(f(L) = \text{if } (\ L = \langle\rangle\ ) \text{ then } e \text{ else first_of}(L) \blacklozenge f(\text{rest_of}(L)) \text{ fi }) $

```
S ← f(L) ◀▶ begin  var N:ℤ*, res:ℤ;
                   N ← L;
                   res ← e;
                   while N ≠ ⟨⟩
                      do  res ← res ♦ first_of(N);
                          N ← rest_of(N)
                      od;
                   S ← res
            end
```

Of course, this rule can be further abstracted; there is nothing special about the type $\mathbb{Z}$.

❑

For obvious reasons, 'analogy' is also known as 'abstraction and re-instantiation' [re-use and inheritance of software design].

When developing software, we make use of intrinsic properties of data types (most notably the operations and methods on and between data types) and of functions and predicates that are used in the specification.

Abstraction may be viewed as a kind of parameterisation, but not just the kind of parameter found in sub-programs (procedures or functions) of conventional procedural programming examples.

The notions of abstraction and analogy are difficult to grasp (until they suddenly become 'obvious'), yet examples are very common. To formalise the concept only makes it seem harder. We shall be content to mention it, in passing, when suitable examples occur.

3.3 'Eureka' Processes

Constructing any non-trivial program involves very many small parts. If any part of the construction is not formally justified, then the correctness of the entire program is compromised. But how do we manage all this detail? We have a quandary. Are there any 'work-arounds'?

One approach is to re-use existing program segments. This is essentially what object-oriented programming is all about; we can abstract (as in Section 3.2.4) from existing program (or segment) designs and — in some sense — parameterise related specifications and implementations. These can be collected together to form higher-level classes (of objects and functions that act upon them). Essentially this is a generalisation of our presentation of types, a generalisation which we shall not investigate in this text. The closest we get to the topic is investigating the formal link between existing designs and the designs we require. This is studied in Chapter 6.

Another approach can be described as a 'sideways' derivation instead of working 'down' from a specification — in a purely constructive way — or working 'upwards' by trying to verify that code does actually satisfy a specification. Alternatively, when presented with a problem, whether an entire problem or just a small 'sub-computation', for which we can 'see' a solution/implementation[24], we write down a set of rules which we want to be true of the implementation. We must then show that each rule is consistent with the specification, that for any input/data value exactly one rule is applicable, and that there is an appropriate notion of reduction. From these rules, we can routinely construct a converging recursive implementation.

This technique, which we will not define formally, can typically be used within the split or combine phases of a divide-and-conquer design, or for an entire higher level calculation. We illustrate the technique by a sequence of examples.

[24] There may also be cases where a function is defined or specified (inductively) by such a set of rules, e.g. the factorial function defined by $(n=0) \quad fact(n) \Leftrightarrow 1$
$(n>1) \quad fact(n) \Leftrightarrow n * fact(n\text{-}1)$

We are really trying to justify using guesswork, but in a way that does not compromise our formal derivation procedure. The computational procedures that we use will be realised as recursive functions. One step in the procedure corresponds to a single function evaluation.

To do this, and this may well also utilise one of the strategies[25] introduced in Section 3.2, we must relate our guess to the specification[26]. We do this by considering different 'cases'; sufficient to cover *all* eventualities (and, to avoid the possibility of introducing ambiguity[27], these cases should be disjoint and hence only one rule is applicable in any given situation). Moreover, application of a non-terminal rule (i.e., one which requires further application of the same process) must employ an appropriate 'reduction' between the current and 'next' parameter values so as to guarantee convergence of the recursion.

We start our sequence of examples by revisiting some of the calculations discussed in the Introduction, Chapter 0. But, because these examples use *operators*, we insert here a description of how the idea works on a *function*. Also, since it is timely, we relate these 'simple[28]' recursive *functions* to parameterless recursive *procedures*.

To clarify and emphasize the link between the rules (the conditions for which are disjoint and allow for all valid situations) and an implementation design, consider the following scenario for the definition of $f: X \rightarrow Y$:

$(p(x))$ $\quad f(x) \blacktriangleleft\!\!\blacktriangleright g(x)$ $\quad$ (a)

$(q(x))$ $\quad f(x) \blacktriangleleft\!\!\blacktriangleright f(\,h(x)\,)$ $\quad$ (b)

$(r(x))$ $\quad f(x) \blacktriangleleft\!\!\blacktriangleright m(\,f(\,k(x)\,)\,)$ $\quad$ (c)[29]

Following on from the properties of the guarding conditions for these rules, for a given input value only one condition will hold at each stage of the computation. Hence, a definite sequence of rule applications is determined; in this case this will be an ordered progression of (b) and (c) rules followed by a single application of (a).

[25] Principally, problem reduction.

[26] In the initial examples this is traditional calculation. More general situations will be considered later.

[27] Allowing the introduction of ambiguity may not cause problems. Indeed, it may be useful to have another degree of non-determinism, but this would require construction of a proof that *all* possible derived calculations were correct. This is something that we do not wish to consider here.

[28] By 'simple' we mean that in their evaluation we do not need to 'remember' values after they have been used once. And functions which produce duplicate or 'partial' copies of the input (and hence may circumvent this restriction) are disallowed within these rules. The net effect is to produce functions which can be evaluated sequentially.

[29] More complex configurations are possible but our narrative applies only to 'simple' cases where the right-hand side expression involves a single occurrence of *f*.

The rules could be combined into a single composite rule or, with what amounts almost only to a change in punctuation, the implementation

$$f \triangleq (\lambda x{:}X)\ (\text{ if } p(x) \text{ then } g(x)$$
$$\text{else\_if } q(x) \text{ then } f(\ h(x)\ )$$
$$\text{else } m(\ f(\ k(x)\ )\ ) \text{ fi }\ )$$

— the correctness of which follows immediately.

Notice also that since we use call-by-value with functions, simple recursive embeddings of functions (such as those used here) can be replaced by recursive schemes using a parameterless *procedure*. To do this, we make the passing of parameters and results explicit. First identify the types of the functions used in the implementation scheme above.

$f{:}\ X \rightarrow Y$
$g{:}\ X \rightarrow Y$
$h{:}\ X \rightarrow X$
$k{:}\ X \rightarrow X$
$m{:}Y \rightarrow Y$

Then we replace $y \leftarrow f(x)$

by $s \leftarrow x$; proc-f; $y \leftarrow t$ with $s{:}X$ and $t{:}Y$ declared as locals.

The construction of the procedure proc-f, which embodies f, follows in a straightforward fashion as

$$\text{proc-}f \triangleq \text{ if } p(s) \text{ then } t \leftarrow g(s)$$
$$\text{else\_if } q(s) \text{ then } s \leftarrow h(s);\ \text{proc-}f$$
$$\text{else } s \leftarrow k(s);\ \text{proc-}f;\ t \leftarrow m(t)$$
$$\text{fi}$$

In each case (p, $\neg p \wedge q$, $\neg p \wedge \neg q$) the input value s yields the output value t.

Apart from a single instance of s and t there is no need to generate new local versions on each recursive call (as would be the case with f, even though it has no local data, new space is required to hold the input parameter on every recursive invocation). This may be very important in some situations, and these procedures can be usefully employed when 'changes to data' are required. We shall say more about this when we meet specific applications.

Now for the promised examples.

Example 3.13 This example concerns the 'div' operation/function[30].

Recall the specification, which we can now write more formally,

$\mathbb{Z}$ div $\mathbb{Z} \rightarrow \mathbb{Z}$ (the type, and indication of the infix syntax)
pre-div($\langle n,d \rangle$) $\triangleq d \neq 0$
post-div($\langle n,d \rangle$, q) $\triangleq (\exists r{:}\mathbb{Z})(\, n = q*d + r \wedge 0 \leq r < d\,)$

i.e., n div d represents $n \div d$ (integer division)

$n \div d = q$ (and r is the remainder),

So, for example $11 \div 4 = 2$

since $11 = 2*4 + 3$

Notice that $\mathbb{Z}$ is actually a structured type and hence we could use structural decomposition:

$$7 = \underbrace{1 + 1 + 1 + 1}_{4} + \underbrace{1 + 1 + 1}_{3}$$

But you might regard this as rather 'over the top'. So let's just think of numbers in the usual way; and we will simplify matters even more and restrict the type to

$$\mathbb{P} \text{ div } \mathbb{N} \rightarrow \mathbb{P}$$

(although what follows could be easily adapted to cope with negative values as well).

Now for the intuitive guess. It may be an informed guess, but it is a guess nevertheless.

We take three cases, $n<d$, $n=d$ and $n>d$. Clearly, these are distinct and cover all eventualities for possible, legal, values of n and d.

If $n<d$ then we suggest that $q = 0$ and $r = n$,
if $n=d$ then $q=1$ and $r=0$

[30] In an attempt to help distinguish items within expressions, we shall arbitrarily adopt the convention of using italic text for user-defined function names and plain text for (infix) operators.

and otherwise[31], when $n > d$, let $n = s + t$ (with $s \geq 0$ and $t \geq 0$), so that

$$n \text{ div } d \;=\; s \text{ div } d \;+ t \text{ div } d$$

and

$$(s+t) \text{ div } d \;=\; s \text{ div } d \;+ t \text{ div } d$$

Before we can use these equalities as transformation rules, we must check that they are correct wrt the specification[32].

If $n<d$, and $q=0$ (and $r=n$), then

$$\begin{aligned} q{*}d + r &= 0{*}d + n \\ &= 0 + n \\ &= n \end{aligned}$$

and

$$0 \leq r < d \Leftrightarrow 0 \leq n < d$$

This is as required so

$(n<d)$ $\quad n \text{ div } d$ ◀▶ 0 $\qquad\qquad$ is a valid rule.

Similarly, if $n=d$, $q=1$ and $r=0$

then $\quad q{*}d + r \;=\; 1{*}n + 0$
$\qquad\qquad\qquad\;\; = n$

and

$$0 \leq r < d \Leftrightarrow 0 \leq 0 < d$$

so

$(n=d)$ $\quad n \text{ div } d$ ◀▶ 1 $\qquad\qquad$ is valid.

But what about the '$n>d$' case?
Notice that

$$(5 + 4) \text{ div } 4 \;=\; 2$$

and

$$5 \text{ div } 4 \;+\; 4 \text{ div } 4 \;=\; 1 + 1 \;=\; 2$$

which is correct.

But

$$6 \text{ div } 4 \;+\; 3 \text{ div } 4 \;=\; 1 + 0 \;=\; 1$$

and

$$6 + 3 \;=\; 5 + 4$$

---

[31] This is wrong. We must find this out and devise a correct replacement.

[27] The specification involves equalities ('=') and hence we shall use '=' in the calculations. Alternatively, we could have used '◀▶' and deduced that if a ◀▶ b, then $a = b$ (◀▶ True).

So the answers may be different when we decompose n in different ways; it is not *always* true that

$$(s+t) \text{ div } d \;=\; s \text{ div } d \;+\; t \text{ div } d$$

But if we had not seen a counter-example, we might have believed[33] that the relationship was (*always*) valid and, erroneously, that

$$((s+t) > d) \qquad (s+t) \text{ div } d \;\leftrightarrow\; s \text{ div } d + t \text{ div } d$$

was a valid rule.

So, what rule can we use? Can we show why this, over simplistic, version is wrong? This might help us find a fix.

Let's work it out.

Assume that

$$(s+t) \text{ div } d = q \qquad \text{(and remainder is } r\text{),}$$

$$s \text{ div } d = q_1 \qquad \text{(and remainder is } r_1\text{)}$$

and

$$t \text{ div } d = q_2 \qquad \text{(and remainder is } r_2\text{)}$$

i.e.,

$$s+t = q*d + r \qquad \text{and} \quad 0 \le r < d$$

$$s = q_1*d + r_1 \qquad \text{and} \quad 0 \le r_1 < d$$

$$t = q_2*d + r_2 \qquad \text{and} \quad 0 \le r_2 < d$$

So,

$$\begin{aligned} q*d + r &= q_1*d + r_1 \;+\; q_2*d + r_2 \\ &= (q_1 + q_2)*d \;+\; (r_1 + r_2) \end{aligned}$$

Therefore

$$(s+t) \text{ div } d \;=\; s \text{ div } d \;+\; t \text{ div } d$$

providing that

$$0 \le r_1 + r_2 < d$$

But

$$0 \le r_1 < d \text{ and } 0 \le r_2 < d$$

so

$$0 \le r_1 + r_2 < 2*d \qquad (\text{not} < d)$$

Our rule would work if we could ensure that

$$0 \le r_1 + r_2 < d$$

One way to achieve this would be to make $r_2 = 0$, i.e., to insist that t was an *exact* multiple of d.

---

[33] This is exactly the trap into which traditional testing falls. "We haven't found a case where it goes wrong, therefore we deduce that it always works." Clearly, this is logical nonsense.

To choose $q_2 = 0$ would get us nowhere since it would make $t = 0$ and hence

$$\begin{aligned} s \text{ div } d &\Leftrightarrow (s+t) \text{ div } d \\ &\Leftrightarrow s \text{ div } d + t \text{ div } d \\ &\Leftrightarrow s \text{ div } d + 0 \text{ div } d \\ &\Leftrightarrow s \text{ div } d + 0 \\ &\Leftrightarrow s \text{ div } d \end{aligned}$$

which makes no progress.

Reducing $(s+t)$ to s with $t \neq 0$ guarantees convergence. So taking $q_2 = 1$[34], then:

$$\begin{aligned} t &= 1 * d + 0 \\ &= d \end{aligned}$$

and

$$\begin{aligned} n &= s + t \\ &= s + d \end{aligned}$$

so

$$s = n - d$$

Putting this together, since $n > d$ and $s = n - d$, it follows that $s > 0$.

If $n \text{ div } d = q$ (with remainder r), what is $s \text{ div } d$? i.e., $(n-d) \text{ div } d$

$$\begin{aligned} n - d &= (q*d + r) - d \\ &= (q-1)*d + r \qquad \text{and } 0 \leq r < d \end{aligned}$$

Thus

$$\begin{aligned} (n-d) \text{ div } d &= q - 1 \\ &= n \text{ div } d - 1 \end{aligned}$$

Our final rule is therefore

$$(n>d) \qquad n \text{ div } d \Leftrightarrow (n-d) \text{ div } d + 1$$

Collecting these together[35],

$$\begin{aligned} &(n<d) \qquad n \text{ div } d \Leftrightarrow 0 \\ &(n=d) \qquad n \text{ div } d \Leftrightarrow 1 \\ &(n>d) \qquad n \text{ div } d \Leftrightarrow (n-d) \text{ div } d + 1 \end{aligned}$$

[The '<' and '=' rules are terminal and hence must satisfy the specification directly. The '>' rule is an intermediate rule, and its validity follows from the fact that if the 'smaller' evaluation of div is correct then so is the 'larger' one as given in the rule. This is another hidden form of induction.]

---

34 Other choices are possible, and we shall use some of these to great effect later.

35 As always, under appropriate conditions, the rules may be applied in either direction. Notice, however, that in order to fully evaluate *n* div *d*, the rules must ultimately be applied left to right.

Factoring these together, we can immediately define a correct (and converging) recursive implementation:

n div d ≜ if $n<d$ then 0
    else if $n=d$ then 1
        else $(n-d)$ div d + 1
        fi
    fi

Notice that, as with all recursive implementations, we need to ensure convergence. Here the positive integer parameter n is reduced to $n-d$ until we reach an exit case (not necessarily zero; although a more complicated measure that does reach zero can be invented, there is no necessity for this).

[Notice that we only allow call by value, and using recursive functions requires new 'local' space to be allocated on each call. However, this space is only used to pass data into an expression evaluation and, in simple cases like this where there is only a single embedded function call, once that call is invoked, the space is never accessed again. We can avoid this by first setting up the initial parameter values and then using a parameterless recursive *procedure* that accesses and changes what it sees as 'global' variables. Applying this to our current example yields

$\langle x, y, q\rangle \leftarrow \langle n, d, 0\rangle$; div_proc

where:

div-proc ≜ if $x < y$ then $q \leftarrow 0$ (or skip)
    else if $x = y$ then $q \leftarrow 1$
        else $x \leftarrow x - y$; div_proc; $q \leftarrow q + 1$
        fi
    fi]

❑

Example 3.14 We can use the same approach to compute the remainder of performing division. We can even calculate both at the same time.

We denote the remainder of dividing n by d by n mod d (which is spoken as "n modulo d").

So 11 mod 4 = 3 (11 = 2*4 + 3)
(more generally $n = q*d + r$ with $0 \leq r < d$)

The functions / operations div and mod are related by the identity

$$n = (n \text{ div } d) * d + n \text{ mod } d$$

Once we have div, we can easily calculate mod by using this relationship. Alternatively, as in the previous example, we can derive a set of rules for its *direct* computation.

Such a set of rules is

$$
\begin{array}{ll}
(n<d) & n \text{ mod } d \blacklozenge n \\
(n=d) & n \text{ mod } d \blacklozenge 0 \\
(n>d) & n \text{ mod } d \blacklozenge (n-d) \text{ mod } d
\end{array}
$$

Justification of these rules is straightforward and left as an exercise to the reader.

[You may regard this as tedious and unnecessary detail, but such working is all part of establishing familiarity with the problem under consideration. Detail of this nature is required *somewhere* within the computation; we are merely bringing it out into the open and making it explicit early in the programming process.]

Now we can combine the sets of rules to give

$$
\begin{array}{ll}
(n<d) & \langle n \text{ div } d , n \text{ mod } d\rangle \blacklozenge \langle 0, n\rangle \\
(n=d) & \langle n \text{ div } d , n \text{ mod } d\rangle \blacklozenge \langle 1, 0\rangle \\
(n>d) & \langle n \text{ div } d , n \text{ mod } d\rangle \blacklozenge \langle (n-d) \text{ div } d + 1, (n-d) \text{ mod } d \rangle
\end{array}
$$

or, inventing a new function (a new function name),

$$
\begin{array}{l}
div\_mod: \mathbb{P} \times \mathbb{N} \rightarrow \mathbb{P} \times \mathbb{P} \\
div\_mod: \langle n , d\rangle \mapsto \langle n \text{ div } d , n \text{ mod } d\rangle
\end{array}
$$

where

$$
\begin{array}{ll}
(n<d) & div\_mod(n,d) \blacklozenge \langle 0, n\rangle \\
(n=d) & div\_mod(n,d) \blacklozenge \langle 1, 0\rangle \\
(n>d) & div\_mod(n,d) \blacklozenge div\_mod((n-d),d) + \langle 1, 0\rangle
\end{array}
$$

In the $(n>d)$ rule the '+' is componentwise addition over $\mathbb{P} \times \mathbb{P}$, defined by

$$\langle x, y\rangle + \langle a, b\rangle \triangleq \langle x + a, y + b\rangle$$

Again, a recursive implementation follows immediately from these rules:

```
div_mod(n,d) ≜ if n<d then ⟨0, n⟩
               else  if n=d then ⟨1, 0⟩
                     else div_mod((n−d),d) + ⟨1, 0⟩
                     fi
               fi
```

Extraction of the individual components can be achieved simultaneously by the assignment

$$\langle q, r\rangle \leftarrow div\_mod(n,d)$$

[Again we can use a recursive procedure so, as a further illustration

$$\langle x, y, q, r\rangle \leftarrow \langle n, d, 0, 0\rangle;\ \text{div\_mod\_proc}$$

where:

```
div_mod_proc ≜  if x < y then ⟨q, r⟩ ← ⟨0, x⟩
                else if x = y  then ⟨q, r⟩ ← ⟨1, 0⟩
                     else x ← x − y; div_mod_proc; q ← q + 1
                     fi
                fi                                   ]
```

❑

Example 3.15 We now return to the 'greatest common divisor' example discussed in Chapter 0. Recall the following

$gcd(m, n{:}\mathbb{N}) \triangleq$ the largest $i{:}\mathbb{N}$ such that $i|m$ and $i|n$.

"the function *gcd* ... ($\triangleq$) is defined to be ... ($i|m$) i divides m and ... ."

With the reasoning given in Chapter 0, we have rules

$(m{=}n)$ $\quad gcd(m, n) \blacktriangleleft\!\blacktriangleright n$ $\qquad$ which is OK

and

$gcd(m, n) \blacktriangleleft\!\blacktriangleright gcd(n, m)$ $\qquad$ which makes no progress.

However, we also had

$$gcd(m{+}n, n) \blacktriangleleft\!\blacktriangleright gcd(m, n)$$

We can use this, together with the 'swapping' rule to give

$(m{<}n)$ $\quad gcd(m, n) \blacktriangleleft\!\blacktriangleright gcd(m, n{-}m)$

and

$(m{>}n)$ $\quad gcd(m, n) \blacktriangleleft\!\blacktriangleright gcd(m{-}n, n)$

These are not cyclic *per se*, but may step up or down, including up, down, up ..., etc., and hence not converge. However, we can pick out the rules we want so as to yield a finite non-repeating sequence of intermediate expressions which will evaluate the *gcd* function; we simply use the rules that strictly reduce the sum of the parameters as necessary until an exit case is reached.

Hence, we have

$$
\begin{aligned}
gcd(m, n) \triangleq \text{ if } m=n \text{ then } n \\
\text{else if } m>n \text{ then } gcd(m-n, n) \\
\text{else } gcd(m, n-m) \\
\text{fi} \\
\text{fi}
\end{aligned}
$$

which is a slight modification of the earlier version.

❑

In recent examples, we have seen some (perfectly valid) 'funny functions' and unusual ways of combining functions, their parameters, and their results. Likewise, some of the manipulations in the following example may seem rather strange, but they are perfectly valid; stick with us. It all falls out nicely in the end.

Example 3.16 This example uses the Fibonacci function, $fib:\mathbb{P} \rightarrow \mathbb{N}$. This is a function which you may have seen before. It is defined inductively by the following set of rules and is particularly interesting to us because on the face of things the direct method of calculation — by program — is rather involved and possibly inefficient.

$$
\begin{aligned}
& fib(0) \;◆\; 1 \\
& fib(1) \;◆\; 1 \\
(n>1) \quad & fib(n) \;◆\; fib(n-1) + fib(n-2)
\end{aligned}
$$

Using these rules, we can calculate

$fib(0), fib(1), fib(2), fib(3), fib(4)$, etc.

to obtain the (we hope) familiar Fibonacci sequence

1, 1, 2, 3, 5, 8, 13, 21, etc.

The rules also give rise to a correct, convergent, implementation:

$$
\begin{aligned}
fib(n) \triangleq \text{ if } n=0 \lor n=1 \text{ then } 1 \\
\text{else } fib(n-1) + fib(n-2) \\
\text{fi}
\end{aligned}
$$

but using this, as it stands, involves much repeated calculation/evaluation.

Clearly, it is possible, by hand-crafting the program code, to save intermediate values and avoid much of the duplicated effort, but can we achieve the same effect *systematically* by using some 'eureka' function(s) which then fits with our simple (even simplistic) way of handling recursion? Yes!

One possibility is as follows. Notice that in the non-trivial cases we use two earlier (smaller!) evaluations of *fib*; so let's invent a new function, *fib*2, which gives both of these values from a single parameter. We define

$$fib2 : \mathbb{N} \rightarrow \mathbb{N} \times \mathbb{N} \qquad \text{(with pre-}fib2(n) \triangleq n>1)$$

by

$$fib2 : n \mapsto \langle fib(n-1),\ fib(n-2)\rangle$$

It would then follow that $fib(n) = x + y$ where $\langle x, y\rangle = fib2(n)$

How does this help?

Well, for $n>2$ we have

$$\begin{aligned} fib2(n) &\Leftrightarrow \langle fib(n-1),\ fib(n-2)\rangle \\ &\Leftrightarrow \langle fib(n-2) + fib(n-3),\ fib(n-2)\rangle \\ &\Leftrightarrow \langle x + y, x\rangle \\ &\qquad \text{where: } \langle x, y\rangle = fib2(n-1) \end{aligned}$$

So, with a little 'housekeeping' and addition, we can compute $fib2(n)$ from $fib2(n-1)$. This looks peculiar because the function *fib*2 takes a single argument and delivers a result having 2 components, rather than 1. We can make the situation look more 'normal' not by removing it but by including an extra function, of type: $\mathbb{P} \times \mathbb{P} \rightarrow \mathbb{P} \times \mathbb{P}$. We call it *update*. Perhaps predictably, we define *update* by

$$\text{update}(\langle x, y\rangle) \triangleq \langle x + y, x\rangle \quad \text{over } \mathbb{P} \times \mathbb{P}.$$

Then

$$\begin{aligned} &(n=2) \qquad fib2(n) \Leftrightarrow \langle 1, 1\rangle \\ &(n>2) \qquad fib2(n) \Leftrightarrow update(fib2(n-1)) \end{aligned}$$

See how this works for $n = 5$:

$$\begin{aligned} fib(5) &\Leftrightarrow x + y \\ \text{where } \langle x, y\rangle &\Leftrightarrow fib2(5) \\ &\Leftrightarrow update(fib2(4)) \\ &\Leftrightarrow update(update(fib2(3))) \\ &\Leftrightarrow update(update(update(fib2(2)))) \\ &\Leftrightarrow update(update(update(\langle 1, 1\rangle))) \\ &\Leftrightarrow update(update(\langle 2, 1\rangle)) \\ &\Leftrightarrow update(\langle 3, 2\rangle) \\ &\Leftrightarrow \langle 5, 3\rangle \end{aligned}$$

and

$$x + y = 8$$

Hence we can construct a recursive implementation scheme based on our new rules for *fib*2:

$$fib2(n) \triangleq \text{if } n = 2 \text{ then } \langle 1, 1 \rangle \text{ else } update(fib2(n-1)) \text{ fi};$$

$$update(\langle x, y \rangle) \triangleq \langle x + y, x \rangle$$

and

$$fib(n) \triangleq \text{if } n < 2 \text{ then } 1 \text{ else } x + y \text{ fi} \quad \text{where: } \langle x, y \rangle = fib2(n-1)$$

Before leaving this example, notice that:

$$(n > 2) \qquad fib2(n) \;\blacklozenge\; update^{n-2}(fib2(2))$$

so, for suitably large values of n, we could take bigger jumps and use, say

$$up2 \qquad (\text{i.e., } up^2 \triangleq update \circ update$$
$$\blacklozenge\; (\lambda \langle x, y \rangle)(\langle 2*x + y,\; x + y \rangle))$$

Thus, for instance

$$up2(\langle 1, 1 \rangle) \;\blacklozenge\; \langle 2*1 + 1, 1 + 1 \rangle$$
$$\blacklozenge\; \langle 3, 2 \rangle$$

and we miss out the "$\langle 2, 1 \rangle$" term in the earlier evaluation sequence.

We shall return to such possibilities in Chapter 4.

❑

Finally, we have an examplethat *is* mathematical but not *arithmetical*.

Example 3.17 The *merge* function. Recall its specification.

$$merge: \mathbb{Z}^* \times \mathbb{Z}^* \rightarrow \mathbb{Z}^*$$
$$\text{pre-}merge(\langle N_1, N_2 \rangle) \triangleq ascending(N_1) \wedge ascending(N_2)$$
$$\text{post-}merge(\langle N_1, N_2 \rangle, N) \triangleq ascending(N) \wedge$$
$$\text{bag\_of}(N) = \text{bag\_of}(N_1) \uplus \text{bag\_of}(N_2)$$

We change the names of the variables just to keep the expressions slightly simpler.

Consider $merge(P,Q)$.

It would seem *reasonable* that

$$merge(P,\langle\rangle) = P$$
$$merge(\langle\rangle,Q) = Q$$

and[36]

$$merge(P,\langle x\rangle) = insert(x,P)$$
$$merge(\langle x\rangle,Q) = insert(x,Q)$$

where

$$insert: \mathbb{Z}\times\mathbb{Z}^* \rightarrow \mathbb{Z}^*$$
$$\text{pre-}insert(\langle x,L\rangle) \triangleq ascending(L)$$
$$\text{post-}insert(\langle x,L\rangle,N) \triangleq ascending(N) \wedge$$
$$bag\_of(N) = bag\_of(L) \uplus \{\!\{x\}\!\}$$

and[37], if P and Q are split at productive[38] and *corresponding* places,

$$merge(P_1{}^\frown P_2, Q_1{}^\frown Q_2) = merge(P_1,Q_1){}^\frown merge(P_2,Q_2).$$

As always, if we wish to make use of these five identities as *rules*, they must be checked. To illustrate we take $merge(P,\langle\rangle) \blacklozenge P$.

Given the assumption that $\text{pre-}merge(\langle P,\langle\rangle\rangle)$ ($\triangleq ascending(P)$) is True, it follows that

$$\text{post-}merge(\langle P,\langle\rangle\rangle,P) \blacklozenge ascending(P) \wedge$$
$$bag\_of(P) = bag\_of(P) \uplus bag\_of(\langle\rangle)$$
$$\blacklozenge \text{ True} \wedge bag\_of(P) = bag\_of(P) \uplus \varnothing$$
$$\blacklozenge bag\_of(P) = bag\_of(P)$$
$$\blacklozenge \text{ True}$$

Similarly, for $merge(P,\langle x\rangle) \blacklozenge insert(x,P)$ to be valid we have to show that

$$\text{post-}merge(\langle P,\langle x\rangle\rangle,Q) = \text{post-}insert(\langle x,P\rangle,Q) \text{ is True.}$$

This is straightforward:

$$\text{post-}merge(\langle P,\langle x\rangle\rangle,Q) = \text{post-}insert(\langle x,P\rangle,Q)$$

$\blacklozenge$ $(ascending(Q) \wedge bag\_of(Q) = bag\_of(P) \uplus bag\_of(\langle x\rangle))$
      $= (ascending(Q) \wedge bag\_of(Q) = bag\_of(P) \uplus \{\!\{x\}\!\})$

$\blacklozenge$ $(ascending(Q) \wedge bag\_of(Q) = bag\_of(P) \uplus \{\!\{x\}\!\})$
      $= (ascending(Q) \wedge bag\_of(Q) = bag\_of(P) \uplus \{\!\{x\}\!\})$

$\blacklozenge$ True

---

[36] Actually the singleton forms are not needed in what follows, but investigation of such cases is a reasonable step in the evolution of designs.

[37] Likewise, we shall not use this form directly, but it is a reasonable situation to consider when investigating the current problem.

[38] So that the break point does not fall outside of the original lists and hence the new sub-problems really are smaller. We call this 'double-split' and use it within the next set of exercises.

So the first four identities hold (those concerning the cases when at least one of the lists is empty or a singleton). Instead of tackling the last one directly, we will use the same idea but avoid a general split and consider (in the cases when P and Q are not empty) the suitability of first_of(P) and first_of(Q) as values to split Q and P, respectively.

Suppose that $P = \langle x \rangle \frown A$ and $Q = \langle y \rangle \frown B$. If $x \leq y$, then the first element of $merge(P,Q)$ ought to be x and we should have $merge(P,Q) = \langle x \rangle \frown merge(A,Q)$, and if $x > y$, then surely $merge(P,Q) = \langle y \rangle \frown merge(P,B)$.

We check the first of these,

$(x \leq y)$

post-$merge(\langle P,Q \rangle, \langle x \rangle \frown merge(A,Q))$

◆

post-$merge(\langle \langle x \rangle \frown A, \langle y \rangle \frown B \rangle, \langle x \rangle \frown merge(A,Q))$

◆ using the definition of post-merge and Q ◆ $\langle y \rangle \frown B$

$ascending(\langle x \rangle \frown merge(A,\langle y \rangle \frown B)) \wedge$
$\text{bag\_of}(\langle x \rangle \frown merge(A,\langle y \rangle \frown B)) = \text{bag\_of}(\langle x \rangle \frown A) \uplus \text{bag\_of}(\langle y \rangle \frown B)$

◆

$ascending(\langle x \rangle \frown \text{merge}(A,\langle y \rangle \frown B)) \wedge$
$\text{bag\_of}(\langle x \rangle) \uplus \text{bag\_of}(A) \uplus \text{bag\_of}(\langle y \rangle \frown B)$
$= \text{bag\_of}(\langle x \rangle) \uplus \text{bag\_of}(A) \uplus \text{bag\_of}(\langle y \rangle \frown B)$

◆

$ascending(\langle x \rangle \frown merge(A,\langle y \rangle \frown B)) \wedge \text{True}$

◆

$ascending(\langle x \rangle \frown merge(A,\langle y \rangle \frown B))$

If $A = \langle \rangle$, then $merge(A,\langle y \rangle \frown B) = \langle y \rangle \frown B$ and $x \leq y$ so $\langle x \rangle \frown \langle y \rangle \frown B$ is *ascending*:
i.e.,

◆ $ascending(\langle x \rangle \frown \langle y \rangle \frown B)$ ◆ True

Otherwise, $x \leq$ first_of(A) since $\langle x \rangle \frown A$ is *ascending* and hence

first_of(merge($A,\langle y \rangle \frown B$)) is either y (and $x \leq y$) or first_of(A)

and

$merge(A,\langle y \rangle \frown B)$ is *ascending*, therefore so is $\langle x \rangle \frown merge(A,\langle y \rangle \frown B)$,

and again

◆ $ascending(\langle x \rangle \frown merge(A,\langle y \rangle \frown B))$

◆ True

These identities can therefore give rise to rules and, putting all this together

```
merge(P,Q) ◆ if P = ⟨⟩ V Q = ⟨⟩                          -- see[39]
             then P⌢Q
             else if first_of(P) ≤ first_of(Q)
                  then ⟨first_of(P)⟩⌢merge(rest_of(P),Q)
                  else ⟨first_of(Q)⟩⌢merge(P,rest_of(Q))
                  fi
             fi
```

This is a recursive functional design (which converges using $\#X * \#Y$ as a measure on *merge*(X,Y)) that can subsequently be transformed into an iterative procedural scheme such as

```
merge(P,Q) ≙ (var A,B,C:ℤ*;
                ⟨A,B⟩ ← ⟨P,Q⟩;
                C ← ⟨⟩;
                while A ≠ ⟨⟩ Λ B ≠ ⟨⟩                      --see[40]
                do  if first_of(A) ≤ first_of(B)
                    then  C ← C⌢⟨first_of(A)⟩; A ← rest_of(A)
                    else  C ← C⌢⟨first_of(B)⟩; B ← rest_of(B)
                    fi
                od;
                [result ←] C⌢A⌢B  )
```

Details of this transformation are not included here, but corresponding details will be given for similar transformations in Chapter 4.

❑

Exercises

3.2 Construct a specification for '*double-split*', splitting two integer lists at *corresponding* places.

Summary So we now have a collection of general tactics for the creation of a program design linked to a formal specification, either by forward synthesis, by retrospective checking, or by 'sideways' inspiration in the form of a 'eureka' step. Along the way we have included quite a few examples. More examples and exercises will be included in later chapters, but first we consider the problem of removing recursion and the possibility of replacing it by more familiar constructs.

---

39 This is the *sequential or* operator. If a is True, then we ignore b in the evaluation of $a \vee b$.

40 The sequential *and*. By a variant of de Morgan's Law, $\neg(a \vee b)$ ◆ $\neg a \wedge \neg b$.

Chapter 4
Recursion Removal

Using the techniques of the previous chapter, we have a 'functional' program. The essence of a functional program is the expressing of a calculation in the form of a function call, $f(x)$ say, which delivers 'the answer' when given an input value x. The program can thus be represented by a function definition/declaration followed by a function call:

$$f(x) \triangleq \ldots ;$$
$$f(x)$$

In a more relational form, in which y explicitly represents the answer/result/output we may write

$$y = f(x) \qquad (\Leftrightarrow \text{True}).$$

Within this form of program, we have assumed that x has been given its value before commencing the real computation (we shall continue to assume this for some considerable time), that the central computation corresponds to the evaluation of $f(x)$, and that the value of x is never changed. Thus we can regard it as a constant. The value y has also been treated as a constant, which is unknown and which satisfies the various properties given in the specification. We now move on to a representation of the calculation in which delivery of the 'answer' to y is made explicit.

Conversion into a procedural program then gives us the command

$$y \leftarrow f(x)$$

after which, of course, $y = f(x) \Leftrightarrow \text{True}$.

This is the first instance of a 'variable' having a value assigned to it — of a 'variable' changing value. Here the 'variable' y is given a value *once*, and so far this is the *only* assignment in the program. We now introduce other assignments, which will be derived by transformations and are used to control the program execution (the evaluation of the function).

To run functional programs[1], the execution system needs to be able to evaluate recursive functions with complex types of input and output. Certain kinds of recursion can be systematically replaced by iterative constructs (such as "while" and "repeat"), and then the function evaluation is achieved effectively by (a sequence of) state changes resulting from the execution of a sequence of commands.

Put more generally, if $x{:}X$ and $y{:}Y$ are the names associated with the input and output, then the command

$$y \leftarrow f(x)$$

acts on the pair of values $\langle x,y \rangle$ of type $X \times Y$ and results in changing the value of y. In an even more general situation, a command is of type $S \rightarrow S$, where S can be thought of as a composite data type consisting of all the "variables" used in (this part of) the program. Of course, it may not be reasonable to change x (the "input"), but we shall return to that issue when we discuss input/output (I/O) and communication in Chapter 12.

Procedural programs perform calculations by causing (internal) state changes. Assuming that all proper I/O is dealt with at the outer-most block of the program, all other actions can be thought of as acting on some state S. (However, S itself never changes. It always has the same components, the same names, but the values associated with its components usually *do* change, so we need to devise special conventions to distinguish 'old' and 'new' values of the same variable. Other specification notations, such as Z and VDM, need these from the outset. We shall defer consideration of *specified* changes until the final chapter.)

We systematically generate the principal assignment statements so as to indicate the explicit placing of appropriate results in certain named locations[2]. Other assignment statements are used to store intermediate calculations and are often introduced within recursion removal rules. They may be optimised by the application of other transformation rules, if this is needed. But this is not our immediate concern.

---

[1] Note that *our* functional programs make very little use of the high-level operations (on functions) that occur in other 'proper' functional languages. Here they are merely used as an intermediate design tool.

[2] The concept of (constant) locations, the contents of which may be changed, is one of the, few, notions which are central to software engineering. The concept is not a difficult one but is often misunderstood. On the other hand, the concept of a variable, the value of which actually changes, is very rare in most mathematics but is often confused with 'unknown' constants, which are commonplace.

So, we have a single assignment statement and (in general) a recursive subroutine that computes *f*. The recursion can now be replaced by iteration, but this is not always easy and may not always be desirable. Here we focus on two related transformations which cover many common situations.

They give rise to programs involving *while* loops. Consequently, we need to know how such loops work. To do this formally, we need to consider the semantics — the meanings — of procedural programs; however, so as not to get seriously diverted to looking at programming languages rather than programs, we shall use flowcharts to indicate how program segments are related.

4.1 Tail Recursion

Changing signatures (e.g., moving from $X \to Y$ to $X \times Y \to X \times Y$) often allows procedures — derived from functions — to be transformed into a tail-recursive form and then to a *while* loop. We shall derive the rule for removal of tail recursion from the flowchart semantics of the *while* loop. Then we can use the appropriate rules whenever the recursive call is embedded (in the conditional specification) in certain common ways. These are proper transformation rules and hence are reversible. We shall find it convenient (and much easier) to derive them 'in reverse'. And we shall initially also use a diagrammatic representation[3] rather than a textual one.

Let S be the state (of 'current' variables) and consider the composite command

while B do C od:$S \to S$

with	$C{:}S \to S$	where C is a programming language command
and	$B{:}S \to \mathbb{B}$	where B is a programming language 'test'.

To make annotations easier, we label "while B do C od" by W, as in Figure 4.1.

Now unfold,(i.e., unwrap) the diagram so as not to pass through the original B test for a second time. This means that we have to duplicate the test within the flow diagram in Figure 4.2.

[3] The manipulations that we shall perform with these diagrams (either conventional flowcharts or data-flow diagrams) can be explained algebraically by using expressions to describe sets of execution paths through the charts, but we shall stick with diagrammatic reasoning, which is probably easier in the first instance. The formal justification here is similar to the way that equivalence of grammars is defined by the equality of the languages they generate. Two flowcharts are (strongly) equivalent if they generate equivalent sets of operation/test traces.

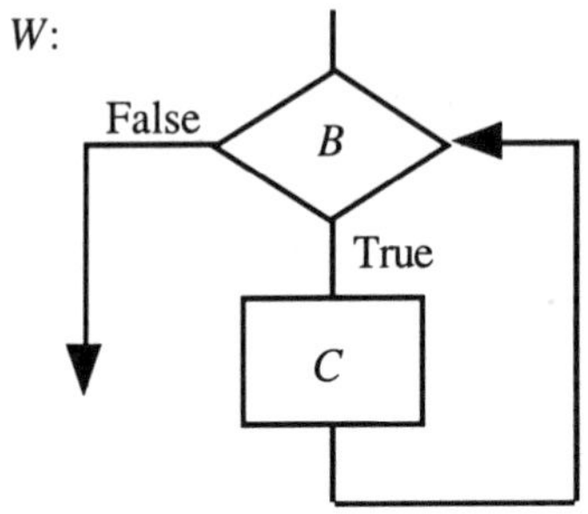

Figure 4.1

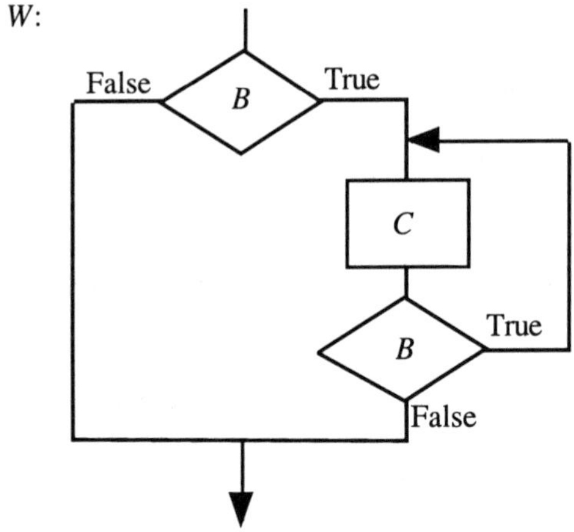

Figure 4.2

Both of these flowcharts give rise to the set of trace sequences starting:

$\neg B$, $B, C, \neg B$, $B, C, B, C, \neg B$, etc.;

i.e.,

B is False (do nothing and end),

or

B is True, do *C* (in the current state), then *B* is False (end)

or

B is True, do *C* (in the current state), then *B* is True,
do *C* (in the now current state), then *B* is False (end)

or

...

Now unfold again to give Figure 4.3.

W:

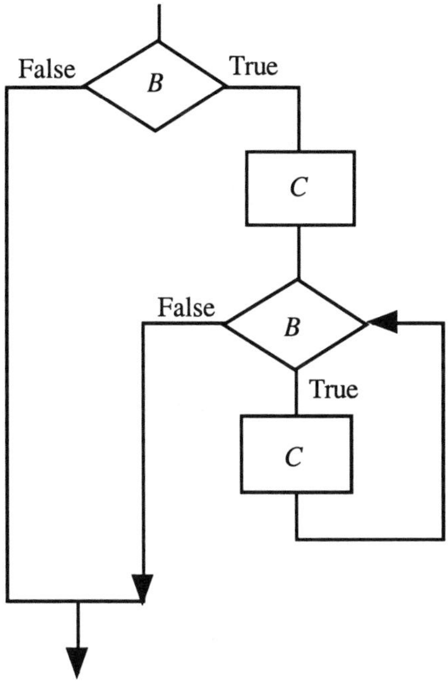

Figure 4.3

Clearly, this could go on forever, but notice now that we can fold (exactly the same idea as with functions but now in flowcharts; see Figure 4.4).

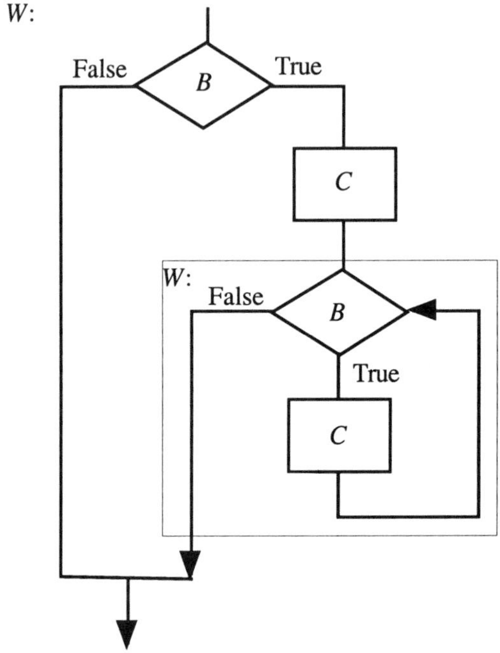

Figure 4.4

So W reappears. This is a recursive characterisation of a *while* loop! It is called ***tail recursive*** because the embedded W occurs as the *last* proper[4] element in one of the computational paths through this flowchart for W. Performing a fold operation gives Figure 4.5.

[4] A 'proper' element, a 'proper' command, is one which can (in appropriate circumstances) cause a change in state.

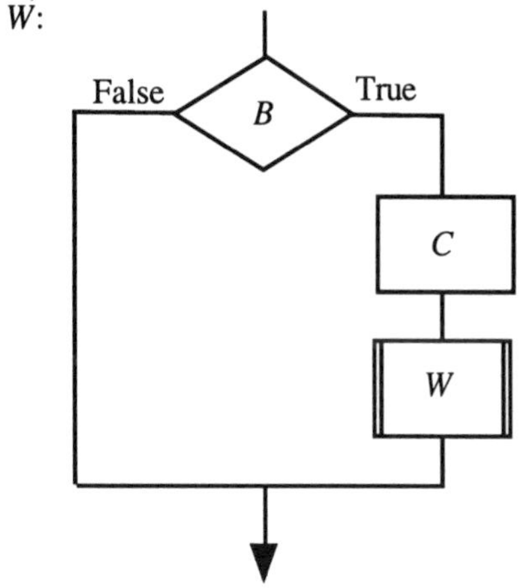

Figure 4.5

Hence, coding the (structured) flowchart and using conditional commands, we get

W ◆ if B then C; W else skip fi

or

W ◆ if B then C; W fi

where 'skip'[5] is the 'do nothing', 'change nothing', command acting on S.

But

$W \triangleq$ while B do C od

so we have the conditional rules

($W \equiv$ while B do C od)[6]

W ◆ if B then C; W fi

($W \equiv$ if B then C; W fi)

W ◆ while B do C od

And it works in an almost identical fashion for the general case where the 'else' branch of the conditional command need not be 'skip'. Take the construct labelled W_1 as in Figure 4.6.

[5] So 'skip' is the identity element wrt the operator ';' in the algebra of flowcharts.

[6] '≡' denotes the so-called strong equivalence of flowcharts. For any given initial state, the corresponding sequences of test outcomes and commands executed through each flowchart are the same, and when defining a new flowchart segment (using $W \triangleq$ ...) we automatically get a rule (W ◆ ...) as expected.

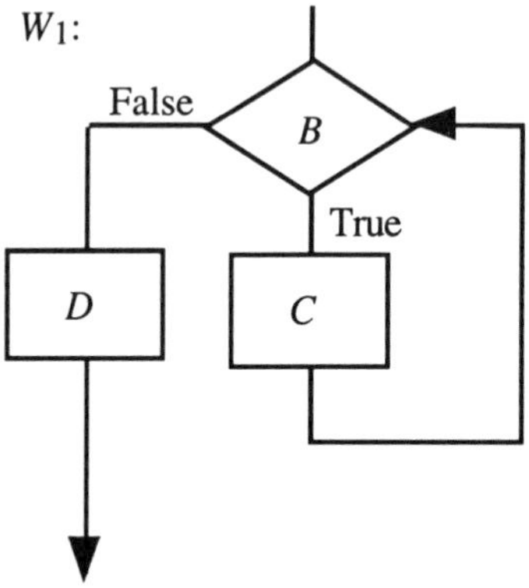

Figure 4.6

Now unfold by introducing another copy of *B* (as in Figure 4.7), but do *not* coalesce the 2 copies of *D*!

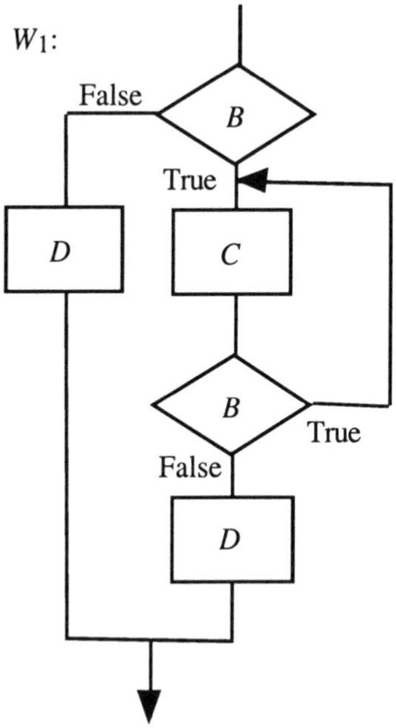

Figure 4.7

Then unfold further and introduce another copy of C, as in Figure 4.8.

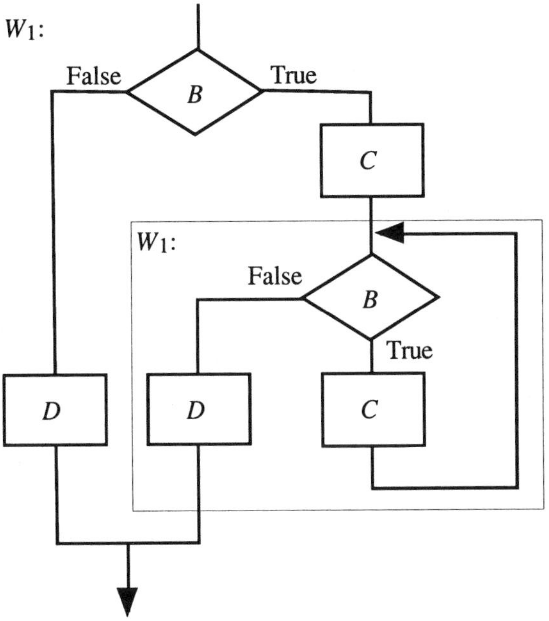

Figure 4.8

And then fold W_1 as in Figure 4.9.

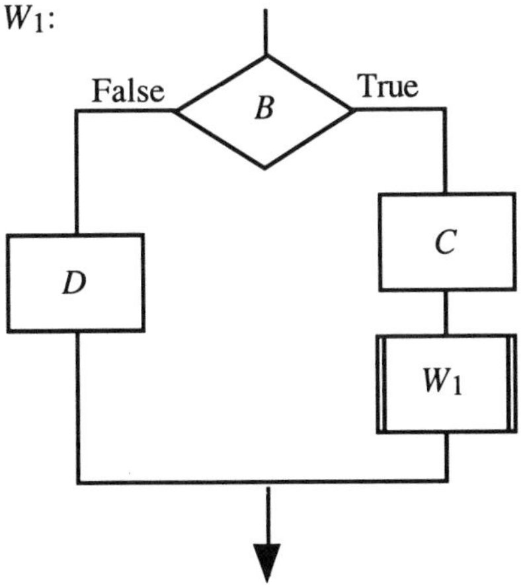

Figure 4.9

So

$$W_1 \blacktriangleleft\!\blacktriangleright \text{ if } B \text{ then } C;\ W_1 \text{ else } D \text{ fi}$$

[Notice that the flowchart *equation*

$$W_1 \equiv \text{if } B \text{ then } C;\ W_1 \text{ else } D \text{ fi}$$

is satisfied by

while B do C od; D

i.e.,

while B do C od; $D \equiv$ if B then C; while B do C od; D else D fi

As already stated, it will be sufficient to reason about these equivalences by reference to flowchart manipulations. These can all be re-expressed using an extended regular algebra. Indeed, we could go further and use denotational semantics, a mathematical framework for defining the meaning of programming languages. However, this takes us well away from our main area of study, and we shall be content to stay with our Program Design Language, PDL, rather than more complex languages.]

So,

if $W_1 \equiv$ if B then C; W_1
else D fi

then we can use the rule

$$W_1 \blacktriangleleft\!\blacktriangleright \text{ while } B \text{ do } C \text{ od};\ D.$$

Exercises

4.1 Take the "repeat C until B" command as defined by the flowchart in Figure 4.10 and, by using unfold/fold manipulations, derive an equivalent form in which the iteration is performed by a "while ... do ... od" construct.

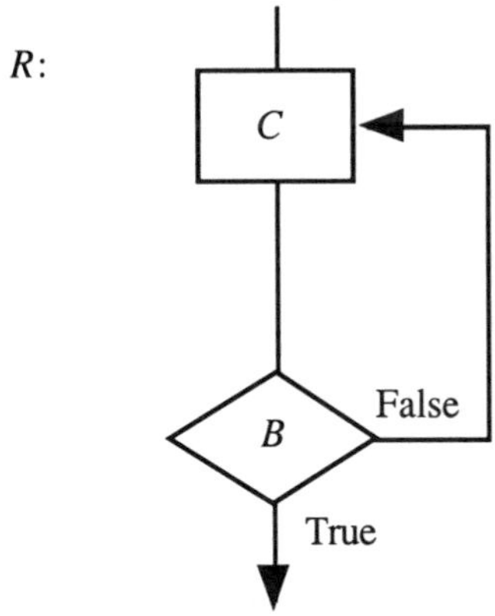

Figure 4.10

4.2 Derive a recursive formulation of the "repeat ... until ..." construct.

❑

Now let's try to manipulate the the *while* construct 'in reverse' and without pictures. Suppose we have derived the legal (and correct) command

$$y \leftarrow f(x)$$

where

$$f \triangleq (\lambda x{:}X)\ (\text{ if } p(x) \text{ then } g(x) \text{ else } f(h(x)) \text{ fi })$$

so

$$f(x) \Leftrightarrow (\lambda x{:}X)\ (\text{ if } p(x) \text{ then } g(x) \text{ else } f(h(x)) \text{ fi })\ (x)$$

and

$$f(x) \Leftrightarrow \text{ if } p(x) \text{ then } g(x) \text{ else } f(h(x)) \text{ fi}$$

Then

$y \leftarrow f(x)$

◆

$y \leftarrow$ (if $p(x)$
then $g(x)$
else $f(h(x))$ fi)

◆ factoring 'if' through '$\leftarrow$'

if $p(x)$ then $y \leftarrow g(x)$
else $y \leftarrow f(h(x))$ fi

We assume that we do not need to preserve x (treat it as a local variable)

◆ W_1 not only corresponds to $y \leftarrow f(x)$ but also includes $x \leftarrow$?
where ? is an unknown value[7]

if $p(x)$ then $y \leftarrow g(x)$
else $x \leftarrow h(x)$;
$y \leftarrow f(x)$ fi

[Ignoring the type information associated with commands, we have the
[substitutions B ◆ $\neg p(x)$
[C ◆ $x \leftarrow h(x)$; *and* $(y \leftarrow y)$
◆ [D ◆ $y \leftarrow g(x)$; *and* $(x \leftarrow x)$
[into the rule (see Figure 4.9)
[
[($W_1 \equiv$ if B then C; W_1 else D fi) W_1 ◆ while B do C od; D
[and this gives:

while $\neg p(x)$ do $x \leftarrow h(x)$ od;
$y \leftarrow g(x)$

and f has gone, it is no longer referenced and its definition/declaration can be removed.

The corresponding scheme that preserves the 'input' value x is derived from the form

$y = f(x)$ ◆ $(\exists v{:}X)(\ y = f(v)$ where: $v = x\ )$

or

$v \leftarrow x$; [v is a new local variable
$y \leftarrow f(v)$

We can then change the new local variable v without 'corrupting' x.

[7] Yes, this *can* be found, but it does not generally correspond to a requirement *within* the specification.

This gives us a rule for the removal of tail recursion, replacing it with a *while* loop. Formally

if $f{:}X \rightarrow Y$
$f(x) \triangleq$ if $p(x)$
then $g(x)$
else $f(h(x))$
fi

where $p{:}X \rightarrow \mathbb{B}$
$g{:}X \rightarrow Y$
$h{:}X \rightarrow X$

and $(\forall x{:}X)(\exists n{:}\mathbb{P})\ (p(h^n(x))$

we can replace $y \leftarrow f(x)$

by:

```
begin  var v:X;
          v ← x;
          while ¬p(v)
             do v ← h(v)
             od;
          y ← g(v)
end
```

Expressed as a parameterised transformation rule[8,9], this is

$(\lambda X{::}\text{Type}, Y{::}\text{Type})$
$(\lambda f{:}X \rightarrow Y)\ (\lambda p{:}X \rightarrow \mathbb{B})\ (\lambda g{:}X \rightarrow Y)\ (\lambda h{:}X \rightarrow X)$
$(\forall x{:}X)(f(x) =$ if $p(x)$ then $g(x)$ else $f(h(x))$ fi) — see[10]
$(\forall x{:}X)(\exists n{:}\mathbb{P})\ (p(h^n(x)))$ — ditto

```
y ← f(x)  ◆  begin  var v:X;
                        v ← x;
                        while ¬p(v)
                              do v ← h(v)
                              od;
                        y ← g(v)
             end
```

[8] Eight similar rules can be found in *Program Construction*, by R G Stone and D J Cooke, CUP, Cambridge (1987), but we shall only consider the two major rules here. The other rule concerns "associative recursion".

[9] Assuming that *f* is total.

[10] These are conditions governing the applicability of this rule. If the function *f* is not total (i.e., if it's pre-condition is not identically True) then the body of this condition should be modified to

(pre-$f(x) \Rrightarrow (f(x) =$ if $p(x)$ then $g(x)$ else $f(h(x))$ fi))

and then the resultant procedural code would only be safe when the initial value of x was known to satisfy pre-*f*, so the condition (pre-$f(x)$) must also be satisfied. This is one of many variants which can be used, but to consider them here would only be a distraction.

[This looks very complicated, but that is only because of its high degree of parameterisation, which enables the basic rule to be applied in many situations. The central rule is

$$
\begin{array}{lll}
y \leftarrow f(x) & \blacktriangleleft\!\blacktriangleright & \text{begin var } v{:}X; \\
 & & \quad v \leftarrow x; \\
 & & \quad \text{while } \neg p(v) \\
 & & \qquad \text{do } v \leftarrow h(v) \\
 & & \qquad \text{od;} \\
 & & \quad y \leftarrow g(v) \\
 & & \text{end}
\end{array}
$$

but this can be applied to any function f (of type $X \rightarrow Y$) that is defined using a template of the form

$$(\lambda x)(\text{ if } p(x) \text{ then } g(x) \text{ else } f(h(x)) \text{ fi })$$

into which functions p, g and h (of types $X \rightarrow \mathbb{B}$, $X \rightarrow Y$, and $X \rightarrow X$, respectively) may be substituted and all this for some types X and Y.

So this is very general indeed.

The condition "$(\exists n{:}\mathbb{P})(p(h^n(x)))$" guarantees convergence / termination of the loop. It must be related to a measure m as follows:

$$
\begin{array}{lll}
 & m{:}X \rightarrow \mathbb{P} & \\
 & m(x) = 0 & \text{iff } p(x) \quad (\text{i.e., } p(x) \Leftrightarrow \text{True}) \\
\text{and} & m(h(x)) < m(x) & \text{otherwise}
\end{array}
$$

(Recall that the function h is sometimes called a ***reduction*** function for reasons that are now obvious.)

In fact, we could define m by

$$m(x) \triangleq 0 \text{ iff } p(x)$$

and

$$m(h(x)) \triangleq m(x) - 1$$

Then, for input value x, $m(x) = n$, where n is the depth of recursion (equal to the number of iterations of the resulting loop) required for the evaluation of f. We do not need to know the value of n, but merely that there is such a value.

Before going on, we give an example. This is necessarily simple and somewhat artificial. Tail recursion, as we shall see below, often occurs in a function that is not the one which we originally set out to compute. Anyway, here goes.

Example 4.1

Suppose that we have the specification

$$
\begin{aligned}
&all\_2 : \mathbb{Z}^* \rightarrow \mathbb{B} \\
&\text{pre-}all\_2(L) \triangleq \text{True} \\
&\text{post-}all\_2(L,b) \triangleq b \Leftrightarrow (\forall n : \mathbb{N}) \\
&\qquad\qquad (n \leq \#L \Rrightarrow^{11} (\forall x : \mathbb{Z})(x \text{ in } L \text{ at } n \Rightarrow (x = 2)))
\end{aligned}
$$

where

$$x \text{ in } L \text{ at } n \triangleq (\exists N, M : \mathbb{Z}^*)(L = N \frown \langle x \rangle \frown M \wedge \#N = n-1)$$

So $all\_2(L)$ gives the value True only if all the elements of L are equal to the number 2. Now suppose that, somehow, we have found the solution

```
b ⇔ if L = ⟨⟩ then True
    else if first_of(L) ≠ 2 then False
                   else all_2(rest_of(L)
         fi
    fi
```

◆ re-arrange into the appropriate form.

```
b ⇔ if L = ⟨⟩ ∨ first_of(L) ≠ 2
    then  if L = ⟨⟩ then True else False fi
    else all_2(rest_of(L))
    fi
```

So we have

```
all_2(L) ◆ if L = ⟨⟩ ∨ first_of(L) ≠ 2
           then if L = ⟨⟩ then True else False fi
           else all_2(rest_of(L))
           fi
```

and then we can replace $b \leftarrow all\_2(L)$

by

```
begin var v:ℤ*;
      v ← L;
      while ¬(v = ⟨⟩ ∨ first_of(v) ≠ 2)
        do v ← rest_of(v) od;
      b ← (if v = ⟨⟩ then True else False fi)
end
```

[11] Notice that using the Boolean implication might invite us to find the *n*th item of a list which does not have *n* elements.

A suitable measure is the length of L and

$$\#(\langle\rangle) = 0$$

otherwise

$$\#(\text{rest\_of}(L)) < \#L$$

❑

[Notice that the other component of the exit condition can only cause the recursion to exit prematurely — a consequence of the conditional logic operators. This and examples with a similar structure can in fact be tackled more directly using the notation of Chapter 5.]

4.2 Associative Recursion

Here the occurrence of the recursive call is not the last operation in the 'recursive arm' of the conditional but is followed by a further function (or operation) which is *associative* — hence the name. The associativity allows 'the answer' to be computed 'backwards' i.e., in the opposite direction from that given by the recursion.

Suppose we have the situation

$$\begin{aligned}
&f\colon X \to Y \\
&f(x) \triangleq \text{if } p(x) \\
&\qquad\quad \text{then } g(x) \\
&\qquad\quad \text{else } h(f(k(x)), \ell(x)) \\
&\qquad\quad \text{fi}
\end{aligned}$$

where

$$\begin{aligned}
&p\colon X \to \mathbb{B} \\
&g\colon X \to Y \\
&k\colon X \to X \\
&\ell\colon X \to Y \\
&h\colon Y \times Y \to Y
\end{aligned}$$

h is associative (i.e., $(\forall a,b,c{:}Y)\ (\ h(a, h(b, c)) = h(h(a, b), c)\ )$

and

$$(\forall x{:}X)\ (\exists n{:}\mathbb{P})\ (p(k^n(x))).$$

Here we derive a version of the program that embodies a tail recursion and hence we can extract a *while* version. This is a common approach to handling certain kinds of (non-tail-recursive) recursion.

First look at the (conditional) data-flow segments for some values of x. We need to go down two levels so as to include two occurrences of the function h. With only a single instance, we cannot make use of its associativity. The first diagram (Figure 4.11) is trivial and relates to the situation when $p(x)$ is True.

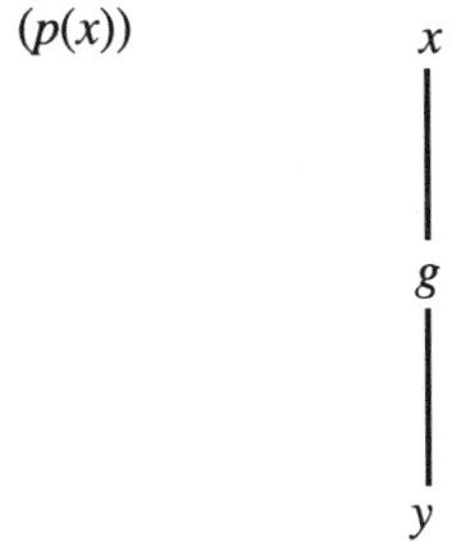

Figure 4.11

When $p(x)$ is False, we have the — downwards — data flow as in Figure 4.12. Here, we introduce two new functions on either side of the dotted line, with as much non-recursive processing as possible within the *init* (initialise?) function. Notice the types of $init{:}X \rightarrow X \times Y$ and $final{:}X \times Y \rightarrow Y$, more complex than the type of f.

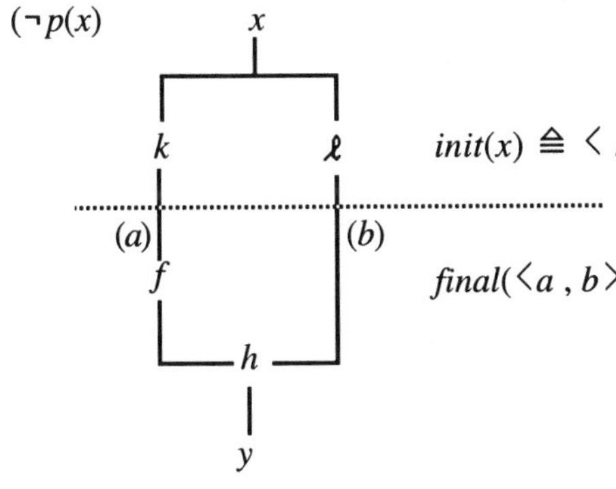

$$init(x) \triangleq \langle\, k(x)\ ,\ \ell(x) \,\rangle$$

$$final(\langle a\ ,\ b \rangle) \triangleq h(\,f(a)\ ,\ b)$$

Figure 4.12

and again,

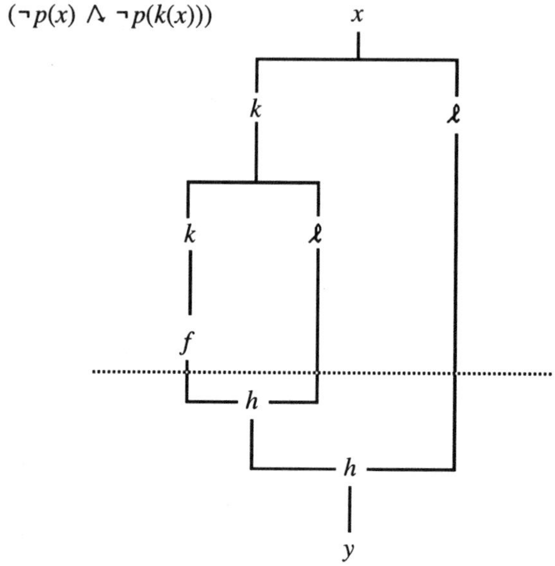

Figure 4.13

With the associativity of h (see Figure 4.14), this can be restructured to give Figure 4.15. Now we can re-introduce *init* and *final*, and introduce the new function *change* to cope with the intermediate calculation.

Writing down the function *change* (of type $X \times Y \rightarrow X \times Y$) from the diagram (in Figure 4.15) we have:

$$change(\langle a,b \rangle) \triangleq \langle\, k(a)\, ,\, h(\ell(a),\, b)\, \rangle$$

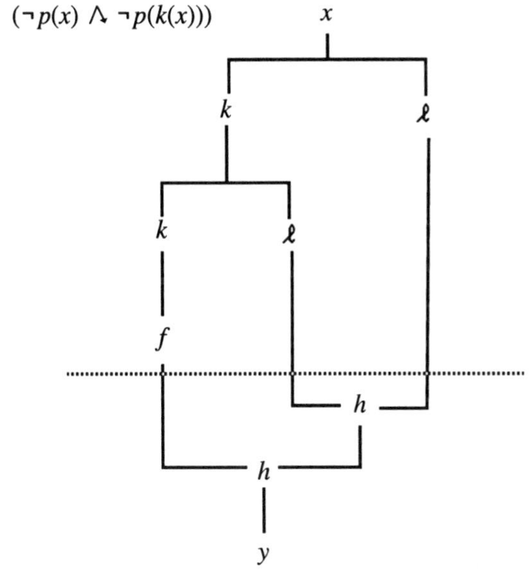

Figure 4.14

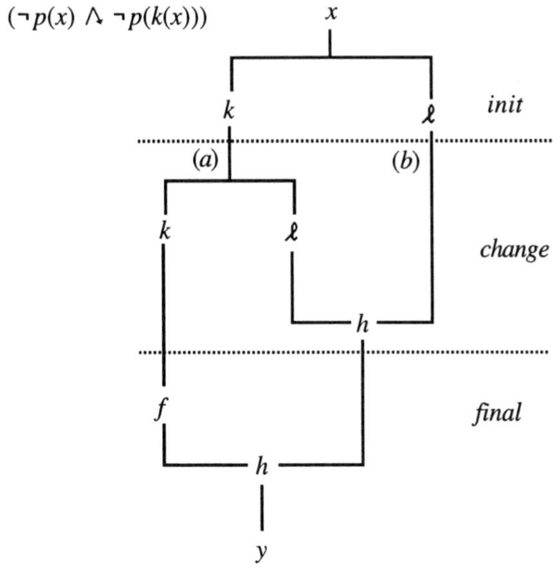

Figure 4.15

We can now use this new function, together with *init* and *final*, and the associativity of h, to extract a tail-recursive function (but it is not f), which can then be transformed into a *while* loop as before.

Recall $f{:}X \to Y$, $init{:}X \to X \times Y$ and $final{:}X \times Y \to Y$, so unfolding and folding as appropriate, we get

$f(x)$ ◆ if $p(x)$
then $g(x)$
else $final(init(x))$
fi

where: $final(\langle a,b \rangle)$

◆

$h(f(a), b)$

◆

$h($ if $p(a)$
then $g(a)$
else $final(init(a))$
fi) , $b)$

◆

$h($ if $p(a)$
then $g(a)$
else $h(f(k(a)), \ell(a))$
fi , $b)$

◆

if $p(a)$
then $h(g(a), b)$
else $h(h(f(k(a)), \ell(a)), b)$
fi

◆ h is associative

if $p(a)$
then $h(g(a), b)$
else $h(f(k(a)), h(\ell(a), b))$
fi

◆

if $p(a)$
then $h(g(a), b)$
else $final(k(a), h(\ell(a), b))$
fi

◆

if $p(a)$
then $h(g(a), b)$
else $final(change(\langle a, b \rangle))$
fi

So

```
final(⟨a,b⟩) ◀▶ if p(a)
                 then h(g(a), b)
                 else final(change(⟨a, b⟩))
                 fi
```

This *is* tail recursion. It converges (terminates, exits) since

$(\neg p(a))$ $\qquad$ $change(\langle a,b \rangle$ ◀▶ $\langle\ k(a), h(\ell(a), b)\ \rangle$

and in a finite number of moves k reduces its parameter value 'a' to a situation where $p(a)$ is True.

The function *final*, and delivery of its result to *y*, can be transformed directly into

```
while ¬p(a)
        do ⟨a, b⟩ ← change(⟨a, b⟩) od;
y ← h(g(a),b)
```

So the full iterative scheme for the calculation of *f* and its delivery is

```
if p(x)
then y ← g(x)
else  begin var a:X,b:Y;
          ⟨a, b⟩ ←  init(x);
          while ¬p(a)
               do ⟨a, b⟩ ← change(⟨a, b⟩) od;
          y ← h(g(a), b)
      end
fi
```

or, without the newly defined functions,

```
if p(x)
then y ← g(x)
else  begin var a:X,b:Y;
          ⟨a, b⟩ ←  ⟨k(x), ℓ(x)⟩;
          while ¬p(a)
               do ⟨a, b⟩ ← ⟨ k(a) , h(ℓ(a), b) ⟩ od;
          y ← h(g(a), b)
      end
fi
```

The (parameterised) rule[12] is therefore

$(\lambda X{::}\text{Type}, Y{::}\text{Type})$
$\quad(\lambda f{:}X\to Y)\ (\lambda p{:}X\to\mathbb{B})\ (\lambda g{:}X\to Y)\ (\lambda k{:}X \to X)\ (\lambda \ell{:}X \to Y)\ (\lambda h{:}Y\times Y \to Y)$

$\quad(\forall x{:}X)\ (f(x) = \text{if } p(x) \text{ then } g(x) \text{ else } h(f(k(x)), \ell(x)) \text{ fi})$
$\quad(\forall a,b,c{:}Y)\ (h(a, h(b, c)) = h(h(a,b), c)$
$\quad(\forall x{:}X)\ (\exists n{:}\mathbb{P})\ (p(k^n(x)))$

```
y ← f(x)  ◆  begin  if p(x)
                    then y ← g(x)
                    else   begin var a:X,b:Y;
                           ⟨a,b⟩ ← ⟨k(x),ℓ(x)⟩;
                           while ¬p(a)
                               do ⟨a,b⟩ ← ⟨ k(a), h(ℓ(a),b) ⟩ od;
                           y ← h(g(a),b)
                           end
                    fi
             end
```

The recursive definition of the factorial function is one which involves associative recursion. Here we use it to show how the recursive version evaluates the product from left to right, whereas the iterative version evaluates from right to left.

```
fact(x) ≜ if x = 0
          then 1
          else mult(fact(x−1),x)
          fi
```

For the recursive evaluation of *fact*(4), we have:

fact(4) ◆ *fact*(3) *4

◆ (*fact*(2) * 3) *4

◆ ((*fact*(1) *2) *3) *4

◆ (((*fact*(0) *1) *2) *3) *4

◆ (((1 * 1) *2) *3) *4

[12] Assuming that *f* is total.

Pattern matching with the names given in the rule, we have

$f \triangleq fact$
$p(x) \triangleq x = 0$ i.e., $p \triangleq \lambda x.(x = 0)$
$g(x) \triangleq 1$
$k(x) \triangleq x-1$
$\ell(x) \triangleq x$
$h(y_1,y_2) \triangleq y_1*y_2$ i.e., $mult(y_1,y_2)$

Now substituting these into the recursion removal rule we get

```
begin if x = 0
      then y ← 1
      else begin var a:ℙ,b:ℙ ;
                 ⟨a, b⟩ ← ⟨x–1, x⟩;
                 while a ≠ 0
                     do ⟨a, b⟩ ← ⟨ a–1 , a*b ⟩ od;
                 y ← 1*b
                 end
      fi
end
```

This 'executes' to give

initial x is 4 (≠ 0, so)

a	b
3	4
2	3*4
1	2 * (3 * 4)
0	1 * (2 * (3 * 4))

and the final value of y is 1 * (1 * (2* (3 * 4)))

Clearly, the two expressions for the final value of y are equivalent, but only because * is associative.

[Note that although this is a valid iterative scheme for the calculation of the factorial function, it is not the only one. We have been 'guided' to this design by the recursive structure of the specification. Starting from a more general representation allows us to synthesise another design, as we shall see in Chapter 5.]

One variation on associative recursion (actually it is a special instance of it) is of particular importance later. It is applicable when the associative function has an identity element, which we shall call e. This then allows us to remove one instance of the test in the iterative scheme and perform other simplifications to give

$(\lambda X{::}\text{Type}, Y{::}\text{Type})$
$\quad(\lambda f{:}X \to Y)\ (\lambda p{:}X \to \mathbb{B})\ (\lambda g{:}X \to Y)\ (\lambda k{:}X \to X)\ (\lambda \ell{:}X \to Y)\ (\lambda h{:}Y \times Y \to Y)$
$\quad(\forall x{:}X)\ (f(x) = \text{if } p(x) \text{ then } g(x) \text{ else } h(f(k(x)), \ell(x)) \text{ fi })$
$\quad(\forall a,b,c{:}Y)\ (h(a, h(b, c)) = h(h(a,b),c))$
$\quad(\exists e{:}Y)(\forall z{:}Y)(h(z,e) = z \wedge h(e,z) = z)$
$\quad(\forall x{:}X)\ (\exists n{:}\mathbb{P})\ (p(k^n(x)))$

```
y ← f(x)  ◆  begin  var a:X,b:Y;
                    ⟨a,b⟩ ← ⟨x,e⟩;
                    while ¬p(a)
                             do ⟨a,b⟩ ← ⟨ k(a), h(ℓ(a),b) ⟩ od;
                    y ← h(g(a),b)
             end
```

Although this text is not intended to concentrate on transformations *per se*, it is instructive to see how the existence of the identity element $e{:}Y$ (wrt h) gives rise to this transformation, which is a simplification of the previous rule.

The derivation is as follows. Starting with the current form, we get the progression

```
begin  if p(x)
       then y ← g(x)
       else  begin var a:X,b:Y;
             ⟨a,b⟩ ← ⟨ k(x), ℓ(x) ⟩;
             while ¬p(a)
                   do ⟨a,b⟩ ← ⟨ k(a) , h(ℓ(a),b) ⟩ od;
             y ← h(g(a),b)
             end
       fi
end
```

◆ $g(x)$ ◆ $h(g(x),e)$ and $\ell(x)$ ◆ $h(\ell(x),e)$

```
begin  if p(x)
       then y ← h(g(x),e)
       else  begin var a:X,b:Y;
             ⟨a,b⟩ ← ⟨ k(x), h(ℓ(x),e) ⟩;
             while ¬p(a)
                  do ⟨a,b⟩ ← ⟨ k(a) , h(ℓ(a),b) ⟩ od;
             y ← h(g(a),b)
             end
       fi
end
```

◆ widen the scope of a and b

```
begin  var a:X,b:Y;
       if p(x)
       then y ← h(g(x),e)
       else
             ⟨a,b⟩ ← ⟨ k(x), h(ℓ(x),e) ⟩;
             while ¬p(a)
                  do ⟨a,b⟩ ← ⟨ k(a) , h(ℓ(a),b) ⟩ od;
             y ← h(g(a),b)
       fi
end
```

◆ promote (advance) assignments to a and b, and use them to achieve common forms of expression assigned to y.

```
begin  var a:X,b:Y;
       ⟨a,b⟩ ← ⟨x,e⟩;
       if p(a)
       then y ← h(g(a),b)
       else
             ⟨a,b⟩ ← ⟨ k(a), h(ℓ(a),b) ⟩;
             while ¬p(a)
                  do ⟨a,b⟩ ← ⟨ k(a), h(ℓ(a),b) ⟩ od;
             y ← h(g(a),b)
       fi
end
```

◆ Now swap the branches of the if-then-else so as to give repeated conditions leading to the body of the while, and factor out the common trailing command from both branches of if-then-else.

```
begin  var a:X,b:Y;
       ⟨a,b⟩ ← ⟨x,e⟩;
       if ¬p(a)
       then
              ⟨a,b⟩ ← ⟨ k(a), h(ℓ(a),b) ⟩;
              while ¬p(a)
                    do ⟨a,b⟩ ← ⟨ k(a),h(ℓ(a),b) ⟩ od
       else skip
       fi;
       y ← h(g(a),b)
end
```

◆ Next combine the sequencing (';') and the while to give

```
begin  var a:X,b:Y;
       ⟨a,b⟩ ← ⟨x,e⟩;
       if ¬p(a)
       then
              repeat ⟨a,b⟩ ← ⟨ k(a),h(ℓ(a), b) ⟩
              until p(a)
       else skip
       fi;
       y ← h(g(a),b)
end
```

◆ Finally combine the if ... then ... else ... fi and the repeat to give

```
begin  var a:X,b:Y;
       ⟨a,b⟩ ← ⟨x,e⟩;
              while ¬p(a)
                    do ⟨a,b⟩ ← ⟨ k(a),h(ℓ(a),b) ⟩ od
       y ← h(g(a),b)
end
```

4.3 Up and Down Iteration

Tail-recursive functions effectively work by 'counting down' until we reach some small value for which the function can be evaluated directly. So, for instance, we might perform some calculation on a list and 'reduce' the current operand value until we reach the empty list or a singleton. Notice that in such cases we could not construct longer lists from smaller ones, and hence certain calculations *have* to be computed in this way.

Others may be computed in the reverse direction, and for some functions we have a choice. In Section 3.3, we admitted the possibility (either via 'eureka' inspiration or by the use of induction) of functions defined by rules of the form

$$(n = 0) \qquad f(n) \;◆\; a$$
$$(n > 0) \qquad f(n) \;◆\; g(f(n-1))$$

where $f{:}\mathbb{P} \to X$ and $g{:}X \to X$.

Clearly, with sufficient 'space', f is computable for any value of $\mathbb{P}$; but it is not tail-recursive, and g is not associative (it is of the wrong type for us even to consider the possibility). But, f can be calculated iteratively. We demonstrate how to do this (and hence present another recursive-to-iterative transformation rule). We do this directly rather than trying to derive some other, related, tail-recursive function.

Our justification is based on the sequence of values

$$a,\ g(a),\ g^2(a),\ g^3(a),\ g^4(a),\ \ldots\ ,\ g^m(a),\ \ldots$$

Then $\quad f(n) = g^n(a)$

(and $f(0) = g^0(a) = a$ using the usual notation).

So, starting with a and applying g to it n times, we get the required result. This immediately gives the design:

$y \leftarrow f(n)$

◆

```
begin var v:X,m:ℙ;
      ⟨v,m⟩ ← ⟨a,0⟩;
      while m < n
            do ⟨v,m⟩ ← ⟨g(v), m + 1⟩ od;
      y ← v
end
```

Either by initialisation or by subsequent iteration, after every assignment to v and m the property $v = g^m(a)$ holds (this is *a* loop invariant), and the value of $n - m$ is reduced by 1. Of course, when $n = m$, then $v = g^n(a)$ (i.e., $f(n)$), which is then assigned to y. These facts are a specific instance of what has to be deduced when we seek to verify loops directly. Here the construction is straightforward and simple; in general this is certainly not the case.

So, we have a mechanism for 'counting up' to the required operand value, n. We shall take this as another 'rule'. Its formal proof involves arguments about state changes, which we are striving to avoid. The reader who is concerned about this apparent flaw in our logic is invited either to regard this simply as another 'given' rule or to delay using it until (much) later.

[To obtain the loop invariant introduced in Section 2.6, we need to add (more properly, to *retain*) a little more information. Recall that upon exit from the loop we must reach a state that, together with the state values on loop entry, satisfies the appropriate post-condition. The link between these two invariants is the Boolean exit condition, and the fact that we are, in this instance, counting *up* using the variable m. We have

$$invar(\langle v, m\rangle) \triangleq v = g^m(a) \wedge m \leq n.$$

Initially

$$\langle v, m\rangle = \langle a, 0\rangle$$

so

$$v = g^0(a) = a \wedge 0 \leq n .$$

On loop exit

$\neg(m < n)$ and, since m was incremented by 1 on each iteration, we know that $m=n$, and therefore

$$y = v = g^n(a) = f(n)$$

Hence

$$\text{post-}f(\langle n,y\rangle) \Leftrightarrow y = f(n) \qquad \text{and the result is correct.}$$

In general, we want to find 'invar' given the post-condition and information about the 'counter'. The technique used here is sometimes referred to as 'replacing a constant (here, n) with a variable (here, m)'. Details are perhaps better considered not in general but with respect to each problem in isolation, following the inspiration that suggested the 'eureka' idea.]

[Also in the above scheme, the quantity v may be regarded as the 'result_so_far' and m as pertaining to the 'data_remaining'. This is a form which, either directly or in some slight variant, will often be seen in the sequel. Elsewhere it is known as 'signature rotation'; we change the signature of the original calculation, $X \rightarrow Y$, into $X \times Y \rightarrow X \times Y$ with, where possible (i.e., when such a rotation can usefully be applied), suitable initialisation of the Y field — from a trivial version of the problem — and consequential extraction of the result from the final value in this field. Typically, and of no mathematical significance, we may use $Y \times X$ as above, which is similar in layout to the high-level form $y \leftarrow f(x)$, so, reading left to right, the result is set to a function of the input.]

Before going on, we give an alternative version of the same calculation which 'counts down'.

Again

$f(n) \triangleq$ if $n = 0$ then a
              else $g(f(n - 1))$ fi

Adopting the notion of a recursive procedure from Section 3.3,

$\langle x, y \rangle \leftarrow \langle n, a \rangle$; proc_f; [result $\leftarrow y$]

where

proc_f $\triangleq$ if $x = 0$ then skip
              else $\langle x, y \rangle \leftarrow \langle x - 1, g(y) \rangle$;
                  proc_f fi

We can then extract the rule

$y \leftarrow f(n)$

◆

begin var x:$\mathbb{P}$;
    $\langle x,y \rangle \leftarrow \langle n,a \rangle$;
    while $x \neq 0$
        do $\langle x,y \rangle \leftarrow \langle x - 1, g(y) \rangle$ od
end

Here x decreases and y 'accumulates', so the invariant is slightly more complicated.

On the mth iteration of the while loop, we have

$0 \leq x \leq n \qquad x + m = n \qquad y = g^m(a)$

Thus, when

$m = 0 \qquad x = n \qquad y = a$

and when

$m = n \qquad x = 0 \qquad y = g^n(a)$

So, we can use $0 \leq x \leq n \;\wedge\; y = g^{(n-x)}(a)$ as the loop invariant.

Now to another example.

Example 4.2 Recall the Fibonacci function $fib:\mathbb{P} \to \mathbb{N}$ discussed in example 3.16. It was defined inductively by the rules

$$\begin{array}{lrl} & fib(0) & \Leftrightarrow\ 1 \\ & fib(1) & \Leftrightarrow\ 1 \\ (n > 1) & fib(n) & \Leftrightarrow\ fib(n-1) + fib(n-2) \end{array}$$

and subsequently (when $n > 1$) implemented using the functions

$$fib(n) \triangleq x + y \quad \text{where} \quad \langle x,y\rangle = fib2(n)$$

where

$$\begin{array}{l} fib2(n) \triangleq \text{if } n = 2 \text{ then } \langle 1,1\rangle \\ \qquad\qquad\qquad\qquad \text{else } update(fib2(n-1)) \\ \qquad\qquad\quad \text{fi} \end{array}$$

with

$$update(\langle x, y\rangle) \triangleq \langle x + y, x\rangle$$

The rules governing *fib*2 are

$$\begin{array}{lll} (n=2) & fib2(n) & \Leftrightarrow\ \langle 1,1\rangle \\ (n>2) & fib2(n) & \Leftrightarrow\ update(fib2(n-1)) \end{array}$$

Hence (the form of rules for) *fib*2 is appropriate for this treatment and we can devise a reasoned implementation counting upwards from 2. In the new implementation, m is the counter and we work with the triple $\langle m, a, b\rangle$ for which $a = fib(m-1) \land b = fib(m-2) \land m \leq n$ is the invariant. Check the extremal values of $m = 2$ and $m = n$.

Directly from the rules, we have

```
begin  var m,a,b,c,d:ℕ;
       ⟨m,a,b⟩ ← ⟨2,1,1⟩;
       while m < n
              do ⟨m,a,b⟩ ← ⟨m + 1,c,d⟩
                                    where: ⟨c,d⟩ = update(⟨a,b⟩)
              od;
       [ result ← ] ⟨a,b⟩
end
```

which simplifies on the removal (unfolding) of *update* to give:

```
begin  var m,a,b:ℕ;
       ⟨m,a,b⟩ ← ⟨2,1,1⟩;
       while m < n
              do ⟨m,a,b⟩ ← ⟨m + 1,a + b,a⟩ od;
       [ result ← ] ⟨a,b⟩
end
```

And repeating the previous evaluation (Example 3.16), we get the progression

$$\langle 2,1,1\rangle$$
$$\langle 3,2,1\rangle$$
$$\langle 4,3,2\rangle$$
$$\langle 5,5,3\rangle$$

The right-most pair $\langle 5,3\rangle$ in the last triple is the value of *fib*2(5), from which we can obtain the answer to the original calculation we sought, *fib*(5) = 5+3 = 8.

We can combine the code for *fib*2 within a routine for *fib* to give the following code:

```
begin  var m,a,b:ℕ;
       if n < 2
       then [ result ← ]  1
       else  ⟨m,a,b⟩ ← ⟨2,1,1⟩;
             while m < n
                   do ⟨m,a,b⟩ ← ⟨m + 1,a + b,a⟩ od;
             [ result ← ]  a + b
       fi
end
```

❑

Now to a more complex (certainly much more complex-looking) example, the combined division_modulo function of Example 3.14.

Example 4.3 We restate the specification and the rules for the *div_mod* function.

$$div\_mod\colon \mathbb{P} \times \mathbb{N} \rightarrow \mathbb{P} \times \mathbb{P}$$
$$\text{pre-}div\_mod(\langle n,d\rangle) \triangleq \text{True}$$
$$\text{post-}div\_mod(\langle n,d\rangle,\langle q,r\rangle) \triangleq n = q*d + r \;\wedge\; 0 \le r < n$$

and

$$(n<d) \qquad div\_mod(n.d) \Leftrightarrow \langle 0, n\rangle$$
$$(n=d) \qquad div\_mod(n,d) \Leftrightarrow \langle 1, 0\rangle$$
$$(n>d) \qquad div\_mod(n,d) \Leftrightarrow div\_mod((n-d), d) + \langle 1,0\rangle$$

First notice that since the '+' operation on pairs is associative, we could use associative recursion removal; however, we shall not do that here.

Notice also that the rules can be combined and simplified to give

$$(n<d) \qquad div\_mod(n, d) \Leftrightarrow \langle 0,n\rangle$$
$$(n\ge d) \qquad div\_mod(n, d) \Leftrightarrow div\_mod((n-d), d) + \langle 1,0\rangle$$

We now build a 'counting up' implementation using m to count from 0 in steps of d until $m + d > n$; i.e, while $m + d \le n$. [We shall ignore r until we have the final value for q.]

The counter, together with the results and the operand values, gives a rather fearsome 5-tuple: $\langle m, n, d, q, r\rangle$. Even though the values of n and d never change, we retain them so as to see how the working is carried through. We can sideline them later. The invariant[13] satisfied by a corresponding set of values is

$$m = q*d + r \;\wedge\; 0 = r \;\wedge\; m \le n$$

The initial 5-tuple is $\langle 0, n, d, 0, 0\rangle$, and the invariant clearly holds for this. We increment q as much as possible and then find the appropriate r.

From the '≥' rule we get

$$(m + d \ge d) \quad div\_mod(m + d, d) \Leftrightarrow div\_mod(m, d) + \langle 1, 0\rangle$$

i.e.,

$$(m \ge 0) \quad div\_mod(m + d, d) \Leftrightarrow div\_mod(m, d) + \langle 1, 0\rangle$$

13 We did say that these invariants could get quite complex. Remember that attempting to construct an iterative loop directly from a specification (and that requires that we find such invariants) was rather difficult. Here at least we have some clues from the recursive version and the associated rules.

Hence, if

$$div\_mod(m, d) = \langle q,r \rangle$$

then

$$\begin{aligned} div\_mod(m+d, d) &= div\_mod(m, d) + \langle 1,0 \rangle \\ &= \langle q,r \rangle + \langle 1,0 \rangle \\ &= \langle q+1,r \rangle \end{aligned}$$

So, providing that we stop when we should, each intermediate incremental step is of the form

$$\langle m, n,d,q,r \rangle \leftarrow \langle m+d,n,d,q+1,r \rangle$$

which preserves the invariant.

The difference between m and n (i.e., $n-m$) decreases until we can use the '$n<d$' rule with n replaced by $n-m$:

$$((n-m)<d) \qquad div\_mod((n-m), d) \ \blacktriangleleft\!\blacktriangleright \ \langle 0, n-m \rangle$$

This delivers the proper value for r, which added to m give n. But, in the same move, r is set to $n-m$, and m is set to $m + r$ $(= m + (n - m) = n)$.
Then,

$$0 \leq r = n - m < d$$

After executing the corresponding assignment, namely:

$$\langle m,n,d,q,r \rangle \leftarrow \langle n,n,d,q,n-m \rangle$$

we have

$$n = q*d + r \quad \wedge \quad 0 \leq r < d \qquad (\wedge \quad m = n)$$

which is what is required of the complete calculation. Hence we have the code

```
div_mod(n, d) ≙
      begin  var m, q, r:ℙ;
             ⟨m,n,d,q,r⟩ ← ⟨0,n,d,0,0⟩;
             while m < n+d
                    do ⟨m,n,d,q,r⟩ ← ⟨m+d,n,d,q+1,r⟩ od;
             ⟨m,n,d,q,r⟩ ← ⟨n,n,d,q,n−m⟩;
             [ result ← ] ⟨q,r⟩
      end
```

which simplifies to

```
div_mod(n, d) ≜
      begin  var m, q, r:ℙ;
             ⟨m,q⟩ ← ⟨0,0⟩;
             while m < n+d
                   do ⟨m,q⟩ ← ⟨m+d,q+1⟩ od;
             r ← n−m;
             [ result ← ] ⟨q,r⟩
      end
```

(Note that the final value of m is not required.)

❑

Notice that, in this case, we could also 'count down' to give the following code, which we quote without any formal derivation:

```
div_mod(n, d) ≜
      begin  var m, q, r:ℙ;
             ⟨m,q⟩ ← ⟨n,0⟩;
             while m ≥ d
                   do ⟨m,q⟩ ← ⟨m−d,q+1⟩ od;
             r ← m;
             [ result ← ] ⟨q,r⟩
      end
```

Of course, counting up with m from 0 to n is the same as counting down from n to 0, so we should expect that there are going to be ways of relating these computation schemes. That leads on to the fascinating topic of program transformation; however, we shall not go very far down that path. We are merely scratching the surface of the subject; our main aim is deriving one (any) iterative scheme from a recursive one.

4.4 Speeding up Iterations

As noted on several occasions, the efficiency of a program is of secondary importance to its correctness. However, following on from the previous examples in this chapter (and rules from Examples 3.14 and 3.16), we take a quick look at how faster iterative schemes may be constructed.

Recall that from the rules

$$(n<d) \qquad div\_mod(n, d) \;\blacktriangleleft\!\blacktriangleright\; \langle 0,n \rangle$$
$$(n\geq d) \qquad div\_mod(n, d) \;\blacktriangleleft\!\blacktriangleright\; div\_mod((n-d), d) + \langle 1,0 \rangle$$

we can obtain the simplest(?) implementation of *div_mod*(n, d):

```
begin  var m, q, r:ℙ;
       ⟨m,q⟩ ← ⟨n,0⟩;
       while m ≥ d
              do ⟨m,q⟩ ← ⟨m−d,q+1⟩ od;
       r ← m;
       [ result ← ] ⟨q,r⟩
end
```

But other rules can be derived. Suppose $n \geq 2*d$.

Then,

$$(n \geq 2*d) \qquad div\_mod(n, d) \;\blacktriangleleft\!\blacktriangleright\; div\_mod((n-d), d) + \langle 1,0 \rangle$$

and, since $n - d \geq d$

$$\blacktriangleleft\!\blacktriangleright\; div\_mod(((n-d)-d), d) + \langle 1,0 \rangle + \langle 1,0 \rangle$$

$$\blacktriangleleft\!\blacktriangleright\; div\_mod((n-2*d), d) + \langle 2,0 \rangle$$

So, we have another rule

$$(n \geq 2*d) \qquad div\_mod(n, d) \;\blacktriangleleft\!\blacktriangleright\; div\_mod((n-2*d), d) + \langle 2,0 \rangle$$

Plugging this into the implementation scheme gives

```
       ⟨m,q⟩ ← ⟨n,0⟩;
       while m ≥ 2*d
              do ⟨m,q⟩ ← ⟨m−2*d,q+2⟩ od;
       r ← m;
       [ result ← ] ⟨q,r⟩
```

But this is wrong since it can yield a remainder between d and $2*d$. We need to check whether further processing is necessary. This can be done in several ways, one of which (which may not be the simplest but uses previous work, and can be generalised) is

$\langle m,q\rangle \leftarrow \langle n,0\rangle$;
while $m \geq 2*d$
    do $\langle m,q\rangle \leftarrow \langle m-2*d,q+2\rangle$ od;
while $m \geq d$
    do $\langle m,q\rangle \leftarrow \langle m-d,q+1\rangle$ od;
$r \leftarrow m$;
[result $\leftarrow$] $\langle q,r\rangle$

in which the second loop iterates either once or not at all.

We shall not give any technical definitions of (computational) complexity but, to indicate the kinds of gains made by this scheme, consider the number of adjustments made to the value of q within the two schemes. For larger and larger values of n, this number of assignments in the second version comes closer and closer to being half of those in the first scheme.

Provided that we have adequate end sections for ensuring that the q is large enough and r is within the right bounds, we can carry this idea further and have implementations such as

$\langle m,q\rangle \leftarrow \langle n,0\rangle$;
while $m \geq 3*d$
    do $\langle m,q\rangle \leftarrow \langle m-3*d,q+3\rangle$ od;
while $m \geq d$
    do $\langle m,q\rangle \leftarrow \langle m-d,q+1\rangle$ od;
$r \leftarrow m$;
[result $\leftarrow$] $\langle q,r\rangle$

and

$\langle m,q\rangle \leftarrow \langle n,0\rangle$;
while $m \geq 5*d$
    do $\langle m,q\rangle \leftarrow \langle m-5*d,q+5\rangle$ od;
while $m \geq 2*d$
    do $\langle m,q\rangle \leftarrow \langle m-2*d,q+2\rangle$ od;
while $m \geq d$
    do $\langle m,q\rangle \leftarrow \langle m-d,q+1\rangle$ od;
$r \leftarrow m$;
[result $\leftarrow$] $\langle q,r\rangle$

Notice that we do not need to revisit the question of rule validity (and hence the correctness of our design). Essentially the working is the same except for using a larger value in place of the original d, a multiple of d.

Notice also that with these — big step — designs we need to include a final loop to ensure that the remainder is less than d (and hence the decrement in that loop is d, $1*d$). To gain the maximum benefit from the initial loop (in which the decrement is $k*d$), we require k to be as large as possible, but of course k depends on the input value d.

(In reverse order) the step size – as a multiple of d – in a succession of loops might be

1, 2, 3, 4, ... k for some k.

or

1, 2, 3, 5, 8, ... from the Fibonacci series!

or

1, 2, 4, 8, ...

i.e.,

$2^0, 2^1, 2^2, 2^3, \ldots 2^k$ for some (other) k.

Moreover, using the last sequence and the largest possible value of k (such that $2^k \le d$) means that each of the 'lower' loops will be executed at most once.

Given some value d:$\mathbb{N}$, this initial value of k can be computed by

$k \leftarrow 0$;
while $2^{k+1}*d < n$ do $k \leftarrow k+1$ od

Example 4.4 Let's see how we can apply this idea to *div_mod*. First we need to parameterize our *div_mod* function by k. We call this *quick_div_mod* and abbreviate as *QDM*.

Its rules are as follows:

$(n<d)$	$QDM(n,d,k)$ ◆	$\langle 0,n \rangle$
$(n \ge 2^k*d)$	$QDM(n,d,k)$ ◆	$QDM(n-2^k*d,d,k-1) + \langle 2^k,0 \rangle$
$(n < 2^k*d, k \ne 0)$	$QDM(n,d,k)$ ◆	$QDM(n,d,k-1)$

To see how this works, consider the calculation of *div_mod*(121, 3):

$k = 0$	$2^1 * 3 = 6 < 121$
$k = 1$	$2^2 * 3 = 12 < 121$
$k = 2$	$2^3 * 3 = 24 < 121$
$k = 3$	$2^4 * 3 = 48 < 121$
$k = 4$	$2^5 * 3 = 96 < 121$
$k = 5$	$2^6 * 3 = 192 \geq 121$

So we start the main calculation with $k = 5$,

$QDM(121, 3, 5)$

$\Leftrightarrow$ $(121 \geq 2^5 * 3)$

$QDM(121 - 2^5 * 3, 3, 5-1) \; + \; \langle 2^5, 0 \rangle$

$\Leftrightarrow$

$QDM(121 - 96, 3, 5-1) \; + \; \langle 2^5, 0 \rangle$

$\Leftrightarrow$

$QDM(25, 3, 4) \; + \; \langle 32, 0 \rangle$

$\Leftrightarrow$ $(25 < 2^4 * 3)$

$QDM(25, 3, 3) \; + \; \langle 32, 0 \rangle$

$\Leftrightarrow$ $(25 \geq 2^3 * 3)$

$QDM(25 - 2^3 * 3, 3, 2) \; + \; \langle 2^3, 0 \rangle \; + \; \langle 32, 0 \rangle$

$\Leftrightarrow$

$QDM(1, 3, 2) \; + \; \langle 8, 0 \rangle \; + \; \langle 32, 0 \rangle$

$\Leftrightarrow$ $(1 < 2^2 * 3)$

$QDM(1, 3, 1) \; + \; \langle 8, 0 \rangle \; + \; \langle 32, 0 \rangle$

$\Leftrightarrow$ $(1 < 2^1 * 3)$

$QDM(1, 3, 0) \; + \; \langle 8, 0 \rangle \; + \; \langle 32, 0 \rangle$

$\Leftrightarrow$ $(1 < 3)$

$\langle 0, 1 \rangle \; + \; \langle 8, 0 \rangle \; + \; \langle 32, 0 \rangle$

$\Leftrightarrow$

$\langle 40, 1 \rangle$

and $121 \div 3$ is 40 remainder 1, which is correct.

Intermediate working uses the 6-tuple $\langle m, n, d, k, q, r \rangle$, where k has been externally declared and initialised and acts as a decreasing control variable, m is effectively the 'data still to process', n and d are the input values, and r collects the remaining value of m.

On removing all the components which cause no changes, the main loop of our calculation is

begin var $m, q, r{:}\mathbb{P}$;
  $\langle m,q\rangle \leftarrow \langle n,0\rangle$;
  while $k \geq 0$
    do if $m \geq 2^k{*}d$ then $\langle m,q\rangle \leftarrow \langle m - 2^k{*}d, q + 2^k\rangle$ fi;
    $k \leftarrow k - 1$
    od;
  $r \leftarrow m$;
  [result $\leftarrow$] $\langle q,r\rangle$
end

❑

Example 4.5 Now back to the Fibonacci function, $fib{:}\mathbb{P} \rightarrow \mathbb{N}$ discussed in Examples 3.16 and 4.2. For $(n \geq 2)$ it was implemented by

$$fib(n) \triangleq x+y \quad \text{where: } \langle x,y\rangle = fib2(n-1)$$

and

$$fib2(n) \triangleq \text{if } n = 2 \text{ then } \langle 1,1\rangle \text{ else } update(fib2(n-1)) \text{ fi}$$

and

$$update(\langle x,y\rangle) \triangleq \langle x+y, x\rangle$$

A possible iterative implementation of $fib2(n)$ was

begin var $m,a,b,c,d{:}\mathbb{N}$;
  $\langle m,a,b\rangle \leftarrow \langle 2,1,1\rangle$;
  while $m \leq n+1$
    do $\langle m,a,b\rangle \leftarrow \langle m+1,c,d\rangle$
      where: $\langle c,d\rangle = update(\langle a,b\rangle)$
    od;
  [result $\leftarrow$] $\langle a,b\rangle$
end

We also defined

$up2$ (i.e., $up^2 \triangleq update \circ update$
$\Leftrightarrow (\lambda \langle x,y\rangle)(\langle 2{*}x+y, x+y\rangle))$

Thus, using *up*2 as much as possible and not letting the value of m overshoot n, we have

```
begin  var m,a,b,c,d:ℕ;
       ⟨m,a,b⟩ ← ⟨2,1,1⟩;
       while m ≤ n+2
              do ⟨m,a,b⟩ ← ⟨m+2,c,d⟩
                                       where: ⟨c,d⟩ = up2(⟨a,b⟩)
              od;
       while m ≤ n+1
              do ⟨m,a,b⟩ ← ⟨m+1,c,d⟩
                                       where: ⟨c,d⟩ = update(⟨a,b⟩)
              od;
       [ result ← ] ⟨a,b⟩
end
```

Check that you understand the reasons for the bounding conditions on the two while loops.

This simplifies to

```
begin  var m,a,b:ℕ;
       ⟨m,a,b⟩ ← ⟨2,1,1⟩;
       while m ≤ n+2
              do ⟨m,a,b⟩ ← ⟨m+2,2*a+b,a+b⟩
              od;
       while m ≤ n+1
              do ⟨m,a,b⟩ ← ⟨m+1,a+b,a⟩
              od;
       [ result ← ] ⟨a,b⟩
end
```

❑

4.5 Recursive Procedures

We have seen how certain recursive functions used within program derivation can be realised as parameterless Procedures[14]. Here we shall apply some of the 'recursion-to-iteration' technology developed for certain classes of functions to these procedures. The first kind of procedure considered are those that are tail-recursive. Having handled tail-recursive functions (and the link between a function call, which is an *expression*, and an assignment *command*, which embodied such a call), the corresponding transformation of procedures is very easy. As before, we work backwards and justify the transformation by a sequence of equivalent flowcharts.

[14] But only certain forms of parameterless procedures.

Consider the procedure p defined by

$$p \triangleq \text{if } b \text{ then } q \text{ else } r; p \text{ fi}$$

where: b:State $\rightarrow \mathbb{B}$
and p,q,r:State $\rightarrow$ State

It is reasonable to assume that p may be implemented by a *while* loop given by the scheme

while $\neg b$ do r od; q

but we must check (justify) this assumption. We do this by collecting together the progression of transformations given earlier. They are presented in Figure 4.16.

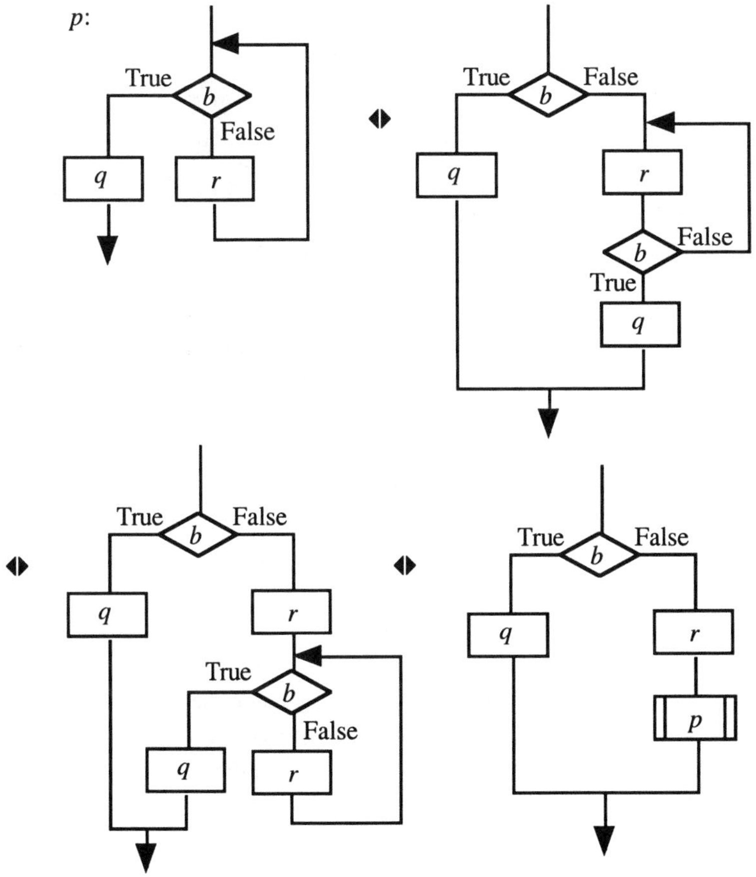

Figure 4.16

Hence

$$p \blacktriangleleft\!\!\blacktriangleright \text{ if } b \text{ then } q \text{ else } r;\, p \text{ fi}$$

and the assumed realisation holds.

Therefore, we have the rule

p where: $p \triangleq \text{if } b \text{ then } q \text{ else } r;\, p \text{ fi}$

$\blacktriangleleft\!\!\blacktriangleright$

while $\neg b$ do r od; q

The other form of (parameterless) recursive procedure that we shall consider again follows from the 'simple' form given in Section 3.3.

Suppose now that

$$p \triangleq \text{if } b \text{ then } q \text{ else } r;\, p;\, s \text{ fi}$$

where: $b{:}\text{State} \to \mathbb{B}$
and $p,q,r,s{:}\text{State} \to \text{State}$

All terminating recursions (and those are the only ones in which we are interested) give rise to calculations of the form

$$x \mapsto s^n \circ q \circ r^n(x) \qquad \text{for some } n{:}\mathbb{P}.$$

The two parts of the calculation that surround the recursive call (r and s) must be repeated the same number of times. To facilitate this requirement, we introduce a local counter, i. Using i, we can count up and then down as in the scheme

$i \leftarrow 0$; if b then q
else r; $i \leftarrow i+1$; p; $i \leftarrow i-1$; s fi

$\blacktriangleleft\!\!\blacktriangleright$

$i \leftarrow 0$; p

where: $p \blacktriangleleft\!\!\blacktriangleright$ if b then q
else r; $i \leftarrow i+1$; p; $i \leftarrow i-1$; s fi

With this construction, the value of i when we reach the end is zero and has its highest value when we execute q. So now we can split the entire calculation approximately in half and, continuing to re-use names for related (but slightly different) functions

◀▶

$i \leftarrow 0$; p; while $i \neq 0$ do $i \leftarrow i - 1$; s od

where: p ◀▶ if b then q
else r; $i \leftarrow i + 1$; p fi

But now p is tail-recursive so, finally, we have

◀▶

$i \leftarrow 0$;
while $\neg b$ do r; $i \leftarrow i + 1$ od;
q;
while $i \neq 0$ do $i \leftarrow i - 1$; s od

Summary We have studied the important phenomenon of tail recursion and the commonly occurring 'pattern' of associative recursion. Most recursive designs can be transformed into one of these two forms (and hence ultimately to tail recursion), but the way this is achieved may not be easy to justify. However, such matters are not our concern here. We have also seen how transformations can be used to speed up the resultant iterative forms. Again this is not always easy but is consistent with the philosophy of "get it right, and then make it fast". Finally, we have showed how certain notions from recursion can be applied to procedures rather than functions.

Chapter 5
Quantifications

One criticism that has in the past been levelled at formal methods is that they are difficult to scale up to large problems. Of course, some problems are more complicated than others, but it is often the case that specifiers of software think in terms of units which are too small. Many specifications can be expressed using *big* data items but in a way that does not unduly constrain their subsequent refinement down to an implementation. Using the constructions detailed in this chapter requires you to view problems more abstractly, but they facilitate application of powerful refinement rules which give shorter, more immediate, derivation sequences. The price that must be paid for using *these* rules is that the designs produced are constrained; they have a certain structure and may be less efficient (at run time) than more tailored designs.

Most sets, relations and functions used to specify software and systems are not defined explicitly, element by element, but are represented implicitly by means of formulae — usually terms expressed as combinations of 'variables', or predicates expressing selection criteria. This not only allows big sets to be represented in a more compact fashion but can be very useful when synthesising software designs (code!). We seek a more general, less biased, way of representing (derived) sets, relations and functions.

Overtly logical specifications often don't need recursion, but others do. We have already seen the Fibonacci function, $Fib{:}\mathbb{P} \to \mathbb{N}$, usually defined (inductively) by

$$\begin{aligned} Fib(0) &\triangleq 1 \\ Fib(1) &\triangleq 1 \\ Fib(n+2) &\triangleq Fib(n) + Fib(n+1) \qquad \text{for values of } n \geq 0. \end{aligned}$$

Some would say that this function was inherently recursive. Perhaps it is, but other functions can easily be represented in other ways. These can be regarded either as non-recursive or as (implicitly) *very* recursive — you will see later what we mean. It is also important to recognise the connection between the structure of data and the structure of associated 'standard' program designs. They are *not* the same (they can't be) but they are *related*.

5.0 Overview

In Section 5.1, we look at more ways of defining composite values (sets, etc.), and then, in Section 5.2, we consider how more complicated values may be derived using 1-place and 2-place functions (and hidden away in here we have the operations known elsewhere as quantifiers or quantifications). It turns out that certain of these constructions are particularly useful in program development because they map directly onto the design structures encountered in Section 3.2.3.1. We look at these in Section 5.3. Then, somewhat retrospectively, in Section 5.4 we look at manipulation rules for quantifications. These include rules for manipulating 'for all' and 'there exists'. They complement the rules introduced in Chapter 1 and are given more fully in the Appendix.

5.1 Defining Composite Values

Where we cannot, or do not wish to, write a set explicitly by giving all its elements in a display like

$$\{\ \ ,\ \ ,\ \ ,\ \ ,\ldots,\ \ \}$$

we may be able to stipulate how to generate the elements from a 'term' by evaluating it for all values of certain variables that satisfy a given condition. We shall develop an extended and more general notation through a sequence of examples.

First we consider the expression $\{\, n \mid n{:}\mathbb{N} \mid (1 < n \le 5) \vee (10 \le n \le 12) \,\}$

This represents the set of all natural numbers n for which the predicate

$(1 < n \le 5) \vee (10 \le n \le 12)$ holds,

and is the same as

$$\{\, 2,3,4,5,10,11,12 \,\}$$

The symbolic representations are not unique and may be abbreviated.

So $\{\, n \mid n{:}\mathbb{N} \mid 1 \le n \le 4 \,\}$

◀▶

$\{\, n{:}\mathbb{N} \mid 1 \le n \le 4 \,\}$

◀▶

$\{\, n{:}1..4 \,\}$

◀▶

$1..4$

Similarly,

$\{ n \mid n{:}\mathbb{N} \mid (\exists m{:}\mathbb{N})(n = 2*m) \}$

◆

$\{ n{:}\mathbb{N} \mid (\exists m{:}\mathbb{N})(n = 2*m) \}$

— the set of even natural numbers

and $\{ n^2 \mid n{:}\mathbb{N} \mid \text{True} \}$

◆

$\{ n^2 \mid n{:}\mathbb{N} \}$

— the set of square naturals

and $\{ n + n^2 \mid n{:}\mathbb{N} \}$

◆

$\{ 2,6,12,20,.... \}$

The general form is

{ *term* (using variables) | *variable* names and types
| *condition* (using variables) }

read as

the set of all ... where ... and ... .

If the *term* is a single variable and/or the *condition* is 'True', then these components and the associated '|' may be omitted as in the examples.

But what about

$\{ n^2 \mid n{:}\mathbb{Z} \mid {}^{-}3 \leq n \leq 3 \}$?

This generates the set

$\{ 0,1,4,9 \}$

If we require duplicate entries — caused by the *term* giving the same answer for two or more values of n which satisfy the *condition* — then we must use *bags*. The notation extends in the expected way.

$\{\!\!\{ n^2 \mid n{:}\mathbb{Z} \mid {}^{-}3 \leq n \leq 3 \}\!\!\}$

◆

$\{\!\!\{ 9,4,1,0,1,4,9 \}\!\!\}$

◆

$\{\!\!\{ 0,1,1,4,4,9,9 \}\!\!\}$

So,

$⦃$ *term* | *variables* | *condition* $⦄$

is the bag of values obtained by evaluating the *term* for all values of the quoted (bound) *variables* for which the *condition* holds. In general, the *term* and the *condition* will be expressions that involve the quoted variables, but other (free) variables may be included, and the bound variables need not occur in the *term* or *condition*. Certain constraints must be imposed on the components of this construction to ensure that its evaluation is finite, but more on this later.

5.2 Derived Composite Values

New sets and bags, and lists, can be generated from existing ones by means of functions and algebraic operations (which we shall often write as functions so as not to require extra notation). There are two major ways in which this is done.

5.2.1 1-place Functions

Suppose $f{:}X \to Y$ is a function and $S{:}\mathfrak{F}(X)$ is a set. We define a new function, *set-f*, so that

$$set\text{-}f{:}\mathfrak{F}(X) \to \mathfrak{F}(Y) \quad \text{and} \quad set\text{-}f(S) \triangleq \{\ f(x) \mid x{:}X \mid x \in S\ \}$$

set-f simply applies the function f to each element of the set. Of course, the set used here, S, has nothing to do with the definition of *set-f*, so we should more properly write

$$set\text{-}f \triangleq (\lambda S{:}\mathfrak{F}(X))\ (\{\ f(x) \mid x{:}X \mid x \in S\ \}).$$

So, if $f{:}x \mapsto x^2$, $X \triangleq \mathbb{Z}$ and $V \triangleq 1..4$

then,
$$\begin{aligned} set\text{-}f(V) &\Leftrightarrow (\lambda S{:}\mathfrak{F}(X))\ (\{\ f(x) \mid x{:}X \mid x \in S\ \})\ (V) \\ &\Leftrightarrow \{\ f(x) \mid x{:}X \mid x \in V\ \} \\ &\Leftrightarrow \{\ f(x) \mid x{:}X \mid x \in 1..4\ \} \\ &\Leftrightarrow \{\ f(1), f(2), f(3), f(4)\ \} \\ &\Leftrightarrow \{\ 1,4,9,16\ \} \end{aligned}$$

And notice that if $T \triangleq {}^{-}4\ ..+4$

then, $set\text{-}f(T) \Leftrightarrow \{\ 0,1,4,9,16\ \}$.

We have the same 'problem' as before, but this is circumvented by using

$$bag\text{-}f \triangleq (\lambda S{:}\mathfrak{F}(X))\,(\,\{\!\!\{\, f(x) \mid x{:}X \mid x{\in}S \,\}\!\!\}\,)$$

so

$$bag\text{-}f(T) \iff \{\!\!\{\, 16, 9, 4, 1, 0, 1, 4, 9, 16 \,\}\!\!\}$$

Note that, if no confusion arises, the name *f* may be used in place of *set-f* or *bag-f*. Then the interpretation of $f(A)$ depends on the *type* of A.

We can apply the same construction to other structured collections of data, but only lists will be considered here. The idea is again simple: just apply the function to each element in the list to obtain a list of results (in the corresponding order). Instead of defining the new function directly, we define it axiomatically.

If $f{:}X{\to}Y$ then $list\text{-}f{:}X^*{\to}Y^*$, so that

$$list\text{-}f(\langle\rangle) \iff \langle\rangle$$
$$list\text{-}f(\langle x\rangle) \iff \langle f(x)\rangle$$

and

$$list\text{-}f(L_1{}^\frown L_2) \iff list\text{-}f(L_1){}^\frown list\text{-}f(L_2)$$

Hence, using the same function $f{:}x{\mapsto}x^2$

$$list\text{-}f(\langle 1,2,3\rangle) \iff \langle\, 1^2, 2^2, 3^2 \,\rangle$$
$$\iff \langle\, 1, 4, 9 \,\rangle$$

'*list-f*' can also be written as f^* (or, when the lists are non-empty, as f^+), so that if we have $h{:}X \to Y$, then it follows[1] that $h^*{:}X^* \to Y^*$ and $h^+{:}X^+ \to Y^+$.

Notice that the rule

$$list\text{-}f(L_1{}^\frown L_2) \iff list\text{-}f(L_1){}^\frown list\text{-}f(L_2)$$

fits directly with the structural decomposition tactic and gives the familiar data-flow diagram in Figure 5.1. This is the real motivation for making this sideways (or even backward) move to link specifications and 'devide and conquer' design strategies. Notice the relationship between the 'split' and 'combine' phases in the designs that follow, namely a reverse $^\frown$ and a forward $^\frown$.

[1] This notation is not accidental but reflects the common usage of superscript + and * in theoretical Computer Science.

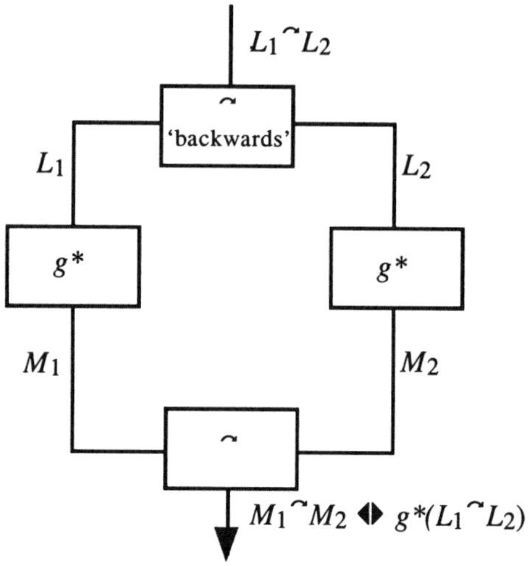

Figure 5.1

A less obvious but perhaps potentially more useful example is:

$f_1: \mathbb{Z} \to \mathbb{B} \qquad f_1: z \mapsto (z\ is\_odd)$

then $\quad f_1*(\langle 1..4 \rangle)$

◆

$f_1*(\langle 1,2,3,4 \rangle)$

◆

$\langle$True,False,True,False$\rangle$

When a function of type $X \to Y$ is applied to a list of type $X*$, the resultant operation is often called a *mapping*[2] — it translates, it 'maps', the X elements to Y elements (and of course X and Y may or may not be the same!).

5.2.2 2-place Functions

A more important situation occurs when we wish to *combine* the elements in a set, say of type $\mathfrak{F}(X)$, to give a result of type X. This is potentially very powerful but, in contrast to the above situation we cannot use just *any* function of the appropriate type; the functions must satisfy certain conditions. We explain the need for these conditions by considering a simple example.

[2] This is another instance of an over-worked word. Be careful: the word 'mapping' is also used for a total function (i.e., a function having the pre-condition True).

We wish to add together all the elements of a finite set of integers. Instead of using the addition operator directly, we name the function *plus*, simply to assist with the naming of the induced functions.

Let

$$plus: \mathbb{Z} \times \mathbb{Z} \rightarrow \mathbb{Z}$$
$$plus: \langle x,y \rangle \mapsto x+y$$

Now if $S \triangleq \{a,b,c,d\}:\mathfrak{F}(\mathbb{Z})$,
we want to define *set-plus* so that

$$set\text{-}plus(S) \Leftrightarrow a+b+c+d.$$

Set-plus is to be a *function* (of type $\mathfrak{F}(\mathbb{Z}) \rightarrow \mathbb{Z}$). The order in which the elements of the set are presented and the order in which we perform the operation (here, addition) must not affect the result. Hence we require properties (i) and (ii):

(i) $((a + b) + c) + d$

$\Leftrightarrow$

$(a + (b + c)) + d$ etc.

We require that the order of calculation does not affect the result. So *plus* must be ***associative***.

i.e., $plus(plus(x,y),z) \Leftrightarrow plus(x,plus(y,z))$

(ii) Since the elements of a set need not be considered in any specific order, we also need *plus* to be ***commutative***;

i.e., $plus(x,y) \Leftrightarrow plus(y,x)$

So the order in which the elements is presented does not affect the calculation.
and, finally, we require that

(iii) because we may wish to apply this to an empty data set,

$set\text{-}plus(\emptyset) \Leftrightarrow 0$

where 0 is the ***identity*** for *plus*, i.e., $(\forall x:\mathbb{Z})\ \ plus(x,0) = x$.

With these properties, *plus* is called a ***quantifier***.

Using *plus* (and *set-plus*, and 0) as our model, the properties which give an axiomatic definition of *set-plus* are as follows:

$$
\begin{aligned}
\textit{set-plus}(\emptyset) &\Leftrightarrow 0\\
\textit{set-plus}(\{x\}) &\Leftrightarrow x\\
\textit{plus}(\textit{set-plus}(S \cup T), \textit{set-plus}(S \cap T)) &\Leftrightarrow \textit{plus}(\textit{set-plus}(S), \textit{set-plus}(T))
\end{aligned}
$$

The last rule looks rather complex, but with $S \triangleq \{2,3,4\}$ and $T \triangleq \{2,3,5\}$ all it amounts to is

$$14 \quad + \quad 5 \quad = \quad 9 \quad + \quad 10$$

If $S \cap T = \emptyset$, then this rule becomes more useful. Hence, as a conditional rule, we have

$$(S \cap T = \emptyset) \qquad \textit{set-plus}(S \cup T) \Leftrightarrow \textit{plus}(\textit{set-plus}(S), \textit{set-plus}(T))$$

Diagrammatically, we have the familiar shape shown in Figure 5.1.

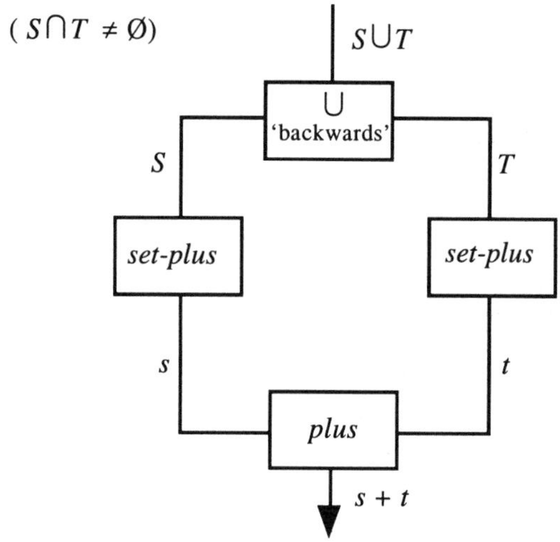

Figure 5.2

With bags, the situation is slightly different (and always simpler)

$$
\begin{aligned}
\textit{bag-plus}(\emptyset) &\Leftrightarrow 0\\
\textit{bag-plus}(\{\!|x|\!\}) &\Leftrightarrow x\\
\textit{bag-plus}(S \uplus T) &\Leftrightarrow \textit{plus}(\textit{bag-plus}(S), \textit{bag-plus}(T))
\end{aligned}
$$

— when two bags are united ($\uplus$'ed), there is no loss of data values.

Again notice the 'shape' of the last unconditional rule (as shown in Figure 5.3).

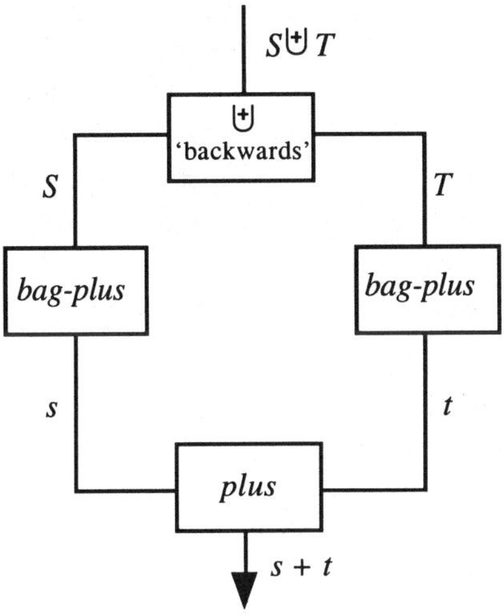

Figure 5.3

Here, *split* and *combine* are not the same operation (once forward and once in reverse), but the *split* is derived automatically and the *combine* operation is related to the overall operation (here *bag-plus*) in a systematic way.

This is sufficiently important to give rise to new notation.

$$bag\text{-}plus(\{\!\!\{ x \mid x{:}\mathbb{Z} \mid x \in S \}\!\!\})$$

is written

$$(\, plus\ x \mid x{:}\mathbb{Z} \mid x \in S\ )$$

This notation is inspired by the 'linearisation' of $\sum_{1 \le x \le n} x^2$

We start with

$$(\ \Sigma\ x^2 \text{ where } 1 \le x \le n\ )$$

where x is local, and we include a local declaration of its type

$$(\ \Sigma\ x^2 \mid\ x{:}\mathbb{Z} \text{ where } 1 \le x \le n\ )$$

then get rid of the Σ symbol, which is really addition, to give[3]

$$(\ +\ x^2 \mid\ x{:}\mathbb{Z} \text{ where } 1 \le x \le n\ )$$

and finally tidy up the syntax by removing the word 'where'

$$(\ +\ x^2 \mid\ x{:}\mathbb{Z} \mid 1 \le x \le n\ )$$

This is (intentionally) similar to the extended set and bag notations used earlier.

3 We use the infix operator symbol as a prefix. Binary function names will similarly be used as unary indications of induced bag operations — quantifiers.

As might be expected, there is a list version of this construction. Again we use *plus* as the basic example. The list version will be called *plus**. Notice that there can be no possibility of confusing this with the earlier definition of *f**. In that situation, *f* was a *monadic* function — it acted upon a single input value. Here *plus* is diadic, its type being $\mathbb{Z} \times \mathbb{Z} \rightarrow \mathbb{Z}$, and the $^+$ 'decoration' can be used in cases where inputs are restricted to being non-empty.

Again we can characterise $plus^*:\mathbb{Z}^* \rightarrow \mathbb{Z}$ axiomatically:

$$
\begin{aligned}
plus^*(\langle\,\rangle) &\;◀▶\; 0 \\
plus^*(\langle x \rangle) &\;◀▶\; x \\
plus^*(L^\frown M) &\;◀▶\; plus(plus^*(L), plus^*(M))
\end{aligned}
$$

Notice that from the third rule we can infer that *plus* must be associative. This follows automatically since

$$
\begin{aligned}
plus(plus(a, b), c) &\;◀▶\; plus(plus(plus^*(\langle a \rangle), plus^*(\langle b \rangle)), plus^*(\langle c \rangle)) \\
&\;◀▶\; plus(plus^*(\langle a, b \rangle), plus^*(\langle c \rangle)) \\
&\;◀▶\; plus^*(\langle a, b \rangle^\frown \langle c \rangle) \\
&\;◀▶\; plus^*(\langle a, b, c \rangle) \\
&\;◀▶\; plus^*(\langle a \rangle^\frown \langle b, c \rangle) \\
&\;◀▶\; plus(plus^*(\langle a \rangle), plus^*(\langle b, c \rangle)) \\
&\;◀▶\; plus(plus^*(\langle a \rangle), plus(plus^*(\langle b \rangle), plus^*(\langle c \rangle))) \\
&\;◀▶\; plus(a, plus(b, c))
\end{aligned}
$$

Hence, *plus* is associative and we get the same answer (as we should) regardless of how this list is split. Working in the opposite direction, we demonstrate this in the case of non-trivial splitting.

Consider the list $L^\frown M^\frown N$, where L, M, N are non-empty, and suppose that $plus^*(L)$ ◀▶ ℓ and $plus^*(M)$ ◀▶ m and $plus^*(N)$ ◀▶ n.

Then

$$
\begin{aligned}
plus^*((L^\frown M)^\frown N) &\;◀▶\; plus(plus^*(L^\frown M), plus^*(N)) \\
&\;◀▶\; plus(plus(plus^*(L), plus^*(M)), plus^*(N)) \\
&\;◀▶\; plus(plus(\ell, m), n) \\
&\;◀▶\; plus(\ell, plus(m, n)) \\
&\;◀▶\; plus(plus^*(L), plus(plus^*(M), plus^*(N)) \\
&\;◀▶\; plus(plus^*(L), plus^*(M^\frown N)) \\
&\;◀▶\; plus^*(L^\frown(M^\frown N))
\end{aligned}
$$

Obviously, this can also be deduced, directly and simply, from the associativity of the concatenation operator on lists ($(L^\frown M)^\frown N \Leftrightarrow L^\frown(M^\frown N)$), so the upshot is that the output can be decomposed in exactly the same way as the input.

Abstracting from this example, the rules for g^* (generated from an associative function $g{:}X \times X \to X$) with identity e are

$$g^*(\langle\rangle) \Leftrightarrow e \qquad \text{where } (\forall x{:}X)\,(g(x,e) = x \wedge g(e,x) = x)$$
$$g^*(\langle x \rangle) \Leftrightarrow x$$
$$g^*(L^\frown M) \Leftrightarrow g(g^*(L), g^*(M))$$

Notice also that if we have a situation in which empty lists are not sensible (e.g., *max* — you cannot find the maximal element of an empty list of integers!) then we would use the notation g^+, based on $g{:}X \times X \to X$ and here, of course, we don't need to pay heed to any 'empty list' rule.

Now we can use quantifiers and induced list operations to give more abstract (and non-recursive?) specifications of familiar calculations. Remember that the way recursion is included in a specification biases the design.

So, for example,

$$fact(n) \triangleq mult^+(\langle 1..n \rangle)$$
$$\Leftrightarrow (\, mult\ i \mid i{:}\mathbb{Z} \mid 1 \le i \le n \,) \qquad \text{where } mult(x,y) \triangleq x * y$$

We can also use induced operations to give unbiased definitions of other common functions which hitherto have had to be characterised axiomatically or by means of recursion, so

$$\#(S) \triangleq (\, +1 \mid i{:}X \mid i \in S \,) \qquad \text{where } S{:}\mathfrak{F}(X)$$

and

$$\#(L) \triangleq (\, +1 \mid L_1, L_2{:}X^*, x{:}X \mid L = L_1{}^\frown\langle x \rangle^\frown L_2 \,) \quad \text{where } L{:}X^*.$$

Try these on small values of S and L.

5.3 Application to Program Development

So, if we can manipulate a given specification (post-condition) into the form of a quantifier or a * or $^+$ function (perhaps with additional pre- and post-processing functions), we can routinely and quickly extract a correct 'divide and conquer' design. Of course, since many intermediate stages are combined (and hidden), alternative variations are denied to the programmer, and the possible forms of program that result are restricted. [See, for example, the sorting program design in

Section 7.4.] That is the price that must be paid for using 'big' transformation rules. The derived form of program may be susceptible to further (code level) transformations, but these cannot reverse any strict refinements (reductions) made earlier in the program synthesis.

5.3.1 1-place Functions

Recall the recursion removal rule which utilises an associative combination function with an identity element:

$(\lambda X{::}\text{Type}, Y{::}\text{Type})$
$(\lambda f{:}X\rightarrow Y)\ (\lambda p{:}X\rightarrow \mathbb{B})\ (\lambda g{:}X\rightarrow Y)\ (\lambda k{:}X \rightarrow X)\ (\lambda \ell{:}X \rightarrow Y)\ (\lambda h{:}Y\times Y \rightarrow Y)$

$(\forall x{:}X)(f(x) = \text{if } p(x) \text{ then } g(x) \text{ else } h(f(k(x)), \ell(x)) \text{ fi })$
$(\forall a,b,c{:}Y)\ (h(a,h(b,c)) = h(h(a,b),c)$
$(\exists e{:}Y)(\forall y{:}Y)(h(y,e) = y \wedge h(e,y) = y)$
$(\exists n{:}\mathbb{P})\ (p(k^n(x)))$

$y \leftarrow f(x)$ ◆ begin var $a{:}X, b{:}Y$;
$\langle a,b \rangle \leftarrow \langle x,e \rangle$;
while $\neg p(a)$
do $\langle a,b \rangle \leftarrow \langle\, k(a), h(\ell(a),b)\, \rangle$ od;
$y \leftarrow h(g(a),b)$
end

We seek to employ this rule to derive a more specialised rule for the computation of $F^*{:}X^* \rightarrow Y^*$ (say), where $F{:}X \rightarrow Y$ (so F is monadic).

From the required identities for induced functions, we know that

$$F^*(\langle\rangle) \;◆\; \langle\rangle$$
$$F^*(\langle x\rangle) \;◆\; \langle F(x)\rangle$$
$$F^*(L \frown M) \;◆\; F^*(L) \frown F^*(M).$$

Now, arbitrarily opting to process lists from left to right,

if $L \neq \langle\rangle$ then $F^*(L)$ ◆ $F^*(\langle \text{first\_of}(L)\rangle) \frown F^*(\text{rest\_of}(L))$
◆ $\langle F(\text{first\_of}(L))\rangle \frown F^*(\text{rest\_of}(L))$

so, pattern matching with the general rule, we need to replace

X	by	X^*
Y	by	Y^*
f	by	F^*

	$p(x)$	by	$x = \langle\rangle$
	$g(x)$	by	$\langle\rangle$
	$\ell(x)$	by	$\langle F(\text{first\_of}(x))\rangle$
	$h(x,y)$[4]	by	$y \frown x$
	$k(x)$	by	$\text{rest\_of}(x)$
and hence	e	by	$\langle\rangle$

to give

```
y ← F*(x)  ◆  begin  var a:X*,b:Y*;
                  ⟨a,b⟩ ← ⟨x,⟨⟩⟩;
                  while a ≠ ⟨⟩
                     do ⟨a,b⟩ ← ⟨ rest_of(a), b⁀⟨F(first_of(a))⟩ ⟩ od;
                  y ← b
              end
```

The fully parameterised version is

$(\lambda X::\text{Type}, Y::\text{Type})$
$\quad(\lambda F:X \to Y)$
$\quad\quad(F^*(\langle\rangle) = \langle\rangle)$
$\quad\quad(\forall x:X)\ (F^*(\langle x\rangle) = \langle F(x)\rangle)$
$\quad\quad(\forall L,M:X^*)\ (F^*(L \frown M) = F^*(L) \frown F^*(M).$

```
M ← F*(L)  ◆  begin  var N:X*,P:Y*;
                  ⟨N,P⟩ ← ⟨L,⟨⟩⟩;
                  while N ≠ ⟨⟩
                     do ⟨N,P⟩ ← ⟨ rest_of(N), P⁀⟨F(first_of(N))⟩ ⟩ od;
                  M ← P
              end
```

So, given a specification/design of a function in the form of an F^* function induced from a monadic function F, there is a simple implementation derived by application of a single rule. Of course, another implementation which works from right to left can similarly be derived from a rule which embodies the front_of and last_of functions.

---

[4] Notice that if we had a function q where $q(x,y) \triangleq h(y,x)$ and h was associative, then q would also be associative. Check this.

5.3.2 2-place Functions

Following similar substitutions into the general scheme, we can obtain an implementation rule for the calculation of $G^*:X^* \rightarrow X$, where $G:X^2 \rightarrow X$ is an associative function with (a two-sided[5]) identity element e. The rules applicable to G^* are

$$G^*(\langle\rangle) \;◆\; e$$
$$G^*(\langle x\rangle) \;◆\; x$$
$$G^*(L \frown M) \;◆\; G(G^*(L), G^*(M)).$$

Again forcing a left-to-right evaluation regime, we get

$$(L \neq \langle\rangle) \qquad G^*(L) \;◆\; G(G^*(\langle \text{first\_of}(L)\rangle), G^*(\text{rest\_of}(L)))$$
$$◆\; G(\text{first\_of}(L), G^*(\text{rest\_of}(L))).$$

Hence we require the (parallel) substitutions to replace

	X	by	X^*
	Y	by	X
	f	by	G^*
	$p(x)$	by	$x = \langle\rangle$
	$\ell(x)$	by	first_of(x)
	$h(x,y)$	by	$G(y, x)$
	$k(x)$	by	rest_of(x)
and	$g(\langle\rangle)$	by	e

to give

$y \leftarrow G^*(x)$ ◆ begin var a:X^*,b:X;
    $\langle a,b\rangle \leftarrow \langle x,e\rangle$;
    while $a \neq \langle\rangle$
        do $\langle a,b\rangle \leftarrow \langle$ rest_of(a), $G(b$, first_of(a))$\rangle$ od;
    $y \leftarrow b$
end

[5] That is, $(\forall y{:}X)(G(y,e) = y \wedge G(e,y) = y)$.

The fully parameterised version is

$(\lambda X::\text{Type})$
$(\lambda G:X^2 \rightarrow X)$
$(\forall a,b,c:X)\ (G(a, G(b, c)) = G(G(a,b), c)$
$(\exists e:X)(\forall y:X)(G(y,e) = y \wedge G(e,y) = y)$
$(G^*(\langle\rangle) = e)$
$(\forall x:X)\ (G^*(\langle x \rangle) = x$
$(\forall L,M:X^*)\ (G^*(L^\frown M) = G(G^*(L), G^*(M)\ ).$

```
y ← G*(L) ◆ begin var N:X*,b:X;
               ⟨N,b⟩ ← ⟨L,e⟩;
               while N ≠ ⟨⟩
                 do ⟨N,b⟩ ← ⟨ rest_of(N), G(b, first_of(N))⟩ ⟩ od;
               y ← b
             end
```

Recall the *listmax* function studied extensively in Chapter 3. Although this function cannot be applied to the empty list, similar processing can be used to give an implementation design very quickly.

Notice that

$listmax(L:\mathbb{Z}^+)$ ◆ $(\ max^+(x) \mid x:\mathbb{Z} \mid x \text{ in } L\ )$
$listmax(\langle a \rangle)$ ◆ a

and

$listmax(\langle a, b \rangle)$ ◆ if $a<b$ then b else a fi
◆ $max(a, b)$.

Even though *max* is associative (and commutative), it has no identity element, so the derivation given above cannot be used, but the same ideas are applicable. Before studying the next section, try to justify the following replacement based on left-to-right evaluation.

```
y ← listmax(L) ◆ begin var N:ℤ*, v:ℤ;
                   v ← first_of(L); N ← rest_of(L);
                   while N ≠ ⟨⟩
                     do ⟨N, v⟩ ← ⟨rest_of(N), max(v, first_of(N))⟩ od;
                   y ← v
                 end
```

5.3.3 An Extended Example: The Factorial Function

Although it might seem surprising that we use this example, it is in keeping with our aim of focusing on techniques applied to familiar and well-understood problems, rather that having to spend time explaining the problem.

The factorial function has been the butt of recursive ridicule ever since stacks were invented. Nevertheless, it is well-known and a useful example. We shall use it to demonstrate the derivation of three designs. Moreover, we shall intentionally not make use of all the properties of multiplication and hence increase the utility of the underlying transformations. Additionally, we use The factorial function as another illustration of how to work out some of the details from scratch rather than simply quoting powerful high-level rules. The mathematical manipulations are illustrated in part by data-flow diagrams (DFDs).

For $n{:}\mathbb{N}$

(we exclude fact(0), which must be equal to 1 because 1 is the multiplicative identity and 0 is associated with an empty data list — see below. But it is not always easy to convince readers about this, even mathematicians; so we avoid having 0 as a legitimate input.)

$$fact(n) \triangleq 1*2*...*n$$

'*' is a quantifier (being associative, commutative and having 1 as identity) so we can write

$$fact(n) \triangleq (*i \mid i{:}\mathbb{N} \mid 1 \leq i \leq n)$$

or, to avoid using the prefix '*' symbol for multiplication, we introduce the name *mult*, so

$$fact(n) \triangleq (mult\ i \mid i{:}1..n)$$

Subsequently, we shall only use the associativity of *mult*, which is of type

$\mathbb{N}^2 \to \mathbb{N}$ (i.e., two natural numbers in and one out)

Partly for emphasis and partly because it is very useful, we introduce an induced list operation

$$mult^{+}{:}\mathbb{N}^{+} \to \mathbb{N}$$

Remember, $\mathbb{N}^{+}$ is the set/type/class of non-empty lists of naturals.

We are going to calculate *fact*(n) by explicit multiplication of numbers in the list

$$\langle 1,2, \ldots ,n\rangle \quad \text{so} \quad fact(n) \Leftrightarrow mult^+(\langle 1,2, \ldots ,n\rangle)$$

and $mult^+$ obeys the following rules:

$$mult^+(\langle x\rangle) \Leftrightarrow x$$
$$mult^+(L_1 {}^\frown L_2) \Leftrightarrow mult(\ mult^+(L_1)\ ,\ mult^+(L_2)\ ) \qquad \text{where } L_1,L_2{:}\mathbb{N}^+$$

The general 'divide and conquer' strategy applied to this problem yields the DFD in Figure 5.4,

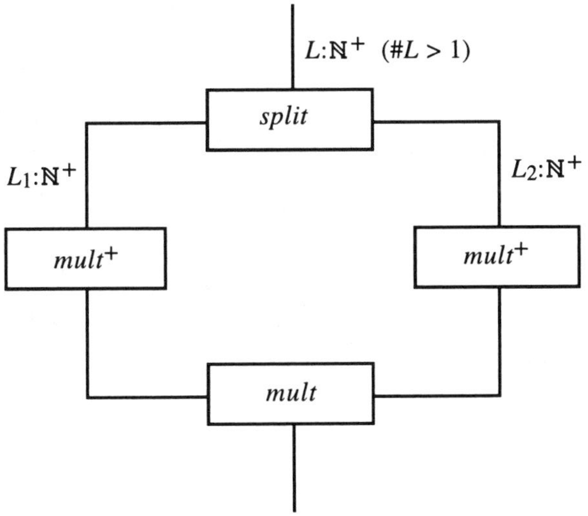

Figure 5.4

with $split{:}\mathbb{N}^+ \rightarrow \mathbb{N}^+ \times \mathbb{N}^+$ and $split(L) = \langle L_1,L_2\rangle$, where $L = L_1{}^\frown L_2$

Notice that *split* is non-deterministic; lots of different implementations are possible, and we shall use three of them. Recall that, when $n{>}1$,

$$fact(n) \Leftrightarrow mult^+(\langle 1,2, \ldots ,n\rangle) \Leftrightarrow mult^+(\langle 1..n\rangle)$$

Now take a *software engineering* decision and particularise (refine!!) *split* to be *split_left*, so

$$split\_left(\langle 1..n\rangle) \triangleq (\langle 1\rangle,\langle 2..n\rangle)$$

(We do this now rather than later purely as an illustration. It would in general be much more desirable to defer such decisions for as long as possible so as to retain the non-determinism and allow choices to be made later.) Using *split_left*, the full DFD for $mult^+(\langle 1..4 \rangle)$ is as in Figure 5.5.

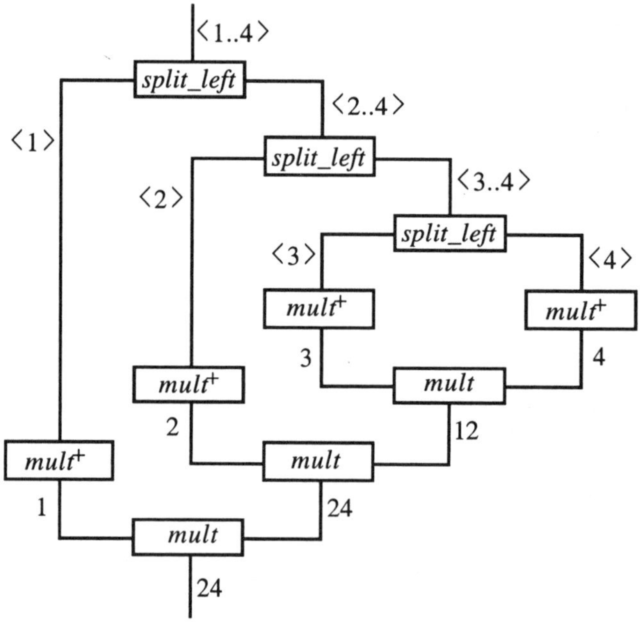

Figure 5.5

The order of evaluation suggested in Figure 5.5 is essentially deterministic, the only variability being the order of executing the four $mult^+$ operations, each of which does no more than extract the integer x from the list $\langle x \rangle$. However, since *mult* is associative, we can 'change the plumbing'. Moreover, by staggering the order of evaluation of the $mult^+$ operations, so as to derive 1, from $\langle 1 \rangle$, *before* *split*ting $\langle 2..4 \rangle$, we get the DFD in Figure 5.6.

Now we express this mathematically and use it to *calculate* an iterative program design. In outline, this goes as follows:

$mult^+(L)$ ◆ if $\#L = 1$ then first_of(L)
else $mult$(first_of(L), $mult^+$(rest_of(L)))
fi

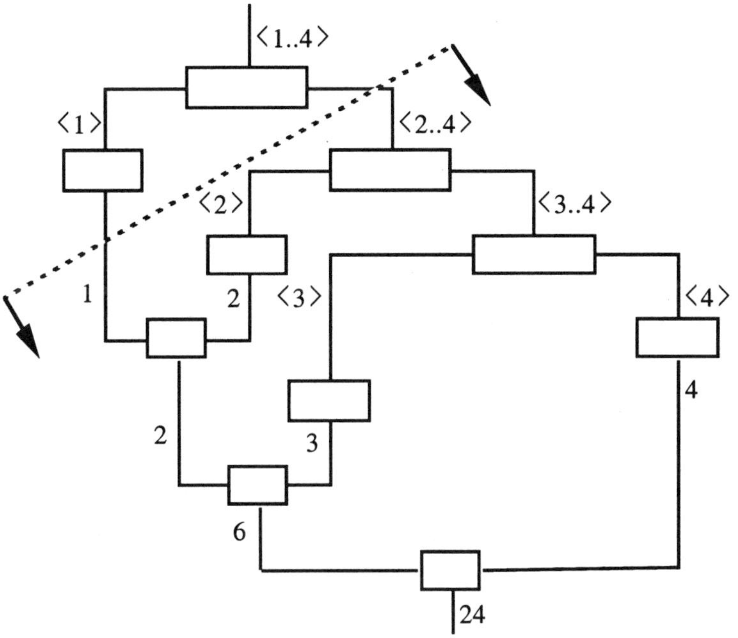

Figure 5.6

We now introduce a new function based on the 'else' branch of the current expression.

Let $\quad finish\_1(x{:}\mathbb{N}, y{:}\mathbb{N}^+) \triangleq mult(x, mult^+(y))$

so

$$
\begin{aligned}
mult^+(L) \Leftrightarrow\ & \text{if } \#L = 1 \text{ then first\_of}(L) \\
& \qquad\quad \text{else } finish\_1(\text{first\_of}(L), \text{rest\_of}(L)) \\
& \text{fi}
\end{aligned}
$$

From this definition of *finish_1*, we can proceed as follows.

If $\#y = 1$, then $y \Leftrightarrow \langle v \rangle$ for some $v{:}\mathbb{N}$, so

$$
\begin{aligned}
finish\_1(x,y) &\Leftrightarrow mult(x, mult^+(y)) \\
&\Leftrightarrow mult(x, mult^+(\langle v \rangle)) \\
&\Leftrightarrow mult(x, v) \\
&\Leftrightarrow mult(x, \text{first\_of}(y))
\end{aligned}
$$

If $\#y > 1$, then y ◀▶ $\langle v \rangle ^\frown w$ for some $v:\mathbb{N}, w:\mathbb{N}^+$ so

$$\begin{aligned}
\mathit{finish_1}(x,y) \;&◀▶\; \mathit{mult}(x,\mathit{mult}^+(y)) \\
&◀▶\; \mathit{mult}(x,\mathit{mult}^+(\langle v \rangle ^\frown w)) \\
&◀▶\; \mathit{mult}(x, \mathit{mult}(\mathit{mult}^+(\langle v \rangle),\mathit{mult}^+(w))) \\
&◀▶\; \mathit{mult}(x, \mathit{mult}(v,\mathit{mult}^+(w))) \\
&◀▶\; \mathit{mult}(\mathit{mult}(x,v), \mathit{mult}^+(w)) \\
&◀▶\; \mathit{mult}(\mathit{mult}(x,\text{first_of}(y)), \mathit{mult}^+(\text{rest_of}(y))) \\
&◀▶\; \mathit{finish_1}(\mathit{mult}(x,\text{first_of}(y)), \text{rest_of}(y))
\end{aligned}$$

which gives

$$\begin{aligned}
\mathit{finish_1}(x,y) \;◀▶\; & \text{if } \#y = 1 \\
& \text{then } \mathit{mult}(x,\text{first_of}(y)) \\
& \text{else } \mathit{finish_1}(\mathit{mult}(x,\text{first_of}(y)), \text{rest_of}(y)) \\
& \text{fi}
\end{aligned}$$

and this converges using $\#y - 1$ as a measure.

This is tail recursion, so we can apply a standard rule to restructure the calculation into the iterative form.

```
begin var u:ℕ, v:ℕ⁺;
      ⟨u,v⟩ ← ⟨x,y⟩;
      while #v ≠ 1
         do ⟨u,v⟩ ← ⟨mult(u,first_of(v)), rest_of(v)⟩
         od;
      mult(u,first_of(v))
end
```

Now, substituting back in $\mathit{mult}^+(L)$ and simplifying, using the programming language rules (such as 'loop pull back' — see Section A.5 in the Appendix), we have:

$$\begin{aligned}
\mathit{mult}^+(L) \;◀▶\; & \text{if } \#L = 1 \text{ then first_of}(L) \\
& \qquad\qquad \text{else } \mathit{mult}(\text{first_of}(L), \mathit{mult}^+(\text{rest_of}(L))) \\
& \text{fi} \\[1em]
◀▶\; & \text{if } \#L = 1 \text{ then first_of}(L) \\
& \qquad\qquad \text{else } \mathit{finish_1}(\text{first_of}(L),\text{rest_of}(L)) \\
& \text{fi}
\end{aligned}$$

◆

```
begin   var u:ℕ, v:ℕ⁺;
[ result ← ] if #L =1  then first_of(L)
                       else
                       ⟨u,v⟩ ← ⟨first_of(L), rest_of(L⟩;
                       while #v ≠ 1
                          do ⟨u,v⟩ ← ⟨mult(u,first_of(v)), rest_of(v)⟩
                          od;
                       mult(u,first_of(v))
             fi
end
```

◆

```
begin   var u:ℕ, v:ℕ⁺;
[ result ← ] if #L =1  then first_of(L)
                       else
                       ⟨u,v⟩ ← ⟨first_of(L), rest_of(L⟩;
                       while #v ≠ 1
                          do ⟨u,v⟩ ← ⟨mult(u,first_of(v)), rest_of(v)⟩
                          od;
                       ⟨u,v⟩ ← ⟨mult(u,first_of(v)), rest_of(v)⟩;
                       u
             fi
end
```

◆

```
begin   var u:ℕ, v:ℕ⁺;
[ result ← ] if #L =1  then first_of(L)
                       else
                       ⟨u,v⟩ ← ⟨first_of(L), rest_of(L⟩;
                       while #rest_of(v) ≠ 0
                          do ⟨u,v⟩ ← ⟨mult(u,first_of(v)), rest_of(v)⟩
                          od;
                       ⟨u,v⟩ ← ⟨mult(u,first_of(v)), rest_of(v)⟩;
                       u
             fi
end
```

◆ by 'loop pull back', legitimately regarding the predicate $\#v \neq 0$ as a function of $\langle u,v \rangle$.

```
begin  var u:ℕ, v:ℕ⁺;
[ result ← ] if #L =1 then first_of(L)
                       else
                       ⟨u,v⟩ ← ⟨first_of(L), rest_of(L⟩;
                       while #v ≠ 0
                          do ⟨u,v⟩ ← ⟨mult(u,first_of(v)), rest_of(v)⟩
                          od;
                       u
             fi
end
```

so

```
fact(n) ≜ begin  var u:ℕ, L, v:ℕ⁺;
               L ← ⟨1..n⟩:ℕ⁺;
               u ← first_of(L);
               v ← rest_of(L);
               while #v ≠ 0
                    do  u ← mult(u, first_of(v));
                        v ← rest_of(v)
                    od;
               [ result ← ] u
          end
```

Of course, we could transform the data-flow diagram for $mult^{+}(\langle 1..n \rangle)$ in other ways. Using a *split-right*, we would arrive at the DFD shown in Figure 5.7. (Again some detail is omitted so as not to detract from the main features — i.e., the shape).

When $n > 1$, we can use the functions 'front_of' and 'last_of' to split $\langle 1..n \rangle$ into $\langle 1..n\text{-}1 \rangle$ and $\langle n \rangle$, and by a similar calculation, we get:

```
mult⁺(L) ◆ if #L = 1 then last_of(L)
                      else finish_2(front_of(L), last_of(L))
           fi
```

where:

```
finish_2(x:ℕ⁺,y:ℕ) ≜ if #x = 1
                      then mult(last_of(x),y)
                      else finish_2(front_of(x),mult(last_of(x),y))
                      fi
```

which then transforms into

$fact(n) \triangleq$ begin var $z{:}\mathbb{N}, L, m{:}\mathbb{N}^+$;
$L \leftarrow \langle 1..n \rangle{:}\mathbb{N}^+$;
$z \leftarrow$ last_of(L);
$m \leftarrow$ front_of(L);
while $\#m \neq 0$
do $z \leftarrow mult$(last_of(m), z);
$m \leftarrow$ front_of(m)
od;
[result $\leftarrow$] z
end

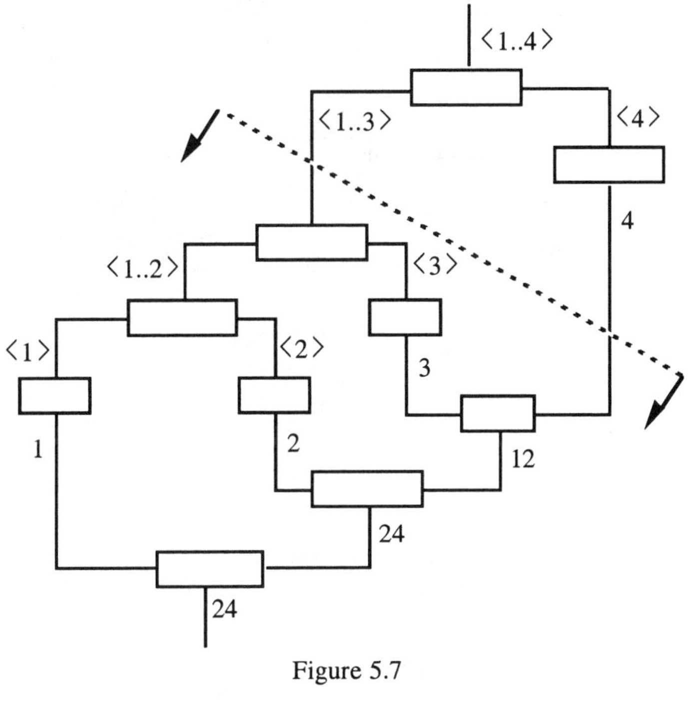

Figure 5.7

The similarity of these two programs is only to be expected; after all, we are simply processing the list in the opposite direction. These two programs can be further transformed and converted so that they do not utilise lists, but this will not always be possible and hence will not be pursued here.

Notice, that we could even use *split_equal*, so.

$$\begin{array}{l} \text{if } \#L > 1 \text{ then } split\_equal(L) = \langle L_1, L_2 \rangle \\ \qquad\qquad \text{where } (2*\#L_1 = \#L \vee 2*\#L_1 = \#L + 1) \wedge L = L_1 \frown L_2 \\ \text{fi} \end{array}$$

This would then give rise to

$$\begin{array}{l} mult^+(L) \triangleq \text{ if } \#L = 1 \text{ then first\_of}(L) \\ \qquad\qquad\qquad\qquad \text{else } mult(mult^+(L_1), mult^+(L_2)) \\ \qquad\qquad\quad \text{fi} \\ \qquad\qquad\qquad\qquad \text{where } \langle L_1, L_2 \rangle = split\_equal(L) \end{array}$$

With our running example, this would give the DFD in Figure 5.8.

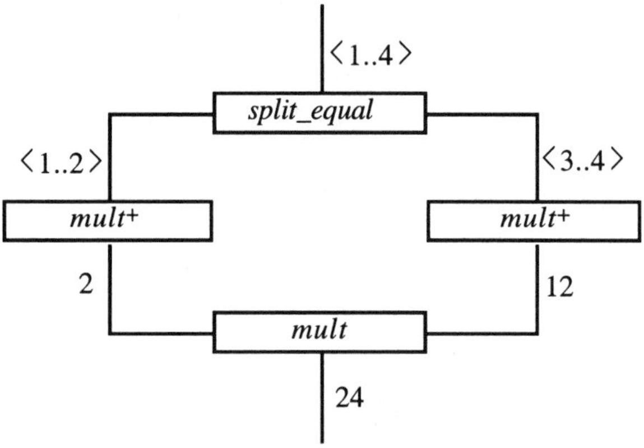

Figure 5.8

Here, the two embedded references to $mult^+$ can be computed in any of the ways so far encountered. In particular, using integer division and *parallel* execution, we could have a program such as

$$\begin{array}{l} fact(n) \triangleq \text{ begin } \text{ var } z1, z2, m{:}\mathbb{N}; \\ \qquad\quad \text{if } n > 1 \text{ then } m \leftarrow n \div 2; \\ \qquad\qquad\qquad (z1 \leftarrow mult^+(\langle 1..m \rangle) \parallel z2 \leftarrow mult^+(\langle m{+}1..n \rangle)); \\ \qquad\qquad\qquad mult(z1, z2) \\ \qquad\qquad \text{else } 1 \\ \qquad\quad \text{fi} \\ \qquad\quad \text{end} \end{array}$$

So, the "shape" in the specification need not be reflected in a resulting design/implementation. We suggest that it is not desirable that the structure of a specification be imposed on any subsequent design and hence it *is* desirable that a specification should have no unnecessary structure; and where a degree of structure is necessary to cope with "size", that structure should be as general as possible.

5.4 Some Rules for Quantifications

Returning to quantifiers proper, we now look at some rules that can be used in their manipulation. Recall that quantifiers are commutative, associative, and have an identity element. In contrast, the induced list operations need to be associative but not necessarily commutative (because the list ordering is often significant), they need to process singleton lists appropriately, and only in the * case need we bother about empty lists. Quantifiers include the operators +, *, $\wedge$ and $\vee$. These are so common as to have new symbols to represent them when used as quantifiers, namely Σ, Π, $\exists$ and $\forall$, but there are many more.

Note also that the familiar logical quantifiers, namely $\exists$ and $\forall$, are derived from $\vee$ and $\wedge$, which are idempotent and hence there is no distinction between the set and bag formulations of these derived operators. In general, however, quantifiers are not idempotent and the formulations yield different answers. The bag version is the one that is appropriate in the general case.

Quantifiers do not just occur as the outer-most operators in a post-condition[6] (giving rise to what the logicians call prenex normal form, which might then be implemented in a straightforward fashion using nested recursions). Elsewhere we need to be able to manipulate in similar ways to all the other algebraic operations.

Let $\circledast$, called 'circled star', be an *arbitrary* quantifier. We write it as an infix binary operator simply to make it easier to read and to see the shape of the surrounding expressions. The type of $\circledast$ is $Y^2 \to Y$, and e is its identity element.

Moreover, take $f{:}X \to Y$ and $s{:}X \to \mathbb{B}$.
Then

$$(\circledast f(x) \mid x{:}X \mid s(x))$$

represents $\circledast$ applied to the elements of the bag

$$\{\!\{ f(x) \mid x{:}X \mid s(x) \}\!\} : \mathcal{B}(Y)$$

to give a result of type Y.

[6] Although they can be manipulated into this form, this is not always a fruitful move.

One way to ensure that this result is well-defined is to stipulate that the number of elements to be combined, using ⊛, be finite. This follows as a matter of course if the set $\{ x{:}X \mid s(x) \}$ is finite, or even more immediately if X is finite.

The set $\{ x{:}X \mid s(x) \}$ is called the ***base***[7] of the quantification. The predicate s can also be thought of as the ***selector*** because it selects the items of type X which are to be included in the base.

(Other restrictions achieve the same effect, but they will not be considered for the general case.)

5.4.1 General Rules

[To avoid technical problems we shall assume that the types used to generate the base of a quantification are both finite and non-empty. So that the form of the rules can be more easily seen, we shall also simplify the notation used. Usually "$x{:}X$" will be omitted, as will the explicit reference to "(x)" in the term and the selector except when necessary to demonstrate the working of the rule.]

In view of the extensive use of the logical quantifiers, we shall not only give the general form of each rule but include an interpretation of a logical instance using both the general syntax introduced above and the more familiar traditional syntax. So as to make the illustrations more meaningful, we point out that, in the logical case, both the selector and the term are predicates (both deliver Boolean results), and they may therefore be 'combined' by using so-called ***trading*** rules. They allow information to be 'traded' between the selector and term. This also allows us to quantify over an entire (finite) type using a single composite term. For universal quantification, we have

$$
\begin{aligned}
(\ \wedge p(x) \mid x{:}X \mid s(x)\ ) &\Leftrightarrow (\ \wedge (s(x) \Rightarrow p(x)) \mid x{:}X \mid \text{True}) \\
&\Leftrightarrow (\forall x{:}X)(s(x) \Rightarrow p(x))
\end{aligned}
$$

or, in a more compact fashion,

$$
\begin{aligned}
(\ \wedge p \mid x{:}X \mid s\ ) &\Leftrightarrow (\ \wedge (s \Rightarrow p) \mid x{:}X \mid \text{True}) \\
&\Leftrightarrow (\forall x{:}X)(s \Rightarrow p)
\end{aligned}
$$

The correspondence for the existential quantifier is

$$
\begin{aligned}
(\ \vee p(x) \mid x{:}X \mid s(x)\ ) &\Leftrightarrow (\ \vee (s(x) \wedge p(x)) \mid x{:}X \mid \text{True}) \\
&\Leftrightarrow (\exists x{:}X)(s(x) \wedge p(x))
\end{aligned}
$$

or

$$
\begin{aligned}
(\ \vee p \mid x{:}X \mid s\ ) &\Leftrightarrow (\ \vee (s \wedge p) \mid x{:}X \mid \text{True}) \\
&\Leftrightarrow (\exists x{:}X)(s \wedge p)
\end{aligned}
$$

---

[7] Some authors call this the range of the quantification, but it is also the domain of the quantification stage of the evaluation; hence the reason for the introduction of new terminology.

Notice that these trading rules are necessary in order to translate the new notation, using the two predicates s and p, into the traditional form which only uses a single predicate. We have

$$(\wedge p \mid x{:}X \mid s) \;\Leftrightarrow\; (\forall x{:}X)(s \Rightarrow p)$$
$$(\vee p \mid x{:}X \mid s) \;\Leftrightarrow\; (\exists x{:}X)(s \wedge p)$$

and

$$(\forall x{:}X)(p) \;\Leftrightarrow\; (\wedge p \mid x{:}X \mid \text{True})$$
$$(\exists x{:}X)(p) \;\Leftrightarrow\; (\vee p \mid x{:}X \mid \text{True})$$

Now for some general rules. We shall not go into lengthy justifications (we can simply take the rules as 'given') but will mention the key properties of bags and Booleans from which they follow, and how they might relate to useful design transformations.

(1) Empty base:

$$(\circledast f(x) \mid \mid \text{False}) \;\Leftrightarrow\; e$$

This follows from

$$\{\!\!\{ f(x) \mid x{:}X \mid \text{False} \}\!\!\} \;\Leftrightarrow\; \emptyset$$

and

$$x \circledast e \;\Leftrightarrow\; x \qquad \text{for all } x{:}X$$

In the logical cases, we have

$$\begin{aligned} (\wedge p(x) \mid x{:}X \mid \text{False}) &\Leftrightarrow (\wedge(\text{False} \Rightarrow p(x)) \mid x{:}X \mid \text{True}) \\ &\Leftrightarrow (\wedge(\text{True}) \mid x{:}X \mid \text{True}) \\ &\Leftrightarrow \text{True} \qquad \text{all answers are True} \end{aligned}$$

so

$$\begin{aligned} (\forall x{:}X)(\text{False} \Rightarrow p(x)) &\Leftrightarrow (\forall x{:}X)(\text{True}) \\ &\Leftrightarrow \text{True} \end{aligned}$$

Similarly,

$$\begin{aligned} (\vee p(x) \mid x{:}X \mid \text{False}) &\Leftrightarrow (\vee(\text{False} \wedge p(x)) \mid x{:}X \mid \text{True}) \\ &\Leftrightarrow (\vee(\text{False}) \mid x{:}X \mid \text{True}) \\ &\Leftrightarrow \text{False} \\ &\qquad \text{there exist no answers which are True} \end{aligned}$$

or, in traditional notation,

$$\begin{aligned} (\exists x{:}X)(\text{False} \wedge p(x)) &\Leftrightarrow (\exists x{:}X)(\text{False}) \\ &\Leftrightarrow \text{False} \end{aligned}$$

(2) One-point rule

This is simply the direct application of the term to a single value.

$(x \setminus E)$[8] $$(\circledast f(x) \mid\mid x{=}E) \;\Leftrightarrow\; f(x)[x \leftarrow E]^{9}$$
$$\Leftrightarrow\; f(E)$$

In the logical cases,

$$(\wedge p(x) \mid\mid x{=}E) \;\Leftrightarrow\; p(E)$$

i.e.,

$$(\forall x{:}X)((x{=}E) \Rightarrow p(x)) \;\Leftrightarrow\; p(E)$$

conditionally evaluate $p(x)$ when $x{=}E$,

$$(\vee p(x) \mid\mid x{=}E) \;\Leftrightarrow\; p(E)$$

i.e.,

$$(\exists x{:}X)((x{=}E) \wedge p(x)) \;\Leftrightarrow\; p(E)$$

rationalisation, using $x{=}E$ to simplify $p(x)$.

The empty and singleton rules are clearly useful to cope with 'trivial' instances of problems. The next rules deal with decomposition. Rule 3 can be used to split the term (from $f \circledast g$ to f and g), and Rule 4 can similarly be used to split the selector.

(3) Re-distribution[10]

If we also have $g{:}X \rightarrow Y$, where $(f \circledast g)(x) \triangleq f(x) \circledast g(x)$, then

$$(\circledast f \mid\mid s) \;\circledast\; (\circledast g \mid\mid s) \;\Leftrightarrow\; (\circledast (f \circledast g) \mid\mid s)$$

This utilises the associativity and commutativity of $\circledast$.

From the general form, we get

$$(\wedge p \mid\mid s) \;\wedge\; (\wedge q \mid\mid s) \;\Leftrightarrow\; (\wedge (p \wedge q) \mid\mid s)$$
$$\Leftrightarrow\; (\wedge (s \Rightarrow (p \wedge q)) \mid\mid \text{True})$$

$$(\forall x{:}X)(s \Rightarrow p) \wedge (\forall x{:}X)(s \Rightarrow q) \;\Leftrightarrow\; (\forall x{:}X)(s \Rightarrow (p \wedge q))$$

and when $s \Leftrightarrow \text{True}$ we get

$$(\forall x{:}X)(p) \wedge (\forall x{:}X)(q) \;\Leftrightarrow\; (\forall x{:}X)(p \wedge q)$$

---

[8] That is "x is not (free for substitution) in E". See the Appendix for a fuller explanation.

[9] $f(x)[x \leftarrow E] \triangleq \lambda x.f(x)\,(E)$, $f(x)$ with x replaced by E.

[10] This is not the terminology used by other authors. We do not use "distributivity" since distributivity — such as the distributivity of * over + or ∧ over ∨ — is not used in the justification of this rule.

and
$$(\vee p \,||\, s) \ \vee \ (\vee q \,||\, s) \ \blacklozenge \ (\vee (p \vee q) \,||\, s)$$
$$\blacklozenge \ (\vee (s \wedge (p \vee q)) \,||\, \text{True})$$

i.e.,
$$(\exists x{:}X)(s \wedge p) \ \vee \ (\exists x{:}X)(s \wedge q) \ \blacklozenge \ (\exists x{:}X)(s \wedge (p \vee q))$$

which then gives,
$$(\exists x{:}X)(p) \ \vee \ (\exists x{:}X)(q) \ \blacklozenge \ (\exists x{:}X)(p \vee q)$$

(4) Base split
If additionally $r{:}X{\rightarrow}\mathbb{B}$, then

$$(\circledast f \,||\, r \wedge s) \circledast (\circledast f \,||\, r \vee s) \ \blacklozenge \ (\circledast f \,||\, r) \circledast (\circledast f \,||\, s)$$

Applied to $\wedge$, this gives

$$(\wedge p \,||\, r \wedge s) \wedge (\wedge p \,||\, r \vee s) \ \blacklozenge \ (\wedge p \,||\, r) \wedge (\wedge p \,||\, s)$$

i.e.,
$$(\forall x{:}X)((r \wedge s) \Rightarrow p) \wedge (\forall x{:}X)((r \vee s) \Rightarrow p) \ \blacklozenge \ (\forall x{:}X)(r \Rightarrow p) \wedge (\forall x{:}X)(s \Rightarrow p)$$

and with $\vee$,
$$(\vee p \,||\, r \wedge s) \vee (\vee p \,||\, r \vee s) \ \blacklozenge \ (\vee p \,||\, r) \vee (\vee p \,||\, s)$$

so
$$(\exists x{:}X)((r \wedge s) \wedge p) \vee (\exists x{:}X)((r \vee s) \wedge p) \ \blacklozenge \ (\exists x{:}X)(r \wedge p) \vee (\exists x{:}X)(s \wedge p)$$

Notice that if $r \wedge s \ \blacklozenge$ False, then we get
$$(\circledast f \,||\, r \vee s) \ \blacklozenge \ (\circledast f \,||\, r) \circledast (\circledast f \,||\, s)$$

which is a variant of the familiar 'divide and conquer' scheme.

The next rule is concerned with breaking off a 'simple' part of the calculation. It may also be regarded as changing the scope of a variable. It is this aspect that is of particular importance in the case of the quantifier $\exists$.

(5) Nesting. If $g:X^2 \to Y$ and $u:X^2 \to \mathbb{B}$,

$$(\circledast g(x,y) \mid x,y:X \mid s(x) \wedge u(x,y)) \quad \Leftrightarrow \quad (\circledast (\circledast g(x,y) \mid y:X \mid u(x,y)) \mid x:X \mid s(x))$$

i.e., $(y \setminus s)$

$$(\circledast g \mid x,y:X \mid s \wedge u) \quad \Leftrightarrow \quad (\circledast (\circledast g \mid y:X \mid u) \mid x:X \mid s)$$

the Boolean versions of which are

$(y \setminus s)$

$$(\wedge p \mid x,y:X \mid s \wedge u) \quad \Leftrightarrow \quad (\wedge (\wedge p \mid y:X \mid u) \mid x:X \mid s)$$

i.e.,

$(y \setminus s)$

$$(\forall x,y:X)((s \wedge u) \Rightarrow p) \quad \Leftrightarrow \quad (\forall x:X)(s \Rightarrow (\forall y:X)(u \Rightarrow p))$$

and

$(y \setminus s)$

$$(\vee p \mid x,y:X \mid s \wedge u) \quad \Leftrightarrow \quad (\vee (\vee p \mid y:X \mid u) \mid x:X \mid s)$$

i.e.,

$(y \setminus s)$ $$(\exists x,y:X)(s \wedge u \wedge p) \quad \Leftrightarrow \quad (\exists x:X)(s \wedge (\exists y:X)(u \wedge p))$$

so the scope of y is changed.

The variable y is not needed in the evaluation of s, so we can deal with it (and the the partial evaluation of u and g) first and the pass then intermediate result — which would be a function — to the outer calculation, which involves s.

Notice also that if $p \Leftrightarrow$ True, then we have the rule

$(y \setminus s)$ $$(\exists x,y:X)(s \wedge u) \quad \Leftrightarrow \quad (\exists x:X)(s \wedge (\exists y:X)(u))$$

which emphasises the change even more clearly, and this also works when x and y are not of the same type.

Carrying on this idea, we can sometimes break a calculation into two parts, each dealing with one variable.

(6) Interchange of dummy variables
If $(y \setminus r)$ and $(x \setminus s)$,
then

$$(\circledast (\circledast g(x,y) \mid y{:}X \mid s(y)) \ \mid x{:}X \mid r(x)) \quad \Leftrightarrow \quad (\circledast (\circledast g(x,y) \mid x{:}X \mid r(x)) \ \mid y{:}X \mid s(y))$$

i.e.,

$$(\circledast \ (\circledast g \mid y{:}X \mid s) \ \mid x{:}X \mid r) \quad \Leftrightarrow \quad (\circledast \ (\circledast g \mid x{:}X \mid r) \ \mid y{:}X \mid s).$$

The logic versions are

$(y \setminus r)$, $(x \setminus s)$

$$(\wedge (\wedge p \mid y{:}X \mid s) \ \mid x{:}X \mid r) \quad \Leftrightarrow \quad (\wedge (\wedge p \mid x{:}X \mid r) \ \mid y{:}X \mid s)$$

i.e.,

$$(\forall x{:}X)(r \Rightarrow (\forall y{:}X)(s \Rightarrow p)) \quad \Leftrightarrow \quad (\forall y{:}X)(s \Rightarrow (\forall x{:}X)(r \Rightarrow p))$$

and

$(y \setminus r)$, $(x \setminus s)$

$$(\vee (\vee p \mid y{:}X \mid s) \ \mid x{:}X \mid r) \quad \Leftrightarrow \quad (\vee (\vee p \mid x{:}X \mid r) \ \mid y{:}X \mid s)$$

i.e.,

$$(\exists x{:}X)(r \wedge (\exists y{:}X)(s \wedge p)) \quad \Leftrightarrow \quad (\exists y{:}X)(s \wedge (\exists x{:}X)(r \wedge p))$$

which again gives us a simpler form

$(y \setminus r)$, $(x \setminus s)$

$$(\exists x{:}X)(r \wedge (\exists y{:}X)(s)) \quad \Leftrightarrow \quad (\exists y{:}X)(s \wedge (\exists x{:}X)(r))$$

(7) Re-naming
This serves only to emphasise the independence and arbitrary nature of appropriately named bound variables.

$(y \setminus f(x),\ y \setminus s(x))$, $(x \setminus f(y),\ x \setminus s(y))$

$$(\circledast f(x) \mid x{:}X \mid s(x)) \quad \Leftrightarrow \quad (\circledast f(y) \mid y{:}X \mid s(y))$$

The logic versions are

$(y \setminus p(x),\ y \setminus s(x))$, $(x \setminus p(y),\ x \setminus s(y))$

$$(\wedge p(x) \mid x{:}X \mid s(x)) \quad \Leftrightarrow \quad (\wedge p(y) \mid y{:}X \mid s(y))$$

i.e.,

$$(\forall x{:}X)(s(x) \Rightarrow p(x)) \quad \Leftrightarrow \quad (\forall x{:}X)(s(x) \Rightarrow p(x))$$

and

$(y \setminus p(x),\ y \setminus s(x))$, $(x \setminus p(y),\ x \setminus s(y))$

$$(\vee p(x) \mid x{:}X \mid s(x)) \quad \Leftrightarrow \quad (\vee p(y) \mid y{:}X \mid s(y))$$

i.e.,

$$(\exists x{:}X)(s(x) \wedge p(x)) \quad ◀▶ \quad (\exists y{:}X)(s(y) \wedge p(y))$$

and, of course,

$$(y \setminus p(x)),\ (x \setminus p(y)) \qquad (\exists x{:}X)(p(x)) \quad ◀▶ \quad (\exists y{:}X)(p(y))$$

5.4.2 Special Rules for Logical Quantifiers

Quantifiers are not just $\wedge$ and $\vee$ (i.e., $\forall$ and $\exists$) but + and * and so on. Of course, $\wedge$ and $\vee$ are special operators that have properties over and above general quantifiers. Consequently, they also satisfy other rules, three of which we give below. Others can be derived by further algebraic manipulation.

Distributivity

Following immediately from the mutual distributivity of $\wedge$ over $\vee$ and vice versa, we have

$$(x \setminus p) \qquad p \vee (\ \wedge q \mid x{:}X \mid r) \quad ◀▶ \quad (\wedge\ (p \vee q) \mid x{:}X \mid r)$$

or

$$(x \setminus p) \quad p \vee (\forall x{:}X)(r(x) \Rightarrow q(x)) \quad ◀▶ \quad (\forall x{:}X)(r(x) \Rightarrow (p \vee q(x)))$$

$$(x \setminus p) \qquad p \wedge (\ \vee q \mid x{:}X \mid r) \quad ◀▶ \quad (\vee\ (p \wedge q) \mid x{:}X \mid r\ )$$

or

$$(x \setminus p) \quad p \wedge (\exists x{:}X)(r(x) \wedge q(x)) \quad ◀▶ \quad (\exists x{:}X)(p \wedge r(x) \wedge q(x))$$

With r ◀▶ True, we have the expected forms

$$(x \setminus p) \qquad p \vee (\forall x{:}X)(q(x)) \quad ◀▶ \quad (\forall x{:}X)(p \vee q(x))$$

and

$$(x \setminus p) \qquad p \wedge (\exists x{:}X)(q(x)) \quad ◀▶ \quad (\exists x{:}X)(p \wedge q(x))$$

which are more scope-change rules.

De Morgan's Laws

Straightforward generalisation of the laws for manipulating simple Boolean expressions gives

$$\neg (\; \vee p \mid x{:}X \mid r) \quad \blacklozenge \quad (\wedge \neg p \mid x{:}X \mid r)$$

or

$$\neg (\exists x{:}X)(\; p \wedge \; r) \quad \blacklozenge \quad (\forall x{:}X)(r \Rightarrow \neg p)$$
$$\blacklozenge \quad (\forall x{:}X)(\neg r \Rightarrow p)$$

and with $r \blacklozenge$ True this gives

$$\neg (\exists x{:}X)(\; p) \quad \blacklozenge \quad (\forall x{:}X)(\neg p)$$

Finally, we have monotonicity.

Monotonicity

This is not an equivalence rule but is based on implication; hence there is a potential loss of information and the rule is not reversible.

If $(\wedge \; (q \Rightarrow \; p) \mid x{:}X \mid r)$, i.e., if $(\forall x{:}X)(r \Rightarrow (q \Rightarrow p))$,
then

$$(\wedge q \mid x{:}X \mid r) \Rightarrow (\wedge p \mid x{:}X \mid r)$$

or

$$(\forall x{:}X)(r \Rightarrow q) \Rightarrow (\forall x{:}X)(r \Rightarrow p)$$

Similarly, if $(\wedge \; (q \Rightarrow p) \mid \mid r)$,
then

$$(\vee q \mid x{:}X \mid r) \Rightarrow (\vee p \mid x{:}X \mid r)$$

or

$$(\exists x{:}X)(r \wedge q) \Rightarrow (\exists x{:}X)(r \wedge p)$$

These might also be expressed as

$(\forall x{:}X)(r \Rightarrow (q \Rightarrow p))$

$$(\forall x{:}X)(r \Rightarrow q) \Rightarrow (\forall x{:}X)(r \Rightarrow p) \quad \blacklozenge \quad \text{True},$$

$(\forall x{:}X)(r \Rightarrow (q \Rightarrow p))$

$$(\exists x{:}X)(r \wedge q) \Rightarrow (\exists x{:}X)(r \wedge p) \quad \blacklozenge \quad \text{True}$$

and

$$(\forall x{:}X)(r \Rightarrow (q \Rightarrow p)) \;\Rightarrow\; (\; (\forall x{:}X)(r \Rightarrow q) \Rightarrow (\forall x{:}X)(r \Rightarrow p) \;)$$

$$(\forall x{:}X)(r \Rightarrow (q \Rightarrow p)) \;\Rightarrow\; (\; (\exists x{:}X)(r \wedge q) \Rightarrow (\exists x{:}X)(r \wedge p) \;)$$

With rules such as these, we can (attempt to) transform specifications into forms more susceptible to divide and conquer strategies. Having said this, the rules which allow changes of name and changes of scope are the most useful.

Summary This very long list of rules for manipulating quantified forms, together with the techniques for handling inductively defined functions (in Chapter 3), give us a large armoury of transformations which lead to mechanistic ways of generating correct implementations of these functions. Of course, in this introductory text, we are not in a position to utilise them all. Hence we have (the beginnings of) a catalogue of construction rules. To put these to full use, we need the facility to carry out the underlying mathematical manipulations, checking for applicability and then correctly making appropriate substitutions (either manually or mechanically). Apart from presenting these rules, the contribution made here (and using the planned web-based supplement) is simply to give more elementary examples and detailed working so that the reader will more fully appreciate the mathematical underpinnings of the principles.

Exercises

5.1 Given that $a \vee b \Leftrightarrow \text{True}$, show that

$$(\ \wedge p\ ||\ s\ ) \Leftrightarrow (\ \wedge p\ ||\ s \wedge a\ )\ \wedge\ (\ \wedge p\ ||\ s \wedge b\ )$$

Chapter 6

Refinement and Re-use

Transformations, by definition, are reversible. Working purely with transformations is therefore essentially about re-arranging information, and without some particular strategies (such as those given in Chapter 3) we run the risk of going round in circles and wasting much effort getting precisely nowhere. Even when our initial specification is deterministic (and hence specifies a single function rather than a *collection* of functions, any one of which would be acceptable in the eyes of the specifier), we may well wish to introduce intermediate non-determinism within the process of deriving a correct implementation of a specified function. This is in line with the software engineering maxim that decisions should be delayed for as long as possible. We have already met a common instance of this in the application of structural splitting to the processing of lists; instead of deciding exactly how a list should be split, we can simply say that L should be split into, say L_1 and L_2, so that $L_1 {}^\frown L_2 \blacktriangleleft\!\!\blacktriangleright L$. For non-trivial lists, there are many ways that this can be done — and therefore we have ***non-determinism***, which must eventually be resolved. Subsequent processing of L_1 and L_2 will generally lose details of these lists, and consequently any attempt to retrieve L and then decompose it in a different way may be impossible. In this small, but very important, chapter we give the essential elements of the theory of Operational Refinement (or Functional Refinement) based on the notion of the progressive reduction of non-determinism. We start with the basic formalisation in Section 6.1.

In Section 6.2, we include a brief digression on the re-use of existing specification/implementation pairs (which might be available from a library of software components that are known to be 'correct').

A second kind of refinement, data refinement, is discussed in Chapter 8.

A closely related issue, discussed in Chapter 10, is the way in which the adjustment of data types can provide a possible way round some of the failures of 'divide and conquer' tactics.

6.1 Operational Refinement

We seek to construct a finite sequence of consistent[1] relations, each of which is 'more deterministic' than its predecessor; the first of these is the given specification, and the last one is essentially an "executable" program scheme. Each of these relations can be regarded as a specification (it *is* a specification of the next relation in the sequence), and hence we could represent the sequence by

$$S_0, S_1, S_2, \dots, S_n$$

for some *finite n*.

However, so as not to cause confusion by apparently changing specifications (i.e., changing the problem) as we move through a synthesis sequence, we shall call the intermediate relations "designs" and restrict usage of the name "specification" to the initial formulation of the problem, either that which is given or which we generate as a sub-problem as the synthesis proceeds.

$$\text{spec-}f = D_0, D_1, D_2, \dots, D_n = f$$

where spec-f is the initial specification and f is (the graph of)[2] an implementation; f is an explicit representation of *one* of the functions specified by spec-f.

6.1.1 On Correctness

Of course. we cannot just have *any* sequence of designs; they must 'link' together in the desired way. Each needs to be 'correct' with respect to earlier ones in the progression. The purpose of this sub-section is to show how this is guaranteed, but first we must clarify exactly what is meant by the correctness of an implementation (with respect to a given specification).

The *idea* is fairly simple: any valid data value should give an acceptable answer. Put more formally, if we are given the specification spec-f:$X \to Y \triangleq$ [pre, post] and an implementation f, then

$$(\forall x{:}X)\ [\text{ if pre}(x) \text{ then post}(x, f(x)) \text{ fi }]$$

i.e.,

$$(\forall x{:}X)\ [\text{ pre}(x) \Rrightarrow^{3} \text{post}(x, f(x))\ ]$$

— "for any ... valid data (x) ... $f(x)$ is acceptable".

---

[1] At the very least, these relations should have the same domain. Read on.

[2] As discussed in Chapter 1, we shall blur the distinction between a function and its graph. Here, the last relation in the sequence is that which includes the pairs $\langle x, f(x)\rangle$ for all x where pre-$f(x)$ = True. The relation is of type $\mathcal{P}(X \times Y)$, whereas the function f is of type $X \to Y$; its *graph* is of type $\mathcal{P}(X \times Y)$.

[3] We need this version of implication because for some $x{:}X \mid \neg\,\text{pre}(x)$ the expression for $f(x)$ may be illegal.

The difficulty here is dealing with the universal quantifier ($\forall$) — just as it is in testing. Instead of trying to get an 'answer' and then checking for its correctness, we seek to *derive* an answer through a sequence of intermediate designs, each of which fits with its predecessor. First we consider a typical intermediate step.

Any design derived from spec-f is of the form

$:X \rightarrow Y$
pre-$f(a) \triangleq$ ...
post-$f(a,b) \triangleq$ ...

but there may be numerous designs.

Clearly, we might have problems with the naming of designs, but we realy need to use names only when discussing the theory. Here names are invented purely for local convenience. In more global terms, D_0 is spec-f and D_n is f for some suitable name f. Consider two specific designs:

$D1{:}X \rightarrow Y$
pre1$(a) \triangleq$ ...
post1$(a,b) \triangleq$ ...

and

$D2{:}X \rightarrow Y$
pre2$(a) \triangleq$ ...
post2$(a,b) \triangleq$ ... — we use simpler names.

$D1$ and $D2$ define relations of type $\mathbb{P}(X \times Y)$, where X is the type of the input values and Y is the type of the outputs. As the transfinement sequence is constructed (so that a transformation or refinement links each of the designs in the D_0 ,..., D_n sequence), we wish to ensure that, at each stage, we can still accept (and process) all the data acceptable at the previous step. We can express this in various ways:

"if we can process x by $D1$ then we can process x by $D2$"

or

$\{\ x{:}X \mid \text{pre1}(x)\ \} \subseteq \{\ x{:}X \mid \text{pre2}(x)\ \}$

or

$\mathcal{D}D1 \subseteq \mathcal{D}D2$ comparing domains.

Pictorially, we can represent this requirement as shown in Figure 6.1.

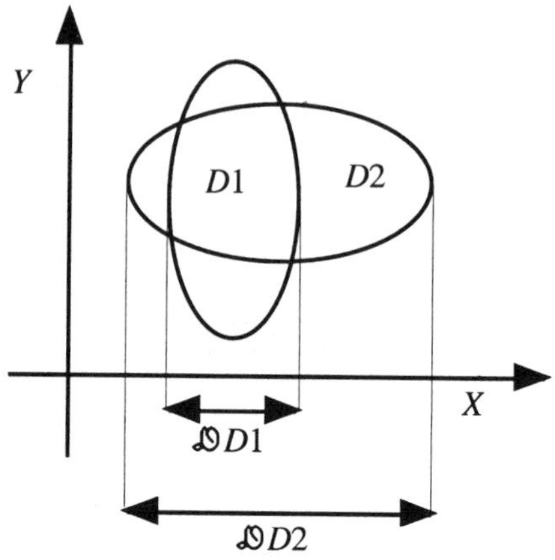

Figure 6.1

But $D1$ also imposes a bound on acceptable $\langle x,y \rangle$ pairs associated with the calculation specified (by $D1$). Clearly, we cannot, now or later, permit extra $\langle x,y \rangle$ pairs to become 'legal' without violating post1. To guarantee this, we demand that for any $x \in \mathcal{D}D1$, a 'result' allowed by $D2$ must have previously been allowed by $D1$. Again this requirement can also be represented in several ways, starting with Figure 6.2.

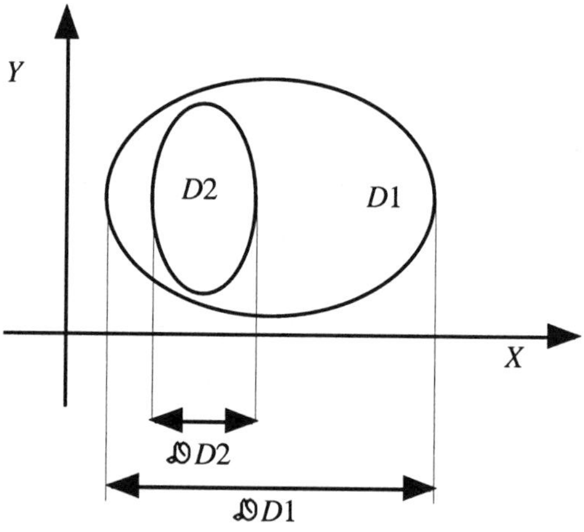

Figure 6.2

Alternatively, we may write

$$D2 \subseteq D1$$

or

$$\{ \langle x,y \rangle : X \times Y \mid \mathrm{pre2}(x) \wedge \mathrm{post2}(x,y) \} \subseteq \{ \langle x,y \rangle : X \times Y \mid \mathrm{pre1}(x) \wedge \mathrm{post1}(x,y) \}$$

from which it follows that

$$\{ x{:}X \mid \mathrm{pre2}(x) \} \subseteq \{ x{:}X \mid \mathrm{pre1}(x) \}$$

i.e.,

$$\mathcal{D}D2 \subseteq \mathcal{D}D1$$

so

$$\mathcal{D}D1 = \mathcal{D}D2$$

Hence

$$(\forall x{:}X)(\ \mathrm{pre1}(x) = \mathrm{pre2}(x))\ ;$$

that is,

$$\mathrm{pre1} = \mathrm{pre2}.$$

Putting these requirements together, we therefore get the situation in Figure 6.3.

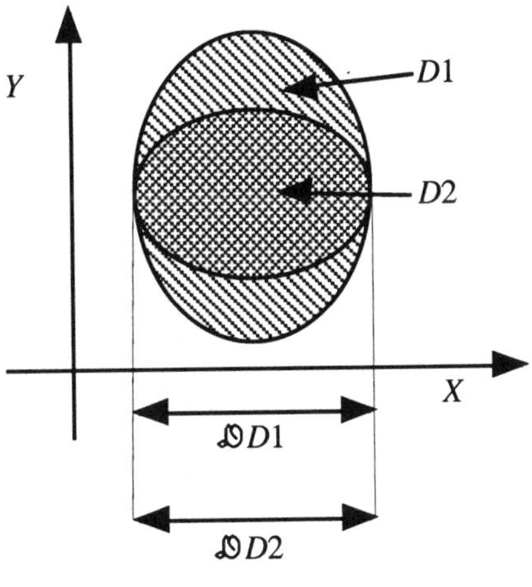

Figure 6.3

We say that design $D2$ is ***consistent*** with the design $D1$ (or, put another way, $D2$ is a ***design refinement*** of $D1$), written $D1 \blacktriangleright D2$ if $\mathrm{pre1} = \mathrm{pre2}$ and, whenever $\mathrm{pre1}(x)$ is True, $\mathrm{post2}(x,y) \Rightarrow \mathrm{post1}(x,y)$; i.e., the set of valid data is the same, and any result delivered by $D2$ is also acceptable to $D1$.

Summarising, all the old data still works and there are no new results.

We say that $D1$ ***refines***, or is refined, to $D2$, and since the pre-conditions are maintained (this condition can be varied when we seek to "re-use" derivations, as inSection 6.2) we also use the "▶" symbol to indicate the relationship between the associated post conditions, namely post1 ▶ post2.

Technically, if $D1{:}X \times Y \triangleq$ [pre, post1] and $D2{:}X \times Y \triangleq$ [pre, post2] and

$$D1 \blacktriangleright D2$$

then we allow ourselves to write

$$\text{post1} \blacktriangleright \text{post2}$$

and treat it as being equivalent to the sequential implication rule

$$(\text{pre}(x) \Rrightarrow (\exists y{:}Y)(\text{post2}(x,y))) \qquad (\forall z{:}Y)(\ \text{post2}(x,z) \Rrightarrow \text{post1}(x,z)\ )$$

The condition required for the application of this rule, namely

$$(\ \text{pre}(x) \Rrightarrow (\exists y{:}Y)(\text{post2}(x,y))\ ),$$

is rather complex, and we really ought to say more about it. It says that the pre-condition for $D1$ is satisfied and that the pair of predicates pre and post2 together form a valid specification. The 'rule' then says that $D2$ is consistent with $D1$. We need all this complication to ensure that we retain not only consistency with $D1$ but keep all the required data values. Without the rule condition, we could use the constant predicate 'False' for post2; this would be consistent but would give us no answers whatsoever. In practice, we shall not need to check this condition but merely ensure that the current pre-condition works for the next post-condition at each stage.

We make one final technical point about design sequences. Given the specification spec-f, an initial design, we shall attempt to find an implementation (a deterministic design), f, which is consistent with the specification, so that spec-$f \blacktriangleright f$. A design D (based on conditions pre and post) is ***deterministic*** if

$$\begin{aligned}&(\forall x{:}X)(\text{pre}(x)\\&\qquad \Rrightarrow (\exists y_1,y_2{:}Y)\\&\qquad\qquad (\text{pre1}(x) \wedge (\text{post}(x,y_1) \wedge \text{post}(x,y_2)) \Rrightarrow (y_1 = y_2)))\end{aligned}$$

So, for any valid data value x, if we (seem to) get results y_1 and y_2, then they are actually equal, so the answer is unique.

6.1.2 Some Properties of Design Refinement

Design refinement is transitive:

if $D1 \blacktriangleright D2$ and $D2 \blacktriangleright D3$ then $D1 \blacktriangleright D3$.

This follows easily from the transitivity of '=' and '$\Rrightarrow$' whence pre1 = pre3 since pre1 = pre2 and pre2 = pre3, and post3 $\Rrightarrow$[4] post1 since post3 $\Rrightarrow$ post2 and post2 $\Rrightarrow$ post1.

So if we consider the specification spec-f and an implementation I (of f) linked by a sequence of intermediate designs, then, with the obvious notation

spec-$f \blacktriangleright I$ i.e., pre-f = pre-I and post-I $\Rrightarrow$ post-f.

As I is deterministic, then for any $x{:}X$ satisfying pre-I there is a unique $y{:}Y$ such that post-$I(x,y)$. As in conventional mathematics, y is usually denoted by $f(x)$.

Putting all of this together,

$$(\forall x{:}X) \qquad \text{pre-}f(x) \Rrightarrow \text{pre-}I(x) \\ \Rrightarrow \text{post-}I(x,f(x)) \\ \Rrightarrow \text{post-}f(x,f(x))$$

and I is a correct implementation of f as specified by spec-f.

The aim of this is to refine/reduce/reify[5] spec-f to another design which is closer to being an implementation (ultimately to achieve a unique answer from each valid input).

Remember that the purpose of the pre-condition is to ensure that answers exist, and each answer, together with associated data, must satisfy the post-condition. From an operational point of view, we need to know that the pre-condition holds before considering the post-conditions. From a mathematical standpoint, the *weakest* pre-condition (*wp*) can be found from the post-condition. In practice, the required pre-condition may be more restrictive.

['$\blacktriangleright$' is also *anti-symmetric* since if $D1 \blacktriangleright D2$ and $D2 \blacktriangleright D1$ then $D1$ and $D2$ are equal, i.e. $D1 \blacktriangleleft\!\blacktriangleright D2$. So the notations correlate in a reasonable fashion.]

---

[4] Here the intent is obvious, but for completeness we give a proper definition:

given $p,q{:}X \to \mathbb{B}$, $\quad (p \Rrightarrow q) \triangleq (\forall x{:}X)(\, p(x) \Rrightarrow q(x)\,)$.

Here $\mathcal{D}$(post3) = $\mathcal{D}$(post1) so

$(\text{post3} \Rrightarrow \text{post1}) \triangleq (\forall x{:}X, y{:}Y))(x \in \mathcal{D}(\text{post3}) \wedge (\text{post3}(x,y) \Rrightarrow \text{post1}(x,y))\,)$

[5] Meaning "to make 'stone like', to fix".

Example 6.1 Consider the following two specifications:

$split$: $X^* \rightarrow X^* \times X^*$
pre-$split(L) \triangleq \#L > 1$
post-$split(L, \langle L_1, L_2 \rangle) \triangleq L = L_1 \frown L_2 \wedge L_1 \neq \langle\rangle \wedge L_2 \neq \langle\rangle$

and

$split\_1$: $X^* \rightarrow X^* \times X^*$
pre-$split\_1(L) \triangleq \#L > 1$
post-$split\_1(L, \langle L_1, L_2 \rangle) \triangleq (\exists x{:}X)(L = L_1 \frown L_2 \wedge L_1 = \langle x \rangle)$

To justify the use of *split*_1 as a refinement of *split* (so *split* ▶ *split*_1), we must check the relationship between the pre- and post-conditions.

Clearly, pre-*split* = pre-*split*_1.

Now assume that $\#L > 1$; then

post-$split\_1(L, \langle L_1, L_2 \rangle)$

$$\Rrightarrow (\exists x{:}X)(L = L_1 \frown L_2 \wedge L_1 = \langle x \rangle)$$

$$\Rrightarrow (\exists x{:}X)(L = L_1 \frown L_2 \wedge L_1 = \langle x \rangle \wedge (\#L_2 + 1) = \#L)$$

$$\Rrightarrow (\exists x{:}X)(L = L_1 \frown L_2 \wedge L_1 = \langle x \rangle \wedge (\#L_2 + 1) > 1)$$

$$\Rrightarrow (\exists x{:}X)(L = L_1 \frown L_2 \wedge L_1 = \langle x \rangle \wedge \#L_2 > 0)$$

$$\Rrightarrow (\exists x{:}X)(L = L_1 \frown L_2 \wedge \#L_1 > 0 \wedge \#L_2 > 0)$$

$$\Rrightarrow (\exists x{:}X)(L = L_1 \frown L_2 \wedge L_1 \neq \langle\rangle \wedge L_2 \neq \langle\rangle)$$

$$\Rrightarrow \text{post-}split(L, \langle L_1, L_2 \rangle)$$

Therefore, we can replace spec-*split* by spec-*split*_1 without the loss of any essential information.

❑

6.1.3 An Alternative View

Suppose we have a design, $D1$, for a function of type $X \rightarrow Y$. If $D1$ is not deterministic, and hence not the graph of an implementation, then we can seek ways of finding a design $D2$ such that $D1 \blacktriangleright D2$ and $D1 \neq D2$. Suppose also that the components of $D1$ and $D2$ are as indicated below:

$D1 : X \rightarrow Y$	and	$D2 : X \rightarrow Y$
$\text{pre}(x) \triangleq \ldots$		$\text{pre}(x) \triangleq \ldots$
$\text{post1}(x,y) \triangleq \ldots$		$\text{post2}(x,y) \triangleq \ldots$

For any value $a{:}X$ for which $\text{pre}(a) \Leftrightarrow \text{True}$, the set $\{\ y{:}Y \mid \text{post1}(a,y)\ \} \neq \emptyset$. (This is, of course, precisely the situation which the pre-condition is intended to guarantee.)

Moreover, since Dl is not deterministic, there is some value $b{:}X$ such that $\text{pre}(b) \Leftrightarrow \text{True}$ and $\#\{\ y{:}Y \mid \text{post1}(b,y)\ \} \geq 2$.

If $D2$ is to be a ***reduction*** (i.e., a *strict* refinement, one which is not reversible as would be the case if $D1 = D2$) we would require at least one value $b{:}X$ satisfying *pre* and the condition

$$\{\ y{:}Y \mid \text{post1}(b,y)\ \} \supset \{\ y{:}Y \mid \text{post2}(b,y)\ \}$$

and hence

$$\#\{\ y{:}Y \mid \text{post1}(b,y)\ \} >^{6} \#\{\ y{:}Y \mid \text{post2}(b,y)\ \}.$$

This gives us an alternative (yet equivalent) way to characterise operational refinement.

If $D1$ is (the graph of) an implementation, then, for all $x{:}X$ where $\text{pre}(x) \Leftrightarrow \text{True}$, the set $\{\ y{:}Y \mid \text{post1}(x,y)\ \}$ is a singleton.

If $D1$ is *not* an implementation but $D1 \blacktriangleright D2$ and $D2$ *is* an implementation, then, for all $x{:}X$ where $\text{pre}(x) \Leftrightarrow \text{True}$, the set $\{\ y{:}Y \mid \text{post2}(x,y)\ \}$ is a singleton and the reduction can be viewed as picking a single value, c, from the set $\{y{:}Y \mid \text{post1}(x,y)\}$ and using it to define $\text{post2}(x,c)$, and hence f.

Explicitly,

$$\text{post2}(x,c) \Leftrightarrow c = f(x).$$

In a more general situation, when $D2$ is not necessarily an implementation, design reduction/refinement may be viewed simply as deriving a non-empty set $\{\ y{:}Y \mid \text{post2}(x,y)\ \}$ by removing elements from the set $\{\ y{:}Y \mid \text{post1}(x,y)\ \}$ for one or more of the values x where $\text{pre}(x) \Leftrightarrow \text{True}$.

[6] But be careful when trying to argue about infinite sets.

This may be achieved more systematically by adding extra constraints to post1 to get post2. Algebraically, for a general x, we may define

$$\text{post2}(x,y) \triangleq \text{post1}(x,y) \wedge p(y) \qquad \text{for some } p{:}Y \to \mathbb{B},$$

provided that

$$(\forall x{:}X)(\ \text{pre}(x) \Rightarrow (\exists y{:}Y)(\ \text{post2}(x,y))\ )$$

If all else fails, find a value of x where

$\#\{\ y{:}Y \mid \text{pre}(x) \wedge \text{post1}(x,y)\ \} > 1$ and then throw away one element, but this could be a very lengthy process.

6.2 Re-using Designs

We now consider a different situation. Suppose that there exists an implementation of design $D3$ and we are invited to use this implementation as a refinement for $D1$. ($D3$ might be in a library of designs.) This would only be possible if the specifications were related in the right way. Look at the relationship indicated in Figure 6.4.

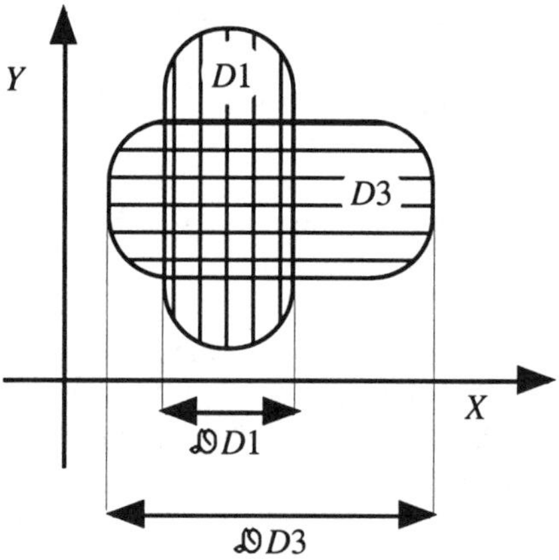

Figure 6.4.

Design $D3$ might be applicable outside the set of values for which we are to produce results in $D1$; we are only concerned with what happens *within* the domain of $D1$.

And the re-use of a design carries with it the re-use of a previously produced derivation sequence (with the appropriate 'contractions' so as to ignore input values that are now not required).

Clearly we require that $\mathcal{D}D1 \subseteq \mathcal{D}D3$
but now it may no longer be the case that

$$D3 \subseteq D1.$$

We need to intersect $D3$ with $\mathcal{D}D1$ which will then limit our consideration to relevant input values.

The modified conditions are

$$\mathcal{D}D1 \subseteq \mathcal{D}D3$$

and

$$D3 \cap (\mathcal{D}D1 \times Y) \subseteq D1$$

or, in logic,

$$(\forall x{:}X)(\mathrm{pre1}(x) \Rightarrow \mathrm{pre3}(x))$$

and

$$(\forall \langle x,y \rangle{:}X \times Y)(\mathrm{pre1}(x) \wedge (\mathrm{post3}(x,y) \Rightarrow \mathrm{post1}(x,y)))$$

Referring to Figure 6.4, we restrict $D3$ to the input values of $D1$. The resultant set (the double hatched area) must be a refinement of $D1$, i.e. a relation (sub-set) with the appropriate domain.

Example 6.2 Over $\mathcal{P}(\mathbb{Z} \times \mathbb{Z})$ so $D1,D3 \subseteq \mathbb{Z} \times \mathbb{Z}$

$$\mathrm{pre3}(x) \triangleq \mathrm{True}$$
$$\mathrm{post3}(x,y) \triangleq x^2 = y$$

and

$$\mathrm{pre1}(x) \triangleq x \geq 0$$
$$\mathrm{post1}(x,y) \triangleq x^2 = y$$

Here, the formulae for the post-conditions are the same but the domain of '$D1$' (the set for which pre1 is True) is restricted to positive integers. Hence, when programming '$D1$' we do not need to cope with negative input values.

❑

Example 6.3 Again, over $\mathcal{P}(\mathbb{Z}\times\mathbb{Z})$,

$$\text{pre3}(n) \triangleq \text{True}$$
$$\text{post3}(n,m) \triangleq \text{if } n < 15 \text{ then } m = n^2 \text{ else } m = n^3 \text{ fi}$$

and

$$\text{pre1}(n) \triangleq 1 \leq n \leq 10$$
$$\text{post1}(n,m) \triangleq m = n^2 \lor m = n$$

The predicates used here are intentionally simple so that the logical inter-relationships are very clear.

	pre1 $\Rrightarrow$ pre3	so the library routine will handle all the required data.
(pre1)	post3 $\Rrightarrow$ post1	so the results from the library routine fit our current specification

That is, the routine, program, which satisfies the specification [pre3, post3] can be used to implement [pre1, post3].

❑

We may also allow 'slight' type adjustments. For instance, in Example 3.17 we showed that in certain situations *insert* could be used to implement *merge*, despite the signatures (types) being different.

Recall the specifications

$$merge:\mathbb{Z}^*\times\mathbb{Z}^* \to \mathbb{Z}^*$$
$$\text{pre-}merge(\langle N_1,N_2\rangle) \triangleq ascending(N_1) \land ascending(N_2)$$
$$\text{post-}merge(\langle N_1,N_2\rangle,N) \triangleq ascending(N) \land \text{bag\_of}(N) = \text{bag\_of}(N_1) \uplus \text{bag\_of}(N_2)$$

and

$$insert:\mathbb{Z}\times\mathbb{Z}^* \to \mathbb{Z}^*$$
$$\text{pre-}insert(\langle x,L\rangle) \triangleq ascending(L)$$
$$\text{post-}insert(\langle x,L\rangle,N) \triangleq ascending(N) \land \text{bag\_of}(N) = \text{bag\_of}(L) \uplus \{\!\!\{x\}\!\!\}$$

Clearly, from $x:\mathbb{Z}^*$ we can construct $\langle x\rangle:\mathbb{Z}^*$ by means of a cast[7]. In general, we cannot take $L:\mathbb{Z}^*$ and derive from it one single integer. (Usually, there are many; there may be none.) However, within the design development presented in Example 3.17, we had the extra constraint on N_1 that $\#N_1 = 1$; therefore a well-defined 'extract' function ($N_1 \mapsto \text{first\_of}(N_1)$) does exist and nothing is lost by the use of

[7] See Section 1.4.10.

insert for *merge*, providing that this extra condition is met. Namely

$$insert(x, L) \blacktriangleleft\!\!\blacktriangleright merge(\langle x \rangle, L)$$

The relationship between the types underlying these two functions is very similar to the notions behind Data Refinement; about which we shall say (a little) more in Chapter 8.

Conclusion

The theory is based on two sequential implications ($\Rrightarrow$), one which preserves valid inputs and the other prevents the creation of new (out of 'spec') results. In practice, we need to ensure that we eventually reach a situation where each valid input has a *unique* output and we have (the graph of) a function rather than a more general binary relation.

We can often achieve this by imposing extra constraints (either by adding, $\wedge$ing, new Boolean terms to the post condition, or by using structural decomposition) providing that these constraints do not remove too many values and hence reduce the domain, which must remain constant.

Part C
Developments

This part is really about examples, illustrations of the application of the theory to some serious problems. Also included are sections on how the basic priciples may be extended, how they may apparently 'fail', and how these failures may be overcome.

Chapter 7
Sorting

Having introduced and illustrated the major construction techniques on some simple problems, we now turn our attention to the more substantial task of sorting. We demonstrate how a selection of different algorithms can be derived from a single specification, but our coverage is by no means exhaustive. Our major concern is the detailed application, and a certain amount of customisation[1], of the general transfinement tactics.

After a preliminary discussion of the problem (in Section 7.1), we shall present the designs in a layered fashion, first obtaining three main high-level approaches (and generating specifications of sub-problems) in Section7.2, and then develop them into more explicit designs in Section 7.3. This scheme is not new[2], although the presentation here is probably more constructive. Finally, in Section 7.4 we show how high level functions, as introduced in Chapter 5, can quickly yield a design for a sorting algorithm, albeit one over which we have little control. In Chapter 9, we return to sorting and take a look at how arrays can be used within the development of more sorting algorithms.

In places, our presentation is given in great detail. At the risk of boring the reader who well-understands the principles, this is done to emphasize points which are often missed by those who are new to formal methods.

7.1 Specification and Initial Discussion

In general, we need knowledge about the problem domain, about the data types used to model the input and output. Here we need to know about lists and integers. Notice first that the type of the input need not be *lists* of integers; if we were solving the problem 'by hand', then we would be given a bag of integers and asked to produce an appropriate list. But bags can not be read as input to programs without their elements being processed in a certain order; hence the input bag must

[1] Such customisation is common and allows us to extend our (very small) set of general tactics by using domain knowledge.

[2] Parts of this chapter (and Chapter 9) closely follow Darlington,J., "A Synthesis of Several Sorting Algorithms", Acta. Informatica (11), 1-30 (1978).

effectively be regarded as a list. Notice that in real applications we would often be required to sort lists of records but, merely to focus on the computational aspects and reduce the amount of text within expressions, we consider lists of *integers* instead of lists of *records* in which there is an integer key. The technical connection is simply that we use $x{:}\mathbb{Z}$ rather than *key* of x where $x{:}record$, and $key{:}\mathbb{Z}$. Arbitrarily we choose to sort the list in *ascending* order from left to right.

We shall presume familiarity with lists and their properties, but a compendium of relevant operations and rules is given in the appendix for completeness. Rules for integers and special rules for lists of integers are similarly included, but we draw attention to the property that any list which is not in ascending order must have an *adjacent* pair of elements which are not in the correct order[3].

Now for the problem. We first give an appropriate specification and then describe it in some detail.

$$\begin{aligned}
&Sort: \mathbb{Z}^* \to \mathbb{Z}^* \\
&\text{pre-}Sort(L) \triangleq \text{True} \\
&\text{post-}Sort(L,N) \triangleq \text{bag_of}(N) = \text{bag_of}(L) \;\wedge\; ascending(N)
\end{aligned}$$

where

$$\begin{aligned}
\text{bag_of}(\langle\rangle) &\Leftrightarrow \emptyset \\
\text{bag_of}(\langle x\rangle) &\Leftrightarrow \{\!\{x\}\!\} \\
\text{bag_of}(L_1 \frown L_2) &\Leftrightarrow \text{bag_of}(L_1) \uplus \text{bag_of}(L_2)
\end{aligned}$$

$$ascending(N) \triangleq (\forall x,y{:}\mathbb{Z})(x \text{ before } y \text{ in } N \Rightarrow x \le y)$$

and

$$x \text{ before } y \text{ in } N \triangleq (\exists N_1,N_2,N_3{:}\mathbb{Z}^*)(\, N = N_1 \frown \langle x\rangle \frown N_2 \frown \langle y\rangle \frown N_3 \,)$$

This specification tells us the properties of the desired output list relative to the given input. The specification is presented in a hierarchical fashion intended to assist in its comprehension, *not* its implementation *per se*. It need not tell us anything about how the result can be obtained.

Here the characterisation of "bag_of" is axiomatic, whereas *ascending* is defined using quantification. This is written in the classical form, but we shall re-express this in some alternative forms that are more amenable to the manipulations required for certain design strategies.

[3] If no adjacent pairs are out of order, then, by the transitivity of '≤', the entire list is in ascending order.

Let's read through the post-condition:

$$\text{post-}sort(L,N) \triangleq \text{bag\_of}(N) = \text{bag\_of}(L) \ \wedge \ ascending(N)$$

The "bag_of" function takes a list and delivers the multi-set, the bag, of the elements contained in the list, so the first part of the post-condition simply says that the lists L and N have exactly the same elements, including duplicates where appropriate. Additionally, the list N must be in ascending order. To complete the specification, we (or someone else) must define what these sub-parts mean.

Our axiomatic definition of "bag_of" is

$$\text{bag\_of}(\langle\rangle) \Leftrightarrow \emptyset$$
— the empty list contains no elements; Ø is the empty bag,

$$\text{bag\_of}(\langle x\rangle) \Leftrightarrow \{\!\!\{x\}\!\!\}$$
— the singleton list yields the singleton bag,

$$\text{bag\_of}(L_1 \frown L_2) \Leftrightarrow \text{bag\_of}(L_1) \uplus \text{bag\_of}(L_2)$$
— list concatenation, $\frown$, translates into bag union, $\uplus$. In bag unions, duplicates are preserved.

Now for *ascending*,

$$ascending(N) \triangleq (\forall x,y{:}\mathbb{Z})(x \text{ before } y \text{ in } N \Rightarrow x \le y)$$

This says that N is *ascending* if, for all integers x and y, if x occurs before y in N, then

$$x \le y$$

and

$$x \text{ before } y \text{ in } N \triangleq (\exists N_1,N_2,N_3{:}\mathbb{Z}^*)(\ N = N_1 \frown \langle x\rangle \frown N_2 \frown \langle y\rangle \frown N_3\ )$$

defines exactly what "x before y in N" means, namely that we can find lists N_1,N_2 and N_3 which when composed with x and y as indicated make up N.

Before going on, let us consider the solvability of the sorting problem. Is it really possible to produce N as a sorted version of an arbitrary finite list L?

We re-arrange the post-condition. First we can get rid of the "before...in..." construction and use a more general conditional quantification syntax from Chapter 5.

So

$$ascending(N) \triangleq (\forall x,y:\mathbb{Z})(x \text{ before } y \text{ in } N \Rightarrow x \leq y)$$

and

$$x \text{ before } y \text{ in } N \triangleq (\exists N_1,N_2,N_3:\mathbb{Z}^*)(\, N = N_1 \frown \langle x \rangle \frown N_2 \frown \langle y \rangle \frown N_3 \,)$$

together become

$$ascending(N) \;◆\; (\, \wedge (x \leq y) \mid x,y:\mathbb{Z}, N_1,N_2,N_3:\mathbb{Z}^* \mid N = N_1 \frown \langle x \rangle \frown N_2 \frown \langle y \rangle \frown N_3 \,)$$

We *and* together, 'conjoin', all the values in the bag derived from the term "$x \leq y$" which are obtained from the set of all 5-tuples $\langle x,y,N_1,N_2,N_3 \rangle$ which satisfy the condition

$$N = N_1 \frown \langle x \rangle \frown N_2 \frown \langle y \rangle \frown N_3.$$

Remember that this set of elements is the *base* of the quantification.

If any elements are 'out of order' then there will be at least one $\langle x,y \rangle$ pair that will cause $x \leq y$ to evaluate to False and hence the *and* (the $\wedge$, the $\forall$) will give False as expected. Otherwise we get True.

[All terminating calculations are completed in a finite number of stages, and all pieces of valid data are also finite. Therefore, we must also either replace infinite types by finite approximations or take other steps to guarantee that the base is finite. In this problem, the input list L is finite so there are no problems due to infinite collections of data.]

Other ways of expressing the *ascending* condition relate to counting the number of elements which are 'out of place'. Such "out of orderness" measures are necessary when applying certain problem-solving strategies, but here we are only concerned with investigating whether the problem is solvable; not in solving it.

[Taking the trouble to investigate a problem and check details is one of the aspects of formal methods that programmers find frustrating. Perhaps this is exacerbated by pressures to produce code quickly, but skipping such details may cause errors. Paying attention to such details is intrinsic to formal methods; without such attention, we cannot guarantee the correctness of the software produced.]

First notice that by using de Morgan's law we can make the following change:

$$(\, \wedge (x \leq y) \mid x,y:\mathbb{Z}, N_1,N_2,N_3:\mathbb{Z}^* \mid N = N_1 \frown \langle x \rangle \frown N_2 \frown \langle y \rangle \frown N_3 \,)$$

◆

$$\neg(\, \vee \; \neg(x \leq y) \mid x,y:\mathbb{Z}, N_1,N_2,N_3:\mathbb{Z}^* \mid N = N_1 \frown \langle x \rangle \frown N_2 \frown \langle y \rangle \frown N_3 \,)$$

That is, it is not the case that there are any $\langle x,y \rangle$ pairs, where x comes before y in N and $x \leq y$ doesn't hold

◆

$$\neg(\ \vee\ \ (x > y)\ \mid\ x,y{:}\mathbb{Z},N_1,N_2,N_3{:}\mathbb{Z}^*\ \mid\ N = N_1 \frown \langle x \rangle \frown N_2 \frown \langle y \rangle \frown N_3\ )$$

Alternatively, instead of simply saying that there are none of these pairs, we could count them and then require that the count be zero.

◆

$$(\ +1 \mid x,y{:}\mathbb{Z},N_1,N_2,N_3{:}\mathbb{Z}^* \mid N = N_1 \frown \langle x \rangle \frown N_2 \frown \langle y \rangle \frown N_3\ \wedge\ (x > y)\ )\ =\ 0$$

In this quantification the "+1" says that we add together all the "1s" we get every time the condition is satisfied. Notice that this not only gives the same answer as before but the expression

$$(\ +1 \mid x,y{:}\mathbb{Z},N_1,N_2,N_3{:}\mathbb{Z}^* \mid N = N_1 \frown \langle x \rangle \frown N_2 \frown \langle y \rangle \frown N_3\ \wedge\ (x > y)\ )$$

gives greater integer values when the list N is more disordered.

For example, for the list $\langle 1,2,5,4,3 \rangle$ we get the value 3, whereas the list $\langle 1,2,5,3,4 \rangle$ gives 2. Moreover, if the list is not ordered and we swap one of its offending (i.e., out of order) pairs, then this quantity is reduced, thus demonstrating that within a finite number of exchanges the list will be sorted and hence the given list, indeed any finite integer list, *can* be sorted. But this claim is not obvious, and even if it were, we would still need to justify it.

Suppose that the list was not in ascending order, that $x > y$ with x before y and that z is some other element in the list. There are three possible positions for z relative to x and y.

(a) ...... z...... x..... .... y..... ....

(b) .... x..... z...... y..... ....

(c) .... x..... .... y..... z...... ....

Consider what happens when we attempt to improve the ordering by exchanging the x and y values in the positions indicated. There are five possible relationships between z and (x and y) in each of the three scenarios above. Scenario (c) is clearly a reflection of (a), so we need only consider (a) and (b). Furthermore, since the relative positions (such as z before x and z before y) do not change in (a) then neither do the contributions (to the "out of order'ness" measure) due to z, but swapping x and y *does* reduce the measure.

Similarly, in the (b) scenario, all the other items in the list stay in place, so we need only consider the contribution to the calculation of

$$(+1 \mid x,y{:}\mathbb{Z}, N_1,N_2,N_3{:}\mathbb{Z}^* \mid N = N_1 \frown \langle x \rangle \frown N_2 \frown \langle y \rangle \frown N_3 \ \wedge \ (x > y) \ )$$

made by a typical element z between x and y.

First we evaluate the z contribution in the unchanged (b) list:

(b) .... x..... z..... y..... ....

When $z < y$ (and thus $z < x$) the contribution is 1
when $z = y$ (and thus $z < x$) the contribution is 1
when $y < z < x$ the contribution is 2
when $z = x$ (and thus $y < z$) the contribution is 1
when $x < z$ (and thus $y < z$) the contribution is 1

Now perform the swap to get:

(b') .... y..... z..... x..... ....

Then,
when $z < y$ (and thus $z < x$) the contribution is 1
when $z = y$ (and thus $z < x$) the contribution is 0
when $y < z < x$ the contribution is 0
when $z = x$ (and thus $y < z$) the contribution is 0
when $x < z$ (and thus $y < z$) the contribution is 1

So the z contribution either remains constant or is reduced. Summing the contributions over possible values and positions of z, the measure therefore, at worst, does not increase. But in the measure, the x—y swap must reduce the sum by 1 so overall there *is* a reduction.

This property could be used as the basis for constructing a sorting algorithm, and later it will be used as such, but at the moment all we are interested only in is showing that the problem *does* have a solution.

Such measures are not just interesting, they are crucial. As part of the synthesis procedure, we shall have cause to introduce recursion, and when this is done we need to ensure that we use a well-ordering, a strict reduction in some characteristic of the problem that uses the positive integers ($\mathbb{P}$). This *guarantees* convergence of recursion. Moreover, if the recursion is transformed into iteration, then that iteration will terminate, *by construction*. This means that, later in the development

development process, there is no need to find loop invariants (and variants) which *are* required in retrospective verification proofs.

7.2. Initial Designs

Our constructive approach to programming now requires that we take the specification and, working within the rules which govern the relevant data types, apply appropriate problem-solving strategies to *reorganise* and *particularise* the specification into a recursive design for an executable program.

Sorting is a fairly simple problem to specify, but it can be implemented in a myriad of different ways (even back in 1973, Knuth[4] filled almost 400 pages on the subject). In this section, we give the initial phases of derivations leading to three major types of sorting algorithms. As will become clear later, concepts introduced within the initial stages of the designs cross over when the lower-level details are considered in Section 7.3 and in Chapter 9.

7.2.1 Problem Reduction

We have just seen that one way of characterising whether the list L is in ascending order is to evaluate the test:

$$(+1 \mid x,y{:}\mathbb{Z}, N_1,N_2,N_3{:}\mathbb{Z}^* \mid N = N_1 \frown \langle x \rangle \frown N_2 \frown \langle y \rangle \frown N_3 \ \wedge\ (x > y)) = 0$$

We already know that, in any unsorted list, swapping an 'out of order' pair of numbers, which need not be adjacent, reduces the left-hand expression in this test.

This leads us immediately to the following design, which uses domain splitting (with the test 'is L ascending') and *any* reduction based on a suitable swapping function. To make the description easier, we define

$$M(N) \triangleq (+1 \mid x,y{:}\mathbb{Z}, N_1,N_2,N_3{:}\mathbb{Z}^* \mid N = N_1 \frown \langle x \rangle \frown N_2 \frown \langle y \rangle \frown N_3 \ \wedge\ (x > y)).$$

So

post-*sort*(L,N)

◆ — using the specification

bag_of(N) = bag_of(L) $\wedge$ *ascending*(N)

[4] Knuth,D.E., The Art of Computer Programming, Vol 3 "Sorting and Searching", Addison-Wesley (1973).

▶

if $ascending(L)$
  then $N = L$
  else $N = sort(improve(L))$
fi

where:
  $improve: \mathbb{Z}^* \rightarrow \mathbb{Z}^*$
  pre-$improve(L) \triangleq \neg\ ascending(L)$
  post-$improve(L,P) \triangleq$ bag_of(P) = bag_of$(L) \wedge M(P) < M(L)$

[Notice that this is *not* a "divide and conquer" strategy so there is no splitting function. This concept of *improv*ing a value so that it becomes closer (in an appropriate sense) to one on which the calculation is trivial is very important. It will be used frequently in what follows, but the measures used to characterise the size of the problem will be specialised to suit the problem under consideration and will often relate only to part of the data.]

We seem merely to be passing the buck. All the real work in this algorithm design is in the *improve* function. This is indeed true, but the shape of this design is fundamental. As will be seen more clearly when we express the design in functional form, it is tail-recursive — on one branch of the conditional structure, the *last* function to be performed is the same function as we are defining (and it occurs *only* there). In this situation, we can immediately replace the recursion by iteration. Variants of this situation effectively explain how all common forms of iteration are related to recursion. Now we return to the current synthesis.

◀▶

[N =] if $ascending(L)$
  then L
  else $sort(improve(L))$
fi

where:
  $improve: \mathbb{Z}^* \rightarrow \mathbb{Z}^*$
  pre-$improve(L) \triangleq \neg\ ascending(L)$
  post-$improve(L,P) \triangleq$ bag_of(P) = bag_of$(L) \wedge M(P) < M(L)$

▶▶ from relational to functional form

[N =] $sort(L)$ where:
  $sort(L) \triangleq$ if $ascending(L)$
    then L
    else $sort(improve(L))$
  fi;
  $improve(L) \triangleq \ldots$

⯈⯈ from functional to procedural form

$$
\begin{array}{l}
\mathit{improve}(L) \triangleq \ldots ; \\
\mathit{sort}(L) \triangleq [\mathit{result} \leftarrow] \;\; \text{if } \mathit{ascending}(L) \\
\qquad\qquad\qquad\qquad\qquad \text{then } L \\
\qquad\qquad\qquad\qquad\qquad \text{else } \mathit{sort}(\mathit{improve}(L)) \\
\qquad\qquad\qquad\qquad\quad \text{fi}; \\
N \leftarrow \mathit{sort}(L)
\end{array}
$$

◆ apply the (tail-) recursion removal rule

$$
\begin{array}{l}
\mathit{improve}(L) \triangleq \ldots ; \\
\mathit{sort}(L) \triangleq \;\; (\text{var } V\text{: } \mathbb{Z}^*; \\
\qquad\qquad\qquad V \leftarrow L; \\
\qquad\qquad\qquad \text{while } \neg\, \mathit{ascending}(V) \\
\qquad\qquad\qquad\qquad \text{do } V \leftarrow \mathit{improve}(V) \\
\qquad\qquad\qquad\qquad \text{od}; \\
\qquad\qquad\qquad \mathit{result} \leftarrow V); \\
N \leftarrow \mathit{sort}(L)
\end{array}
$$

Thus we have a design for an iterative procedural program that is *automatically* correct relative to the given specification. Providing that any subsequent transfinements are performed correctly, the resultant complete program will also be correct and can be optimised by use of other (procedural programming) transformations if efficiency needs to be improved.

So now we have an outline (the outer level) of a program which involves undeveloped segments and we have derived specifications of the remaining parts. We shall look at how the design might be completed once we have investigated other possible initial design steps.

7.2.2 Structural Splitting

Now for a less direct approach. *Arbitrarily* split the list into two parts, sort each separately, and then try to construct the overall answer from the answers to the two parts. This is a classical "divide and conquer" approach using an 'ignorant' split, which does not consider the values present in the list.

The general schema can be depicted by the *data-flow* diagram in Figure 7.1:

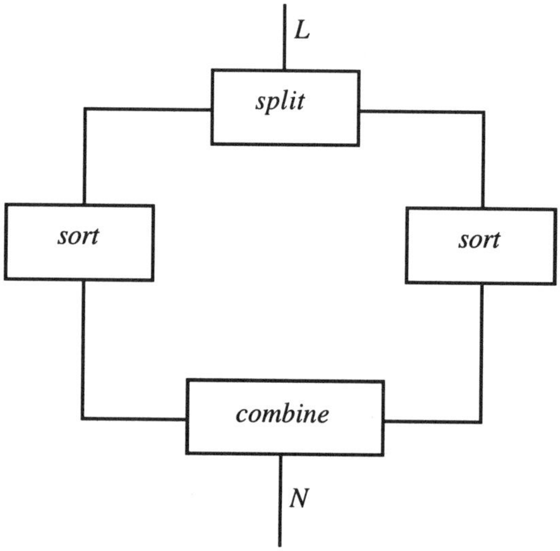

Figure 7.1

The list L is finite (i.e., $\#L$, the length of L, is a finite positive integer). We shall effectively assume that we can sort any list which is 'smaller' than the given one. (This is really hiding a proof/construction by induction.) Splitting L into L_1 and L_2 (so L ◀▶ $L_1 \frown L_2$) gives us $\#L$ ◀▶ $\#L_1 + \#L_2$. In order to make progress, and guarantee convergence/termination of our construction, we need some strictly reducing $\mathbb{P}$-valued measure of the size / complexity / magnitude of the problem. Here we do not use M as in the previous section but the length of the lists. So we must insist that $\#L_1 < \#L$ and $\#L_2 < \#L$; and this in turn means that $\#L_1 \geq 1$, $\#L_2 \geq 1$, and hence $\#L \geq 2$.

Note that if $\#L < 2$, then *ascending*(L) must be True. The set

$$\{\langle x,y,L_3,L_4,L_5\rangle : \mathbb{Z}\times\mathbb{Z}\times\mathbb{Z}^*\times\mathbb{Z}^*\times\mathbb{Z}^* \mid L = L_3 \frown \langle x\rangle \frown L_4 \frown \langle y\rangle \frown L_5\}$$

is clearly empty and hence we have to "and"(to " $\wedge$ ") together zero terms and since "True" is the identity element associated with the " $\wedge$ " operation, *ascending*(L) is True. Thus, if $\#L < 2$ we can show that using L for N is acceptable.

We do this by substituting L for N using $L \Leftrightarrow N$ in the post-$sort(L,N)$ and showing that it evaluates to True.

$$\begin{aligned} \text{post-}sort(L,N) &\Leftrightarrow \text{post-}sort(L,L) \\ &\Leftrightarrow \text{bag\_of}(L) = \text{bag\_of}(L) \;\wedge\; ascending(L) \\ &\Leftrightarrow \text{True} \wedge \text{True} \\ &\Leftrightarrow \text{True} \end{aligned}$$

So, using the predicate ($\#L < 2$) to split the problem domain, a solution starts to emerge which is of the form

$$\text{post-}sort(L,N) \Leftrightarrow \text{if } \#L < 2 \text{ then } N = L \text{ else } \ldots \text{ fi}$$

In the $\#L \geq 2$ case, we now introduce non-empty lists L_1 and L_2 and append the extra condition $L = L_1 {}^\frown L_2$ to the 'else' part of the current design. This does nothing adverse since these new lists are internal to the design. Also notice that since we have a conjunction of conditions, they must all be True and hence we can (later) use one to simplify the others by rationalisation.

So, given L where $\#L \geq 2$, we introduce L_1 and L_2.

Next, we assume that L_1 and L_2 *can* be sorted, i.e., that there exists an *implementation* of sort which works correctly on these shorter lists and hence produces lists N_1 and N_2 such that

$$N_1 = sort(L_1) \text{ and } N_2 = sort(L_2)$$

where

$$\text{post-}sort(L_1,N_1) \Leftrightarrow \text{bag\_of}(N_1) = \text{bag\_of}(L_1) \;\wedge\; ascending(N_1)$$

and

$$\text{post-}sort(L_2,N_2) \Leftrightarrow \text{bag\_of}(N_2) = \text{bag\_of}(L_2) \;\wedge\; ascending(N_2)\,.$$

We avoid explicit justification, but this relies on Burstall's structural induction principle[5] which works by virtue of our suitable measure of 'size'.

The lists N_1 and N_2 can also be included and the design description extended to include their properties.

The main design step is now almost complete. We can refer back to the general (divide and conquer) diagram and append relevant names to the internal data-flow lines as in Figure 7.2. We number the splitting and combination components since we are going to meet many different variants in subsequent designs.

[5] Burstall,R.M., "Proving Properties of Programs by Structural Induction", *Comp. J.* (12), 41-48 (1969).

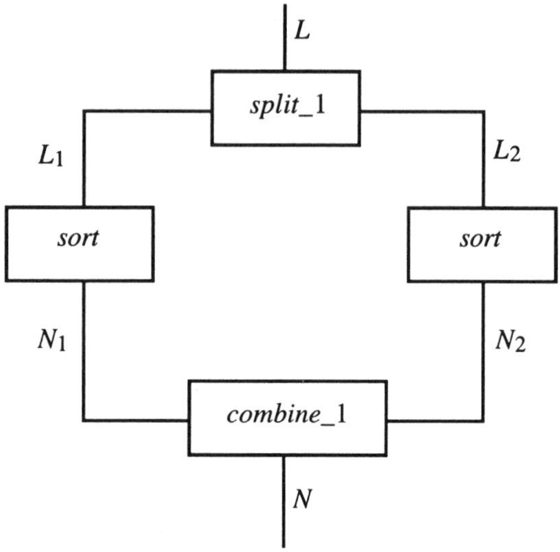

Figure 7.2

If the "divide and conquer" strategy works, then other relationships can be removed. We need to re-organise the information that we now have available into a form that matches Figure 7.2.

$$\begin{array}{l}
\text{bag_of}(N) = \text{bag_of}(L) \;\wedge\; ascending(N) \;\wedge \\
L = L_1 \frown L_2 \;\wedge \\
\text{bag_of}(N_1) = \text{bag_of}(L_1) \;\wedge\; ascending(N_1) \;\wedge \\
\text{bag_of}(N_2) = \text{bag_of}(L_2) \;\wedge\; ascending(N_2)
\end{array}$$

Applying common bag rules

$$\begin{array}{rl}
\text{bag_of}(L) & \Leftrightarrow \text{bag_of}(L_1 \frown L_2) \\
 & \Leftrightarrow \text{bag_of}(L_1) \uplus \text{bag_of}(L_2)
\end{array}$$

where: $L_1, L_2 : \mathbb{Z}^+$, non-empty integer lists.

[The bag union operator does not remove duplicates; no elements are lost.]

and so

$$\begin{array}{rl}
\text{bag_of}(N) & \Leftrightarrow \text{bag_of}(L) \\
 & \Leftrightarrow \text{bag_of}(L_1) \uplus \text{bag_of}(L_2) \\
 & \Leftrightarrow \text{bag_of}(N_1) \uplus \text{bag_of}(N_2)
\end{array}$$

Widening the scope of the local names L_1, L_2, N_1, N_2 — allowed since they are all new — we can lay out the design thus:

$$(\exists L_1,L_2,N_1,N_2{:}\mathbb{Z}^+)(\quad L = L_1 \frown L_2 \wedge$$

$$\text{bag\_of}(N_1) = \text{bag\_of}(L_1) \wedge \quad \text{bag\_of}(N_2) = \text{bag\_of}(L_2) \wedge$$
$$\mathit{ascending}(N_1) \wedge \quad \mathit{ascending}(N_2) \wedge$$

$$\text{bag\_of}(N) = \text{bag\_of}(N_1) \uplus \text{bag\_of}(N_2)$$
$$\wedge\ \mathit{ascending}(N) \quad)$$

which then can be 'boxed' so as reflect the sought after structure, i.e.,

$$(\exists L_1,L_2,N_1,N_2{:}\mathbb{Z}^+)(\quad \boxed{L = L_1 \frown L_2 \wedge}$$

$$\boxed{\begin{array}{l}\text{bag\_of}(N_1) = \text{bag\_of}(L_1) \wedge \\ \mathit{ascending}(N_1) \wedge\end{array}} \quad \boxed{\begin{array}{r}\text{bag\_of}(N_2) = \text{bag\_of}(L_2) \wedge \\ \mathit{ascending}(N_2) \wedge\end{array}}$$

$$\boxed{\begin{array}{c}\text{bag\_of}(N) = \text{bag\_of}(N_1) \uplus \text{bag\_of}(N_2) \\ \wedge\ \text{ascending}(N)\end{array}} \quad)$$

We could now introduce *combine_1* specified as

$$\mathit{combine\_1}{:}\ \mathbb{Z}^* \times \mathbb{Z}^* \to \mathbb{Z}^*$$
$$\text{pre-}\mathit{combine\_1}(\langle N_1,N_2\rangle) \triangleq \mathit{ascending}(N_1) \wedge \mathit{ascending}(N_2)$$
$$\text{post-}\mathit{combine\_1}(\langle N_1,N_2\rangle,N) \triangleq \mathit{ascending}(N) \wedge$$
$$\text{bag\_of}(N) = \text{bag\_of}(N_1) \uplus \text{bag\_of}(N_2)$$

Having done some of the exercises in Chapter 1, the reader might recognise this as the specification of merging two ascending integer lists — hence we rename *combine_1* as *merge*. As with good programming practice, the use of sensible names is to be encouraged. If we were interested in deriving a *single* algorithm, this would also be appropriate here; however, if we tried to do that throughout this chapter we would either run out of sensible names or have to use identifiers that were too long to be easily manipulated in expressions. Inasmuch as this detracts from the readability of some mathematical expressions, we apologise to the reader.

So, in total we have the skeletal design of a *simple merge sort* program:

if $\#L < 2$
then $N = L$
else $(\exists L_1, L_2, N_1, N_2 : \mathbb{Z}^+)$
($\langle L_1, L_2 \rangle = split\_1(L) \wedge$

$N_1 = sort(L_1) \wedge N_2 = sort(L_2) \wedge$

$N = merge(\langle N_1, N_2 \rangle$)
fi

Thus, we have a high-level recursive design for sorting. For this we claim that if *split_1* and *merge* are implemented so as to satisfy their specifications, then this design satisfies the specification for *sort*,

where, for completeness, *split_1* is specified by

$split\_1 : \mathbb{Z}^* \rightarrow \mathbb{Z}^* \times \mathbb{Z}^*$
pre-$split\_1(L) \triangleq \#L \geq 2$
post-$split\_1(L, \langle L_1, L_2 \rangle) \triangleq L = L_1 {}^\frown L_2 \quad \wedge \quad \#L_1 \geq 1 \quad \wedge \quad \#L_2 \geq 1$

The only jobs left to be done with this design are to change the paradigms so as to make the extraction of the result more explicit. We shall not attempt to describe this in general terms but refer the reader back to Chapter 3 and illustrate the paradigm shifts in the course of synthesising the algorithm designs.

Now, putting all the pieces together, the formal presentation of the design derivation for a general merge sort is as follows.

Assuming the pre-condition (i.e., here assuming *nothing* special about L), we have
post-$sort(L,N)$

◆ using the specification

$\text{bag\_of}(N) = \text{bag\_of}(L) \wedge ascending(N)$

◆ partitioning the domain $\mathbb{Z}^*$

if $\#L < 2$
then bag_of(N) = bag_of(L) $\wedge$ *ascending*(N)
else bag_of(N) = bag_of(L) $\wedge$ *ascending*(N)
fi

◆ since when $\#L < 2$, $L = N$ satisfies bag_of(N) = bag_of(L) $\wedge$ *ascending*(N)

Normally we would have to break off here and do a side derivation using the extra assumption that $\#L < 2$. But in this instance we merely use the 'checked' result, which was thought to be 'obvious'.

if $\#L < 2$
then $L = N$
else bag_of(N) = bag_of(L) $\wedge$ *ascending*(N)
fi

▶ This is potentially a strict (i.e., non-reversible) refinement since we use implementations

if $\#L < 2$
then $N = L$
else $(\exists L_1, L_2, N_1, N_2 : \mathbb{Z}^+)$
($\langle L_1, L_2 \rangle = split\_1(L) \wedge$
$N_1 = sort(L_1) \wedge N_2 = sort(L_2) \wedge$
$N = merge(\langle N_1, N_2 \rangle)$)
fi

where: *split_1* and *merge* are realisations (implementations) of

$split\_1 : \mathbb{Z}^* \rightarrow \mathbb{Z}^* \times \mathbb{Z}^*$
pre-*split_1*(L) $\triangleq \#L \geq 2$
post-*split_1*$(L, \langle L_1, L_2 \rangle) \triangleq L = L_1 {}^\frown L_2 \wedge \#L_1 \geq 1 \wedge \#L_2 \geq 1$

and

$merge : \mathbb{Z}^* \times \mathbb{Z}^* \rightarrow \mathbb{Z}^*$
pre-*merge*$(\langle N_1, N_2 \rangle) \triangleq ascending(N_1) \wedge ascending(N_2)$
post-*merge*$(\langle N_1, N_2 \rangle, N) \triangleq ascending(N) \wedge$
bag_of(N) = bag_of(N_1) $\uplus$ bag_of(N_2)

◆ "where" introduction, Motivated by the data-flow diagram.
Moving towards the functional form.

$$
\begin{array}{l}
\text{if } \#L < 2 \\
\quad \text{then } N = L \\
\quad \text{else } (\quad N = merge(\langle N_1,N_2 \rangle) \\
\qquad\qquad\qquad \text{where: } L_1,L_2,N_1,N_2{:}\mathbb{Z}^+ \\
\qquad\qquad\qquad\qquad N_1 = sort(L_1) \wedge N_2 = sort(L_2) \\
\qquad\qquad\qquad\qquad \langle L_1,L_2 \rangle = split\_1(L) \\
\qquad\quad) \\
\text{fi}
\end{array}
$$

◆ factoring out the "=" over the "if-then-else-fi" structure,

$$
\begin{array}{l}
N = \text{if } \#L < 2 \\
\qquad \text{then } L \\
\qquad \text{else } (\quad merge(\langle N_1,N_2 \rangle) \\
\qquad\qquad\qquad \text{where: } L_1,L_2,N_1,N_2{:}\mathbb{Z}^+ \\
\qquad\qquad\qquad\qquad N_1 = sort(L_1) \wedge N_2 = sort(L_2) \\
\qquad\qquad\qquad\qquad \langle L_1,L_2 \rangle = split\_1(L) \\
\qquad\qquad) \\
\qquad \text{fi}
\end{array}
$$

▶▶ in 'functional' form; the 'N =' is not necessary since the answer is the evaluation of the expression "*sort*(L)".

$$
\begin{array}{l}
[\, N = \,] \; sort(L) \text{ where:} \\
\quad sort(L) \triangleq \text{if } \#L < 2 \\
\qquad\qquad \text{then } L \\
\qquad\qquad \text{else } (\exists L_1,L_2,N_1,N_2{:}\mathbb{Z}^+) \\
\qquad\qquad\quad (\quad merge(\langle N_1,N_2 \rangle) \\
\qquad\qquad\qquad\quad \text{where: } N_1 = sort(L_1) \wedge N_2 = sort(L_2) \\
\qquad\qquad\qquad\quad \text{where: } \langle L_1,L_2 \rangle = split\_1(L) \\
\qquad\qquad\quad) \\
\qquad\qquad \text{fi,} \\
\quad split\_1(L) \triangleq \ldots, \\
\quad merge(\langle N_1,N_2 \rangle) \triangleq \ldots
\end{array}
$$

⏩ in procedural form

$$
\begin{array}{l}
split\_1(L) \triangleq \ldots ; \\
merge(\langle N_1,N_2\rangle) \triangleq \ldots ; \\
sort(L) \triangleq \text{if } \#L < 2 \\
\qquad\qquad \text{then } result \leftarrow L \\
\qquad\qquad \text{else } \; (\text{var } L_1,L_2,N_1,N_2{:}\mathbb{Z}^+; \\
\qquad\qquad\qquad\quad \langle L_1,L_2\rangle \leftarrow split\_1(L); \\
\qquad\qquad\qquad\quad N_1 \leftarrow sort(L_1) \parallel N_2 \leftarrow sort(L_2); \\
\qquad\qquad\qquad\quad result \leftarrow merge(\langle N_1,N_2\rangle) \qquad) \\
\qquad\qquad \text{fi}; \\
N \leftarrow sort(L)
\end{array}
$$

Thus, we have an outline of a procedural program with three function declarations, two of which have still to be filled in, and a single assignment statement which involves the function call that kicks the whole calculation into action. The "where" clauses used in the functional form have been replaced by assignments and ordered as dictated, again, by the DFD. Notice the use of "$\parallel$" to indicate the allowed parallel execution of the two sub-sorts and the fact that there are no declarations for L or N and no input or output commands. These components are part of the program which surrounds the calculation, which is our sole concern here.

The completion of the other parts of the design, and consequential simplifications are given in Section 7.3 (or the use of previously constructed — reusable? — implementations of functions).

Notice that if the input list was already in ascending order, adopting the structural splitting tactic would still decompose the list into singletons and then rebuild it to give the output. All this despite the fact that apparently no work was really being done, except passing the list from input to output. All this seems rather poor, but we can always devise a list input which will cause a particular tactic to perform badly. To fully analyse any sorting algorithm requires an extensive probabilistic study. Remember that such considerations are secondary (to ensuring correctness) and will not be studied in this text.

7.2.3 Predicated Splitting (Partitioning)

Recall that a structural split makes use of the (data) structure in which the integers are presented as input. Indeed, in its most elementary form it uses only this structure and totally ignores the actual values present. In marked contrast, the predicate mentioned in the name of the current strategy refers to the integers and not to the structure — the list — which is not used other than as a way of containing the integers. But, of course, by virtue of the problem we are attempting to solve, the list structure of the output is essential.

The general strategy is to take the (bag of) data items and partition them into two bags depending on whether they do (or do not) satisfy a chosen property. The bags are held in lists. In the case of sorting, we take some value x and divide up the numbers in the list into 'lows' (having values "$\leq x$") and the 'highs' (having values "$\geq x$"). Note that x itself need not be in the list, but if it is included (possibly more than once), then it can be placed either in the 'lows' or 'highs'.

So, a new *split*, *split_2*, might be

$$\begin{array}{l} split\_2 \colon \mathbb{Z}^* \to \mathbb{Z}^* \times \mathbb{Z}^* \\ \text{pre-}split\_2(L) \triangleq \text{True} \\ \text{post-}split\_2(L, \langle L_1, L_2 \rangle) \triangleq (\exists x \colon \mathbb{Z}) \\ \qquad (\text{bag\_of}(L) = \text{bag\_of}(L_1) \uplus \text{bag\_of}(L_2) \wedge \\ \qquad\quad (\wedge (y \leq x) \mid y \colon \mathbb{Z} \mid y \text{ in } L_1) \wedge \\ \qquad\quad (\wedge (x \leq y) \mid y \colon \mathbb{Z} \mid y \text{ in } L_2)) \end{array}$$

where

$$(\wedge (y \leq x) \mid y \colon \mathbb{Z} \mid y \text{ in } M) \triangleq (\wedge (y \leq x) \mid M_1, M_2 \colon \mathbb{Z}^*, y \colon \mathbb{Z} \mid M = M_1 \frown \langle y \rangle \frown M_2)$$

As before, all lists of length less than 2 are already sorted, so the pre-condition can be strengthened to reflect this. Notice that, since L is finite, it is always possible to choose a value of x so that it is larger than all the values in L, and hence we would have $L = L_1$ and no progress would be made by such a split.

The simplest way to fix this is to add extra constraints:

$$\begin{array}{l} split\_3 \colon \mathbb{Z}^* \to \mathbb{Z}^* \times \mathbb{Z}^* \\ \text{pre-}split\_3(L) \triangleq \#L \geq 2 \\ \text{post-}split\_3(L, \langle L_1, L_2 \rangle) \triangleq (\exists x \colon \mathbb{Z}) \\ \qquad (\text{bag\_of}(L) = \text{bag\_of}(L_1) \uplus \text{bag\_of}(L_2) \wedge \\ \qquad\quad (\wedge (y \leq x) \mid y \colon \mathbb{Z} \mid y \text{ in } L_1) \wedge \\ \qquad\quad (\wedge (x \leq y) \mid y \colon \mathbb{Z} \mid y \text{ in } L_2) \wedge \\ \qquad\quad \#L_1 \geq 1 \wedge \#L_2 \geq 1) \end{array}$$

Here, once x has been used to obtain L_1 and L_2, it is forgotten about, indeed; if it *is* a member of L, then it is placed in either L_1 or L_2 and may have to be re-sorted later despite our knowing how it relates to all the items in the two new lists.

Later we shall modify the splitting process so as to make use of this information.

So, with *split*_3 we can set off again on the trail of a "divide and conquer" design. For lists having two or more elements, we again have

$(\exists L_1,L_2,N_1,N_2{:}\mathbb{Z}^+)(\quad \langle L_1,L_2\rangle = split\_3(L) \wedge$

$\text{bag\_of}(N_1) = \text{bag\_of}(L_1) \wedge \qquad \text{bag\_of}(N_2) = \text{bag\_of}(L_2) \wedge$
$ascending(N_1) \wedge \qquad ascending(N_2) \wedge$

$N = combine\_3(\langle N_1,N_2\rangle) \;)$

Notice that we could use "merge" for the combine phase but

$y \text{ in } N_1 \Leftrightarrow y \in \text{bag\_of}(N_1)$
$\Leftrightarrow y \in \text{bag\_of}(L_1)$
$\Leftrightarrow y \text{ in } L_1$
$\Rightarrow y \le x$ with the x used in *split*_3

Similarly,

$z \text{ in } N_2 \Leftrightarrow z \in \text{bag\_of}(N_2)$
$\Leftrightarrow z \in \text{bag\_of}(L_2)$
$\Leftrightarrow z \text{ in } L_2$
$\Rightarrow x \le z$ for the *same* x.

and thus $y \text{ in } N_1 \wedge z \text{ in } N_2 \Rightarrow y \le z.$ We will need this later.

Recall the other requirements for *combine*_3, namely

$\text{pre-}combine\_3(\langle N_1,N_2\rangle) \triangleq ascending(N_1) \wedge ascending(N_2)$
$\text{post-}combine\_3(\langle N_1,N_2\rangle,N) \triangleq ascending(N) \wedge$
$\text{bag\_of}(N) = \text{bag\_of}(N_1) \uplus \text{bag\_of}(N_2)$

By virtue of using *split*_3, it would seem reasonable that N could be obtained from N_1 and N_2 by simple concatenation; i.e., $N_1 {}^\frown N_2$. Instead of trying to work this out, we *check* it by substituting into the post-condition and evaluating.

post-*combine*$(\langle N_1, N_2\rangle, N_1 \frown N_2)$

◆

$ascending(N_1 \frown N_2) \wedge \text{bag\_of}(N_1 \frown N_2) = \text{bag\_of}(N_1) \uplus \text{bag\_of}(N_2)$

◆ the second term is a bag axiom and so it is always True.

$ascending(N_1 \frown N_2)$

◆

$(\wedge(a \le b) \mid a,b{:}\mathbb{Z}, N_3, N_4, N_5{:}\mathbb{Z}^* \mid N_1 \frown N_2 = N_3 \frown \langle a\rangle \frown N_4 \frown \langle b\rangle \frown N_5)$

◆ partition the base using 3 cases[6]

[— $\#N_5 \ge \#N_2$

[— $\#N_1 \le \#N_3$

[— $\#N_3 < \#N_1 \;\wedge\; \#N_2 > \#N_5$

$(\wedge(a \le b) \mid a,b{:}\mathbb{Z}, N_3, N_4, N_5{:}\mathbb{Z}^* \mid N_1 \frown N_2 = N_3 \frown \langle a\rangle \frown N_4 \frown \langle b\rangle \frown N_5 \wedge \#N_5 \ge \#N_2) \wedge$[7]

$(\wedge(a \le b) \mid a,b{:}\mathbb{Z}, N_3, N_4, N_5{:}\mathbb{Z}^* \mid N_1 \frown N_2 = N_3 \frown \langle a\rangle \frown N_4 \frown \langle b\rangle \frown N_5 \wedge \#N_1 \le \#N_3) \wedge$

$(\wedge(a \le b) \mid a,b{:}\mathbb{Z}, N_3, N_4, N_5{:}\mathbb{Z}^* \mid N_1 \frown N_2 = N_3 \frown \langle a\rangle \frown N_4 \frown \langle b\rangle \frown N_5 \wedge \#N_3 < \#N_1 \wedge \#N_2 > \#N_5)$

introducing new list names to assist in reasoning (again see Figure 7.3, all ◆ will become clear in the next step) and deleting common end segments of lists in the base expression.

$(\wedge(a \le b) \mid a,b{:}\mathbb{Z}, N_3, N_4, N_6{:}\mathbb{Z}^* \mid N_1 = N_3 \frown \langle a\rangle \frown N_4 \frown \langle b\rangle \frown N_6) \wedge$

[— where $N_5 = N_6 \frown N_2$]

$(\wedge(a \le b) \mid a,b{:}\mathbb{Z}, N_7, N_4, N_5{:}\mathbb{Z}^* \mid N_2 = N_7 \frown \langle a\rangle \frown N_4 \frown \langle b\rangle \frown N_5) \wedge$

[— where $N_3 = N_1 \frown N_7$]

$(\wedge(a \le b) \mid a,b{:}\mathbb{Z}, N_3, N_4, N_5{:}\mathbb{Z}^* \mid N_1 \frown N_2 = N_3 \frown \langle a\rangle \frown N_4 \frown \langle b\rangle \frown N_5 \wedge \#N_3 < \#N_1 \wedge \#N_2 > \#N_5)$

---

[6] See how the named segments relate to each other in Figure 7.3.

[7] See Exercise 5.1 for justification of this move.

$(\#N_5 \geq \#N_2)$ $N_1 \uparrow N_2$

◆▶ $N_3 \char"0303 \langle a \rangle \char"0303 N_4 \char"0303 \langle b \rangle \uparrow \boxed{N_5}$

◆▶ $N_3 \char"0303 \langle a \rangle \char"0303 N_4 \char"0303 \langle b \rangle \uparrow \boxed{N_6 \char"0303 N_2}$

◆▶ $N_1 \uparrow N_2$

$(\#N_1 \leq \#N_3)$ $N_1 \uparrow N_2$

◆▶ $\boxed{N_3} \char"0303 \langle a \rangle \char"0303 N_4 \char"0303 \langle b \rangle \char"0303 N_5$

◆▶ $\boxed{N_1 \char"0303 N_7} \langle a \rangle \char"0303 N_4 \char"0303 \langle b \rangle \char"0303 N_5$

◆▶ $N_1 \uparrow N_2$

$(\#N_3 < \#N_1 \wedge \#N_2 > \#N_5)$ $N_1 \uparrow N_2$

◆▶ $N_3 \char"0303 \langle a \rangle \uparrow \boxed{N_4} \uparrow \langle b \rangle \char"0303 N_5$

◆▶ $N_3 \char"0303 \langle a \rangle \uparrow \boxed{N_8 \char"0303 N_9} \uparrow \langle b \rangle \char"0303 N_5$

◆▶ $N_1 \uparrow N_2$

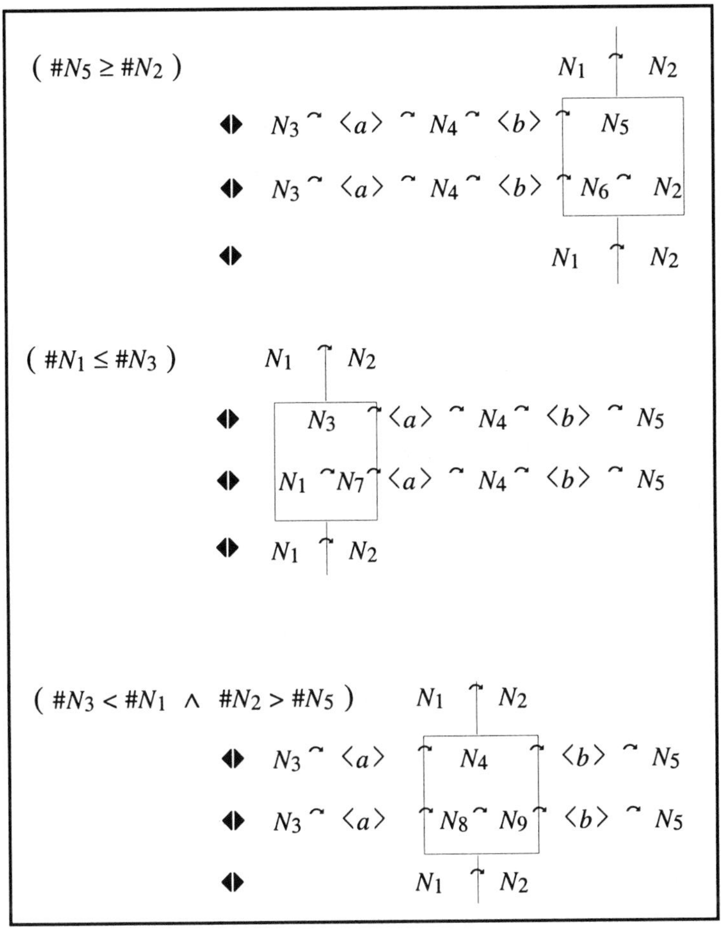

Figure 7.3

◆▶ using the definition of *ascend* and naming parts of N_4,

$ascending(N_1) \wedge ascending(N_2) \wedge$
$(\wedge (a \leq b) \mid a,b : \mathbb{Z}, N_3, N_8, N_9, N_5 : \mathbb{Z}* \mid$
$\qquad\qquad N_1 \char"0303 N_2 = N_3 \char"0303 \langle a \rangle \char"0303 N_8 \char"0303 N_9 \char"0303 \langle b \rangle \char"0303 N_5)$

$[—$ where $N_3 \char"0303 \langle a \rangle \char"0303 N_8 = N_1 \wedge N_9 \char"0303 \langle b \rangle \char"0303 N_5 = N_2$
$\qquad\qquad\qquad$ i.e., a in $N_1 \wedge b$ in $N_2]$

◆▶ and recall that $ascending(N_1)$ and $ascending(N_2)$ are True,
$(\wedge (a \leq b) \mid a,b : \mathbb{Z} \mid a$ in $N_1 \wedge b$ in $N_2)$

⟺

$(\wedge(a \leq b) \mid a,b{:}\mathbb{Z} \mid a \text{ in } L_1 \wedge b \text{ in } L_2)$

⟺ $a \text{ in } L_1 \wedge b \text{ in } L_2 \Rightarrow (\exists x{:}\mathbb{Z})(a \leq x \wedge x \leq b) \Rightarrow (a \leq b)$ for some x

so if $a \text{ in } L_1 \wedge b \text{ in } L_2$ then $a \leq b$ ⟺ True.

$(\wedge(\text{True}) \mid a,b{:}\mathbb{Z} \mid a \text{ in } L_1 \wedge b \text{ in } L_2)$

⟺

True

So our intuition that concatenation would suffice was correct, and the skeletal design for this kind of sort is as follows:

if $\#L < 2$
then $N = L$
else $(\exists L_1,L_2,N_1,N_2{:}\mathbb{Z}^+)$
($\langle L_1,L_2\rangle = split\_3(L) \wedge$
$N_1 = sort(L_1) \wedge N_2 = sort(L_2) \wedge$
$N = N_1 \frown N_2$)
fi

This is known as a *partition sort.*

Having done this 'side work', we can present the derivation as a formal progression and include the appropriate paradigm shifts. These are similar to those in the previous derivation and so will be given in less detail.

This starts in the same way as before:

post-$sort(L,N)$

⟺ using the specification

$\text{bag\_of}(N) = \text{bag\_of}(L) \wedge ascending(N)$

◆ partitioning the domain $\mathbb{Z}^*$

if #$L < 2$
then bag_of(N) = bag_of(L) ∧ *ascending*(N)
else bag_of(N) = bag_of(L) ∧ *ascending*(N)
fi

◆ as before

if #$L < 2$
then $L = N$
else bag_of(N) = bag_of(L) ∧ *ascending*(N)
fi

▶

if #$L < 2$
then $N = L$
else $(\exists L_1, L_2, N_1, N_2 : \mathbb{Z}^+)$
($\langle L_1, L_2 \rangle = split\_3(L) \wedge$
$N_1 = sort(L_1) \wedge N_2 = sort(L_2) \wedge$
$N = N_1 \frown N_2$)
where
$split\_3 : \mathbb{Z}^* \to \mathbb{Z}^* \times \mathbb{Z}^*$
pre-$split\_3(L) \triangleq \#L \geq 2$
post-$split\_3(L, \langle L_1, L_2 \rangle) \triangleq (\exists x : \mathbb{Z})$
(bag_of(L) = bag_of(L_1) ⊎ bag_of(L_2) ∧
$(\wedge (y \leq x) \mid y : \mathbb{Z} \mid y \text{ in } L_1) \wedge$
$(\wedge (x \leq y) \mid y : \mathbb{Z} \mid y \text{ in } L_2) \wedge$
$\#L_1 \geq 1 \wedge \#L_2 \geq 1$)
fi

◆

N = (if #$L < 2$
then L
else ($N_1 \frown N_2$
where: $L_1, L_2, N_1, N_2 : \mathbb{Z}^+$
$N_1 = sort(L_1) \wedge N_2 = sort(L_2)$
$\langle L_1, L_2 \rangle = split\_3(L)$
)
fi)

⏩ into 'functional' form

$[\ N = \ ]$ $\quad sort(L)$ where

$sort(L) \triangleq$ if $\#L < 2$
then L
else ($N_1 {}^\frown N_2$
where: $L_1, L_2, N_1, N_2 : \mathbb{Z}^+$
$N_1 = sort(L_1) \wedge N_2 = sort(L_2)$
$\langle L_1, L_2 \rangle = split\_3(L)$
)
fi,
$split\_3(L) \triangleq \ldots ,$

⏩ into procedural form

$split\_3(L) \triangleq \ldots ;$
$sort(L) \triangleq$ if $\#L < 2$
then $result \leftarrow L$
else (var $L_1, L_2, N_1, N_2 : \mathbb{Z}^+$;
$\langle L_1, L_2 \rangle \leftarrow split\_3(L)$;
$N_1 \leftarrow sort(L_1) \parallel N_2 \leftarrow sort(L_2)$;
$result \leftarrow N_1 {}^\frown N_2$)
fi;
$N \leftarrow sort(L)$

The general layout of this design is superficially similar to the merge sort, but now all the work is concentrated in the splitting phase, about which we shall say more in Section 7.3.3.

Notice how each of the three fundamental designs have introduced recursion as an intermediate form and that all these recursions are different. This observation reinforces the need to avoid recursion in the (initial) specification.

7.3 Complete Designs

With the development machinery available so far, we now try to fill in the parts of the designs to make complete[8] program schemes. We shall use the same broad subdivisions as in the previous section, but now we shall admit the common classifications of the kinds of sorting algorithms obtained, namely exchange sorts, merge sorts, and partition sorts, but be aware that the distinction is often confusing; in array-based implementations of internal (i.e., in store) sorting, most operations are achieved by means of exchanges. We shall follow this up further in Chapter 9.

The length of some derivation sequences might well give rise to alarm. They are so long simply because we are presenting in some detail the manipulation of multi-line expressions — potentially whole programs! Using a suitable software development tool, each step can be likened to performing an edit, but instead of changing (and hence deleting) the original, we must retain it so as to allow the manipulation to be fully appreciated.

7.3.1 Exchange Sorts

Recall that so far we have

```
improve(L) ≙ ... ;
sort(L) ≙  (var V: ℤ*;
                 V ← L;
                 while ¬ascending(V)
                   do V ← improve(V)
                   od;
                 result ← V);
N ← sort(L)
```

To make this scheme complete, we need to devise a design for the *improve* function[9]. As always, we advocate some experimentation to get a feel for the ways in which the problem might be tackled. Of course, in Section 7.1, we discussed the effect of swapping 'out of order' pairs and how performing such exchanges would eventually result in the list being 'sorted'; but how can this idea be harnessed to give an algorithm? Here we shall not go into the numerous different possibilities but consider one straightforward approach — other alternatives will be discussed in Chapter 9. First we remark that within the class of exchange-sorting algorithms, the notion of exchange is generally interpreted as meaning the exchange of *adjacent* pairs of list elements.

[8] Our immediate concern is only to obtain complete designs. Other, slightly more sophisticated, developments are given in Chapter 9.

[9] It would also be reasonable to expect that we also need an implementation of the predicate *ascending*; however, as we shall see, we can side-step the need for this function.

So, what about *improve*(L)? The intention of this function is to take the list L, known not to be *ascending*, and deliver another list, with the same elements, which is 'nearer' to being sorted; to 'improve' the ordering or, put more technically, to use *improve*(L), where $M(improve(L)) < M(L)$ and M is the measure defined in Section 7.2.1. And we know that swapping elements which are relatively out of order lowers the value of M.

We could take a very naive approach as follows.

Since $\neg\, ascending(L)$, we know that we can have

$$L \Leftrightarrow L_1 \frown L_2$$

where

$$L_1 \Leftrightarrow L_3 \frown \langle x \rangle$$
$$L_2 \Leftrightarrow \langle y \rangle \frown L_4$$

and

$$x > y.$$

It is tempting to try and define an implementation of *improve* by

$$improve(L_3 \frown \langle x \rangle \frown \langle y \rangle \frown L_4) \triangleq L_3 \frown \langle y \rangle \frown \langle x \rangle \frown L_4$$

By a repetition of previous arguments, it then follows that

$$M(L_3 \frown \langle y \rangle \frown \langle x \rangle \frown L_4) \quad < \quad M(L_3 \frown \langle x \rangle \frown \langle y \rangle \frown L_4)$$

so

$$M(improve(L_3 \frown \langle x \rangle \frown \langle y \rangle \frown L_4)) \quad < \quad M(L_3 \frown \langle x \rangle \frown \langle y \rangle \frown L_4)$$

and the recursion is guaranteed to terminate in a finite number of moves.

But, a given list L may include several adjacent out-of-order pairs. Thus, the proposed definition of *improve* does not always give a unique answer. To be used as an implementation, it must therefore be made deterministic. But notice also that some work is being duplicated since we effectively have to find an out-of-order pair to be sure that the given list is not *ascending*, and we then forget where this occurs and have to find such a split all over again before we can perform the swap.

One possible modification to this approach is to add the extra condition, namely that L_1 $(= L_3 \frown \langle x \rangle)$ should be *ascending*, and so the x—y pair is the first out-of-order pair, counting from left to right. (We can definitely do this because singleton lists are known to be *ascending* and so this works even if $L_3 = \langle\, \rangle$.) Performing *improve* recursively will then cause y gradually to 'sink' to the appropriate position before the *improve* function moves further up the list.

To see how this might work, consider the sequence of lists in Figure 7.4. At each stage, the two numbers compared (and either interchanged or not) are printed in bold. The result of a comparison leads either to a swap, indicated by a cross, or to no change, indicated by the two vertical parallel lines.

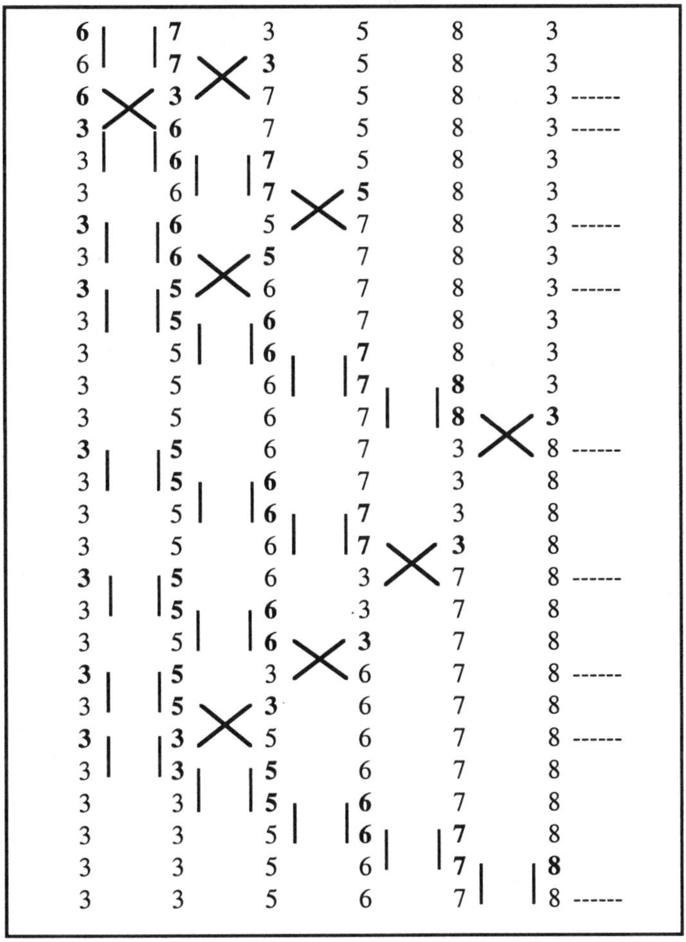

Figure 7.4

The list ⟨6, 7, 3, 5, 8, 3⟩ has six items and requires eight adjacent swaps to become sorted into ascending order[10]. Each such swap comes at the end of what we shall call a 'pass'. Here we show nine passes. The last one does not perform a swap; it cannot since the list is now completely sorted and hence the *ascending* predicate controlling the loop would prevent this pass from being performed — but stay with us!

[10] Not trivial but complex enough to serve as a vehicle for illustrating the differences between the collection of sorting algorithms that we consider.

The end of each pass is indicated by the horizontal lines drawn on the right-hand side of certain lists. Each of these lists is the result of one phase (pass) and hence is also the starting point for the subsequent pass, if any. Any exchange sort (performed by swapping adjacent out-of-order pairs) with this list as input needs eight swaps but lots of other work is done in organisation of the processing. The 27 steps/comparisons are executed in passes of length 2, 1, 3 etc. (A pass of length n involves $n - 1$ 'do nothing' steps followed by a swap or termination of the entire sort. Notice in particular the successive passes of lengths 5, 4, 3, and 2 that drop the second '3' in the list down to its proper position.) We can do better than this, but let's look at this version in detail first.

We call the basic process a *ripple*. This swaps the lowest out-of-order pair (that closest to the left-hand end), otherwise the list is ascending and we are done. We define *ripple* by a set of rules which we want it to obey. (They can be collected together into the usual form of specification, but we do not need this yet.) We consider six different cases for the argument of $ripple{:}\mathbb{Z}^* \to \mathbb{Z}^*$.

(1)		$ripple(\langle\rangle) ◆ \langle\rangle$	end of sort
(2)		$ripple\ (\langle x\rangle) ◆ \langle x\rangle$	end of sort
(3)	$(x \le y)$	$ripple(\langle x, y\rangle) ◆ \langle x, y\rangle$	end of sort
(4)	$(x > y)$	$ripple(\langle x, y\rangle) ◆ \langle y, x\rangle$	end of pass

and, when $L{:}\mathbb{Z}^+$,

(5)	$(x \le y)$	$ripple(\langle x, y\rangle \frown L) ◆ \langle x\rangle \frown ripple(\langle y\rangle \frown L)$	and continue
(6)	$(x > y)$	$ripple(\langle x, y\rangle \frown L) ◆ \langle y, x\rangle \frown L$	end of pass

Here, cases 1, 2 and 3 effectively detect that the list is already in ascending order and that sorting is complete. Notice that rules 1 and 2 are only ever used for empty and singleton lists (not as parts of longer lists) and are included for completeness. They correspond to *sort* in the following way:

$$ripple(L) = sort(L) = L$$

In all other cases, the bag of elements on each side of the rule is the same (as is the case within the specification of *sort*) and, if $ripple(L)$ ◆ N, either $ascending(N)$ or $M(N) < M(L)$ (in fact $M(N) = M(L) - 1$). Applying *ripple* to an arbitrary non-trivial list of integers is achieved by a finite sequence of applications of rule 5 and then either rule 3, 4 or 6. Using rule 3 indicates that no swaps were required and hence the list is sorted; rule 4 corresponds to swapping the end pair, and rule 6 to a swap somewhere before the end. Try these swaps with the example given above; *ripple* should describe the processing of one complete pass. On each step, each rule application, *ripple* either achieves a swap (and hence reduces the M measure) or increases the length of the front part of the list, which is known to be in ascending order. Correspondingly, it also reduces the length of the list parameter in the next invocation of *ripple*, so we could simply use *ripple* in place of *improve* and use the rules which define *ripple* as the basis of an implementation.

$$ripple(L) \triangleq \text{if } L = \langle\,\rangle \text{ then } \langle\,\rangle$$
$$\text{else if } \#L = 1 \text{ then } \langle first\_of(L)\rangle \qquad \text{etc.}$$

and hence we would have

$$ripple(L) \triangleq \dots ;$$
$$sort(\text{L}) \triangleq (\text{var } V\colon \mathbb{Z}*;$$
$$V \leftarrow L;$$
$$\text{while } \neg \, ascending(V)$$
$$\text{do } V \leftarrow ripple(V)$$
$$\text{od};$$
$$\text{result} \leftarrow V);$$
$$N \leftarrow sort(L)$$

But what about an implementation of *ascending*? Notice that on the final application of *ripple*, resulting from the use of rule 3, we know that at that point the list *is* in order and we can use this to circumvent the need for an explicit *ascending* predicate in the program code. Notice also that for a given list L there is some value $n\colon\mathbb{N}$ such that $ripple^n(L) = sort(L)$.

We can achieve such repetitions by using recursion (based on *ripple* but using two parameters so as to hold the part of the intermediate answer to which *ripple* is not applied in rule 5). Call this procedure *exchange* and use the following rule set:

$$exch(A, \langle\,\rangle) \quad \blacklozenge \quad A$$
$$exch(A, \langle x \rangle) \quad \blacklozenge \quad A^\frown\langle x \rangle$$

$(x \le y)$	$exch(A, \langle x, y \rangle) \quad \blacklozenge \quad A^\frown\langle x, y \rangle$	end of sort
$(x > y)$	$exch(A, \langle x, y \rangle) \quad \blacklozenge \quad exch(\langle\,\rangle, A^\frown\langle y, x \rangle)$	end of pass

and, when $L\colon\mathbb{Z}^+$,

$(x \le y)$	$exch(A, \langle x, y \rangle^\frown L) \quad \blacklozenge \quad exch(A^\frown\langle x \rangle, \langle y \rangle^\frown L)$	and continue
$(x > y)$	$exch(A, \langle x, y \rangle^\frown L) \quad \blacklozenge \quad exch(\langle\,\rangle, A^\frown\langle y, x \rangle^\frown L)$	end of pass

To set this all in motion, we simply need to link to *sort* by

$$sort(L) \triangleq exch(\langle\,\rangle, L)$$

This gives the same sequence of lists as *ripple*, but the surrounding code can be greatly simplified to

$$exch(A, B) \triangleq \dots \; ;$$
$$sort(L) \triangleq exch(\langle\,\rangle, L);$$
$$N \leftarrow sort(L)$$

Moreover, the rules for *exch* can be slightly reduced to

$$exch(A, \langle\,\rangle) \; \blacklozenge \; A$$
$$exch(A, \langle x \rangle) \; \blacklozenge \; A^\frown \langle x \rangle$$

and, when $L:\mathbb{Z}^*$,

$$(x \le y) \qquad exch(A, \langle x, y \rangle^\frown L) \; \blacklozenge \; exch(A^\frown \langle x \rangle, \langle y \rangle^\frown L)$$
$$(x > y) \qquad exch(A, \langle x, y \rangle^\frown L) \; \blacklozenge \; exch(\langle\,\rangle, A^\frown \langle y, x \rangle^\frown L)$$

which gives rise to a recursive implementation scheme

$$exch(A, B) \triangleq \; \text{if } \#B < 2 \text{ then } A^\frown B$$
$$\text{else if } x \le y \text{ then } exch(A^\frown \langle x \rangle, \langle y \rangle^\frown C)$$
$$\text{else } exch(\langle\,\rangle, A^\frown \langle y, x \rangle^\frown C)$$
$$\text{where: } B = \langle x, y \rangle^\frown C$$
$$\text{fi}$$
$$\text{fi}$$

Of course, there are many ways in which this idea can be developed, usually to make better use of some property of the list that we have discovered and then 'forgotten'. We shall take this up in Chapter 9.

Exercises

7.1 Before moving on we must say something about the function *exch* and the specification of *sort*. The progression of *exch* evaluations starts with

$$exch(\langle\,\rangle, L) \; \blacklozenge \; sort(L)$$

Henceforth, any instance of $exch(A, B)$ is such that

$$\text{bag\_of}(A) \; \uplus \; \text{bag\_of}(B) = \text{bag\_of}(L) \; \wedge \; ascending(A)$$

(and if both A and B are non-empty, then

$$\text{last\_of } A \; \le \; \text{first\_of } B \quad)$$

Check this and confirm that the intermediate stages 'make progress' by improving the ordering of $A^\frown B$ or by reducing the $\#B$ and hence prove that, on termination, the final result is correct.

❑

7.3.2 Merge Sorts

Here we shall consider the basic merge sort and one simple variation.

7.3.2.1 The Basic Merge Sort

Recall the design obtained so far:

$$
\begin{array}{l}
split\_1(L) \triangleq \ldots ; \\
merge(\langle N_1,N_2\rangle) \triangleq \ldots ; \\
sort(L) \triangleq \text{ if } \#L < 2 \\
\qquad\qquad\quad \text{then } result \leftarrow L \\
\qquad\qquad\quad \text{else } \ (\text{var } L_1,L_2,N_1,N_2{:}\mathbb{Z}^+; \\
\qquad\qquad\qquad\quad \langle L_1,L_2\rangle \leftarrow split\_1(L); \\
\qquad\qquad\qquad\quad N_1 \leftarrow sort(L_1) \parallel N_2 \leftarrow sort(L_2); \\
\qquad\qquad\qquad\quad result \leftarrow merge(\langle N_1,N_2\rangle) \qquad) \\
\qquad\qquad\quad \text{fi}; \\
N \leftarrow sort(L)
\end{array}
$$

Note that *any* non-void-splitting routine will suffice, but we shall not consider that part of the program until later. We can immediately utilise an earlier synthesis to complete the other function that we need.

Substituting the implementation of *merge* from Section 3.3, we have

```
split_1(L) ≙ ... ;
merge(P,Q) ≙ (var A,B,C:ℤ*;
        ⟨A,B⟩ ← ⟨P,Q⟩;
        C ← ⟨⟩;
        while A ≠ ⟨⟩ ∧ B ≠ ⟨⟩
        do  if first_of(A) ≤ first_of(B)
            then  C ← C⌢⟨first_of(A)⟩; A ← rest_of(A)
            else  C ← C⌢⟨first_of(B)⟩; B ← rest_of(B)
            fi
        od;
        result ← C⌢A⌢B);
sort(L) ≙ if #L < 2
          then result ← L
          else (var L1,L2,N1,N2:ℤ+;
                ⟨L1,L2⟩ ← split_1(L);
                N1 ← sort(L1) ‖ N2 ← sort(L2);
                result ← merge(⟨N1,N2⟩)      )
          fi;
N ← sort(L)
```

7.3.3 Partition Sorts

As you can see from the top-level design in Section 7.2.3 (repeated below), most of the work in a partition sort is concentrated in the splitting phase, and devising clever ways to achieve the required splitting is at the heart of algorithms such as *Quicksort*.

```
split_3(L) ≙ ... ;
sort(L) ≙ if #L < 2
          then result ← L
          else (var L1,L2,N1,N2:ℤ+;
                ⟨L1,L2⟩ ← split_3(L);
                N1 ← sort(L1) ‖ N2 ← sort(L2);
                result ← N1⌢N2      )
          fi;
N ← sort(L)
```

where

$$\begin{aligned}
&split_3 \colon \mathbb{Z}^* \to \mathbb{Z}^* \times \mathbb{Z}^* \\
&\text{pre-}split_3(L) \triangleq \#L \geq 2 \\
&\text{post-}split_3(L, \langle L_1, L_2 \rangle) \triangleq (\exists x{:}\mathbb{Z}) \\
&\qquad (\text{bag_of}(L) = \text{bag_of}(L_1) \uplus \text{bag_of}(L_2) \land \\
&\qquad\quad (\land (y \leq x) \mid y{:}\mathbb{Z} \mid y \text{ in } L_1) \land \\
&\qquad\quad (\land (x \leq y) \mid y{:}\mathbb{Z} \mid y \text{ in } L_2) \land \\
&\qquad\quad \#L_1 \geq 1 \land \#L_2 \geq 1 \ )
\end{aligned}$$

So, on the face of it, we need to devise a way of implementing *split*_3. However, before looking at a complete partition sort, we note the following. The x in the specification above is usually called a ***pivot***. It is the value used to separate the high values from the low ones and may or may not be included in the list. (In the specification of *split*_3, if x *is* included in L, then it may be placed either in L_1 or L_2, or both, if it occurs more than once.) Recall also that the clause '$\#L_1 \geq 1 \land \#L_2 \geq 1$' is included so as to guarantee that $\#L_1 < \#L$ and $\#L_2 < \#L$ and hence that the recursive calls of *sort* converge (i.e., the recursion terminates).

If we *insist* that the pivot, x, is an element of the input list L and that only values strictly greater than x are placed in L_2, then we can replace/refine *split*_3 by *split*_4 with the following specification:

$$\begin{aligned}
&split_4 \colon \mathbb{Z}^* \to \mathbb{Z}^* \times \mathbb{Z} \times \mathbb{Z}^* \qquad \text{— this order[11] puts } x \text{ 'in the middle'} \\
&\text{pre-}split_4(L) \triangleq \#L \geq 2 \\
&\text{post-}split_4(L, \langle L_1, x, L_2 \rangle) \triangleq \\
&\qquad (\text{bag_of}(L) = \text{bag_of}(L_1) \uplus \{\!\{x\}\!\} \uplus \text{bag_of}(L_2) \\
&\qquad \land \ (\land (y \leq x) \mid y{:}\mathbb{Z} \mid y \text{ in } L_1) \land \\
&\qquad\quad (\land (x < y) \mid y{:}\mathbb{Z} \mid y \text{ in } L_2) \ )
\end{aligned}$$

Here we have three outputs. Having found x, we can hold on to it and use it within the calculation of the answer by replacing the assignment to the final result of the *sort* routine by

$$result \leftarrow N_1 \frown \langle x \rangle \frown N_2$$

Now x is in its final position, and we have fewer values to sort within the recursive calls. And because $\#L = \#L_1 + 1 + \#L_2$, we see that $\#L_1 < \#L$ and $\#L_2 < \#L$, and hence termination follows without putting lower size constraints on $\#L_1$ and $\#L_2$. With these changes/choices, we move on.

---

[11] The use of this ordering is not essential, but it is a useful indicator to subsequent developments.

7.3.3.1 A Simple Partition Sort

How can we implement *split_4*? The idea which we seek to employ is a simple one. We take the first item in L as the pivot and compare it with each of the remaining elements. We place the tested elements in either the front portion or the rear portion depending on the result of the comparison. We propose some rules[12] for the process $split\_5 : \mathbb{Z} \times \mathbb{Z}^* \times \mathbb{Z}^* \times \mathbb{Z}^* \rightarrow \mathbb{Z}^* \times \mathbb{Z} \times \mathbb{Z}^*$

	$split\_5(x, \langle\rangle, A, B)$ ◀▶ $\langle A, x, B \rangle$	end of splitting
$(x < y)$	$split\_5(x, \langle y \rangle ^\frown N, A, B)$ ◀▶ $split\_5(x, N, A, \langle y \rangle ^\frown B)$	y is 'high'
$(x \geq y)$	$split\_5(x, \langle y \rangle ^\frown N, A, B)$ ◀▶ $split\_5(x, N, \langle y \rangle ^\frown A, B)$	y is 'low'

and we drive this from

$$split\_4(\langle x \rangle ^\frown L) \triangleq split\_5(x, L, \langle\rangle, \langle\rangle)$$

Using the familiar example input, we get

	$split\_4(\langle 6, 7, 3, 5, 8, 3 \rangle)$				
◀▶	$split\_5(6,$	$\langle 7, 3, 5, 8, 3 \rangle,$	$\langle\rangle,$	$\langle\rangle$	$)$
◀▶	$split\_5(6,$	$\langle 3, 5, 8, 3 \rangle,$	$\langle\rangle,$	$\langle 7 \rangle$	$)$
◀▶	$split\_5(6,$	$\langle 5, 8, 3 \rangle,$	$\langle 3 \rangle,$	$\langle 7 \rangle$	$)$
◀▶	$split\_5(6,$	$\langle 8, 3 \rangle,$	$\langle 5, 3 \rangle,$	$\langle 7 \rangle$	$)$
◀▶	$split\_5(6,$	$\langle 3 \rangle,$	$\langle 5, 3 \rangle,$	$\langle 8, 7 \rangle$	$)$
◀▶	$split\_5(6,$	$\langle\rangle,$	$\langle 3, 5, 3 \rangle,$	$\langle 8, 7 \rangle$	$)$
◀▶	$\langle \langle 3, 5, 3 \rangle, 6, \langle 8, 7 \rangle \rangle$				

Notice that in these rules for manipulating $split\_5(x, L, A, B)$ the bag derived from L, A and B is constant, starting with A and B empty and ending with L empty, so elements are conserved. Moreover, only low ($\leq x$) values are appended to A and only high ($> x$) values are appended to B, so, starting as indicated, the final results are as required by the specification of *split_4*. Notice also that the length of the L parameter is progressively reduced and hence the recursive evaluation terminates correctly.

Of course, all this can be expressed mathematically. Do this as an exercise.

[12] Of course, we really only want to use these rules from left to right. They are still valid in the reverse direction but are unproductive.

We now have

```
split_5( x, L, A, B ) ≙ ... ;
split_4(L) ≙ split_5( first_of(L), rest_of(L), ⟨⟩, ⟨⟩ );
sort(L) ≙ if #L < 2
              then result ← L
              else (var x:ℤ,L1,L2,N1,N2:ℤ*;
                      ⟨L1, x, L2⟩ ← split_4(L);
                      N1 ← sort(L1) ∥ N2 ← sort(L2);
                      result ← N1⁀⟨x⟩⁀N2          )
              fi;
N ← sort(L)
```

An implementation of *split_5* follows immediately as

```
split_5( x, L, A, B ) ≙ if L = ⟨⟩
                          then ⟨ A, x, B ⟩
                          else  if x < y
                                then split_5( x,N, A,⟨y⟩⁀B )
                                else split_5( x,N, ⟨y⟩⁀A,B )
                                      where: L = ⟨y⟩⁀N
                                fi
                          fi
```

We can then combine some of these routines together[13] to give

```
split_5( x, L, A, B ) ≙ ... ;
sort(L) ≙ if #L < 2
            then result ← L
            else (var x:ℤ,L1,L2:ℤ*;
                  ⟨L1, x, L2⟩ ← split_5( first_of(L), rest_of(L), ⟨⟩, ⟨⟩ );
                  result ← sort(L1)⁀⟨x⟩⁀sort(L2)          )
            fi;
N ← sort(L)
```

[13] Here the possible parallel execution of the recursive calls of *sort* is implicit (by virtue of the independence of the evaluation of sub-expressions within the expression '$sort(L_1)^\frown\langle x\rangle^\frown sort(L_2)$'.

Notice that when all intermediate rules for a function (such as *split_5*, above) are of the form

$$(c) \qquad f(x) \;\blacklozenge\; f(h(x))$$

— where h merely calculates the 'new' parameters form the 'old' ones and does not involve further instances of f — the function f can be factored over the conditionals so as to be (explicitly) tail recursive. Hence we can achieve the iterative design:

```
split_5( x, L, A, B ) ≙     ( var M, C, D: ℤ*
                        <M, C, D> ← <L, A, B>;
                        while M ≠ <>
                        do
                              if x < first_of M
                              then D ← <first _of M>⁀D
                              else C ← <first _of M>⁀C
                              fi;
                              M ← rest _of M
                        od;
                        result ← <C, x, D>;  )
```

This transformation can be routinely carried out in all similar situations. However we shall normally not utilise this step but concentrate on those aspects which are more specific to a given example.

So much for traditional approaches to these familiar sorting techniques. To finish this chapter, we have something rather different.

7.4 A Quick Design

This chapter has included much detail; this has been done so as to emphasise the need to pay great attention to aspects of program synthesis which must be followed through very carefully. It is this attention to detail which characterises formal methods and which also causes many programmers to despair at the amount of effort (and care!) that is necessary[14]. We have already mentioned that, with appropriate tools, many of these construction steps can be performed very quickly; but can we do something else; can we take short cuts? Can we use the 'big' operators of Chapter 5?

[14] Focussing on the construction phase, rather than the subsequent analysis and correction of errors, means that the costing of software can be done more accurately. Empirical evidence supports claims that overall software costs are greatly reduced by this approach.

The answer is "yes". Below we show how this works for sorting. [Using such powerful rules does indeed give us *a* design, but it also denies us the possibility of fine tuning which might be done when developing an algorithm in smaller steps; hence the need for the major segment of this chapter.]

The result of the sorting process is a value of type $\mathbb{Z}*$, and this suggests that the final step might be achieved by an induced function $f*$ of type $X* \rightarrow \mathbb{Z}*$ derived from an associative binary function $f{:}\mathbb{Z}* \times \mathbb{Z}* \rightarrow \mathbb{Z}*$.
So what does this say about X? Well, the result delivered by $f*$ is a *sort*ed list and hence so are both inputs of f and $X \triangleq \mathbb{Z}*$. But, all lists of length 1 *are* ascending, so we might reasonably search for a function f such that

$$sort(L) \triangleq f* \circ g*(L)$$

where $g{:}\mathbb{Z} \rightarrow \mathbb{Z}*$ is defined by $g{:}x \mapsto \langle x \rangle$.

Then

$$g*{:}\mathbb{Z}* \rightarrow (\mathbb{Z}*)*$$

and, for example,

$$\begin{aligned} g*(\langle a, b, c\rangle) &\Leftrightarrow \langle\ g(a),\ g(b),\ g(c)\ \rangle \\ &\Leftrightarrow \langle\ \langle a\rangle, \langle b\rangle, \langle c\rangle\ \rangle. \end{aligned}$$

The required properties of $f*$ and $g*$ (as induced list operators) are

$$\begin{aligned} f*(\langle\rangle) &\Leftrightarrow \langle\rangle \\ f*(\langle L\rangle) &\Leftrightarrow L \\ f*(L^\frown M) &\Leftrightarrow f(\,f*(L), f*(M)\,) \end{aligned}$$

and

$$\begin{aligned} g*(\langle\rangle) &\Leftrightarrow \langle\rangle \\ g*(\langle x\rangle) &\Leftrightarrow \langle\ g(x)\ \rangle \\ g*(L^\frown M) &\Leftrightarrow g*(L)^\frown g*(M)\,. \end{aligned}$$

Clearly, our g function satisfies the requirements, but what about f? We can actually calculate f as follows.

Take two sorted lists L and M, and assume that $sort \triangleq f^* \circ g^*$;

then

$$
\begin{array}{ll}
 & f(L, M) \\
\Leftrightarrow & \qquad\qquad (ascending(N)) \quad sort(N) \Leftrightarrow N \\
 & f(\, sort(L), sort(M)\,) \\
\Leftrightarrow & f(\, f^* \circ g^*(L), f^* \circ g^*(M)\,) \\
\Leftrightarrow & f(\, f^*(g^*(L)), f^*(g^*(M))\,) \\
\Leftrightarrow & f^*(\, g^*(L) \frown g^*(M)\,) \\
\Leftrightarrow & f^*(\, g^*(L \frown M)\,) \\
\Leftrightarrow & f^* \circ g^*(L \frown M)\,) \\
\Leftrightarrow & sort(L \frown M)\,)
\end{array}
$$

so we must have

$$
\begin{array}{l}
f{:}\mathbb{Z}^* \times \mathbb{Z}^* \to \mathbb{Z}^* \\
\text{pre-}f(\langle L,M \rangle) \triangleq ascending(L) \wedge ascending(M) \\
\text{post-}f(\langle L,M \rangle, N) \triangleq \; N = sort(L \frown M)
\end{array}
$$

$$
\begin{array}{ll}
\Leftrightarrow & ascending(N) \wedge \\
 & \text{bag\_of}(N) = \text{bag\_of}(L \frown M) \\
 & \\
\Leftrightarrow & ascending(N) \wedge \\
 & \text{bag\_of}(N) = \text{bag\_of}(L) \uplus \text{bag\_of}(M)
\end{array}
$$

(f is in fact *merge*, but we shall not pay particular regard to this observation. We do, however, need to check that f is associative. This is left as an exercise.)

The * functions can now be directly implemented by the schemes

$$
\begin{array}{l}
g^*(L) \triangleq (\ \text{var } V{:}\mathbb{Z}^*, R{:}(\mathbb{Z}^*)^*; \\
\qquad V \leftarrow L;\ R \leftarrow \langle\rangle; \\
\qquad \text{while } V \neq \langle\rangle \\
\qquad\quad \text{do } R \leftarrow R \frown \langle\langle \text{first\_of}(V) \rangle\rangle;\ V \leftarrow \text{rest\_of}(V) \text{ od}; \\
\qquad \text{result} \leftarrow R\,)
\end{array}
$$

and

$$
\begin{array}{l}
f^*(L) \triangleq (\ \text{var } V{:}(\mathbb{Z}^*)^*, R{:}\mathbb{Z}^*; \\
\qquad V \leftarrow L;\ R \leftarrow \langle\rangle; \\
\qquad \text{while } V \neq \langle\rangle \\
\qquad\qquad \text{do } R \leftarrow f(R, \text{first\_of}(V));\ V \leftarrow \text{rest\_of}(V) \text{ od}; \\
\qquad \text{result} \leftarrow R)
\end{array}
$$

To complete the program design, we need to give a declaration for f (this too we leave as an exercise) and the link

$$sort(L) \triangleq f^*(\ g^*(L)).$$

This should all work by construction but, so as to justify this claim, we provide the following calculations.

$$
\begin{array}{ll}
 & f^* \circ g^*(\langle\rangle) \\
\Leftrightarrow & f^*(\langle\rangle) \\
\Leftrightarrow & \langle\rangle \\
\Leftrightarrow & sort(\langle\rangle)
\end{array}
$$

$$
\begin{array}{ll}
 & f^* \circ g^*(\langle x\rangle) \\
\Leftrightarrow & f^*(\langle g(x)\rangle) \\
\Leftrightarrow & f^*(\langle\langle x\rangle\rangle) \\
\Leftrightarrow & \langle x\rangle \\
\Leftrightarrow & sort(\langle x\rangle)
\end{array}
$$

and

$$
\begin{array}{ll}
 & f^* \circ g^*(L^\frown M) \\
\Leftrightarrow & f^*(\ g^*(L)^\frown g^*(M)\ ) \\
\Leftrightarrow & f(\ f^* \circ g^*(L), f^* \circ g^*(M)\ ) \\
\Leftrightarrow & f(\ sort(L), sort(M)\ ) \\
\Leftrightarrow & f(\ A, B\ ) \qquad \text{where:} \quad A = sort(L) \ \text{ and } \ B = sort(M) \\
\Leftrightarrow & C \\
 & \qquad \text{and} \quad \text{bag\_of}(C) = \text{bag\_of}(A) \uplus \text{bag\_of}(B) \\
 & \qquad\qquad \wedge\ ascending(C) \\
\Leftrightarrow & C \\
 & \qquad \text{where:} \quad \text{bag\_of}(C) = \text{bag\_of}(L) \uplus \text{bag\_of}(M) \\
 & \qquad\qquad \wedge\ ascending(C) \\
\Leftrightarrow & C \\
 & \qquad \text{where:} \quad \text{bag\_of}(C) = \text{bag\_of}(L^\frown M) \\
 & \qquad\qquad \wedge\ ascending(C) \\
\Leftrightarrow & sort(L^\frown M)
\end{array}
$$

So, the construction does indeed give the right answer and time spent in reorganising the specification into the appropriate form allows us to rapidly derive an implementation scheme.

Chapter 8
Data Refinement

It is not our intention that this book should be about algorithms, but merely the correctness concerns associated with algorithms and how they may be addressed hand-in-hand with the construction/derivation/generation of implementations. Another topic that comes into play when addressing more complex problems (apart from the characterization and measurement of complexity) is that of Data Structures. So far we have taken the stance that any data type (structure?) that is used within a problem specification is also available in PDL. This may not be so and hence, if we wish to model the problem structure directly in the solution, we may have to provide a bespoke implementation of an 'abstract' type within our implementation/program. In general terms, this chapter considers the replacement, the refinement[1] of data structures.

We do not study data structures here. The ways in which they are constructed and used is more properly part of a traditional (and introductory) course on programming — a course on coding (on how to talk to the computer). However, we should point out that the basic purpose of data structures is to store data in ways that facilitate its easy processing. As such, the storage and retrieval regimes go (again) hand-in-hand. It is silly to even suggest that incompatible computation and storage techniques should be used together (for instance, referring back to the problem of sorting in Chapter 7, the use of conventional arrays to hold lists that are to be merged). On the other hand, arrays may well be an appropriate storage structure in which to perform exchange sorts.

In Section 8.1, we briefly discuss the relationship between external data types (as given in the signature part of the specification) and internal storage structures. We then move to the main part of the chapter (Section 8.2) to consider the translation from one data structure to another. Here, in order to avoid the need to address more complex issues which could only be undertaken in an extensive study of data structures (which we have already declared as 'out of bounds' for us), we restrict consideration to cases that are structurally very similar but have interpretations and rules that are very different. Finally, as a link to further (or previous) study by the reader, we mention the potential benefits of using other, existing or purpose-built, data structures.

[1] This is *not* the common notion of data refinement, but the underlying concepts are very similar.

8.1 On 'Internal' Data Types

The structure (the types) of the inputs and outputs of a specified function is fixed 'by the customer' and cannot be changed without referring back to him/her. On the other hand, how (intermediate) data is represented and held internally can be determined by the programmer. To facilitate the calculations — to hold relevant data in a form that is easy to access and manipulate — is, as already noted, the real rationale for such structures. Remember that a specification should be about the problem, not about any potential solution *per se.* Internal structures may therefore be different from the types used within the signature of the specification (which we assume can already be represented in the system — but these usually only amount to linked records[2]) or in the post-condition. The study of data structures, and the potentially contradictory demands of space, speed and readability, is a whole topic on its own. We will not delve into it except in the next section, to show how the changing of data types can be used to good effect.

8.2 Changing Data Types

Operational refinement (as presented in Section 6.1) ultimately results in the removal of unnecessary calculations (i.e., the calculation of alternative answers where only one is required for each valid data value). On the other hand, data refinement is concerned with removing unnecessary data[3] and generally storing the remaining data in a more appropriate/convenient way — possibly in a newly invented data type/structure. Of course, this data type will be derived using the basic types and constructors described in Chapter 1, and these give rise to rules appropriate for their manipulation.

Suppose that we have some function f calculated by a sequence of smaller calculations f_1, f_2, etc., with intermediate results d_2, d_3, etc., as depicted in Figure 8.1. The idea behind data refinement is that we can 'translate' each of the values d_1, d_2, etc., into a reduced (less detailed?) form so, for example, $a_1 \blacktriangleleft\!\blacktriangleright \mathit{reduce}(d_1)$ and similar translations exist for d_2, d_3, etc. And the function *reduce* must be applicable to all possible values that can occur in the sequence $d_1, d_2, \ldots, d_n$.

Figure 8.1

[2] The way in which they are linked effectively defines (the structure of) these new, internal, structures.

[3] This might not be simply the deletion of individual data values but may involve the 're-coding' of information into different data values. The essential point is that we may not be able to retrieve *all* the original data by reversing the process; however, *enough* information to solve the problem *can* be extracted.

Suppose that there are functions g_1, g_2, etc., which act on the a values in a way that corresponds to the f functions acting on d_1, d_2, etc., as in Figure 8.2.

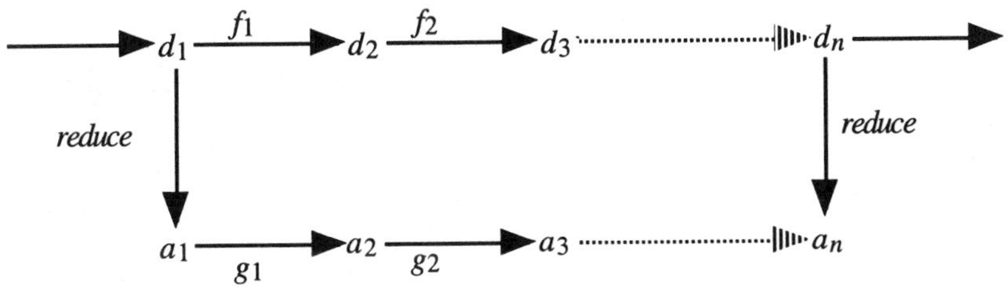

Figure 8.2

We make two observations. Firstly, whichever route we take from d_1 to a_n, we want to get the same answer; in particular, for any value d_1, we require that

$$reduce \circ f(d_1) \Leftrightarrow g \circ reduce(d_1)$$

where $d_n \Leftrightarrow f(d_1)$ and $a_n \Leftrightarrow g(a_1)$,
and $f \triangleq f_{n-1} \circ f_{n-2} \circ \ldots \circ f_2 \circ f_1$, and similarly for g.

And, since d_n is the answer to the original calculation, it should contain no redundant information; therefore a_n should hold exactly the same information as d_n, but it may be in a different form. We therefore have the possibility of the computation sequence as set out in Figure 8.3.

We can also translate at any intermediate stage (for example $reduce(d_2) = a_2$), and hence many other paths from a_1 to d_n are possible.

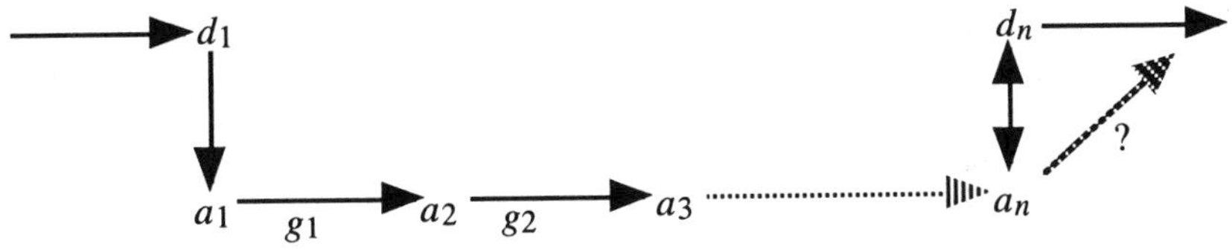

Figure 8.3

The hope here is that the g functions, deduced from the corresponding f functions so as to fit with the *reduce* (or *trans*late) function, are easier to carry out because they have less information to manipulate and those manipulations are somehow easier to perform.

Of course, the reduction steps of d_1 to a_1 (and d_2 to a_2, etc.) can coincide with other refinement strategies, so this might give us nothing 'new'; however, we should be aware of the possibility of information loss.

But we do not need to delve into data structures which have more complicated 'shapes', we can adequately illustrate the concept of data refinement by reference to structures which, on paper, look like lists. These are sets, bags, lists and (1-dimensional) arrays. We consider explicit representations of finite examples of such 'structures'.

Textually, sets, bags, lists and (the contents of) arrays[4] are all *written* as lists, albeit with different bracketing. We now itemise some of the important differences.

When translating from:

(a) a set to a list — we impose an ordering (and in reverse, we must delete duplicates)

(b) a bag to a list — we again impose an ordering (in reverse, there is no problem)

> [Note that these translations *to* lists are not well-defined since many list orderings are possible and legal. Without some explicit ordering process, the 'translation' is not a proper function. However, since every time we write down a sequential representation we use a list, there is no problem. Similarly, storing a set or bag sequentially already gives us such an order that can be used directly in the translation into a list.]

(c) a set to a bag — is OK (but again in the reverse direction we must delete duplicates) and

(d) a list (L) to an array (A)

providing that $\#L < \#A$ translation is easy, but (in PDL, and many programming languages) the bounds of A, p and q, say, are generally fixed when A is created/declared. Here, 'growing' A by appending X values to either end is not always possible. If $\#L = \#A$ and L is mapped directly to A using the straightforward[5] translation, then the array version of

$$L \leftarrow (\text{rest\_of } L)^\frown\langle\text{first\_of } L\rangle$$

requires that *all* elements of A be 'moved'. This is an overhead, which hardly seems to be a computational gain.

[4] The contents of one of these array *is* a list.

[5] Rather than a more complex 'circular' implementation scheme.

Despite the similarities between these four structures, they each have certain individual characteristics. So, using proper notations, we can now get more formal.

Taking X as the generic base type and $x{:}X$ as an arbitrary element, typical predicates and (interrogatory) functions which must be 'translated' appropriately include:

(a) a finite set S is declared as $S{:}\mathfrak{F}(X)$
and "is x in S?" is represented by $x \in S$

(b) a bag B is declared as $B{:}\mathfrak{B}(X)$
and "how many x's in B?" by $x\#S$

(c) a list L is declared as $L{:}X^*$
and "is x in L?"
by $(\exists L_1,L_2,{:}X^*)(L = L_1 {}^\frown \langle x \rangle {}^\frown L_2)$

and, if x in L,
"where is (the first instance of) x in L?" by $\#L_1{+}1$
where: $(\exists L_1,L_2,{:}X^*)(L = L_1 {}^\frown \langle x \rangle {}^\frown L_2)$
and $\neg (x \text{ in } L_1)$, and

(d) an array A denoted by A: array $[p..q]$ of X
(or $A[p..q]{:}X^n$, where $n = q - p + 1$)

then
"x in A" is represented by $(\exists i{:}\mathbb{Z})(\, p \leq i \leq q \wedge A[i] = x)$
and, if x in A then
"where is the first instance of x in A?" by i

where: $(A[i] = x \wedge (\forall j{:}\mathbb{Z})(\, p \leq j < i \wedge A[j] \neq x)\,)$

In sets and bags the order of elements is insignificant, but removing or ignoring any ordering can be difficult to achieve. Often, it is the case that some ordering (perhaps induced from an ordering on X if such an ordering is available or can be devised) can usefully be employed when either counting duplicates or ensuring that there are none. (This has nothing to do with translations between these types, but merely the *storing* of sets and bags.) Usually, sets and bags *are* stored as lists, and the implicit ordering used by this regime can usefully be employed in subsequent translation.

[Note that once we have a *trans*lation function of type $X \rightarrow Y$, it must also preserve operations. Suppose that *bop* is a binary operation on X, and *mop* is a monadic operation on X. We require that *bop'* and *mop'* be corresponding operations on Y values.

The correspondence required is explicitly given by the rules

$$trans(x_1\ bop\ x_2)\ \blacktriangleleft\!\blacktriangleright\ trans(x_1)\ bop'\ \text{trans}(x_2)$$

and

$$trans(mop\ x)\ \blacktriangleleft\!\blacktriangleright\ mop'(trans(x))$$

These rules must apply to 'all' of X. (At least, to that part of X that we require them to. They need to be applicable to all legal situations which arise when performing calculations in type X.)

But perhaps they do not yield all values in Y, and hence we cannot expect that the inverse *relation*, $trans^{-1}$, will be a function. And even if $trans^{-1}$ is a function, it may not always be the case that

$$trans^{-1} \circ trans(x)\ \blacktriangleleft\!\blacktriangleright\ x \qquad \text{for all the } x{:}X \text{ that we need.}$$

But the other way round, $trans \circ trans^{-1}(y,)$ may not even be possible or legal for arbitrary $y{:}Y$, and the rule

$$trans \circ trans^{-1}(y)\ \blacktriangleleft\!\blacktriangleright\ y \qquad \text{may be a complete non-starter.}$$

However, if both of these rules are universally valid, then the translation is totally reversible and should be very easy to perform — both forwards and backwards. It also follows that we are not likely to gain much benefit from the translation. In effect, we have a data *transformation* rather than a proper reduction. (The distinction is the same as the operational transformation/reduction discussed in Chapter 6.)]

We now concentrate on one specific and important translation, the translation from a list to a 1-dimensional array. Despite the fact that the contents of such an array is a list, there are major differences between them. We should expect that these are mainly concerned with the fact that lists can grow, at either end, and arrays do not normally have this property. In the reverse direction, arrays cannot shrink, but we may be able to map a list onto *part* of an array, and this leaves some space for subsequent expansion.

Suppose (either by working in situations where this cannot arise or by planning) that we can avoid 'running out of space'. Let's look at how list operations might relate to operations on a corresponding array.

Specifically, suppose that A is bounded by (indices) p and q and that we wish to translate the list L (where $\#L \leq p - q + 1$) onto part of A. Or, put another way, we load a contiguous part of A with (the values of) L.

So, with $a,b{:}\mathbb{Z}$, we have the following correspondences:

L	maps to	$A[a..b]$	providing that $p \leq a \leq b \leq q$
$L = \langle\rangle$	to	$a > b$	
$\#L = 1$	to	$a = b$	
$\#L$	to	$b - a + 1$	

and, providing that $a \leq b$,

first_of L	to	$A[a]$
last_of L	to	$A[b]$
rest_of L	to	$A[a+1..b]$

and

front_of L	to	$A[a..b-1]$

Further, if $M \frown N$ is a sublist of L,

i.e., $L = L_1 \frown M \frown N \frown L_2$

with M as $A[I..J]$
and N as $A[J+1..K]$ where: $a \leq I \leq J \leq K \leq b$

then, when $I \leq J$, the assignment

$$\langle M, N\rangle \leftarrow \langle \text{front\_of } M, \langle \text{last\_of } M\rangle \frown N\rangle$$

may be implemented, within A, simply by: $J \leftarrow J - 1$

And, similarly, when $J \leq K$,

$$\langle M, N\rangle \leftarrow \langle M \frown \langle \text{first\_of } N\rangle, \text{rest\_of } N\rangle$$

by: $J \leftarrow J + 1$

But other operations can be fairly complex within either data type; for example, swapping the left-most element of M and the right-most element of N is achieved by

$$\langle M, N\rangle \leftarrow \langle\langle \text{last\_of } N\rangle \frown (\text{rest\_of } M), (\text{front\_of } N) \frown \langle \text{first\_of } M\rangle\rangle$$

providing that ($I \leq J$ and $J+1 \leq K$)

and the array version is

$$\langle A[I], A[K]\rangle \leftarrow \langle A[K], A[I]\rangle$$

Now we look at some specific examples.

Example 8.1

Recall Exercise 3.6, in which we derived a recursive scheme for finding the maximum value, m, in a non-empty list, L, of integers. This was

$$
\begin{aligned}
&Listmax(L) \triangleq (\text{if } \#L < 2 \text{ then first\_of}(L) \\
&\qquad\qquad\qquad\qquad\qquad \text{else } Listmax(reduce(L)) \text{ fi}); \\
&reduce(\langle x,y \rangle ^\frown C) \triangleq \langle \text{if } x \leq y \text{ then } y \text{ else } x \text{ fi} \rangle ^\frown C; \\
&m \leftarrow Listmax(L)
\end{aligned}
$$

Removing the recursion, we can delete the *Listmax* function and use the rule

```
        m ← Listmax(L)
◆
        begin  var v:ℤ*;
                    v ← L;
                    while #v ≥ 2
                       do v ← reduce(v)
                       od;
                    m ← first_of(v)
        end
```

where:

$$reduce(\langle x,y \rangle ^\frown C) \triangleq \langle \text{if } x \leq y \text{ then } y \text{ else } x \text{ fi} \rangle ^\frown C.$$

Coding this directly into an array-based scheme – providing that $\#L \leq \#A$ – we have

```
        A[1..n] ← ℤⁿ:L;                [or A ← ℤⁿ:L ]           (⁶)
        ⟨a,b⟩ ← ⟨1,n⟩;
        while a < b
           do
              if A[a] ≤ A[a+1]
                 then skip
                 else A[a+1] ← A[a]
              fi;
              a ← a+1
           od;
        m ← A[a]
```

❑

[6] Although not used in this example, the reverse transformation would be $L \leftarrow \mathbb{Z}^*{:}A[p..q]$ or $L \leftarrow \mathbb{Z}^*{:}A$. In both cases, ordering is preserved so as to ensure 'well-definedness'.

This solves the problem but also may corrupt the (initial contents of the) array. Of course, this does not matter since the specification[7] does not require this, but, by way of investigating the potential of using arrays, we consider some variants of this problem and its solution.

Example 8.2

Notice that within the version above, the 'largest so far' element is moved up the array from left to right and is eventually in $A[n]$ (and $a = b = n$).

Recall that we used the first two elements of L simply because they were easy to access. Alternatively, we could use the end elements, in which case we would define *reduce* as

$$reduce(\langle x\rangle \frown C \frown \langle y\rangle) \triangleq \text{if } x \geq y \text{ then } \langle x\rangle \frown C \text{ else } \langle y\rangle \frown C \text{ fi.}$$

With the same lead in as before, this would give rise to

```
while a < b
    do
       if A[a] ≥ A[b]
         then skip
         else ⟨A[a], A[b]⟩ ← ⟨A[b], A[a]⟩
       fi;
       b ← b−1
    od;
m ← A[a]
```

Now we have a swap rather than a simple over-write but, at the end of processing, $A[1..n]$ holds a shuffled copy of L, which might be useful in other situations. But, of course, we are doing more work than is required by the original problem statement.

❑

[7] Since we 'call by value', the input cannot be changed. However, the array A is an internal item, initialised by L, and it is A, not L, that is corrupted – but in a controlled way that we can exploit.

Example 8.3
A final variant, not deduced from the original scheme, uses indexing, which, of course, is a feature of arrays not directly available in lists.

$\langle a,b \rangle \leftarrow \langle 1,n \rangle$;
$i \leftarrow a$; $\langle m,i \rangle \leftarrow \langle A[i], i+1 \rangle$;
while $i \leq b$
  do
    if $m \leq A[i]$
      then $m \leftarrow A[i]$
      else skip
    fi;
    $i \leftarrow i+1$
  od;
[result $\leftarrow$] m

Upon exit, $A[1..n]$ remains unchanged; we have done no (extra, unnecessary?) work in moving items around. And we could modify the central loop to

while $i \leq b$
  do
    if $m \leq A[i]$
      then $m \leftarrow A[i]$; $j \leftarrow i$
      else skip
    fi;
    $i \leftarrow i+1$
  od   with j initialised to 1.

And, if $j \neq 1$ on exit, we could apply the assignment

$$\langle A[1], A[j] \rangle \leftarrow \langle A[j], A[1] \rangle$$

and place a maximal value in the $A[1]$ position, but even this may not be required.

❑

Loading an array, or part of an array, with values from a given list is a classic example of a situation in which the input (the list) is left unchanged — as it should be if it is the input to a function — but once its value(s) is (are) placed in the array, we can manipulate and *move* the data in our search for the 'answer'.

Hence, as in the next example, we can utilise (tail-recursive) parameterless procedures naturally and to great effect. We shall not cross-refer all the details, but the reader may find it useful to have a quick re-read of the beginning of Section 3.3 and Section 4.5.

Example 8.4
In Chapter 7 (Section 7.3.1), we derived a recursive implementation for an exchange sort using lists. This worked as shown in Figure 8.4 (and Figure 7.4), and the code[8] was as follows:

$$
\begin{aligned}
&exch(C, D) \triangleq \text{ if } \#D < 2 \text{ then } C^\frown D \\
&\qquad\qquad\qquad \text{else if } x \le y \text{ then } exch(C^\frown\langle x\rangle, \langle y\rangle^\frown E) \\
&\qquad\qquad\qquad\qquad\qquad\qquad \text{else } exch(\langle\rangle, C^\frown\langle y, x\rangle^\frown E) \\
&\qquad\qquad\qquad\qquad\qquad\qquad\qquad\qquad \text{where: } D = \langle x, y\rangle^\frown E \\
&\qquad\qquad\qquad\qquad \text{fi} \\
&\qquad\qquad\qquad \text{fi;} \\
&sort(L) \triangleq exch(\langle\rangle, L)
\end{aligned}
$$

We now move to an array-based scheme. Here L is loaded into $A[1..n]$, C into $A[i..j]$, and D into $A[p..q]$, the indices being global. The *exch* function can then be translated into a recursive procedure, *exchp*, and linked to *sort* as

$$
\begin{aligned}
&exchp \triangleq \text{ if } q - p + 1 < 2 \text{ then skip} \\
&\qquad\qquad \text{else if } A[p] \le A[p+1] \\
&\qquad\qquad\qquad \text{then } \langle j, p\rangle \leftarrow \langle j+1, p+1\rangle;\ exchp \\
&\qquad\qquad\qquad \text{else } \langle A[p], A[p+1]\rangle \leftarrow \langle A[p+1], A[p]\rangle; \\
&\qquad\qquad\qquad\qquad \langle i, j, p\rangle \leftarrow \langle 1, 0, 1\rangle;\ exchp \\
&\qquad\qquad\qquad \text{fi} \\
&\qquad\qquad \text{fi;} \\
&sort(L) \triangleq A[1..n] \leftarrow L;\ \langle i, j, p, q\rangle \leftarrow \langle 1, 0, 1, n\rangle;\ exchp
\end{aligned}
$$

from which we can move easily to an iterative version of *sort*:

$$
\begin{aligned}
&A[1..n] \leftarrow L;\ \langle j, p\rangle \leftarrow \langle 0, 1\rangle; \\
&\text{while } n - p \ge 1 \\
&\quad \text{do if } A[p] \le A[p+1] \\
&\qquad \text{then } \langle j, p\rangle \leftarrow \langle j+1, p+1\rangle \\
&\qquad \text{else } \langle A[p], A[p+1]\rangle \leftarrow \langle A[p+1], A[p]\rangle; \\
&\qquad\qquad \langle j, p\rangle \leftarrow \langle 0, 1\rangle \\
&\qquad \text{fi} \\
&\quad \text{od}
\end{aligned}
$$

❑

[8] We have used different identifiers so that A can be used to name the underlying array in the sequel.

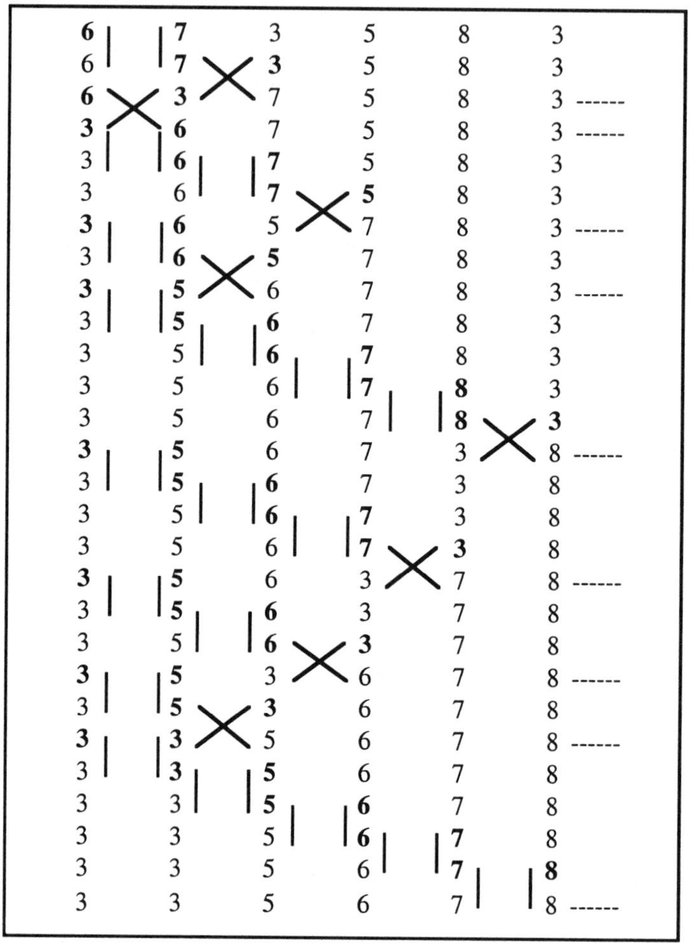

Figure 8.4

The move from a set $S{:}\mathfrak{F}(X)$ to its size $\#S{:}\mathbb{P}$ is typical of a genuine possible loss of information that we might encounter.

We now turn to a familiar example (and one in which the translation function is everywhere invertible, so there is no actual loss of information but merely a change in representation) which we last saw in the guise of a list. We start with the design for the calculation of the factorial function obtained in Chapter 4.

Example 8.5 The Factorial Function (continued)
Earlier, we derived schemes for the calculation of factorials based on the rule

$$fact(n) \blacktriangleleft\!\blacktriangleright mult^{+}(\langle 1..n \rangle)$$

and two designs for the function $mult^{+}$, given by

```
mult+(L) ≜ begin [...]
             z ← first_of(L);
             M ← rest_of(L);
             while #M ≠ 0
                   do z ← mult(z,first_of(M));
                      M ← rest_of(M)
                   od;

             z
           end
```

and

```
mult+(L) ≜ begin [...]
             z ← last_of(L);
             M ← front_of(L);
             while #M ≠ 0
                   do z ← mult(last_of(M),z);
                      M ← front_of(M)
                   od;

             z
           end
```

Of course, this is a very special, unusual, situation where the list holds a run of consecutive integer values. So, instead of using the list M (= $\langle p..q \rangle$), say, we can simply use integer variables p and q. All the references to M must then be changed, and we achieve the more familiar versions of the factorial calculation.

The core of this 'left-to-right' design becomes

```
z ← 1; p ← 2; q ← n;
while p ≤ q
      do z ← z * p; p ← p + 1
      od;
z
```

which optimises to

$$
\begin{array}{l}
z \leftarrow 1;\ p \leftarrow 2; \\
\text{while } p \leq n \\
\qquad \text{do } z \leftarrow z * p;\ p \leftarrow p + 1 \\
\qquad \text{od}; \\
z
\end{array}
$$

Likewise, the core of the 'right-to-left' program scheme becomes

$$
\begin{array}{l}
z \leftarrow n;\ p \leftarrow 1;\ q \leftarrow n - 1; \\
\text{while } p \leq q \\
\qquad \text{do } z \leftarrow q * z;\ q \leftarrow q - 1 \\
\qquad \text{od}; \\
z
\end{array}
$$

which then gives

$$
\begin{array}{l}
z \leftarrow n;\ q \leftarrow n - 1; \\
\text{while } 1 \leq q \\
\qquad \text{do } z \leftarrow q * z;\ q \leftarrow q - 1 \\
\qquad \text{od}; \\
z
\end{array}
$$

These are the familiar algorithms for calculating factorials. They both follow quite routinely from our initial abstract specification, but it is not very easy to transform one final version into the other.

❑

Notice that when using operational/design refinement the calculations are manipulated in a compositional fashion (i.e., we can change the content of any 'box' without the need to change any other parts of the DFD). In contrast, to gain maximum benefit from *data* refinement, it *cannot* be compositional; if we change the way in which one piece of software stores data, then we must also change the way in which other software retrieves it.

8.3 Where to Next?

Knowing that you want to use arrays in your final implementation may well influence the way in which you use and organise lists. Indeed, we shall see examples of this in the next chapter.

The ability to use other structures (and to create new ones appropriate to the task in hand) opens up many possibilities to process the data in either a more 'natural' way, perhaps mirroring some 'non-computer' solution, or in a more 'abstract' fashion driven by the dictates of the computation and, at a lower level, looking nothing like the original problem.

Any study of data structures will include examples of common structures and their use in well-known algorithms. But once the methods for the creation of such structures (at the level of space allocation, pointer manipulation, etc.) have been covered, it is desirable that an algorithm and any data structures be developed together. It therefore follows that there is little general theory linking algorithms to data structures; each example has to be developed individually.

We have already mentioned that certain processes and certain storage regimes do not mix well. The example cited was the use of arrays and sorting by the merging of ordered lists. A special case of merging is insertion. Suppose we have an ordered sequence of integers on which we need to perform insertions and deletions. If we store the integers in a simple 1-dimensional array (rather than in an array indexed indirectly via a secondary array which determines the ordering of items in the first), then performing either an insertion or a deletion requires that we 'shuffle' some of the array contents either to make space for a new value or to close up what would otherwise be a gap in the array.

Now consider (briefly and only in outline) the storing of an ordered list of integers in a tree rather than in an array. We input the list and construct the tree by inserting the integers into the tree one at a time as they are read. Hence, the shape of the tree is determined by the order of the input list. If the given list was in (ascending or descending) numerical order, the tree would be completely one-sided with the top item, the root, being the first read and the last being the only leaf node, as far away as possible from the root and the tree being of maximum height. So reading the list $\langle 7, 9, 10, 20, 30 \rangle$ from left to right gives the tree in Figure 8.5.

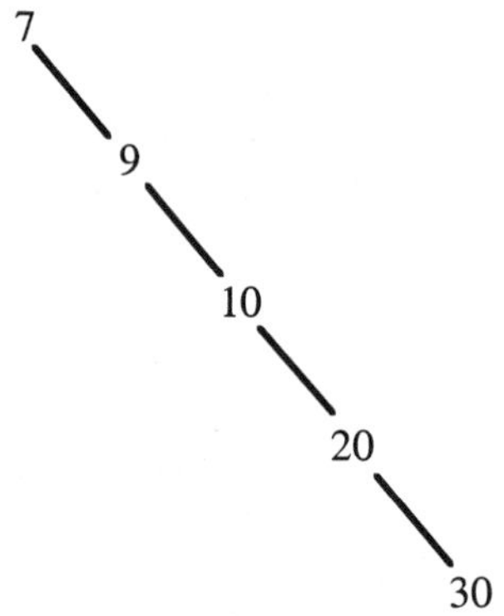

Figure 8.5

With input ⟨ 9, 20, 7, 10, 30⟩, we would get the tree depicted in Figure 8.6.

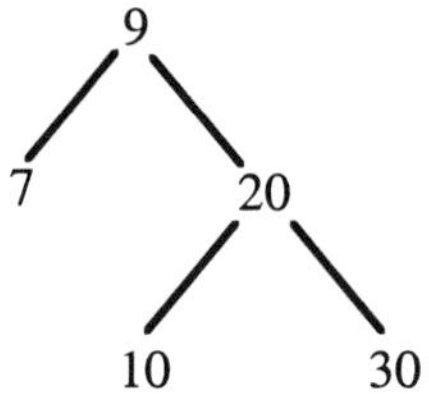

Figure 8.6

The second of these (Figure 8.6) may well be regarded as 'better', basically because it is 'lower' and hence the elements can be reached, from the root (the 'top', in computing, trees are generally drawn upside-down), in fewer moves. Of course, we can balance the tree (periodically or on every update, i.e., insertion or deletion) to lessen the height as much as possible. Figure 8.6 might therefore be regarded as a balanced version of Figure 8.5, although the tree in Figure 8.7 might be more usually expected. Of course, there are others, and in some cases we may wish to leave 'gaps' to aid subsequent processing.

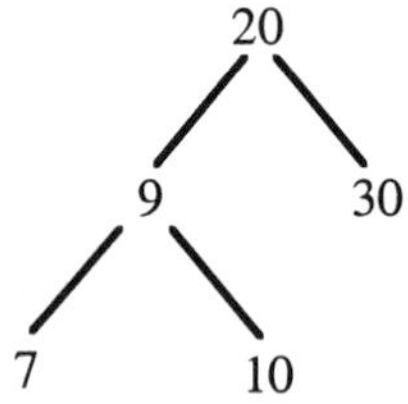

Figure 8.7

Using a tree, insertion is easy; we simply grow another leaf and link it appropriately, as shown by the insertion of '8' into Figure 8.6 to give Figure 8.8. We do not need to shuffle existing elements of an array to make room.

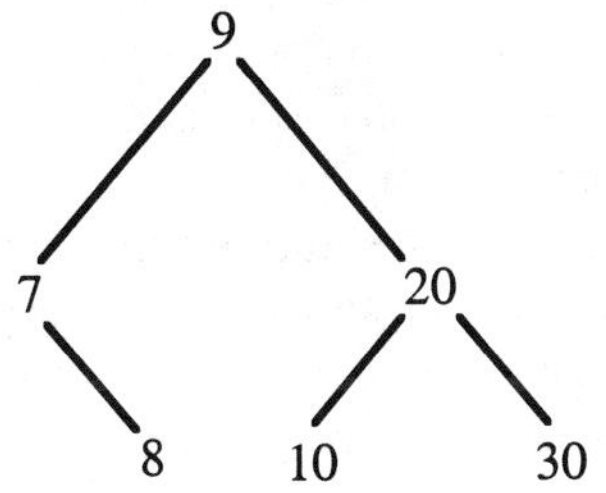

Figure 8.8

Deletions are also easy but not quite so straightforward[9]. Removing a leaf node is simple. Deletion of '10' from Figure 8.8 yields the tree in Figure 8.9.

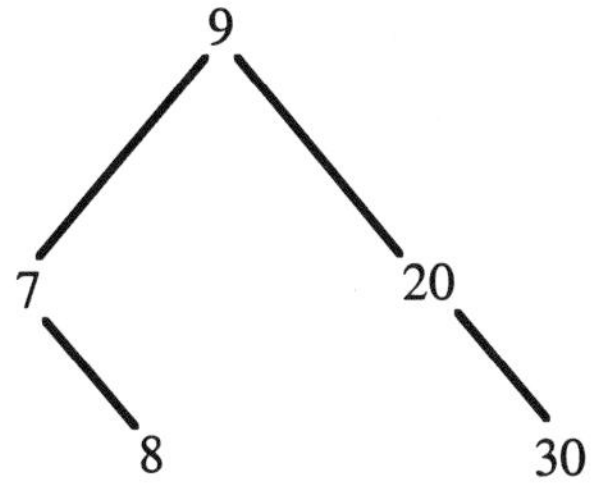

Figure 8.9

However, deletion of any non-leaf value requires reorganisation within the tree so as to prevent other values from being 'cut off'. This can usually be achieved in different ways, even with these small examples. Deleting the value '20' from the tree in Figure 8.8 can give either of the two trees depicted in Figure 8.10.

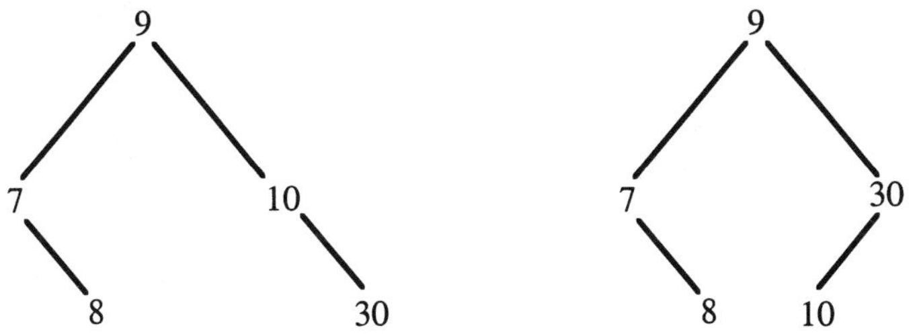

Figure 8.10

[9] The kind of tree used here cannot handle empty lists but a simple variant, which only holds data at leaf nodes, will cope with this *and* obviate the need to delete values held at internal nodes — another 'problem' with our simple trees — as we shall soon see.

That was a brief digression into the possible use of a certain kind of tree data structure and is as far as we go. Remember, once you have understood the common structures you can (and probably should) invent your own to fit the given situation. But remember, particularly when considering computational complexity (the 'cost' of performing a computation, another subject that we do not consider here but which is very important - that accessing data from structures involves extra cost. These costs that are often ignored. The indexing of an array, or the following of a list pointer, to reach the required element is not free. Moreover, the cost can be dependent not only on the structure of your program (and the structures you used) but the way that such structures are implemented and accessed by the system software and even the characteristics of the underlying hardware.

Chapter 9

Sorting Revisited

We now present some variants of the high-level designs given in Chapter 7. We shall use the same broad sub-divisions used there, namely exchange sorts, merge sorts and partition sorts — but beware that the distinction is often confusing, and that in array based implementations most operations are achieved by means of exchanges.

9.1 Exchange Sorts

In Section 7.3.1, we took the general 'reduction' tactic in the form of

$$
\begin{array}{ll}
\mathit{improve}(L) \triangleq \ldots ; & \\
\mathit{sort}(L) \triangleq & (\text{var } V\text{: } \mathbb{Z}^*; \\
& \quad V \leftarrow L; \\
& \quad \text{while} \neg \mathit{ascending}(V) \\
& \quad\quad\quad \text{do } V \leftarrow \mathit{improve}(V) \\
& \quad\quad\quad \text{od}; \\
& \quad \text{result} \leftarrow V); \\
N \leftarrow \mathit{sort}(L) &
\end{array}
$$

and provided a full implementation based on the function *ripple*, in which we moved through the list from left to right, testing the order of adjacent pairs and either finding none to be out of order or, on encountering the first out-of-order pair, we swapped the two elements and started back at the left end, processing the altered list.

From *ripple*, we obtained *exch*, and linked it to the sort problem by

$$
\begin{array}{l}
\mathit{exch}(A, B) \triangleq \ldots ; \\
\mathit{sort}(L) \triangleq \mathit{exch}(\langle\rangle, L); \\
N \leftarrow \mathit{sort}(L)
\end{array}
$$

where *exch* is subject to the rules

$$exch(A, \langle \rangle) \;\blacklozenge\; A$$
$$exch(A, \langle x \rangle) \;\blacklozenge\; A^\frown \langle x \rangle$$

and, when $L:\mathbb{Z}^*$,

$$(x \leq y) \qquad exch(A, \langle x, y \rangle ^\frown L) \;\blacklozenge\; exch(A^\frown \langle x \rangle, \langle y \rangle ^\frown L)$$
$$(x > y) \qquad exch(A, \langle x, y \rangle ^\frown L) \;\blacklozenge\; exch(\langle \rangle, A^\frown \langle y, x \rangle ^\frown L)$$

From these rules, we routinely obtained the implementation design:

$$exch(A, B) \;\triangleq\; \text{if } \#B < 2 \text{ then } A^\frown B$$
$$\text{else if } x \leq y \text{ then } exch(A^\frown \langle x \rangle, \langle y \rangle ^\frown C)$$
$$\text{else } exch(\langle \rangle, A^\frown \langle y, x \rangle ^\frown C)$$
$$\text{where: } B = \langle x, y \rangle ^\frown C$$
$$\text{fi}$$
$$\text{fi}$$

We now develop this idea in two related ways. First, we continue each '*ripple*' all the way up the list and hence may swap more than one mis-ordered pair in a single pass; we call this function *full_ripple*. Alternatively, we could, on finding a number that is lower than its predecessor, let it 'sink' all the way back to its 'correct' position in the segment to the left of the current exchange and then proceed up the list as in the previous algorithm.

So, we turn our attention to '*full_ripple*'.

Starting with the same initial list of integers, we have the progression depicted in Figure 9.1.

Again, the last pass changes nothing and could be used to affirm that the resultant list satisfies the *ascending* condition.

The rules for *full_ripple* are

(1)		$full\_ripple(\langle \rangle) \;\blacklozenge\; \langle \rangle$	end of sort
(2)		$full\_ripple(\langle x \rangle) \;\blacklozenge\; \langle x \rangle$	end of sort
(3)	$(x \leq y)$	$full\_ripple(\langle x, y \rangle) \;\blacklozenge\; \langle x, y \rangle$	end of pass
(4)	$(x > y)$	$full\_ripple(\langle x, y \rangle) \;\blacklozenge\; \langle y, x \rangle$	end of pass

and, when $L:\mathbb{Z}^+$,

(5) $\quad (x \leq y) \quad full\_ripple(\langle x, y \rangle ^\frown L) \;\blacklozenge\; \langle x \rangle ^\frown full\_ripple(\langle y \rangle ^\frown L)$
$$\text{and continue}$$

(6) $\quad (x > y) \quad full\_ripple(\langle x, y \rangle ^\frown L) \;\blacklozenge\; \langle y \rangle ^\frown full\_ripple(\langle x \rangle ^\frown L)$
$$\text{and continue}$$

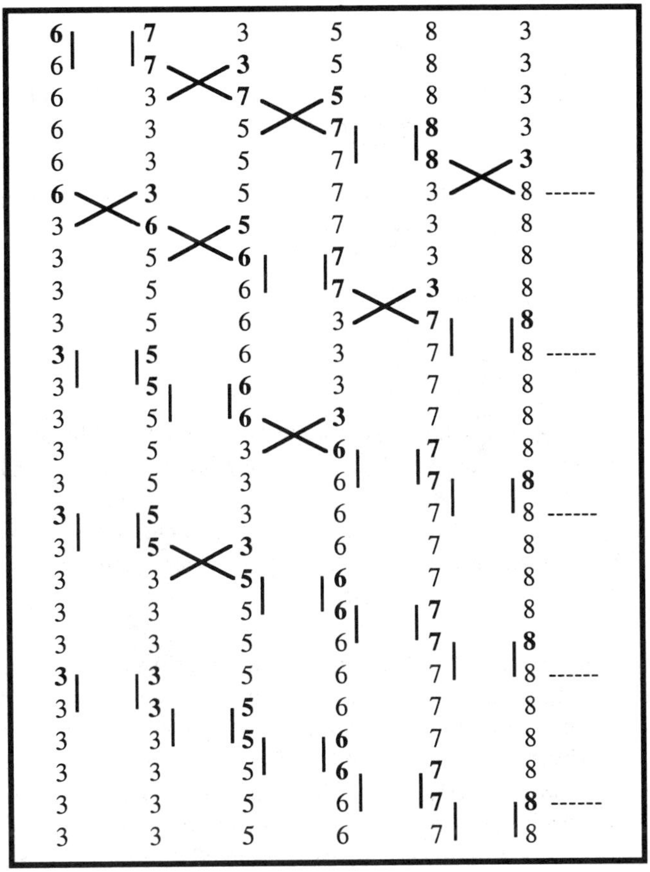

Figure 9.1

This is very similar to *ripple*, but for non-trivial inputs each pass only terminates with rules 3 or 4. These rules always place the larger of x and y at the right-hand end. In rules 5 and 6 (applied left to right), the larger value of x and y is carried forward to the next evaluation of *full_ripple*, moving the value to the right. Hence, after a complete pass, the right-most value is maximal. This can be used to great effect in the variant of 'exchange' based on *full_ripple*.

We call this *exch*(ange)_2, and its rules are

$$\begin{array}{lll} & exch\_2(A, \langle\,\rangle) \blacktriangleleft\!\blacktriangleright A & \text{end of sort} \\ & exch\_2(A, \langle x\rangle) \blacktriangleleft\!\blacktriangleright A \frown \langle x\rangle & \text{end of sort} \\ (x \le y) & exch\_2(A, \langle x, y\rangle) \blacktriangleleft\!\blacktriangleright exch\_2(\langle\,\rangle, A \frown \langle x\rangle) \frown \langle y\rangle & \text{end of pass} \\ (x > y) & exch\_2(A, \langle x, y\rangle) \blacktriangleleft\!\blacktriangleright exch\_2(\langle\,\rangle, A \frown \langle y\rangle) \frown \langle x\rangle & \text{end of pass} \end{array}$$

and, when $L{:}\mathbb{Z}^+$,

$$\begin{array}{lll} (x \le y) & exch\_2(A, \langle x, y\rangle \frown L) \blacktriangleleft\!\blacktriangleright exch\_2(A \frown \langle x\rangle, \langle y\rangle \frown L) & \text{and continue} \\ (x > y) & exch\_2(A, \langle x, y\rangle \frown L) \blacktriangleleft\!\blacktriangleright exch\_2(A \frown \langle y\rangle, \langle x\rangle \frown L) & \text{and continue} \end{array}$$

which is driven from the link

$$sort(L) \triangleq exch\_2(\langle\,\rangle, L)$$

We can see that not only are the bags of integers preserved by all the rules but that, when a pass is started, within $exch\_2(A, B)$ the only elements appended to A are ones of equal or lesser value than some element remaining in B. Hence each pass results in placing a maximal element at the right-hand end of the list, and only the 'front_of' portion of the current list is processed further. How this copes with our standard example list is shown in Figure 9.2.

Once the maximal elements have been moved into position (here one on each pass, but in other examples this could be many more), then we move back to the beginning and start processing again with the revised lisf. Holding the list in an array, we can easily note the position of the 'last' swap on each pass; this gives us what is generally called a ***bubble sort***, but we shall not pursue this possibility. However, notice that, presented with a list of length n that is already in ascending order, *exch_2* will still perform $n - 1$ passes, each confirming the correct position of just one element and never changing the list at all. This is indicated by the 'staircase' in Figure 9.2.

The processing of all non-empty lists terminates with the singleton rule with $A = \langle\,\rangle$. The empty rule is also only applicable when $A = \langle\,\rangle$.

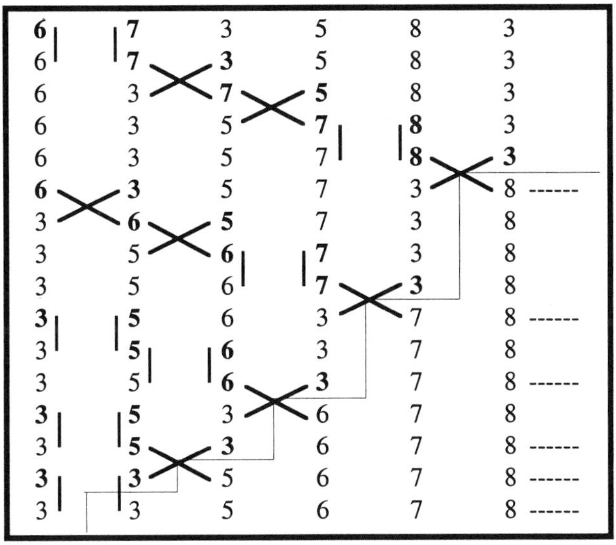

Figure 9.2

Hence we have, as another complete exchange sorting program

```
exch_2(A, B) ≜ if #B < 2 then A⌢B
               else if #B = 2
                    then if x ≤ y
                         then exch_2(⟨⟩, A⌢⟨x⟩)⌢⟨y⟩
                         else exch_2(⟨⟩, A⌢⟨y⟩)⌢⟨x⟩
                                                where:  B = ⟨x, y⟩
                         fi
                    else if x ≤ y
                         then exch_2(A⌢⟨x⟩, ⟨y⟩⌢C)
                         else exch_2(A⌢⟨y⟩, ⟨x⟩⌢C)
                                                where:  B = ⟨x, y⟩⌢C
                         fi
                    fi
               fi;
sort(L) ≜ exch_2(⟨⟩, L);
N ← sort(L)
```

which can be further simplified.

Next we essentially apply the same technique, twice, in opposite directions. We move high values up the list and, on encountering a small value, we move it down. We avoid further explanation and merely present the rules for the exchange function, *exch_3*:

$$exch\_3(A, \langle\rangle) \;◆\; A \qquad \text{end of sort}$$
$$exch\_3(A, \langle x\rangle) \;◆\; sink(A, x) \qquad \text{end of sort}$$

and, when $L{:}\mathbb{Z}^*$,

$$(x \le y) \quad exch\_3(A, \langle x, y\rangle \frown L) \;◆\; exch\_3(A \frown \langle x\rangle, \langle y\rangle \frown L) \qquad \text{and continue}$$
$$(x > y) \quad exch\_3(A, \langle x, y\rangle \frown L) \;◆\; exch\_3(B, \langle x\rangle \frown L) \qquad \text{and continue}$$

where: $B = sink(A, y)$

and *sink* satisfies the rules:

$$sink(\langle\rangle, y) \;◆\; \langle y\rangle$$
$$(a \le y) \quad sink(X \frown \langle a\rangle, y) \;◆\; X \frown \langle a\rangle \frown \langle y\rangle$$
$$(a > y) \quad sink(X \frown \langle a\rangle, y) \;◆\; sink(X, y) \frown \langle a\rangle$$

As before, this is driven by

$$sort(L) \triangleq exch\_3(\langle\rangle, L)$$

With the usual example list, we get the following progression of evaluation steps:

$sort(\langle 6, 7, 3, 5, 8, 3\rangle)$

◆

$exch\_3(\langle\rangle, \langle 6, 7, 3, 5, 8, 3\rangle)$

◆

$exch\_3(\langle 6\rangle, \langle 7, 3, 5, 8, 3\rangle)$

and $sink(\langle 6\rangle, 3)$

◆ $sink(\langle\rangle, 3) \frown \langle 6\rangle$

◆ $\langle 3\rangle \frown \langle 6\rangle$

◆ $\langle 3,6\rangle$

◆

$exch\_3(\langle 3,6\rangle, \langle 7, 5, 8, 3\rangle)$

and $sink(\langle 3,6\rangle, 5)$

◆ $sink(\langle 3\rangle, 5) \frown \langle 6\rangle$

◆ $\langle 3\rangle \frown \langle 5\rangle \frown \langle 6\rangle$

◆ $\langle 3,5,6\rangle$

$\Leftrightarrow$

$exch\_3(\langle 3,5,6\rangle, \langle 7, 8, 3\rangle)$

$\Leftrightarrow$

$exch\_3(\langle 3,5,6,7\rangle, \langle 8, 3\rangle)$

and

$sink(\langle 3,5,6,7\rangle, 3)$

$\Leftrightarrow$

$sink(\langle 3,5,6\rangle, 3)^\frown\langle 7\rangle$

$\Leftrightarrow$

$sink(\langle 3,5\rangle, 3)^\frown\langle 6,7\rangle$

$\Leftrightarrow$

$sink(\langle 3\rangle, 3)^\frown\langle 5,6,7\rangle$

$\Leftrightarrow$

$\langle 3\rangle^\frown\langle 3\rangle^\frown\langle 5,6,7\rangle$

$\Leftrightarrow$

$\langle 3,3,5,6,7\rangle$

$\Leftrightarrow$

$exch\_3(\langle 3,3,5,6,7\rangle, \langle 8\rangle)$

$\Leftrightarrow$

$exch\_3(\langle 3,3,5,6,7,8\rangle, \langle\,\rangle)$

$\Leftrightarrow$

$\langle 3,3,5,6,7,8\rangle$

These two functions can be incorporated in yet another sorting program as

```
exch_3(A, B) ≜ if #B = 0 then A
               else if #B = 1
                    then sink(A, first_of B)
                    else if x≤y
                         then exch_3(A⁀<x>, <y>⁀C)
                         else exch_3(sink(A, y), <x>⁀C)
                                       where: B = <x, y>⁀C
                         fi
                    fi
               fi;
sort(L) ≜ exch_3(<>, L);
sink(A, y) ≜ if #A = 0 then <y>
             else if a ≤ y
                  then  A⁀<y>
                  else  sink(X, y)⁀<a>
                                where: A = X⁀<a>
                  fi
             fi;
N ← sort(L)
```

This is not the only way of describing (coding) this particular process using *sink*. Using a different intermediate function name (so as to try to avoid confusion), we could use the following linking rules

$$sort(L) \;\blacklozenge\; exch\_4(\langle\rangle, L)$$
$$exch\_4(A, \langle\rangle) \;\blacklozenge\; A$$

and

$$exch\_4(A, \langle x\rangle \frown B) \;\blacklozenge\; exch\_4(C, B)$$
$$\text{where:} \quad C = sink(A, x)$$

with the same *sink* rules as before. Here, all the relational testing (between list elements) is done by *sink*, so the *exch_4* rules are much simpler.

Another possibility involves alternating full sweeps through the middle section of the list, moving a high number to the right and then back in the opposite direction. moving a low number to the left, and back sweeping to the right. At each stage, at least one (high or low) moves to the correct position (possibly more than one) and the middle segment of unsorted values gets smaller. This gives rise to a sorting technique know as the ***Cocktail Shaker***. We leave the formulation of rules and the derivation of an algorithm as an exercise to the reader.

9.2 Merge Sorts

We shall now present some simple variations on the basic merge sort.

Recall the design obtained so far

```
split_1(L) ≙ ... ;
merge(⟨N1,N2⟩) ≙ (var A,B,C:ℤ*;
                  ⟨A,B⟩ ← ⟨N1,N2⟩;
                  C ← ⟨⟩;
                  while A ≠ ⟨⟩ ∧ B ≠ ⟨⟩
                  do  if first_of(A) ≤ first_of(B)
                      then  C ← C⌢⟨first_of(A)⟩; A ← rest_of(A)
                      else  C ← C⌢⟨first_of(B)⟩; B ← rest_of(B)
                      fi
                  od;
                  result ← C⌢A⌢B);
sort(L) ≙ if #L < 2
          then result ← L
          else (var L1,L2,N1,N2:ℤ+;
               ⟨L1,L2⟩ ← split_1(L);
               N1 ← sort(L1) ‖ N2 ← sort(L2);
               result ← merge(⟨N1,N2⟩)      )
          fi;
N ← sort(L)
```

where *split*_1 is specified by

$split\_1: \mathbb{Z}^* \rightarrow \mathbb{Z}^* \times \mathbb{Z}^*$
pre-$split\_1(L) \triangleq \#L \geq 2$
post-$split\_1(L, \langle L_1, L_2 \rangle) \triangleq L = L_1 {}^\frown L_2 \quad \wedge \quad \#L_1 \geq 1 \quad \wedge \quad \#L_2 \geq 1$

First note that *any* non-void *split*ting routine will suffice, and it is the choice of splitting strategy which dictates how different *merge* sorts work. Such choices may also facilitate specialisations in the *merge* function, as we shall see.

9.2.1 Variants of the Merge Sort

This basic design of a merge sort can be refined (particularised) in several ways. For instance, *split*_1 may be replaced[1] by a deterministic version, as in

$$\begin{aligned}
&split_6: \mathbb{Z}^{+} \rightarrow \mathbb{Z}^{+} \times \mathbb{Z}^{+} \\
&\text{pre-}split_6(L) \triangleq \#L \geq 2 \\
&\text{post-}split_6(L, \langle L_1, L_2 \rangle) \triangleq L = L_1 {}^\frown L_2 \ \wedge \ \#L_1 = 1
\end{aligned}$$

With this version, the left-hand sorting sub-process involves no calculation and the *merge* becomes an insertion, giving us what is classically regarded as an ***insertion sort***. We now present a reasoned derivation of this algorithm.

Using the familiar "first_of" and "rest_of" operations, a useful rearrangement of post-*split*_6 would seem to be

$$L_1 = \langle \text{first\_of}(L) \rangle \ \wedge \ L_2 = \text{rest\_of}(L)$$

As always, we should check. First notice that $\#L \geq 2 \Rightarrow \#L \geq 1$, so the first_of and rest_of functions are defined and we can apply the conditional rule

$$(\#L \geq 1) \qquad \langle \text{first\_of}(L) \rangle {}^\frown \text{rest\_of}(L) \Leftrightarrow L$$

So, substituting $\langle \text{first\_of}(L) \rangle$ for L_1 and rest_of(L) for L_2 in the post-condition, we get

$$\begin{aligned}
& \text{post-}split_6(L, \langle \langle \text{first_of}(L) \rangle, \text{rest_of}(L) \rangle) \\
\Leftrightarrow\ & L = \langle \text{first_of}(L) \rangle {}^\frown \text{rest_of}(L) \ \wedge \ \#\langle \text{first_of}(L) \rangle = 1 \\
\Leftrightarrow\ & L = L \ \wedge \ 1 = 1 \\
\Leftrightarrow\ & \text{True} \qquad\qquad \text{i.e., the solution checks out OK}
\end{aligned}$$

---

[1] Note that although the signature of *split*_6 is more restrictive than that of *split*_1, this is still a refinement since the restriction imposed by pre-*split*_1 and post-*split*_1 forces the input and outputs to be non-empty lists.

Substituting back into the merge sort scheme gives

⏩ $split\_6(L) \triangleq \ldots ;$
$merge(\langle N_1,N_2 \rangle) \triangleq \ldots ;$ — NB see[2]
$sort(L) \triangleq$ if $\#L < 2$
then result $\leftarrow L$
else (var $L_1,L_2,N_1,N_2:\mathbb{Z}^+$;
$\langle L_1,L_2 \rangle \leftarrow split\_6(L)$;
$N_1 \leftarrow sort(L_1) \parallel N_2 \leftarrow sort(L_2)$;
result $\leftarrow merge(\langle N_1,N_2 \rangle)$)
fi;
$N \leftarrow sort(L)$

But now $\#L_1 = 1$ and so $sort(L_1) = L_1$. In fact, the implementation of *split_6* is so simple that it can be removed altogether to give

◆ $merge(\langle N_1,N_2 \rangle) \triangleq \ldots ;$
$sort(L) \triangleq$ if $\#L < 2$
then result $\leftarrow L$
else (var $N_2:\mathbb{Z}^+$;
$N_2 \leftarrow sort(\text{rest\_of}(L))$;
result $\leftarrow merge(\langle\langle \text{first\_of}(L)\rangle,N_2 \rangle)$)
fi;
$N \leftarrow sort(L)$

And *merge* can now be simplified since we know its first argument is always of length 1,

$$merge\_1:\mathbb{Z}^* \times \mathbb{Z}^* \rightarrow \mathbb{Z}^*$$
$$\text{pre-}merge\_1(\langle N_1,N_2 \rangle) \triangleq \#N_1 = 1 \land ascending(N_2)$$
$$\text{post-}merge\_1(\langle N_1,N_2 \rangle,N) \triangleq ascending(N) \land \text{bag\_of}(N) = \text{bag\_of}(N_1) \uplus \text{bag\_of}(N_2)$$

2 Although this is the formally correct notation, we shall accept the conventional, but strictly illegal, shorthand by writing the function with two parameters, like '$merge(N_1,N_2)$', rather than a single parameter that happens to be a pair. A transformation tool might require the syntax to be more strict.

Since N_1 is always of the form $\langle x \rangle$, $merge\_1$ can sensibly be re-written as $insert$ where $insert(\langle x,N_2 \rangle) \triangleq merge\_1(\langle\langle x \rangle,N_2 \rangle)$ and, as before,

$$insert{:}\mathbb{Z}\times\mathbb{Z}^* \to \mathbb{Z}^*$$
$$\text{pre-}insert(\langle x,N_2 \rangle) \triangleq ascending(N_2)$$
$$\text{post-}insert(\langle x,N_2 \rangle,N) \triangleq ascending(N) \land$$
$$\text{bag\_of}(N) = \text{bag\_of}(N_1) \uplus \{\!\!\{x\}\!\!\}$$

to give

◆ $\qquad insert(x,N_2) \triangleq \dots$;
$\qquad sort(L) \triangleq$ if $\#L < 2$
$\qquad\qquad\qquad$ then result $\leftarrow L$
$\qquad\qquad\qquad$ else result $\leftarrow insert(\text{first\_of}(L), sort(\text{rest\_of}(L))$)
$\qquad\qquad\qquad$ fi;
$\qquad N \leftarrow sort(L)$

Finally, to complete this version of *sort*, we need an implementation scheme for *insert*. First let's change the names in the specification of *insert*. Obviously, this makes no technical difference, but may make it easier to see what is happening, i.e., *insert x* into *L* giving *N*:

$$insert{:}\mathbb{Z}\times\mathbb{Z}^* \to \mathbb{Z}^*$$
$$\text{pre-}insert(\langle x,L \rangle) \triangleq ascending(L)$$
$$\text{post-}insert(\langle x,L \rangle,N) \triangleq ascending(N) \land$$
$$\text{bag\_of}(N) = \text{bag\_of}(L) \uplus \{\!\!\{x\}\!\!\}$$

It would seem reasonable to require that *insert* satisfies a set of rules such as those given below. Check that these make sense[3] and that they are consistent with the specification given above.

$$insert(x,\langle\,\rangle) \quad◆\quad \langle x \rangle$$

$(x \le y)$ $\qquad\qquad insert(x,\langle y \rangle) \quad◆\quad \langle x,y \rangle$
$(x > y)$ $\qquad\qquad insert(x,\langle y \rangle) \quad◆\quad \langle y,x \rangle$
and, with $L_1,L_2{:}\mathbb{Z}^+$,
$(x \le \text{first\_of}(L_2))$ $\qquad insert(x,L_1\!^\frown\!L_2) \quad◆\quad insert(x,L_1)\!^\frown\!L_2$
$(x > \text{first\_of}(L_2))$ $\qquad insert(x,L_1\!^\frown\!L_2) \quad◆\quad L_1\!^\frown\!insert(x,L_2)$

---

[3]   Notice also that these rules guarantee convergence of $insert(x, L)$ using $\#L$ as the measure.

But here the breakpoint between L_1 and L_2 is arbitrary, and hence the rules cannot be used directly in an implementation design. An alternative set of rules is

$$insert(x,\langle\rangle) \;◆\; \langle x\rangle$$

$(x \le y)$ $\quad insert(x,\langle y\rangle) \;◆\; \langle x,y\rangle$

$(x > y)$ $\quad insert(x,\langle y\rangle) \;◆\; \langle y,x\rangle$

and, with $L_2{:}\mathbb{Z}^+$,

$(x \le y)$ $\quad insert(x,\langle y\rangle ^\frown L_2) \;◆\; \langle x\rangle ^\frown \langle y\rangle ^\frown L_2$

$(x > y)$ $\quad insert(x,\langle y\rangle ^\frown L_2) \;◆\; \langle y\rangle ^\frown insert(x,L_2)$

And these reduce to

$$insert(x,\langle\rangle) \;◆\; \langle x\rangle$$

and, with $L_2{:}\mathbb{Z}^*$,

$(x \le y)$ $\quad insert(x,\langle y\rangle ^\frown L_2) \;◆\; \langle x\rangle ^\frown \langle y\rangle ^\frown L_2$

$(x > y)$ $\quad insert(x,\langle y\rangle ^\frown L_2) \;◆\; \langle y\rangle ^\frown insert(x,L_2)$

So

```
insert(x,L) ◆ if L = ⟨⟩ then ⟨x⟩
                         else if x ≤ first_of(L)
                              then ⟨x⟩⁀L
                              else ⟨first_of(L)⟩⁀insert(x,rest_of(L))
                              fi
              fi
```

◆ making the two "then" clauses the same to allow their combination

```
insert(x,L) ◆ if L = ⟨⟩ then ⟨x⟩⁀L
                         else if x ≤ first_of(L)
                              then ⟨x⟩⁀L
                              else ⟨first_of(L)⟩⁀insert(x,rest_of(L))
                              fi
              fi
```

◆ combine the two "if" constructs

```
insert(x,L) ◆ if L = ⟨⟩ ∨ x ≤ first_of(L)
              then ⟨x⟩⁀L
              else ⟨first_of(L)⟩⁀insert(x,rest_of(L))
              fi
```

Applying the associative recursion removal rule, we get

$$
\begin{array}{l}
insert(x,L) \triangleq (\text{var } N_0{:}\mathbb{Z}^*, L_0{:}\mathbb{Z}^*; \\
\quad N_0 \leftarrow \langle\rangle; \\
\quad L_0 \leftarrow L; \\
\quad \text{while } \neg(L_0 = \langle\rangle \vee x \le \text{first\_of}(L_0)) \\
\quad\quad \text{do } N_0 \leftarrow N_0 \frown \langle \text{first\_of}(L_0) \rangle; \\
\quad\quad\quad L_0 \leftarrow \text{rest\_of}(L_0) \\
\quad\quad \text{od}; \\
\quad\quad \text{result} \leftarrow N_0 \frown \langle x \rangle \frown L_0 \\
\quad); \\
sort(L) \triangleq \text{if } \#L < 2 \text{ then result} \leftarrow L \\
\quad\quad \text{else result} \leftarrow insert(\text{ first\_of}(L), sort(\text{rest\_of}(L))) \\
\quad \text{fi}; \\
N \leftarrow sort(L)
\end{array}
$$

Note that by virtue of the recursion at the top level and the use of first_of and rest_of, the insertion here effectively works in reverse, taking the last element in the list, placing it in the output, and progressively inserting the elements into that list by working backwards through the input. Obviously, the synthesis can be done just as well using the functions *last_of* and *front_of*, where, when $\#L \ge 1$,

$$\text{front\_of}(L) \frown \langle \text{last\_of}(L) \rangle \Leftrightarrow L$$

[And notice that in these derivations we have purposely avoided corrupting the input list.]

We now have what is generally know as an ***Insertion Sort***.

Other list decompositions based on size can be used. These include

$$
\begin{array}{l}
split\_7{:}\ \mathbb{Z}^+ \rightarrow \mathbb{Z}^+ \times \mathbb{Z}^+ \\
\text{pre-}split\_7(L) \triangleq \#L \ge 2 \\
\text{post-}split\_7(L, \langle L_1, L_2 \rangle) \triangleq L = L_1 \frown L_2 \wedge \quad \#L_1 = \#L \div 2
\end{array}
$$

which breaks the list as equally as possible. or

$$
\begin{array}{l}
split\_8{:}\ \mathbb{Z}^+ \rightarrow \mathbb{Z}^+ \times \mathbb{Z}^+ \\
\text{pre-}split\_8(L) \triangleq \#L \ge n \\
\text{post-}split\_8(L, \langle L_1, L_2 \rangle) \triangleq L = L_1 \frown L_2 \wedge \quad \#L_1 = n
\end{array}
$$

for some specific value of n. Both these variants are better suited to multi-processor systems when a division of effort is desired.

Alternatively, the initial problem domain can be split using the predicate *ascending*(L).

if *ascending*(L) then $N = L$
else *split* L at a point where it is not ascending
fi

This requires that *split* becomes

$$\begin{array}{l}
split_9\colon \mathbb{Z}^* \to \mathbb{Z}^+ \times \mathbb{Z}^+ \\
\text{pre-}split_9(L) \triangleq \neg ascending(L) \\
\text{post-}split_9(L, \langle L_1, L_2 \rangle) \triangleq (\exists L_3, L_4{:}\mathbb{Z}^*, x, y{:}\mathbb{Z}) \\
\qquad (L = L_1 {}^\frown L_2 \wedge \\
\qquad\ \ L_1 = L_3 {}^\frown \langle x \rangle \wedge \\
\qquad\ \ L_2 = \langle y \rangle {}^\frown L_4 \wedge \\
\qquad\ \ x > y)
\end{array}$$

which could be used recursively to break the original list into ascending runs. No sub-lists would be re-sorted unnecessarily, and this gives rise to a *"minimal" merge sort*. Notice that we could also impose a non-parallel structure on the algorithm by adding a further restriction (refinement) within *split_9* by insisting that "*ascending*(L_1)" also holds.

$$\begin{array}{l}
split_10\colon \mathbb{Z}^* \to \mathbb{Z}^+ \times \mathbb{Z}^+ \\
\text{pre-}split_10(L) \triangleq \neg ascending(L) \\
\text{post-}split_10(L, \langle L_1, L_2 \rangle) \triangleq (\exists L_3, L_4{:}\mathbb{Z}^*, x, y{:}\mathbb{Z}) \\
\qquad (L = L_1 {}^\frown L_2 \wedge \\
\qquad\ \ L_1 = L_3 {}^\frown \langle x \rangle \wedge \\
\qquad\ \ L_2 = \langle y \rangle {}^\frown L_4 \wedge \\
\qquad\ \ x > y \wedge \\
\qquad\ \ ascending(L_1))
\end{array}$$

With this specification, it is quite straightforward to devise an appropriate set of rules which a deterministic function should obey and hence extract a functional program design.

9.3 Partition Sorts

In contrast with merge sorts, where all work is essentially done in the combine phase, in partition sorts, the computational effort is concentrated in the splitting phase. Devising clever ways to achieve the required split is at the heart of algorithms such as *Quicksort* and others.

As may be expected, this design can also be refined in several ways. The most obvious is to require that one of L_1 or L_2 be a singleton list and therefore does not need sorting. Making an appropriate refinement to the splitting phase, to *split*_3, gives

$$
\begin{aligned}
&split\_11: \mathbb{Z}^* \to \mathbb{Z}^* \times \mathbb{Z}^* \\
&\text{pre-}split\_11(L) \triangleq \#L \geq 2 \\
&\text{post-}split\_11(L,\langle\langle x\rangle,L_2\rangle) \triangleq \quad (\text{bag\_of}(L) = \{\!|x|\!\} \uplus \text{bag\_of}(L_2) \\
&\qquad\qquad \wedge\ (\wedge(x \leq y) \mid y{:}\mathbb{Z} \mid y \text{ in } L_2\ )
\end{aligned}
$$

This simplifies to

$$
\begin{aligned}
&split\_11: \mathbb{Z}^* \to \mathbb{Z}^* \times \mathbb{Z}^* \\
&\text{pre-}split\_11(L) \triangleq \#L \geq 2 \\
&\text{post-}split\_11(L,\langle\langle x\rangle,L_2\rangle) \triangleq (\text{bag\_of}(L) = \{\!|x|\!\} \uplus \text{bag\_of}(L_2) \\
&\qquad\qquad \wedge\ x = (min\ y \mid y{:}\mathbb{Z} \mid y \text{ in } L\ )\ )
\end{aligned}
$$

where:

$$min(x,y) \triangleq \text{if } x \leq y \text{ then } x \text{ else } y \text{ fi}$$

A possible refinement of *split*_11 is simply to remove x from L, leaving the remaining elements, in their original order, in L_2. If x is in L (as it must be from the specification of *split*_11) then there are lists L_3 and L_4, say, such that

$$L = L_3 \frown \langle x\rangle \frown L_4$$

We call the new version *split*_12. Note that *split*_11 ▶ *split*_12.

$$
\begin{aligned}
&split\_12: \mathbb{Z}^* \to \mathbb{Z}^* \times \mathbb{Z}^* \\
&\text{pre-}split\_12(L) \triangleq \#L \geq 2 \\
&\text{post-}split\_12(L,\langle\langle x\rangle,L_2\rangle) \triangleq (\exists L_3,L_4{:}\mathbb{Z}^*) \\
&\qquad\qquad (\ L = L_3 \frown \langle x\rangle \frown L_4\ \wedge \\
&\qquad\qquad\ \ L_2 = L_3 \frown L_4\ \wedge \\
&\qquad\qquad\ \ x = (min\ y \mid y{:}\mathbb{Z} \mid y \text{ in } L\ )\ )
\end{aligned}
$$

We can then further refine *split*_12 by insisting that the x extracted from L is the first encountered, from left to right. This gives *split*_13

$$
\begin{aligned}
& split\_13: \mathbb{Z}^* \to \mathbb{Z}^* \times \mathbb{Z}^* \\
& \text{pre-}split\_13(L) \triangleq \#L \geq 2 \\
& \text{post-}split\_13(L, \langle\langle x\rangle, L_2\rangle) \triangleq (\exists L_3, L_4{:}\mathbb{Z}^*) \\
& \qquad\qquad (L = L_3 {}^\frown \langle x\rangle {}^\frown L_4 \wedge \\
& \qquad\qquad\;\; L_2 = L_3 {}^\frown L_4 \wedge \\
& \qquad\qquad\;\; \neg x \text{ in } L_3 \wedge \\
& \qquad\qquad\;\; x = (min\ y \mid y{:}\mathbb{Z} \mid y \text{ in } L)\ )
\end{aligned}
$$

The idea is to move a minimal element to the left end whilst leaving the remaining elements in their original positions. Unfortunately, if, as is commonly done, the lists are held in arrays, then we cannot simply leave gaps, and the elements would have to be shuffled up[4]. An alternative refinement of *split*_11 (but not of *split*_13!) in which at most a single swap is required[5] is as follows

$$
\begin{aligned}
& split\_14: \mathbb{Z}^* \to \mathbb{Z}^* \times \mathbb{Z}^* \\
& \text{pre-}split\_14(L) \triangleq \#L \geq 2 \\
& \text{post-}split\_14(L, \langle\langle x\rangle, L_2\rangle) \triangleq \\
& \qquad (x = (min\ y \mid y{:}\mathbb{Z} \mid y \text{ in } L\ ) \wedge \\
& \qquad (L = \langle x\rangle {}^\frown L_2 \vee \\
& \qquad (\exists y{:}\mathbb{Z}, L_3, L_4{:}\mathbb{Z}^*)(\ L = \langle y\rangle {}^\frown L_3 {}^\frown \langle x\rangle {}^\frown L_4 \wedge \\
& \qquad\qquad L_2 = L_3 {}^\frown \langle y\rangle {}^\frown L_4 \wedge \\
& \qquad\qquad \neg x \text{ in } L_3\ )\ )\ )
\end{aligned}
$$

So, either we perform a single swap (which reduces the out-of-order measure, $M(\langle x\rangle {}^\frown L_2) < M(L)$), or $x = y$ and the problem reduces to sorting L_2 and $\#L_2 < \#L$.

Before putting *split*_14 into the general structure for a partition sort, we need to calculate an implementation of *split*_14. We could start in the usual way by considering the possible forms of the input list L, but it will soon become clear that the place where L is divided by x, (i.e., L_3 and L_4) is important. It is therefore convenient to reformulate *split*_14 so as to combine the two alternatives (currently combined using '$\vee$') into a conditional form. This reflects the necessary ordering of the sub-components, namely, identify the minimum value, locate where it is, and then split the list accordingly.

[4] And even using lists, this is not particularly easy.

[5] If our lists consisted of 'large' records instead of simply integers (effectively the keys of such records), then swapping list elements might be expensive and this would be a *significant* consideration.

We derive a design for *split*_14 in two different ways, the first of which is intentionally gradual.

Hence

$$\begin{aligned}
split_14(L) \;\blacktriangleleft\!\blacktriangleright\; & \text{if } L_3 = \langle\,\rangle \\
& \text{then } \langle\langle x\rangle, L_4\rangle \\
& \text{else } \langle\langle x\rangle, \text{rest_of}(L_3)^\frown\langle\text{first_of}(L_3)\rangle^\frown L_4\rangle \\
& \text{fi} \\
& \qquad\qquad \text{where: } \langle L_3, L_4\rangle = partition_1(L, x) \\
& \qquad\qquad \text{where: } x = (min\ y \mid y{:}\mathbb{Z} \mid y \text{ in } L\ )
\end{aligned}$$

and

$$\begin{aligned}
& partition_1{:}\ \mathbb{Z}^*\times\mathbb{Z} \to \mathbb{Z}^*\times\mathbb{Z}^* \\
& \text{pre-}partition_1(\langle L,x\rangle) \triangleq\ x \text{ in } L \\
& \text{post-}partition_1(\langle L,x\rangle,\langle L_3,L_4\rangle) \triangleq L = L_3{}^\frown\langle x\rangle^\frown L_4 \land \\
& \qquad\qquad\qquad\qquad \neg x \text{ in } L_3\ \ )
\end{aligned}$$

Viewed computationally, the list L has to be visited twice, once to determine x and then again essentially to find L_3. This can be avoided by having the partitioning function find the minimum as well as using it in the decomposition of L.

Hence

$$\begin{aligned}
split_14(L) \;\blacktriangleleft\!\blacktriangleright\; & \text{if } L_3 = \langle\,\rangle \\
& \text{then } \langle\langle x\rangle, L_4\rangle \\
& \text{else } \langle\langle x\rangle, \text{rest_of}(L_3)^\frown\langle\text{first_of}(L_3)\rangle^\frown L_4\rangle \\
& \text{fi} \\
& \qquad\qquad \text{where: } \langle L_3, x, L_4\rangle = partition_2(L)
\end{aligned}$$

and

$$\begin{aligned}
& partition_2{:}\ \mathbb{Z}^* \to \mathbb{Z}^*\times\mathbb{Z}\times\mathbb{Z}^* \\
& \text{pre-}partition_2(L) \triangleq\ \neg L = \langle\,\rangle \\
& \text{post-}partition_2(L,\langle L_3,x,L_4\rangle) \triangleq (\ x = (min\ y \mid y{:}\mathbb{Z} \mid y \text{ in } L\ ) \land \\
& \qquad\qquad\qquad L = L_3{}^\frown\langle x\rangle^\frown L_4 \land \\
& \qquad\qquad\qquad \neg x \text{ in } L_3\ \ )
\end{aligned}$$

Now we set about computing a recursive design for *partition_2*. First note some simple rules which hold for an implementation of *partition_2*.

$(a{:}\mathbb{Z})$ $\quad partition\_2(\langle a\rangle) \;\Leftrightarrow\; \langle\langle\rangle, a, \langle\rangle\rangle$ — see[6]

$(P,Q{:}\mathbb{Z}^+)$

$(p \le q)$ $\quad partition\_2(P\frown Q) \;\Leftrightarrow\; \langle P_1, p, P_2\frown Q\rangle$ — ditto

$(q<p)$ $\quad partition\_2(P\frown Q) \;\Leftrightarrow\; \langle P\frown Q_1, q, Q_2\rangle$

where: $partition\_2(P) = \langle P_1, p, P_2\rangle \wedge partition\_2(Q) = \langle Q_1, q, Q_2\rangle$

Since the 'input' in each of these cases is a non-empty lists (and hence the pre-partition condition holds), these rules are justified by substitution into post-*partition_2*.

post-$partition\_2(\langle a\rangle, \langle\langle\rangle, a, \langle\rangle\rangle)$

$\Leftrightarrow$

$(a = (min\ y \mid y{:}\mathbb{Z} \mid y \text{ in } \langle a\rangle) \wedge$
$\langle a\rangle = \langle\rangle\frown\langle a\rangle\frown\langle\rangle \wedge$
$\neg a \text{ in } \langle\rangle)$

$\Leftrightarrow$ — $(min\ y \mid y{:}\mathbb{Z} \mid y \text{ in } \langle a\rangle) \Leftrightarrow min⦃a⦄ \Leftrightarrow a$
— $a \text{ in } \langle\rangle \Leftrightarrow$ False

True

and, if $p \le q$ then, with $P,Q{:}\mathbb{Z}^+$,

post-$partition\_2(P\frown Q, \langle P_1, p, P_2\frown Q\rangle)$

$\Leftrightarrow$

$(p = (min\ y \mid y{:}\mathbb{Z} \mid y \text{ in } P\frown Q) \wedge$
$P\frown Q = P_1\frown\langle p\rangle\frown P_2\frown Q \wedge$
$\neg p \text{ in } P_1)$

where: $partition\_2(P) = \langle P_1, p, P_2\rangle$
$\wedge\ partition\_2(Q) = \langle Q_1, q, Q_2\rangle$
$\wedge\ (min\ y \mid y{:}\mathbb{Z} \mid y \text{ in } P\frown Q) =$
$min((min\ y \mid y{:}\mathbb{Z} \mid y \text{ in } P), (min\ y \mid y{:}\mathbb{Z} \mid y \text{ in } Q))$

$\Leftrightarrow$ post-$partition\_2(P, \langle P_1, p, P_2\rangle) \Rightarrow \neg p \text{ in } P_1$

$(p = min(p,q)) \wedge$
$P\frown Q = P\frown Q)$

$\Leftrightarrow$

True

[6] These rules are parameterised by a (of type $\mathbb{Z}$) and by P and Q (of type $\mathbb{Z}^+$, the non-empty elements of $\mathbb{Z}^*$), respectively.

So, using these rules, we get

$$\begin{aligned}
partition_2(L) \blacktriangleleft\!\!\blacktriangleright\ & \text{if } \#L = 1 \text{ then } \langle\langle\rangle, \text{first_of}(L), \langle\rangle\rangle \\
& \quad \text{else if first_of}(L) \le q \\
& \quad\quad \text{then } \langle\langle\rangle, \text{first_of}(L), Q\rangle \\
& \quad\quad \text{else} \langle\langle\text{first_of}(L)\rangle ^\frown Q_1, q, Q_2\rangle \\
& \quad\quad \text{fi} \\
& \text{fi} \\
& \quad\quad \text{where: } \langle Q_1, q, Q_2\rangle = partition_2(\text{rest_of}(L))
\end{aligned}$$

We need now to introduce an 'improvement' function to calculate *partition_2*. Explicitly, in $improve\_2(R_1,r,R_2, Q)$ we want to improve R_1,r,R_2; Q is the remaining data. The type of *improve_2* is

$$\mathbb{Z}^* \times \mathbb{Z} \times \mathbb{Z}^* \times \mathbb{Z}^* \to \mathbb{Z}^* \times \mathbb{Z} \times \mathbb{Z}^*$$

Basic requirements for such a function include

$$improve\_2(R_1,r,R_2, \langle\rangle) \blacktriangleleft\!\!\blacktriangleright\ partition\_2(T) \quad \text{for some } T{:}\mathbb{Z}^+$$

so $\quad improve\_2(\langle\rangle, r, \langle\rangle, \langle\rangle) \blacktriangleleft\!\!\blacktriangleright\ \langle\langle\rangle, r, \langle\rangle\rangle$

and, if $Q \ne \langle\rangle$,

$$improve\_2(R_1,r,R_2, Q) \blacktriangleleft\!\!\blacktriangleright\ partition\_2(T ^\frown Q)$$

$$\text{where: } improve\_2(R_1,r,R_2, \langle\rangle) = partition\_2(T)$$

The triple $\langle R_1, r, R_2\rangle$ represents 'the answer so far', before we move on to consider Q, which is reduced until it becomes empty.

i.e.,

$$\begin{aligned}
improve_2(R_1,r,R_2,Q) \blacktriangleleft\!\!\blacktriangleright\ & \text{if } r \le q \text{ then } \langle R_1, r, R_2 ^\frown Q\rangle \\
& \quad \text{else } \langle R_1 ^\frown \langle r\rangle ^\frown R_2 ^\frown Q_1, q, Q_2\rangle \\
& \text{fi} \\
& \quad \text{where: } partition_2(Q) = \langle Q_1, q, Q_2\rangle
\end{aligned}$$

It therefore follows that

$$partition\_2(L) \blacktriangleleft\!\!\blacktriangleright\ improve\_2(\langle\rangle, \text{first\_of}(L), \langle\rangle, \text{rest\_of}(L))$$

By assumption $L \ne \langle\rangle$ so we can start with the triple $\langle\langle\rangle, \text{first\_of}(L), \langle\rangle\rangle$ and improve it by using the remaining elements, i.e., rest_of(L), and, when there are no more elements left, we have

$$improve\_2(R_1,r,R_2, \langle\rangle) \blacktriangleleft\!\!\blacktriangleright\ \langle R_1, r, R_2\rangle$$

These are used for starting and ending the calculation. In the simplest case, they collapse to give

partition_2($\langle a \rangle$) ◀▶ *improve_2*($\langle\rangle$, a, $\langle\rangle$, $\langle\rangle$)

and for intermediate stages we need:

improve_2($R_1, r, R_2, P^\frown Q$) ◀▶ if $r \le p$
then *improve_2*($R_1, r, R_2{}^\frown P, Q$)
else *improve_2*($R_1{}^\frown\langle r \rangle^\frown R_2{}^\frown P_1, p, P_2, Q$)
fi
where: *partition_2*(P) = $\langle P_1, p, P_2 \rangle$

These can be verified by substitution.

Putting them to use, we get:

improve_2(R_1, r, R_2, Q)

◀▶

if $Q = \langle\rangle$ then $\langle R_1, r, R_2 \rangle$
else if $r \le$ first_of(Q)
then *improve_2*($R_1, r, R_2{}^\frown\langle$first_of($Q$)$\rangle$, rest_of($Q$))
else *improve_2*($R_1{}^\frown\langle r \rangle^\frown R_2$,first_of($Q$),$\langle\rangle$,rest_of($Q$))
fi
fi

◀▶

if $Q = \langle\rangle$ then $\langle R_1, r, R_2 \rangle$
else *improve_2*(X_1, x, X_2, rest_of(Q))
fi
where: $\langle X_1, x, X_2 \rangle$ = if $r \le$ first_of(Q)
then $\langle R_1, r, R_2{}^\frown\langle$first_of($Q$)$\rangle\rangle$
else$\langle R_1{}^\frown\langle r \rangle^\frown R_2$,first_of($Q$),$\langle\rangle\rangle$
fi

This *is* tail-recursive and can be replaced by an iterative procedural scheme that can be used directly in *partition_2* and subsequently in *split_14*, which is a refinement of *split_3*. Making the appropriate substitutions and removing the trivial recursive call within sort (since it only sorts a singleton list), we get

```
improve_2(R1,r,R2,Q) ≜
    (var X1:ℤ*,x:ℤ,X2,Y:ℤ*;
        ⟨X1,x,X2,Y⟩ ← ⟨R1,r,R2,Q⟩;
        while ¬( Y = ⟨⟩)
        do ⟨X1,x,X2,Y⟩ ←
                if x ≤ first_of(Y)
                then ⟨X1,x,X2⌢⟨first_of(Y)⟩, rest_of(Y)⟩
                else⟨ X1⌢⟨x⟩⌢X2,first_of(Y),⟨⟩, rest_of(Y)⟩
                fi
        od;
        result ← ⟨X1,x,X2⟩
    );
partition_2(L) ≜ improve_2(⟨⟩ , first_of(L) , ⟨⟩, rest_of(L) )
split_14(L) ≜ (var L3:ℤ*,x:ℤ,L4:ℤ*;
            ⟨L3,x,L4⟩ ← partition_2(L);
            result ← if L3 = ⟨⟩
                     then ⟨⟨x⟩,L4⟩
                     else ⟨⟨x⟩, rest_of(L3)⌢⟨first_of(L3)⟩⌢L4⟩
                     fi );
sort(L) ≜ if #L < 2
        then result ← L
        else (var L2:ℤ+,x:ℤ;
                ⟨⟨x⟩,L2⟩ ← split_14(L);
                result ← ⟨x⟩⌢sort(L2)      )
        fi;
N ← sort(L)
```

[An alternative and more direct 'derivation' of the same implementation design is via a eureka step. As is always the case with such tactics, the explanation of the underlying inspiration is not always easy — except in the mind of its creator. Since the idea behind this eureka step is the same as the calculation just presented, we shall not even try to give another explanation. We merely quote a set of appropriate rules in terms of an intermediate function F.

Lowest finds the position of the (first instance of the) lowest value within a non-empty list of integers without actually performing any exchanges. All the types can be deduced from the list and integer operators used, so (for simplicity of presentation) we omit any explicit indication.

$$Lowest(L) \Leftrightarrow F(\langle\rangle, x, \langle\rangle, N) \quad \text{where: } L = \langle x\rangle^\frown N$$

$$\begin{array}{ll} (N=\langle\rangle) & F(A, \ell, B, N) \Leftrightarrow \langle A, \ell, B\rangle \\ (\ell \le y) & F(A, \ell, B, N) \Leftrightarrow F(A, \ell, B^\frown\langle y\rangle, M) \\ (\ell > y) & F(A, \ell, B, N) \Leftrightarrow F(A^\frown\langle \ell\rangle^\frown B, y, \langle\rangle, M) \\ & \qquad \text{where: } N = \langle y\rangle^\frown M \end{array}$$

Here the invariant of $F(A, \ell, B, N)$ is

$$\begin{array}{l} L = A^\frown\langle \ell\rangle^\frown B^\frown N \\ \wedge\ \ell = (min\ y \mid y{:}\mathbb{Z} \mid y \text{ in } A^\frown\langle \ell\rangle^\frown B) \\ \wedge\ \neg(\ell \text{ in } A) \end{array}$$

and $\#N$ reduces to zero, thus guaranteeing termination.

Immediately this yields the iterative implementation scheme for *Lowest*:

```
begin  var A, B, N: ℤ*, ℓ:ℤ;
       ⟨A, ℓ, B, N⟩ ← ⟨⟨⟩ , first_of(L), ⟨⟩, rest_of(L)⟩;
       while N ≠ ⟨⟩
       do  if ℓ ≤ first_of(N)
           then ⟨A,ℓ,B,N⟩ ← ⟨A,ℓ,B⁀⟨first_of(N)⟩,rest_of(N)⟩
           else ⟨A,ℓ,B,N⟩ ← ⟨A⁀⟨ℓ⟩⁀B,first_of(N), ⟨⟩, rest_of(N)⟩
           fi
       od;
       result ← ⟨A,ℓ,B⟩
end
```

This then simplifies to

```
begin  var A, B, N: ℤ*, ℓ:ℤ;
       ⟨A,ℓ,B,N⟩ ← ⟨⟨⟩ ,first_of(L),⟨⟩,rest_of(L)⟩;
       while N ≠ ⟨⟩
       do  if ℓ ≤ first_of(N)
           then B ← B⁀⟨first_of(N)⟩
           else ⟨A,ℓ,B⟩ ← ⟨A⁀⟨ℓ⟩⁀B,first_of(N),⟨⟩⟩
           fi; N ← rest_of(N)
       od;
       result ← ⟨A,ℓ,B⟩
end
```

Therefore, we have

$Lowest(L) \triangleq$ begin var A,B,N: $\mathbb{Z}^*, \ell:\mathbb{Z}$;
$\langle A,\ell,B,N\rangle \leftarrow \langle\langle\rangle$, first_of$(L)$, $\langle\rangle$, rest_of$(L)\rangle$;
while $N \neq \langle\rangle$
do if $\ell \leq$ first_of(N)
then $B \leftarrow B^\frown\langle$first_of$(N)\rangle$
else $\langle A,\ell,B\rangle \leftarrow \langle A^\frown\langle\ell\rangle^\frown B$, first_of$(N)$, $\langle\rangle\rangle$
fi; $N \leftarrow$ rest_of(N)
od;
result $\leftarrow \langle A,\ell,B\rangle$
end;
$sort(L) \triangleq$ if $\#L < 2$
then result $\leftarrow L$
else (var L_1,L_2:$\mathbb{Z}^*$,x:$\mathbb{Z}$;
$\langle L_1,x,L_2\rangle \leftarrow Lowest(L)$;
result $\leftarrow \langle x\rangle^\frown sort($rest_of$(L_1)^\frown\langle$first_of$(L_1)\rangle^\frown L_2)$)
fi;
$N \leftarrow sort(L)$

which, apart from changes in internal 'variable' names[7] and some factorization, is the same as the scheme already obtained.]

[Note also that if there is little expense associated with swapping[8], then we need not preserve the order of the list segment that does not contain the (first encountered) minimal element. So, working from the specification of *split*_11, we can use the simpler set of rules

$select(L)$ ◂▸ $F(\, x, \langle\rangle, N\,)$
where: $L = \langle x\rangle^\frown N$

$(N=\langle\rangle)$ $F(\,\ell, A, N\,)$ ◂▸ $\langle \ell, A\rangle$
$(\ell \leq y)$ $F(\,\ell, A, N\,)$ ◂▸ $F(\,\ell, A^\frown\langle y\rangle, M\,)$
$(\ell > y)$ $F(\,\ell, A, N\,)$ ◂▸ $F(\,y, A^\frown\langle \ell\rangle, M\,)$
where: $N = \langle y\rangle^\frown M$

Here the invariant now uses bags but is essentially the same, and again convergence is controlled by the size of N.

---

7 We have made no attempt to unify the sets of names used within design segments and strongly advise the use of whatever names are deemed appropriate. Of course, a certain software house may have guidelines for such matters, but it often helps to clarify local concerns to use (very) different names within the body of a function declaration and not those used in the surrounding 'calling' context.

8 Or the program uses 'pseudo' pointers that are swapped, rather than the actual data values.

Routinely we can extract the following implementation scheme:

```
select(L) ≜ begin var A,N: ℤ*, ℓ:ℤ;
                ⟨ℓ,A,N⟩ ← ⟨ first_of(L), ⟨⟩,rest_of(L)⟩;
                   while N ≠ ⟨⟩
                   do if ℓ ≤ first_of(N)
                      then A ← A⌢⟨first_of(N)⟩
                      else ⟨ℓ,A⟩ ← ⟨first_of(N),A⌢⟨ℓ⟩⟩
                      fi; N ← rest_of(N)
                   od;
                   result ← ⟨ℓ,A⟩
                end;
sort(L) ≜ if #L < 2
          then result ← L
          else (var L2:ℤ*,x:ℤ;
                ⟨x,L2⟩ ← select(L);
                result ← ⟨x⟩⌢sort(L2) )
          fi;
N ← sort(L)
```

We shall now break off this digression and return to our main thread of development.]

Combining the functions schemes *improve_2*, *partition_2*, *split_14* and *sort*, we have, after substitution and renaming

$sort(L) \triangleq$ if $\#L < 2$
then result $\leftarrow L$
else (var $L_2{:}\mathbb{Z}^+, x{:}\mathbb{Z}, X_1{:}\mathbb{Z}^*, X_2, Y{:}\mathbb{Z}^*$;
$\langle X_1, x, X_2, Y\rangle \leftarrow \langle\langle\rangle$,first_of(L) , $\langle\rangle$,rest_of(L) $\rangle$;
while $\neg(Y = \langle\rangle)$
do $\langle X_1, x, X_2, Y\rangle \leftarrow$
if $x \leq$ first_of(Y)
then $\langle X_1, x, X_2 {}^\frown \langle$first_of($Y$)$\rangle$,rest_of($Y$)$\rangle$
else $\langle X_1 {}^\frown \langle x\rangle {}^\frown X_2$, first_of($Y$), $\langle\rangle$, rest_of(Y)$\rangle$
fi
od;
$L_2 \leftarrow$ if $X_1 = \langle\rangle$ then X_2
else rest_of(X_1)$^\frown\langle$first_of(X_1)$\rangle^\frown X_2$
fi;
result $\leftarrow \langle x\rangle^\frown sort(L_2)$)
fi;
$N \leftarrow sort(L)$

Now, without all the detailed explanation, we superimpose the lists onto an array A. The basic idea is that A should hold the composite list

$$X_1{}^\frown\langle x\rangle^\frown X_2{}^\frown Y$$

(This composite list is of fixed length, so storing in an array is a reasonable idea.)

Recall the convention that $A[i..j]$ is empty if $i>j$. So, initially, if $\#L = n$

X_1 is held in	$A[1..0]$
x	$A[1]$
X_2	$A[2..1]$
Y	$A[2..n]$

More generally, representing a segment of L with subscripts running from a to b,

X_1 is held in	$A[a..I-1]$
x	$A[I]$
X_2	$A[I+1..J-1]$
Y	$A[J..b]$

We can then translate (as in Chapter 8)[9] the list scheme above to give

```
sort(a,b) ≙ if b≤a
              then skip
              else (var I,J:ℤ;
                    I←a; J←a+1;
                    while J≤b
                        do if A[I] > A[J] then I←J fi;
                        J←J+1
                        od;
                    if I≠a then ⟨A[I],A[a]⟩←⟨A[a],A[I]⟩ fi;
                    sort(a+1,b)  )
            fi;
A[1..n] ← L;
sort(1,n);
N ← A[1..n]
```

and then the tail recursion can be replaced by an iteration to yield the familiar algorithm

```
sort(a,b) ≙ (var a1:ℤ;
              a1 ← a;
              while a1<b
              do (var I,J:ℤ;
                    I←a1; J←a1+1;
                    while J≤b
                        do if A[I] > A[J] then I←J fi;
                        J←J+1
                        od;
                    if I≠a1 then ⟨A[I],A[a1]⟩←⟨A[a1],A[I]⟩ fi;
                    a1←a1+1)
              od)
```

So we select (the first instance of) the smallest integer in L and use it to make a list; L_2 is the list of remaining elements and is processed in the same way. This is called a ***selection sort***.

An alternative development, which is not strictly a refinement of the traditional partition *split* but illustrates how the characteristics of individual problems can be used to tailor general techniques.

[9] Notice that not only is there a type change here, but the new version of *sort* is a procedure, not a function. Also, a suitable declaration of the array needs to be included.

Recall

$split\_3: \mathbb{Z}^* \to \mathbb{Z}^* \times \mathbb{Z}^*$
pre-$split\_3(L) \triangleq \#L \geq 2$
post-split_3$(L, \langle L_1, L_2 \rangle) \triangleq (\exists x{:}\mathbb{Z})$
$(\ \text{bag\_of}(L) = \text{bag\_of}(L_1) \uplus \text{bag\_of}(L_2) \wedge$
$(\wedge (y \leq x) \mid y{:}\mathbb{Z} \mid y \text{ in } L_1\ ) \wedge$
$(\wedge (x \leq y) \mid y{:}\mathbb{Z} \mid y \text{ in } L_2\ ) \wedge$
$\#L_1 \geq 1 \ \wedge\ \#L_2 \geq 1\ )$

in which the value of x is effectively lost once we have passed this phase. Why not retain it? Remove it from the intermediate processing and place it — in the right place — in the combine phase. Of course, this means that we can no longer demand that $\#L_1 \geq 1 \wedge \#L_2 \geq 1$, but that does not matter since the 'removal' of x[10] will ensure that $\#L_1 < \#L$ and $\#L_2 < \#L$.

We therefore have

$split\_15: \mathbb{Z}^* \to \mathbb{Z}^* \times \mathbb{Z} \times \mathbb{Z}^*$
pre-$split\_15(L) \triangleq \#L \geq 2$
post-$split\_15(L, \langle L_1, x, L_2 \rangle) \triangleq$
$(\text{bag\_of}(L) = \text{bag\_of}(L_1) \uplus \{\!\{x\}\!\} \uplus \text{bag\_of}(L_2) \wedge$
$(\wedge (y \leq x) \mid y{:}\mathbb{Z} \mid y \text{ in } L_1\ ) \wedge (\wedge (x \leq y) \mid y{:}\mathbb{Z} \mid y \text{ in } L_2\ )\ )$

This is *not* a refinement of *split*_3; it can't be because the signatures are different.

We then get the overall design for the sort:

if $\#L < 2$
then $N = L$
else $(\exists L_1, L_2, N_1, N_2{:}\mathbb{Z}^*, x{:}\mathbb{Z})$
$(\quad \langle L_1, x, L_2 \rangle = split\_15(L) \ \wedge$
$N_1 = sort(L_1) \quad \wedge \quad N_2 = sort(L_2)$
$\wedge \quad N = N_1 \frown \langle x \rangle \frown N_2 \quad)$
fi

(Notice that restricting L_1 to $\langle\rangle$ would give us a reformulation of a *selection sort*, particularly if we were to add the extra constraint that $\neg (x \text{ in } L_1)$.)

10 The pivot of the (partition) sort.

Allowing empty values for L_1 and L_2 and targeting the implementation at array usage — trying to avoid deletions and insertions in favour of swaps — leads us in the direction of Quicksort. But beware, the literature contains many different algorithms named Quicksort. We are not quite there yet. Before giving a derivation of (one version of) Quicksort, we consider some more simplistic implementation schemes.

First we make the remark that, since we know nothing special about the lists that we are being asked to sort, and hence the ordering of the input list is 'random', *any* choice of the value x (now known to be *in* L) is as good as any other. Therefore, without any loss of generality, we can use the first element in L.

A possible starting point for an implementation of *split*_15 is the following set of rules involving the subsidiary function F:

$$split\_15(L{:}\mathbb{Z}^+) \;\blacklozenge\; F(x, \langle\rangle, \langle\rangle, N) \qquad \text{where: } L = \langle x\rangle^\frown N$$

$$\begin{array}{ll} (N=\langle\rangle) & F(x,A,B,N) \;\blacklozenge\; \langle A, x, B\rangle \\ (y<x) & F(x,A,B,\langle y\rangle^\frown M) \;\blacklozenge\; F(x,\langle y\rangle^\frown A,B,M) \\ (x\le y) & F(x,A,B,\langle y\rangle^\frown M) \;\blacklozenge\; F(x,A,\langle y\rangle^\frown B,M) \end{array}$$

Here the invariant for $F(x,A,B,N)$ is

$$(\text{bag\_of}(L) = \text{bag\_of}(A) \uplus \{\!\!\{x\}\!\!\} \uplus \text{bag\_of}(B) \uplus \text{bag\_of}(N) \;\wedge\; (\wedge(y<x) \mid y{:}\mathbb{Z} \mid y \text{ in } A) \wedge (\wedge(x\le y) \mid y{:}\mathbb{Z} \mid y \text{ in } B))$$

and again $\#N$ reduces to zero, thus guaranteeing termination.

As an alternative, we could re-order the parameters and use

$$split\_15(L{:}\mathbb{Z}^+) \;\blacklozenge\; G(x, \langle\rangle, N, \langle\rangle) \qquad \text{where: } L = \langle x\rangle^\frown N$$

$$\begin{array}{ll} (N=\langle\rangle) & G(x,A,N,B) \;\blacklozenge\; \langle A, x, B\rangle \\ (y<x) & G(x,A,\langle y\rangle^\frown M,B) \;\blacklozenge\; G(x,A^\frown\langle y\rangle,M,B) \\ (x\le y) & G(x,A,\langle y\rangle^\frown M,B) \;\blacklozenge\; G(x,A,M,\langle y\rangle^\frown B) \end{array}$$

There is no mathematical difference between these two rule sets, but notice the convenient 'sliding' of the value y between the third and second parameters in the $(y < x)$ rule, particularly if they were held in consecutive segments in an array. However, the same could not be said of the transfer of y in the $(x \le y)$ rule. But we can make some concession to this situation with yet another set of rules.

Suppose

$$split\_15(L{:}\mathbb{Z}^+) \;\blacktriangleleft\!\!\blacktriangleright\; H(x,\langle\rangle,N,\langle\rangle) \quad \text{where: } L=\langle x\rangle^\frown N$$

$$\begin{array}{lrcl}
(N=\langle\rangle) & H(x,A,N,B) & \blacktriangleleft\!\!\blacktriangleright & \langle A,x,B\rangle \\
(y<x)^{11} & H(x,A,\langle y\rangle^\frown M,B) & \blacktriangleleft\!\!\blacktriangleright & H(x,A^\frown\langle y\rangle,M,B) \\
(x\le y,\, x\le z) & H(x,A,\langle y\rangle^\frown M^\frown\langle z\rangle,B) & \blacktriangleleft\!\!\blacktriangleright & H(x,A,\langle y\rangle^\frown M,\langle z\rangle^\frown B)
\end{array}$$

So now we 'slipped z from the third parameter to the forth, but what about the 'other' case, when $x\le y$, and $x>z$? Clearly what has to happen is that y has to go to B and z to A. This can be done with a single exchange, and we get

$$(x\le y, x>z) \quad H(x,A,\langle y\rangle^\frown M^\frown\langle z\rangle,B) \;\blacktriangleleft\!\!\blacktriangleright\; H(x,A^\frown\langle z\rangle,M,\langle y\rangle^\frown B)$$

These rules provide the essence of Quicksort[12], all that is needed to allow the output triple to fit directly into the calling scenario is to replace the $N=\langle\rangle$ rule by two slightly more specialised rules, namely

$$(N=\langle\rangle, A=\langle\rangle) \quad H(x,A,N,B) \;\blacktriangleleft\!\!\blacktriangleright\; \langle A,x,B\rangle$$

and

$$(N=\langle\rangle, A\ne\langle\rangle) \quad H(x,A,N,B) \;\blacktriangleleft\!\!\blacktriangleright\; \langle\langle y\rangle^\frown D,x,B\rangle \quad \text{where: } A=D^\frown\langle y\rangle$$

The reason for this final manipulation is to ensure that x is in the appropriate position in the implied list derived from

$$\langle x\rangle^\frown D^\frown\langle y\rangle$$

with the least amount of swapping. Remember that all the elements in $D^\frown\langle y\rangle$ are less than x but we know nothing about the order within that list; hence we do as little work as possible and perform a single exchange to give

$$\langle y\rangle^\frown D^\frown\langle x\rangle$$

Of course, if x is the minimal value, then there is nothing to be done.

---

11 The conditions used here force a particular order of application. Other orders are possible, as indeed is ambiguity, but we want the rules to guarantee deterministic evaluation.

12 In the original version Hoare started off with a random selection of the x element, but we have argued that this is not necessary. He also allowed for multiple x values to be returned in the A segment and within a longer 'all x' segment, as well as in the B segment.

From these rules, we have

```
split_15(L:ℤ⁺) ≜
   begin var x,ℤ,A,N,B:ℤ*;
   ⟨x,A,N,B⟩ ← ⟨first_of(L),⟨⟩,rest_of(L),⟨⟩⟩;
   while N ≠ ⟨⟩
    do  if first_of(N) < x
        then ⟨x,A,N,B⟩ ← ⟨x,A⌢⟨first_of(N)⟩,rest_of(N),B⟩
        else_if x ≤ last_of(N)
        then ⟨x,A,N,B⟩ ← ⟨x,A,front_of(N),⟨last_of(N)⟩⌢B⟩
        else ⟨x,A,N,B⟩
             ← ⟨x,A⌢⟨last_of(N)⟩, front_of(rest_of(N)),⟨first_of(N)⟩⌢B⟩
        fi
    od;
   result ←  if A = ⟨⟩
             then ⟨A,x,B⟩
             else ⟨⟨last_of(A)⟩⌢front_of(A),x,B⟩
             fi
   end;
   sort(L) ≜ ( result ← if #L < 2
                        then N = L
                        else (var L1,L2,N1,N2:ℤ*,x:ℤ;
                              ⟨L1,x,L2⟩ ← split_15(L);
                              (N1 ← sort(L1) ∥ N2 ← sort(L2));
                              N1⌢⟨x⟩⌢N2 )
                        fi;  )
```

Before the last transformation, we simplify *split*_15 slightly and rename A and B as C and D. This gives

```
split_15(L:ℤ⁺) ≜
   begin var x,ℤ,C,N,D:ℤ*;
   ⟨x,C,N,D⟩ ← ⟨first_of(L),⟨⟩,rest_of(L),⟨⟩⟩;
   while N ≠ ⟨⟩
    do  if first_of(N) < x
        then ⟨C,N⟩ ← ⟨C⌢⟨first_of(N)⟩,rest_of(N)⟩
        else_if x ≤ last_of(N)
        then ⟨N,D⟩ ← ⟨ front_of(N),⟨last_of(N)⟩⌢D⟩
        else ⟨C,N,D⟩
             ← ⟨C⌢⟨last_of(N)⟩, front_of(rest_of(N)),⟨first_of(N)⟩⌢D⟩
        fi
    od;
```

```
result ← if C = ⟨ ⟩
             then ⟨C, x, D⟩
             else ⟨⟨last_of(C)⟩⌢front_of(C), x, D⟩
             fi
end
```

Finally, we map the list L onto the array $A[1 .. \#L]$, whence the functions become procedures and we have

```
split_15(a, b:ℤ) ≜
  begin var x,ℤ ,I,J:ℤ ;
            " in the main computation, we hold N in A[I .. J],
                                       C in A[a+1 .. I-1], D in A[J+1 .. b] "
  x ← A[a]; ⟨I,J⟩ ← ⟨ a+1,b⟩;
  while I ≤ J
   do if A[I] < x
      then I ← I+1
      else_if x ≤ A[J]
      then J ← J−1
      else ⟨A[I] ,A[J]⟩  ←  ⟨A[J] ,A[I]⟩;
           I ← I+1; J ← J−1
      fi
   od;                   " we simply deliver the index of the pivot in n "
  if I−1 < a+1
      then n ← a
      else ⟨A[a] ,A[I−1]⟩  ←  ⟨A[I−1] ,A[a]⟩;
           n ← I−1
  fi
  end;
  sort(a,b) ≜( if b ≤ a
                then skip
                else (var n:ℤ)
                       (split_15(a,b);
                       (sort(a,n−1) ‖ sort(n + 1,b)) )
                fi );
   A[1..n] ← L;
   sort(1,n);
   N ← A[1..n]
```

Finally, we mention a variant of Quicksort (of which there are many, some in which the pivot is changed — for a 'better' one — as the algorithm proceeds). Here the pivot 'bounces' up and down within the list. Again we use the first element as the pivot but at the end it is already in the required position, so the last part of the previous scheme can be omitted. [We are not advocating this as an improvement. We have said nothing about the relative complexity and efficiency of the various computation schemes — such considerations fall outside the scope of this book.]

We only give sets of evaluation rules (their subsequent to give program designs is quite straightforward) and include them merely as a further example of this form of algorithm development.

Here we use two functions $K1$ and $K2$, which have slightly different signatures.

$$split\_15(L{:}\mathbb{Z}^{+}) \blacktriangleleft\!\blacktriangleright K1(\langle\rangle, x, N, \langle\rangle) \quad \text{where: } L = \langle x\rangle^\frown N$$

$$\begin{array}{lrl}
(N=\langle\rangle) & K1(A,x,N,B) & \blacktriangleleft\!\blacktriangleright \langle A, x, B\rangle \\
(x \le y) & K1(A,x,Q^\frown\langle y\rangle,B) & \blacktriangleleft\!\blacktriangleright K1(A,x,Q,\langle y\rangle^\frown B) \\
(x > y) & K1(A,x,Q^\frown\langle y\rangle,B) & \blacktriangleleft\!\blacktriangleright K2(A^\frown\langle y\rangle,Q,x,B)
\end{array}$$

$$\begin{array}{lrl}
(N=\langle\rangle) & K2(A,N,x,B) & \blacktriangleleft\!\blacktriangleright \langle A, x, B\rangle \\
(z \le x) & K2(A,\langle z\rangle^\frown Q,x,B) & \blacktriangleleft\!\blacktriangleright K2(A^\frown\langle z\rangle,Q,x,B) \\
(z > x) & K2(A,\langle z\rangle^\frown Q,x,B) & \blacktriangleleft\!\blacktriangleright K1(A,x,Q,\langle z\rangle^\frown B)
\end{array}$$

With these rules, the usual input list gives rise to the following progression, presented as a 'concatenation' of the parameters in order with the pivot underlined:

$$\begin{array}{ccccccccccccccc}
A & | & x & | & & & & & N & & & & & | & B \\
 & | & \underline{6} & | & 7 & & 3 & & 5 & & 8 & & 3 & | & \\
 & & 3 & | & 7 & & 3 & & 5 & & 8 & | & \underline{6} & | & \\
 & & 3 & | & \underline{6} & | & 3 & & 5 & & 8 & | & 7 & & \\
 & & 3 & | & \underline{6} & | & 3 & & 5 & | & 8 & & 7 & & \\
 & & 3 & & 5 & | & 3 & | & \underline{6} & | & 8 & & 7 & & \\
 & & 3 & & 5 & & 3 & | & \underline{6} & | & 8 & & 7 & &
\end{array}$$

So, there we are; in two chapters we have presented quite a few ways of sorting a list of integers (all developed from a single specification using formally justified steps). Yet we have barely scratched the surface of the subject. Much more can be done using other more complicated data structures. But that, as they say, is another book.

Chapter 10
Failures and Fixes

Transformations, by definition, are reversible. Working purely with transformations is therefore essentially about re-arranging information without loss. When reducing one design to another (and hence moving strictly closer to a deterministic implementation), we intentionally discard certain possibilities. We must take care not to remove anything essential.

Of course, there might be a more fundamental problem — we may have been asked to do something impossible; the given problem may be insoluble. In the context of program derivation, this means that we need to address the specification (Section 10.1).

Our formulation of (operational) refinement ensures that the pre-conditions are preserved so that the same data is valid before and after a refinement step; but other (hidden) refinements are embedded within some design tactics. These do not yield errors as such but cause the tactic to fail. There is no general solution to this problem; we must reach a productive compromise that loses an acceptable amount of the original information. This is discussed in Section 10.2.

So, in this chapter, a *failure* refers to an attempt to solve an insoluble problem[1] or an attempt to apply an inappropriate tactic (in which we lose some necessary information).

Here, failure does not mean that there is an error, a failure, in the theory; but, there is an error in the initial specification or in the application of the theory.

Consequently, to rectify such a 'failure' requires that we reverse the design process (even as far as the creation of the specification) and adopt a different tactic or, after consultation with the 'customer', adjust the specification.

It is important to realise that these failures are detected within the transfinement process. We cannot reach a situation where an implementation fails because of a logical flaw in the derivation process.

[1] Insoluble (unsolvable) in the sense that it cannot be solved for all legitimate inputs.

10.1 Inadequate Pre-Conditions

For technical (mathematical) reasons, it is *impossible*[2] to determine whether an arbitrary specification is satisfiable[3] (i.e., whether it does actually specify an implementable, non-void[4], function. Although we can usually justify that a data value, x, satisfying the pre-condition, *does* admit the existence of an acceptable result, y, so that $\langle x,y\rangle$ satisfies the post-condition, it is theoretically possible that the search for such a y fails. When this happens, our manipulations simply fail to yield an answer. This is very frustrating, but the failure prevents us from producing an incorrect program design.

In practice, when this happens, it identifies a set of illegal input values, and this leads to (negotiations with the customer and) revision of the specifications.

[Of course, since we are not insisting on *weakest* pre-conditions (WPs), the pre-condition may be stronger than that dictated by the post-condition and hence any pre-condition may, if agreeable with the 'customer', be strengthened providing that it does not equate to 'False' and hence deny *any* possible implementation.]

Recall that the purpose of a pre-condition is to identify those input values for which it is possible (and for which we *wish*) to compute the function. Suppose that we *do not know*, or cannot easily find, the pre-condition. It is tempting to write.

$$\text{pre-}f(x) \triangleq (\exists y{:}Y)(\text{post-}f(x,y))$$

That is, if x satisfies the pre-condition, then there is some value y — and there may be more than one — such that $\langle x, y\rangle$ satisfies the post-condition.

But of course this would not be right; it is a circular argument.

Essentially there are two problems related to the specification

$$\begin{aligned}&f{:}X \to Y\\&\text{pre-}f(x) \triangleq \text{True}\\&\text{post-}f(x, y) \triangleq \ldots\end{aligned}$$

(1) For a given x, is there a value y such that post-$f(x, y)$ = True?
(2) If one or more such values exist, *find* one of them.

---

[2] This is provably impossible. It is not simply that nobody has managed to solve this (general) problem yet; they never can.

[3] Of course, for many specific problems (in fact, the vast majority of 'real' specifications that you will encounter), it *is* possible.

[4] A function other than the empty function, the function with an empty domain.

Without a proper pre-condition, we cannot confidently simply embark on the program synthesis process and try to deduce an answer since there might not be one. This is rather like slipping from the type $\mathbb{B}$ to $\mathbb{E}$, trying to evaluate some decision procedure and getting the answer "unknown".

In trying to cope[5] with the specification above, let us take the pre-condition as a working assumption (an informed 'guess') and consider the modified specification.

$$
\begin{aligned}
& f'\!:X \rightarrow Y \times \mathbb{B} \\
& \text{pre-}f'(x) \triangleq \text{True} \\
& \text{post-}f'(x, \langle y, b \rangle) \triangleq \quad b = (\exists y{:}Y)(\text{post-}f(x,y)) \\
& \qquad\qquad\qquad\qquad \wedge \text{ if } b \text{ then post-}f(x,y) \\
& \qquad\qquad\qquad\qquad\qquad \text{else } y = \mathit{any\_value}{:}Y \ \text{ fi}
\end{aligned}
$$

This is *not* the same problem; f' *is* not the *same* function as f, although it is closely related. Assuming that we can apply some useful techniques, such as splitting or reduction, then the synthesis for a design for f' can proceed as normal.

If it transpires that that the resultant implementation design always delivers True for the Boolean component, then the pre-condition for f was adequate, and if, as here, the pre-condition was identically True, the calculation is said to be ***robust***. (i.e., it will deliver a valid result for *any* input of type X). In general, this will not be the case, and we have to compute f' and use a 'rig' of the form

$$
\begin{aligned}
& \langle y, b \rangle \qquad \leftarrow f'(x); \\
& \text{if } b \text{ then } y \\
& \qquad \text{else "calculation of } f(x) \text{ failed" fi}
\end{aligned}
$$

This is the best we can do.

10.2 Failures in Structural Splitting

Of the different 'divide and conquer' tactics, structural splitting is perhaps the one most likely to 'fail'. We cannot always simply apply the structural splitting strategy and expect that a valid, correct, program design will just 'fall out'. There are many different reasons why this might be so; sometimes the structure of the problem — and the structure of the input — might simply not be susceptible to this approach. However, it will often be the case that the method *almost* works, and it is to these situations that we wish to alert the reader. Recall that in structural splitting we break up the data, perform calculations on the parts, and then try to deduce the final answer by combining the answers to the sub-calculations. Since

[5] The construction outlined above *can* be applied to situations where the pre-condition is not assumed to be identically True, but we shall make this simplification for the sake of presentation.

deduce the final answer by combining the answers to the sub-calculations. Since the splitting phase can be reversed (so as to retrieve the original input values), there would seem to be no possibility that any information could be lost. Information *isn't* lost during splitting, but it can be lost within the following sub-calculations. A way to circumvent this problem is to retain more information in the 'answer' — thus solving a different problem — and extract the desired result at the very end. We now discuss this situation by means of one extended example.

10.2.1 Loss of Vital Information

Example 10.1 To illustrate the problem, recall the *all_same* specification from Example 3.9:

$$\begin{aligned}&all\_same{:}\mathbb{Z}^* \to \mathbb{B}\\ &\text{pre-}all\_same(L) \triangleq \text{True}\\ &\text{post-}all\_same(L,b) \triangleq b \Leftrightarrow (\exists x{:}\mathbb{Z})(\forall y{:}\mathbb{Z})(y \text{ in } L \Rightarrow x = y)\end{aligned}$$

Using straightforward structural splitting, we would proceed as follows. With input $\langle 2, 3\rangle$ we would get $\langle 2\rangle$ and $\langle 3\rangle$, each of which yields the intermediate answer 'True'. We must then combine these values to give the final result (for *all_same*($\langle 2, 3\rangle$)), which we want to be 'False'. But working with input $\langle 2, 2\rangle$, we get the same intermediate values and now require the overall result to be 'True'. Clearly, there is no *combine* function that is consistent with

$$\langle \text{True}, \text{True}\rangle \mapsto \text{True}$$

and

$$\langle \text{True}, \text{True}\rangle \mapsto \text{False}$$

This conflict arises because *all_same* delivers a Boolean result; it tells us whether or not all the elements of a singleton list are the same (and of course they are since there is only one), but it does not tell us what that element is. We have thrown away information which we might have retained, but the specification did not *allow* us to retain it.

In this problem (and in general), we can solve the problem — and hence perform the required calculation using the same splitting technique — by solving a slightly 'wider' problem and then using its result to solve *all_same*.

To focus attention on the essential 'loss of information', we modify *all_same* so as to have the signature $\mathbb{Z}^+ \to \mathbb{B}$ (i.e., we deny the empty list as valid input; it is easily handled on its own). We shall call this new variant *NAS*, *new_all_same*.

The promised 'internal' function has the specification

$$g: \mathbb{Z}^{+} \rightarrow \mathbb{B} \times (\mathbb{Z} \cup \{\text{Undefined}\})$$
$$\text{pre-}g(\, L\,) \triangleq \text{True}$$
$$\begin{aligned}\text{post-}g(\, L, \langle b, z\rangle\,) \triangleq (\exists x{:}\mathbb{Z})(\ &\text{if } (\forall y{:}\mathbb{Z})(y \text{ in } L \Rightarrow x = y)\\ &\text{then } \langle b, z\rangle = \langle \text{True}, x\rangle\\ &\text{else } \langle b, z\rangle = \langle \text{False, Undefined}\rangle \text{ fi }) \end{aligned}$$

Then

$$NAS(L) \ \blacktriangleleft\!\blacktriangleright\ b \qquad \text{where:} \ \ (\exists z{:}\ \mathbb{Z} \cup \{\text{Undefined}\})(\, g(L) = \langle b, z\rangle)$$

We do not need the z part of the answer in the *final* result, but we *do* need it in the intermediate steps.

Now, with input $\langle 2, 3\rangle$ we have:

$$\begin{aligned} g(\langle 2, 3\rangle) \ &\blacktriangleleft\!\blacktriangleright\ g(\langle 2\rangle ^\frown \langle 3\rangle)\\ &\blacktriangleleft\!\blacktriangleright\ \mathit{combine}(\, g(\langle 2\rangle), g(\langle 3\rangle)\,)\\ &\blacktriangleleft\!\blacktriangleright\ \mathit{combine}(\langle \text{True}, 2\rangle, \langle \text{True}, 3\rangle) \end{aligned}$$

Here *combine* has more input (more information) and can be defined by

$$\begin{aligned}\text{combine: } (\langle b_1, z_1\rangle, \langle b_2, z_2\rangle) \mapsto\ & \text{if } (b_1 \wedge b_2) \mathbin{\Lambda} (z_1 =^{6} z_2) \text{ then } \langle \text{True}, z_1\rangle\\ & \qquad \text{else } \langle \text{False, Undefined}\rangle \text{ fi}\end{aligned}$$

So, we obtain

$$\begin{aligned} g(\langle 2, 3\rangle) \ &\blacktriangleleft\!\blacktriangleright\ \mathit{combine}(\langle \text{True}, 2\rangle, \langle \text{True}, 3\rangle)\\ &\blacktriangleleft\!\blacktriangleright\ \text{if } (\text{True} \wedge \text{True}) \mathbin{\Lambda} (2 = 3) \text{ then } \langle \text{True}, 2\rangle\\ &\qquad\qquad \text{else } \langle \text{False, Undefined}\rangle \text{ fi}\\ &\blacktriangleleft\!\blacktriangleright\ \text{if True } \mathbin{\Lambda} (2 = 3) \text{ then } \langle \text{True}, 2\rangle\\ &\qquad\qquad \text{else } \langle \text{False, Undefined}\rangle \text{ fi}\\ &\blacktriangleleft\!\blacktriangleright\ \langle \text{False, Undefined}\rangle \end{aligned}$$

whereas

$$\begin{aligned} g(\langle 2, 2\rangle) \ &\blacktriangleleft\!\blacktriangleright\ \mathit{combine}(\langle \text{True}, 2\rangle, \langle \text{True}, 2\rangle)\\ &\blacktriangleleft\!\blacktriangleright\ \text{if True } \mathbin{\Lambda} (2 = 2) \text{ then } \langle \text{True}, 2\rangle\\ &\qquad\qquad \text{else } \langle \text{False, Undefined}\rangle \text{ fi}\\ &\blacktriangleleft\!\blacktriangleright\ \langle \text{True}, 2\rangle \end{aligned}$$

❑

---

[6] Remember that Undefined = Undefined $\blacktriangleleft\!\blacktriangleright$ Undefined, but this situation should never arise.

We have suggested one way to handle the *all_same* failure, but can we find a general fix for this and similar failures? The answer is that if the problem is amenable to structural splitting, then this approach will provide a framework for its calculation. We describe a general construction, which saves *all* the available information, so it must work. (By keeping *all* the available information, the technique succeeds but we apparently gain nothing.) However, we do not usually need all this information and we can therefore — once we know that the technique works — remove any information that is not used. Here goes.

Suppose that we have a specification of a function with signature

$$f: X^+ \to Y$$

[Again, if we were asked to deal with $f: X^* \to Y$, then we would need to handle $f(\langle\rangle)$ as a special case.]

Now construct

p^+ where $p: X \to X^+ \times Y$ defined by $p(x) \triangleq \langle\langle x\rangle, f(\langle x\rangle)\rangle$

q^+ where $q:(X^+ \times Y)^2 \to (X^+ \times Y)$ (see[7])

defined by $q(\langle\langle L_1,y_1\rangle,\langle L_2,y_2\rangle\rangle) \triangleq \langle L_1 \frown L_2, amalgamate(y_1, y_2, L_1, L_2)\rangle$

and

r where $r: X^+ \times Y \to Y$ is defined by $r(\langle L,y\rangle) \triangleq y$.

To complete this construction, we need a definition of the function

$$amalgamate: Y \times Y \times X^+ \times X^+ \to Y.$$

Notice that using the definition

$$amalgamate(y_1, y_2, L_1, L_2) \triangleq f(L_1 \frown L_2)$$

we get

$r \circ q^+ \circ p^+(L) \Leftrightarrow f(L)$ for any non-empty L, so this combination of functions 'works' in the sense that it gives the required answer.

However, in order to benefit from this rather complicated way of going about things, we need a definition of *amalgamate* which utilises y_1 and y_2 as *much* as possible and L_1 and L_2 as *little* as possible. To be of practical use, the calculation at the heart of *amalgamate* must be 'simpler' than f; it must be able to utilise the values y_1 and y_2 to some extent. [If we don't need to use L_1 and L_2 at all, then a straightforward structural split would have worked.]

---

[7] p^+ and q^+ are list functions induced from p and q — see Sections 5.3.2 and 5.3.3.

Example 10.2 We won't attempt a general discussion of the relationship between *amalgamate* and f (it is far too difficult) but we walk through this construction as it can be applied to *all_same*.

Recall the specification

$$all\_same : \mathbb{Z}^* \to \mathbb{B}$$
$$\text{pre-}all\_same(L) \triangleq \text{True}$$
$$\text{post-}all\_same(L,b) \triangleq b = (\exists x:\mathbb{Z})(\forall y:\mathbb{Z})(y \text{ in } L \Rightarrow x = y)$$

First notice that $all\_same(\langle\rangle) \blacktriangleleft\!\!\blacktriangleright \text{True}$

— check this by formal substitution into the specification.

Secondly, for any $n:\mathbb{Z}$,

$$p(\langle n\rangle) \blacktriangleleft\!\!\blacktriangleright \langle \langle n\rangle, \text{True} \rangle$$

This follows from $all\_same(\langle n\rangle) \blacktriangleleft\!\!\blacktriangleright \text{True}$ which again needs checking.

Now, by way of illustration, consider the input $\langle 1, 2, 3\rangle$, then

$$p^+(\langle 1, 2, 3\rangle) \blacktriangleleft\!\!\blacktriangleright \langle \begin{array}{l} \langle \langle 1\rangle, \text{True} \rangle, \\ \langle \langle 2\rangle, \text{True} \rangle, \\ \langle \langle 3\rangle, \text{True} \rangle \end{array} \rangle$$

The function q[8] now takes two items in this list and combines them. Typically we have

$$(\langle L_1 , b_1\rangle , \langle L_2 , b_2\rangle)$$

If b_1 and b_2 are True (i.e. $all\_same(L_1)$ and $all\_same(L_2)$ are True), then we need to refer back to L_1 and L_2 and check if the common value in L_1 is the same as the common value in L_2. We can do this by evaluating

$$\text{first\_of}(L_1) = \text{first\_of}(L_2).$$

Of course, if either b_1 or b_2 are False we need not consult the lists L_1 and L_2. This suggests that we might be able to use the definition

$$amalgamate(b_1, b_2, L_1, L_2) \triangleq (b_1 \wedge b_2) \wedge (\text{first-of}(L_1) = \text{first\_of}(L_2)).$$

[8] Which must be associative in order that $g+$ be well-defined.

[Again this has to be checked[9] by showing that for $L_1,L_2:\mathbb{Z}^+$

$$\text{post-}all\_same(L_1 \frown L_2, (all\_same(L_1) \wedge all\_same(L_2)) \\ \wedge (\text{first-of}(L_1) = \text{first\_of}(L_2))\ ) \Leftrightarrow \text{True}\ ]$$

We can then use the standard implementation schemes for p^* and q^* (applied to p^+ and q^+) as given in Section 5.3.2. Superficially this solution is very similar to our earlier version (Example 10.1) despite the more general approach. However, we can now refine the data types involved to save only a single value from each list and use the modified functions

p^+ where $p:\mathbb{Z} \to \mathbb{Z} \times \mathbb{B}$ is defined by $p(x) \triangleq \langle x,\text{True}\rangle$

q^+ where $q:(\mathbb{Z} \times \mathbb{B})^2 \to (\mathbb{Z} \times \mathbb{B})^2$

is defined by $q(\langle\langle z_1,b_1\rangle,\langle z_2,b_2\rangle\rangle) \triangleq \langle z_1,\ (b_1 \wedge b_2) \wedge (z_1 = z_2)\rangle$

and

r where $r:\mathbb{Z} \times \mathbb{B} \to \mathbb{B}$ is defined by $r(\langle z,b\rangle) \triangleq b$.

And now we *are* back to the same solution. Of course, we need to ensure that we have not lost too much of the information which was present in the original lists.

❑

Exercises

10.1 Try this construction with the following specification:

within_10
type: $\mathbb{Z}^* \to \mathbb{B}$
pre-*within_10*$(L) \triangleq$ True
post-*within_10*$(L,b) \triangleq b \Leftrightarrow (\exists x:\mathbb{Z})\ (\forall n:\mathbb{Z})\ (n \text{ in } L \Rightarrow diff(n,x) \leq 5)$

where

$$diff(x,y) \triangleq \text{if } x \geq y \text{ then } x - y \text{ else } y - x \text{ fi}$$

Following the construction above, see if you can reduce the data so as to use

$p:\mathbb{Z} \to \mathfrak{F}(\mathbb{Z}) \times \mathbb{B}$
where $p(x) \triangleq \langle\ x-5\,..\,x+5\ ,\ \text{True}\ \rangle$

and

$$g(\ \langle\ S_1, b_1\ \rangle\ ,\ \langle\ S_2, b_2\ \rangle\ ) \triangleq \langle\ S_1 \cap S_2\ ,\ (b_1 \wedge b_2) \wedge (S_1 \cap S_2 \neq \emptyset)\ \rangle.$$

❑

9 This calculation, together with the definition of p^+ and induction on the length of lists, guarantees the correctness of $r \circ q^+ \circ p^+$.

Chapter 11

Further Examples

Having spent many pages looking at various ways in which a single specification can give rise to numerous designs and implementations, we now turn our attention to two further examples which illustrate different aspects of algorithm design. These are two important, if unfamiliar, problems that can be represented pictorially. We could follow them through right down to the level of complete PDL implementations; however, we shall stop at an earlier stage in the synthesis. Here we are less concerned with details than the basic approach — the smaller sub-calculations that are generated as we proceed can be tackled in the same way as earlier examples.

Remember that essentially what we are doing is 'inventing' algorithms, and here we shall describe the process by giving informal presentations of formal syntheses. We shall be content with giving a detailed presentation of the *problems* — sufficient to draw out the computationally significant aspects — construct a usable specification, derive an initial high-level design, and then indicate how one might proceed further.

Much of what is presented in this chapter might well be described as problem manipulation (refinement) *prior* to software development and guided by the availability of certain techniques and a desire to utilise more powerful functions such as quantifications.

In Section 11.1, we consider a geometric problem, the so-called (2-dimensional) convex hull problem. This does not employ any advanced mathematics but is explained and discussed in terms of pictures. The example is included so as to illustrate how the problem-solving ideas might be applied in non-software contexts and then modelled in software. Indeed, the way in which the data for this problem is represented presents an additional level of complication in formulating an adequate specification.

Next, in Section 11.2, we look at topological sorting. This is a classical problem which, despite its name, is based not on the order properties of integers (or any other subset of real numbers) but on the implied orderings within the data set. It is important in our context because the simplistic initial specification leads to the possibility of failure (i.e., the problem may not be soluble for an arbitrary but 'valid' data set). The (signature of the) initial problem can be changed to overcome this difficulty and provide a robust algorithm — one whose pre-condition is "True" — and from which a solution to the initial problem can be extracted, if one exists.

To conclude this chapter, we include a discussion of some related 'extremal' problems. These are presented in a somewhat abstract context, but they relate to many practical problems involving the extraction of (usually maximal) sequences of related data elements within structures. In keeping with our wish not to move into the realm of (specialized) data structure, we restrict our examples to integer lists and arrays.

11.1 The 2-D Convex Hull

This problem involves real numbers. For our purposes, this is *not* important; the structure of the algorithm (not the accuracy of the arithmetic) *is* the important factor.

First we must explain exactly what the problem is. It is essentially a geometric problem (see Figure 11.1), and whilst we do not expect many readers to be particularly interested in geometry, it is a non-trivial yet easy-to-understand problem, the overall structure of which mirrors many other, complex and not easily visualised, problems which a software engineer might encounter.

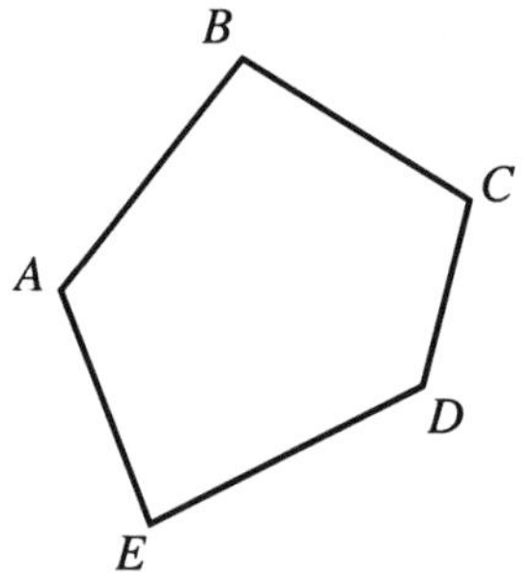

Figure 11.1

Given a non-empty finite set of points in a "2-dimensional" plane (pairs of real numbers), we have to find the smallest convex polygon (the hull) which includes these points. A convex polygon is one that has no 'hollows'; put another way, all its internal angles are less than 180°.

The polygon in Figure 11.1 is convex, whereas the one in Figure 11.2 is concave (the opposite of convex). The internal angle ZYX (measured clockwise from YZ to YX) in Figure 11.2 is clearly bigger than 180°, the 'straight' angle.

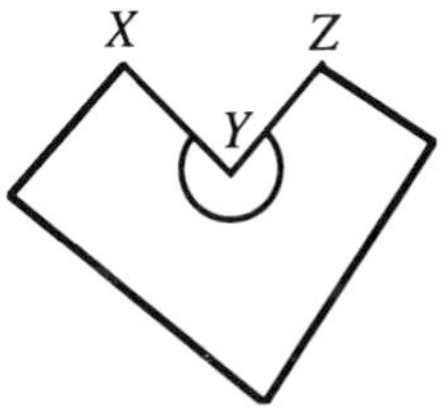

Figure 11.2

So given the set of points $\{a, b, c\}$ as depicted in Figure 11.3, they can be enclosed by a (convex) polygon as shown.

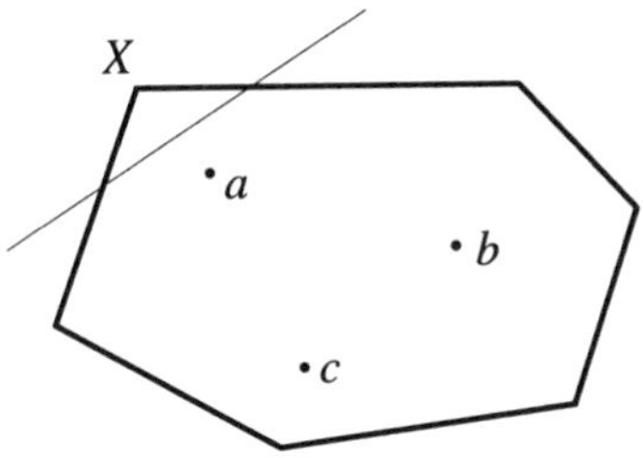

Figure 11.3

The convex polygon in Figure 11.3 is clearly not the smallest (either measured by area or by the length of its perimeter) since we can chop off the corner X and get a valid smaller polygon, provided that all the given points are still 'inside'.

In fact, using domain knowledge, we can reformulate the specification (not change it in the sense that it specifies something different). Doing this not only provides us with a more manageable specification but also assists in the construction of a solution[1].

[1] Of course, the specifier and the implementor are generally *not* the same person, but it is the specifier who has the domain knowledge. We do not presume that the implementor knows more than what he can deduce from the specification and the rules associated with the relevant data types.

Now consider the corner X of the polygon, annotated as in Figure 11.4, and suppose, as shown, that a is the only given point in the triangle XYZ. This choice is only to render the following discussion fairly simple; more complex situations have to be considered in a succession of smaller steps. First notice that we can remove the triangle XYW and achieve a smaller polygon which still contains all the given points by replacing the vertex (corner) X by W. [For future reference this might be regarded as 'swinging' the line YX clockwise about Y to YW, so that it passes through a.] Now continue rotating the line aW about the point a to get the edge aZ and hence replace W by a, giving an even smaller polygon.

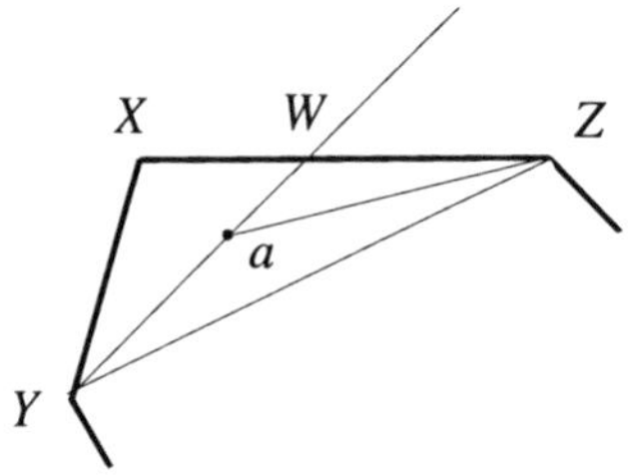

Figure 11.4

Applying the same argument to any vertex of the (current) polygon which is not included in the given set eventually gives us a polygon that is 'shrink wrapped' about the given set of points. This leads us to a reformulation of the problem:

> Given a non-empty finite set of points, find a subset of these points that defines a convex polygon which contains all of the given points.

So, a polygon can be represented by a set of points, but why not use a list, of the vertices — ordered so as to traverse the polygon in a clockwise direction (say)? Moreover, doing this, none of the given points will ever be to the left of this direction of travel. We could even decide to start the list with the vertex having the most 'westerly', most 'northern' vertex. Put a little more formally, if any point d has co-ordinates $\langle d_x, d_y \rangle$, then we seek the point with the greatest y co-ordinate, and, if there is more than one, then we select the one which has the least (most negative) x co-ordinate. Using this representation, the polygon depicted in Figure 11.5 can be encoded as the list $\langle c, a, b, d, e \rangle$. This selection of a start point may be useful in certain situations, but we shall not insist upon this; an appropriate list can always be found by cycling the elements of the list.

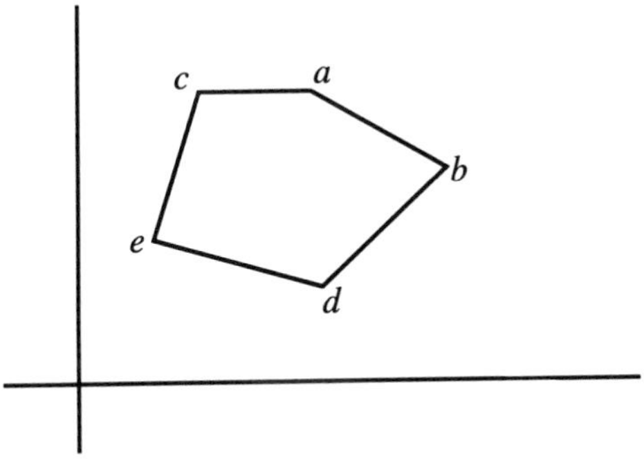

Figure 11.5

So the formal specification is

$$
\begin{aligned}
&CHull: \mathfrak{F}(point) \rightarrow poly \\
&\text{pre-}CHull(S) \triangleq \text{True} \\
&\text{post-}CHull(S,P) \triangleq \mathfrak{F}(point){:}P \subseteq S \\
&\qquad\qquad \wedge\ convex(P) \wedge \neg(\exists x{:}point)(x \in S \wedge x\ outside\ P)
\end{aligned}
$$

where

$$
\begin{aligned}
&point \triangleq \mathbb{R} \times \mathbb{R} \\
&poly \triangleq point^{+} \\
&convex(P{:}poly) \triangleq (\#P \leq 2) \vee (\forall a,b,c{:}point,\ L,M{:}point^{*}) \\
&\qquad ((P = L \frown \langle a, b, c\rangle \frown M) \\
&\qquad \vee (\ b = \text{first\_of}(P) \\
&\qquad\quad \wedge\ c = \text{first\_of}(\text{rest\_of}(P)) \\
&\qquad\quad \wedge\ a = \text{last\_of}(P)\ ) \\
&\qquad \vee (\ a = \text{last\_of}(\text{front\_of}(P)) \\
&\qquad\quad \wedge\ b = \text{last\_of}(P) \\
&\qquad\quad \wedge\ c = \text{first\_of}(P)\ ) \\
&\qquad \Rightarrow \text{angle } cba < 180^{\circ})
\end{aligned}
$$

and

$$
\begin{aligned}
&x\ outside\ P \triangleq (\exists a,b{:}point,\ L,M{:}point^{*}) \\
&\qquad ((P = L \frown \langle a, b\rangle \frown M) \\
&\qquad \vee (\ b = \text{first\_of}(P) \\
&\qquad\quad \wedge\ a = \text{last\_of}(P)\ ) \\
&\qquad \Rightarrow \text{angle } bxa < 180^{\circ})
\end{aligned}
$$

We will not use any of these details, but those of you who know some co-ordinate geometry can check them out. Suffice it to say that the convexity condition represents the situation in Figure 11.6 and that the "outside'ness" predicate corresponds to Figure 11.7. Throughout this problem, the way that angles are written is crucial so that the angle ZYX relates to the arc between YZ and YX, again moving clockwise.

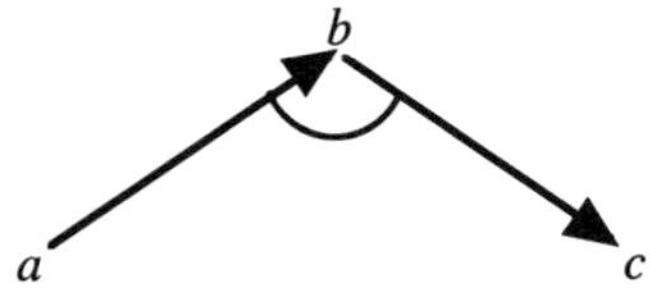

Figure 11.6

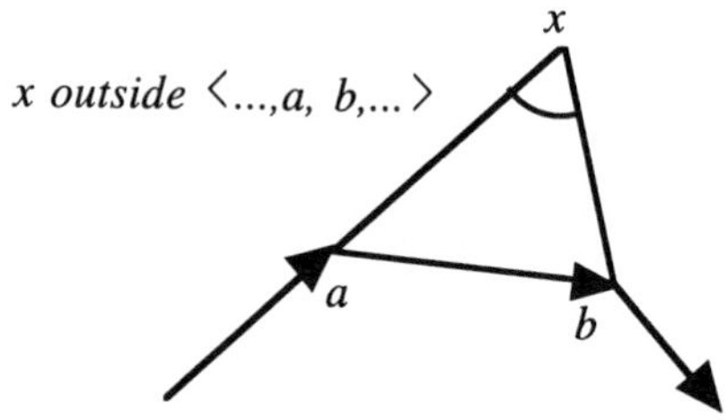

Figure 11.7

So, the post-condition tells us that the (corners of the) convex polygon P consists of a subset of the points in S and that none of the points in S lie outside of P.

[These conditions can be used to check the correctness of each stage of algorithm construction; however, an easier approach is to ensure that these conditions are used within the actual construction steps.]

A traditional structural splitting tactic can now be applied to this problem, dividing the set S, achieving convex hulls for each subset, and then combining pairs of hulls to give the required composite hull. And the specification of the necessary *combine* function is immediate:

$$\begin{aligned}
&\textit{combine}: \textit{poly} \times \textit{poly} \to \textit{poly}\\
&\text{pre-}\textit{combine}(\langle H,L\rangle) \triangleq \textit{convex}(H) \wedge \textit{convex}(L)\\
&\text{post-}\textit{combine}(\langle H,L\rangle, N) \triangleq \textit{convex}(N)\\
&\qquad\qquad \wedge\ \mathfrak{F}(\textit{point}){:}N \subseteq (\mathfrak{F}(\textit{point}){:}H \cup \mathfrak{F}(\textit{point}){:}L)\\
&\quad \wedge\ \neg(\exists x{:}\textit{point})(x \in (\mathfrak{F}(\textit{point}){:}H \cup \mathfrak{F}(\textit{point}){:}L) \wedge x \textit{ outside } N)
\end{aligned}$$

How to construct a design for the implementation of this function is less obvious from the specification but can be deduced more easily by reference to pictorial representations of the possible situations. [Again we shall skip the detailed mathematical calculations. Although these only amount to finding the slopes of lines — the ratios of differences in co-ordinates — and distances, they serve only to cloud the main issues and add extra confusion for those readers who are not confident in this area of mathematics.] Firstly, we can dispose of the trivial case.

$CHull(\{x\})$ ◆ $\langle x \rangle$

This has to be checked by substitution.

For the more complex cases, let us represent the smaller hulls by ovals indicating their general shape and relative position. The hulls are, by definition convex so this is not unreasonable. There are four basic ways in which a pair of hulls can be related. These are shown in Figure 11.8. Also included in the diagrams are extra line segments indicating how the composite hull is achieved.

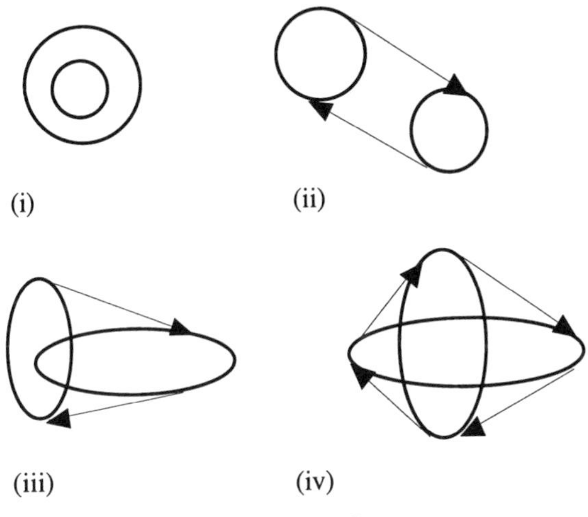

Figure 11.8

In each case, the resultant hull can be found by starting at the 'most westerly, most northern' point of the two hulls (which gives the start of the composite) and taking the initial direction as being from west to east. Now we build up the list of points by selecting from two possible next points. (Actually, it is more correct to say that one of these might be rejected.) These may be two points from the same hull or one point from either. A typical situation is indicated in Figure 11.9.

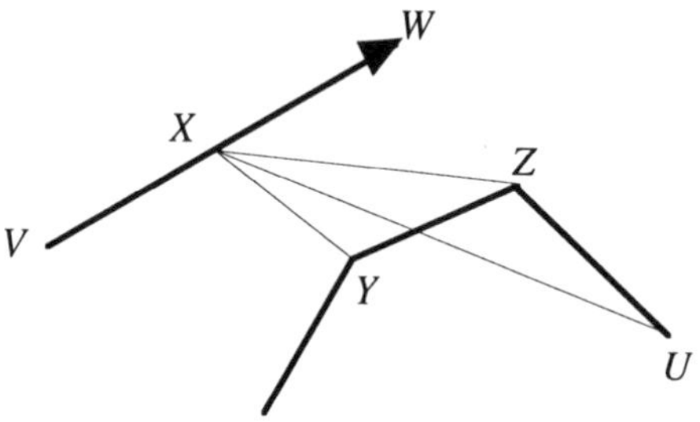

Figure 11.9

Suppose that we are at X and that VW indicates the current direction of traversal. Y is a possible next point, and Z is the point to be considered afterwards. Angle WXY is greater than angle WXZ so we skip Y (it might be required later!) and now examine the acceptability of Z for inclusion in the resultant hull. Again look at the next point in the hull (the hull that includes Y, Z and U ...). Angle WXZ is less than angle WXU, so now we can include Z, and the current direction of travel becomes XZ, and so on. This guarantees that no points are outside of the final hull, that the resultant polygon is convex (and therefore *is* a hull), and that all the corners of the resultant hull are corners of the given hulls.

We'll stop there. The shape of the algorithms which follow are typical "divide and conquer" designs. One possible twist is to consider the input set one point at a time — and derive an incremental calculation — either the point will be internal and not affect the 'result so far' or will be included in this polygon and perhaps cause some other corners to be deleted. In order to pursue the construction of one of these algorithms to a complete design, we need to have sufficient domain knowledge; at the level of detail indicated here and be given all the necessary information within the specification.

Notice also that the *combine* function is almost a quantifier (we do not have empty inputs so the identity rules are not required) and hence a re-formulation based on the associativity of *combine* is also possible.

11.2 Topological Sort

This is a classical programming problem related to scheduling — typically the scheduling of very many tasks within a large project. Here we are not concerned with any specific project, so we shall describe the general situation in a pictorial fashion. [In practice, diagrams are often used by engineers to 'see' what is going on, so recourse to pictures is not a great deviation from reality.]

11.2.1 Experimentation

Imagine you have a (very) large number of, typically small, assembly tasks. Associated with each task there will usually be certain resources — such as manpower, time, specialised equipment — that are needed in order that the task may be undertaken. (These attributes are required for subsequent processing, documentation, determination of *critical paths* etc. associated with the overall project. However, they are not relevant to the current problem and we shall ignore them; they can be added later if required.)

Each task (each activity) may be regarded as a 'connection' between two events (i.e., two situations) and can be represented by the ordered pair $\langle x,y \rangle$, where x and y are events. The situation x indicates that all the pre-requisites for the current task have been done (so that it is now ***enabled***); y corresponds to the situation when this task has been carried out and hence some other tasks may be enabled[2]. A complete, but small, project may be represented as in Figure 11.10.

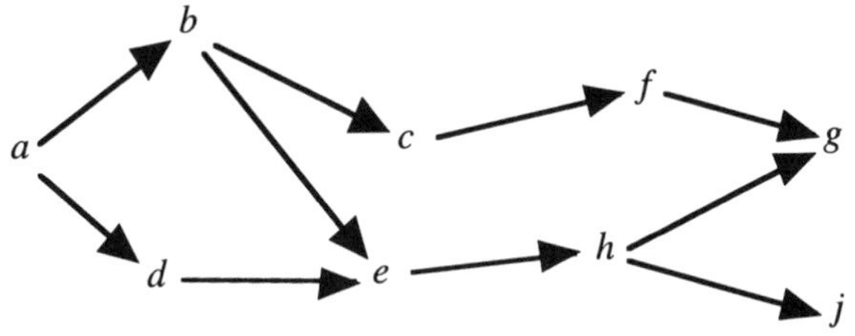

Figure 11.10

A more realistic project may involve several hundred events, and these will usually be numbered (but the numerical values would not be significant, merely a convenient way of generating lots of new names). Moreover, the diagrams would probably not be very neat, the 'start' and 'finish' (which are poor terms anyway as we shall see) may not be unique, and they may not be easy to find just by looking — after all, the diagram is unlikely to fit on a single sheet of paper.

Essentially the diagram depicts a *partial* order. It merely says that certain pairs of events must occur in a prescribed order. For example, both b and d 'come before' e, but c and e are unrelated so it may be the case that c comes before e, or that e comes before c, or that they coincide or overlap in time. The diagram is a directed graph (or ***digraph***) and may be represented as a set, G, of arrows where

$$G \triangleq \{ \langle a,b \rangle , \langle a,d \rangle , \langle b,c \rangle , \langle b,e \rangle , \langle c,f \rangle , \langle d,e \rangle , \langle e,h \rangle , \langle f,g \rangle , \langle h,g \rangle , \langle h,j \rangle \}$$

[2] There is an alternative formulation which roughly relates to swapping activities and events. Instead of dwelling on such terms, we want to get to the diagrams, and the mathematical formulation, as quickly as possible; they are easier to deal with.

Here G is small; a corresponding picture is easy to draw, the set is easy to write down, and we can view it in its entirety. For more complex processes, it is often convenient not to use the original structure of G but to 'flatten' the graph onto a straight line as in Figure 11.11.

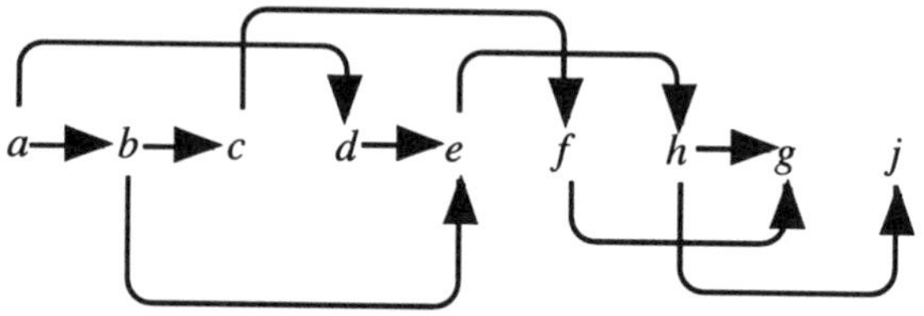

Figure 11.11

From this figure, we simply carry forward the list $\langle a, b, c, d, e, f, h, g, j \rangle$ and forget about the arrows. But notice that here, and in general, there is more than one permissible answer. Another ordering consistent with G is as shown in Figure 11.12.

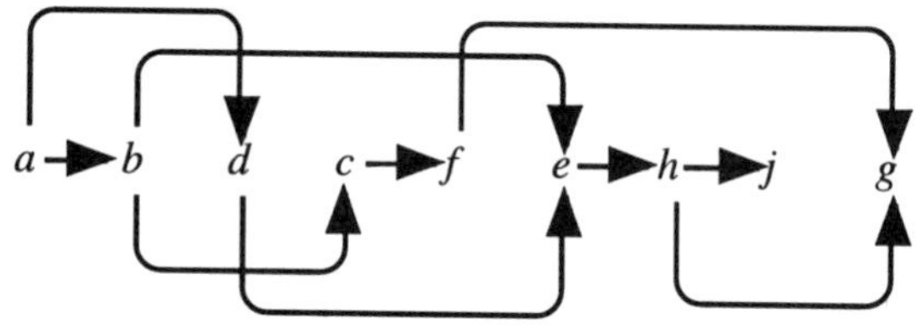

Figure 11.12

In each of these diagrams, we have retained all the arrows and merely moved the nodes (the letters representing the events) around and twisted the arrows appropriately. In the final version, all the arrows point from left to right. That is the essence of what we are trying to achieve in what is called a ***topological sort*** — to derive a linear ordering of the nodes which is consistent with the arrows in the given graph.

You may be able to see that this problem is not always soluble. (Don't worry if you can't; we shall presume for the moment that it *is* and identify the flaw in this belief as we try to synthesise a program to solve the problem. And then we shall fix it.)

So the input is a digraph[3] (i.e., a set of points and a set of arrows) but not just *any* set of arrows. Each arrow must link two distinct elements from the given set of points. (We can have a point x which is not used in the identification of any arrow,

[3] In this chapter, we shall always be concerned with directed graph structures, but the terms graph, digraph and directed graph will be used interchangeably.

but the $\langle y,z \rangle$ only makes sense if y and z are points in the given graph.) If a digraph satisfies this property, then we shall say that it is *well_defined* and hence we can write down an initial attempt at a specification of a topological sort called *T_Sort*0.

Let *Node* be a set (the type) of node names, and then define

$$Arrow \triangleq Node \times Node$$

and a directed graph $\quad Dg \triangleq \mathcal{F}(Node) \times \mathcal{F}(Arrow)$

A topological sort can then be specified by

$$\begin{array}{l} T\_Sort0\text{: } Dg \rightarrow Node^* \\ \text{pre-}T\_Sort0(D) \triangleq well\_defined(D) \\ \text{post-}T\_Sort0(\langle N,A \rangle,L) \triangleq (\mathcal{B}(Node){:}L = \mathcal{B}(Node){:}N) \\ \qquad\qquad \wedge\ (\forall x,y{:}Node)(\langle x,y \rangle \in A \Rightarrow x\ before\ y\ in\ L) \end{array}$$

where

$$\begin{array}{l} well\_defined(\langle N,A \rangle) \triangleq \\ \qquad (\forall x,y{:}Node)(\langle x,y \rangle \in A \Rightarrow (x \in N \wedge y \in N \wedge x \neq y)) \end{array}$$

$$x\ before\ y\ in\ L \triangleq (\exists L1,L2,L3\text{: } Node^*)\ (L = L1 ^\frown \langle x \rangle ^\frown L2 ^\frown \langle y \rangle ^\frown L3)$$

In pre-*T_Sort*0, we have no need to refer to the components of D, but in the post-condition it is convenient to represent D by its components N and A (nodes and arrows). If we had not done this, we would have had to introduce local names N and A and to add a clause "$D = \langle N,A \rangle$" within the definition of the post-condition. Many variants such as this are possible. The particular form used is largely a matter of taste, but we shall always strive to increase readability.

The post-condition here says that the list L includes exactly the same elements as the set of nodes N in the graph D. Since N is a set, it has no repeats. Using the "$\mathcal{B}$:" ("bag of") cast ensures that $\#L = \#N$ and that there are no repeats in L. Additionally, as it says very directly, if x—y is an arrow in D, then x comes before y in L.

OK, so how can we set about solving this problem. How can we *calculate* the answer? First notice that reduction is not going to work. Reducing A — removing arrows from the input — will permit more variation in L. Removing *all* arrows in A will permit *any* ordering of the elements in L, but A is supposed to constrain the ordering of L. Reducing N — throwing away nodes (and therefore also throwing away any arrows that link those nodes) — would also necessitate throwing away elements in the output list L, and again this contradicts the specification. If we cannot 'reduce' the problem, then perhaps we could apply a "divide and conquer" strategy but first we consider small versions of the problem which would not be amenable to sub-division.

Let's *play* with the problem and take cases where $\#N = 0, 1, 2$ or 3.

If $\#N = 0$, then $N = \emptyset$, $A = \emptyset$ and $L = \langle\rangle$. This must follow since $\#L = \#N$, so $L = \langle\rangle$. We must also have $A = \emptyset$ since $A = \emptyset \iff \#A = 0$; if $\#A \neq 0$ (i.e., $\#A > 0$), then there would be some $\langle x,y\rangle \in A$ with *x before y in L*, and thus we would need to have $\#L \geq 2$, which is not True. So the input must be $\langle\emptyset,\emptyset\rangle$, and this gives the output $L = \langle\rangle$. Check this piece of reasoning by substitution into the specification.

$$\text{pre-}T\_Sort0(\langle\emptyset,\emptyset\rangle)$$

$$\iff$$

$$\textit{well-defined}(\langle\emptyset,\emptyset\rangle)$$

$$\iff$$

$$(\forall x,y{:}Node)(\langle x,y\rangle \in \emptyset \Rightarrow (x \in \emptyset \wedge y \in \emptyset \wedge x \neq y))$$

$$\iff$$

$$(\forall x,y{:}Node)(\text{False} \Rightarrow (x \in \emptyset \wedge y \in \emptyset \wedge x \neq y))$$

$$\iff$$

$$(\forall x,y{:}Node)(\text{True})$$

$$\iff$$

$$\text{True}$$

and

$$\text{post-}T\_Sort0(\langle\emptyset,\emptyset\rangle,\langle\rangle)$$

$$\iff$$

$$(\mathcal{B}(Node){:}\langle\rangle = \mathcal{B}(Node){:}\emptyset) \wedge (\forall x,y{:}Node)(\langle x,y\rangle \in \emptyset \Rightarrow x \textit{ before } y \textit{ in } \langle\rangle)$$

$$\iff$$

$$(\{\!\!\{\ \}\!\!\} = \{\!\!\{\ \}\!\!\}) \wedge (\forall x,y{:}Node)(\langle x,y\rangle \in \emptyset \Rightarrow x \textit{ before } y \textit{ in } \langle\rangle)$$

$$\iff$$

$$\text{True} \wedge (\forall x,y{:}Node)(\langle x,y\rangle \in \emptyset \Rightarrow x \textit{ before } y \textit{ in } \langle\rangle)$$

$$\iff$$

$$(\forall x,y{:}Node)(\text{False} \Rightarrow x \textit{ before } y \textit{ in } \langle\rangle)$$

$$\iff$$

$$(\forall x,y{:}Node)(\text{True})$$

$$\iff$$

$$\text{True}$$

Similarly, if $\#N = 1$, then $N = \{z\}$ for some z:*Node*, $A = \emptyset$, and $L = \langle z \rangle$.

$\#N = 1 \Rightarrow A = \emptyset$ by the previous argument, and so we have

$$\text{pre-}T\_Sort0(\langle \{z\},\emptyset \rangle)$$
$$\Leftrightarrow$$
$$well\text{-}defined(\langle \{z\},\emptyset \rangle)$$
$$\Leftrightarrow$$
$$(\forall x,y{:}Node)(\langle x,y \rangle \in \emptyset \Rightarrow (x \in \{z\} \wedge y \in \{z\} \wedge x \neq y))$$
$$\Leftrightarrow$$
$$(\forall x,y{:}Node)(\text{False} \Rightarrow (x \in \{z\} \wedge y \in \{z\} \wedge x \neq y))$$
$$\Leftrightarrow$$
$$(\forall x,y{:}Node)(\text{True})$$
$$\Leftrightarrow$$
$$\text{True}$$

Notice also that

$$(x \in \{z\} \wedge y \in \{z\} \wedge x \neq y)$$
$$\Leftrightarrow$$
$$(x = z \wedge y = z \wedge x \neq y)$$
$$\Leftrightarrow$$
$$(x = z \wedge y = z \wedge x \neq z)$$
$$\Leftrightarrow$$
$$(x = z) \wedge (y = z) \wedge \neg(x = z)$$
$$\Leftrightarrow$$
$$\text{False}$$

We don't actually need to know this, but it illustrates the kind of reasoning commonly found in graph problems.

We *do* need

$$\text{post-}T\_Sort0(\langle \{z\},\emptyset \rangle,\langle z \rangle)$$
$$\Leftrightarrow$$
$$(\mathfrak{B}(Node){:}\langle z \rangle = \mathfrak{B}(Node){:}\{z\}) \wedge (\forall x,y{:}Node)(\langle x,y \rangle \in \emptyset \Rightarrow x \textit{ before } y \textit{ in } \langle z \rangle)$$
$$\Leftrightarrow$$
$$(\{\!|z|\!\} = \{\!|z|\!\}) \wedge (\forall x,y{:}Node)(\langle x,y \rangle \in \emptyset \Rightarrow x \textit{ before } y \textit{ in } \langle z \rangle)$$
$$\Leftrightarrow$$
$$\text{True} \wedge (\forall x,y{:}Node)(\langle x,y \rangle \in \emptyset \Rightarrow x \textit{ before } y \textit{ in } \langle z \rangle)$$
$$\Leftrightarrow$$
$$(\forall x,y{:}Node)(\langle x,y \rangle \in \emptyset \Rightarrow x \textit{ before } y \textit{ in } \langle z \rangle)$$

◆▶
   $(\forall x,y:Node)(\text{False} \Rightarrow x \text{ before } y \text{ in } \langle z \rangle)$

◆▶
   $(\forall x,y:Node)(\text{True})$

◆▶
   True

Involving a little more calculation but still straightforward, if $\#N = 2$, then $N = \{x,y\}$ for two distinct values $x,y:Node$. Then we may still have $A = \emptyset$, in which case either $L = \langle x,y \rangle$ or $L = \langle y,x \rangle$ would do. However, if we   had $A = \{\langle x,y \rangle\}$ (say), then $L = \langle x,y \rangle$ would be the only answer.

So, taking the latter alternative,

   $\text{pre-}T\_Sort0(\langle \{x,y\},\{\langle x,y \rangle\} \rangle)$

◆▶
   $well\_defined(\{x,y\},\{\langle x,y \rangle\})$

◆▶
   $(\forall a,b:Node)(\langle a,b \rangle \in \{\langle x,y \rangle\} \Rightarrow (a \in \{x,y\} \land b \in \{x,y\} \land a \neq b))$

◆▶
   $(\forall a,b:Node)$
     $(a = x \land b = y) \Rightarrow ((a = x \lor a = y) \land (b = x \lor b = y) \land a \neq b)$

Then, assuming that x,y are distinct $Nodes$ and $(a = x \land b = y)$, so the rules a◆▶x, b◆▶y, $a = x$ ◆▶ True, and $b = y$ ◆▶ True hold, we have

   $((a = x \lor a = y) \land (b = x \lor b = y) \land a \neq b)$

◆▶
   $((\text{True} \lor a = y) \land (b = x \lor \text{True}) \land x \neq y)$

◆▶
   $(\text{True} \land \text{True} \land \text{True})$

◆▶
   True

so

   $(a = x \land b = y) \Rightarrow ((a = x \lor a = y) \land (b = x \lor b = y) \land a \neq b)$
◆▶
   True

From which it follows that

   $\text{pre-}T\_Sort0(\langle \{x,y\},\{\langle x,y \rangle\} \rangle)$

◆▶
   $well\_defined(\{x,y\},\{\langle x,y \rangle\})$

◆

$(\forall a,b{:}Node)(\langle a,b\rangle \in \{\langle x,y\rangle\} \Rightarrow (a \in \{x,y\} \wedge b \in \{x,y\} \wedge a \neq b))$

◆

$(\forall a,b{:}Node)$
$\quad (a = x \wedge b = y) \Rightarrow ((a = x \vee a = y) \wedge (b = x \vee b = y) \wedge a \neq b)$

◆

$(\forall a,b{:}Node)(\text{True})$

◆

True

and then

post-$T\_Sort0(\langle\{x,y\},\{\langle x,y\rangle\}\rangle,\langle x,y\rangle)$ — see[4]

◆

$(\mathfrak{B}(Node){:}\langle x,y\rangle = \mathfrak{B}(Node){:}\{x,y\})$
$\quad \wedge (\forall a,b{:}Node)(\langle a,b\rangle \in \{\langle x,y\rangle\} \Rightarrow a \textit{ before } b \textit{ in } \langle x,y\rangle)$

◆

$(\{\!|x,y|\!\} = \{\!|x,y|\!\})$
$\quad \wedge (\forall a,b{:}Node)(\langle a,b\rangle \in \{\langle x,y\rangle\} \Rightarrow a \textit{ before } b \textit{ in } \langle x,y\rangle)$

◆

$\text{True} \wedge (\forall a,b{:}Node)(\langle a,b\rangle \in \{\langle x,y\rangle\} \Rightarrow a \textit{ before } b \textit{ in } \langle x,y\rangle)$

◆

$(\forall a,b{:}Node)(\langle a,b\rangle \in \{\langle x,y\rangle\} \Rightarrow a \textit{ before } b \textit{ in } \langle x,y\rangle)$

◆

$(\forall a,b{:}Node)((a = x \wedge b = y) \Rightarrow a \textit{ before } b \textit{ in } \langle x,y\rangle)$

Again we take $x,y{:}Node$ to be distinct and assume $(a = x \wedge b = y)$ so the rules a◆x and b◆y hold; then

$a \textit{ before } b \textit{ in } \langle x,y\rangle$

◆

$x \textit{ before } y \textit{ in } \langle x,y\rangle$

◆

$(\exists L_1,L_2,L_3{:}Node^*)\ (\langle x,y\rangle = L_1 \frown \langle x\rangle \frown L_2 \frown \langle y\rangle \frown L_3)$

◆

True

since $\langle x,y\rangle = \langle\rangle \frown \langle x\rangle \frown \langle\rangle \frown \langle y\rangle \frown \langle\rangle$

Thus, referring back to the main calculation,

post-$T\_Sort0(\langle\{x,y\},\{\langle x,y\rangle\}\rangle,\langle x,y\rangle)$

◆

$(\forall a,b{:}Node)((a = x \wedge b = y) \Rightarrow a$ before b in $\langle x,y\rangle)$

---

[4] Notice the different types involved here. The values all use the names x and y, but the first is a *set* of *Nodes*, the second is a *set* of *arrows*, and the last is a *list*.

⟺

$(\forall a,b:Node)(\text{True})$

⟺

True

So this answer works. What we have done here is traditional verification, but we only advocate this for a very simple instance of a problem. (It is usually quicker and involves less effort than synthesising an answer.)

We are not going to work through the case when $\#N = 3$, but we shall *discuss* the problem. Notice that if $N = \{x,y,z\}$ and $A = \emptyset$, then there are six different possibilities for L, namely

$$\langle x,y,z\rangle\ ,\ \langle y,z,x\rangle\ ,\langle z,x,y\rangle\ ,\langle z,y,x\rangle\ ,\langle y,x,z\rangle\ ,\langle x,z,y\rangle\ .$$

If we had $A = \{\langle x,y\rangle\}$, this would reduce to three, $\langle x,y,z\rangle,\langle z,x,y\rangle$ and $\langle x,z,y\rangle$, and so on. As mentioned before, there is in general not a unique solution but many. So as to make the non-deterministic nature of the specification more apparent, we can reformulate it as follows. We shall give the specification and then discuss it (i.e., *read* it).

$$
\begin{array}{l}
T\_Sort1\text{: } Dg \to Node^* \\
\text{pre-}T\_Sort1(D) \triangleq well\_defined(D) \\
\text{post-}T\_Sort1(\langle N,A\rangle,L) \triangleq \\
\quad (\exists Lset\text{: } \mathcal{F}(Node^*)) \\
\quad\quad (Lset = \{\ell\text{: } Node^* \mid \ (\mathcal{B}(Node)\text{:}\ell = \mathcal{B}(Node)\text{:}N) \\
\quad\quad\quad\quad\quad\quad \wedge\ (\forall x,y\text{:}Node)(\langle x,y\rangle \in A \Rightarrow x \textit{ before } y \textit{ in } \ell)\} \\
\quad\quad \wedge\ L \in Lset\ )
\end{array}
$$

Here *Lset* is the set of all *Node* lists having the same elements as N and being ordered in a way that is consistent with all the arrows in A. The 'answer' L is then chosen freely from *Lset*. [Note that this is a *specification*. It is not our intention to actually derive *Lset* as part of the *calculation* of L.] Referring back to the situation where $N = \{x,y,z\}$, suppose now that $A = \{\langle x,y\rangle,\langle x,z\rangle\}$; then the choices for L reduce to $\langle x,y,z\rangle$ and $\langle x,z,y\rangle$. So far, so good, but what happens if we now include $\langle y,x\rangle$ in A? This does not fit with either of the remaining two alternatives. The set *Lset* is empty and no 'correct' value for L can be found; the problem is insoluble.

Drawing a picture (Figure 11.13) with the elements of N joined up appropriately, the problem is obvious.

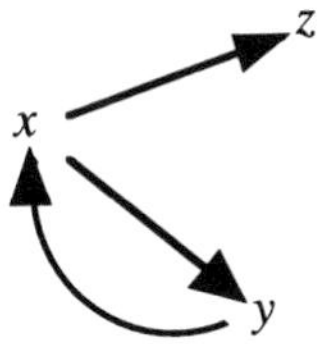

Figure 11.13

There is a *loop*, albeit a very tight loop. So we can't put x before y and then y before x in L. Rremember that L can include only a single copy of x. In fact, a directed graph D can only be topologically sorted if it contains no loops.

So the pre-condition ought to include a clause which says that D cannot contain loops, but this is equivalent to saying that D can be topologically sorted and hence we have a circular argument. We cannot check that the problem is soluble before trying — and possibly failing — to solve it. We need to check that D can be topologically sorted as we go along. We modify the specification to reflect this extra facet of the problem.

11.2.2 A Proper Formulation

Following the discussion above, we add an extra output, a Boolean which indicates whether we have been successful in our attempt to perform a topological sort on the given digraph.

$$
\begin{aligned}
&T\_Sort\text{: } Dg \rightarrow Node^* \times \mathbb{B}\\
&\text{pre-}T\_Sort(D) \triangleq well\_defined(D)\\
&\text{post-}T\_Sort(\langle N,A\rangle,\langle L,sortable\rangle) \triangleq\\
&\qquad (\exists Lset\text{: } \mathfrak{F}(Node^*))\\
&\qquad\quad (Lset = \{\ell : Node^* \mid \; (\mathfrak{B}(Node)\text{:}\ell = \mathfrak{B}(Node)\text{:}N)\\
&\qquad\qquad\qquad\qquad \wedge\ (\forall x,y\text{:}Node)(\langle x,y\rangle \in A \Rightarrow x \; before \; y \; in \; \ell)\}\\
&\qquad\quad \wedge\ ((Lset = \emptyset \wedge \neg sortable) \;\vee\; (L \in Lset \wedge sortable))\;)
\end{aligned}
$$

So, if $T\_Sort(D) = \langle L,s\rangle$ and s = True, then the search for a consistent listing of the nodes in D was successful and L is one such listing; otherwise, the search failed. Note that if $Lset = \emptyset$ then *any* list will do for L and the answer is $\langle L,\text{False}\rangle$.

When $\#N \leq 1$ we have $A = \emptyset$ and hence A cannot contain arrows which cause the 'sorting' to fail.

Exercises

11.1 Show by substitution that $\langle\langle\rangle,\text{True}\rangle$ is a solution for $T\_Sort(\langle\emptyset,\emptyset\rangle)$.

11.2 Similarly, show that if $D = \langle\{x\},\emptyset\rangle$ for some $x{:}Node$ then $\langle\langle x\rangle,\text{True}\rangle$ is an acceptable result for $T\_Sort(D)$.

❑

Now for $D = \langle N,A\rangle$, where $\#N > 1$, the associated data-flow diagram is as in Figure 11.14.

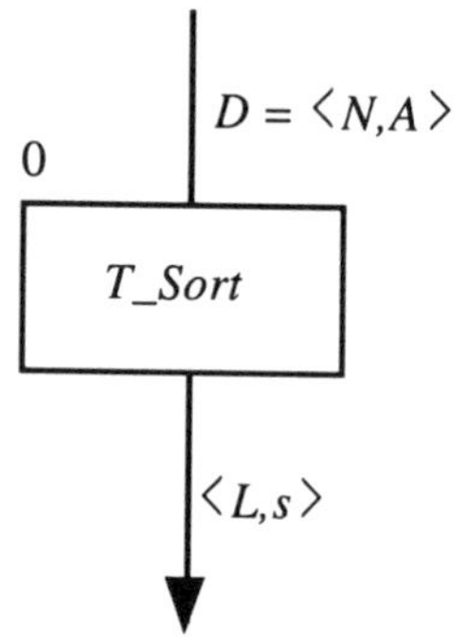

Figure 11.14

We want to split D into D_1 and D_2 to give L_1 and L_2, from which we can construct L. The classical structure, suitably labelled, is given in Figure 11.15.

The specifications of boxes (2) and (3) are the same as box (0) but with different, smaller, parameters. But how do we specify what goes on in boxes (1) and (4) so that the new four-box combination is consistent with box (0)?

Consider the possibilities of what to do with an arrow $\langle x,y\rangle$ in A (in D). Recall that we require that x should come before y in L. If $\langle x,y\rangle$ is put into D_1, then x will come before y in L_1, and therefore the *combine* phase must preserve this ordering — which knows nothing about x and y, only L_1 — so

$$x \textit{ before } y \textit{ in } L_1 \Rightarrow x \textit{ before } y \textit{ in } L$$

Similarly, for the case when $\langle x,y\rangle$ is placed in D_2, we then require that

$$x \textit{ before } y \textit{ in } L_2 \Rightarrow x \textit{ before } y \textit{ in } L$$

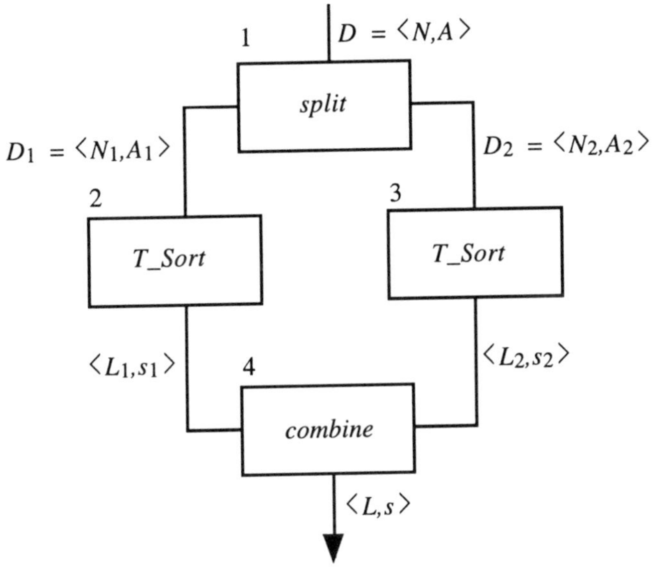

Figure 11.15

To satisfy both these requirements, L would have to be the result of overlapping L_1 and L_2 (preserving the orderings on L_1 and L_2). But now suppose that $\langle x,y \rangle \in D$ with $x \in N_1$ and $y \in N_2$ as in Figure 11.16.

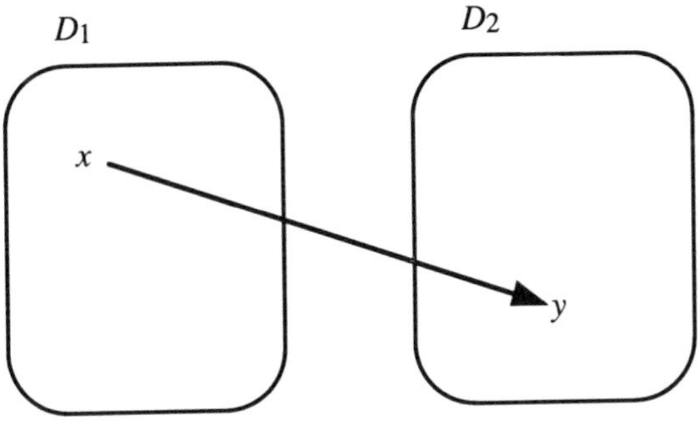

Figure 11.16.

This would give x in L_1 and y in L_2, as in Figure 11.17.

The only way to guarantee that x comes before y in L, regardless of where x occurs in L_1 or where y occurs in L_2, is to concatenate L_2 *after* L_1 (i.e., to require that $L = L_1 {}^\frown L_2$). Of course, concatenation satisfies the "bag_of" requirements.

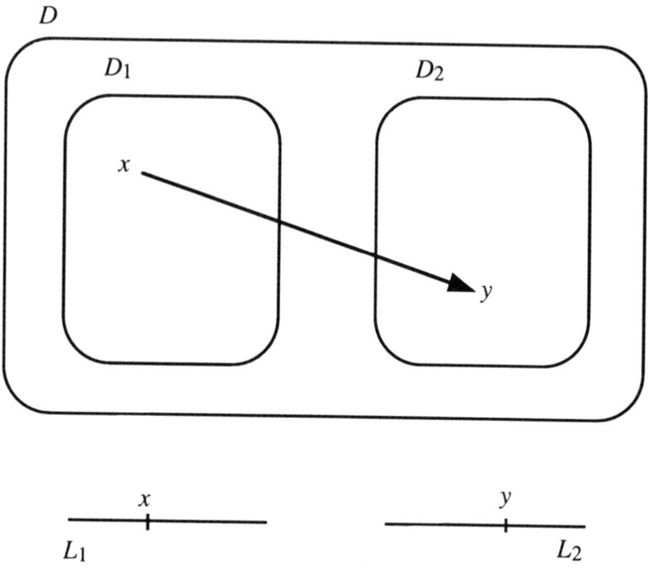

Figure 11.17

Now for a "eureka step. There is nothing automatic about this; we have to "invent" a way of breaking up D and then constructing L. Although we are trying to use one of the common strategies, the details will vary from problem to problem. The idea — the intuition behind the eureka step — is that

$$L = L_1 \frown L_2$$

so that if x in L_1 and y in L_2 then we would require that either $\langle x,y \rangle \in A$ (and x *is* before y in L, so that's OK), or $\langle x,y \rangle \notin A$ (which is again OK), but not that $\langle y,x \rangle \in A$ (because then "x before y in L" would be False).

Put the other way around

if $\langle x,y \rangle \in A$	then	x,y in L_1
	or	x,y in L_2
	or	x in L_1 and y in L_2

would be OK, *for now*.

(The actual ordering of x and y when both are in L_1 or both are in L_2 will be determined later, when the corresponding sub-graphs are 'sorted'.)

So we need a non-trivial mixed strategy. A simple arbitrary splitting of the node set N, to give N_1, N_2, etc., independently of A, will not work in general. Obviously, we require that

$$\begin{aligned} \text{bag\_of}(L) &= \text{bag\_of}(L_1) \uplus \text{bag\_of}(L_2) \\ &= \text{bag\_of}(N) \end{aligned}$$

The specification of *split* is of similar complexity to *T_Sort* and will involve a selection from a set of possibilities.

There are three cases, $\#N = 0{,}1$ or more, but only the third demands special attention. We attempt to define a *split*ting function as follows:

$$\begin{aligned}
&split0{:}Dg \rightarrow Dg \times Dg \\
&\text{pre-}split0(D) \triangleq well_defined(D) \\
&\text{post-}split0(D,\langle D_1,D_2\rangle) \triangleq \\
&\qquad (\exists Dpairs{:}\mathfrak{F}(Dg^2)) \\
&\qquad\quad (Dpairs = \{\langle\langle N_1,A_1\rangle,\langle N_2,A_2\rangle\rangle{:}Dg^2 | \\
&\qquad\qquad N_1 \cup N_2 = N \wedge \\
&\qquad\qquad N_1 \cap N_2 = \emptyset \wedge \\
&\qquad\qquad N_1 \neq \emptyset \wedge N_2 \neq \emptyset \wedge \\
&\qquad\qquad A_1 \subseteq A \wedge A_2 \subseteq A \wedge \\
&\qquad\qquad (\forall x,y{:}Node)(\langle x,y\rangle \in A \\
&\qquad\qquad\qquad \Rightarrow (\langle x,y\rangle \in A_1 \vee \langle x,y\rangle \in A_2 \vee \\
&\qquad\qquad\qquad\quad (x \in N_1 \wedge y \in N_2)))\ \} \\
&\qquad\quad \wedge \langle D_1,D_2\rangle \in Dpairs\ )
\end{aligned}$$

We divide N into N_1 and N_2 (without losing or duplicating any Nodes) so that arrows in A either link *Nodes* in N_1 (and are put into A_1) or link Nodes in N_2 (and are put into A_2), or start in N_1 and end in N_2, in which case they are thrown away. Providing that all the Nodes in N_1 are placed before those of N_2 in the resultant list, then their purpose has been achieved.

Of course, as we have seen, attempting a split like this might fail, so this specification is *wrong* since it does not allow failure. If *split* fails, then *any* list will be a valid output component for *T_Sort*, and this can be specified (or not) elsewhere.

Hence we have

$$
\begin{array}{l}
split{:}Dg \rightarrow Dg \times Dg \times \mathbb{B} \\
\text{pre-}split(D) \triangleq well\_defined(D) \\
\text{post-}split(D,\langle D_1,D_2,splittable\rangle) \triangleq \\
\quad (\exists Dpairs{:}\mathfrak{F}(Dg^2)) \\
\quad\quad (Dpairs = \{\langle\langle N_1,A_1\rangle,\langle N_2,A_2\rangle\rangle{:}Dg^2 \mid \\
\quad\quad\quad\quad N_1 \cup N_2 = N \wedge \\
\quad\quad\quad\quad N_1 \cap N_2 = \emptyset \wedge \\
\quad\quad\quad\quad N_1 \neq \emptyset \wedge N_2 \neq \emptyset \wedge \\
\quad\quad\quad\quad A_1 \subseteq A \wedge A_2 \subseteq A \wedge \\
\quad\quad\quad\quad (\forall x,y{:}Node)(\langle x,y\rangle \in A \\
\quad\quad\quad\quad\quad \Rightarrow (\langle x,y\rangle \in A_1 \vee \langle x,y\rangle \in A_2 \vee \\
\quad\quad\quad\quad\quad\quad (x \in N_1 \wedge y \in N_2)))\ \} \\
\quad\quad \wedge\ \text{if } Dpairs = \emptyset \\
\quad\quad\quad \text{then } \langle D_1,D_2\rangle = \langle\langle\emptyset,\emptyset\rangle,\langle\emptyset,\emptyset\rangle\rangle \wedge splittable = \text{False} \\
\quad\quad\quad \text{else } \langle D_1,D_2\rangle \in Dpairs \wedge splittable = \text{True} \\
\quad\quad\quad \text{fi })
\end{array}
$$

so we (attempt to) calculate suitable pairs of sub-graphs and, if successful, deliver one such pair and say that the search was successful or deliver empty graphs and "False".

To match this splitting function, we need a suitable *combine* function. Based on our earlier discussion, this ought to be

$$
\begin{array}{l}
combine{:}\ (Node^* \times \mathbb{B})^2 \rightarrow (Node^* \times \mathbb{B}) \\
\text{pre-}combine(\langle\langle L_1, s_1\rangle,\langle L_2, s_2\rangle\rangle) \triangleq \text{True} \\
\text{post-}combine(\langle\langle L_1, s_1\rangle,\langle L_2, s_2\rangle\rangle, \langle L, s\rangle) \\
\quad\quad\quad\quad \triangleq \langle L, s\rangle = \langle L_1 {}^\frown L_2, s_1 \wedge s_2\rangle
\end{array}
$$

So we get a proper answer only if both of the subgraphs were sortable and then the answer is computed by concatenating the intermediate lists in the appropriate order.

But is this right? Or does it just seem reasonable? Can we legitimately replace box 0 (of Figure 11.14) by the combination depicted in Figure 11.15?

As always, this needs to be checked — by substitution and evaluation. This is quite routine, even if long and more involved than anything encountered earlier. We leave it as an exercise.

As before, we can refine *split* so as to break off a single element at a time and obtain an incremental calculation. Doing this suggests a re-structuring of the way in which the digraph is held in order to facilitate the location of valid 'next' points and their subsequent processing (i.e., their 'removal' from the graph and appending to the end of the output list that represents the polygon, the hull). Details of how this might be done are not difficult but rather lengthy.

A re-formulation in terms of a quantification based on *combine* (here concatenation) is another possibility. Obviously by virtue of the investigations we have carried out, this leads to a rapid, though 'inefficient' implementation design.

11.3 Some Extremal Problems

Here we consider a few related problems which involve finding the largest / smallest values in, and (the length of) the longest / shortest segments of, lists and arrays which have certain properties. We start by revisiting an old friend, the *listmax* function, and collecting together a few techniques that we have encountered along the way. We shall then look at how *listmax* can be developed to deal with so-called segment problems. The program designs developed here only deliver an extreme value or the length of an extremal segment, not the position of the value or segment. The designs can, however, be augmented so that these factors can be incorporated in the output, but we don't do that; we concentrate on the simpler and more central aspects of the calculations.

Example 11.1 Recall the definition of *listmax*:

$$LMAX(L{:}\mathbb{Z}^{+}) \triangleq (\max i \mid i{:}\mathbb{Z} \mid i \text{ in } L)$$

where $\mathbb{Z} \max \mathbb{Z} \to \mathbb{Z}$ and $x \max y \triangleq$ if $x \leq y$ then y else x fi.
vWe use a further name change, to *LMAX*, to emphasise similarities and differences in the various routines that follow and to avoid 'decorations' which may be distracting.

We are going to lift implementations of *LMAX* from sets of rules[5], of which there are many.

(a)
$$LMAX(\langle x\rangle) \;\Leftrightarrow\; x$$
$$(x \le y)\quad LMAX(\langle x,y\rangle ^\frown N) \;\Leftrightarrow\; LMAX(\langle y\rangle ^\frown N)$$
$$(x > y)\quad LMAX(\langle x,y\rangle ^\frown N) \;\Leftrightarrow\; LMAX(\langle x\rangle ^\frown N)$$

or

(b)
$$LMAX(\langle x\rangle) \;\Leftrightarrow\; x$$
$$LMAX(\langle x,y\rangle ^\frown N) \;\Leftrightarrow\; \text{if } x \le y \text{ then } LMAX(\langle y\rangle ^\frown N) \text{ else } LMAX(\langle x\rangle ^\frown N) \text{ fi}$$

or

(c)
$$LMAX(\langle x\rangle) \;\Leftrightarrow\; x$$
$$LMAX(\langle x,y\rangle ^\frown N) \;\Leftrightarrow\; LMAX(\langle x \max y\rangle ^\frown N)$$

The 'max' operation is associative, so, with certain provisos, we could utilise quantification rules, but not directly; hence we adopt the current eureka approach. vUsing 'results_so_far and data_remaining' tuples as in Section 4.3, we devise a local function $F{:}\mathbb{Z}\times\mathbb{Z}^* \to \mathbb{Z}$ which satisfies the following rules:

$$LMAX(\langle y\rangle ^\frown N) \;\Leftrightarrow\; F(\langle y, N\rangle)$$
$$F(\langle v, \langle\,\rangle\rangle) \;\Leftrightarrow\; v$$
$$F(\langle x, \langle y\rangle ^\frown M\rangle) \;\Leftrightarrow\; F(\langle x \max y, M\rangle)$$

or, equivalently,

$$LMAX(\langle y\rangle ^\frown N) \;\Leftrightarrow\; F(\langle y, N\rangle)$$
$$(N = \langle\,\rangle)\quad F(\langle v, N\rangle) \;\Leftrightarrow\; v$$
$$(N = \langle y\rangle ^\frown M)\quad F(\langle x, N\rangle) \;\Leftrightarrow\; F(\langle x \max y, M\rangle)$$

These lead to the design

```
begin var maxval:ℤ, N:ℤ*;
        ⟨maxval, N⟩ ← ⟨first_of L, rest_of L⟩;
        while N ≠ ⟨⟩
                do ⟨maxval, N⟩
                        ← ⟨maxval max first_of N, rest_of N⟩ od;
        [ result ← ] maxval
end
```

❑

[5] The reader might well ask why this was not done earlier. The earlier work with this function was done primarily as a vehicle to describe various derivation techniques. Also, following the 'rules' approach yields certain designs. There is bias built into the rules from the outset. Certain designs are therefore denied to us.

Example 11.2 By analogy (see Section 3.2.4) we can quickly derive *LMIN*, which finds the minimal element of $L{:}\mathbb{Z}^{+}$. Its definition is

$$LMIN(L{:}\mathbb{Z}^{+}) \triangleq (\ \min i \mid i{:}\mathbb{Z} \mid i \text{ in } L\ )$$

where $\mathbb{Z} \min \mathbb{Z} \to \mathbb{Z}$ and $x \min y \triangleq \text{if } x \geq y \text{ then } y \text{ else } x \text{ fi}$

This is implemented by

```
begin  var minval:ℤ, N:ℤ*;
         ⟨minval, N⟩ ← ⟨first_of L, rest_of L⟩;
         while N ≠ ⟨ ⟩
                  do ⟨minval, N⟩
                           ← ⟨minval min first_of N, rest_of N⟩ od;
         [ result ← ] minval
end
```

In passing, notice that the following design would also be correct:

```
begin  var maxval:ℤ, N:ℤ*;
         ⟨maxval, N⟩ ← ⟨first_of L, rest_of L⟩;
         while N ≠ ⟨ ⟩
                  do ⟨maxval, N⟩
                           ← ⟨maxval min first_of N, rest_of N⟩ od;
         [ result ← ] maxval
end
```

❑

Following our earlier observations on program readability, notice that the use of the identifier *maxval* is perfectly valid and completely misleading to the human reader. We could obviously include comments that would also be misleading — take care, and try to use helpful names.

Example 11.3 Now for the array version of *LMAX* which we call *AMAX*. Suppose we have an array *A* of integers indexed from *p* to *q*. This could be declared as

$$A\text{: array } p..q \text{ of } \mathbb{Z}$$

or, more usually,

$$A[p..q]{:}\mathbb{Z} \qquad \text{with } p \leq q$$

Then, following the style of *LMAX*,

$$AMAX(A\text{: array } p..q \text{ of } \mathbb{Z}) \triangleq AMAX(A[p..q]) \qquad \text{by convention,}$$

where $AMAX(A[p..q]) \triangleq (\ \max A[i] \mid i{:}\mathbb{Z} \mid p \leq i \wedge i \leq q\ )$

and again $\mathbb{Z}$ max $\mathbb{Z} \rightarrow \mathbb{Z}$ with x max $y \triangleq$ if $x \leq y$ then y else x fi.

As in the list case, but this time having to cope with array indices, we have another subsidiary function, again called F (but that name will eventually disappear), with the following rules:

$$AMAX(A[p..q]) \quad \Leftrightarrow \quad F(\langle A[p], A[p+1..q]\rangle)$$
$$(i > j) \qquad F(\langle v, A[i..j]\rangle) \quad \Leftrightarrow \quad v$$
$$(i \leq j) \qquad F(\langle v, A[i..j]\rangle) \quad \Leftrightarrow \quad F(\langle v \text{ max } A[i], A[i+1..j]\rangle)$$

This can be encoded in a similar fashion as

```
begin  var maxval:ℤ, i,j:ℤ;
       ⟨maxval, i, j⟩ ← ⟨A[p], p+1, q⟩;
       while i ≤ j
       do ⟨maxval, i, j⟩ ← ⟨maxval max A[i], i+1, j⟩ od;
       [ result ← ] maxval
end
```

and, as j never changes value but is always equal to q, we can simplify to give

```
begin  var maxval:ℤ, i:ℤ;
       ⟨maxval, i⟩ ← ⟨A[p], p+1⟩;
       while i ≤ q
       do ⟨maxval, i⟩ ← ⟨maxval max A[i], i+1⟩ od;
       [ result ← ] maxval
end
```

❑

Example 11.4 We now move on to segment problems. The first is to find the length of the longest segment within the integer array, $A[p..q]$, in which all the elements have the value a. It will be convenient to refer to such a segment as a *run*. We shall tackle the problem in two parts, two levels. [By using some of the quantification rules, some shortcuts can be taken, but we shall not do this. Again we stress the basic nature of the presentation. With the basics included herein, the reader who goes on to further study will be able to pull all these threads together and formulate more powerful rules and transformations.]

The overall definition is

$$(\text{ max } (j-i+1) \mid i,j:\mathbb{Z} \mid \quad (\wedge (A[k] = a) \mid k:\mathbb{Z} \mid i \leq k \leq j\ )\ )$$

where $A[k]$ is only defined for values of k such that $p \leq k \leq q$, or, alternatively and equivalently,

$$(\max m \mid i,m{:}\mathbb{Z} \mid \quad (\wedge (A[k] = a) \mid k{:}\mathbb{Z} \mid i \le k \le i+m-1 \,)\ )$$

Other variants are possible. We could find the lengths of appropriate runs and then find the maximum of these. Following the lead of the previous examples, and taking the inner-most problem first, we find the first (reading from left to right) maximal[6] 'all a's' run. After that, we can find the first such list in the remaining section of the array — if any — and retain the maximum of their two lengths. We already know how to do this, so first things first.

At the risk of over-parameterisation, we introduce $FMR(A[p..q],a)$ to denote the First Maximal Run of a's in the array $A[p..q]$. Again we introduce a function having these components, and called F for no particular reason, and the result, ℓ (which will eventually be set to the maximal length of the run) as parameters.

First we establish the link and then propose rules[7] for the evaluation of F.

	$FMR(A[p..q], a)$	◆	$F(\langle a, 0, A, p, q\rangle)$
$(i>j)$	$F(\langle a, \ell, A, i, j\rangle)$	◆	ℓ
$(i\le j,\ \ell=0, A[i]\ne a)$	$F(\langle a, \ell, A, i, j\rangle)$	◆	$F(\langle a, \ell, A, i+1, j\rangle)$
$(i\le j,\ \ell=0, A[i]=a)$	$F(\langle a, \ell, A, i, j\rangle)$	◆	$F(\langle a, 1, A, i+1, j\rangle)$
$(i\le j,\ \ell\ne 0, A[i]=a)$	$F(\langle a, \ell, A, i, j\rangle)$	◆	$F(\langle a, \ell+1, A, i+1, j\rangle)$
$(i\le j,\ \ell\ne 0, A[i]\ne a)$	$F(\langle a, \ell, A, i, j\rangle)$	◆	ℓ

We start with $\ell=0$ and move through the array by incrementing i. If we encounter an a, we set ℓ to one and keep incrementing it until we either get to the end of A or find a non-a element. In either situation, the answer is the current value of ℓ.

By inspection, the rules can be reduced to

	$FMR(A[p..q], a)$	◆	$F(\langle a, 0, A, p, q\rangle)$
$(i>j)$	$F(\langle a, \ell, A, i, j\rangle)$	◆	ℓ
$(i\le j,\ \ell=0, A[i]\ne a)$	$F(\langle a, \ell, A, i, j\rangle)$	◆	$F(\langle a, \ell, A, i+1, j\rangle)$
$(i\le j, A[i]=a)$	$F(\langle a, \ell, A, i, j\rangle)$	◆	$F(\langle a, \ell+1, A, i+1, j\rangle)$
$(i\le j,\ \ell\ne 0, A[i]\ne a)$	$F(\langle a, \ell, A, i, j\rangle)$	◆	ℓ

[6] Obviously, any run contains a single "a", but we should not conclude that the length of the run is 1 until we have found that we are at the end of the array or that the next item is not a.

[7] The rules used here involve complex conditions. Remember that in such cases the commas should be interpreted as $\wedge$s and the conditions evaluated sequentially until either the end is reached or one term fails.

Notice that we exit from the loop when

$$(i>j) \vee (i \leq j \wedge \ell \neq 0 \wedge A[i] \neq a)$$

so we continue when

$$(i \leq j) \wedge (i>j \vee \ell=0 \vee A[i]=a),$$

which simplifies to

$$(i \leq j) \wedge (\ell=0 \vee A[i]=a),$$

and the code for this follows as

```
begin var i,j,ℓ:ℤ;
    ⟨a, ℓ, A, i, j⟩ ← ⟨a, 0, A, p, q⟩;
    while i ≤ j ∧ (ℓ=0 ∨ A[i]=a)
    do    if A[i]=a
          then ⟨a, ℓ, A, i, j⟩ ← ⟨a, ℓ+1, A, i+1, j⟩
          else ⟨a, ℓ, A, i, j⟩ ← ⟨a, ℓ, A, i+1, j⟩
          fi
    od;
    [ result ← ] ℓ
end
```

And this simplifies to

```
begin var i,ℓ:ℤ;
    ⟨ℓ, i⟩ ← ⟨0, p⟩;
    while i ≤ q ∧ (ℓ=0 ∨ A[i]=a)
    do    if A[i]=a then ℓ ← ℓ+1 fi;
          i ← i+1
    od;
    [ result ← ] ℓ
end
```

In the wider context of calculating the length of the maximal run, it will be convenient to know the exit value of i. Hence we have

```
begin var i,ℓ:ℤ;
    ⟨ℓ, i⟩ ← ⟨0, p⟩;
    while i ≤ q ∧ (ℓ=0 ∨ A[i]=a)
    do if A[i]=a then ℓ ← ℓ+1 fi; i ← i+1 od;
    [ result ← ] ⟨ℓ, i⟩
end
```

Henceforth we can regard this as the code for the function *FMR*2, which takes input p (representing the array segment $A[p..q]$) and delivers ℓ (the length of the first maximal 'all *a*s' segment within $A[p..i-1]$) and, for subsequent use, the value of i[8]. We also assume that all other referenced data values are delivered by the surrounding context.

We can now use this design together with that from the previous *AMAX* problem to draw up a set of rules for *MAXRUN*. Here the situation is slightly different in that the given array may not contain any a values and hence the maximum run length may be zero.

Again, we start with the full problem (including all the necessary but constant data items) and prune down the implementation scheme later on.

We begin with a set of rules for *MAXRUN*. In the subsidiary — and temporary — function G, the result parameter, m, represents the length of the maximal run in the segment of the array so far processed by *FMR*.

$$
\begin{array}{lrcl}
 & MAXRUN(A[p..q]) & \Longleftrightarrow & G(\langle 0, A, p, q\rangle) \\
(i>j) & G(\langle m, A, i, j\rangle) & \Longleftrightarrow & m \\
(i\le j) & G(\langle m, A, i, j\rangle) & \Longleftrightarrow & G(\langle m \max \ell, A, k, j\rangle) \\
 & & & \quad \text{where: } \langle \ell, k\rangle = FMR2(i)
\end{array}
$$

Hence the design follows mechanically as

```
begin  var i,j,k,ℓ,m:ℤ;
    ⟨m, A, i, j⟩ ← ⟨0, A, p, q⟩;
          while i ≤ j
          do ⟨m, A, i, j⟩ ← ⟨m  max ℓ, A, k, j⟩
                                      where: ⟨ℓ, k⟩ = FMR2(i)

          od;
    [ result ← ] m
end
```

[8] This value of i is either $q+1$ or the start of a 'non-a sequence' following an a.

which expands[9] and rationalises, first to

```
begin var i,j,k,ℓ,m:ℤ; var ii, pp,ℓℓ:ℤ;
    ⟨m, A, i, j⟩ ← ⟨0, A, p, q⟩;
        while i ≤ j
        do      pp ← i;
                ⟨ℓℓ, ii⟩ ← ⟨0, pp⟩;
                while ii ≤ q ∧ (ℓℓ=0 ∨ A[ii]=a)
                do if A[ii]=a then ℓℓ ← ℓℓ+1 fi; ii ← ii+1 od:
                ⟨ℓ, k⟩ ← ⟨ℓℓ, ii⟩;
        ⟨m, A, i, j⟩ ← ⟨m max ℓ, A, k, j⟩
        od;
    [ result ← ] m
end
```

and then to

```
begin var i,ℓ,m:ℤ;
    ⟨m, i⟩ ← ⟨0, p⟩;
        while i ≤ q
        do  ℓ ← 0;
            while i ≤ q ∧ (ℓ=0 ∨ A[i]=a)
            do if A[i]=a then ℓ ← ℓ+1 fi; i ← i+1 od;
        m ← m max ℓ
        od;
    [ result ← ] m
end
```

❑

Of course, the controlling conditions of the two while loops in Example 11.4 are related and the two loops can be combined. The way this is done is similar to the merging of nested quantifications in Chapter 5. Again, we resist the temptation to get involved with more transformations.

A characteristic of the previous example was that the key property, $A[i]=a$, did not depend on other elements in the array. We now turn to a slight variation where there *is* a dependence.

---

[9] The variables local to *FMR*2 have been given new 'double' names and their scope widened, and the input/output assignments have been made explicit.

Example 11.5 Consider the problem, given an integer array $A[p..q]$, where $p \leq q$ of finding

$$(\max m \mid i,m{:}\mathbb{Z} \mid \\ (\ \vee\ (\wedge(A[k]=a) \mid k{:}\mathbb{Z} \mid i \leq k \leq i+m-1\ ) \mid a{:}\mathbb{Z} \mid \text{True}\ )\ )$$

Picking the bones out of this, we have to find the maximum length of runs in the array in which all the elements are equal to some value a, but the a need not be the same for all runs.

Since '=' is transitive, we can simply test all elements in the potential run with the first element of that run. Hence we could use the specification

$$(\ \max m \mid i,m{:}\mathbb{Z} \mid\ (\wedge(A[k]=A[i]) \mid k{:}\mathbb{Z} \mid i \leq k \leq i+m-1\ )\ )$$

Of course, since $p \leq q$, the array is non-void, so there are values in the array and every element is part of a run (of values equal to itself), so the problem is soluble. Moreover, for the element $A[i]$ with $p < i < q$, it will be necessary to compare it with $A[i-1]$ and $A[i+1]$ to determine whether it is part of an 'equal value' segment of length greater than one.

The solution is rather like that for *AMAX*. If a segment is not empty, then get the first and try to 'grow' the maximal run which starts there.

When considering the segment $A[i..j]$ where $i \leq j$, we take the ith element as the common value for which we seek the first maximal run length. Using subsidiary functions similar to those in the previous example, we have

$(p \leq q)$	$FMR3(A[p..q])$	◆	$F(\langle A[p], 1, A, p+1, q\rangle)$
$(i > j)$	$F(\langle c, \ell, A, i, j\rangle)$	◆	$\langle \ell, i\rangle$
$(i \leq j, A[i]=c)$	$F(\langle c, \ell, A, i, j\rangle)$	◆	$F(\langle c, \ell+1, A, i+1, j\rangle)$
$(i \leq j, A[i] \neq c)$	$F(\langle c, \ell, A, i, j\rangle)$	◆	$\langle \ell, i\rangle$

*FMR*3 delivers run length ℓ and 'next' i, which, as before, is either the start of the next run or $q + 1$,

and the code for this follows as

```
begin var c,i,j,ℓ:ℤ;
      ⟨c, ℓ, A, i, j⟩ ← ⟨A[p], 1, A, p+1, q⟩;
      while i ≤ j ∧ A[i]=c
      do   ⟨c, ℓ, A, i, j⟩ ← ⟨c, ℓ+1, A, i+1, j⟩     od;
      [ result ← ] ⟨ℓ, i⟩
end
```

Here we have combined the two loops in the previous scheme, which is easier to do here because of there being fewer conditions. The use of the sequential 'and' again reflects the order of nesting in the earlier design (in Example 11.4) and prevents the attempt to access $A[i]$ when i has overshot the end of the array.

As usual, we can simplify this to give

begin var $c, i, \ell : \mathbb{Z}$;
  $\langle c, \ell, i \rangle \leftarrow \langle A[p], 1, p+1 \rangle$;
  while $i \leq q \ \wedge\!\!\!\!\cdot\ A[i] = c$
  do $\langle \ell, i \rangle \leftarrow \langle \ell+1, i+1 \rangle$ od;
  $[\ result \leftarrow]\ \langle \ell, i \rangle$
end

We can then utilize the previous derivation of *MAXRUN*. With the subsidiary function G, in which the parameter, m, represents the length of the maximal run in the segment of the array so far processed by *FMR*4,

$$MAXRUN(A[p..q]) \ \blacklozenge\ G(\langle 0, A, p, q \rangle)$$

$$(i > j) \quad G(\langle m, A, i, j \rangle) \ \blacklozenge\ m$$

$$(i \leq j) \quad G(\langle m, A, i, j \rangle) \ \blacklozenge\ G(\langle m \max \ell, A, k, j \rangle)$$

where: $\langle \ell, k \rangle = FMR4(i)$

Where $FMR4(i) \triangleq FMR3(A[i..q])$,
other, constant, values being taken from the context.

Mechanically, we have

begin var $i, j, k, \ell, m : \mathbb{Z}$;
  $\langle m, A, i, j \rangle \leftarrow \langle 0, A, p, q \rangle$;
    while $i \leq j$
    do $\langle m, A, i, j \rangle \leftarrow \langle m \max \ell, A, k, j \rangle$
      where: $\langle \ell, k \rangle = FMR4(i)$
    od;
  $[\ result \leftarrow]\ m$
end

The corresponding assembly of the full design follows as before but is quite involved, so we include an intermediate version:

```
begin  var c,i,j,k,ℓ,m:ℤ; var ii, ℓℓ:ℤ;
    ⟨m, A, i, j⟩ ← ⟨0, A, p, q⟩;
        while i ≤ j
        do      ⟨c, ℓℓ, ii⟩ ← ⟨A[i], 1, i+1⟩;
                while ii ≤ q  ∧  A[ii]=c
                do      ⟨ℓℓ, ii⟩ ← ⟨ℓℓ+1, ii+1⟩      od;
                ⟨ℓ, k⟩ ←  ⟨ℓℓ, ii⟩;
        ⟨m, A, i, j⟩ ← ⟨m max ℓ, A, k, j⟩
        od;
    [ result ← ] m
end
```

and ultimately we have

```
begin  var c,i,ℓ,m:ℤ;
    ⟨m, i⟩ ← ⟨0, p⟩;
        while i ≤ q
        do  ⟨c, ℓ, i⟩ ← ⟨A[i], 1, i+1⟩;
            while i ≤ q  ∧  A[i]=c
            do ⟨ℓ, i⟩ ← ⟨ℓ+1, i+1⟩  od;
        m ← m max ℓ
        od;
    [ result ← ] m
end
```

❑

Example 11.6. We now turn to the segment problem where the test for inclusion in the run *does* need the value of the previous element (if there is one of course). The run condition here is that the elements are increasing, using the relation '≤', so the specification is

$$(\max j-i+1 \mid i,j:\mathbb{Z} \mid \\ \wedge\, (\,(k=j) \vee (A[k] \le A[k+1]\,)\mid k:\mathbb{Z} \mid i \le k \le j\,)\ )$$

and removing the upper limit, j, and using the 'length', m, we have:

$$(\max m \mid i,m:\mathbb{Z} \mid \\ \wedge\, (\,(k = i+m-1\,) \vee (A[k] \le A[k+1]\,)\ )\ \mid k:\mathbb{Z} \mid i \le k \le i+m-1\,)\,)$$

Following the thread of earlier examples but noting that we need to retain the immediately preceding element, we have the rules

$(p \le q)$	$FMR5(A[p..q])$	◆	$F(\langle A[p], 1, A, p+1, q\rangle)$
$(i > j)$	$F(\langle c, \ell, A, i, j\rangle)$	◆	$\langle \ell, i\rangle$
$(i \le j, c \le A[i])$	$F(\langle c, \ell, A, i, j\rangle)$	◆	$F(\langle A[i], \ell+1, A, i+1, j\rangle)$
$(i \le j, c > A[i])$	$F(\langle c, \ell, A, i, j\rangle)$	◆	$\langle \ell, i\rangle$

The code for this follows as

```
begin  var c,i,j,ℓ:ℤ;
     ⟨c, ℓ, A, i, j⟩ ← ⟨A[p], 1, A, p+1, q⟩;
     while i ≤ j  ∧  c ≤ A[i]
     do  ⟨c, ℓ, A, i, j⟩ ← ⟨A[i], ℓ+1, A, i+1, j⟩      od;
     [ result ← ] ⟨ℓ, i⟩
end
```

We can then embed this code into the *MAXRUN* design to give

```
begin  var c,i,ℓ,m:ℤ;
     ⟨m, i⟩ ← ⟨0, p⟩;
          while i ≤ q
          do  ⟨c, ℓ, i⟩ ← ⟨A[i], 1, i+1⟩;
               while i ≤ q  ∧  c ≤ A[i]
               do  ⟨c, ℓ, i⟩ ← ⟨A[i], ℓ+1, i+1⟩   od;
               m ← m max ℓ
          od;
     [ result ← ] m
end
```

❑

Example 11.7. Finally we have a problem in which we have to compare potentially all other elements in the array in order to determine the validity of each single element within a run. We seek the length of the maximal run within the array $A[p..q]$ (which may be void, empty) in which all elements are different. Using the property that we need only compare an element $A[j]$ with elements $A[k]$ when $j < k$, we have the problem definition

$$(\max m \mid i,m{:}\mathbb{Z} \mid$$
$$(\ \wedge\ (\ (j = k)^{10} \vee (A[j] \ne A[k])\ )\ \mid j,k{:}\mathbb{Z}\ \mid\ i \le j \le k \le i+m-1\ )\ )$$

[10] This term is to cater for the possibility of runs of length 1.

This is more complicated than the problems in which we need only to make local comparisons within each run. But there are also similarities, such as the way in which we obtain the maximal run length, that we shall employ.

Again, for the 'inner' calculation, we use a eureka step, which we try to explain as follows.

Suppose we know that the segment X has no duplicates and hence is a valid run. This could be the whole of $A[p..q]$, or X could be extended to a maximal run or it could be followed immediately by a value already in X. It is this last case which is most significant. Consider the situation depicted below

```
<----          X          ---->
A[i]          A[j]          A[k]
               a             a
           <----              Y              ---->
```

So, $X = A[i \,..\, k{-}1]$.

If, when searching through X for a (the value at $A[k]$), we find it at $A[j]$, then X is a maximal run and its length is $k - i$. The next run, Y, starts at $j + 1$; moreover, we already know that the segment $A[j + 1 \,..\, k]$ has no duplicates, and hence we need only start searching for duplicates in Y from $A[k + 1]$ onwards — unless we already at the end of the array. We now translate these ideas into rules.

We use the function $FMR6$, which takes the array and delivers the length (ℓ) of the first maximal run having no duplicate values, the array index (j), where the subsequent run starts (if appropriate), and the index (k) in the next run, where we should start searching for duplicates, but in the order j, k, ℓ.

$$FMR6(A[p..q]) \blacktriangleleft\!\blacktriangleright F(\langle A, p, p, p, 0, q\rangle)$$

$(k>q)$ $\quad F(\langle A, i, j, k, \ell, q\rangle) \blacktriangleleft\!\blacktriangleright \langle j, k, \ell\rangle$

exit at the end of the array; the final value of j is of no significance.

$(k\leq q, j=k)$ $\quad F(\langle A, i, j, k, \ell, q\rangle) \blacktriangleleft\!\blacktriangleright F(\langle A, i, i, k+1, \ell+1, q\rangle)$

no duplicates so far, including $A[k]$, so extend X and reset j to i

$(k\leq q, j<k, A[j]\neq A[k])$ $\quad F(\langle A, i, j, k, \ell, q\rangle) \blacktriangleleft\!\blacktriangleright F(\langle A, i, j+1, k, \ell, q\rangle)$

no duplicate so increment j

$(k\leq q, j<k, A[j]=A[k])$ $\quad F(\langle A, i, j, k, \ell, q\rangle) \blacktriangleleft\!\blacktriangleright \langle j+1, k+1, \ell\rangle$

end of run detected, so deliver ℓ and set new values of j and k for next run

[Notice that throughout these rules $i \leq j \leq k$. This will be a useful fact later.]

Routinely we have

```
begin var i,j,k,ℓ:ℤ;
      ⟨A, i, j, k, ℓ, q⟩ ← ⟨A, p, p, p, 0, q⟩;
      while k ≤ q ∧ ((j=k) ∨ ((j<k) ∧ (A[j]≠A[k])))¹¹
      do if j=k
         then ⟨A, i, j, k, ℓ, q⟩ ← ⟨A, i, i, k + 1, ℓ + 1, q⟩
         else ⟨A, i, j, k, ℓ, q⟩ ← ⟨A, i, j + 1, k, ℓ, q⟩
         fi;
      od;
      [result ←] if k ≤ q then ⟨j + 1, k + 1, ℓ⟩
                          else ⟨j, k, ℓ⟩ fi
end
```

As might be expected, this simplifies to, say

```
begin var i,j,k,ℓ:ℤ;
      ⟨i, j, k, ℓ⟩ ← ⟨p, p, p, 0⟩;
      while k ≤ q ∧ ((j=k) ∨ (A[j]≠A[k]))
      do if j=k
         then ⟨j, k, ℓ⟩ ← ⟨i, k + 1, ℓ + 1⟩
         else ⟨j, k, ℓ⟩ ← ⟨j + 1, k, ℓ⟩
         fi;
      od;
      [result ←] if k ≤ q then ⟨j + 1, k + 1, ℓ⟩
                          else ⟨j, k, ℓ⟩ fi
end
```

For the outer, maximum, calculation we have

```
begin var i,j,k,ℓ,m:ℤ;
      ⟨m, i, k⟩ ← ⟨0, p, p⟩;
            while i ≤ q
            do ⟨m, i, k⟩ ← ⟨m max ℓ, j, k⟩
                             where: ⟨j, k, ℓ⟩ = FMR7¹²(⟨i, k⟩)
            od;
      [result ←] m
end
```

[11] Since $j \leq k$ and $(j = k) \Rightarrow (A[j] = A[k])$, this simplifies to $(j = k) \vee (A[j] \neq A[k])$.

[12] Here $FMR7(\langle i, k\rangle)$ is like $FMR6(A[i..q])$, but here we know that the segment $A[i..k-1]$ contains no duplicate values and hence we should start looking for duplicates at $A[k]$. Hence we can define $FMR7(\langle i, k\rangle) \triangleq F(\langle A, i, i, k, k-i, q\rangle)$. Hence we need to modify the initialisation step to give the appropriate start value to ℓ.

Putting the parts together, we have

```
begin var i,j,k,ℓ,m:ℤ;
    ⟨m, i, k⟩ ← ⟨0, p, p⟩;
    while i ≤ q
    do  ⟨j, ℓ⟩ ← ⟨i, k – i⟩;
        while k ≤ q ∧ ((j=k) ∨ (A[j]≠A[k]))
        do  if j=k
              then ⟨j, k, ℓ⟩ ← ⟨i, k + 1, ℓ + 1⟩
              else ⟨j, k, ℓ⟩ ← ⟨j + 1, k, ℓ⟩
              fi;
        od;
        if k ≤ q then ⟨j, k⟩ ← ⟨j + 1, k + 1⟩ fi
        ⟨m, i⟩ ← ⟨m max ℓ, j⟩
    od;
    [ result ← ] m
end
```

❑

Well that was quite involved and is certainly complicated enough for an introductory text. Hopefully the reader can see that by breaking a problem down into layers and using eureka steps motivated by "divide-and-conquer" and/or reduction techniques, we can devise solutions to some quite complex problems. Applying the full force of transformation to the resulting designs can then make them more efficient whilst retaining their correctness.

Chapter 12
On Interactive Software

This book has focussed on the specification and design of programs which carry out computations (i.e., situations where, given suitable data, we compute an appropriate result and deposit it in a named location that was hitherto unused).

Clearly, there is more to software than this. The software segments which have been built from formal specifications (of functions) are themselves of absolutely no use on their own, despite the fact that virtually all software will include such computational segments. One glaring omission is that our program designs have no input or output statements, and none of the specifications have included the possibility of making *changes*[1] to the contents of named locations. These two features are in fact instances of the same general characteristic and are easily dealt with (Section 12.1). In one fell swoop, we can bridge the gap between the specification and implementation of *functions* and the corresponding process applied to *operations*[2].

The *requirements* of a computation are simply that eventually[3] (in some finite time) it completes its task, places the result in the expected location,and does this in such a way as to guarantee that the data and result are related as dictated by the specification. How long it takes to achieve this is not part of the specification — indeed, the duration of the computation depends not only on the software but on the hardware on which it runs.

So-called operational requirements are often regarded as being outside the province of software design since they depend on factors over which the software engineer has no control. In isolation, all we can ask is that the software is built so as to meet its ("functional") specification and then check to see whether it is fast enough, or that it fits into a certain size memory. Both these requirements *may* be attainable

[1] Of course, there was a reason for this simplification: it meant that until we synthesised iterations from recursive constructs, no values (in named locations) were changed — everything was constant, and there were no side effects, which made the work much easier.

[2] Computationally, operations are code sequences which can actually *change* the contents of named components within the system. They are also called *procedures*.

[3] This is not even mentioned in almost all texts dealing with algorithm construction. In contrast, when addressing the needs of computing systems, time and temporal concerns are of great importance.

by using a faster processor and/or more memory. On the other hand, if hardware resources are fixed, we can *always* determine a period of time in which a given computation cannot be completed. Unlike the notion of correctness, which can be preserved as we proceed with the synthesis process, there is no accompanying theory that allows software designs to get faster and converge to the optimum. (Indeed, the optimum might well be achieved by going through a whole sequence of designs with very poor performance but which allow for subsequent transformations to be applied and an optimum design obtained.)

Just as most specifications generated by customers are 'over specifications' — they ask for more than they need and include much irrelevant information — requirements of software systems often include substantial tolerances so as to allow for 'slack'.

For example, suppose that we are asked to carry out tasks *A* and *B* sequentially and within a total time of 10 seconds. One possibility is to ask that both *A* and *B*, are each completed within 5 seconds. This preserves design independence[4] between *A* and *B*; the time associated with performing *A* should not depend on *B* or vice versa, but this higher-level design step puts, perhaps unreasonable, constraints on both. Alternatively, we could simply go away and build both and see how long they take. If the time is less than 10 seconds, then all is well, but what do we do if the composite task takes too long? (This is one of the main reasons why software should do only what is asked of it and no more, and why specifications and requirements should ask for only what is necessary, and no more!)

The logical relationship between the requirements of a system and a specification of what actions it is to perform is not unlike that between the specification of software and a correct implementation of it, but it is more complex. In Section 12.2, we briefly discuss some of the factors involved in this aspect of (software) system design. That section is included so as to provide a bridge between what might reasonably be called "Constructing Correct Software Systems" rather than the contents of this book which really addresses the "Construction of Correct Software Components".

[4] In a more technical discussion, this notion of independence would be called *compositionality*; apart from information passed via declared interfaces, the development of one part of the system should be independent of the details pertaining to the design of other parts.

12.1 Specifications Involving Change

We have only considered specifications (of computational algorithms) of the form

$f_1 : X \to Y$

i.e., f_1
type: $X \to Y$

etc.

The specification links a given value of $x{:}X$ to acceptable values of $y{:}Y$. The variable x is considered as the input, and its value is accessed but not changed. The variable y, which represents the result, has no initial value, and the specification characterises the non-empty set of values (dependent upon the given value of $x \in \mathcal{D}\,f_1$) from which one is assigned to y. This is therefore not a *change* of value. Notice also that changing the input value of a function is expressly forbidden.

As we shall see below, it *is* possible to write specifications that indicate that values, such as x here, are allowed or required to change. But these are *specified* changes rather than 'housekeeping' changes introduced to control or support the computation. Primarily, we are concerned with the specification of software in terms of external observations, and we consider several possibilities.

Because the concept of input and output operations is familiar to the reader, we shall start our discussion of matters related to state changes by addressing the specification of these operations. Notice also that we have previously only considered the evaluation of functions that have been *enabled* (i.e., functions whose data values are known to satisfy the corresponding pre-condition). We now move to situations where functions (and operations) might become disabled by the actions of other system components.

12.1.1 Specification of Input/Output

Suppose now that x is taken from a list of type X^* (x is the first element of the list) and y is placed at the back of a list of type Y^*. Here, the lists may be regarded as *external* queues of data values and results, respectively.

The type of this related computation is *not* $X^* \to Y^*$. The input list is still available after the calculation but has been changed. Likewise the output list is *changed* rather than initialised. More properly, the type might be

$$X^* \times Y^* \to X^* \times Y^*$$

[Compare this with the use of $X \times Y$ as part of the underlying types in the design of iterative procedural designs for a computation of type $X \to Y$.]

Not only do 'input' and 'output' have the same structure, but there is a stronger connection: they have the same variables, the input is an X list and a Y list, and the output consists of updated (changed!) versions of the *same* lists. To indicate the correspondence between initial and final values, the final value of the 'name' is decorated with dash/prime.

Instead of writing

$$\text{type: } X^* \times Y^* \to X^* \times Y^*$$

to indicate that the same names occur 'on both sides', we write

$$\text{states: } X^* \times Y^*$$

Eventually, we will move to the situation where, in a state, names stay fixed but the values which they have can change.

Assuming that pre-f_1 is identically True, we can then write

$$
\begin{array}{l}
f_2 \\
\text{states: } X^* \times Y^* \\
\text{pre-}f_2(\langle xs,ys\rangle) \triangleq xs \neq \langle\,\rangle \\
\text{post-}f_2(\langle xs,ys\rangle,\langle xs',ys'\rangle) \triangleq \quad ys' = ys \frown \langle f_1(\text{first\_of}(xs))\rangle \\
\qquad\qquad\qquad\qquad\qquad\qquad\quad \wedge\ xs' = \text{rest\_of}(xs)
\end{array}
$$

or, to separate out the different phases,

$$
\begin{array}{llll}
\multicolumn{4}{l}{\text{post-}f_2(\langle xs,ys\rangle,\langle xs',ys'\rangle) \triangleq} \\
\quad (\exists x{:}X,\ y{:}Y) & & & \\
\qquad (& & xs = \langle x\rangle \frown xs' & [\textit{read}]^{5} \\
 & \wedge & y = f_1(x) & [\textit{calculate}] \\
 & \wedge & ys' = ys \frown \langle y\rangle \quad) & [\textit{write}]
\end{array}
$$

Here x, y are local variables and f_1 is as specified by pre-f_1 and post-f_1.

$xs = \langle x\rangle \frown xs'$

is the 'get input' phase.

[5] As will be seen in Figure 12.1, the underlying order of evaluation is determined by the three clauses and there is no need for sequential Boolean operators; but using them to emphasize the ultimately necessary ordering does no harm.

It is a *communication*. It accesses an 'external' variable, xs, and in this case xs has its value changed. [Notice the more compact, but less explicit, form used here rather than using the first_of and rest_of functions. Note also the possibility of other agencies changing external values, such as xs being given extra input values, possibly by the user?]

$$y = f_1(x)$$

is the calculation phase. It uses only local variables and determines the value of y.

$$ys' = ys \frown \langle y \rangle$$

is another communication[6]. It changes the value of ys to ys'.

Now, provided that the condition pre-f_1, is satisfied, the central computation can't fail since the variables x and y are local. The value of x has been found, the value of y will be generated, and no other process can access or change these values. Moreover, if the computation is interrupted[7] for a finite period, the calculation will still give a valid answer.

'Correctness' of the communications can, in general, only be guaranteed if we have only a single process (here, a single program) and a single processor. In this situation, if the pre-condition '$xs \neq \langle\rangle$' holds at the beginning of the computation, then it will remain True until it is changed (to xs') as the implementation of f_2 is executed. In particular xs *has* at least one element, so the evaluation of rest_of(xs) will not fail.

However, if other processes exist and one seeks to read from xs, then the possibility arises that the list xs may have been accessed, and emptied, between the times when f_2 was ***enabled*** (i.e., pre-f_2 is known to be True) and f_2 was evaluated. We need to prevent such a possibility. This could be done by demanding that no interrupts be allowed between a successful pre-check and a call of the routine. To reduce the extent to which this constraint affects other processes, we need only apply the restriction to the 'get input' phase. In fact, we can reduce the restriction even further and allow interrupts, providing that (all) the data accessed in this phase is protected (is made 'private' — albeit temporarily).

---

6 So as to demonstrate the range of possibilities, we shall now give several different operations using the same embedded calculation. In Section 12.1.2, we shall give the relationship between function evaluations and common read and write operations.

7 The possibility of interrupts is another factor that needs to be taken into account when dealing with more complex systems but, apart from a brief discussion in Section 12.2, it lies outside the scope of the current text.

Returning to our specification and now allowing a more general pre-f_1 condition (i.e. not identically True),

f_3

states: $X^* \times Y^*$

pre-$f_3(\langle xs,ys\rangle) \triangleq xs \neq \langle\rangle \;\wedge\; \text{pre-}f_1(\text{first\_of}(xs))$

post-$f_3(\langle xs,ys\rangle, \langle xs', ys'\rangle) \triangleq$

$(\exists x{:}X, y{:}Y)$ (*get_input*, with private data
$\wedge$ *calculate*
$\wedge$ *write*)

where *get_input*, *calculate*, and *write* are as before.

[Recall that the $\wedge$ connective is the lazy/sequential/conditional 'and' that is defined axiomatically by

$$\text{True} \wedge P \Leftrightarrow P \qquad\qquad \text{False} \wedge P \Leftrightarrow \text{False}$$

Over Boolean values $\wedge$ is exactly the same as $\wedge$ but, as in the case above, P may not always be defined.]

Still with the assumption that *write* never fails, we can go further.

f_4

states: $X^* \times Y^*$

type: $\rightarrow \mathbb{B}$ [8] — there is no input 'parameter'

pre-$f_4(\langle xs,ys\rangle) \triangleq$ True

post-$f_4(\langle xs,ys\rangle,\langle xs',ys'\rangle,b) \triangleq$

$$b \Leftrightarrow (\exists x{:}X, y{:}Y)(\;(\mathit{get\_input}1 \wedge \mathit{calculate} \wedge \mathit{write})\;)$$

where

$$\mathit{get\_input}1 \Leftrightarrow (xs \neq \langle\rangle \;\wedge\; \text{pre-}f_1(\text{first\_of}(xs)) \wedge xs = \langle x\rangle^\frown xs')$$

and

$$\mathit{write} \Leftrightarrow ys' = ys^\frown\langle y\rangle$$

f_4 is more properly 'try to do f_3'. If it delivers True, then the lists xs and ys are changed appropriately. If it delivers False, then the *get_input*1 was not enabled (meaning here that xs had a first element and it was suitable as data for f_1), and we usually require that no changes are made to xs and ys. Of course, the '$b \Leftrightarrow$' part of the specification not only delivers a result but ensures that the post-f_4 condition evaluates to True (as is required by any enabled specification). Unfortunately, when b is False, it also allows xs' and ys' to assume *any* values, and this may not be what is desired.

8 Notice here that the signature has been extended to include an output as well as a state change and is written as $(X^* \times Y^*) \rightarrow ((X^* \times Y^*) \times \mathbb{B})$. In the next variation, this output is absorbed into the state.

Using the lazy 'or' operation, we fix this[9] — but we shall greatly improve the notation later.

*f*5
states: $X^* \times Y^* \times \mathbb{B}$
pre-*f*5($\langle xs,ys,b\rangle$) $\triangleq$ True
post-*f*5($\langle xs,ys,b\rangle,\langle xs',ys',b'\rangle$) $\triangleq$

$$(get\_input1 \wedge calculate \wedge write \wedge b')$$
$$\vee\ (\neg get\_input1 \wedge xs' = xs \wedge ys' = ys \wedge \neg b')$$

In a correct implementation, if *get_input*1 succeeds, then so will *calculate* and *write,* and *b* will be set to True. If it fails, then the values of *xs* and *ys* are preserved and the final value of *b* (i.e., *b*') is False.

To cut down on the duplication of text within the specification, we now introduce a name for the state (and names of the components within the state) and write

*f*6
states: S ($\triangleq$ $\{xs{:}X^*,\ ys{:}Y^*,\ b{:}\mathbb{B}\}$)[10]
pre-*f*6 $\triangleq$ True
post-*f*6 $\triangleq$ $(get\_input1 \wedge calculate \wedge write \wedge b')$

$$\vee\ (\neg get\_input1 \wedge S' = S[b' \mapsto \text{False}])$$

The last clause being read as *S*' (the new value of *S*) is as the original but with its *b* component (i.e.< *b*') set to False. This and related notations are very useful when the state has many components but only a few change.

These specifications all relate to the processing of one specific element from the list *xs* (or an attempt to do this). This requirement — to process only one element — is a *system* design decision. Alternatively, it may be required to process the entire list sequentially so as to absorb *all* of *xs* and fill *ys* with the results of the embedded calculation. Hence the data objects communicated are of type X^* and Y^*, rather than *X* and *Y*.

[9] And, to defer details of *x* and *y*, we avoid them by replacing *x* by first_of(*xs*) and equating *xs*' with rest_of(*xs*) and so on.

[10] This notation needs explaining. Although superficially *S* looks like a set, we really want to use it as a 'lookup' function — but to write it out in full is very inconvenient. The domain of *S*, $\mathcal{D}S$, is a set of names, and *S* is a mapping from those names to their current values. Applying *S* to one of these names gives a value of the appropriate type so, for example, $S(xs){:}X^*$. If $S(xs) = \langle a, b, c\rangle$, then $(xs \mapsto \langle a, b, c\rangle) \in S$. The construction $S[xs \mapsto \langle\rangle]$ would then represent a new function which is identical to *S* except that it maps *xs* to the empty list. Of course, any other value could be used. Also, using *S*' to denote the new value of *S*, rather than writing $S' = S[xs \mapsto \langle\rangle]$, we would use $S[xs' \mapsto \langle\rangle]$ instead, thus emphasising that the *new* value of *xs* is $\langle\rangle$.

f_7
states: $xs{:}X^*,\ ys{:}Y^*$
pre-$f_7 \triangleq (\forall x{:}X)(x \text{ in } xs \Rightarrow \text{pre-}f_1(x))$
$\quad\quad \wedge\ ys = \langle\rangle$
post-$f_7 \triangleq xs' = \langle\rangle$
$\quad\quad \wedge\ ys' = f_1{}^*(xs)$

Recall that $f_1{}^*$ indicates that f_1 is applied to each element of its argument and the list structure of the input is preserved in the output.

Again, allowing interference can cause problems in a multi-process system. Since $ys = \langle\rangle$ in the pre-condition and this property is needed to ensure that the *write* phase works correctly, the easiest way to guarantee non-interference is to stipulate

f_7 with private data

which would bar access to *xs* and *ys* (and the changing of their values) by other processes.

Note that breaking down of f_7 into a sequence of operations as in f_6 is a *software design* task. To include this within an initial specification of the software may amount to over-specification.

Expressing f_7 in terms of the three phases used earlier would give

f_8
states: $xs{:}X^*,\ ys{:}Y^*$
pre-$f_8 \triangleq (\forall x{:}X)(x \text{ in } xs \Rightarrow \text{pre-}f_1(x)) \wedge ys = \langle\rangle$
post-$f_8 \triangleq (\exists loc\_xs{:}X^*,\ loc\_ys{:}Y^*)$
$\quad\quad (\ loc\_xs = xs \wedge xs' = \langle\rangle$
$\quad\quad \wedge\ loc\_ys = f_1{}^*(loc\_xs)$
$\quad\quad \wedge\ ys' = ys \frown loc\_ys)$

The data-flow diagram for the post-condition is given in Figure 12.1.

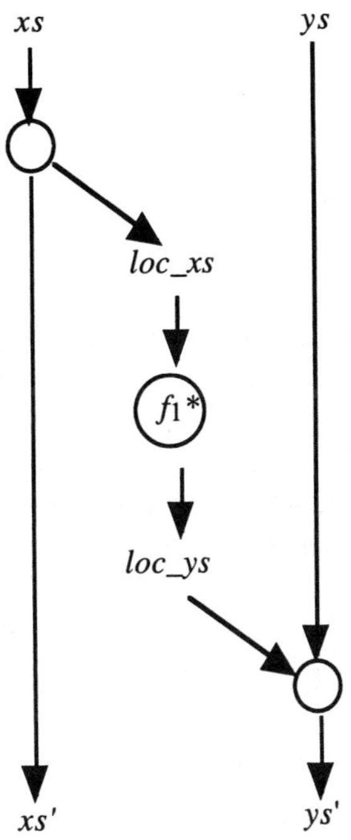

Figure 12.1

The structure of the diagram indicates that, without loss of generality, we could have written

$$
\begin{aligned}
& (loc\_xs = xs \land xs' = \langle\rangle) \\
\land \quad & (loc\_ys = f_1{*}(loc\_xs)) \\
\land \quad & (ys' = ys \frown loc\_ys)
\end{aligned}
$$

12.1.2 Conventional 'Communications'

Clearly, the variations in the ways in which we can incorporate f_1 as the only computational element within an operation are numerous. Great care is needed when specifying such operations, particularly in regard to which 'variables' have their final values determined by f_1, which have to retain their initial values, and which have undetermined final values.

We need to distinguish between the notions of *looking*, and *taking*, and *showing* and *giving*.

Notwithstanding previous variations in notation used to represent states, we adopt the following:

$$S \triangleq \{input{:}X^*,\ output{:}Y^*,\ x{:}X,\ \ldots.\}$$

This is shorthand for the proper version of S, which is a function from names to values. In the display above $x{:}X$ represents $x{:}name \mapsto ?{:}X$ which means that x is a *name* that, in the state S, maps to the value '?' and which is of type X. So the domain of (the function) S is the set $\{input, output, x, \ldots\}$ and, overloading the use of S to represent both the function and its domain, we allow the use of notation such as $x \in S$ when we really mean $x \in \mathcal{D}\, S$.

This is consistent with earlier footnotes and, in particular, if x is a specific name in S and y is an arbitrary name in S, then the value of x in state S (usually written simply as 'x') is more properly $S(x)$, and after the state update $S' = S[x \mapsto v]$, or $S' = S[x' \mapsto v]$, to emphasize that the value of x in S' has (potentially) changed from that in state S.

$S'(x) = v$ and, providing that y is different from x, $S'(y) = S(y)$,
— so the new value of y is equal to the old one.

We can then specify

read_into(x) $x \in S$
State: S
type: x:name →
pre-*read_into* $\triangleq$ $input \neq \langle\,\rangle$ i.e., $S(input) \neq \langle\,\rangle$
post-*read_into* $\triangleq$ $S' = S[input' \mapsto \text{rest\_of}(input),\ x' \mapsto \text{first\_of}(input)]$

This is a *get* operation, a data value is taken from the *input* list and passed to x.

A similar but different situation is a non-destructive read, which merely 'looks' and copies

copy_into(x) $x \in S$
State: S
type: x:name →
pre-*copy_into* $\triangleq$ $input \neq \langle\,\rangle$
post-*copy_into* $\triangleq$ $S' = S[x' \mapsto \text{first\_of}(input)]$

In the opposite direction, we can have

$write\_from(x)$ $\quad\quad\quad\quad x \in S$
State: S
type: x:name $\rightarrow$
pre-$write\_from \triangleq$ 'enough space in $output$'
post-$write\_from \triangleq S' = S[output' \mapsto output \frown \langle x \rangle]$

and

$display\_in(y)$ $\quad\quad\quad\quad y \in S$
State: S
type: y:name $\rightarrow$
pre-$display\_in \triangleq$ ...
post-$display\_in \triangleq S' = S[y' \mapsto$ 'some computed value'$]$

But here the scope of y *must* extend beyond the current portion. This feature has elsewhere been called a ***beacon***, a value that can be seen from afar. It may have 'global' scope, but its value can only be changed by its 'owner'.

Using the same kind of notation, we can express the function call derived from '$y = f(x)$' as an operation having the specification

State: S
type: x:X, y:name $\rightarrow$
pre $\triangleq$ pre-$f(x)$
post $\triangleq T' = T[y' \mapsto z]$ $\quad$ where post-$f(x, z)$, and $T = S \cup \{x, y\}$

Having got this far, we can even specify such statements as the (integer) assignment '$x \leftarrow x + 1$', by

State: S
type: x:name
pre $\triangleq x \neq \bot_{\mathbb{Z}}$
post $\triangleq S' = S[x' \mapsto x + 1]$ $\quad$ or $\quad$ $S[x' \mapsto S(x) + 1]$

where $\bot_{\mathbb{Z}}$ represents the undefined integer value. Think of it as a place where an integer can be stored, but there is none there at the moment.

12.1.3 The Enabling of Computations

Potentially, the use of $\wedge$ connectives causes problems when we attempt to remove restrictions so as to allow multi-processing. Ideally, we should have expressions of the form

$$A \wedge B \wedge C \wedge \ldots$$

such that A is a predicate involving only the initial state and that if A succeeds (i.e., gives the value True) then so does B and C etc., (so, A enables $B \wedge C \wedge \ldots$). Then, if A fails, there is no implied state change — but *any* is possible — and the result is False. On the other hand, if A yields True, then the entire expression is True and the state change is, perhaps non-deterministically, determined by B, C etc. Relating this discussion to specifications, we observe two facts. Firstly, so as to avoid unintentional arbitrary values, some other disjunctive clause in the specification must guarantee that *some* action is possible, and the post-condition therefore yields True. Secondly, A logically includes all the necessary 'pre-conditions' for B, C etc.; it *enables* them. But this should not imply circularity such as the need to evaluate B in working out A.

To fix this problem, we could write

$$\begin{array}{ll} & (A \wedge B \wedge C \wedge \ldots\ ) \\ \vee & \\ & (\neg A \wedge S' = S) \end{array}$$

so if A is True then the action specified by $B \wedge C \wedge \ldots$ is enabled, but now it is the *only* action enabled and it must be carried out.

12.2 Pertaining to (Software) Systems

When designing systems, (systems in which software, in the form of programs and processes, is embedded, often as a controller), it is usually not appropriate to start by identifying *what* the system should do, but rather *why* such a system is required. Given a set of (operational) requirements, deciding upon the components (the hardware, etc.) and how they should act is itself part of the design process. Where computers are involved, this includes deciding upon what actions should be undertaken when certain conditions hold and including these in the specification of the software. How best to do this is still the subject of much research, although techniques do exist for handling certain common (and relatively simple) situations. Here, as a parting shot, we merely mention some of the factors which need to be considered and some mathematical notations which can be used.

So, in developing software systems there are three 'levels' which might be considered, in reverse (i.e., bottom-up) order, these are:

	implementation,	which tells the software how to perform each action;
	specification,	which says what actions are to performed (and when)
and	requirements,	which says why the system is needed.

The last two of these deserve closer investigation. (Implementation can be derived from segments of the specification as described in the earlier chapters.)

12.2.1 System Requirements

The kind of computer-based system for which software is required includes not only those systems that comprise a computer with end-user peripherals but also systems that have components other than a computer and its human users. Obvious examples from outside the professional orbit of most computer scientists and software engineers include:

- a railway crossing system (for a flat road/rail intersection), and
- an intelligent domestic heating system — to achieve and maintain a certain temperature range over a given period each day.

It is desirable that the requirements are described in terms of externally observable characteristics (i.e., nothing to do with a possible system design). Actually deciding to have traffic lights and railway signals and then calculating where they should be positioned is all part of the design process and should not be included in the statement of requirements.

Classically the requirements of a system have two components, a *safety* requirement, in which we state the 'bad' situations that should never arise, and a *liveness* requirement, that something 'good' should happen.

Safety

Henceforth bad things don't happen
(for all, future, time from "now" ...)

Liveness

Eventually desired outcomes are achieved

But processes conceptually go on for ever, so the liveness requirement needs to hold starting at any time in the future andso the liveness requirement becomes

Henceforth, eventually ...

The liveness ensures that we make progress[11].

Theoretically, this is all we need, but often we wish to say something more about how the system should run. (This therefore encroaches on specification as opposed to requirements.) For instance, we may wish to stipulate that the system should not "pause" for an unreasonable amount of time. Notice how time now comes into play so for instance the logical clause "$x > y$" now no longer means that x is greater than y, for ever. Since x and y may change in value "$x > y$" means that "$x > y$" *now*. To convey the old meaning we now have to write

henceforth $(x > y)$

or, in symbols,

$\Box\ (x > y)$

[x and y are now effectively functions of time, so

$\Box\ (x > y)$ can be thought of as[12] $(\forall t\text{:Time})\ (t > \text{now} \Rightarrow x(t) > y(t))$]

Similarly,

eventually $x > y$

is written

$\Diamond\ (x > y)$ and is like $(\exists t\text{:Time})\ (t > \text{now} \Rightarrow x(t) > y(t))$

As might be expected, there is a whole bunch of mathematical rules involving these new operators and which can be used to investigate consistency of a specification with a statement of requirements.

Additionally, we might want one particular activity or requirement to take priority over another, and we can add extra clauses which dictate priorities within the requirements. For example, we might wish that the system be obliged to take one course of action in preference to another, even though both are enabled and the system could hitherto do either.

---

[11] Within many systems, we have situations when nothing happens (or at least nothing seems to happen). But in order to make progress — to the next stage and eventually to the goal — we must insist that there is only a finite delay before the next change. This is often called ***stuttering***.

[12] These possible characterisations of $\Box$ and $\Diamond$ suppose a linear model of time. This may not be appropriate if each 'processor' has its own clock. We say no more.

Referring to the railway crossing example, these different aspects of requirements can be illustrated by

- safety — at most one vehicle should be on the crossing at any time
- liveness — eventually all vehicles that approach the crossing should pass over it.
- priority — (providing that it is safe to do so) we give priority to trains.

12.2.2 Specifying Systems

As noted above, 'design' of a system involves determining how it should interact with its environment, what components are required, what activities the system should carry out and how these should be sequenced, and specifying the control software. (And for this design to be correct, it must be shown to be consistent with the given statement of requirements.)

The requirements of an interactive system can be expressed in the form

henceforth P[13] $\wedge$ eventually Q

or, in symbols,

$$\Box P \wedge \Diamond Q$$

In a 'simple' system, which can be regarded as moving from one state to another in a (perhaps infinite) sequence, a specification of the system reduces to the specification of the state changes. Such a specification then satisfies the system requirements if every state can be shown to have the property P and from that state, providing that all subsequent system activity is correct, we can reach (in a finite time) another state in which Q holds.

In more complex (multi-processing) systems, we may never truly reach a time when no processing is taking place, and hence we cannot take a snapshot of the 'current' state at *any* time. Consequently, relating specification to requirements of one of these systems is less straightforward, but it can be done.

The specification of a software system consists of the specification of a number of processes, and each process may be defined by the reactions[14] that it can undertake, the conditions under which such reactions are allowed (i.e., when they are enabled),

[13] This means that at all time steps (when we are allowed and able to *see* the relevant information — so, for example, we cannot access values part of the way through the execution of a program command — P has to hold). On the other hand, as in traditional computation, we work towards Q. Q does not hold until we get to the 'end' (if ever). Verification and 'correctness by construction' for interactive systems is therefore more involved than for pure calculations.

[14] An action instigated by some (external) stimulus that can change (part of) the state of the system.

and a structure that dictates the acceptable orders of execution when more than one is enabled. Indeed, an implementation of such a system may well have many processors and hence parallel and distributed processing may be possible. The specification should be independent of this possibility and be equally applicable to single- or multi-processor implementations or to (computer) systems where the available processing power changes dynamically.

The software specification might be so detailed as to look like a 'pseudo program'. Whilst this may be regarded as cheating, it is often the case that the interactions are so complex as to dictate more detail than might seem necessary. Although any details not strictly required can be removed by transformations, it is desirable that these specifications be as abstract as possible.

The specification of a software system includes a (finite and/or fixed?) set of ("input" — "calculate" — "output") programs. When appropriate, each program has to be enabled (this effectively this means that its pre-condition must be satisfied) and then selected (indicating that the system is now required to perform the associated action). These two aspects correspond to the permission/obligation primitives of deontic logic. Within the specification, there may be temporal and "timing" constraints; these are clearly related to the classical connectives of predicate calculus together with notions of sequencing.

Although sequences of mathematical formulae — specifying an enabling condition, its preamble, and subsequent 'calculation' — are useful for verification purposes, it is often more convenient for design purposes to represent system specifications graphically[15].

Once enabled, a calculation acting only on local data cannot fail, and (pure) communications do not change atomic data values but merely the way in which they are held in various data structures. It is therefore reasonable to link the pre-condition of a calculation to the pre-condition of the preceding communication (if there is one). This almost amounts to the suggestion of building specifications of more complex (reactive) software out of communication/computation pairs. Such a strategy would facilitate the generation of sequences of interactions and fit closely with the philosophy of specifying software in terms of visible external actions and hidden internal actions. The only slight variation on the notion of such pairs is that the communication must 'deliver' data suitable for the following computation, thus avoiding an enforced pause in processing or logical backtracking in an elaboration of the specification.

[15] One formalism which copes with all the aspects of requirements to which we have alluded is "Statecharts". For details, the reader is referred to, Harel, D., "Statecharts: A Visual Formalism for Complex Systems", Science of Computer Programming, 8 (1987).

Hence, in much the same way as the specification of a function may be identified with the predicate

$$\text{pre-}f(x) \wedge \text{post-}f(x,y)$$

we have for the input phase[16]

$$suitable\_data\_available \wedge get\_it \wedge compute$$

and for the output phase

$$suitable\_data\_available \wedge write\_it \wedge \text{skip}.$$

['Skip' is the identity process, it involves no change in state, and its predicate delivers the value True. It is the identity relation on the set of states and could be omitted. It is included here merely to show adherence to the emerging 'standard' pattern. Elsewhere it is needed for logical completion so that 'all clauses do something even if it is the identity operation'.]

The general structure of a functional specification of the (reactive) software component of a complex system might be

$$\begin{aligned}\Box\,(\quad & (cond_1 \wedge preamble_1 \wedge calc_1)\\ \vee\ & (cond_2 \wedge preamble_2 \wedge calc_2)\\ \vee\ & \ldots\\ \vee\ & (cond_n \wedge preamble_n \wedge calc_n)\,)\end{aligned}$$

and again we could use lazy operators to enforce priorities.

On each 'pass' at least one of the conditions $cond_1$ to $cond_n$ must be True, indicating enabled actions (the preamble of which handles communication and is followed by a pure, non-communicating, calculation).

Operationally, one of the enabled actions is begun. The preamble *must* be carried out *next* and hence does not permit interference by any other processing; the calculation is then done using the data passed on by the preamble, and so on.

---

[16] With suitable restrictions on accessibility to data; this can be done with the 'next' operator, $\bigcirc$.

Unfortunately, there may be complications (which must be handled by the conditions):

- the actions may be ranked so as to indicate priorities (using $\vee\!\!\nearrow$, for example);

- at run time there may be more than one processor available;

- one process (running on one processor) may be interrupted by another, and then subsequently resumed;

- similarly, one process might be aborted by another, in which case data extracted in its preamble will be lost.

In certain cases, when two reactions apparently have equal status, we might wish to indicate that neither one should be given preferential treatment — that they should be treated 'fairly'. This is difficult to do without effectively counting their activations and trying to keep the respective counts as equal as possible, another factor that we might be asked to consider in the system design.

As you will gather, there is more to software systems than mere calculation (performed by algorithms). But at least we have made a start, and being able to generate correct algorithms — being able to guarantee that all the algorithms we generate *are* correct — is a contribution which can be employed in all but pure communication software.

Appendix
Transformation Digest

A.0 Re-write Rule Conventions

Any definition may be used as a rewrite rule, perhaps within a progression of unfold / fold steps, so we have a general conditional meta rule:

$$(x \triangleq y) \qquad x \; ◆ \; y$$

Conditional rules that involve complex conditions involving a sequence of conjuncts, such as

$$(a \wedge b) \qquad x \; ◆ \; y$$

can be represented in abbreviated form as

$$(a, b) \qquad x \; ◆ \; y$$

so the condition / guard $(a \wedge b \wedge c \wedge \dots)$ can be written as $(a, b, c, \dots)$.

A.1 Data Manipulation Rules

Following some general rules, the rest are ordered by type.

There are some generic properties associated with functions that can be expressed as the highly parameterised rules

$$\begin{array}{l} (\lambda X::\text{Type}, Y::\text{Type}) \\ \quad (\lambda f : X \to Y) \\ \quad\quad (\lambda x, y : X) \\ \quad\quad\quad (x = y) \qquad\qquad f(x) \; ◆ \; f(y) \end{array}$$

$$\begin{array}{l} (\lambda X::\text{Type}, Y::\text{Type}) \\ \quad (\lambda f, g : X \to Y) \\ \quad\quad (\lambda x : X) \\ \quad\quad\quad (f = g) \qquad\qquad f(x) \; ◆ \; g(x) \end{array}$$

$(\lambda X{::}\text{Type}, Y{::}\text{Type})$
$\quad(\lambda f,g{:}X \to Y)$
$\quad\quad((\mathcal{D}f = \mathcal{D}g) \wedge (\forall x{:}X)(x \in \mathcal{D}f \wedge (f(x) = g(x)))$
$\quad\quad\quad f \;◆\; g$

$(\lambda X{::}\text{Type}, Y{::}\text{Type})$
$\quad(\lambda f{:}X \to Y)$
$\quad\quad(\lambda x{:}X)\,(f(x))\,y \;◆\; f(y)$

$(\lambda X{::}\text{Type}, Y{::}\text{Type})$
$\quad(\lambda f{:}X \to Y)$
$\quad\quad(\lambda x{:}X)\,(f(x))\,x \;◆\; f(x)$

("text" = "text") ◆ True

where "text" represents a valid
— well-formed — expression
other than Unknown.

(Unknown = Unknown) ◆ Unknown

Brackets can be used with all types so as to clarify or disambiguate the linear/textual form associated with a particular structure/type tree.

(Meta-) rules generally involve 'variables' which can be instantiated to a constant using the λ-substitution mechanism. Once appropriate substitutions have been carried out and we have a rule which only involves known constants, it is of little further interest, and its use to evaluate expressions is simply referred to as 'arithmetic', even if there are no numbers present.

Of course, the correctness of all such rules must be checked, but we presume that this has been done as part of the system implementation.

A.1.1 The Type $\mathbb{B}$

Type/Class $\mathbb{B}$ (Boolean)

values $\mathbb{B}$ ($\triangleq$ {True,False})

operations:

$$\text{True} \rightarrow \mathbb{B}$$
$$\text{False} \rightarrow \mathbb{B}$$
$$\neg\mathbb{B} \rightarrow \mathbb{B}$$
$$\mathbb{B} \wedge \mathbb{B} \rightarrow \mathbb{B}$$
$$\mathbb{B} \vee \mathbb{B} \rightarrow \mathbb{B}$$
$$\mathbb{B} \Rightarrow \mathbb{B} \rightarrow \mathbb{B}$$
$$\mathbb{B} \Leftrightarrow \mathbb{B} \rightarrow \mathbb{B}$$

rules: ($\lambda a,b,c{:}\mathbb{B}$)

$a \vee b \blacktriangleleft\!\blacktriangleright b \vee a$	$\vee$ is commutative
$a \vee a \blacktriangleleft\!\blacktriangleright a$	$\vee$ is idempotent
$a \vee (b \vee c) \blacktriangleleft\!\blacktriangleright (a \vee b) \vee c$	$\vee$ is associative
$a \vee \text{False} \blacktriangleleft\!\blacktriangleright a$	False is an identity element for the $\vee$ operation
$a \vee (\neg a) \blacktriangleleft\!\blacktriangleright \text{True}$	
$a \vee \text{True} \blacktriangleleft\!\blacktriangleright \text{True}$	True is a null element for $\vee$
$a \wedge b \blacktriangleleft\!\blacktriangleright b \wedge a$	$\wedge$ is commutative
$a \wedge a \blacktriangleleft\!\blacktriangleright a$	$\wedge$ is idempotent
$a \wedge (b \wedge c) \blacktriangleleft\!\blacktriangleright (a \wedge b) \wedge c$	$\wedge$ is associative
$a \wedge \text{True} \blacktriangleleft\!\blacktriangleright a$	True is an identity element for the $\wedge$ operation
$a \wedge (\neg a) \blacktriangleleft\!\blacktriangleright \text{False}$	
$a \wedge \text{False} \blacktriangleleft\!\blacktriangleright \text{False}$	False is a null element for $\wedge$
$\neg\text{True} \blacktriangleleft\!\blacktriangleright \text{False}$	
$\neg\text{False} \blacktriangleleft\!\blacktriangleright \text{True}$	
$\neg\neg a \blacktriangleleft\!\blacktriangleright a$	involution
$a \wedge (b \vee c) \blacktriangleleft\!\blacktriangleright (a \wedge b) \vee (a \wedge c)$	$\wedge$ distributes over $\vee$
$a \vee (b \wedge c) \blacktriangleleft\!\blacktriangleright (a \vee b) \wedge (a \vee c)$	$\vee$ distributes over $\wedge$
$a \vee (a \wedge b) \blacktriangleleft\!\blacktriangleright a$	absorption law
$a \wedge (a \vee b) \blacktriangleleft\!\blacktriangleright a$	absorption law
$\neg(a \wedge b) \blacktriangleleft\!\blacktriangleright (\neg a \vee \neg b)$	deMorgan's law
$\neg(a \vee b) \blacktriangleleft\!\blacktriangleright (\neg a \wedge \neg b)$	deMorgan's law

$$\begin{aligned}
a \Rightarrow b &\;\blacktriangleleft\!\blacktriangleright\; (\neg a) \vee (a \wedge b) \\
a \Rightarrow b &\;\blacktriangleleft\!\blacktriangleright\; (\neg a) \vee b \\
a \Leftrightarrow b &\;\blacktriangleleft\!\blacktriangleright\; (a \Rightarrow b) \wedge (b \Rightarrow a) \\
a \Leftrightarrow b &\;\blacktriangleleft\!\blacktriangleright\; (a \wedge b) \vee (\neg a \wedge \neg b)
\end{aligned}$$

$$\begin{aligned}
a &\;\Leftrightarrow\; a && (\blacktriangleleft\!\blacktriangleright\ \text{True}) \\
a \Leftrightarrow b &\;\blacktriangleleft\!\blacktriangleright\; b \Leftrightarrow a && \\
((a \Leftrightarrow b) \wedge (b \Leftrightarrow c)) &\;\Rightarrow\; (a \Leftrightarrow c) && (\blacktriangleleft\!\blacktriangleright\ \text{True}) \\
a &\;\Rightarrow\; a && (\blacktriangleleft\!\blacktriangleright\ \text{True}) \\
(a \Rightarrow b) \wedge (b \Rightarrow a) &\;\blacktriangleleft\!\blacktriangleright\; (a \Leftrightarrow b) && \\
((a \Rightarrow b) \wedge (b \Rightarrow c)) &\;\Rightarrow\; (a \Rightarrow c) && (\blacktriangleleft\!\blacktriangleright\ \text{True})
\end{aligned}$$

$$\begin{aligned}
a \wedge b &\;\Rightarrow\; a \\
a &\;\Rightarrow\; a \vee b
\end{aligned}$$

$$\begin{aligned}
(\text{True} \Rightarrow b) &\;\blacktriangleleft\!\blacktriangleright\; b \\
(\text{False} \Rightarrow b) &\;\blacktriangleleft\!\blacktriangleright\; \text{True} \\
(a \Rightarrow \text{True}) &\;\blacktriangleleft\!\blacktriangleright\; \text{True} \\
(a \Rightarrow \text{False}) &\;\blacktriangleleft\!\blacktriangleright\; \neg a
\end{aligned}$$

$$\begin{aligned}
(a \Rightarrow b) &\;\blacktriangleleft\!\blacktriangleright\; (\neg b \Rightarrow \neg a) && \\
(a \Rightarrow b) &\;\Rightarrow\; (a \Rightarrow (b \vee c)) && (\blacktriangleleft\!\blacktriangleright\ \text{True}) \\
(a \Rightarrow b) &\;\Rightarrow\; ((a \wedge c) \Rightarrow b) && (\blacktriangleleft\!\blacktriangleright\ \text{True}) \\
((a \Rightarrow b) \wedge (\neg a \Rightarrow \neg b)) &\;\blacktriangleleft\!\blacktriangleright\; (a \Leftrightarrow b) &&
\end{aligned}$$

$$(a \Rightarrow b) \qquad a \;\blacktriangleleft\!\blacktriangleright\; a \wedge b$$

$$(a \Rightarrow b) \qquad b \;\blacktriangleleft\!\blacktriangleright\; a \vee b$$

$$(a \wedge (a \Rightarrow b) \wedge b) \;\blacktriangleleft\!\blacktriangleright\; a \wedge (a \Rightarrow b)$$

$$(a \wedge b) \Leftrightarrow \text{True} \;\blacktriangleleft\!\blacktriangleright\; (a \Leftrightarrow \text{True}) \wedge (b \Leftrightarrow \text{True})$$

$$a \wedge b \;\blacktriangleleft\!\blacktriangleright\; a \wedge (a \Rightarrow b)$$

$$(a \Leftrightarrow b) \qquad a \;\blacktriangleleft\!\blacktriangleright\; b$$

A.1.2 Extended Logic and Conditional Expressions

Type/Class Generic Conditionals
(λW::Type,X::Type,Y::Type)
values $\mathbb{B}$ ($\triangleq$ {True,False}), $\mathbb{E}$ ($\triangleq$ {True,False,Unknown}), W, X ($X \neq \mathbb{E}$), Y
operations:

$$\mathbb{B} \mathbin{\dot\wedge} \mathbb{E} \rightarrow \mathbb{B}$$
$$\mathbb{B} \mathbin{\dot\vee} \mathbb{E} \rightarrow \mathbb{B}$$
$$\mathbb{B} \Rrightarrow \mathbb{E} \rightarrow \mathbb{B}$$
$$\text{if } \mathbb{B} \text{ then } \mathbb{E} \text{ else } \mathbb{E} \text{ fi} \rightarrow \mathbb{B}$$
$$\text{if } \mathbb{B} \text{ then } \mathbb{B} \text{ else } \mathbb{B} \text{ fi} \rightarrow \mathbb{B}$$
$$\text{if } \mathbb{B} \text{ then } \mathbb{E} \text{ fi} \rightarrow \mathbb{B}$$
$$\text{if } \mathbb{B} \text{ then } X \text{ else } X \text{ fi} \rightarrow X$$

rules: ($\lambda a,b,b_1,b_2,c$:$\mathbb{B}$, p,q,r,p_1,q_1,p_2,q_2:$\mathbb{E}$, x,y,z:X, w:W, f:$X \rightarrow Y$, g:$W \times X \rightarrow Y$).

$$\text{True} \mathbin{\dot\wedge} a \;\blacktriangleleft\!\blacktriangleright\; a$$
$$\text{False} \mathbin{\dot\wedge} p \;\blacktriangleleft\!\blacktriangleright\; \text{False}$$

$$\text{True} \mathbin{\dot\vee} p \;\blacktriangleleft\!\blacktriangleright\; \text{True}$$
$$\text{False} \mathbin{\dot\vee} a \;\blacktriangleleft\!\blacktriangleright\; a$$

$$a \mathbin{\dot\wedge} b \;\blacktriangleleft\!\blacktriangleright\; a \wedge b \qquad \text{note } b{:}\mathbb{B}$$
$$a \mathbin{\dot\vee} b \;\blacktriangleleft\!\blacktriangleright\; a \vee b \qquad \text{note } b{:}\mathbb{B}$$

$$a \mathbin{\dot\wedge} (p \mathbin{\dot\wedge} q) \;\blacktriangleleft\!\blacktriangleright\; (a \mathbin{\dot\wedge} p) \mathbin{\dot\wedge} q \text{note } p{:}\mathbb{E}$$
$$a \mathbin{\dot\wedge} (b \mathbin{\dot\wedge} q) \;\blacktriangleleft\!\blacktriangleright\; (a \wedge b) \mathbin{\dot\wedge} q \text{note } b{:}\mathbb{B}$$

$$a \wedge (b \mathbin{\dot\wedge} p) \;\blacktriangleleft\!\blacktriangleright\; (a \wedge b) \mathbin{\dot\wedge} p$$

$$a \mathbin{\dot\wedge} (p \vee q) \;\blacktriangleleft\!\blacktriangleright\; (a \mathbin{\dot\wedge} p) \vee (a \mathbin{\dot\wedge} q) \qquad \text{—see}^{1}$$
$$(a \vee b) \mathbin{\dot\wedge} p \;\blacktriangleleft\!\blacktriangleright\; (a \mathbin{\dot\wedge} p) \vee (b \mathbin{\dot\wedge} p)$$

$$(a \mathbin{\dot\wedge} p) \wedge (b \mathbin{\dot\wedge} q) \;\blacktriangleleft\!\blacktriangleright\; (a \wedge b) \mathbin{\dot\wedge} (p \wedge q)$$
$$(a \mathbin{\dot\vee} p) \vee (b \mathbin{\dot\vee} q) \;\blacktriangleleft\!\blacktriangleright\; (a \vee b) \mathbin{\dot\vee} (p \vee q)$$

$$(a \mathbin{\dot\wedge} p) \vee (\neg a \mathbin{\dot\wedge} b \mathbin{\dot\wedge} p) \;\blacktriangleleft\!\blacktriangleright\; (a \vee b) \mathbin{\dot\wedge} p$$

$$(a \mathbin{\dot\wedge} p) \wedge (\neg a \mathbin{\dot\wedge} q) \;\blacktriangleleft\!\blacktriangleright\; \text{False}$$

$$(a \mathbin{\dot\wedge} p) \vee (b \mathbin{\dot\wedge} q) \Rrightarrow (a \vee b) \mathbin{\dot\wedge} (p \vee q)$$

[1] Here p and q are of type $\mathbb{E}$ and $\mathbb{B} \subseteq \mathbb{E}$ so $p \vee q$ is only defined when p is True or False and q is True or False, and then we use the $\mathbb{B} \vee \mathbb{B} \rightarrow \mathbb{B}$ operation.

$$(a \land b) \lor (p \land q) \Rightarrow (a \lor p) \land (b \lor q)$$

$$\neg(a \land p) \blacktriangleleft\!\blacktriangleright (\neg a \lor \neg p)$$
$$\neg(a \lor p) \blacktriangleleft\!\blacktriangleright (\neg a \land \neg p)$$

$$a \Rrightarrow p \blacktriangleleft\!\blacktriangleright (\neg a) \lor (a \land p)$$
$$a \Rrightarrow p \blacktriangleleft\!\blacktriangleright (\neg a) \lor p$$

$$\text{True} \Rrightarrow b \blacktriangleleft\!\blacktriangleright b$$
$$\text{False} \Rrightarrow p \blacktriangleleft\!\blacktriangleright \text{False}$$

$$(a \Rrightarrow b) \land (b \Rrightarrow a) \blacktriangleleft\!\blacktriangleright (a \Leftrightarrow b)$$
$$((a \Rrightarrow b) \land (b \Rrightarrow c)) \Rightarrow (a \Rrightarrow c)$$

$$\text{if } b \text{ then } p \text{ else } q \text{ fi} \blacktriangleleft\!\blacktriangleright (b \land p) \lor (\neg b \land q)$$
$$\text{if } b \text{ then } p \text{ else } q \text{ fi} \blacktriangleleft\!\blacktriangleright (b \Rrightarrow p) \land (\neg b \Rrightarrow q)$$
$$\text{if } b \text{ then } p \text{ fi} \blacktriangleleft\!\blacktriangleright \text{if } b \text{ then } p \text{ else True fi}$$
$$\text{if } b \text{ then } a \text{ else } a \text{ fi} \blacktriangleleft\!\blacktriangleright a$$
$$\text{if } b \text{ then } x \text{ else } x \text{ fi} \blacktriangleleft\!\blacktriangleright x$$

$$\text{if } a \text{ then } b \text{ else } c \text{ fi} \blacktriangleleft\!\blacktriangleright \text{if } \neg a \text{ then } c \text{ else } b \text{ fi}$$

$$(\text{if } b \text{ then } p_1 \text{ else } q_1 \text{ fi}) \land (\text{if } b \text{ then } p_2 \text{ else } q_2 \text{ fi})$$
$$\blacktriangleleft\!\blacktriangleright (\text{if } b \text{ then } (p_1 \land p_2) \text{ else } (q_1 \land q_2) \text{ fi})$$

$$\text{if } b \text{ then } (\text{if } b \text{ then } p \text{ else } q \text{ fi}) \text{ else } r \text{ fi} \blacktriangleleft\!\blacktriangleright \text{if } b \text{ then } p \text{ else } r \text{ fi}$$

$$\text{if } b_1 \text{ then } p \text{ else } (\text{if } b_2 \text{ then } p \text{ else } q \text{ fi}) \text{ fi} \blacktriangleleft\!\blacktriangleright \text{if } (b_1 \lor b_2) \text{ then } p \text{ else } q \text{ fi}$$

$$\text{if } p \land q \text{ then } a \text{ else } (\text{if } p \text{ then } b \text{ else } c \text{ fi}) \text{ fi}$$
$$\blacktriangleleft\!\blacktriangleright \text{if } p \text{ then } (\text{if } q \text{ then } a \text{ else } b \text{ fi}) \text{ else } c \text{ fi}$$

$$f(\text{if } b \text{ then } x \text{ else } y \text{ fi}) \blacktriangleleft\!\blacktriangleright \text{if } b \text{ then } f(x) \text{ else } f(y) \text{ fi}$$

$$z = (\text{if } b \text{ then } x \text{ else } y \text{ fi}) \blacktriangleleft\!\blacktriangleright \text{if } b \text{ then } (z = x) \text{ else } (z = y) \text{ fi}$$

$$g(w, \text{if } b \text{ then } x \text{ else } y \text{ fi}) \blacktriangleleft\!\blacktriangleright \text{if } b \text{ then } g(w,x) \text{ else } g(w,y) \text{ fi}$$

A.1.3 Integers

Type/Class $\mathbb{Z}$

values $\mathbb{Z}$ ($\triangleq$ {.., $^-2$, $^-1$, 0, 1, 2, ,...}), $\mathbb{P}$ ($\triangleq$ { 0, 1, 2, ,...}), $\mathbb{B}$

operations:

$$
\begin{aligned}
0 &\rightarrow \mathbb{Z}\\
1 &\rightarrow \mathbb{Z}\\
\mathbb{Z} + \mathbb{Z} &\rightarrow \mathbb{Z}\\
{}^-\mathbb{Z} &\rightarrow \mathbb{Z}\\
\mathbb{Z} - \mathbb{Z} &\rightarrow \mathbb{Z}\\
\mathbb{Z} * \mathbb{Z} &\rightarrow \mathbb{Z}\\
\mathbb{Z} \div \mathbb{Z} &\rightarrow \mathbb{Z}\\
\mathbb{Z} \leq \mathbb{Z} &\rightarrow \mathbb{B}\\
\mathbb{Z} < \mathbb{Z} &\rightarrow \mathbb{B}\\
\mathbb{Z} = \mathbb{Z} &\rightarrow \mathbb{B}\\
\mathbb{Z} \geq \mathbb{Z} &\rightarrow \mathbb{B}\\
\mathbb{Z} > \mathbb{Z} &\rightarrow \mathbb{B}\\
\mathbb{Z} \neq \mathbb{Z} &\rightarrow \mathbb{B}
\end{aligned}
$$

rules: ($\lambda a,b,c,d{:}\mathbb{Z}$)

$$
\begin{aligned}
a + 0 &\blacktriangleleft\!\blacktriangleright a\\
a + b &\blacktriangleleft\!\blacktriangleright b + a\\
(a + b) + c &\blacktriangleleft\!\blacktriangleright a + (b + c)\\
a + {}^-a &\blacktriangleleft\!\blacktriangleright 0\\
a - b &\blacktriangleleft\!\blacktriangleright a + ({}^-b)
\end{aligned}
$$

$$
\begin{aligned}
a * 1 &\blacktriangleleft\!\blacktriangleright a\\
a * (b + c) &\blacktriangleleft\!\blacktriangleright (a * b) + (a * c)\\
a * b &\blacktriangleleft\!\blacktriangleright b * a\\
a * (b * c) &\blacktriangleleft\!\blacktriangleright (a * b) * c\\
a * 0 &\blacktriangleleft\!\blacktriangleright 0
\end{aligned}
$$

$\neg(a = 0)$ $\qquad a*b = a*c \blacktriangleleft\!\blacktriangleright b = c$

$$(a * b) = 0 \Rightarrow (a = 0) \vee (b = 0)$$

$\neg(b = 0)$ $\qquad (a \div b) = c \blacktriangleleft\!\blacktriangleright (\exists d{:}\mathbb{Z})(a = (b * c) + d \wedge (\ (0 \leq d \wedge d < b) \vee (b < d \wedge d \leq 0)))$

$$
\begin{aligned}
a &\leq a && (\blacktriangleleft\!\blacktriangleright \text{True})\\
a &\leq a + 1 (\blacktriangleleft\!\blacktriangleright \text{True}) &&\\
a &< a + 1 && (\blacktriangleleft\!\blacktriangleright \text{True})
\end{aligned}
$$

$(0 \leq a \wedge 0 \leq b)$ $\qquad 0 \leq (a + b) \qquad (\blacktriangleleft\!\blacktriangleright \text{True})$

$(0 \leq a \wedge 0 \leq b)$ $\qquad 0 \leq (a*b) \qquad (\blacktriangleleft\!\blacktriangleright \text{True})$

$$a \le b \Leftrightarrow 0 \le (b - a)$$
$$a < b \Leftrightarrow 0 < (b - a)$$
$$a = b \Leftrightarrow (a \le b) \wedge (b \le a)$$
$$a \ge b \Leftrightarrow b \le a$$
$$a < b \Leftrightarrow (a \le b) \wedge (a \ne b)$$
$$a > b \Leftrightarrow b < a$$
$$a \ne b \Leftrightarrow \neg(a = b)$$

$$a \le b \wedge b \le c \Rightarrow a \le c \qquad (\Leftrightarrow \text{True})$$
$$a \le b \Leftrightarrow a + c \le b + c$$
$$a \le b \wedge c \le d \Rightarrow a + c \le b + d \qquad (\Leftrightarrow \text{True})$$
$$(0 < c) \qquad a \le b \Leftrightarrow a * c \le b * c$$
$$(d < 0) \qquad a \le b \Leftrightarrow a * d \ge b * d$$

$$(a = b) \qquad a \Leftrightarrow b$$

A.1.4 Sets

Type/Class Generic Sets
$(\lambda X::\text{Type})$ $(\lambda Y::\text{Type})$
values X, $\mathcal{P}(X)$, $\mathcal{P}(Y)$, $\mathcal{P}(X \times Y)$, $\mathbb{B}$
operations:

$$\varnothing \to \mathcal{P}(X)$$
$$\{X\} \to \mathcal{P}(X)$$
$$X \in \mathcal{P}(X) \to \mathbb{B}$$
$$X \notin \mathcal{P}(X) \to \mathbb{B}$$
$$\mathcal{P}(X) \cup \mathcal{P}(X) \to \mathcal{P}(X)$$
$$\mathcal{P}(X) \cap \mathcal{P}(X) \to \mathcal{P}(X)$$
$$\mathcal{P}(X) \setminus \mathcal{P}(X) \to \mathcal{P}(X)$$
$$\mathcal{P}(X) \subset \mathcal{P}(X) \to \mathbb{B} \qquad \text{(strict subset)}$$
$$\mathcal{P}(X) \subseteq \mathcal{P}(X) \to \mathbb{B}$$
$$\mathcal{P}(X) \in \mathcal{P}(\mathcal{P}(X)) \to \mathbb{B}$$
$$\mathcal{P}(X) \supset \mathcal{P}(X) \to \mathbb{B} \qquad \text{(strict superset)}$$
$$\mathcal{P}(X) \supseteq \mathcal{P}(X) \to \mathbb{B} \qquad \text{(superset)}$$
$$\mathcal{P}(X) = \mathcal{P}(X) \to \mathbb{B}$$
$$\mathcal{P}(X) \ne \mathcal{P}(X) \to \mathbb{B}$$
$$\#\mathcal{F}(X) \to \mathbb{P} \qquad \text{(size of a finite set)}$$
$$\mathcal{P}(X) \times \mathcal{P}(Y) \to \mathcal{P}(X \times Y)$$

rules: $(\lambda x, y{:}X, A, B, C{:}\mathcal{P}(X), D, E{:}\mathcal{F}(X))$

$$x \in \varnothing \Leftrightarrow \text{False}$$
$$x \in \{y\} \Leftrightarrow x = y$$
$$x \in (A \cap B) \Leftrightarrow (x \in A) \wedge (x \in B)$$
$$x \in (A \cup B) \Leftrightarrow (x \in A) \vee (x \in B)$$

$$x \in (A \setminus B) \Leftrightarrow (x \in A) \wedge (x \notin B)$$
$$(x \notin A) \Leftrightarrow \neg(x \in A)$$

$$A \cup B \Leftrightarrow B \cup A$$
$$A \cup A \Leftrightarrow A$$
$$A \cup (B \cup C) \Leftrightarrow (A \cup B) \cup C$$
$$A \cup \emptyset \Leftrightarrow A$$

$$A \cup (X \setminus A) \Leftrightarrow X$$
$$A \cup X \Leftrightarrow X$$

$$A \cap B \Leftrightarrow B \cap A$$
$$A \cap A \Leftrightarrow A$$
$$A \cap (B \cap C) \Leftrightarrow (A \cap B) \cap C$$
$$A \cap X \Leftrightarrow A$$

$$A \cap (X \setminus A) \Leftrightarrow \emptyset$$
$$A \cap \emptyset \Leftrightarrow \emptyset$$
$$(X \setminus X) \Leftrightarrow \emptyset$$
$$(X \setminus \emptyset) \Leftrightarrow X$$
$$X \setminus (X \setminus A) \Leftrightarrow A$$

$$A \cap (B \cup C) \Leftrightarrow (A \cap B) \cup (A \cap C)$$
$$A \cup (B \cap C) \Leftrightarrow (A \cup B) \cap (A \cup C)$$

$$A \cup (A \cap B) \Leftrightarrow A$$
$$A \cap (A \cup B) \Leftrightarrow A$$

$$X \setminus (A \cap B) \Leftrightarrow (X \setminus A) \cup (X \setminus B)$$
$$X \setminus (A \cup B) \Leftrightarrow (X \setminus A) \cap (X \setminus B)$$

$$A \subseteq B \Leftrightarrow (\forall x{:}X)((x \in A) \Rightarrow (x \in B))$$
$$(A \subseteq B) \qquad (x \in A) \Rightarrow (x \in B)$$
$$A \supseteq B \Leftrightarrow B \subseteq A$$
$$A \subseteq B \Leftrightarrow A \in \mathcal{P}(B)$$
$$A \subseteq B \Leftrightarrow (X \setminus B) \subseteq (X \setminus A)$$

$$(A \subseteq B) \qquad (A \cap C) \subseteq (B \cap C)$$
$$(A \subseteq B) \qquad (A \cup C) \subseteq (B \cup C)$$
$$(A \subseteq B) \qquad A \times C \subseteq B \times C \qquad \text{etc.}$$
$$(A \subseteq B) \qquad C \times A \subseteq C \times B \qquad \text{etc.}$$

$$A = B \Leftrightarrow A \subseteq B \wedge B \subseteq A$$
$$A \neq B \Leftrightarrow \neg(A = B)$$

$$
\begin{aligned}
A \subset B &\Leftrightarrow A \subseteq B \land B \neq A \\
A \supset B &\Leftrightarrow B \subset A
\end{aligned}
$$

$$
\begin{aligned}
A &\subseteq A \\
A \subseteq B \land B \subseteq C &\Rightarrow A \subseteq C
\end{aligned}
$$

$$
\begin{aligned}
(A = B) \qquad\qquad A &\Leftrightarrow B \\
(A \subseteq B) \qquad\qquad A \cap B &\Leftrightarrow A \\
(A \subseteq B) \qquad\qquad A \cup B &\Leftrightarrow B
\end{aligned}
$$

$$
\begin{aligned}
\#\emptyset &\Leftrightarrow 0 \\
\#\{x\} &\Leftrightarrow 1 \\
\#D + \#E &\Leftrightarrow \#(D \cup E) + \#(D \cap E)
\end{aligned}
$$

A.1.5 Bags

Type/Class Generic Bags
$(\lambda X{::}\text{Type})$
values $X, \mathfrak{B}(X), \mathbb{B}, \mathbb{P}$
operations:

$$
\begin{aligned}
\emptyset &\rightarrow \mathfrak{B}(X) \\
\{\!\!\{X\}\!\!\} &\rightarrow \mathfrak{B}(X) \\
\mathfrak{B}(X) \uplus \mathfrak{B}(X) &\rightarrow \mathfrak{B}(X) \\
\mathfrak{B}(X) \cap \mathfrak{B}(X) &\rightarrow \mathfrak{B}(X) \\
\mathfrak{B}(X) \setminus \mathfrak{B}(X) &\rightarrow \mathfrak{B}(X) \\
\mathfrak{B}(X) \subseteq \mathfrak{B}(X) &\rightarrow \mathbb{B} \\
\mathfrak{B}(X) = \mathfrak{B}(X) &\rightarrow \mathbb{B} \\
\#\mathfrak{B}(X) &\rightarrow \mathbb{P} \\
X\#\mathfrak{B}(X) &\rightarrow \mathbb{P} \\
\min(\mathbb{P}, \mathbb{P}) &\rightarrow \mathbb{P} \\
\mathbb{P} \text{ minus } \mathbb{P} &\rightarrow \mathbb{P} \\
X \in \mathfrak{B}(X) &\rightarrow \mathbb{B} \\
X \notin \mathfrak{B}(X) &\rightarrow \mathbb{B}
\end{aligned}
$$

rules: $(\lambda x, y{:}X, m, n{:}\mathbb{P}, A, B, C{:}\mathfrak{B}(X))$

$$
\begin{aligned}
x\#\emptyset &\Leftrightarrow 0 \\
x\#\{\!\!\{y\}\!\!\} &\Leftrightarrow \text{if } x = y \text{ then } 1 \text{ else } 0 \text{ fi} \\
x\#(B \uplus C) &\Leftrightarrow (x\#B) + (x\#C)
\end{aligned}
$$

$$
\begin{aligned}
x \in B &\Leftrightarrow (x\#B > 0) \\
x \notin B &\Leftrightarrow (x\#B = 0)
\end{aligned}
$$

$$
\begin{aligned}
\#\emptyset &\Leftrightarrow 0 \\
\#\{\!\!\{y\}\!\!\} &\Leftrightarrow 1 \\
\#(B \uplus C) &\Leftrightarrow \#B + \#C
\end{aligned}
$$

$$x\#(B \cap C) \quad \blacklozenge \quad \min(x\#B, x\#C)$$
$$x\#(B \setminus C) \quad \blacklozenge \quad (x\#B) \text{ minus } (x\#C)$$

$$m \text{ minus } n \quad \blacklozenge \quad \text{if } n \leq m \text{ then } m - n \text{ else } 0 \text{ fi}$$
$$\min(m,n) \quad \blacklozenge \quad \text{if } n \leq m \text{ then } n \text{ else } m \text{ fi}$$

$$x \in A \quad \blacklozenge \quad (x\#A) > 0$$

$$A \subseteq B \quad \blacklozenge \quad (\forall x{:}X)((x\#A) \leq (x\#B))$$

$(A \subseteq B)$ $\qquad\qquad (x\#A) \leq (x\#B)$

$$A = B \quad \blacklozenge \quad \forall x{:}X((x\#A) = (x\#B))$$

$(A = B)$ $\qquad\qquad (x\#A) = (x\#B)$

$(A = B)$ $\qquad\qquad A \blacklozenge B$

$$A \uplus B \quad \blacklozenge \quad B \uplus A$$
$$A \uplus \varnothing \quad \blacklozenge \quad A$$
$$(A \uplus B) \uplus C \quad \blacklozenge \quad A \uplus (B \uplus C)$$

$$A \cap B \quad \blacklozenge \quad B \cap A$$
$$A \cap A \quad \blacklozenge \quad A$$
$$A \cap \varnothing \quad \blacklozenge \quad \varnothing$$
$$(A \cap B) \cap C \quad \blacklozenge \quad A \cap (B \cap C)$$

$$(A \uplus B) \cap (A \uplus C) \quad \blacklozenge \quad A \uplus (B \cap C)$$

A.1.6 Lists

Type/Class Generic lists
$(\lambda X{::}\text{Type})$
values $X, X^*, \mathbb{P}, \mathbb{B}$
operations:

$$\langle \rangle \rightarrow X^*$$
$$\langle X \rangle \rightarrow X^*$$
$$X^* \frown X^* \rightarrow X^*$$
$$\#X^* \rightarrow \mathbb{P}$$
$$X \text{ in } X^* \rightarrow \mathbb{B}$$

$$X^* \text{ is\_empty} \rightarrow \mathbb{B}$$
$$X^* \text{ is\_atomic} \rightarrow \mathbb{B}$$

$$\text{first\_of}(X^*) \rightarrow X$$
$$\text{rest\_of}(X^*) \rightarrow X^*$$
$$\text{last\_of}(X^*) \rightarrow X$$
$$\text{front\_of}(X^*) \rightarrow X^*$$

$$X^* = X^* \rightarrow \mathbb{B}$$

rules: $(\lambda x,y{:}X,\ L,M,N,A,B,C,D{:}X^*,p{:}X \to \mathbb{B})$

	$(L ^\frown M) ^\frown N$	$\Leftrightarrow \ L ^\frown (M ^\frown N)$
	$L ^\frown \langle\,\rangle$	$\Leftrightarrow \ L$
	$\langle\,\rangle ^\frown L$	$\Leftrightarrow \ L$
	$\#\langle\,\rangle$	$\Leftrightarrow \ 0$
	$\#\langle x \rangle$	$\Leftrightarrow \ 1$
	$\#(L ^\frown M)$	$\Leftrightarrow \ \#L + \#M$
	$\#L = 0$	$\Leftrightarrow \ L = \langle\,\rangle$
	$x \text{ in } \langle\,\rangle$	$\Leftrightarrow \ \text{False}$
	$x \text{ in } \langle y \rangle$	$\Leftrightarrow \ x = y$
	$x \text{ in } L ^\frown M$	$\Leftrightarrow \ x \text{ in } L \ \vee \ x \text{ in } M$
	$\langle\,\rangle \text{ is\_empty}$	$\Leftrightarrow \ \text{True}$
	$\langle x \rangle \text{ is\_empty}$	$\Leftrightarrow \ \text{False}$
	$L ^\frown M \text{ is\_empty}$	$\Leftrightarrow \ L \text{ is\_empty} \ \wedge \ M \text{ is\_empty}$
	$L \text{ is\_atomic}$	$\Leftrightarrow \ (\exists z{:}X)(L = \langle z \rangle)$
$\neg(L = \langle\,\rangle)$	L	$\Leftrightarrow \ \langle \text{first\_of}(L) \rangle ^\frown \text{rest\_of}(L)$
$\neg(L = \langle\,\rangle)$	L	$\Leftrightarrow \ \text{front\_of}(L) ^\frown \langle \text{last\_of}(L) \rangle$
$\neg(L = \langle\,\rangle)$	$\#L$	$\Leftrightarrow \ 1 + \#\text{rest\_of}(L)$
	$\langle\,\rangle = \langle\,\rangle$	$\Leftrightarrow \ \text{True}$
	$\langle\,\rangle = \langle x \rangle ^\frown L$	$\Leftrightarrow \ \text{False}$
$\neg(L = \langle\,\rangle) \wedge \neg(M = \langle\,\rangle)$	$L = M$	$\Leftrightarrow \ \text{first\_of}(L) = \text{first\_of}(M) \ \wedge \ \text{rest\_of}(L) = \text{rest\_of}(M)$
	$L = M$	$\Leftrightarrow \ M = L$
$(L = M)$	L	$\Leftrightarrow \ M$
	$(\forall x{:}X)((x \text{ in } L ^\frown M) \Rightarrow p(x))$	$\Leftrightarrow \ (\forall x{:}X)(x \text{ in } L \Rightarrow p(x)) \ \wedge \ (\forall x{:}X)(x \text{ in } M \Rightarrow p(x))$
	$(\forall x{:}X)((x \text{ in } L ^\frown M))$	$\Leftrightarrow \ (\forall x{:}X)(x \text{ in } L) \wedge (\forall x{:}X)(x \text{ in } M)$
$(A ^\frown B = C ^\frown D \wedge \#A = \#C)$	B	$\Leftrightarrow \ D$
$(A ^\frown B = C ^\frown D \wedge \#B = \#D)$	A	$\Leftrightarrow \ C$
$(A = B \wedge C = D)$	$A ^\frown C$	$\Leftrightarrow \ B ^\frown D$

A.1 7 Common Conversion Functions

Type/Class
(λX::Type, Y::Type)
values $X, \mathcal{P}(X), \mathfrak{F}(X), \mathfrak{B}(X), \mathcal{P}(Y), X^*, \mathbb{B}, \mathbb{P}$
operations:

$$\text{“}\mathbb{P}\text{:” } \mathbb{B} \to \mathbb{P}$$
$$\text{“}\mathcal{P}(X)\text{:” } \mathfrak{F}(X) \to \mathcal{P}(X)$$
$$\text{“}\mathfrak{B}(X)\text{:” } \mathfrak{F}(X) \to \mathfrak{B}(X)$$
$$\text{“}\mathcal{P}(Y)\text{:” } \mathcal{P}(X) \to \mathcal{P}(Y)$$
$$\text{“}\mathfrak{B}(X)\text{:” } X^* \to \mathfrak{B}(X)$$
$$\min(\mathbb{P},\mathbb{P}) \to \mathbb{P}$$
$$\max(\mathbb{P},\mathbb{P}) \to \mathbb{P}$$

rules: ($\lambda a,b{:}\mathbb{B}, x{:}X, m,n{:}\mathbb{P}, A,B{:}\mathfrak{F}(X), C,D{:}\mathcal{P}(X), L,M{:}X^*$)

$$\text{“}\mathbb{P}\text{:” True} \Leftrightarrow 1$$
$$\text{“}\mathbb{P}\text{:” False} \Leftrightarrow 0$$
$$\text{“}\mathbb{P}\text{:” } a \wedge b \Leftrightarrow \min(\text{“}\mathbb{P}\text{:” } a, \text{“}\mathbb{P}\text{:” } b)$$
$$\text{“}\mathbb{P}\text{:” } a \vee b \Leftrightarrow \max(\text{“}\mathbb{P}\text{:” } a, \text{“}\mathbb{P}\text{:” } b)$$

$$\min(m,n) \Leftrightarrow \text{if } n \le m \text{ then } n \text{ else } m \text{ fi}$$
$$\max(m,n) \Leftrightarrow \text{if } n \le m \text{ then } m \text{ else } n \text{ fi}$$

$$\text{“}\mathcal{P}(X)\text{:” } \emptyset : \mathfrak{F}(X) \Leftrightarrow \emptyset : \mathcal{P}(X)$$
$$\text{“}\mathcal{P}(X)\text{:” } \{x\} : \mathfrak{F}(X) \Leftrightarrow \{x\} : \mathcal{P}(X)$$
$$\text{“}\mathcal{P}(X)\text{:” } A \cup B : \mathfrak{F}(X) \Leftrightarrow \text{“}\mathcal{P}(X)\text{:” } A : \mathfrak{F}(X) \cup \text{“}\mathcal{P}(X)\text{:” } B : \mathfrak{F}(X)$$

$$\text{“}\mathfrak{B}(X)\text{:” } \emptyset : \mathfrak{F}(X) \Leftrightarrow \emptyset : \mathfrak{B}(X) \qquad (\Leftrightarrow \{\!\!\{\}\!\!\})$$
$$\text{“}\mathfrak{B}(X)\text{:” } \{x\} : \mathfrak{F}(X) \Leftrightarrow \{\!\!\{x\}\!\!\}$$

$$(\text{“}\mathfrak{B}(X)\text{:” } A \cup B : \mathfrak{F}(X)) \uplus (\text{“}\mathfrak{B}(X)\text{:” } A \cap B : \mathfrak{F}(X))$$
$$\Leftrightarrow (\text{“}\mathfrak{B}(X)\text{:” } A : \mathfrak{F}(X)) \uplus (\text{“}\mathfrak{B}(X)\text{:” } B : \mathfrak{F}(X))$$

$$(X \subseteq Y) \qquad \text{“}\mathcal{P}(Y)\text{:” } \emptyset : \mathcal{P}(X) \Leftrightarrow \emptyset : \mathcal{P}(Y)$$
$$(X \subseteq Y) \qquad \text{“}\mathcal{P}(Y)\text{:” } \{x\} : \mathcal{P}(X) \Leftrightarrow \{x\} : \mathcal{P}(Y)$$
$$(X \subseteq Y) \qquad \text{“}\mathcal{P}(Y)\text{:” } C \cup D : \mathcal{P}(X) \Leftrightarrow \text{“}\mathcal{P}(Y)\text{:” } C : \mathcal{P}(X) \cup \text{“}\mathcal{P}(Y)\text{:” } D : \mathcal{P}(X)$$

$$\text{“}\mathfrak{B}(X)\text{:” } \langle\rangle \Leftrightarrow \emptyset \qquad (\Leftrightarrow \{\!\!\{\}\!\!\})$$
$$\text{“}\mathfrak{B}(X)\text{:” } \langle x \rangle \Leftrightarrow \{\!\!\{x\}\!\!\}$$
$$\text{“}\mathfrak{B}(X)\text{:” } L \frown M \Leftrightarrow \text{“}\mathfrak{B}(X)\text{:” } L \uplus \text{“}\mathfrak{B}(X)\text{:” } M$$

A.1.8 Quantifier rules

$(\lambda X{::}\mathrm{Type}, \lambda Y{::}\mathrm{Type})(Y\circledast\ Y \to Y, f{:}X \to Y, s{:}X \to \mathbb{B}, p{:}X \to \mathbb{B})$

Trading rules:

$$(\ \wedge p \mid x{:}X \mid s\ ) \Leftrightarrow (\ \wedge(s \Rightarrow p) \mid x{:}X \mid \mathrm{True})$$
$$(\ \vee p \mid x{:}X \mid s\ ) \Leftrightarrow (\ \vee(s \wedge p) \mid x{:}X \mid \mathrm{True})$$

$$(\ \wedge p \mid x{:}X \mid s\ ) \Leftrightarrow (\forall x{:}X)(s \Rightarrow p)$$
$$(\ \vee p \mid x{:}X \mid s\ ) \Leftrightarrow (\exists x{:}X)(s \wedge p)$$

$$(\forall x{:}X)(\ p\ ) \Leftrightarrow (\ \wedge p \mid x{:}X \mid \mathrm{True}\ )$$
$$(\exists x{:}X)(\ p\ ) \Leftrightarrow (\ \vee p \mid x{:}X \mid \mathrm{True}\ )$$

Empty base: $(\ \circledast f(x) \mid \mid \mathrm{False}\ ) \Leftrightarrow \boldsymbol{e}$

$$(\ \wedge p(x) \mid x{:}X \mid \mathrm{False}\ ) \Leftrightarrow \mathrm{True}$$
$$(\forall x{:}X)(\mathrm{False} \Rightarrow p(x)) \Leftrightarrow \mathrm{True}$$

$$(\ \vee p(x) \mid x{:}X \mid \mathrm{False}\ ) \Leftrightarrow \mathrm{False}$$

$$(\exists x{:}X)(\mathrm{False} \wedge p(x)) \Leftrightarrow \mathrm{False}$$

One-point rules:

$(x \setminus E)$[2]

$$(\ \circledast f(x) \mid \mid x = E\ ) \Leftrightarrow f(x)[x \leftarrow E]^{3} \Leftrightarrow f(E)$$

$$(\ \wedge p(x) \mid \mid x = E\ ) \Leftrightarrow p(E)$$
$$(\forall x{:}X)((x = E) \Rightarrow p(x)) \Leftrightarrow p(E)$$

$$(\ \vee p(x) \mid \mid x = E\ ) \Leftrightarrow p(E)$$
$$(\exists x{:}X)((x = E) \wedge p(x)) \Leftrightarrow p(E)$$

Re-distribution:

If $g{:}X \to Y$, and $(f \circledast g)(x) \triangleq f(x) \circledast g(x)$, then

$$(\ \circledast f \mid \mid s\ )\ \circledast\ (\ \circledast g \mid \mid s\ ) \Leftrightarrow (\ \circledast(f \circledast g) \mid \mid s\ )$$

$$(\ \wedge p \mid \mid s\ ) \wedge (\ \wedge q \mid \mid s\ ) \Leftrightarrow (\ \wedge(s \Rightarrow (p \wedge q)) \mid \mid \mathrm{True}\ )$$
$$(\forall x{:}X)(s \Rightarrow p) \wedge (\forall x{:}X)(s \Rightarrow q) \Leftrightarrow (\forall x{:}X)(s \Rightarrow (p \wedge q))$$

---

[2] That is, "x is not (free for substitution) in E". See Section A.3 in the Appendix for a fuller explanation.

[3] $f(x)[x \leftarrow E] \triangleq \lambda x.f(x)\ (E)$, $f(x)$ with x replaced by E.

$$(\forall x{:}X)(p) \wedge (\forall x{:}X)(q) \quad \blacklozenge \quad (\forall x{:}X)(p \wedge q)$$
$$(\vee p\,||\,s) \vee (\vee q\,||\,s) \quad \blacklozenge \quad (\vee(s \wedge (p \vee q))\,||\,\text{True})$$

$$(\exists x{:}X)(s \wedge p) \vee (\exists x{:}X)(s \wedge q) \quad \blacklozenge \quad (\exists x{:}X)(s \wedge (p \vee q))$$
$$(\exists x{:}X)(p) \vee (\exists x{:}X)(q) \quad \blacklozenge \quad (\exists x{:}X)(p \vee q)$$

Base split:

If $r{:}X \to \mathbb{B}$, then

$$(\circledast f\,||\,r \wedge s) \circledast (\circledast f\,||\,r \vee s) \quad \blacklozenge \quad (\circledast f\,||\,r) \circledast (\circledast f\,||\,s)$$

$$(\wedge p\,||\,r \wedge s) \wedge (\wedge p\,||\,r \vee s) \quad \blacklozenge \quad (\wedge p\,||\,r) \wedge (\wedge p\,||\,s)$$

$$(\forall x{:}X)((r \wedge s) \Rightarrow p) \wedge (\forall x{:}X)((r \vee s) \Rightarrow p)$$
$$\blacklozenge \quad (\forall x{:}X)(r \Rightarrow p) \wedge (\forall x{:}X)(s \Rightarrow p)$$

$$(\vee p\,||\,r \wedge s) \vee (\vee p\,||\,r \vee s) \quad \blacklozenge \quad (\vee p\,||\,r) \vee (\vee p\,||\,s)$$

$$(\exists x{:}X)((r \wedge s) \wedge p) \vee (\exists x{:}X)((r \vee s) \wedge p)$$
$$\blacklozenge \quad (\exists x{:}X)(r \wedge p) \vee (\exists x{:}X)((s \wedge p)$$

Nesting:

If $g{:}X^2 \to Y$ and $u{:}X^2 \to \mathbb{B}$

$$(\circledast g(x,y)\,|\,x,y{:}X\,|\,s(x) \wedge u(x,y)) \quad \blacklozenge \quad (\circledast (\circledast g(x,y)\,|\,y{:}X\,|\,u(x,y))\,|\,x{:}X\,|\,s(x))$$

$(y \setminus s)$ $\quad (\circledast g\,|\,x,y{:}X\,|\,s \wedge u) \quad \blacklozenge \quad (\circledast (\circledast g\,|\,y{:}X\,|\,u)\,|\,x{:}X\,|\,s)$

$(y \setminus s)$ $\quad (\wedge p\,|\,x,y{:}X\,|\,s \wedge u) \quad \blacklozenge \quad (\wedge (\wedge p\,|\,y{:}X\,|\,u)\,|\,x{:}X\,|\,s)$

$(y \setminus s)$ $\quad (\forall x,y{:}X)((s \wedge u) \Rightarrow p) \quad \blacklozenge \quad (\forall x{:}X)(s \Rightarrow (\forall y{:}X)(u \Rightarrow p))$

$(y \setminus s)$ $\quad (\vee p\,|\,x,y{:}X\,|\,s \wedge u) \quad \blacklozenge \quad (\vee (\vee p\,|\,y{:}X\,|\,u)\,|\,x{:}X\,|\,s)$

$(y \setminus s)$ $\quad (\exists x,y{:}X)(s \wedge u \wedge p) \quad \blacklozenge \quad (\exists x{:}X)(s \wedge (\exists y{:}X)(u \wedge p))$

$(y \setminus s)$ $\quad (\exists x,y{:}X)(s \wedge u) \quad \blacklozenge \quad (\exists x{:}X)(s \wedge (\exists y{:}X)(u))$

Interchange of dummy variables:

$(y \setminus r),\ (x \setminus s)$
$$(\circledast (\circledast g(x,y)\,|\,y{:}X\,|\,s(y))\,|\,x{:}X\,|\,r(x))$$
$$\blacklozenge \quad (\circledast (\circledast g(x,y)\,|\,x{:}X\,|\,r(x))\,|\,y{:}X\,|\,s(y))$$

$(y \setminus r),\ (x \setminus s)$
$$(\circledast (\circledast g\,|\,y{:}X\,|\,s)\,|\,x{:}X\,|\,r) \quad \blacklozenge \quad (\circledast (\circledast g\,|\,x{:}X\,|\,r)\,|\,y{:}X\,|\,s)$$

$(y \setminus r), (x \setminus s)$
$$(\wedge (\wedge p \,|\, y{:}X \,|\, s) \,|\, x{:}X \,|\, r) \; \blacklozenge \; (\wedge (\wedge p \,|\, x{:}X \,|\, r) \,|\, y{:}X \,|\, s)$$

$(y \setminus r), (x \setminus s)$
$$(\forall x{:}X)(r \Rightarrow (\forall y{:}X)(s \Rightarrow p)) \; \blacklozenge \; (\forall y{:}X)(s \Rightarrow (\forall x{:}X)(r \Rightarrow p))$$

$(y \setminus r), (x \setminus s)$
$$(\vee (\vee p \,|\, y{:}X \,|\, s) \,|\, x{:}X \,|\, r) \; \blacklozenge \; (\vee (\vee p \,|\, x{:}X \,|\, r) \,|\, y{:}X \,|\, s)$$

$(y \setminus r), (x \setminus s)$
$$(\exists x{:}X)(r \wedge (\exists y{:}X)(s \wedge p)) \; \blacklozenge \; (\exists y{:}X)(s \wedge (\exists x{:}X)(r \wedge p))$$

$(y \setminus r), (x \setminus s)$ $(\exists x{:}X)(r \wedge (\exists y{:}X)(s)) \; \blacklozenge \; (\exists y{:}X)(s \wedge (\exists x{:}X)(r))$

Re-naming:

$(y \setminus f(x)$ and $s(x))$, $(x \setminus f(y)$ and $s(y))$
$$(\circledast f(x) \,|\, x{:}X \,|\, s(x)) \; \blacklozenge \; (\circledast f(y) \,|\, y{:}X \,|\, s(y))$$

$(y \setminus f(x)$ and $s(x))$, $(x \setminus f(y)$ and $s(y))$
$$(\wedge p(x) \,|\, x{:}X \,|\, s(x)) \; \blacklozenge \; (\wedge p(y) \,|\, y{:}X \,|\, s(y))$$

$(y \setminus f(x)$ and $s(x))$, $(x \setminus f(y)$ and $s(y))$
$$(\forall x{:}X)(s(x) \Rightarrow p(x)) \; \blacklozenge \; (\forall x{:}X)(s(x) \Rightarrow p(x))$$

$(y \setminus f(x)$ and $s(x))$, $(x \setminus f(y)$ and $s(y))$
$$(\vee p(x) \,|\, x{:}X \,|\, s(x)) \; \blacklozenge \; (\vee p(y) \,|\, y{:}X \,|\, s(y))$$

$(y \setminus f(x)$ and $s(x))$, $(x \setminus f(y)$ and $s(y))$
$$(\exists x{:}X)(s(x) \wedge p(x)) \; \blacklozenge \; (\exists y{:}X)(s(y) \wedge p(y))$$

$(y \setminus p(x))$, $(x \setminus p(y))$ $(\exists x{:}X)(p(x)) \; \blacklozenge \; (\exists y{:}X)(p(y))$

Distributivity:

$(x \setminus p)$ $p \vee (\wedge q \,|\, x{:}X \,|\, r) \; \blacklozenge \; (\wedge (p \vee q) \,|\, x{:}X \,|\, r)$

$(x \setminus p)$ $p \vee (\forall x{:}X)(r(x) \Rightarrow q(x)) \; \blacklozenge \; (\forall x{:}X)(r(x) \Rightarrow (p \vee q(x)))$

$(x \setminus p)$ $p \wedge (\vee q \,|\, x{:}X \,|\, r) \; \blacklozenge \; (\vee (p \wedge q) \,|\, x{:}X \,|\, r)$

$(x \setminus p)$ $p \wedge (\exists x{:}X)(r(x) \wedge q(x)) \; \blacklozenge \; (\exists x{:}X)(p \wedge r(x) \wedge q(x))$

$(x \setminus p)$ $p \vee (\forall x{:}X)(q(x)) \; \blacklozenge \; (\forall x{:}X)(p \vee q(x))$

$(x \setminus p)$ $p \wedge (\exists x{:}X)(q(x)) \; \blacklozenge \; (\exists x{:}X)(p \wedge q(x))$

DeMorgan's Laws:

$$\neg (\lor p \mid x{:}X \mid r) \; \blacklozenge \; (\land \neg p \mid x{:}X \mid r)$$
$$\neg (\exists x{:}X)(p \land r) \; \blacklozenge \; (\forall x{:}X)(r \Rightarrow \neg p)$$

$$\neg (\exists x{:}X)(p) \; \blacklozenge \; (\forall x{:}X)(\neg p)$$

Monotonicity:

$$(\land (q \Rightarrow p) \mid x{:}X \mid r) \quad (\land q \mid x{:}X \mid r) \Rightarrow (\land p \mid x{:}X \mid r)$$
$$(\forall x{:}X)(r \Rightarrow (q \Rightarrow p)) \quad (\forall x{:}X)(r \Rightarrow q) \Rightarrow (\forall x{:}X)(r \Rightarrow p)$$

$$(\land (q \Rightarrow p) \mid\mid r) \quad (\lor q \mid x{:}X \mid r) \Rightarrow (\lor p \mid x{:}X \mid r)$$
$$(\land (q \Rightarrow p) \mid\mid r) \quad (\exists x{:}X)(r \land q) \Rightarrow (\exists x{:}X)(r \land p)$$

$$(\forall x{:}X)(r \Rightarrow (q \Rightarrow p)) \quad (\forall x{:}X)(r \Rightarrow q) \Rightarrow (\forall x{:}X)(r \Rightarrow p) \qquad (\blacklozenge \text{ True})$$
$$(\forall x{:}X)(r \Rightarrow (q \Rightarrow p)) \quad (\exists x{:}X)(r \land q) \Rightarrow (\exists x{:}X)(r \land p) \; (\blacklozenge \text{ True})$$

$$(\forall x{:}X)(r \Rightarrow (q \Rightarrow p)) \Rightarrow ((\forall x{:}X)(r \Rightarrow q) \Rightarrow (\forall x{:}X)(r \Rightarrow p))$$
$$(\forall x{:}X)(r \Rightarrow (q \Rightarrow p)) \Rightarrow ((\exists x{:}X)(r \land q) \Rightarrow (\exists x{:}X)(r \land p))$$

A.2 Quantifier Properties

Of all the properties which might be possessed by operations, three are of special importance since they are characteristic properties of quantifiers. Suppose that we have an infix binary operator $\otimes$ acting on type T. The three properties are that $\otimes$ has an identity (let's call it $\boldsymbol{e}$) that $\otimes$ is commutative, and most importantly that $\otimes$ is associative. Notice how associativity effectively rotates the tree.

$$(e\_is\_id\_for(\otimes)) \triangleq (\forall x{:}T) \quad x \otimes e = x \;\wedge\; e \otimes x = x$$
$$(is\_comm(\otimes)) \triangleq (\forall x,y{:}T) \quad x \otimes y = y \otimes x$$
$$(is\_assoc(\otimes)) \triangleq (\forall x,y,z{:}T) \quad (x \otimes y) \otimes z = x \otimes (y \otimes z)$$

These give rise to the obvious manipulation rules as depicted in Figure A1.

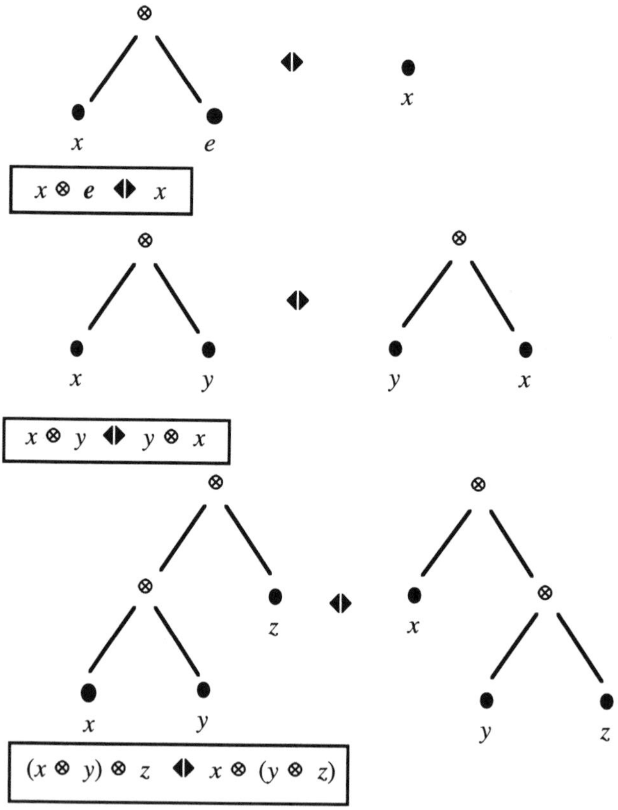

Figure A1

A.3 'Not Occurs in'

The predicate ($x \setminus p$), spoken as "x does not occur in p", is used as a condition in many transformation rules to indicate that the name x does not occur as a *free* variable within the expression p. A full definition based on the possible syntactic form for p could be given — but it is not really necessary. Put simply, if x is not used within the expression (that defines) p then $x \setminus p$ ◆ True. The only apparent exception to this is when x is used as a bound variable within p.

That is, $x \setminus (\exists x{:}X)(q(x))$ ◆ True

Here, the x in '$\exists x{:}X$' is a new x, and since

$$(\exists x{:}X)(q(x)) \;◆\; (\exists y{:}X)(q(y))$$

we have

$$x \setminus (\exists y{:}X)(q(y)) \;◆\; \text{True}$$

the validity of which is easier to appreciate.

Other constructs which use bound variables include:

$(\forall x{:}X)(\ldots)$
$(\lambda x{:}X)(\ldots)$
$\{ x{:}X \mid \ldots \}$
$(\ldots . \mid x{:}X \mid \ldots)$
and begin var $x{:}X$; ... end — or (var $x{:}X$; ...).

A.4 On PDL Structure

A PDL program consists of a sequence of (function) declarations followed by a sequence of statements, separated by semicolons.

Typically, the declaration of a function f of type $X \rightarrow Y$ is of the form

$f(x$ [$:X$]$)$ ≜ [deliver Y:] begin var w:W;
...
[result ←] *expression*
end

The segments in [...] brackets can be omitted, and (...) can be used instead of begin ... end.

Alternatively — and more properly but less commonly — we can write

f ≜ (λx [$:X$]) ([deliver Y:] begin ... end).

The formal syntax[4], given in BNF, is as follows:

⟨PROG⟩ ::= ⟨BLOCK⟩

⟨BLOCK⟩[5] ::= begin ⟨DECS⟩ ; ⟨STMTS⟩ end |
begin ⟨STMTS⟩ end

⟨DECS⟩ ::= ⟨DEC⟩ ; ⟨DECS⟩ |
⟨DEC⟩

⟨DEC⟩ ::= var ⟨IDENTS⟩ : ⟨TYPE⟩ |
⟨IDENT⟩ (⟨IDENTS⟩) ≜ ⟨EXP⟩ |
⟨IDENT⟩ (⟨IDENTS⟩) ≜ (⟨EXP⟩) |
⟨IDENT⟩ (⟨IDENTS⟩) ≜ ⟨BLOCK⟩ |
⟨IDENT⟩ ≜ ⟨BLOCK⟩[6] |
var ⟨IDENT⟩ [⟨TYPES⟩] : ⟨TYPE⟩

⟨IDENTS⟩ ::= ⟨IDENT⟩ , ⟨IDENTS⟩ |
⟨IDENT⟩

⟨IDENT⟩ ::= *a string of letters, digits and the symbol "_", starting with a letter*

[4] Of most of the PDL language.

[5] And we can use "(...)" instead of "begin ... end".

[6] Or any statement except a 'goto' statement or a compond statement containing a 'goto' statement.

```
⟨TYPES⟩ ::= ⟨TYPE⟩ , ⟨TYPES⟩  |
            ⟨TYPE⟩

⟨TYPE⟩ ::= the type indicators given in Chapter 1.

⟨STMTS⟩ ::= ⟨STMT⟩ ; ⟨STMTS⟩  |
            ⟨STMT⟩

⟨STMT⟩ ::= ⟨IDENT⟩ : ⟨STMT⟩  |
           ⟨BLOCK⟩  |
           ⟨STMT⟩ ‖ ⟨STMT⟩  |
           skip  |
           ⟨IDENT⟩ ← ⟨EXP⟩  |
           ⟨IDENT⟩ [ ⟨EXPS⟩ ] ← ⟨EXP⟩  |
           ⟨IDENTS⟩ ← ⟨EXPS⟩  |
           if ⟨EXP⟩ then ⟨STMT⟩ else ⟨STMT⟩ fi  |
           if ⟨EXP⟩ then ⟨STMT⟩ fi  |
           if ⟨EXP⟩ then ⟨STMT⟩ else_if
             ⟨EXP⟩ then ⟨STMT⟩ else ⟨STMT⟩ fi  |
           while ⟨EXP⟩ do ⟨STMT⟩ od  |
           repeat ⟨STMT⟩ until ⟨EXP⟩  |
           goto ⟨IDENT⟩  |
           result ← ⟨EXP⟩  |
           ⟨IDENT⟩ ( ⟨EXPS⟩ )  |
           ⟨IDENT⟩

⟨EXPS⟩ ::= ⟨EXP⟩ , ⟨EXPS⟩  |
           ⟨EXP⟩

⟨EXP⟩ ::= ⟨IDENT⟩ ( ⟨EXPS⟩ )  |
          if ⟨EXP⟩ then ⟨EXP⟩ else ⟨EXP⟩ fi  |
          ⟨EXP⟩ where: ⟨EXP⟩  |
          if ⟨EXP⟩ then ⟨EXP⟩
                   else_if ⟨EXP⟩ then ⟨EXP⟩ else ⟨EXP⟩ fi  |
          ⟨CAST⟩: ⟨EXP⟩  |
          any well-formed expression using the types defined in Chapter 1

⟨CAST⟩ ::= ⟨TYPE⟩
```

We also have comments and assertions. These may be placed before or after statements.

⟨COMMENT⟩ ::= *any sequence of characters (other than quotation marks) delimited by " and "*

⟨ASSERTION⟩ ::= "$" ⟨EXP⟩ "$" |
"$" "assert" ⟨EXP⟩ "$"

A.4.1 Scope and Parameters

'Variables' referenced within a block but not declared within that block are those declared within the smallest surrounding block. Within function and procedure calls, that block is a block surrounding the call rather than the declaration. Notice also that parameters are passed by value and are therefore constants which cannot be changed within a function or procedure.

A.5 PDL Transformation Rules

Here follows a collection of rules for transforming PDL code.

Of course, all the names used within these rules can be changed by making appropriate substitutions, but, so as to keep the presentation simple, in most cases we have not included explicit parameterizations.

$\langle x_1, x_2, \ldots, x_n \rangle \leftarrow \langle e_1, e_2, \ldots, e_n \rangle$

◆▶

$t_1 \leftarrow e_1;$
$t_2 \leftarrow e_2;$
...
$t_n \leftarrow e_n;$
$x_1 \leftarrow t_1;$
$x_2 \leftarrow t_2;$
....
$x_n \leftarrow t_n$

$(x \setminus b)$

$x \leftarrow a;$
$x \leftarrow b$

◆▶

$x \leftarrow b$

$x \leftarrow y;$
$z \leftarrow exp(x)$

◆▶

$x \leftarrow y;$
$z \leftarrow exp(y)$

$((y \setminus a) \wedge (x \setminus b))$

$x \leftarrow a;$
$y \leftarrow b$

◆▶

$y \leftarrow b;$
$x \leftarrow a$

S; skip

◆

S

---

skip; S

◆

S

$(y \setminus p)$ if p then $y \leftarrow a; S$
else $y \leftarrow a; T$ fi

◆

$y \leftarrow a$; if p then S
else T fi

---

if p then S else T fi

◆

if $\neg p$ then T else S fi

---

if p then $S; T$ else $Q; T$ fi

◆

if p then S else Q fi; T

$y \leftarrow$ (if p
then g
else h fi)

◆

if p then $y \leftarrow g$
else $y \leftarrow h$ fi

---

if p then while p do S od fi

◆

while p do S od

---

if p then repeat S until $\neg p$ fi

◆

while p do S od

---

repeat S until p

◆

S; while $\neg p$ do S od

---

loop pull back:

while $p(f(x))$
do $x \leftarrow f(x)$ od:
$x \leftarrow f(x)$

◆

while $p(x)$
do $x \leftarrow f(x)$ od

($W \equiv$ while B do C od; D)
W ◆ if B then C; W else D fi

($W \equiv$ if B then C; W else D fi)
W ◆ while B do C od; D

---

begin var x ...
S;
$x \leftarrow a$
end

◆

begin var x ...
S
end

($v \neq \perp_X$)[7]
$v \leftarrow v$ ◆ skip

---

[7] Where v: $X \cup \{\perp_X\}$ and $\perp_X$ denotes a declared but, as yet, unassigned X value. All our types should have a domain structure that includes such an element. But we have avoided including this minor complication since such values should not occur in any 'proper' program synthesis.

Removal of tail recursion:

λX:: Type, Y:: Type)
  $(\lambda f\colon X \to Y)\ (\lambda p\colon X \to \mathbb{B})\ (\lambda g\colon X \to Y)\ (\lambda h\colon X \to X)$
  $(\forall x{:}X)(\text{pre-}f(x) \Rightarrow (f(x) = \text{if } p(x) \text{ then } g(x) \text{ else } f(h(x)) \text{ fi}))$
  $(\text{pre-}f(x))$
  $(\exists n{:}\mathbb{P})\ (p(h^n(x)))$

```
y ← f(x)  ◆  begin  var v: X;
                    v ← x;
                    while ¬p(v)
                        do v ← h(v)
                        od;
                    y ← g(v)
             end
```

Removal of associative recursion:

$(\lambda X$:: Type, Y:: Type)
  $(\lambda f{:}X \to Y)\ (\lambda p{:}X \to \mathbb{B})\ (\lambda g{:}X \to Y)\ (\lambda k{:}X \to X)\ (\lambda \ell{:}X \to Y)\ (\lambda h{:}Y \times Y \to Y)$
  $(\forall x{:}X)(\text{pre-}f(x) \Rightarrow (f(x) = \text{if } p(x) \text{ then } g(x) \text{ else } h(f(k(x)), \ell(x)) \text{ fi}))$
  $(\forall a,b,c{:}Y)\ (h(a, h(b, c)) = h(h(a, b), c)$
  $(\text{pre-}f(x))$
  $(\exists n{:}\mathbb{P})\ (p(k^n(x)))$

```
y ← f(x)  ◆  begin  var a:X, b:Y;
                    if p(x)
                    then y ← g(x)
                    else  begin var a:X, b:Y;
                          ⟨a, b⟩ ← ⟨k(x), ℓ(x)⟩;
                          while ¬p(a)
                              do ⟨a, b⟩ ← ⟨ k(a), h(ℓ(a), b) ⟩ od;
                          y ← h(g(a), b)
                          end
                    fi
             end
```

Associative recursion with identity:

$(\lambda X{::}\text{Type}, Y{::}\text{Type})$
$(\lambda f{:}X \to Y)\ (\lambda p{:}X \to \mathbb{B})\ (\lambda g{:}X \to Y)\ (\lambda k{:}X \to X)\ (\lambda \ell{:}X \to Y)\ (\lambda h{:}Y \times Y \to Y)$
$(\forall x{:}X)(f(x) = \text{ if } p(x) \text{ then } g(x) \text{ else } h(f(k(x)), \ell(x)) \text{ fi})$
$(\forall a,b,c{:}Y)\ (h(a, h(b, c)) = h(h(a,b), c)$
$(\exists e{:}Y)(\forall y{:}Y)(h(y,e) = y \wedge h(e,y) = y)$
$(\exists n{:}\mathbb{P})\ (p(k^n(x)))$

```
y ← f(x)  ◆  begin  var a:X, b:Y;
                    ⟨a,b⟩ ← ⟨x,e⟩;
                    while ¬p(a)
                          do ⟨a,b⟩ ← ⟨k(a), h(ℓ(a),b)⟩ od;
                    y ← h(g(a),b)
             end
```

Bibliography

Baber, R L, *Error-Free Software*, Wiley, Chichester, England (1991).
Translated from the German edition dated 1990.

Backhouse, R C, *Program Construction and Verification*,
Prentice-Hall, Englewood Cliffs, NJ (1986).

Backhouse, R C, *Program Construction*, Wiley, Chichester, England (2003).

Dahl, O-J, *Verifiable Programming*,
Prentice-Hall, Englewood Cliffs, NJ ((1992).

Dijkstra, E W, *A Discipline of Programming*,
Prentice-Hall, Englewood Cliffs, NJ ((1976).

Dijkstra, E W and Feijen, W H J, *A Method of Programming*,
Addison-Wesley, Reading, MA (1988).

Gries, D, *The Science of Programming*, Springer-Verlag, New York (1981).

Gries, D and Schneider, F B, *A Logical Approach to Discrete Math(s)*,
Springer-Verlag, New York (1994).

Hehner, E C R, *A Practical Theory of Programming*,
Springer-Verlag, New York (1993).

Jones, C B, *Software Development: A Rigorous Approach*,
Prentice-Hall, Englewood Cliffs, NJ ((1980).

Jones, C B, *Systematic Software Development using VDM*, 2nd edition,
Prentice-Hall, Englewood Cliffs, NJ ((1990).

Kaldewaij, A, *Programming: The Derivation of Algorithms*,
Prentice-Hall, Englewood Cliffs, NJ ((1990).

Morgan, C, *Programming from Specifications*, 3rd edition available from http://web.comlab.ox.ac.uk/oucl/publications/books/PfS/

Partsch, H A, *Specification and Transformation of Programs*, Springer-Verlag, Heidelberg (1990).

Stone, R G and Cooke, D J, *Program Construction*, CUP, Cambridge (1987).

Windeknecht, T G, *Logical Derivation of Computer Programs*, Intellect, Exeter (1999).

Index

absorption 68
abstraction 203, 205
action 457
actual parameter 58
additive inverse 98
algorithm extraction 161ff
(for) all, $\forall$ 56
alternation 147, 149
analogy 203
and, $\wedge$ 66
and then, $\wedge$ 46
array subscript 134
assertions 139
assignment command 137, 140
associative recursion 238
associativity 46, 52, 67, 181, 273, 277
atom 104

bag
  bag of X, $\mathfrak{B}(X)$ 101ff, 482ff
  intersection, $\cap$ 101
  number of instances of x in (bag) b, $x\#b$ 102
  size, $\#b$ 102
  sub-bag, $\subseteq$ 102
  union, $\uplus$ 101
base 292
  base split rule 295, 487
beacon 465
binary relation 37
Boolean quantifiers 76
Boolean type, $\mathbb{B}$ 40, 66ff, 71, 475ff
bound variable 76
bubble sort 378

Cartesian product, $X \times Y$ 38
cast 95, 108, 111
changes (of state) 31, 224, 455, 457
checking 172
cocktail shaker sort 382
coercion, see cast
combine 272
command 128
  proper 228
comments 139
communication 459
commutativity 52, 67, 273
complement 69
  uniqueness 69
composite values 268
  derived 270
(functional) composition, $g \circ f$ 45
compositionality 456
concatenation 104
condition 269
conditional 132
conditional and, $\wedge$ 78
conditional expressions 83
  with arbitrary types 89
conditional implication, $\Rightarrow$ 82
conditional or, $\vee$ 78
conditional rule 54
conjunctive form 115
consistency 305
contextual correctness 154
conventional communications 463

convergence 164, 236
conversion functions 485
convex hull 418
correctness 302
    contextual 154
    partial 151
    relative 154
    total 150
correctness theorem 162

dash 458
data
    refinement 357
    structures 357
    types 61
    types and transformations 114
data-flow diagram 326
de Morgan's Law 93, 303, 489
declaration, *a* is a quantity of type *X*, *a*:*X* 15
    definition, ≜ 15
(problem) decomposition 182
decoration 458
deduction 72
(is) defined to be, ≜ 39
(program) derivation 154
derived composite values 270
design
    program 155
    refinement 305
    re-using 310
    tactics 169
detected failure 409
deterministic 163, 306
(program) development 277
difference 56, 92
digraph 425
disabled 457
(re-) distribution rule 294
distributivity 67, 92, 298, 488
divide and conquer 169
divides, | (local usage) 15

does not occur in, \ 117
domain of a function or binary relation 43
domain partitioning 202
domain rule 148
down recursion 249
(interchange of) dummy variables 297

$\mathbb{E}$, extended set of truth values 56, 78ff, 477ff
(is an) element of, ∈ 38
(is not an) element of, ∉ 39
else_if 109
embedded conditional expressions 86
empty base quantifier rule 293, 486
empty set, Ø 92
enabling 457, 459, 466
equality test 55
(flowchart) equation 232
equational reasoning 51
equivalence 72
    strong 225
eureka process 206
exchange sorts 375
existential 116
existential quantifier 44
(there) exists, ∃ 44
explicit 163
(tree representation of an) expression 63
extended (3-valued) logic, $\mathbb{E}$ 78
extremal problems 439

factorization 68
(tactic) failure 409
failures in structural splitting 411
False 40, 66
file 108
finite subsets of *X*, $\mathfrak{F}(X)$ 93
first_of 104
flowchart 128
    equation 232
    program 130

folding 57, 118, 164
for all, ∀ 56
formal parameter 58
front_of 104
function 35, 43
    conversion functions 485
    functional composition, f of g, f over g, $g \circ f$ 45
    list functions f^*, f^+ 271
    total function 47
    type transfer functions 111
    1-place functions 270, 278
    2-place functions 272, 280
functional 163

get input 458
giving 464
go-on, ";" 132
graph 46
    of a function 46

height (of a tree) 371

(specification of) I/O 457
idempotent 70
identity 273, 280
if
    (else_) if 109
    if and only if, *iff*, ⇔ 48, 72
    if ... then ... else ... fi 46, 83
    if $x{:}A$ then ... 109
    if ... then ... fi 86
implication, *implies*, ⇒ 72
improving 324
"in" 104
independent 170
indices 363
induced operations 110
induction 187, 326
    structural 327
inequalities 99
infix operator 62

insertion sort 384, 388
instantiation 59, 203
(re-) instantiation 205
integers, integer type, $\mathbb{Z}$ 19, 51, 61, 62, 96ff, 479ff
    division 101
    positive, $\mathbb{P}$ 97
interactive software 455
interchange of dummy variables 297, 487-8
interrupt 459
intersection, ∩ 92
(additive) inverse 98
involution 70
iteration 147, 150
(speeding up) iterations 257

join 140

key 108, 318

lambda notation 57, 59
last_of 104
leaf node 371
let 138
LFP 14, 127, 164
list functions, f^*, f^+ 271
list operations 103, 483-4
list types X^* and X^+ 103ff, 110, 483-4
liveness 457, 469
locus of control 128
Logic, Functions, Procedures, see LFP
logical types 66
    extended (3-valued) logic, $\mathbb{E}$ 78
logical-functional-procedural, see LFP
looking 464
(while) loop 228
loop pull-back 286
loss of vital information 412

maplet, ↦ 43
mapping 47, 272

measure 165
  of problem size 176
merge sorts 383
  minimal 389
mixed strategies 201
Modus Ponens 74
monotonicity 299, 489
multiplication 98

natural numbers, ℕ 15, 97
negate 98
negative 52, 63
nesting rule 296, 487
non-determinism 301
non-empty X lists, X^+ 105
not, ¬ 66
not an element of, ∉ 39
(does) "not occur in" 117, 491
n-tuple 107
null rules 68
number of instances of x in (bag) b, $x\#b$ 102

object-oriented programming 206
one-point rule 294, 486
operational refinement 302
or, ∨ 66
ordered pair 38
or else, $\bar{\vee}$ 78
orthogonal 170

parameter 139
  actual 58
  formal 58
  passing by value 139
parameterisation 204, 206
parameterless procedure 208
partial correctness 151
partition sort 390
partitioning 333
  domain 203
PDL 4, 134

PDL (continued)
  syntax 492ff
  transformations 495ff
pivot 349, 402
positive integers, ℙ 97
post-check 132
post-condition 140
post-fix operator 60
powerset, $\mathcal{P}(X)$ 41, 92
pre-check 132
pre-condition 139
  weakest, *wp* 45
predicate 40
predicated splitting 201, 333
pre-fix operator 60
prenex normal form 291
prime 458
priority 469
problem
  decomposition 182
  reduction 176, 323
  (measure of) size 176
procedural programming 127
procedures 455
  parameterless 208
  recursive 262
(eureka) process 206
program
  derivation 154
  design 155
  development 277
  flowchart 130
Program Design Language, see PDL
programming 125
  object-oriented 206
proper command 228
(constructive) proof 171
proof obligation 147

quantifier 116, 267ff, 273
  Boolean 76
  empty base rule 293
  existential 44

quantifier (continued)
logical quantifier rules 298
one-point rule 294
properties 490
rules 291, 486ff
universal 56
Quicksort 403, 404

range 44
rule 149
rational numbers, $\mathbb{Q}$ 107
rationalisation 115
rationalise 194
real numbers, $\mathbb{R}$ 107
record 32, 107, 108
recursion 164ff, 223ff
associative 238
down 249
introduction 163
procedures 262
removal 163, 223
tail 225, 228
up 249
re-distribution rule 294
reduce 165, 307
reduction 236, 309
problem 175, 323
refine 306, 307
refinement 172, 301ff
data 357
design 305
operational 302
strict 309
reflexivity 54
reify 307
re-instantiation 205
re-naming rule 297, 488
repeat ... until ... 132
requirements 455, 467
rest_of 104
re-use 206, 301
re-using designs 310
re-write rules 59

robustness 1, 7, 139, 411, 418
root 371
rules
base split 295
conditional 54
conditional on a definition 56
domain 148
empty base 293, 486
logical quantifier 298
nesting 296, 487
one-point 294, 486
quantification 291, 486ff
range 149
re-distribution 294, 486-7
renaming 297, 488
rewrite 54
trading rules 486

safety 467, 469
(*is the*) *same as*, ◆ 51
same (type and) value 55
scope 116, 139
selection sort 401
selector 292
set(s), $\mathcal{P}(X)$ 91, 480ff
set difference, \ 56
set notation 39
(set of finite) sets, $\mathfrak{F}(X)$ 93, 94
sequencing 147
sequential and, $\wedge$ 78
sequential implication, $\Rrightarrow$ 82
sequential or, $\vee$ 78
showing 464
(unexpected) side effects 128

signature 62
singleton, atom 104
size (= count), # 165
size of bag *b*, #*b* 102
(measure of problem) size 176
skip 229
sort(ing algorithm)s 317ff, 375ff
basic merge 347

Sorts (continued)
bubble 378
cocktail shaker 382
exchange 341, 375
insertion 384, 388
merge 347, 383
minimal merge 389
partition 337, 348, 390
selection 401
source of a (binary) relation or function 41
specification 37, 41, 47
of I/O 457
specifying systems 469
speeding up iterations 257
splitting
predicated 201, 333
structural 185, 326
state 458
state changes 143, 224
statement, command 128
(mixed) strategies 201
strong equivalence 225
structural induction 327
structural splitting 185, 326
failures 411
structured program 132, 145, 147
stuttering 468
sub-bag 102
sub-program 131
sub-range, $x..y$ 20, 110
subset, $\subset$, $\subseteq$ 38, 91
substitution 57
type 59
subtraction 98
sub-types 110
such that, | 39
symmetric 54
systems 466

tactic failure 409
tail recursion 225, 228
taking 464
target of a (binary) relation or function 41
term 269
termination 165, 236
test 140
(A) to B, function type 40
tolerances 456
topological sort 424
total correctness 150
total function, mapping 47
trace sequences 226
trading 292
trading rules 486
transfine 161
transformations 473ff
transitive 53
translation 203
tree 371
representation of an expression 63
True 40, 66
(n-) tuple 107
types
(A) to B, function type 40
$\mathfrak{B}(X)$, see bags
$\mathbb{B}$, see Boolean
data type 61
$\mathbb{E}$, see extended logic
$\mathfrak{F}(X)$, see finite sets
function type 40
list types X^* and X^+ 110
$\mathbb{N}$, see natural numbers
$\mathbb{P}$, see positive integers
$\mathfrak{P}(X)$, see power sets
$\mathbb{Q}$, see rationals
$\mathbb{R}$, see real numbers
sub-type 110
substitution 59
transfer functions 111
(variant) enquiry 109
union 109
(x is of) type X, $x{:}X$ 39
$\mathbb{Z}$, see integers

Undefined value (of type) 56, 78, 465
unexpected side effects 128
unfolding 164
union, ∪ 92
union types 109
uniqueness of complements 69
universal quantifier, ∀ 56, 116
Unknown value 78
up recursion 249

values
    composite 268
    derived composite values 270
variables
    interchange of dummy variables
        297, 487-8
    quoted 270
verification 145, 146
(loss of) vital information 412

weakest pre-condition, *wp* 45, 307
well-ordering 152
where 138
while ... do ... od 132
while loop 228
widen 112
wider (problem) 412
wp, see weakest pre-condition
(re-) write rule 54

ℤ, see integers